D0601810

# THE FIREFLY
# FRENCH/ENGLISH
# VISUAL DICTIONARY

Jean-Claude **Corbeil**
Ariane **Archambault**

FIREFLY BOOKS

# A FIREFLY BOOK

Published by Firefly Books Ltd. 2004

Copyright © 2004 QA International

First Printing

Publisher Cataloging-in-Publication Data  (U.S.)
Corbeil, Jean-Claude.
    The Firefly French - English visual dictionary / Jean-Claude Corbeil, Ariane Archambeault.—1st ed.
    [592] p. : col. ill. ;  cm.
    Includes index.
    Summary: A comprehensive general reference visual dictionary featuring terms in English and French.  Includes sections on astronomy, geography, the animal and vegetable kingdoms, human biology, the home, clothing and accessories, art and architecture, communication, transportation, energy, science, society and sports.
    ISBN 1-55297-950-4
    1. Picture dictionaries, French.  2. Picture dictionaries, English.
    3. French language – Dictionaries – English.  4. English language – Dictionaries – French.  I. Archambeault, Ariane.  II. Title.
    443.21 dc22    PC2629.C67   2004

National Library of Canada Cataloguing in Publication
Corbeil, Jean-Claude, 1932-
    The Firefly French/English visual dictionary / Jean-Claude Corbeil, Ariane Archambeault.
    Text in English and French.
    Includes index.
    ISBN 1-55297-950-4
    1. Picture dictionaries, French.  2. Picture dictionaries, English.
    3. French language–Dictionaries–English.  4. English language–Dictionaries–French.  I. Archambault, Ariane, 1936-  II. Title.
    AG250.C66373 2004    443'.17    C2004-901312-2

Published in the United States in 2004 by
Firefly Books (U.S.) Inc.
P.O. Box 1338, Ellicott Station
Buffalo, New York 14205

Published in Canada in 2004 by
Firefly Books Ltd.
66 Leek Crescent
Richmond Hill, Ontario L4B 1H1

Cover design: Gareth Lind

Printed in Singapore

## ACKNOWLEDGMENTS

Our deepest gratitude to the individuals, institutions, companies and businesses that have provided us with the latest technical documentation for use in preparing The Firefly French/English Visual Dictionary.

Arcand, Denys (réalisateur); Association Internationale de Signalisation Maritime; Association canadienne des paiements (Charlie Clarke); Association des banquiers canadiens (Lise Provost); Automobiles Citroën; Automobiles Peugeot; Banque du Canada (Lyse Brousseau); Banque Royale du Canada (Raymond Chouinard, Francine Morel, Carole Trottier); Barrett Xplore inc.; Bazarin, Christine;Bibliothèque du Parlement canadien (Service de renseignements); Bibliothèque nationale du Québec (Jean-François Palomino); Bluechip Kennels (Olga Gagne); Bombardier Aéronautique; Bridgestone-Firestone; Brother (Canada); Canadien National; Casavant Frères ltée; C.O.J.O. ATHENES 2004 (Bureau des Médias Internationaux); Centre Eaton de Montréal; Centre national du Costume (Recherche et de Diffusion); Cetacean Society International (William R. Rossiter); Chagnon, Daniel (architecte D.E.S. – M.E.Q.); Cohen et Rubin Architectes (Maggy Cohen); Commission Scolaire de Montréal (École St-Henri); Compagnie de la Baie d'Hudson (Nunzia Iavarone, Ron Oyama); Corporation d'hébergement du Québec (Céline Drolet); École nationale de théâtre du Canada (Bibliothèque); Élevage Le Grand Saphir (Stéphane Ayotte); Énergie atomique du Canada ltée; Eurocopter; Famous Players; Fédération bancaire française (Védi Hékiman); Fontaine, PierreHenry (biologiste); Future Shop; Garaga; Groupe Jean Coutu; Hôpital du Sacré-Cœur de Montréal; Hôtel Inter-Continental; Hydro-Québec; I.P.I.Q. (Serge Bouchard); IGA Barcelo; International Entomological Society (Dr. Michael Geisthardt); Irisbus; Jérôme, Danielle (O.D.); La Poste (Colette Gouts); Le Groupe Canam Manac inc.; Lévesque, Georges (urgentologue); Lévesque, Robert (chef machiniste); Manutan; Marriot Spring Hill suites; MATRA S.A.; Métro inc.; ministère canadien de la Défense nationale (Affaires publiques); ministère de la Défense, République Française; ministère de la Justice du Québec (Service de la gestion immobilière – Carol Sirois); ministère de l'Éducation du Québec (Direction de l'équipement scolaire- Daniel Chagnon); Muse Productions (Annick Barbery); National Aeronautics and Space Administration; National Oceanic and Atmospheric Administration; Nikon Canada inc.; Normand, Denis (consultant en télécommunications); Office de la langue française du Québec (Chantal Robinson); Paul Demers & Fils inc.; Phillips (France); Pratt & Whitney Canada inc.; Prévost Car inc.; Radio Shack Canada ltée; Réno-Dépôt inc.; Robitaille, Jean-François (Département de biologie, Université Laurentienne); Rocking T Ranch and Poultry Farm (Pete and Justine Theer); RONA inc.; Sears Canada inc.; Secrétariat d'État du Canada : Bureau de la traduction ; Service correctionnel du Canada; Société d'Entomologie Africaine (Alain Drumont); Société des musées québécois (Michel Perron); Société Radio-Canada; Sony du Canada ltée; Sûreté du Québec; Théâtre du Nouveau Monde; Transports Canada (Julie Poirier); Urgences-Santé (Éric Berry); Ville de Longueuil (Direction de la Police); Ville de Montréal (Service de la prévention des incendies); Vimont Lexus Toyota; Volvo Bus Corporation; Yamaha Motor Canada Ltd.

QA International wishes to extend a special thank you to the following people for their contribution to The Firefly French/English Visual Dictionary:

Jean-Louis Martin, Marc Lalumière, Jacques Perrault, Stéphane Roy, Alice Comtois, Michel Blais, Christiane Beauregard, Mamadou Togola, Annie Maurice, Charles Campeau, Mivil Deschênes, Jonathan Jacques, Martin Lortie, Raymond Martin, Frédérick Simard, Yan Tremblay, Mathieu Blouin, Sébastien Dallaire, Hoang Khanh Le, Martin Desrosiers, Nicolas Oroc, François Escalmel, Danièle Lemay, Pierre Savoie, Benoît Bourdeau, Marie-Andrée Lemieux, Caroline Soucy, Yves Chabot, Anne-Marie Ouellette, Anne-Marie Villeneuve, Anne-Marie Brault, Nancy Lepage, Daniel Provost, François Vézina, Brad Wilson, Michael Worek, Lionel Koffler, Maraya Raduha, Dave Harvey, Mike Parkes, George Walker and Anna Simmons.

 The Firefly French/English Visual Dictionary was created and produced by
**QA International**
329, rue de la Commune Ouest, 3e étage
Montréal (Québec) H2Y 2E1 Canada
T 514.499.3000  F 514.499.3010
**www.qa-international.com**

EDITORIAL STAFF

Publisher: Jacques Fortin

Authors: Jean-Claude Corbeil and Ariane Archambault

Editorial Director: François Fortin

Editor-in-Chief: Serge D'Amico

Graphic Design: Anne Tremblay

PRODUCTION

Mac Thien Nguyen Hoang

Guylaine Houle

TERMINOLOGICAL RESEARCH

Jean Beaumont

Catherine Briand

Nathalie Guillo

ILLUSTRATIONS

Art Direction: Jocelyn Gardner

Jean-Yves Ahern

Rielle Lévesque

Alain Lemire

Mélanie Boivin

Yan Bohler

Claude Thivierge

Pascal Bilodeau

Michel Rouleau

Anouk Noël

Carl Pelletier

LAYOUT

Pascal Goyette

Janou-Ève LeGuerrier

Véronique Boisvert

Josée Gagnon

Karine Raymond

Geneviève Théroux Béliveau

DOCUMENTATION

Gilles Vézina

Kathleen Wynd

Stéphane Batigne

Sylvain Robichaud

Jessie Daigle

DATA MANAGEMENT

Programmer: Daniel Beaulieu

Nathalie Fréchette

REVISION

Marie-Nicole Cimon

PREPRESS

Sophie Pellerin

Kien Tang

Tony O'Riley

**Jean-Claude Corbeil** is an expert in linguistic planning, with a world-wide reputation in the fields of comparative terminology and socio-linguistics. He serves as a consultant to various international organizations and governments.

**Ariane Archambault**, a specialist in applied linguistics, has taught foreign languages and is now a terminologist and editor of dictionaries and reference books.

# Introduction to
## *the Firefly French/English Visual Dictionary*

### A DICTIONARY FOR ONE AND ALL

*The Firefly French/English Visual Dictionary* uses pictures to define words. With thousands of illustrations and thousands of specialist and general terms, it provides a rich source of knowledge about the world around you.

Designed for the general reader and students of language, *The Firefly French/English Visual Dictionary* responds to the needs of anyone seeking precise, correct terms for a wide range of objects. Using illustrations enables you to "see" immediately the meaning of each term.

You can use *The Firefly French/English Visual Dictionary* in several ways:

**By going from an idea to a word.** If you are familiar with an object but do not know the correct name for it, you can look up the object in the dictionary and you will find the various parts correctly named.

**By going from a word to an idea.** If you want to check the meaning of a term, refer to the index where you will find the term and be directed to the appropriate illustration that defines the term.

**For sheer pleasure.** You can flip from one illustration to another or from one word to another, for the sole purpose of enjoying the illustrations and enriching your knowledge of the world around us.

### STRUCTURE

*The Firefly French/English Visual Dictionary* is divided into CHAPTERS, outlining subjects from astronomy to sports.

More complex subjects are divided into THEMES; for example, the Animal Kingdom chapter is divided into themes including insects and arachnids, mollusks, and crustaceans.

The TITLES name the object and, at times, the chief members of a class of objects are brought together under the same SUBTITLE.

The ILLUSTRATIONS show an object, a process or a phenomenon, and the most significant details from which they are constructed. It serves as a visual definition for each of the terms presented.

### TERMINOLOGY

Each word in *The Firefly French/English Visual Dictionary* has been carefully chosen and verified. Sometimes different words are used to name the same object, and in these cases the word most commonly used was chosen.

## COLOR REFERENCE

On the spine and back of the book this identifies and accompanies each theme to facilitate quick access to the corresponding section in the book.

## TITLE

It is highlighted in English, and the French equivalent is placed underneath in smaller characters. If the title runs over a number of pages, it is printed in gray on the pages subsequent to the first page on which it appears.

## SUB-THEME

Most themes are subdivided into sub-themes. The sub-theme is given both in English and in French.

## NARROW LINES

These link the word to the item indicated. Where too many lines would make reading difficult, they have been replaced by color codes with captions or, in rare cases, by numbers.

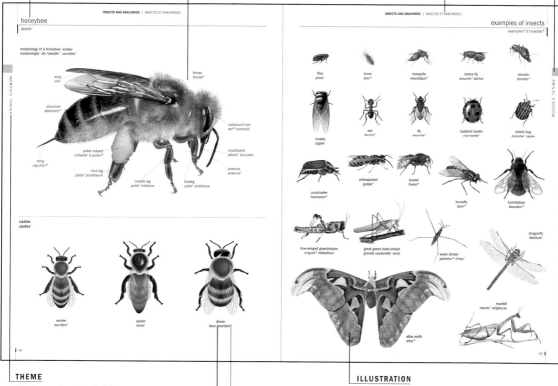

honeybee
*abeille*

morphology of a honeybee: worker
*morphologie* de l'abeille* : ouvrière*

thorax
*thorax*

wing
*aile*

abdomen
*abdomen*

compound eye
*œil* composé*

pollen basket
*corbeille* à pollen*

mouthparts
*pièces* buccales*

sting
*aiguillon*

hind leg
*patte* postérieure*

antenna
*antenne*

middle leg
*patte* médiane*

foreleg
*patte* antérieure*

castes
*castes*

worker
*ouvrière*

queen
*reine*

drone
*faux bourdon*

ANIMAL KINGDOM

examples of insects
*exemples* d'insectes*

flea
*puce*

louse
*pou*

mosquito
*moustique*

tsetse fly
*mouche* tsé-tsé*

termite
*termite*

cicada
*cigale*

ant
*fourmi*

fly
*mouche*

ladybird beetle
*coccinelle*

shield bug
*punaise* rayée*

cockchafer
*hanneton*

yellowjacket
*guêpe*

hornet
*frelon*

horsefly
*taon*

bumblebee
*bourdon*

bow-winged grasshopper
*criquet* mélodieux*

great green bush-cricket
*grande sauterelle* verte*

water strider
*patineur* d'eau*

dragonfly
*libellule*

atlas moth
*atlas*

mantid
*mante* religieuse*

ANIMAL KINGDOM

## THEME

It is always unilingual, in English.

## ILLUSTRATION

It serves as the visual definition for the terms associated with it.

## GENDER INDICATION

F: feminine M: masculine N: neuter

The gender of each word in a term is indicated.

The characters shown in the dictionary are men or women when the function illustrated can be fulfilled by either. In these cases, the gender assigned to the word depends on the illustration; in fact, the word is either masculine or feminine depending on the sex of the person.

## TERM

Each term appears in the index with a reference to the pages on which it appears. It is given in both languages, with English as the main index entry.

# Contents

# List of chapters

ASTRONOMY

# solar system

système<sup>M</sup> solaire

**outer planets**
*planètes<sup>F</sup> externes*

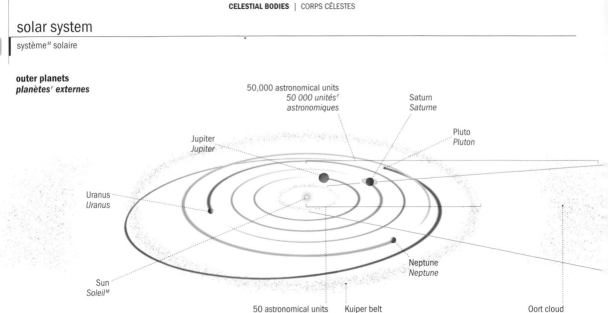

50,000 astronomical units
*50 000 unités<sup>F</sup>
astronomiques*

Saturn
*Saturne*

Jupiter
*Jupiter*

Pluto
*Pluton*

Uranus
*Uranus*

Neptune
*Neptune*

Sun
*Soleil<sup>M</sup>*

50 astronomical units
*50 unités<sup>F</sup> astronomiques*

Kuiper belt
*ceinture<sup>F</sup> de Kuiper*

Oort cloud
*nuage<sup>M</sup> de Oort*

# planets and moons

planètes<sup>F</sup> et satellites<sup>M</sup>

Deimos
*Deimos*

Phobos
*Phobos*

Moon
*Lune<sup>F</sup>*

Venus
*Vénus*

Jupiter
*Jupiter*

Mercury
*Mercure*

Earth
*Terre<sup>F</sup>*

Mars
*Mars<sup>M</sup>*

Io
*Io*

Callisto
*Callisto*

Europa
*Europe*

Ganymede
*Ganymède*

Sun
*Soleil<sup>M</sup>*

solar system

**inner planets**
*planètes*[F] *internes*

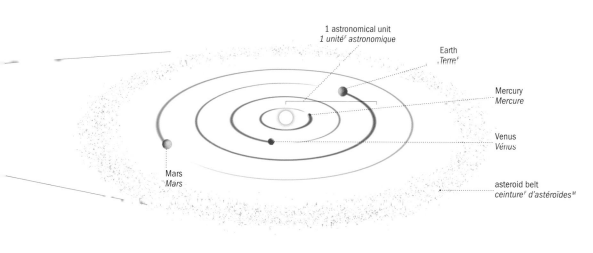

1 astronomical unit
*1 unité*[F] *astronomique*

Earth
*Terre*[F]

Mercury
*Mercure*

Venus
*Vénus*

Mars
*Mars*

asteroid belt
*ceinture*[F] *d'astéroïdes*[M]

planets and moons

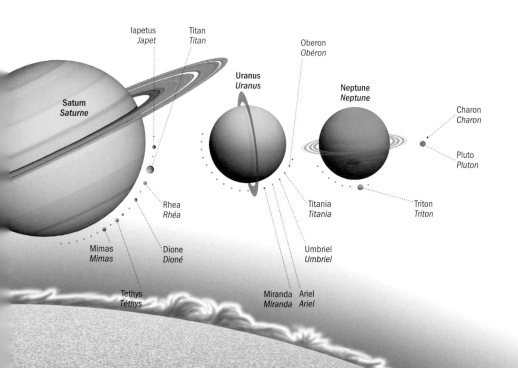

Iapetus
*Japet*

Titan
*Titan*

Oberon
*Obéron*

Uranus
*Uranus*

Neptune
*Neptune*

Charon
*Charon*

Saturn
*Saturne*

Pluto
*Pluton*

Rhea
*Rhéa*

Titania
*Titania*

Triton
*Triton*

Mimas
*Mimas*

Dione
*Dioné*

Umbriel
*Umbriel*

Tethys
*Téthys*

Miranda
*Miranda*

Ariel
*Ariel*

3

# Sun

Soleil[M]

**structure of the Sun**
*structure[F] du Soleil[M]*

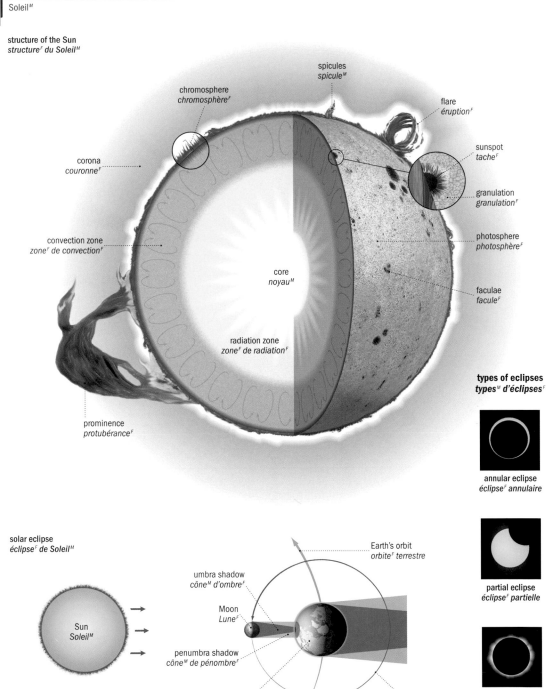

spicules
*spicule[M]*

chromosphere
*chromosphère[F]*

flare
*éruption[F]*

corona
*couronne[F]*

sunspot
*tache[F]*

granulation
*granulation[F]*

convection zone
*zone[F] de convection[F]*

photosphere
*photosphère[F]*

core
*noyau[M]*

faculae
*facule[F]*

radiation zone
*zone[F] de radiation[F]*

prominence
*protubérance[F]*

**types of eclipses**
*types[M] d'éclipses[F]*

annular eclipse
*éclipse[F] annulaire*

**solar eclipse**
*éclipse[F] de Soleil[M]*

Earth's orbit
*orbite[F] terrestre*

umbra shadow
*cône[M] d'ombre[F]*

Moon
*Lune[F]*

Sun
*Soleil[M]*

penumbra shadow
*cône[M] de pénombre[F]*

Earth
*Terre[F]*

Moon's orbit
*orbite[F] lunaire*

partial eclipse
*éclipse[F] partielle*

total eclipse
*éclipse[F] totale*

# Moon
*Lune*[F]

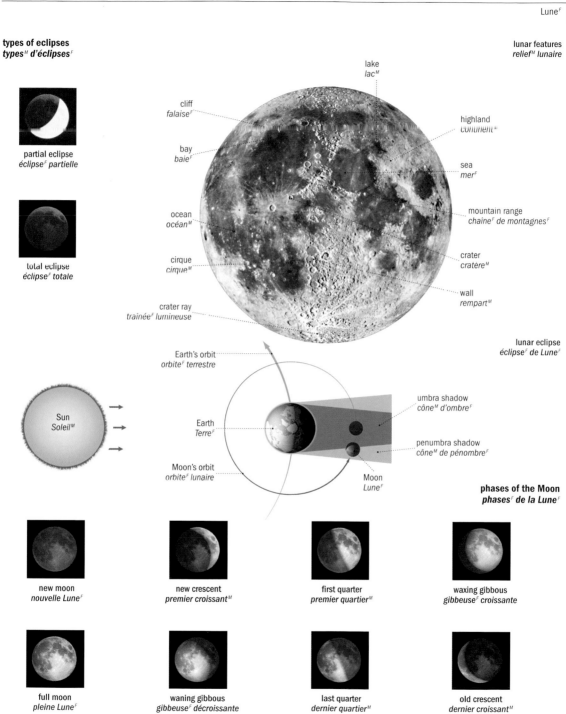

**types of eclipses**
*types*[M] *d'éclipses*[F]

partial eclipse
*éclipse*[F] *partielle*

total eclipse
*éclipse*[F] *totale*

**lunar features**
*relief*[M] *lunaire*

lake
*lac*[M]

cliff
*falaise*[F]

bay
*baie*[F]

ocean
*océan*[M]

cirque
*cirque*[M]

crater ray
*trainée*[F] *lumineuse*

highland
*continent*[M]

sea
*mer*[F]

mountain range
*chaîne*[F] *de montagnes*[F]

crater
*cratère*[M]

wall
*rempart*[M]

**lunar eclipse**
*éclipse*[F] *de Lune*[F]

Earth's orbit
*orbite*[F] *terrestre*

Sun
*Soleil*[M]

Earth
*Terre*[F]

Moon's orbit
*orbite*[F] *lunaire*

umbra shadow
*cône*[M] *d'ombre*[F]

penumbra shadow
*cône*[M] *de pénombre*[F]

Moon
*Lune*[F]

**phases of the Moon**
*phases*[F] *de la Lune*[F]

new moon
*nouvelle Lune*[F]

new crescent
*premier croissant*[M]

first quarter
*premier quartier*[M]

waxing gibbous
*gibbeuse*[F] *croissante*

full moon
*pleine Lune*[F]

waning gibbous
*gibbeuse*[F] *décroissante*

last quarter
*dernier quartier*[M]

old crescent
*dernier croissant*[M]

# galaxy

galaxie[F]

**Milky Way**
*Voie[F] Lactée*

Milky Way (seen from above)
*Voie[F] Lactée (vue[F] de dessus[M])*

Milky Way (side view)
*Voie[F] Lactée (vue[F] de profil[M])*

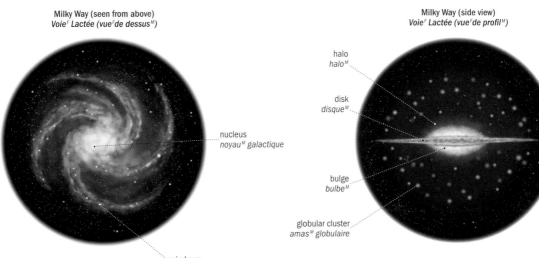

halo
*halo[M]*

disk
*disque[M]*

nucleus
*noyau[M] galactique*

bulge
*bulbe[M]*

globular cluster
*amas[M] globulaire*

spiral arm
*bras[M] spiral*

# comet

comète[F]

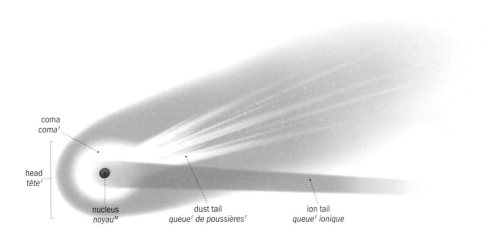

coma
*coma[F]*

head
*tête[F]*

nucleus
*noyau[M]*

dust tail
*queue[F] de poussières[F]*

ion tail
*queue[F] ionique*

# Hubble space telescope

télescope*M* spatial Hubble

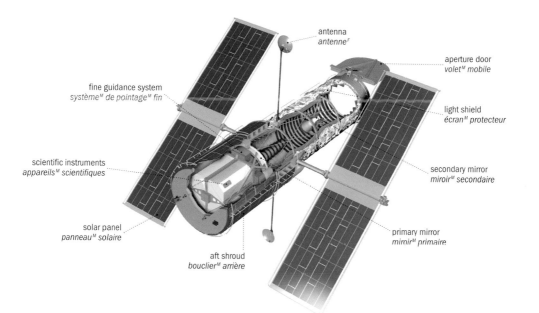

antenna
antenne*F*

aperture door
volet*M* mobile

fine guidance system
système*M* de pointage*M* fin

light shield
écran*M* protecteur

scientific instruments
appareils*M* scientifiques

secondary mirror
miroir*M* secondaire

solar panel
panneau*M* solaire

primary mirror
miroir*M* primaire

aft shroud
bouclier*M* arrière

# astronomical observatory

observatoire*M* astronomique

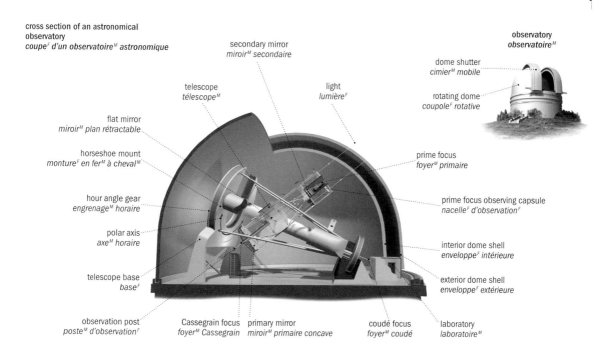

cross section of an astronomical observatory
coupe*F* d'un observatoire*M* astronomique

secondary mirror
miroir*M* secondaire

light
lumière*F*

observatory
observatoire*M*

dome shutter
cimier*M* mobile

rotating dome
coupole*F* rotative

telescope
télescope*M*

flat mirror
miroir*M* plan rétractable

prime focus
foyer*M* primaire

horseshoe mount
monture*F* en fer*M* à cheval*M*

hour angle gear
engrenage*M* horaire

prime focus observing capsule
nacelle*F* d'observation*F*

polar axis
axe*M* horaire

interior dome shell
enveloppe*F* intérieure

telescope base
base*F*

exterior dome shell
enveloppe*F* extérieure

observation post
poste*M* d'observation*F*

Cassegrain focus
foyer*M* Cassegrain

primary mirror
miroir*M* primaire concave

coudé focus
foyer*M* coudé

laboratory
laboratoire*M*

# refracting telescope

lunette<sup>F</sup> astronomique

ASTRONOMY

finderscope
chercheur<sup>M</sup>

cradle
bride<sup>F</sup> de fixation<sup>F</sup>

main tube
tube<sup>M</sup>

dew shield
pare-soleil<sup>M</sup>

eyepiece
oculaire<sup>M</sup>

eyepiece holder
tube<sup>M</sup> porte-oculaire<sup>M</sup>

star diagonal
oculaire<sup>M</sup> coudé

focusing knob
bouton<sup>M</sup> de mise<sup>F</sup> au point<sup>M</sup>

azimuth fine adjustment
réglage<sup>M</sup> micrométrique (azimut<sup>M</sup>)

altitude fine adjustment
réglage<sup>M</sup> micrométrique (latitude<sup>F</sup>)

fork
fourche<sup>F</sup>

tripod accessories shelf
plateau<sup>M</sup> pour accessoires<sup>M</sup>

declination setting scale
cercle<sup>M</sup> de déclinaison<sup>F</sup>

azimuth clamp
vis<sup>F</sup> de blocage<sup>M</sup> (azimut<sup>M</sup>)

altitude clamp
vis<sup>F</sup> de blocage<sup>M</sup> (latitude<sup>F</sup>)

right ascension setting scale
cercle<sup>M</sup> d'ascension<sup>F</sup> droite

counterweight
contrepoids<sup>M</sup>

tripod
trépied<sup>M</sup>

cross section of a refracting telescope
coupe<sup>F</sup> d'une lunette<sup>F</sup> astronomique

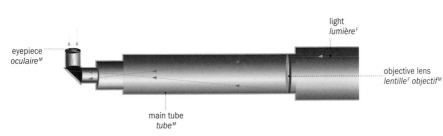

eyepiece
oculaire<sup>M</sup>

light
lumière<sup>F</sup>

objective lens
lentille<sup>F</sup> objectif<sup>M</sup>

main tube
tube<sup>M</sup>

# reflecting telescope

télescope<sup>M</sup>

finderscope
chercheur<sup>M</sup>

cycpiccc
oculaire<sup>M</sup>

cradlc
bride<sup>F</sup> de fixation<sup>F</sup>

support
support<sup>M</sup> de fixation<sup>F</sup>

main tube
tube<sup>M</sup>

focusing knob
bouton<sup>M</sup> de mise<sup>F</sup> au point<sup>M</sup>

declination setting scale
cercle<sup>M</sup> de déclinaison<sup>F</sup>

right ascension setting scale
cercle<sup>M</sup> d'ascension<sup>F</sup> droite

azimuth clamp
vis<sup>F</sup> de blocage<sup>M</sup> (azimut<sup>M</sup>)

azimuth fine adjustment
réglage<sup>M</sup> micrométrique (azimut<sup>M</sup>)

altitude clamp
vis<sup>F</sup> de blocage<sup>M</sup> (latitude<sup>F</sup>)

altitude fine adjustment
réglage<sup>M</sup> micrométrique
(latitude<sup>F</sup>)

**cross section of a reflecting telescope**
coupe<sup>F</sup> d'un télescope<sup>M</sup>

eyepiece
oculaire<sup>M</sup>

secondary mirror
miroir<sup>M</sup> secondaire

concave primary mirror
miroir<sup>M</sup> primaire concave

light
lumière<sup>F</sup>

main tube
tube<sup>M</sup>

# spacesuit

scaphandre*M* spatial

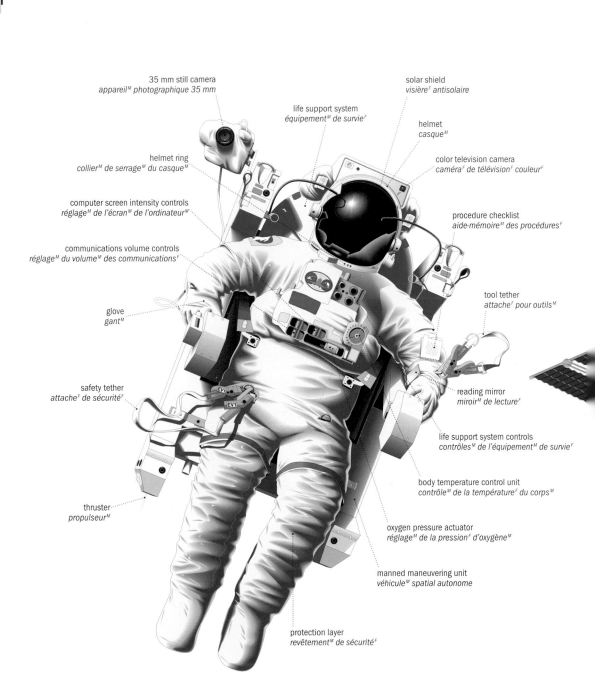

35 mm still camera
*appareil*M *photographique 35 mm*

solar shield
*visière*F *antisolaire*

life support system
*équipement*M *de survie*F

helmet
*casque*M

helmet ring
*collier*M *de serrage*M *du casque*M

color television camera
*caméra*F *de télévision*F *couleur*F

computer screen intensity controls
*réglage*M *de l'écran*M *de l'ordinateur*M

procedure checklist
*aide-mémoire*M *des procédures*F

communications volume controls
*réglage*M *du volume*M *des communications*F

tool tether
*attache*F *pour outils*M

glove
*gant*M

safety tether
*attache*F *de sécurité*F

reading mirror
*miroir*M *de lecture*F

life support system controls
*contrôles*M *de l'équipement*M *de survie*F

thruster
*propulseur*M

body temperature control unit
*contrôle*M *de la température*F *du corps*M

oxygen pressure actuator
*réglage*M *de la pression*F *d'oxygène*M

manned maneuvering unit
*véhicule*M *spatial autonome*

protection layer
*revêtement*M *de sécurité*F

# international space station

station<sup>F</sup> spatiale internationale

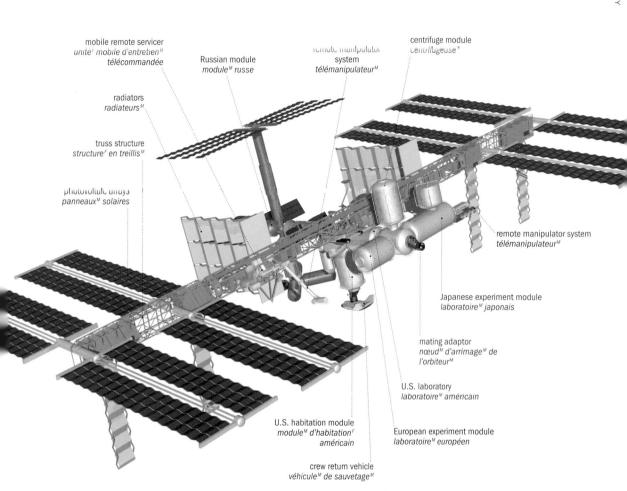

mobile remote servicer
*unité* mobile d'entretien<sup>M</sup>
*télécommandée*

Russian module
*module<sup>M</sup> russe*

remote manipulator
system
*télémanipulateur<sup>M</sup>*

centrifuge module
*centrifugeuse*

radiators
*radiateurs<sup>M</sup>*

truss structure
*structure<sup>F</sup> en treillis<sup>M</sup>*

photovoltaic arrays
*panneaux<sup>M</sup> solaires*

remote manipulator system
*télémanipulateur<sup>M</sup>*

Japanese experiment module
*laboratoire<sup>M</sup> japonais*

mating adaptor
*nœud<sup>M</sup> d'arrimage<sup>M</sup> de
l'orbiteur<sup>M</sup>*

U.S. laboratory
*laboratoire<sup>M</sup> américain*

U.S. habitation module
*module<sup>M</sup> d'habitation<sup>F</sup>
américain*

European experiment module
*laboratoire<sup>M</sup> européen*

crew return vehicle
*véhicule<sup>M</sup> de sauvetage<sup>M</sup>*

# space shuttle

navette<sup>F</sup> spatiale

**space shuttle at takeoff**
*navette<sup>F</sup> spatiale au décollage<sup>M</sup>*

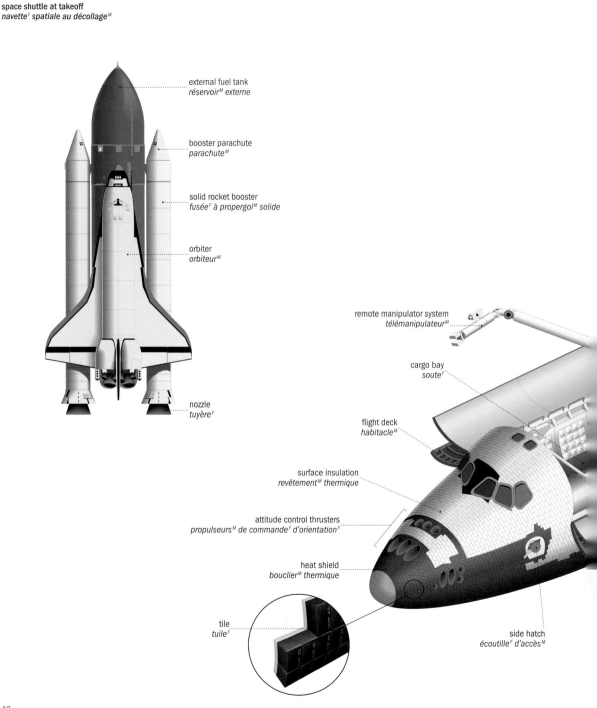

external fuel tank
*réservoir<sup>M</sup> externe*

booster parachute
*parachute<sup>M</sup>*

solid rocket booster
*fusée<sup>F</sup> à propergol<sup>M</sup> solide*

orbiter
*orbiteur<sup>M</sup>*

nozzle
*tuyère<sup>F</sup>*

remote manipulator system
*télémanipulateur<sup>M</sup>*

cargo bay
*soute<sup>F</sup>*

flight deck
*habitacle<sup>M</sup>*

surface insulation
*revêtement<sup>M</sup> thermique*

attitude control thrusters
*propulseurs<sup>M</sup> de commande<sup>F</sup> d'orientation<sup>F</sup>*

heat shield
*bouclier<sup>M</sup> thermique*

tile
*tuile<sup>F</sup>*

side hatch
*écoutille<sup>F</sup> d'accès<sup>M</sup>*

orbiter
*orbiteur*^M

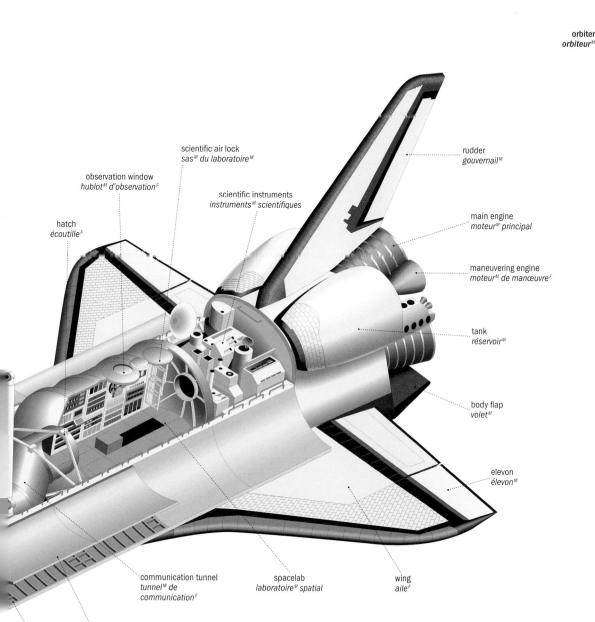

scientific air lock
*sas*^M *du laboratoire*^M

observation window
*hublot*^M *d'observation*^F

scientific instruments
*instruments*^M *scientifiques*

hatch
*écoutille*^F

rudder
*gouvernail*^M

main engine
*moteur*^M *principal*

maneuvering engine
*moteur*^M *de manœuvre*^F

tank
*réservoir*^M

body flap
*volet*^M

elevon
*élevon*^M

communication tunnel
*tunnel*^M *de
communication*^F

spacelab
*laboratoire*^M *spatial*

wing
*aile*^F

radiator panel
*panneau*^M *de refroidissement*^M

cargo bay door
*porte*^F *de la soute*^F

# configuration of the continents

configuration<sup>F</sup> des continents<sup>M</sup>

planisphere
*planisphère*<sup>M</sup>

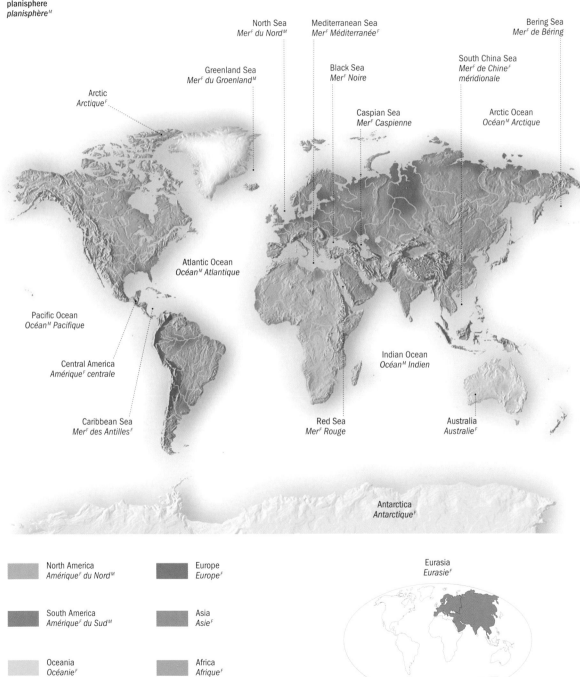

North Sea
*Mer<sup>F</sup> du Nord*<sup>M</sup>

Mediterranean Sea
*Mer<sup>F</sup> Méditerranée*<sup>F</sup>

Bering Sea
*Mer<sup>F</sup> de Béring*

Greenland Sea
*Mer<sup>F</sup> du Groenland*<sup>M</sup>

Black Sea
*Mer<sup>F</sup> Noire*

South China Sea
*Mer<sup>F</sup> de Chine*<sup>F</sup>
*méridionale*

Arctic
*Arctique*<sup>F</sup>

Caspian Sea
*Mer<sup>F</sup> Caspienne*

Arctic Ocean
*Océan*<sup>M</sup> *Arctique*

Atlantic Ocean
*Océan*<sup>M</sup> *Atlantique*

Pacific Ocean
*Océan*<sup>M</sup> *Pacifique*

Central America
*Amérique*<sup>F</sup> *centrale*

Indian Ocean
*Océan*<sup>M</sup> *Indien*

Caribbean Sea
*Mer<sup>F</sup> des Antilles*<sup>F</sup>

Red Sea
*Mer<sup>F</sup> Rouge*

Australia
*Australie*<sup>F</sup>

Antarctica
*Antarctique*<sup>F</sup>

North America
*Amérique*<sup>F</sup> *du Nord*<sup>M</sup>

Europe
*Europe*<sup>F</sup>

Eurasia
*Eurasie*<sup>F</sup>

South America
*Amérique*<sup>F</sup> *du Sud*<sup>M</sup>

Asia
*Asie*<sup>F</sup>

Oceania
*Océanie*<sup>F</sup>

Africa
*Afrique*<sup>F</sup>

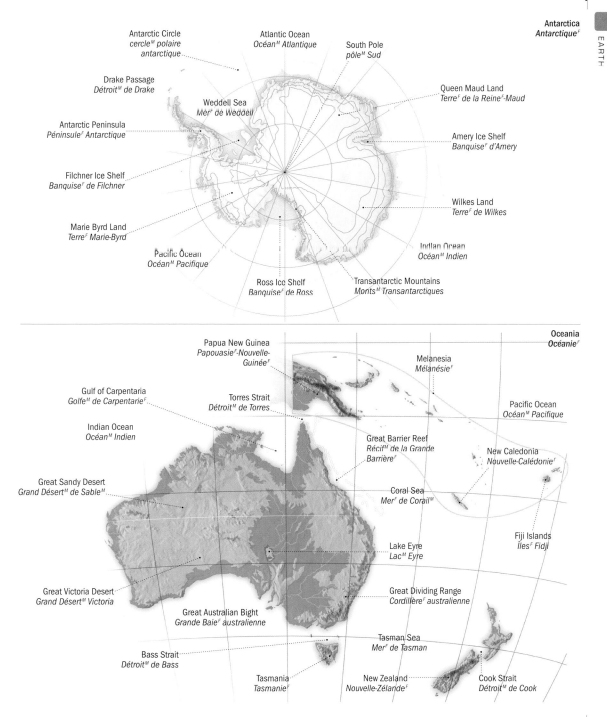

Antarctic Circle
cercle<sup>M</sup> polaire
antarctique

Drake Passage
Détroit<sup>M</sup> de Drake

Weddell Sea
Mer<sup>F</sup> de Weddell

Atlantic Ocean
Océan<sup>M</sup> Atlantique

South Pole
pôle<sup>M</sup> Sud

Antarctica
Antarctique<sup>F</sup>

Queen Maud Land
Terre<sup>F</sup> de la Reine<sup>F</sup>-Maud

Antarctic Peninsula
Péninsule<sup>F</sup> Antarctique

Amery Ice Shelf
Banquise<sup>F</sup> d'Amery

Filchner Ice Shelf
Banquise<sup>F</sup> de Filchner

Wilkes Land
Terre<sup>F</sup> de Wilkes

Marie Byrd Land
Terre<sup>F</sup> Marie-Byrd

Pacific Ocean
Océan<sup>M</sup> Pacifique

Indian Ocean
Océan<sup>M</sup> Indien

Ross Ice Shelf
Banquise<sup>F</sup> de Ross

Transantarctic Mountains
Monts<sup>M</sup> Transantarctiques

Papua New Guinea
Papouasie<sup>F</sup>-Nouvelle-
Guinée<sup>F</sup>

Melanesia
Mélanésie<sup>F</sup>

Oceania
Océanie<sup>F</sup>

Gulf of Carpentaria
Golfe<sup>M</sup> de Carpentarie<sup>F</sup>

Torres Strait
Détroit<sup>M</sup> de Torres

Pacific Ocean
Océan<sup>M</sup> Pacifique

Indian Ocean
Océan<sup>M</sup> Indien

Great Barrier Reef
Récif<sup>M</sup> de la Grande
Barrière<sup>F</sup>

New Caledonia
Nouvelle-Calédonie<sup>F</sup>

Great Sandy Desert
Grand Désert<sup>M</sup> de Sable<sup>M</sup>

Coral Sea
Mer<sup>F</sup> de Corail<sup>M</sup>

Fiji Islands
Îles<sup>F</sup> Fidji

Great Victoria Desert
Grand Désert<sup>M</sup> Victoria

Lake Eyre
Lac<sup>M</sup> Eyre

Great Dividing Range
Cordillère<sup>F</sup> australienne

Great Australian Bight
Grande Baie<sup>F</sup> australienne

Tasman Sea
Mer<sup>F</sup> de Tasman

Bass Strait
Détroit<sup>M</sup> de Bass

Tasmania
Tasmanie<sup>F</sup>

New Zealand
Nouvelle-Zélande<sup>F</sup>

Cook Strait
Détroit<sup>M</sup> de Cook

## configuration of the continents

**North America**
*Amérique<sup>F</sup> du Nord<sup>M</sup>*

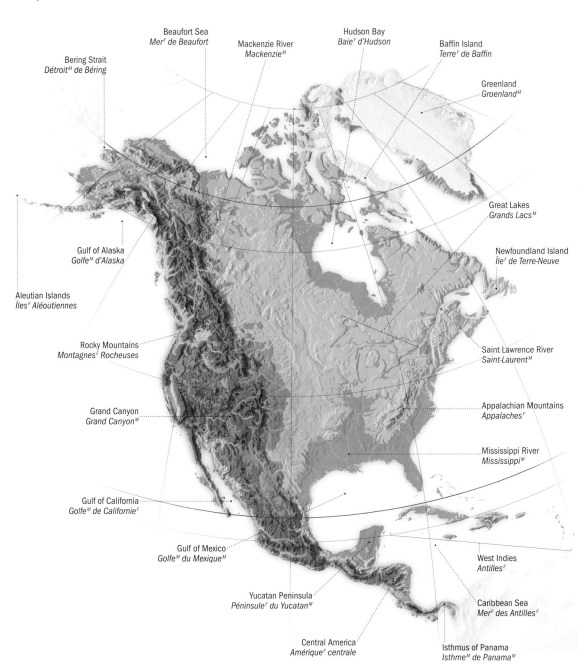

Beaufort Sea
*Mer<sup>F</sup> de Beaufort*

Mackenzie River
*Mackenzie<sup>M</sup>*

Hudson Bay
*Baie<sup>F</sup> d'Hudson*

Baffin Island
*Terre<sup>F</sup> de Baffin*

Bering Strait
*Détroit<sup>M</sup> de Béring*

Greenland
*Groenland<sup>M</sup>*

Gulf of Alaska
*Golfe<sup>M</sup> d'Alaska*

Great Lakes
*Grands Lacs<sup>M</sup>*

Aleutian Islands
*Îles<sup>F</sup> Aléoutiennes*

Newfoundland Island
*Île<sup>F</sup> de Terre-Neuve*

Rocky Mountains
*Montagnes<sup>F</sup> Rocheuses*

Saint Lawrence River
*Saint-Laurent<sup>M</sup>*

Grand Canyon
*Grand Canyon<sup>M</sup>*

Appalachian Mountains
*Appalaches<sup>F</sup>*

Mississippi River
*Mississippi<sup>M</sup>*

Gulf of California
*Golfe<sup>M</sup> de Californie<sup>F</sup>*

Gulf of Mexico
*Golfe<sup>M</sup> du Mexique<sup>M</sup>*

West Indies
*Antilles<sup>F</sup>*

Yucatan Peninsula
*Péninsule<sup>F</sup> du Yucatan<sup>M</sup>*

Caribbean Sea
*Mer<sup>F</sup> des Antilles<sup>F</sup>*

Central America
*Amérique<sup>F</sup> centrale*

Isthmus of Panama
*Isthme<sup>M</sup> de Panama<sup>M</sup>*

**South America**
*Amérique<sup>F</sup> du Sud<sup>M</sup>*

Orinoco River
*Orénoque<sup>M</sup>*

Amazon River
*Amazone<sup>F</sup>*

Gulf of Panama
*Golfe<sup>M</sup> de Panama<sup>M</sup>*

Equator
*équateur<sup>M</sup>*

Andes Cordillera
*Cordillère<sup>F</sup> des Andes<sup>M</sup>*

Lake Titicaca
*Lac<sup>M</sup> Titicaca*

Atacama Desert
*Désert<sup>M</sup> d'Atacama*

Paraná River
*Paraná<sup>M</sup>*

Patagonia
*Patagonie<sup>F</sup>*

Falkland Islands
*Îles<sup>F</sup> Falkland*

Tierra del Fuego
*Terre<sup>F</sup> de Feu<sup>M</sup>*

Cape Horn
*Cap<sup>M</sup> Horn*

Drake Passage
*Détroit<sup>M</sup> de Drake*

## configuration of the continents

**Europe**
*Europe*[F]

Barents Sea
*Mer*[F] *de Barents*

Ural Mountains
*Monts*[M] *Oural*[M]

Lake Ladoga
*Lac*[M] *Ladoga*

Kola Peninsula
*Péninsule*[F] *de Kola*

Volga River
*Volga*[F]

Gulf of Bothnia
*Golfe*[M] *de Botnie*[F]

Norwegian Sea
*Mer*[F] *de Norvège*[F]

Dnieper River
*Dniepr*[M]

Iceland
*Islande*[F]

North Sea
*Mer*[F] *du Nord*[M]

Scandinavian Peninsula
*Péninsule*[F] *Scandinave*

Baltic Sea
*Mer*[F] *Baltique*[F]

Irish Sea
*Mer*[F] *d'Irlande*[F]

Atlantic Ocean
*Océan*[M] *Atlantique*

English Channel
*Manche*[F]

Vistula River
*Vistule*[F]

Alps
*Alpes*[F]

Black Sea
*Mer*[F] *Noire*

Iberian Peninsula
*Péninsule*[F] *Ibérique*

Strait of Gibraltar
*Détroit*[M] *de Gibraltar*

Pyrenees
*Pyrénées*[F]

Danube River
*Danube*[M]

Balkan Peninsula
*Péninsule*[F] *des Balkans*[M]

Carpathian Mountains
*Carpates*[F]

Mediterranean Sea
*Mer*[F] *Méditerranée*[F]

Adriatic Sea
*Mer*[F] *Adriatique*

Aegean Sea
*Mer*[F] *Égée*

Asia
*Asie^F*

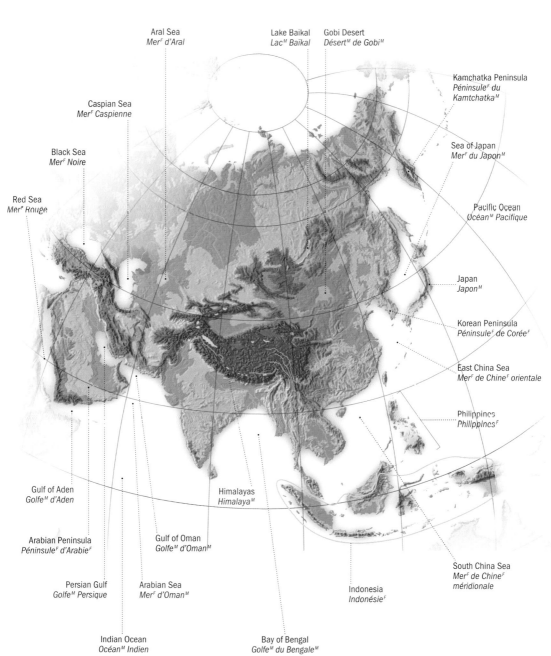

Aral Sea
*Mer^F d'Aral*

Lake Baikal
*Lac^M Baïkal*

Gobi Desert
*Désert^M de Gobi^M*

Kamchatka Peninsula
*Péninsule^F du Kamtchatka^M*

Caspian Sea
*Mer^F Caspienne*

Sea of Japan
*Mer^F du Japon^M*

Black Sea
*Mer^F Noire*

Pacific Ocean
*Océan^M Pacifique*

Red Sea
*Mer^F Rouge*

Japan
*Japon^M*

Korean Peninsula
*Péninsule^F de Corée^F*

East China Sea
*Mer^F de Chine^F orientale*

Philippines
*Philippines^F*

Gulf of Aden
*Golfe^M d'Aden*

Himalayas
*Himalaya^M*

Arabian Peninsula
*Péninsule^F d'Arabie^F*

Gulf of Oman
*Golfe^M d'Oman^M*

South China Sea
*Mer^F de Chine^F méridionale*

Persian Gulf
*Golfe^M Persique*

Arabian Sea
*Mer^F d'Oman^M*

Indonesia
*Indonésie^F*

Indian Ocean
*Océan^M Indien*

Bay of Bengal
*Golfe^M du Bengale^M*

configuration of the continents

EARTH

**Africa**
*Afrique*<sup>F</sup>

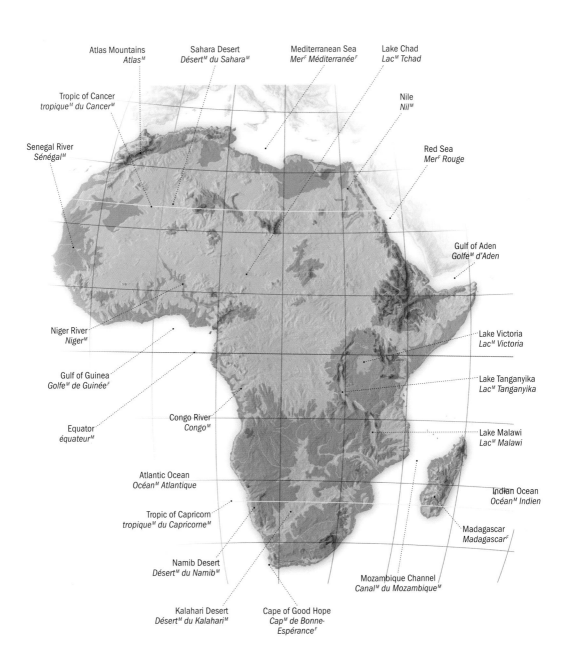

Atlas Mountains
*Atlas*<sup>M</sup>

Sahara Desert
*Désert*<sup>M</sup> *du Sahara*<sup>M</sup>

Mediterranean Sea
*Mer*<sup>F</sup> *Méditerranée*<sup>F</sup>

Lake Chad
*Lac*<sup>M</sup> *Tchad*

Tropic of Cancer
*tropique*<sup>M</sup> *du Cancer*<sup>M</sup>

Nile
*Nil*<sup>M</sup>

Senegal River
*Sénégal*<sup>M</sup>

Red Sea
*Mer*<sup>F</sup> *Rouge*

Gulf of Aden
*Golfe*<sup>M</sup> *d'Aden*

Niger River
*Niger*<sup>M</sup>

Lake Victoria
*Lac*<sup>M</sup> *Victoria*

Gulf of Guinea
*Golfe*<sup>M</sup> *de Guinée*<sup>F</sup>

Lake Tanganyika
*Lac*<sup>M</sup> *Tanganyika*

Congo River
*Congo*<sup>M</sup>

Equator
*équateur*<sup>M</sup>

Lake Malawi
*Lac*<sup>M</sup> *Malawi*

Atlantic Ocean
*Océan*<sup>M</sup> *Atlantique*

Indian Ocean
*Océan*<sup>M</sup> *Indien*

Tropic of Capricorn
*tropique*<sup>M</sup> *du Capricorne*<sup>M</sup>

Madagascar
*Madagascar*<sup>F</sup>

Namib Desert
*Désert*<sup>M</sup> *du Namib*<sup>M</sup>

Mozambique Channel
*Canal*<sup>M</sup> *du Mozambique*<sup>M</sup>

Kalahari Desert
*Désert*<sup>M</sup> *du Kalahari*<sup>M</sup>

Cape of Good Hope
*Cap*<sup>M</sup> *de Bonne-
Espérance*<sup>F</sup>

# cartography

cartographie[F]

**Earth coordinate system**
*coordonnées[F] terrestres*

EARTH

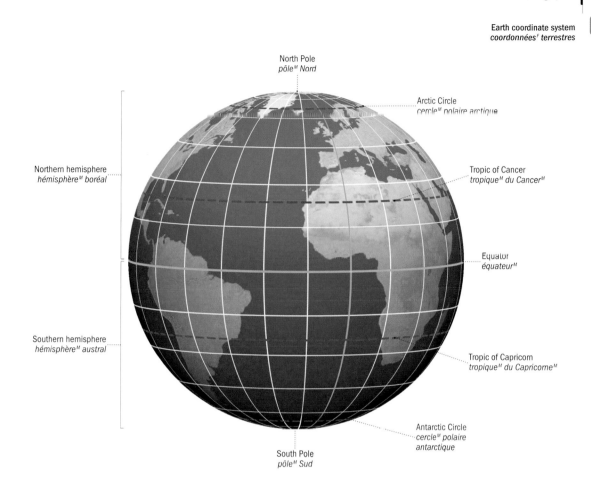

North Pole
*pôle[M] Nord*

Arctic Circle
*cercle[M] polaire arctique*

Tropic of Cancer
*tropique[M] du Cancer[M]*

Northern hemisphere
*hémisphère[M] boréal*

Equator
*équateur[M]*

Southern hemisphere
*hémisphère[M] austral*

Tropic of Capricorn
*tropique[M] du Capricorne[M]*

Antarctic Circle
*cercle[M] polaire antarctique*

South Pole
*pôle[M] Sud*

**hemispheres**
*hémisphères[M]*

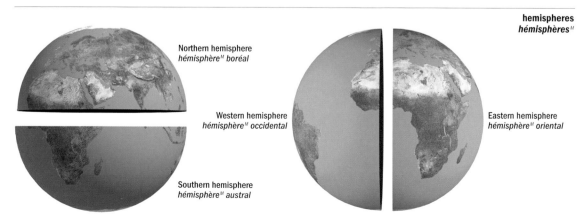

Northern hemisphere
*hémisphère[M] boréal*

Western hemisphere
*hémisphère[M] occidental*

Eastern hemisphere
*hémisphère[M] oriental*

Southern hemisphere
*hémisphère[M] austral*

**grid system**
*divisions<sup>F</sup> cartographiques*

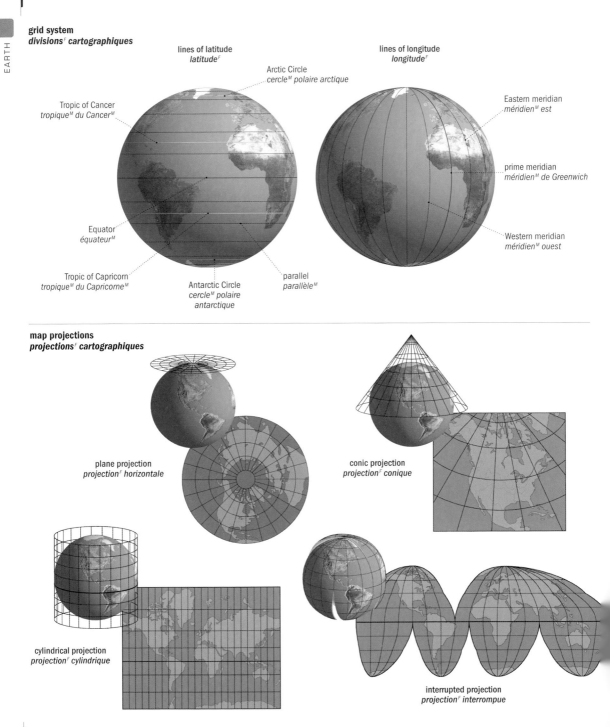

lines of latitude
*latitude<sup>F</sup>*

Arctic Circle
*cercle<sup>M</sup> polaire arctique*

Tropic of Cancer
*tropique<sup>M</sup> du Cancer<sup>M</sup>*

Equator
*équateur<sup>M</sup>*

Tropic of Capricorn
*tropique<sup>M</sup> du Capricorne<sup>M</sup>*

Antarctic Circle
*cercle<sup>M</sup> polaire antarctique*

parallel
*parallèle<sup>M</sup>*

lines of longitude
*longitude<sup>F</sup>*

Eastern meridian
*méridien<sup>M</sup> est*

prime meridian
*méridien<sup>M</sup> de Greenwich*

Western meridian
*méridien<sup>M</sup> ouest*

**map projections**
*projections<sup>F</sup> cartographiques*

plane projection
*projection<sup>F</sup> horizontale*

conic projection
*projection<sup>F</sup> conique*

cylindrical projection
*projection<sup>F</sup> cylindrique*

interrupted projection
*projection<sup>F</sup> interrompue*

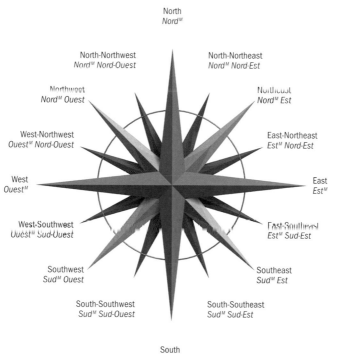

North
Nord<sup>M</sup>

North-Northwest
Nord<sup>M</sup> Nord-Ouest

North-Northeast
Nord<sup>M</sup> Nord-Est

Northwest
Nord<sup>M</sup> Ouest

Northeast
Nord<sup>M</sup> Est

West-Northwest
Ouest<sup>M</sup> Nord-Ouest

East-Northeast
Est<sup>M</sup> Nord-Est

West
Ouest<sup>M</sup>

East
Est<sup>M</sup>

West-Southwest
Ouest<sup>M</sup> Sud-Ouest

East-Southeast
Est<sup>M</sup> Sud-Est

Southwest
Sud<sup>M</sup> Ouest

Southeast
Sud<sup>M</sup> Est

South-Southwest
Sud<sup>M</sup> Sud-Ouest

South-Southeast
Sud<sup>M</sup> Sud-Est

South
Sud<sup>M</sup>

political map
carte<sup>F</sup> politique

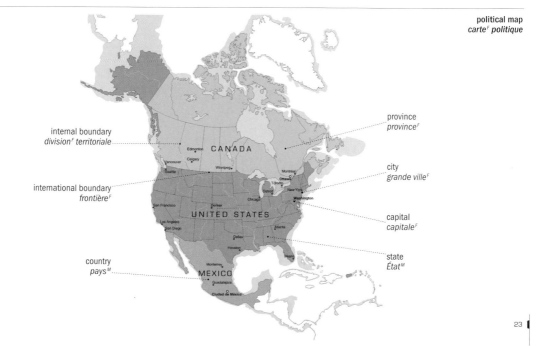

province
province<sup>F</sup>

internal boundary
division<sup>F</sup> territoriale

city
grande ville<sup>F</sup>

international boundary
frontière<sup>F</sup>

capital
capitale<sup>F</sup>

country
pays<sup>M</sup>

state
État<sup>M</sup>

**physical map**
*carte^F physique*

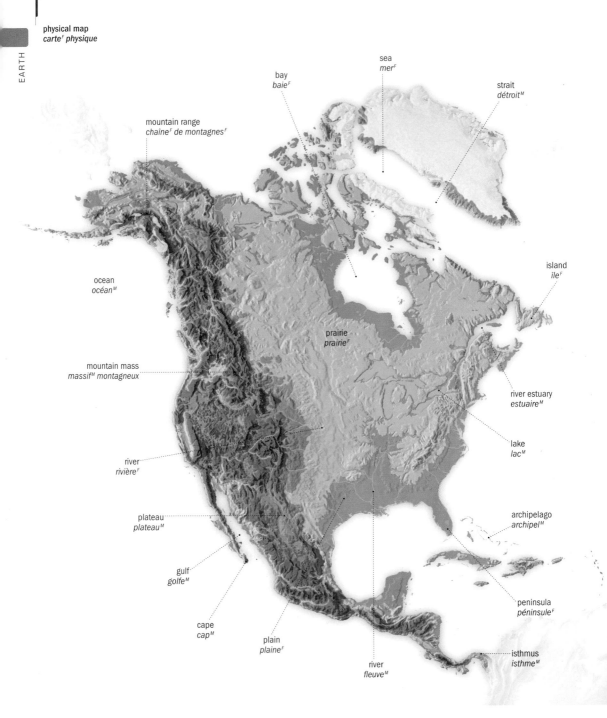

sea
*mer^F*

bay
*baie^F*

strait
*détroit^M*

mountain range
*chaîne^F de montagnes^F*

ocean
*océan^M*

island
*île^F*

prairie
*prairie^F*

mountain mass
*massif^M montagneux*

river estuary
*estuaire^M*

river
*rivière^F*

lake
*lac^M*

plateau
*plateau^M*

archipelago
*archipel^M*

gulf
*golfe^M*

peninsula
*péninsule^F*

cape
*cap^M*

plain
*plaine^F*

isthmus
*isthme^M*

river
*fleuve^M*

railroad line
chemin^M de fer^M

railroad station
gare^F

bridge
pont^M

park
parc^M

suburbs
banlieue^F

cemetery
cimetière^M

river
fleuve^M

monument
monument^M

woods
bois^M

circular route
boulevard^M périphérique

highway
autoroute^F

traffic circle
rond-point^M

district
arrondissement^M

street
rue^F

avenue
avenue^F

public building
édifice^M public

boulevard
boulevard^M

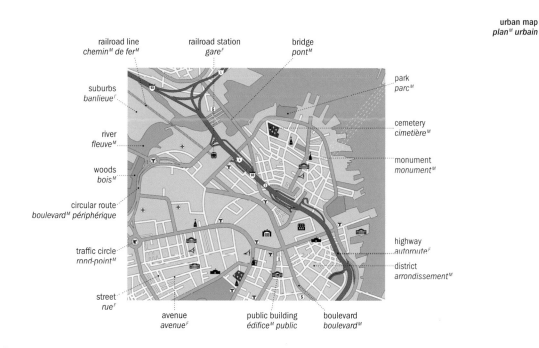

highway number
numéro^M d'autoroute^F

road
route^F

highway
autoroute^F

road number
numéro^M de route^F

rest area
aire^F de repos^M

service area
aire^F de service^M

airport
aéroport^M

national park
parc^M national

belt highway
autoroute^F de ceinture^F

scenic route
parcours^M pittoresque

secondary road
route^F secondaire

point of interest
curiosité^F

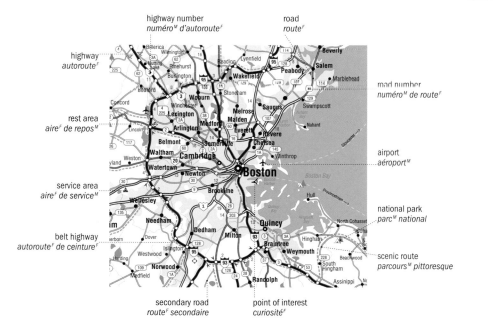

# section of the Earth's crust

coupe<sup>F</sup> de la croûte<sup>F</sup> terrestre

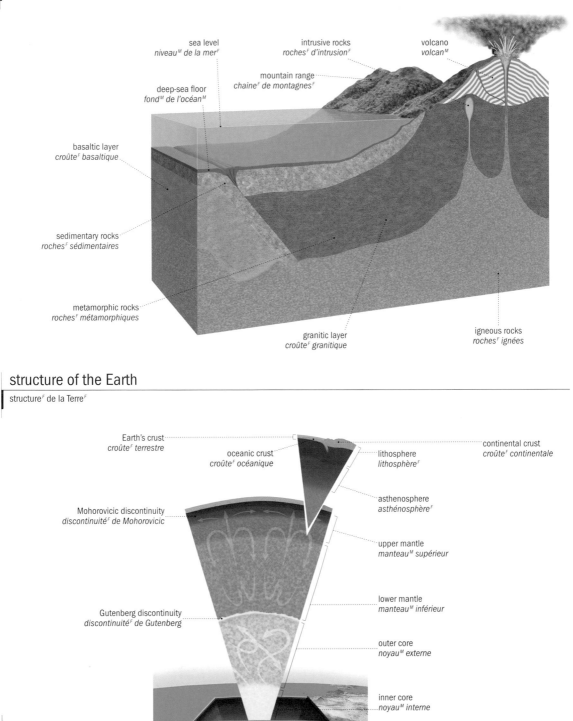

sea level
niveau<sup>M</sup> de la mer<sup>F</sup>

intrusive rocks
roches<sup>F</sup> d'intrusion<sup>F</sup>

volcano
volcan<sup>M</sup>

mountain range
chaîne<sup>F</sup> de montagnes<sup>F</sup>

deep-sea floor
fond<sup>M</sup> de l'océan<sup>M</sup>

basaltic layer
croûte<sup>F</sup> basaltique

sedimentary rocks
roches<sup>F</sup> sédimentaires

metamorphic rocks
roches<sup>F</sup> métamorphiques

granitic layer
croûte<sup>F</sup> granitique

igneous rocks
roches<sup>F</sup> ignées

# structure of the Earth

structure<sup>F</sup> de la Terre<sup>F</sup>

Earth's crust
croûte<sup>F</sup> terrestre

oceanic crust
croûte<sup>F</sup> océanique

continental crust
croûte<sup>F</sup> continentale

lithosphere
lithosphère<sup>F</sup>

Mohorovicic discontinuity
discontinuité<sup>F</sup> de Mohorovicic

asthenosphere
asthénosphère<sup>F</sup>

upper mantle
manteau<sup>M</sup> supérieur

lower mantle
manteau<sup>M</sup> inférieur

Gutenberg discontinuity
discontinuité<sup>F</sup> de Gutenberg

outer core
noyau<sup>M</sup> externe

inner core
noyau<sup>M</sup> interne

## tectonic plates
plaques[F] tectoniques

North American Plate
*plaque[F] nord-américaine*

Cocos Plate
*plaque[F] des îles[F] Cocos*

Caribbean Plate
*plaque[F] des Caraïbes*

Pacific Plate
*plaque[F] pacifique*

Nazca Plate
*plaque[F] Nazca*

Scotia Plate
*plaque[F] Scotia*

South American Plate
*plaque[F] sud-américaine*

African Plate
*plaque[F] africaine*

Eurasian Plate
*plaque[F] eurasiatique*

Philippine Plate
*plaque[F] philippine*

Australian-Indian Plate
*plaque[F] indo-australienne*

Antarctic Plate
*plaque[F] antarctique*

subduction
*subduction[F]*

divergent plate boundaries
*plaques[F] divergentes*

convergent plate
boundaries
*plaques[F] convergentes*

transform plate
boundaries
*plaques[F] transformantes*

## earthquake
séisme[M]

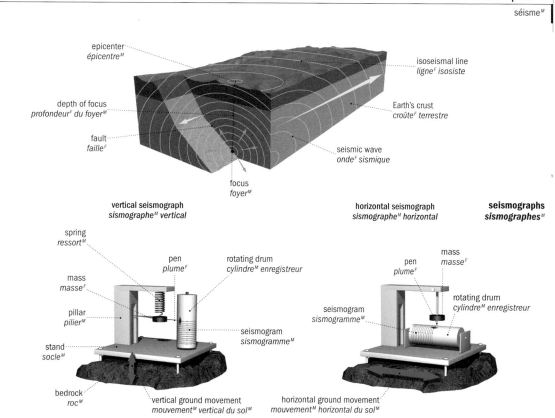

epicenter
*épicentre[M]*

depth of focus
*profondeur[F] du foyer[M]*

fault
*faille[F]*

isoseismal line
*ligne[F] isosiste*

Earth's crust
*croûte[F] terrestre*

seismic wave
*onde[F] sismique*

focus
*foyer[M]*

vertical seismograph
*sismographe[M] vertical*

horizontal seismograph
*sismographe[M] horizontal*

**seismographs**
***sismographes*[M]**

spring
*ressort[M]*

mass
*masse[F]*

pillar
*pilier[M]*

stand
*socle[M]*

bedrock
*roc[M]*

pen
*plume[F]*

rotating drum
*cylindre[M] enregistreur*

seismogram
*sismogramme[M]*

vertical ground movement
*mouvement[M] vertical du sol[M]*

mass
*masse[F]*

pen
*plume[F]*

rotating drum
*cylindre[M] enregistreur*

seismogram
*sismogramme[M]*

horizontal ground movement
*mouvement[M] horizontal du sol[M]*

# volcano

volcan<sup>M</sup>

**volcano during eruption**
*volcan<sup>M</sup> en éruption<sup>F</sup>*

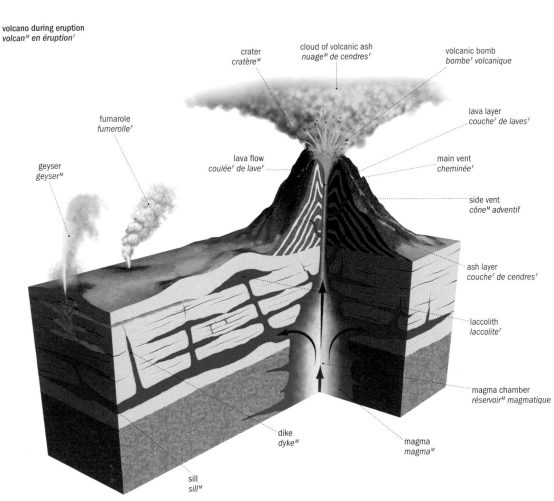

crater
*cratère<sup>M</sup>*

cloud of volcanic ash
*nuage<sup>M</sup> de cendres<sup>F</sup>*

volcanic bomb
*bombe<sup>F</sup> volcanique*

fumarole
*fumerolle<sup>F</sup>*

lava layer
*couche<sup>F</sup> de laves<sup>F</sup>*

geyser
*geyser<sup>M</sup>*

lava flow
*coulée<sup>F</sup> de lave<sup>F</sup>*

main vent
*cheminée<sup>F</sup>*

side vent
*cône<sup>M</sup> adventif*

ash layer
*couche<sup>F</sup> de cendres<sup>F</sup>*

laccolith
*laccolite<sup>F</sup>*

magma chamber
*réservoir<sup>M</sup> magmatique*

dike
*dyke<sup>M</sup>*

magma
*magma<sup>M</sup>*

sill
*sill<sup>M</sup>*

**examples of volcanoes**
*exemples<sup>M</sup> de volcans<sup>M</sup>*

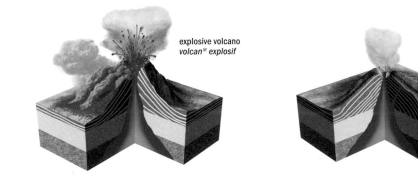

explosive volcano
*volcan<sup>M</sup> explosif*

effusive volcano
*volcan<sup>M</sup> effusif*

# mountain

montagne[F]

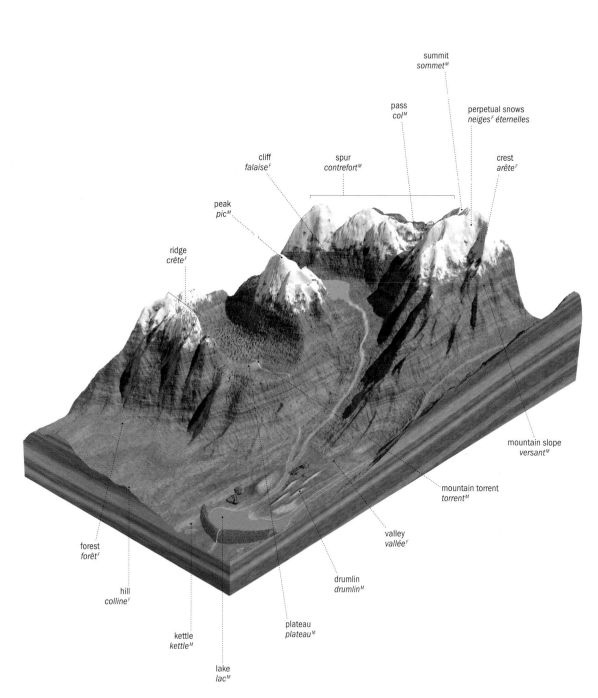

summit
sommet[M]

pass
col[M]

perpetual snows
neiges[F] éternelles

cliff
falaise[F]

spur
contrefort[M]

crest
arête[F]

peak
pic[M]

ridge
crête[F]

mountain slope
versant[M]

mountain torrent
torrent[M]

valley
vallée[F]

forest
forêt[F]

drumlin
drumlin[M]

hill
colline[F]

kettle
kettle[M]

plateau
plateau[M]

lake
lac[M]

# glacier

glacier<sup>M</sup>

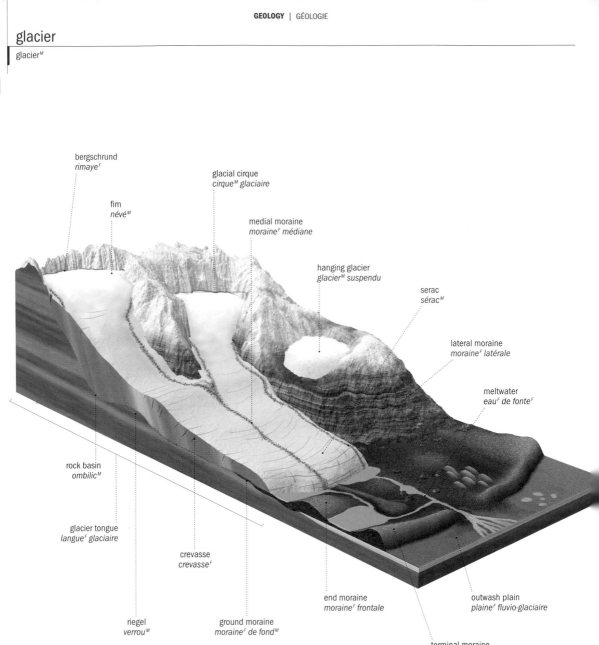

bergschrund
*rimaye*<sup>F</sup>

firn
*névé*<sup>M</sup>

glacial cirque
*cirque*<sup>M</sup> *glaciaire*

medial moraine
*moraine*<sup>F</sup> *médiane*

hanging glacier
*glacier*<sup>M</sup> *suspendu*

serac
*sérac*<sup>M</sup>

lateral moraine
*moraine*<sup>F</sup> *latérale*

meltwater
*eau*<sup>F</sup> *de fonte*<sup>F</sup>

rock basin
*ombilic*<sup>M</sup>

glacier tongue
*langue*<sup>F</sup> *glaciaire*

crevasse
*crevasse*<sup>F</sup>

riegel
*verrou*<sup>M</sup>

ground moraine
*moraine*<sup>F</sup> *de fond*<sup>M</sup>

end moraine
*moraine*<sup>F</sup> *frontale*

outwash plain
*plaine*<sup>F</sup> *fluvio-glaciaire*

terminal moraine
*moraine*<sup>F</sup> *terminale*

# cave
grotte[F]

lapiaz
*lapiaz*[M]

pothole
*aven*[M]

stalactite
*stalactite*[F]

sinkhole
*doline*[F]

gorge
*gorge*[F]

waterfall
*chute*[F]

swallow hole
*gouffre*[M]

gour
*gour*[M]

column
*colonne*[F]

subterranean stream
*rivière*[F] *souterraine*

stalagmite
*stalagmite*[F]

dry gallery
*galerie*[F] *sèche*

resurgence
*résurgence*[F]

water table
*nappe*[F] *phréatique*

# landslides
mouvements[M] de terrain[M]

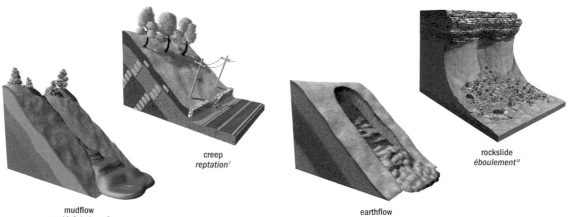

creep
*reptation*[F]

rockslide
*éboulement*[M]

mudflow
*coulée*[F] *de boue*[F]

earthflow
*glissement*[M] *de terrain*[M]

# watercourse

cours<sup>M</sup> d'eau<sup>F</sup>

EARTH

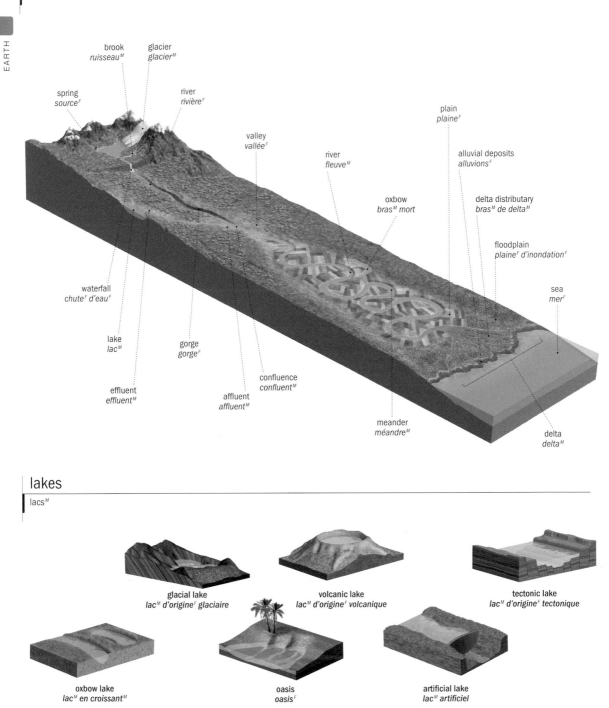

brook
*ruisseau*<sup>M</sup>

glacier
*glacier*<sup>M</sup>

spring
*source*<sup>F</sup>

river
*rivière*<sup>F</sup>

valley
*vallée*<sup>F</sup>

river
*fleuve*<sup>M</sup>

plain
*plaine*<sup>F</sup>

alluvial deposits
*alluvions*<sup>F</sup>

oxbow
*bras*<sup>M</sup> *mort*

delta distributary
*bras*<sup>M</sup> *de delta*<sup>M</sup>

floodplain
*plaine*<sup>F</sup> *d'inondation*<sup>F</sup>

waterfall
*chute*<sup>F</sup> *d'eau*<sup>F</sup>

sea
*mer*<sup>F</sup>

lake
*lac*<sup>M</sup>

gorge
*gorge*<sup>F</sup>

confluence
*confluent*<sup>M</sup>

effluent
*effluent*<sup>M</sup>

affluent
*affluent*<sup>M</sup>

meander
*méandre*<sup>M</sup>

delta
*delta*<sup>M</sup>

# lakes

lacs<sup>M</sup>

glacial lake
*lac*<sup>M</sup> *d'origine*<sup>F</sup> *glaciaire*

volcanic lake
*lac*<sup>M</sup> *d'origine*<sup>F</sup> *volcanique*

tectonic lake
*lac*<sup>M</sup> *d'origine*<sup>F</sup> *tectonique*

oxbow lake
*lac*<sup>M</sup> *en croissant*<sup>M</sup>

oasis
*oasis*<sup>F</sup>

artificial lake
*lac*<sup>M</sup> *artificiel*

# wave
vague<sup>F</sup>

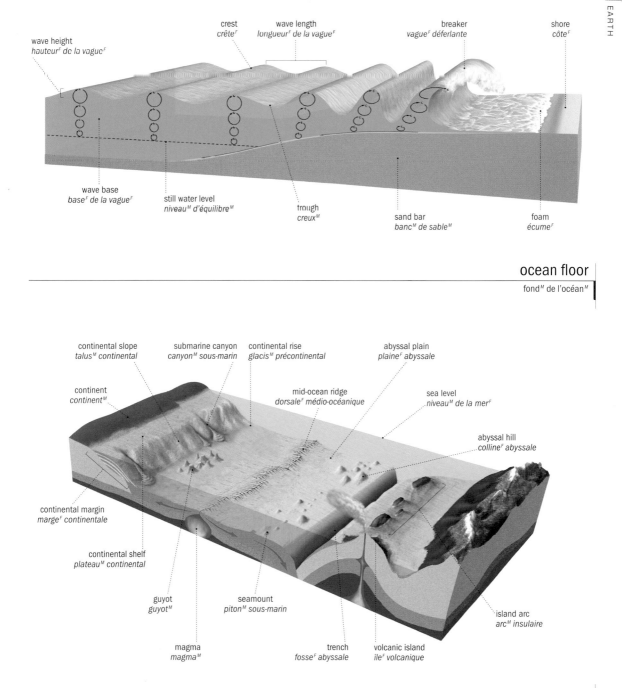

wave height
hauteur<sup>F</sup> de la vague<sup>F</sup>

crest
crête<sup>F</sup>

wave length
longueur<sup>F</sup> de la vague<sup>F</sup>

breaker
vague<sup>F</sup> déferlante

shore
côte<sup>F</sup>

wave base
base<sup>F</sup> de la vague<sup>F</sup>

still water level
niveau<sup>M</sup> d'équilibre<sup>M</sup>

trough
creux<sup>M</sup>

sand bar
banc<sup>M</sup> de sable<sup>M</sup>

foam
écume<sup>F</sup>

# ocean floor
fond<sup>M</sup> de l'océan<sup>M</sup>

continental slope
talus<sup>M</sup> continental

submarine canyon
canyon<sup>M</sup> sous-marin

continental rise
glacis<sup>M</sup> précontinental

abyssal plain
plaine<sup>F</sup> abyssale

continent
continent<sup>M</sup>

mid-ocean ridge
dorsale<sup>F</sup> médio-océanique

sea level
niveau<sup>M</sup> de la mer<sup>F</sup>

abyssal hill
colline<sup>F</sup> abyssale

continental margin
marge<sup>F</sup> continentale

continental shelf
plateau<sup>M</sup> continental

guyot
guyot<sup>M</sup>

seamount
piton<sup>M</sup> sous-marin

island arc
arc<sup>M</sup> insulaire

magma
magma<sup>M</sup>

trench
fosse<sup>F</sup> abyssale

volcanic island
île<sup>F</sup> volcanique

# ocean trenches and ridges

fosses<sup>F</sup> et dorsales<sup>F</sup> océaniques

EARTH

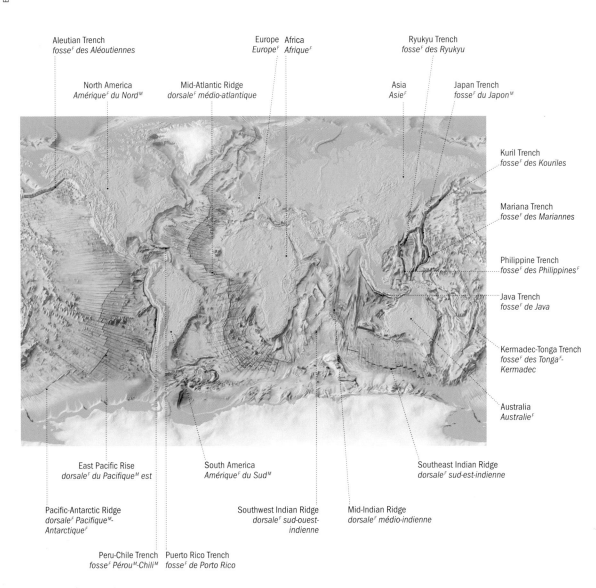

Aleutian Trench
*fosse<sup>F</sup> des Aléoutiennes*

Europe
*Europe<sup>F</sup>*

Africa
*Afrique<sup>F</sup>*

Ryukyu Trench
*fosse<sup>F</sup> des Ryukyu*

North America
*Amérique<sup>F</sup> du Nord<sup>M</sup>*

Mid-Atlantic Ridge
*dorsale<sup>F</sup> médio-atlantique*

Asia
*Asie<sup>F</sup>*

Japan Trench
*fosse<sup>F</sup> du Japon<sup>M</sup>*

Kuril Trench
*fosse<sup>F</sup> des Kouriles*

Mariana Trench
*fosse<sup>F</sup> des Mariannes*

Philippine Trench
*fosse<sup>F</sup> des Philippines<sup>F</sup>*

Java Trench
*fosse<sup>F</sup> de Java*

Kermadec-Tonga Trench
*fosse<sup>F</sup> des Tonga<sup>F</sup>-Kermadec*

Australia
*Australie<sup>F</sup>*

East Pacific Rise
*dorsale<sup>F</sup> du Pacifique<sup>M</sup> est*

South America
*Amérique<sup>F</sup> du Sud<sup>M</sup>*

Southeast Indian Ridge
*dorsale<sup>F</sup> sud-est-indienne*

Pacific-Antarctic Ridge
*dorsale<sup>F</sup> Pacifique<sup>M</sup>-Antarctique<sup>F</sup>*

Southwest Indian Ridge
*dorsale<sup>F</sup> sud-ouest-indienne*

Mid-Indian Ridge
*dorsale<sup>F</sup> médio-indienne*

Peru-Chile Trench
*fosse<sup>F</sup> Pérou<sup>M</sup>-Chili<sup>M</sup>*

Puerto Rico Trench
*fosse<sup>F</sup> de Porto Rico*

# common coastal features

configuration<sup>F</sup> du littoral<sup>M</sup>

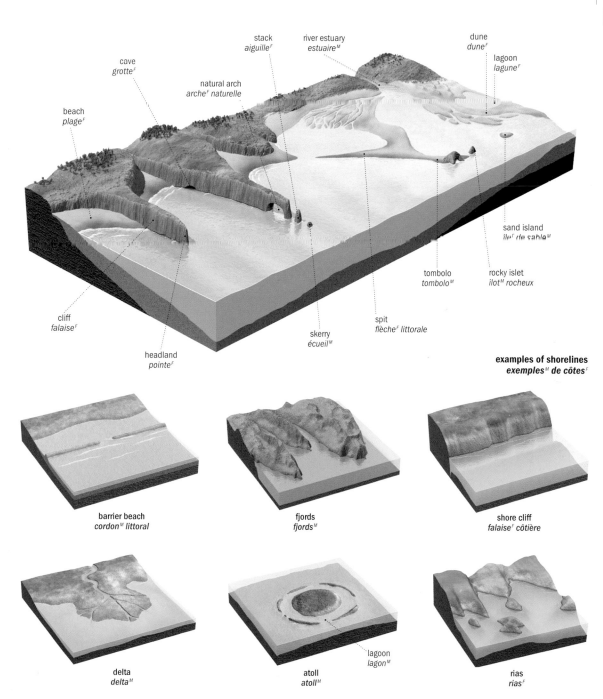

stack
aiguille<sup>F</sup>

river estuary
estuaire<sup>M</sup>

dune
dune<sup>F</sup>

cave
grotte<sup>F</sup>

lagoon
lagune<sup>F</sup>

natural arch
arche<sup>F</sup> naturelle

beach
plage<sup>F</sup>

sand island
île<sup>F</sup> de sable<sup>M</sup>

tombolo
tombolo<sup>M</sup>

rocky islet
îlot<sup>M</sup> rocheux

cliff
falaise<sup>F</sup>

spit
flèche<sup>F</sup> littorale

skerry
écueil<sup>M</sup>

headland
pointe<sup>F</sup>

**examples of shorelines**
*exemples<sup>M</sup> de côtes<sup>F</sup>*

barrier beach
*cordon<sup>M</sup> littoral*

fjords
*fjords<sup>M</sup>*

shore cliff
*falaise<sup>F</sup> côtière*

delta
*delta<sup>M</sup>*

atoll
*atoll<sup>M</sup>*

lagoon
*lagon<sup>M</sup>*

rias
*rias<sup>F</sup>*

35

# desert

désert[M]

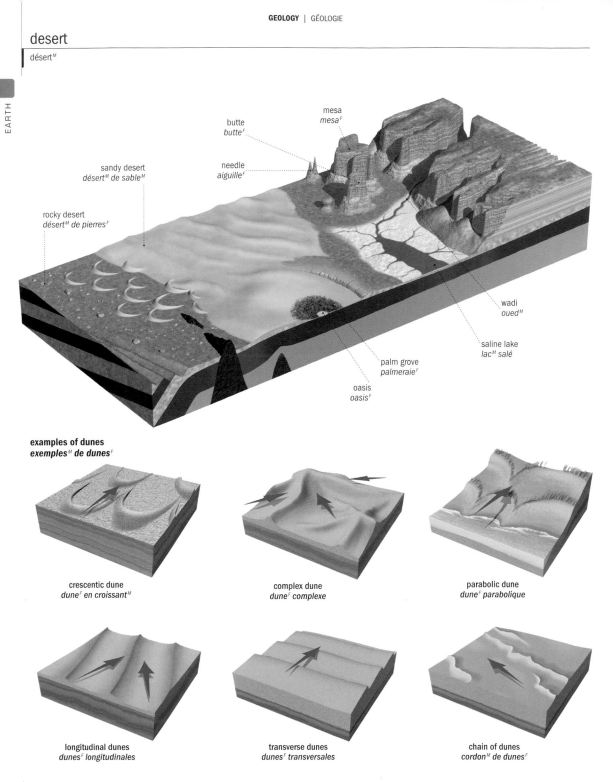

mesa
*mesa*[F]

butte
*butte*[F]

needle
*aiguille*[F]

sandy desert
*désert*[M] *de sable*[M]

rocky desert
*désert*[M] *de pierres*[F]

wadi
*oued*[M]

saline lake
*lac*[M] *salé*

palm grove
*palmeraie*[F]

oasis
*oasis*[F]

**examples of dunes**
*exemples*[M] *de dunes*[F]

crescentic dune
*dune*[F] *en croissant*[M]

complex dune
*dune*[F] *complexe*

parabolic dune
*dune*[F] *parabolique*

longitudinal dunes
*dunes*[F] *longitudinales*

transverse dunes
*dunes*[F] *transversales*

chain of dunes
*cordon*[M] *de dunes*[F]

# profile of the Earth's atmosphere

coupe[F] de l'atmosphère[F] terrestre

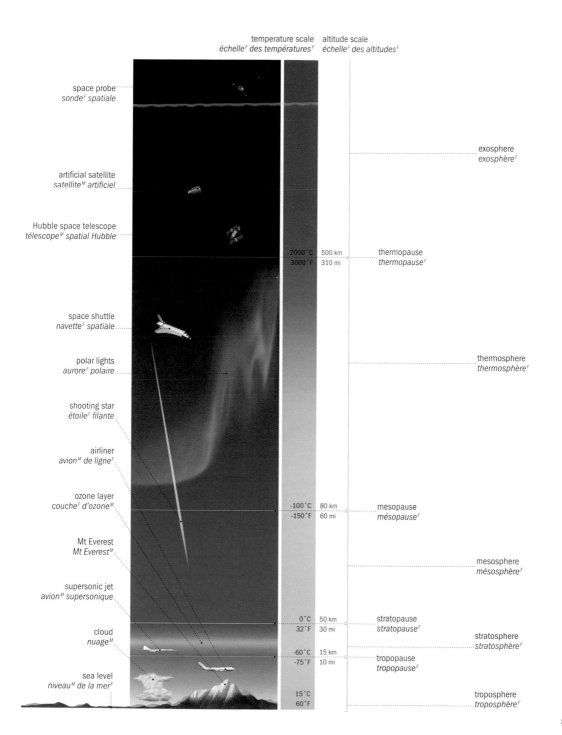

temperature scale  altitude scale
échelle[F] des températures[F]  échelle[F] des altitudes[F]

space probe
sonde[F] spatiale

exosphere
exosphère[F]

artificial satellite
satellite[M] artificiel

Hubble space telescope
télescope[M] spatial Hubble

2000˚C 500 km thermopause
3600˚F 310 mi thermopause[F]

space shuttle
navette[F] spatiale

polar lights
aurore[F] polaire

thermosphere
thermosphère[F]

shooting star
étoile[F] filante

airliner
avion[M] de ligne[F]

ozone layer
couche[F] d'ozone[M]

-100˚C 80 km mesopause
-150˚F 60 mi mésopause[F]

Mt Everest
Mt Everest[M]

mesosphere
mésosphère[F]

supersonic jet
avion[M] supersonique

0˚C 50 km stratopause
32˚F 30 mi stratopause[F]

stratosphere
stratosphère[F]

cloud
nuage[M]

-60˚C 15 km tropopause
-75˚F 10 mi tropopause[F]

sea level
niveau[M] de la mer[F]

15˚C
60˚F

troposphere
troposphère[F]

# seasons of the year

cycle<sup>M</sup> des saisons<sup>F</sup>

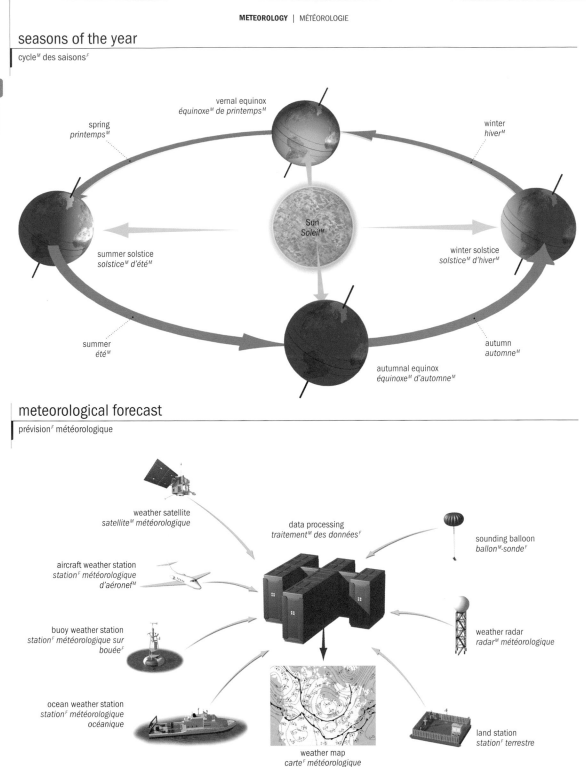

vernal equinox
équinoxe<sup>M</sup> de printemps<sup>M</sup>

spring
printemps<sup>M</sup>

winter
hiver<sup>M</sup>

Sun
Soleil<sup>M</sup>

summer solstice
solstice<sup>M</sup> d'été<sup>M</sup>

winter solstice
solstice<sup>M</sup> d'hiver<sup>M</sup>

summer
été<sup>M</sup>

autumn
automne<sup>M</sup>

autumnal equinox
équinoxe<sup>M</sup> d'automne<sup>M</sup>

# meteorological forecast

prévision<sup>F</sup> météorologique

weather satellite
satellite<sup>M</sup> météorologique

data processing
traitement<sup>M</sup> des données<sup>F</sup>

sounding balloon
ballon<sup>M</sup>-sonde<sup>F</sup>

aircraft weather station
station<sup>F</sup> météorologique
d'aéronef<sup>M</sup>

buoy weather station
station<sup>F</sup> météorologique sur
bouée<sup>F</sup>

weather radar
radar<sup>M</sup> météorologique

ocean weather station
station<sup>F</sup> météorologique
océanique

land station
station<sup>F</sup> terrestre

weather map
carte<sup>F</sup> météorologique

# weather map
carte[F] météorologique

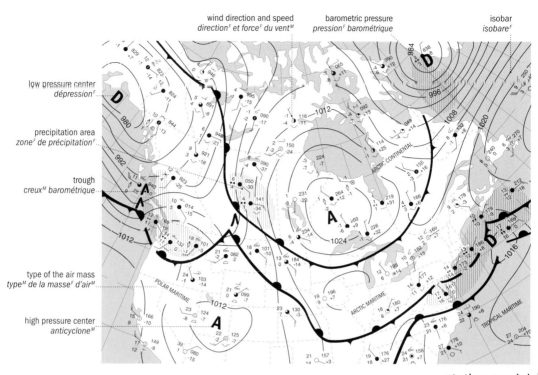

wind direction and speed
direction[F] et force[F] du vent[M]

barometric pressure
pression[F] barométrique

isobar
isobare[F]

low pressure center
dépression[F]

precipitation area
zone[F] de précipitation[F]

trough
creux[M] barométrique

type of the air mass
type[M] de la masse[F] d'air[M]

high pressure center
anticyclone[M]

# station model
disposition[F] des informations[F] d'une station[F]

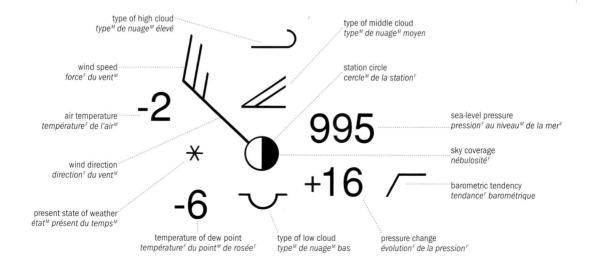

type of high cloud
type[M] de nuage[M] élevé

type of middle cloud
type[M] de nuage[M] moyen

wind speed
force[F] du vent[M]

station circle
cercle[M] de la station[F]

air temperature
température[F] de l'air[M]

sea-level pressure
pression[F] au niveau[M] de la mer[F]

wind direction
direction[F] du vent[M]

sky coverage
nébulosité[F]

barometric tendency
tendance[F] barométrique

present state of weather
état[M] présent du temps[M]

temperature of dew point
température[F] du point[M] de rosée[F]

type of low cloud
type[M] de nuage[M] bas

pressure change
évolution[F] de la pression[F]

# climates of the world

climats<sup>M</sup> du monde<sup>M</sup>

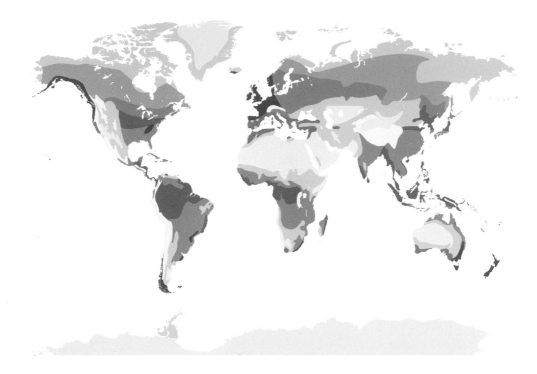

**tropical climates**
*climats<sup>M</sup> tropicaux*

 tropical rain forest
*tropical humide*

tropical wet-and-dry (savanna)
*tropical humide et sec
(savane<sup>F</sup>)*

**dry climates**
*climats<sup>M</sup> arides*

 steppe
*steppe<sup>F</sup>*

desert
*désert<sup>M</sup>*

**cold temperate climates**
*climats<sup>M</sup> tempérés froids*

 humid continental - hot summer
*continental humide, à été<sup>M</sup>
chaud*

humid continental - warm
summer
*continental humide, à été<sup>M</sup>
frais*

subarctic
*subarctique*

**warm temperate climates**
*climats<sup>M</sup> tempérés chauds*

 humid subtropical
*subtropical humide*

 Mediterranean subtropical
*méditerranéen*

 marine
*océanique*

**polar climates**
*climats<sup>M</sup> polaires*

 polar tundra
*toundra<sup>F</sup>*

polar ice cap
*calotte<sup>F</sup> glaciaire*

**highland climates**
*climats<sup>M</sup> de montagne<sup>F</sup>*

highland
*climats<sup>M</sup> de montagne<sup>F</sup>*

# precipitation

précipitations<sup>F</sup>

**winter precipitation**
**précipitations<sup>F</sup>**
**hivernales**

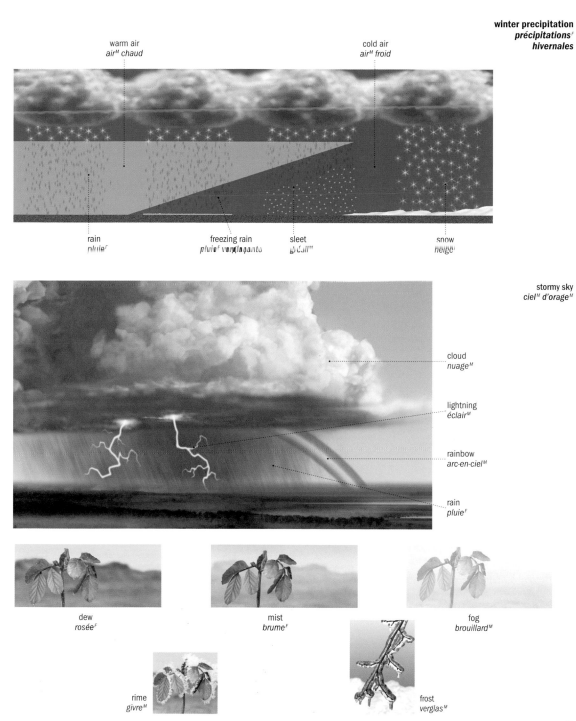

warm air
air<sup>M</sup> chaud

cold air
air<sup>M</sup> froid

rain
pluie<sup>F</sup>

freezing rain
pluie<sup>F</sup> verglaçante

sleet
grésil<sup>M</sup>

snow
neige<sup>F</sup>

**stormy sky**
ciel<sup>M</sup> d'orage<sup>M</sup>

cloud
nuage<sup>M</sup>

lightning
éclair<sup>M</sup>

rainbow
arc-en-ciel<sup>M</sup>

rain
pluie<sup>F</sup>

dew
rosée<sup>F</sup>

mist
brume<sup>F</sup>

fog
brouillard<sup>M</sup>

rime
givre<sup>M</sup>

frost
verglas<sup>M</sup>

# clouds

nuages<sup>M</sup>

EARTH

**high clouds**
*nuages<sup>M</sup> de haute altitude<sup>F</sup>*

**middle clouds**
*nuages<sup>M</sup> de moyenne altitude<sup>F</sup>*

**low clouds**
*nuages<sup>M</sup> de basse altitude<sup>F</sup>*

cirrostratus
*cirro-stratus<sup>M</sup>*

cirrocumulus
*cirro-cumulus<sup>M</sup>*

cirrus
*cirrus<sup>M</sup>*

altostratus
*alto-stratus<sup>M</sup>*

altocumulus
*alto-cumulus<sup>M</sup>*

stratocumulus
*strato-cumulus<sup>M</sup>*

nimbostratus
*nimbo-stratus<sup>M</sup>*

cumulus
*cumulus<sup>M</sup>*

stratus
*stratus<sup>M</sup>*

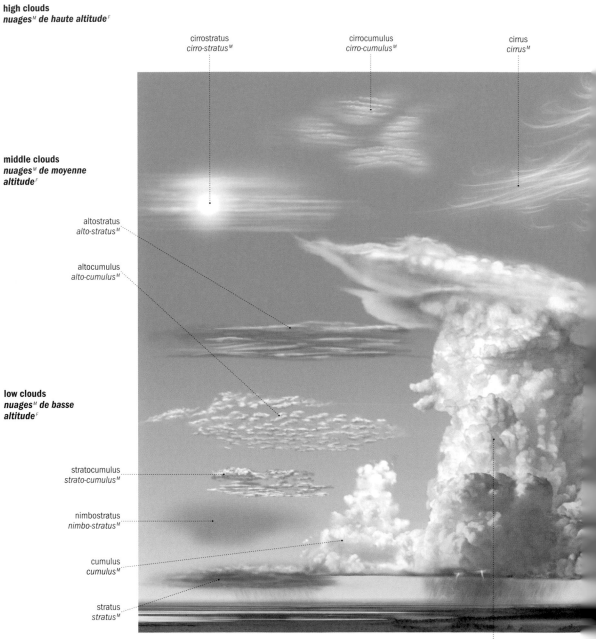

**clouds of vertical development**
*nuages<sup>M</sup> à développement<sup>M</sup> vertical*

cumulonimbus
*cumulo-nimbus<sup>M</sup>*

# tornado and waterspout

tornade*F* et trombe*F* marine

waterspout
trombe*F* marine

wall cloud
mur*M* de nuages*M*

funnel cloud
nuage*M* en entonnoir*M*

debris
buisson*M*

tornado
tornade*F*

# tropical cyclone

cyclone*M* tropical

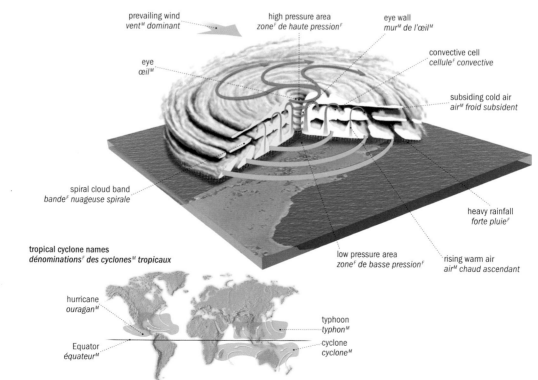

prevailing wind
vent*M* dominant

high pressure area
zone*F* de haute pression*F*

eye wall
mur*M* de l'œil*M*

eye
œil*M*

convective cell
cellule*F* convective

subsiding cold air
air*M* froid subsident

spiral cloud band
bande*F* nuageuse spirale

heavy rainfall
forte pluie*F*

tropical cyclone names
dénominations*F* des cyclones*M* tropicaux

low pressure area
zone*F* de basse pression*F*

rising warm air
air*M* chaud ascendant

hurricane
ouragan*M*

typhoon
typhon*M*

Equator
équateur*M*

cyclone
cyclone*M*

EARTH

# vegetation and biosphere
végétation<sup>F</sup> et biosphère<sup>F</sup>

## vegetation regions
*distribution<sup>F</sup> de la végétation<sup>F</sup>*

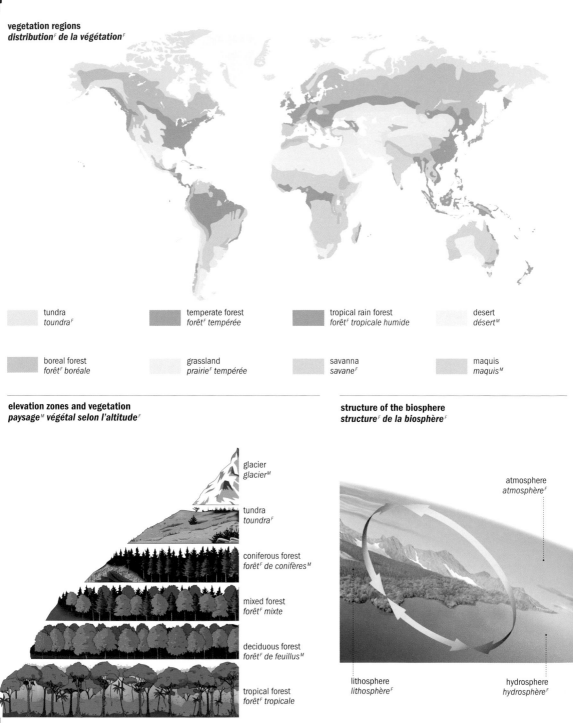

tundra
*toundra<sup>F</sup>*

temperate forest
*forêt<sup>F</sup> tempérée*

tropical rain forest
*forêt<sup>F</sup> tropicale humide*

desert
*désert<sup>M</sup>*

boreal forest
*forêt<sup>F</sup> boréale*

grassland
*prairie<sup>F</sup> tempérée*

savanna
*savane<sup>F</sup>*

maquis
*maquis<sup>M</sup>*

## elevation zones and vegetation
*paysage<sup>M</sup> végétal selon l'altitude<sup>F</sup>*

glacier
*glacier<sup>M</sup>*

tundra
*toundra<sup>F</sup>*

coniferous forest
*forêt<sup>F</sup> de conifères<sup>M</sup>*

mixed forest
*forêt<sup>F</sup> mixte*

deciduous forest
*forêt<sup>F</sup> de feuillus<sup>M</sup>*

tropical forest
*forêt<sup>F</sup> tropicale*

## structure of the biosphere
*structure<sup>F</sup> de la biosphère<sup>F</sup>*

atmosphere
*atmosphère<sup>F</sup>*

lithosphere
*lithosphère<sup>F</sup>*

hydrosphere
*hydrosphère<sup>F</sup>*

# food chain

chaîne^F alimentaire

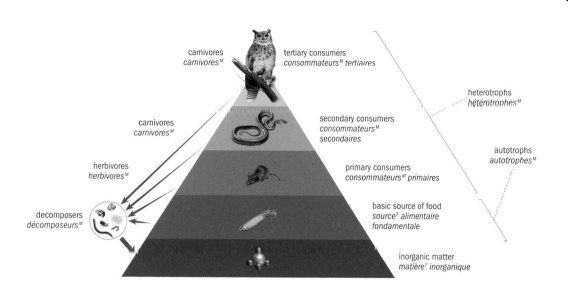

carnivores
carnivores^M

tertiary consumers
consommateurs^M tertiaires

heterotrophs
hétérotrophes^M

carnivores
carnivores^M

secondary consumers
consommateurs^M
secondaires

herbivores
herbivores^M

primary consumers
consommateurs^M primaires

autotrophs
autotrophes^M

decomposers
décomposeurs^M

basic source of food
source^F alimentaire
fondamentale

inorganic matter
matière^F inorganique

# hydrologic cycle

cycle^M de l'eau^F

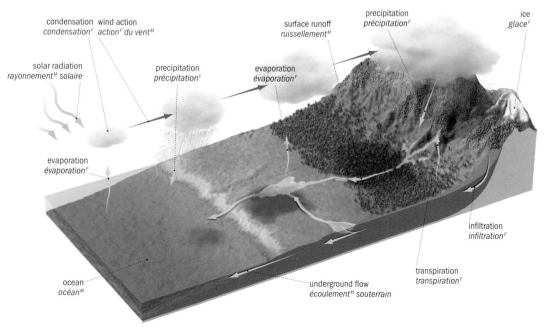

condensation
condensation^F

wind action
action^F du vent^M

surface runoff
ruissellement^M

precipitation
précipitation^F

ice
glace^F

solar radiation
rayonnement^M solaire

precipitation
précipitation^F

evaporation
évaporation^F

evaporation
évaporation^F

infiltration
infiltration^F

transpiration
transpiration^F

ocean
océan^M

underground flow
écoulement^M souterrain

# greenhouse effect

effet<sup>M</sup> de serre<sup>F</sup>

**natural greenhouse effect**
*effet<sup>M</sup> de serre<sup>F</sup> naturel*

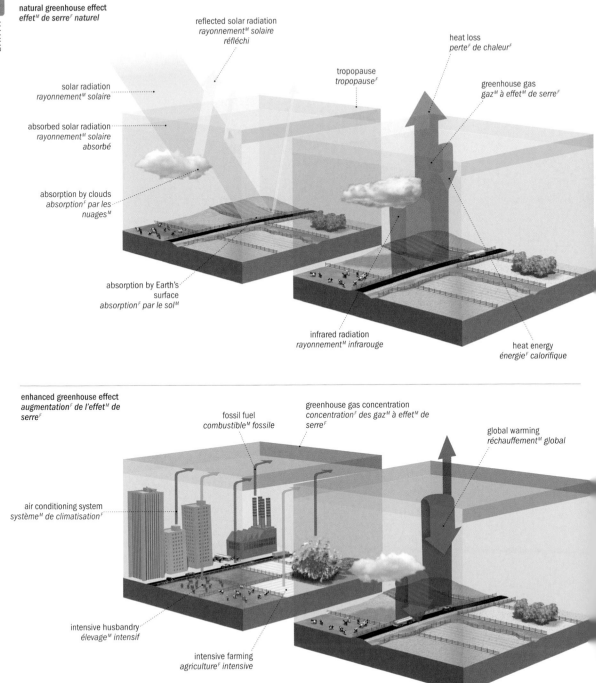

reflected solar radiation
*rayonnement<sup>M</sup> solaire
réfléchi*

heat loss
*perte<sup>F</sup> de chaleur<sup>F</sup>*

tropopause
*tropopause<sup>F</sup>*

greenhouse gas
*gaz<sup>M</sup> à effet<sup>M</sup> de serre<sup>F</sup>*

solar radiation
*rayonnement<sup>M</sup> solaire*

absorbed solar radiation
*rayonnement<sup>M</sup> solaire
absorbé*

absorption by clouds
*absorption<sup>F</sup> par les
nuages<sup>M</sup>*

absorption by Earth's
surface
*absorption<sup>F</sup> par le sol<sup>M</sup>*

infrared radiation
*rayonnement<sup>M</sup> infrarouge*

heat energy
*énergie<sup>F</sup> calorifique*

**enhanced greenhouse effect**
*augmentation<sup>F</sup> de l'effet<sup>M</sup> de
serre<sup>F</sup>*

fossil fuel
*combustible<sup>M</sup> fossile*

greenhouse gas concentration
*concentration<sup>F</sup> des gaz<sup>M</sup> à effet<sup>M</sup> de
serre<sup>F</sup>*

global warming
*réchauffement<sup>M</sup> global*

air conditioning system
*système<sup>M</sup> de climatisation<sup>F</sup>*

intensive husbandry
*élevage<sup>M</sup> intensif*

intensive farming
*agriculture<sup>F</sup> intensive*

## air pollution

pollution<sup>F</sup> de l'air<sup>M</sup>

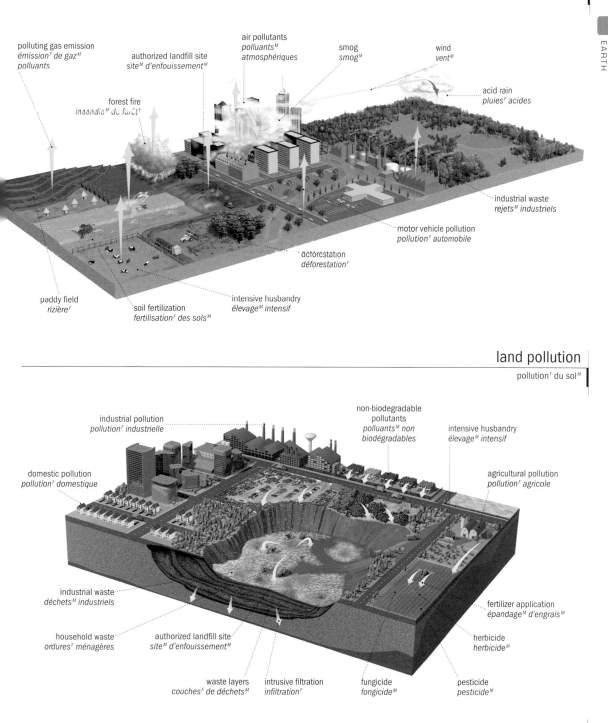

polluting gas emission
émission<sup>F</sup> de gaz<sup>M</sup>
polluants

authorized landfill site
site<sup>M</sup> d'enfouissement<sup>F</sup>

air pollutants
polluants<sup>M</sup>
atmosphériques

smog
smog<sup>M</sup>

wind
vent<sup>M</sup>

forest fire
incendie<sup>M</sup> de forêt<sup>F</sup>

acid rain
pluies<sup>F</sup> acides

industrial waste
rejets<sup>M</sup> industriels

motor vehicle pollution
pollution<sup>F</sup> automobile

déforestation
déforestation<sup>F</sup>

paddy field
rizière<sup>F</sup>

soil fertilization
fertilisation<sup>F</sup> des sols<sup>M</sup>

intensive husbandry
élevage<sup>M</sup> intensif

## land pollution

pollution<sup>F</sup> du sol<sup>M</sup>

industrial pollution
pollution<sup>F</sup> industrielle

non-biodegradable
pollutants
polluants<sup>M</sup> non
biodégradables

intensive husbandry
élevage<sup>M</sup> intensif

domestic pollution
pollution<sup>F</sup> domestique

agricultural pollution
pollution<sup>F</sup> agricole

industrial waste
déchets<sup>M</sup> industriels

household waste
ordures<sup>F</sup> ménagères

authorized landfill site
site<sup>M</sup> d'enfouissement<sup>M</sup>

fertilizer application
épandage<sup>M</sup> d'engrais<sup>M</sup>

herbicide
herbicide<sup>M</sup>

waste layers
couches<sup>F</sup> de déchets<sup>M</sup>

intrusive filtration
infiltration<sup>F</sup>

fungicide
fongicide<sup>M</sup>

pesticide
pesticide<sup>M</sup>

EARTH

# water pollution
pollution<sup>F</sup> de l'eau<sup>F</sup>

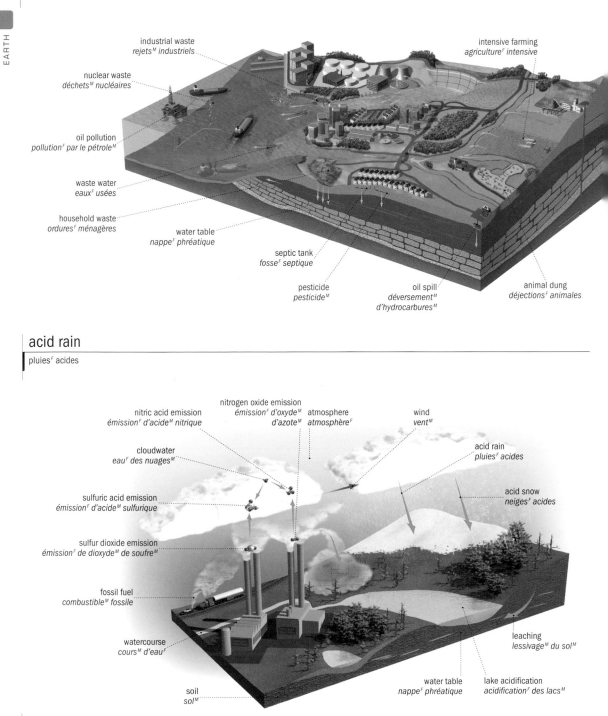

industrial waste
rejets<sup>M</sup> industriels

nuclear waste
déchets<sup>M</sup> nucléaires

oil pollution
pollution<sup>F</sup> par le pétrole<sup>M</sup>

waste water
eaux<sup>F</sup> usées

household waste
ordures<sup>F</sup> ménagères

water table
nappe<sup>F</sup> phréatique

septic tank
fosse<sup>F</sup> septique

pesticide
pesticide<sup>M</sup>

oil spill
déversement<sup>M</sup>
d'hydrocarbures<sup>M</sup>

intensive farming
agriculture<sup>F</sup> intensive

animal dung
déjections<sup>F</sup> animales

# acid rain
pluies<sup>F</sup> acides

nitric acid emission
émission<sup>F</sup> d'acide<sup>M</sup> nitrique

nitrogen oxide emission
émission<sup>F</sup> d'oxyde<sup>M</sup>
d'azote<sup>M</sup>

atmosphere
atmosphère<sup>F</sup>

wind
vent<sup>M</sup>

cloudwater
eau<sup>F</sup> des nuages<sup>M</sup>

acid rain
pluies<sup>F</sup> acides

sulfuric acid emission
émission<sup>F</sup> d'acide<sup>M</sup> sulfurique

acid snow
neiges<sup>F</sup> acides

sulfur dioxide emission
émission<sup>F</sup> de dioxyde<sup>M</sup> de soufre<sup>M</sup>

fossil fuel
combustible<sup>M</sup> fossile

leaching
lessivage<sup>M</sup> du sol<sup>M</sup>

watercourse
cours<sup>M</sup> d'eau<sup>F</sup>

soil
sol<sup>M</sup>

water table
nappe<sup>F</sup> phréatique

lake acidification
acidification<sup>F</sup> des lacs<sup>M</sup>

# selective sorting of waste
tri*[M]* sélectif des déchets*[M]*

EARTH

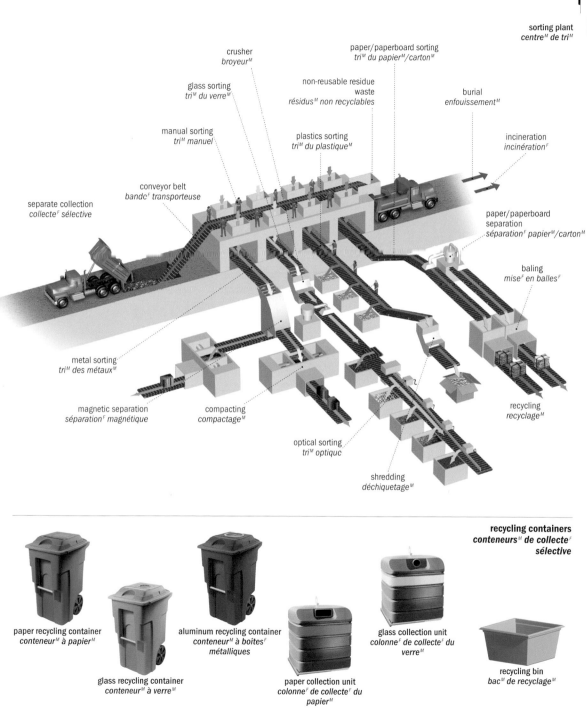

sorting plant
centre*[M]* de tri*[M]*

crusher
broyeur*[M]*

paper/paperboard sorting
tri*[M]* du papier*[M]*/carton*[M]*

glass sorting
tri*[M]* du verre*[M]*

non-reusable residue
waste
résidus*[M]* non recyclables

burial
enfouissement*[M]*

manual sorting
tri*[M]* manuel

plastics sorting
tri*[M]* du plastique*[M]*

incineration
incinération*[F]*

conveyor belt
bande*[F]* transporteuse

separate collection
collecte*[F]* sélective

paper/paperboard
separation
séparation*[F]* papier*[M]*/carton*[M]*

baling
mise*[F]* en balles*[F]*

metal sorting
tri*[M]* des métaux*[M]*

magnetic separation
séparation*[F]* magnétique

compacting
compactage*[M]*

recycling
recyclage*[M]*

optical sorting
tri*[M]* optique

shredding
déchiquetage*[M]*

## recycling containers
conteneurs*[M]* de collecte*[F]*
sélective

paper recycling container
conteneur*[M]* à papier*[M]*

aluminum recycling container
conteneur*[M]* à boites*[F]*
métalliques

glass collection unit
colonne*[F]* de collecte*[F]* du
verre*[M]*

glass recycling container
conteneur*[M]* à verre*[M]*

paper collection unit
colonne*[F]* de collecte*[F]* du
papier*[M]*

recycling bin
bac*[M]* de recyclage*[M]*

# plant cell

cellule<sup>F</sup> végétale

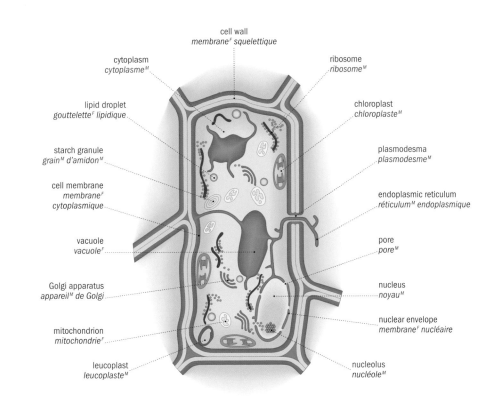

cell wall
*membrane<sup>F</sup> squelettique*

ribosome
*ribosome<sup>M</sup>*

cytoplasm
*cytoplasme<sup>M</sup>*

chloroplast
*chloroplaste<sup>M</sup>*

lipid droplet
*gouttelette<sup>F</sup> lipidique*

plasmodesma
*plasmodesme<sup>M</sup>*

starch granule
*grain<sup>M</sup> d'amidon<sup>M</sup>*

cell membrane
*membrane<sup>F</sup>
cytoplasmique*

endoplasmic reticulum
*réticulum<sup>M</sup> endoplasmique*

vacuole
*vacuole<sup>F</sup>*

pore
*pore<sup>M</sup>*

Golgi apparatus
*appareil<sup>M</sup> de Golgi*

nucleus
*noyau<sup>M</sup>*

nuclear envelope
*membrane<sup>F</sup> nucléaire*

mitochondrion
*mitochondrie<sup>F</sup>*

leucoplast
*leucoplaste<sup>M</sup>*

nucleolus
*nucléole<sup>M</sup>*

# lichen

lichen<sup>M</sup>

**structure of a lichen**
***structure<sup>F</sup> d'un lichen<sup>M</sup>***

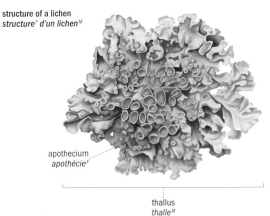

apothecium
*apothécie<sup>F</sup>*

thallus
*thalle<sup>M</sup>*

**examples of lichens**
***exemples<sup>M</sup> de lichens<sup>M</sup>***

crustose lichen
*lichen<sup>M</sup> crustacé*

fruticose lichen
*lichen<sup>M</sup> fruticuleux*

foliose lichen
*lichen<sup>M</sup> foliacé*

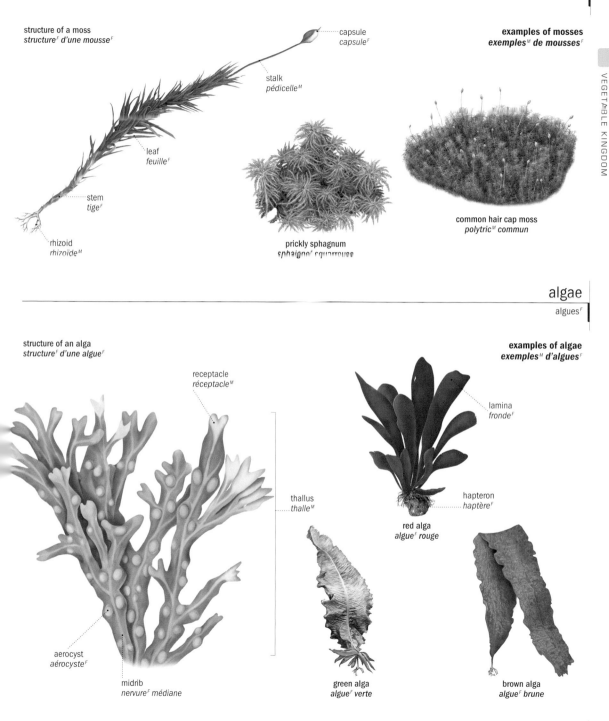

structure of a moss
*structure<sup>F</sup> d'une mousse<sup>F</sup>*

capsule
*capsule<sup>F</sup>*

stalk
*pédicelle<sup>M</sup>*

leaf
*feuille<sup>F</sup>*

stem
*tige<sup>F</sup>*

rhizoid
*rhizoïde<sup>M</sup>*

**examples of mosses**
***exemples<sup>M</sup> de mousses<sup>F</sup>***

common hair cap moss
*polytric<sup>M</sup> commun*

prickly sphagnum
*sphaigne<sup>F</sup> squarreuse*

# algae
algues<sup>F</sup>

structure of an alga
*structure<sup>F</sup> d'une algue<sup>F</sup>*

**examples of algae**
***exemples<sup>M</sup> d'algues<sup>F</sup>***

receptacle
*réceptacle<sup>M</sup>*

lamina
*fronde<sup>F</sup>*

thallus
*thalle<sup>M</sup>*

hapteron
*haptère<sup>F</sup>*

red alga
*algue<sup>F</sup> rouge*

aerocyst
*aérocyste<sup>F</sup>*

midrib
*nervure<sup>F</sup> médiane*

green alga
*algue<sup>F</sup> verte*

brown alga
*algue<sup>F</sup> brune*

# mushroom

champignon[M]

structure of a mushroom
*structure[F] d'un champignon[M]*

cap
*chapeau[M]*

ring
*anneau[M]*

gills
*lamelles[F]*

stem
*pied[M]*

volva
*volve[F]*

spores
*spores[F]*

hypha
*hyphe[M]*

mycelium
*mycélium[M]*

**deadly poisonous
mushroom
*champignon[M] mortel***

**poisonous mushroom
*champignon[M]
vénéneux***

destroying angel
*amanite[F] vireuse*

fly agaric
*fausse oronge[F]*

# fern

fougère[F]

structure of a fern
*structure[F] d'une fougère[F]*

**examples of ferns
*exemples[M] de fougères[F]***

sorus
*sore[M]*

blade
*limbe[M]*

pinna
*pinnule[F]*

frond
*fronde[F]*

petiole
*pétiole[M]*

rhizome
*rhizome[M]*

fiddlehead
*crosse[F]*

adventitious roots
*racines[F] adventives*

tree fern
*fougère[F] arborescente*

trunk
*tronc[M]*

common polypody
*polypode[M] commun*

bird's nest fern
*fougère[F] nid[M] d'oiseau[M]*

**structure of a plant**
*structure<sup>F</sup> d'une plante<sup>F</sup>*

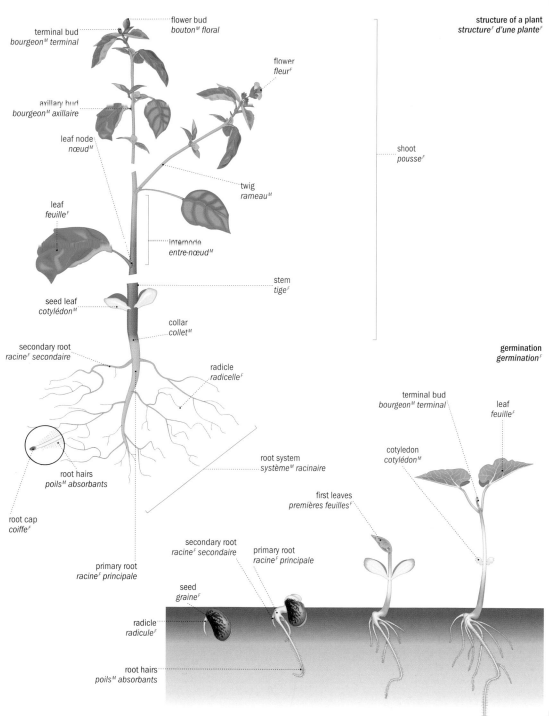

terminal bud
*bourgeon<sup>M</sup> terminal*

flower bud
*bouton<sup>M</sup> floral*

flower
*fleur<sup>F</sup>*

axillary bud
*bourgeon<sup>M</sup> axillaire*

leaf node
*nœud<sup>M</sup>*

shoot
*pousse<sup>F</sup>*

twig
*rameau<sup>M</sup>*

leaf
*feuille<sup>F</sup>*

internode
*entre-nœud<sup>M</sup>*

stem
*tige<sup>F</sup>*

seed leaf
*cotylédon<sup>M</sup>*

collar
*collet<sup>M</sup>*

secondary root
*racine<sup>F</sup> secondaire*

radicle
*radicelle<sup>F</sup>*

**germination**
*germination<sup>F</sup>*

terminal bud
*bourgeon<sup>M</sup> terminal*

leaf
*feuille<sup>F</sup>*

cotyledon
*cotylédon<sup>M</sup>*

root system
*système<sup>M</sup> racinaire*

root hairs
*poils<sup>M</sup> absorbants*

first leaves
*premières feuilles<sup>F</sup>*

root cap
*coiffe<sup>F</sup>*

secondary root
*racine<sup>F</sup> secondaire*

primary root
*racine<sup>F</sup> principale*

primary root
*racine<sup>F</sup> principale*

seed
*graine<sup>F</sup>*

radicle
*radicule<sup>F</sup>*

root hairs
*poils<sup>M</sup> absorbants*

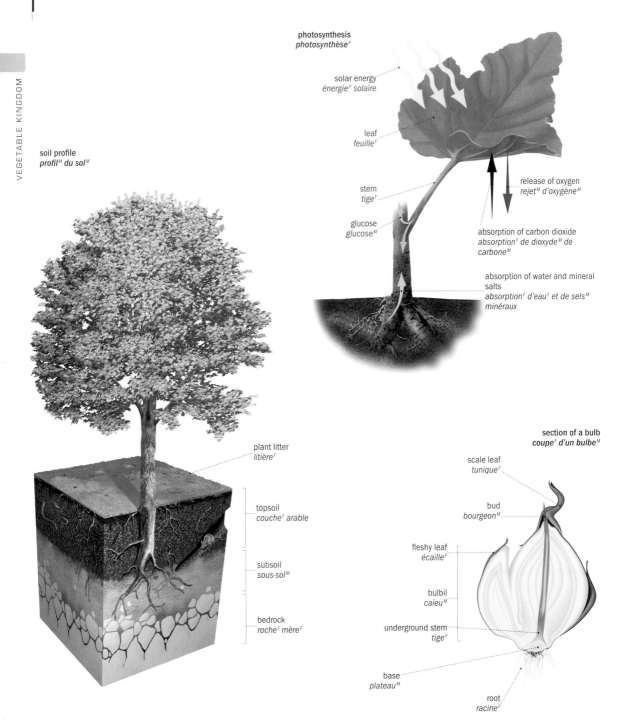

**photosynthesis**
*photosynthèse*<sup>F</sup>

solar energy
*énergie*<sup>F</sup> *solaire*

leaf
*feuille*<sup>F</sup>

stem
*tige*<sup>F</sup>

glucose
*glucose*<sup>M</sup>

release of oxygen
*rejet*<sup>M</sup> *d'oxygène*<sup>M</sup>

absorption of carbon dioxide
*absorption*<sup>F</sup> *de dioxyde*<sup>M</sup> *de carbone*<sup>M</sup>

absorption of water and mineral salts
*absorption*<sup>F</sup> *d'eau*<sup>F</sup> *et de sels*<sup>M</sup> *minéraux*

**soil profile**
*profil*<sup>M</sup> *du sol*<sup>M</sup>

plant litter
*litière*<sup>F</sup>

topsoil
*couche*<sup>F</sup> *arable*

subsoil
*sous-sol*<sup>M</sup>

bedrock
*roche*<sup>F</sup> *mère*<sup>F</sup>

**section of a bulb**
*coupe*<sup>F</sup> *d'un bulbe*<sup>M</sup>

scale leaf
*tunique*<sup>F</sup>

bud
*bourgeon*<sup>M</sup>

fleshy leaf
*écaille*<sup>F</sup>

bulbil
*caïeu*<sup>M</sup>

underground stem
*tige*<sup>F</sup>

base
*plateau*<sup>M</sup>

root
*racine*<sup>F</sup>

VEGETABLE KINGDOM

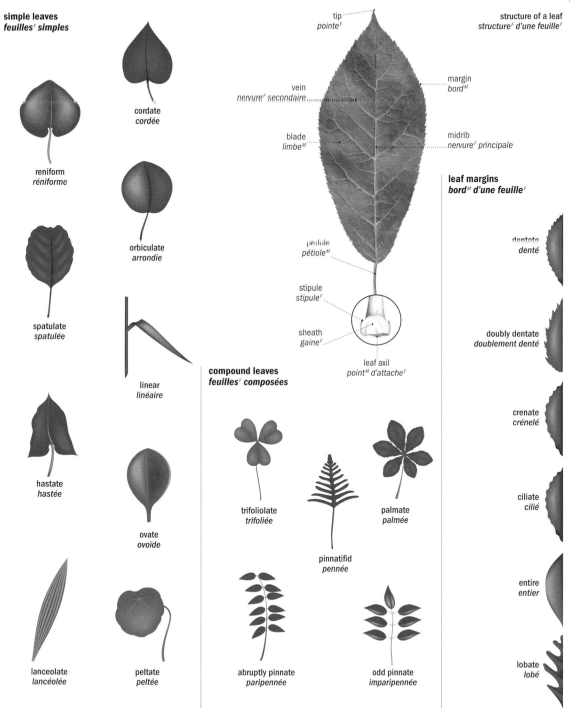

**simple leaves**
*feuilles<sup>F</sup> simples*

cordate
*cordée*

reniform
*réniforme*

orbiculate
*arrondie*

spatulate
*spatulée*

linear
*linéaire*

hastate
*hastée*

ovate
*ovoïde*

lanceolate
*lancéolée*

peltate
*peltée*

structure of a leaf
*structure<sup>F</sup> d'une feuille<sup>F</sup>*

tip
*pointe<sup>F</sup>*

vein
*nervure<sup>F</sup> secondaire*

margin
*bord<sup>M</sup>*

blade
*limbe<sup>M</sup>*

midrib
*nervure<sup>F</sup> principale*

petiole
*pétiole<sup>M</sup>*

stipule
*stipule<sup>F</sup>*

sheath
*gaine<sup>F</sup>*

leaf axil
*point<sup>M</sup> d'attache<sup>F</sup>*

**compound leaves**
*feuilles<sup>F</sup> composées*

trifoliolate
*trifoliée*

palmate
*palmée*

pinnatifid
*pennée*

abruptly pinnate
*paripennée*

odd pinnate
*imparipennée*

**leaf margins**
*bord<sup>M</sup> d'une feuille<sup>F</sup>*

dentate
*denté*

doubly dentate
*doublement denté*

crenate
*crénelé*

ciliate
*cilié*

entire
*entier*

lobate
*lobé*

55

# flower

*fleur*[F]

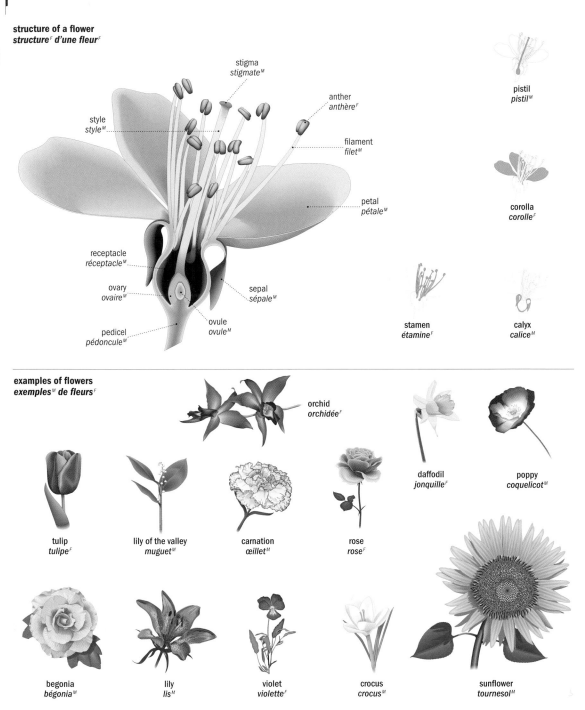

## structure of a flower
## *structure*[F] *d'une fleur*[F]

stigma
*stigmate*[M]

anther
*anthère*[F]

style
*style*[M]

filament
*filet*[M]

petal
*pétale*[M]

receptacle
*réceptacle*[M]

sepal
*sépale*[M]

ovary
*ovaire*[M]

ovule
*ovule*[M]

pedicel
*pédoncule*[M]

pistil
*pistil*[M]

corolla
*corolle*[F]

stamen
*étamine*[F]

calyx
*calice*[M]

## examples of flowers
## *exemples*[M] *de fleurs*[F]

orchid
*orchidée*[F]

daffodil
*jonquille*[F]

poppy
*coquelicot*[M]

tulip
*tulipe*[F]

lily of the valley
*muguet*[M]

carnation
*œillet*[M]

rose
*rose*[F]

begonia
*bégonia*[M]

lily
*lis*[M]

violet
*violette*[F]

crocus
*crocus*[M]

sunflower
*tournesol*[M]

## types of inflorescences
*modes*<sup>M</sup> *d'inflorescence*<sup>F</sup>

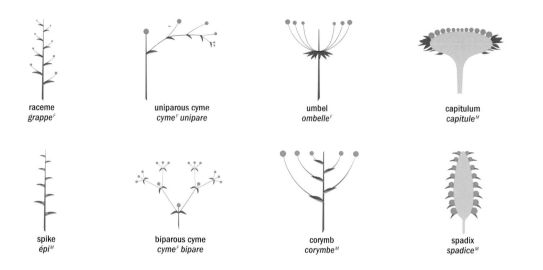

raceme
*grappe*<sup>F</sup>

uniparous cyme
*cyme*<sup>F</sup> *unipare*

umbel
*ombelle*<sup>F</sup>

capitulum
*capitule*<sup>M</sup>

spike
*épi*<sup>M</sup>

biparous cyme
*cyme*<sup>F</sup> *bipare*

corymb
*corymbe*<sup>M</sup>

spadix
*spadice*<sup>M</sup>

# fruit
fruits<sup>M</sup>

## fleshy fruit: stone fruit
*fruit*<sup>M</sup> *charnu à noyau*<sup>M</sup>

technical terms
*termes*<sup>M</sup> *techniques*

section of a peach
*coupe*<sup>F</sup> *d'une pêche*<sup>F</sup>

usual terms
*termes*<sup>M</sup> *familiers*

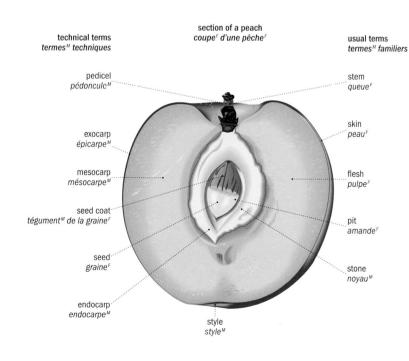

pedicel
*pédoncule*<sup>M</sup>

exocarp
*épicarpe*<sup>M</sup>

mesocarp
*mésocarpe*<sup>M</sup>

seed coat
*tégument*<sup>M</sup> *de la graine*<sup>F</sup>

seed
*graine*<sup>F</sup>

endocarp
*endocarpe*<sup>M</sup>

style
*style*<sup>M</sup>

stem
*queue*<sup>F</sup>

skin
*peau*<sup>F</sup>

flesh
*pulpe*<sup>F</sup>

pit
*amande*<sup>F</sup>

stone
*noyau*<sup>M</sup>

**fleshy fruit: pome fruit**
*fruit$^M$ charnu à pépins$^M$*

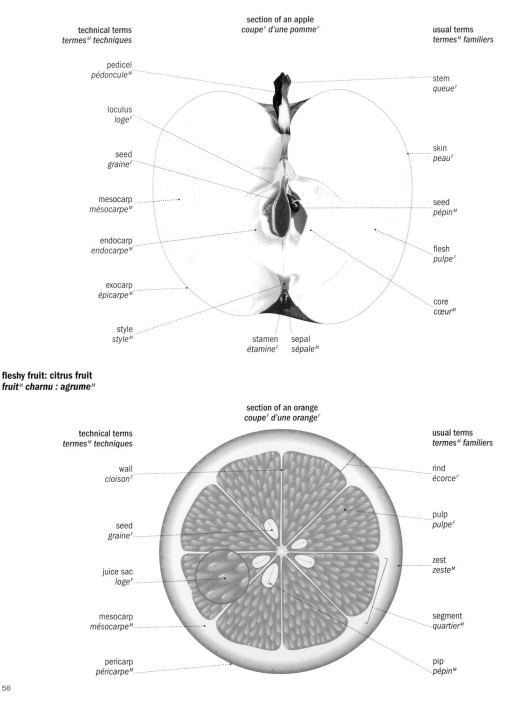

section of an apple
*coupe$^F$ d'une pomme$^F$*

technical terms
*termes$^M$ techniques*

usual terms
*termes$^M$ familiers*

pedicel
*pédoncule$^M$*

stem
*queue$^F$*

loculus
*loge$^F$*

skin
*peau$^F$*

seed
*graine$^F$*

mesocarp
*mésocarpe$^M$*

seed
*pépin$^M$*

endocarp
*endocarpe$^M$*

flesh
*pulpe$^F$*

exocarp
*épicarpe$^M$*

core
*cœur$^M$*

style
*style$^M$*

stamen
*étamine$^F$*

sepal
*sépale$^M$*

**fleshy fruit: citrus fruit**
*fruit$^M$ charnu : agrume$^M$*

section of an orange
*coupe$^F$ d'une orange$^F$*

technical terms
*termes$^M$ techniques*

usual terms
*termes$^M$ familiers*

wall
*cloison$^F$*

rind
*écorce$^F$*

seed
*graine$^F$*

pulp
*pulpe$^F$*

juice sac
*loge$^F$*

zest
*zeste$^M$*

mesocarp
*mésocarpe$^M$*

segment
*quartier$^M$*

pericarp
*péricarpe$^M$*

pip
*pépin$^M$*

VEGETABLE KINGDOM

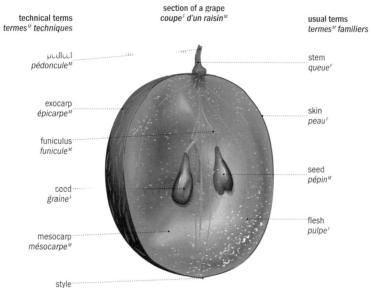

technical terms
*termes*<sup>M</sup> *techniques*

section of a grape
*coupe*<sup>F</sup> *d'un raisin*<sup>M</sup>

usual terms
*termes*<sup>M</sup> *familiers*

pedicel
*pédoncule*<sup>M</sup>

exocarp
*épicarpe*<sup>M</sup>

funiculus
*funicule*<sup>M</sup>

seed
*graine*<sup>F</sup>

mesocarp
*mésocarpe*<sup>M</sup>

style
*style*<sup>M</sup>

stem
*queue*<sup>F</sup>

skin
*peau*<sup>F</sup>

seed
*pépin*<sup>M</sup>

flesh
*pulpe*<sup>F</sup>

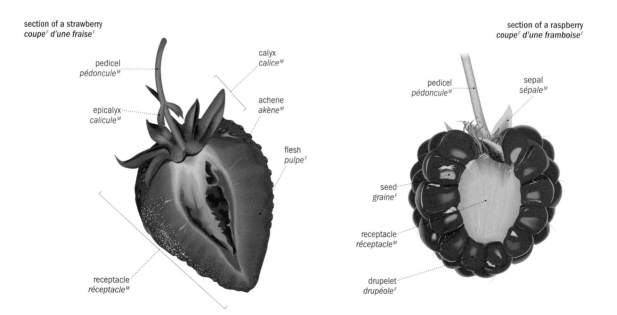

section of a strawberry
*coupe*<sup>F</sup> *d'une fraise*<sup>F</sup>

pedicel
*pédoncule*<sup>M</sup>

epicalyx
*calicule*<sup>M</sup>

calyx
*calice*<sup>M</sup>

achene
*akène*<sup>M</sup>

flesh
*pulpe*<sup>F</sup>

receptacle
*réceptacle*<sup>M</sup>

section of a raspberry
*coupe*<sup>F</sup> *d'une framboise*<sup>F</sup>

pedicel
*pédoncule*<sup>M</sup>

sepal
*sépale*<sup>M</sup>

seed
*graine*<sup>F</sup>

receptacle
*réceptacle*<sup>M</sup>

drupelet
*drupéole*<sup>F</sup>

**dry fruits**
*fruits<sup>M</sup> secs*

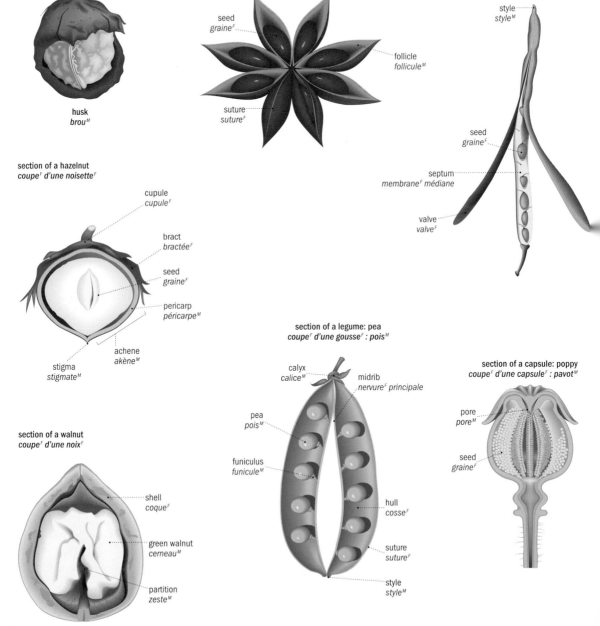

**section of a follicle: star anise**
*coupe<sup>F</sup> d'un follicule<sup>M</sup> : anis<sup>M</sup> étoilé*

seed
*graine<sup>F</sup>*

follicle
*follicule<sup>M</sup>*

suture
*suture<sup>F</sup>*

**section of a silique: mustard**
*coupe<sup>F</sup> d'une silique<sup>F</sup> : moutarde<sup>F</sup>*

style
*style<sup>M</sup>*

seed
*graine<sup>F</sup>*

septum
*membrane<sup>F</sup> médiane*

valve
*valve<sup>F</sup>*

husk
*brou<sup>M</sup>*

**section of a hazelnut**
*coupe<sup>F</sup> d'une noisette<sup>F</sup>*

cupule
*cupule<sup>F</sup>*

bract
*bractée<sup>F</sup>*

seed
*graine<sup>F</sup>*

pericarp
*péricarpe<sup>M</sup>*

achene
*akène<sup>M</sup>*

stigma
*stigmate<sup>M</sup>*

**section of a legume: pea**
*coupe<sup>F</sup> d'une gousse<sup>F</sup> : pois<sup>M</sup>*

calyx
*calice<sup>M</sup>*

midrib
*nervure<sup>F</sup> principale*

pea
*pois<sup>M</sup>*

funiculus
*funicule<sup>M</sup>*

hull
*cosse<sup>F</sup>*

suture
*suture<sup>F</sup>*

style
*style<sup>M</sup>*

**section of a capsule: poppy**
*coupe<sup>F</sup> d'une capsule<sup>F</sup> : pavot<sup>M</sup>*

pore
*pore<sup>M</sup>*

seed
*graine<sup>F</sup>*

**section of a walnut**
*coupe<sup>F</sup> d'une noix<sup>F</sup>*

shell
*coque<sup>F</sup>*

green walnut
*cerneau<sup>M</sup>*

partition
*zeste<sup>M</sup>*

VEGETABLE KINGDOM

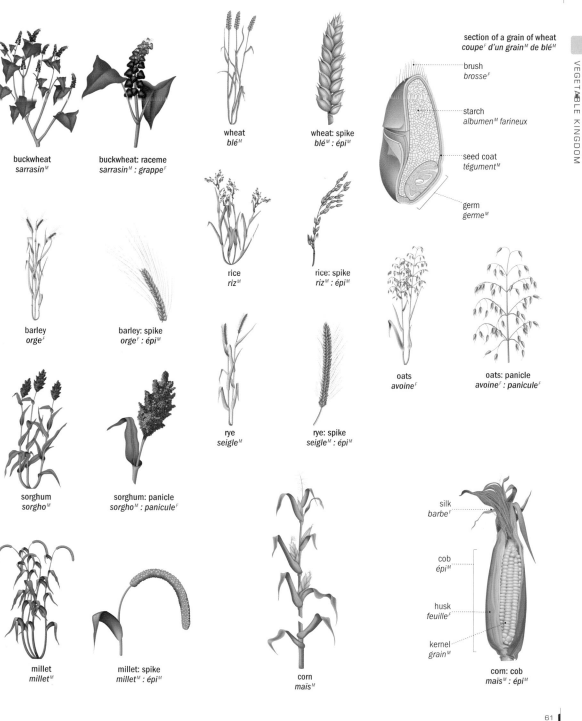

buckwheat
*sarrasin*[M]

buckwheat: raceme
*sarrasin*[M] *: grappe*[F]

wheat
*blé*[M]

wheat: spike
*blé*[M] *: épi*[M]

section of a grain of wheat
*coupe*[F] *d'un grain*[M] *de blé*[M]

brush
*brosse*[F]

starch
*albumen*[M] *farineux*

seed coat
*tégument*[M]

germ
*germe*[M]

barley
*orge*[F]

barley: spike
*orge*[F] *: épi*[M]

rice
*riz*[M]

rice: spike
*riz*[M] *: épi*[M]

oats
*avoine*[F]

oats: panicle
*avoine*[F] *: panicule*[F]

sorghum
*sorgho*[M]

sorghum: panicle
*sorgho*[M] *: panicule*[F]

rye
*seigle*[M]

rye: spike
*seigle*[M] *: épi*[M]

silk
*barbe*[F]

cob
*épi*[M]

husk
*feuille*[F]

kernel
*grain*[M]

millet
*millet*[M]

millet: spike
*millet*[M] *: épi*[M]

corn
*maïs*[M]

corn: cob
*maïs*[M] *: épi*[M]

# grape

*vigne*[F]

VEGETABLE KINGDOM

**bunch of grapes**
*grappe*[F] *de raisins*[M]

**vine stock**
*cep*[M] *de vigne*[F]

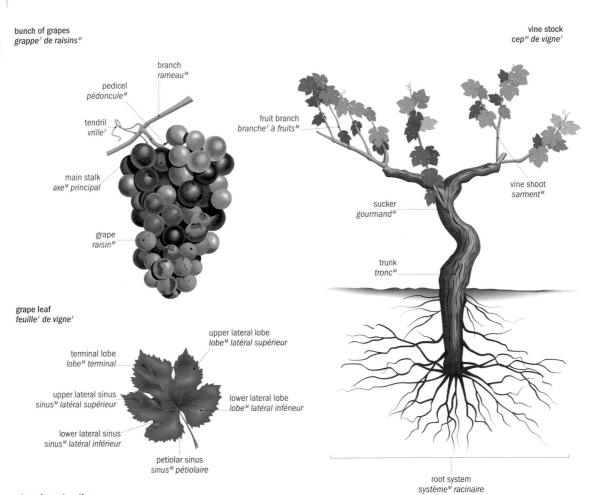

branch
*rameau*[M]

pedicel
*pédoncule*[M]

tendril
*vrille*[F]

fruit branch
*branche*[F] *à fruits*[M]

vine shoot
*sarment*[M]

main stalk
*axe*[M] *principal*

sucker
*gourmand*[M]

grape
*raisin*[M]

trunk
*tronc*[M]

**grape leaf**
*feuille*[F] *de vigne*[F]

upper lateral lobe
*lobe*[M] *latéral supérieur*

terminal lobe
*lobe*[M] *terminal*

upper lateral sinus
*sinus*[M] *latéral supérieur*

lower lateral lobe
*lobe*[M] *latéral inférieur*

lower lateral sinus
*sinus*[M] *latéral inférieur*

petiolar sinus
*sinus*[M] *pétiolaire*

root system
*système*[M] *racinaire*

**steps in maturation**
*étapes*[F] *de maturation*[F]

**flowering**
*floraison*[F]

**fruition**
*nouaison*[F]

**ripening**
*véraison*[F]

**ripeness**
*maturité*[F]

**structure of a tree**
*structure<sup>F</sup> d'un arbre<sup>M</sup>*

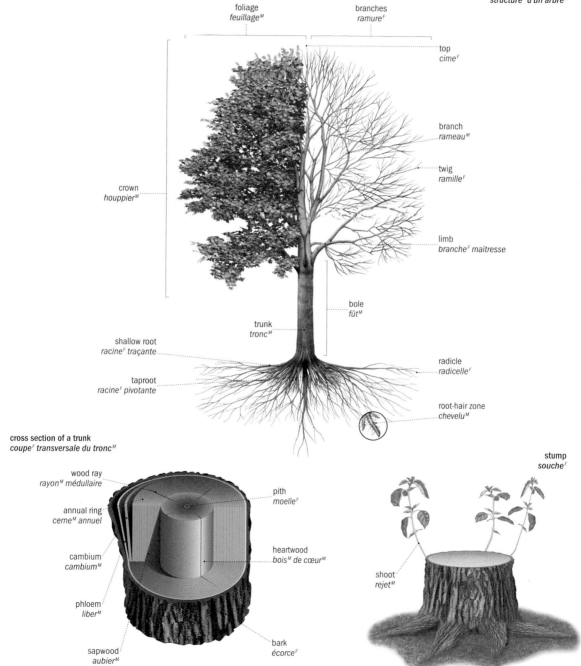

foliage
*feuillage<sup>M</sup>*

branches
*ramure<sup>F</sup>*

top
*cime<sup>F</sup>*

branch
*rameau<sup>M</sup>*

twig
*ramille<sup>F</sup>*

crown
*houppier<sup>M</sup>*

limb
*branche<sup>F</sup> maitresse*

bole
*fût<sup>M</sup>*

trunk
*tronc<sup>M</sup>*

shallow root
*racine<sup>F</sup> traçante*

taproot
*racine<sup>F</sup> pivotante*

radicle
*radicelle<sup>F</sup>*

root-hair zone
*chevelu<sup>M</sup>*

**cross section of a trunk**
*coupe<sup>F</sup> transversale du tronc<sup>M</sup>*

wood ray
*rayon<sup>M</sup> médullaire*

pith
*moelle<sup>F</sup>*

annual ring
*cerne<sup>M</sup> annuel*

cambium
*cambium<sup>M</sup>*

heartwood
*bois<sup>M</sup> de cœur<sup>M</sup>*

phloem
*liber<sup>M</sup>*

sapwood
*aubier<sup>M</sup>*

bark
*écorce<sup>F</sup>*

**stump**
*souche<sup>F</sup>*

shoot
*rejet<sup>M</sup>*

**examples of broadleaved trees**
*exemples*<sup>M</sup> *d'arbres*<sup>M</sup> *feuillus*

oak
*chêne*<sup>M</sup>

birch
*bouleau*<sup>M</sup>

weeping willow
*saule*<sup>M</sup> *pleureur*

poplar
*peuplier*<sup>M</sup>

palm tree
*palmier*<sup>M</sup>

maple
*érable*<sup>M</sup>

beech
*hêtre*<sup>M</sup>

walnut
*noyer*<sup>M</sup>

branch
*rameau*<sup>M</sup>

male cone
*cône*<sup>M</sup> *mâle*

female cone
*cône*<sup>M</sup> *femelle*

cone
*cône*<sup>M</sup>

pine seed
*pignon*<sup>M</sup>

**examples of leaves**
***exemples*<sup>M</sup> *de feuilles*<sup>F</sup>**

fir needles
*aiguilles*<sup>F</sup> *de sapin*<sup>M</sup>

pine needles
*aiguilles*<sup>F</sup> *de pin*<sup>M</sup>

cypress scalelike leaves
*écailles*<sup>F</sup> *de cyprès*<sup>M</sup>

**examples of conifers**
***exemples*<sup>M</sup> *de conifères*<sup>M</sup>**

umbrella pine
*pin*<sup>M</sup> *parasol*<sup>M</sup>

cedar of Lebanon
*cèdre*<sup>M</sup> *du Liban*<sup>M</sup>

fir
*sapin*<sup>M</sup>

spruce
*épicéa*<sup>M</sup> ; *épinette*<sup>F</sup>

larch
*mélèze*<sup>M</sup>

# animal cell

cellule<sup>F</sup> animale

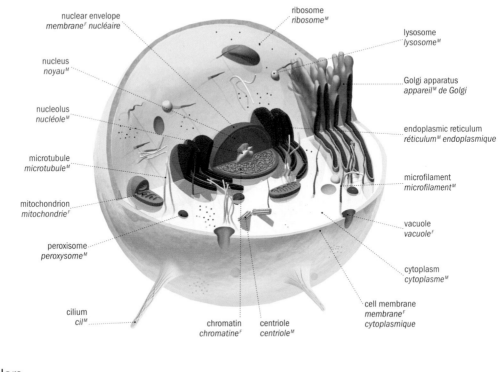

nuclear envelope
*membrane<sup>F</sup> nucléaire*

nucleus
*noyau<sup>M</sup>*

nucleolus
*nucléole<sup>M</sup>*

microtubule
*microtubule<sup>M</sup>*

mitochondrion
*mitochondrie<sup>F</sup>*

peroxisome
*peroxysome<sup>M</sup>*

cilium
*cil<sup>M</sup>*

ribosome
*ribosome<sup>M</sup>*

lysosome
*lysosome<sup>M</sup>*

Golgi apparatus
*appareil<sup>M</sup> de Golgi*

endoplasmic reticulum
*réticulum<sup>M</sup> endoplasmique*

microfilament
*microfilament<sup>M</sup>*

vacuole
*vacuole<sup>F</sup>*

cytoplasm
*cytoplasme<sup>M</sup>*

cell membrane
*membrane<sup>F</sup>
cytoplasmique*

chromatin
*chromatine<sup>F</sup>*

centriole
*centriole<sup>M</sup>*

# unicellulars

unicellulaires<sup>M</sup>

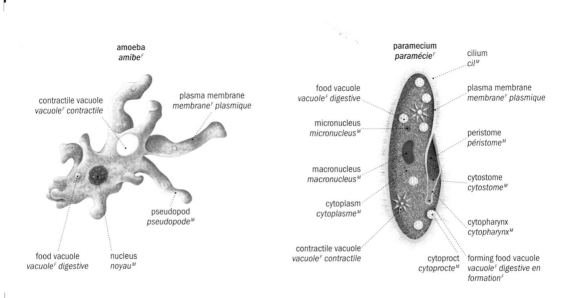

amoeba
*amibe<sup>F</sup>*

paramecium
*paramécie<sup>F</sup>*

contractile vacuole
*vacuole<sup>F</sup> contractile*

plasma membrane
*membrane<sup>F</sup> plasmique*

food vacuole
*vacuole<sup>F</sup> digestive*

cilium
*cil<sup>M</sup>*

plasma membrane
*membrane<sup>F</sup> plasmique*

micronucleus
*micronucleus<sup>M</sup>*

peristome
*péristome<sup>M</sup>*

macronucleus
*macronucleus<sup>M</sup>*

cytostome
*cytostome<sup>M</sup>*

cytoplasm
*cytoplasme<sup>M</sup>*

cytopharynx
*cytopharynx<sup>M</sup>*

pseudopod
*pseudopode<sup>M</sup>*

food vacuole
*vacuole<sup>F</sup> digestive*

nucleus
*noyau<sup>M</sup>*

contractile vacuole
*vacuole<sup>F</sup> contractile*

cytoproct
*cytoprocte<sup>M</sup>*

forming food vacuole
*vacuole<sup>F</sup> digestive en
formation<sup>F</sup>*

# butterfly

papillon<sup>M</sup>

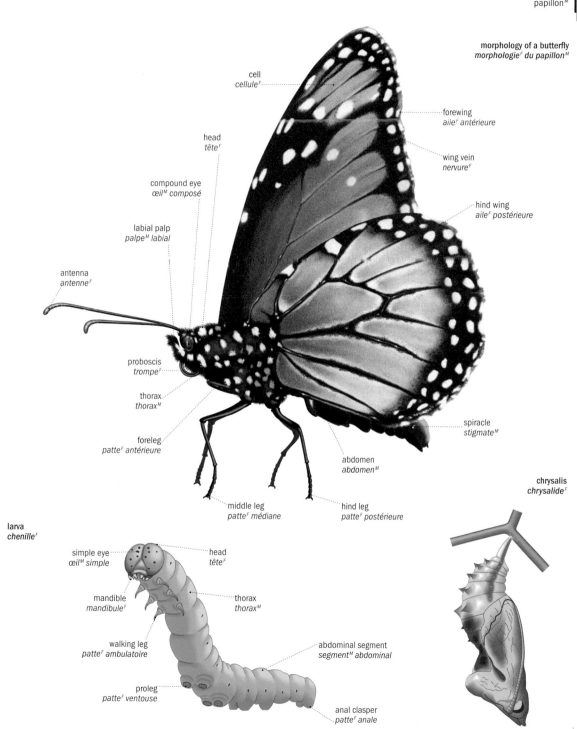

ANIMAL KINGDOM

**morphology of a butterfly**
*morphologie<sup>F</sup> du papillon<sup>M</sup>*

cell
*cellule<sup>F</sup>*

forewing
*aile<sup>F</sup> antérieure*

head
*tête<sup>F</sup>*

wing vein
*nervure<sup>F</sup>*

compound eye
*œil<sup>M</sup> composé*

hind wing
*aile<sup>F</sup> postérieure*

labial palp
*palpe<sup>M</sup> labial*

antenna
*antenne<sup>F</sup>*

proboscis
*trompe<sup>F</sup>*

thorax
*thorax<sup>M</sup>*

spiracle
*stigmate<sup>M</sup>*

foreleg
*patte<sup>F</sup> antérieure*

abdomen
*abdomen<sup>M</sup>*

middle leg
*patte<sup>F</sup> médiane*

hind leg
*patte<sup>F</sup> postérieure*

chrysalis
*chrysalide<sup>F</sup>*

larva
*chenille<sup>F</sup>*

simple eye
*œil<sup>M</sup> simple*

head
*tête<sup>F</sup>*

mandible
*mandibule<sup>F</sup>*

thorax
*thorax<sup>M</sup>*

walking leg
*patte<sup>F</sup> ambulatoire*

abdominal segment
*segment<sup>M</sup> abdominal*

proleg
*patte<sup>F</sup> ventouse*

anal clasper
*patte<sup>F</sup> anale*

# honeybee

abeille<sup>F</sup>

**morphology of a honeybee: worker**
*morphologie<sup>F</sup> de l'abeille<sup>F</sup> : ouvrière<sup>F</sup>*

wing
aile<sup>F</sup>

thorax
*thorax<sup>M</sup>*

abdomen
*abdomen<sup>M</sup>*

compound eye
*œil<sup>M</sup> composé*

pollen basket
*corbeille<sup>F</sup> à pollen<sup>M</sup>*

mouthparts
*pièces<sup>F</sup> buccales*

sting
*aiguillon<sup>M</sup>*

antenna
*antenne<sup>F</sup>*

hind leg
*patte<sup>F</sup> postérieure*

middle leg
*patte<sup>F</sup> médiane*

foreleg
*patte<sup>F</sup> antérieure*

**castes**
*castes<sup>F</sup>*

worker
*ouvrière<sup>F</sup>*

queen
*reine<sup>F</sup>*

drone
*faux bourdon<sup>M</sup>*

# examples of insects

exemples<sup>M</sup> d'insectes<sup>M</sup>

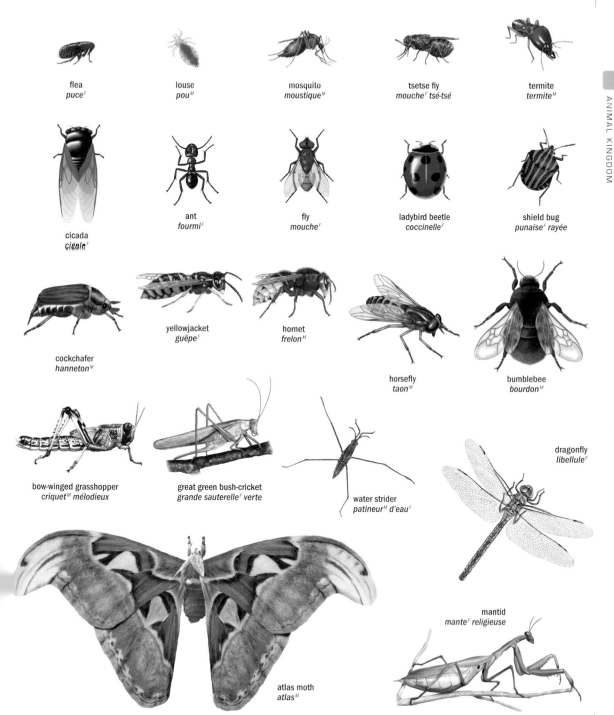

flea
*puce*<sup>F</sup>

louse
*pou*<sup>M</sup>

mosquito
*moustique*<sup>M</sup>

tsetse fly
*mouche*<sup>F</sup> *tsé-tsé*

termite
*termite*<sup>M</sup>

cicada
*cigale*<sup>F</sup>

ant
*fourmi*<sup>F</sup>

fly
*mouche*<sup>F</sup>

ladybird beetle
*coccinelle*<sup>F</sup>

shield bug
*punaise*<sup>F</sup> *rayée*

cockchafer
*hanneton*<sup>M</sup>

yellowjacket
*guêpe*<sup>F</sup>

hornet
*frelon*<sup>M</sup>

horsefly
*taon*<sup>M</sup>

bumblebee
*bourdon*<sup>M</sup>

bow-winged grasshopper
*criquet*<sup>M</sup> *mélodieux*

great green bush-cricket
*grande sauterelle*<sup>F</sup> *verte*

water strider
*patineur*<sup>M</sup> *d'eau*<sup>F</sup>

dragonfly
*libellule*<sup>F</sup>

atlas moth
*atlas*<sup>M</sup>

mantid
*mante*<sup>F</sup> *religieuse*

# spider

araignée<sup>F</sup>

ANIMAL KINGDOM

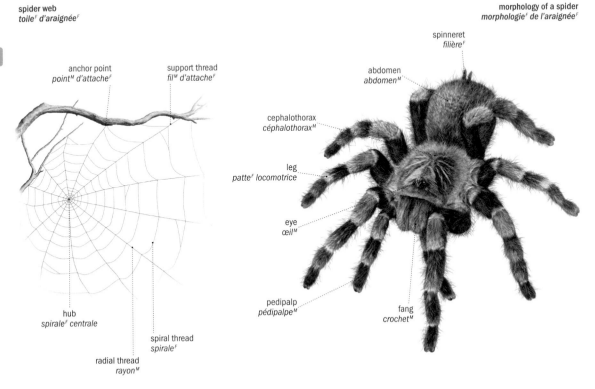

spider web
*toile<sup>F</sup> d'araignée<sup>F</sup>*

morphology of a spider
*morphologie<sup>F</sup> de l'araignée<sup>F</sup>*

anchor point
*point<sup>M</sup> d'attache<sup>F</sup>*

support thread
*fil<sup>M</sup> d'attache<sup>F</sup>*

spinneret
*filière<sup>F</sup>*

abdomen
*abdomen<sup>M</sup>*

cephalothorax
*céphalothorax<sup>M</sup>*

leg
*patte<sup>F</sup> locomotrice*

eye
*œil<sup>M</sup>*

pedipalp
*pédipalpe<sup>M</sup>*

fang
*crochet<sup>M</sup>*

hub
*spirale<sup>F</sup> centrale*

spiral thread
*spirale<sup>F</sup>*

radial thread
*rayon<sup>M</sup>*

# examples of arachnids

exemples<sup>M</sup> d'arachnides<sup>M</sup>

crab spider
*araignée<sup>F</sup>-crabe<sup>M</sup>*

garden spider
*épeire<sup>F</sup>*

scorpion
*scorpion<sup>M</sup>*

tick
*tique<sup>F</sup>*

water spider
*argyronète<sup>F</sup>*

red-kneed tarantula
*mygale<sup>F</sup> du Mexique<sup>M</sup>*

# lobster
homard[M]

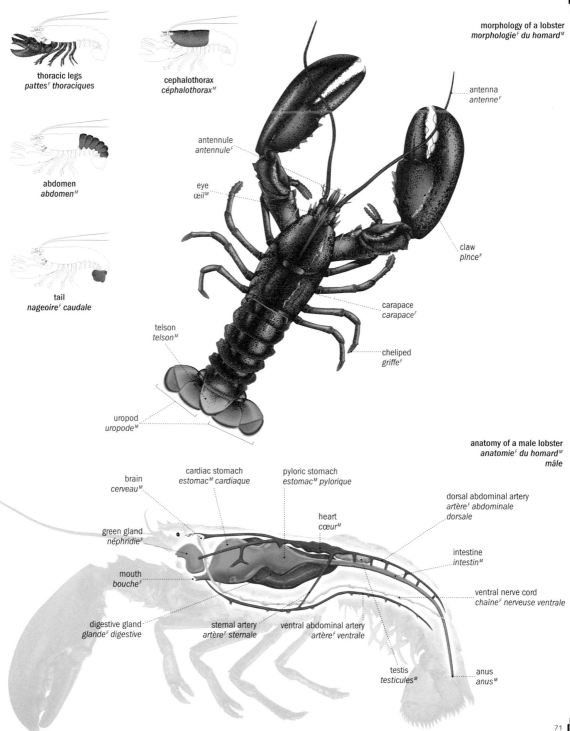

thoracic legs
pattes[F] thoraciques

cephalothorax
céphalothorax[M]

abdomen
abdomen[M]

tail
nageoire[F] caudale

morphology of a lobster
morphologie[F] du homard[M]

antenna
antenne[F]

antennule
antennule[F]

eye
œil[M]

claw
pince[F]

carapace
carapace[F]

cheliped
griffe[F]

telson
telson[M]

uropod
uropode[M]

ANIMAL KINGDOM

anatomy of a male lobster
anatomie[F] du homard[M]
mâle

brain
cerveau[M]

cardiac stomach
estomac[M] cardiaque

pyloric stomach
estomac[M] pylorique

heart
cœur[M]

dorsal abdominal artery
artère[F] abdominale
dorsale

green gland
néphridie[F]

intestine
intestin[M]

mouth
bouche[F]

ventral nerve cord
chaîne[F] nerveuse ventrale

digestive gland
glande[F] digestive

sternal artery
artère[F] sternale

ventral abdominal artery
artère[F] ventrale

testis
testicules[M]

anus
anus[M]

71

# snail

escargot<sup>M</sup>

**morphology of a snail**
*morphologie<sup>F</sup> de l'escargot<sup>M</sup>*

whorl
*tour<sup>M</sup> de coquille<sup>F</sup>*

shell
*coquille<sup>F</sup>*

growth line
*ligne<sup>F</sup> de croissance<sup>F</sup>*

apex
*apex<sup>M</sup>*

head
*tête<sup>F</sup>*

eye
*œil<sup>M</sup>*

foot
*pied<sup>M</sup>*

eyestalk
*tentacule<sup>M</sup> oculaire*

mouth
*bouche<sup>F</sup>*

tentacle
*tentacule<sup>M</sup> tactile*

# octopus

pieuvre<sup>F</sup>

**morphology of an octopus**
*morphologie<sup>F</sup> de la pieuvre<sup>F</sup>*

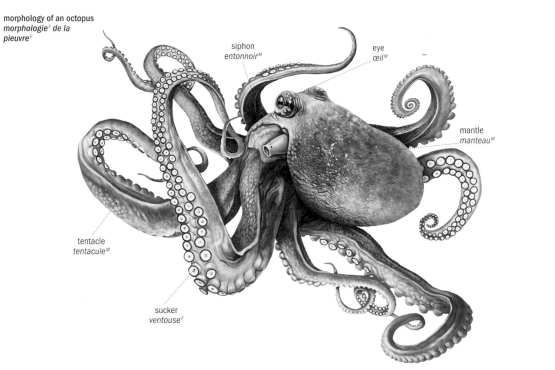

siphon
*entonnoir<sup>M</sup>*

eye
*œil<sup>M</sup>*

mantle
*manteau<sup>M</sup>*

tentacle
*tentacule<sup>M</sup>*

sucker
*ventouse<sup>F</sup>*

# univalve shell

coquillage<sup>M</sup> univalve

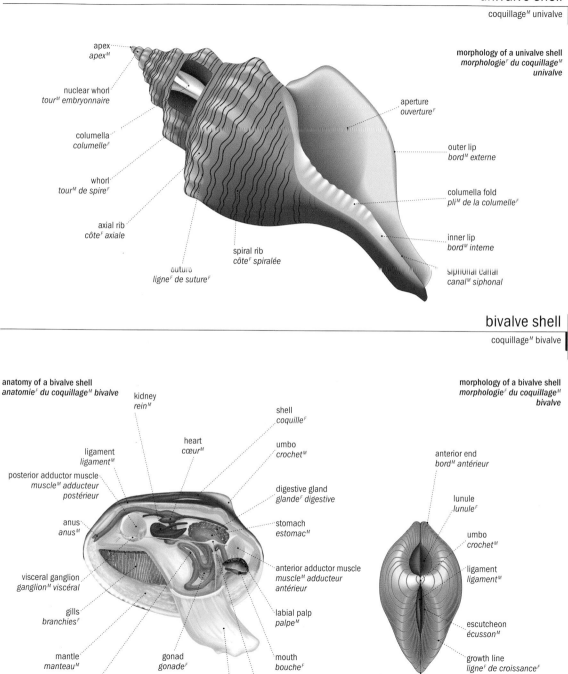

**morphology of a univalve shell**
*morphologie<sup>F</sup> du coquillage<sup>M</sup>
univalve*

apex
*apex<sup>M</sup>*

nuclear whorl
*tour<sup>M</sup> embryonnaire*

columella
*columelle<sup>F</sup>*

whorl
*tour<sup>M</sup> de spire<sup>F</sup>*

axial rib
*côte<sup>F</sup> axiale*

spiral rib
*côte<sup>F</sup> spiralée*

suture
*ligne<sup>F</sup> de suture<sup>F</sup>*

aperture
*ouverture<sup>F</sup>*

outer lip
*bord<sup>M</sup> externe*

columella fold
*pli<sup>M</sup> de la columelle<sup>F</sup>*

inner lip
*bord<sup>M</sup> interne*

siphonal canal
*canal<sup>M</sup> siphonal*

# bivalve shell

coquillage<sup>M</sup> bivalve

**anatomy of a bivalve shell**
*anatomie<sup>F</sup> du coquillage<sup>M</sup> bivalve*

kidney
*rein<sup>M</sup>*

heart
*cœur<sup>M</sup>*

ligament
*ligament<sup>M</sup>*

posterior adductor muscle
*muscle<sup>M</sup> adducteur
postérieur*

anus
*anus<sup>M</sup>*

visceral ganglion
*ganglion<sup>M</sup> viscéral*

gills
*branchies<sup>F</sup>*

mantle
*manteau<sup>M</sup>*

intestine
*intestin<sup>M</sup>*

gonad
*gonade<sup>F</sup>*

foot
*pied<sup>M</sup>*

cerebropleural ganglion
*ganglion<sup>M</sup> cérébropleural*

shell
*coquille<sup>F</sup>*

umbo
*crochet<sup>M</sup>*

digestive gland
*glande<sup>F</sup> digestive*

stomach
*estomac<sup>M</sup>*

anterior adductor muscle
*muscle<sup>M</sup> adducteur
antérieur*

labial palp
*palpe<sup>M</sup>*

mouth
*bouche<sup>F</sup>*

**morphology of a bivalve shell**
*morphologie<sup>F</sup> du coquillage<sup>M</sup>
bivalve*

anterior end
*bord<sup>M</sup> antérieur*

lunule
*lunule<sup>F</sup>*

umbo
*crochet<sup>M</sup>*

ligament
*ligament<sup>M</sup>*

escutcheon
*écusson<sup>M</sup>*

growth line
*ligne<sup>F</sup> de croissance<sup>F</sup>*

valve
*valve<sup>F</sup>*

posterior end
*bord<sup>M</sup> postérieur*

# cartilaginous fish

poisson<sup>M</sup> cartilagineux

**morphology of a female shark**
*morphologie<sup>F</sup> du requin<sup>M</sup> femelle*

snout
*museau<sup>M</sup>*

nostril
*narine<sup>F</sup>*

tooth
*dent<sup>F</sup>*

gill slits
*fentes<sup>F</sup> branchiales*

pectoral fin
*nageoire<sup>F</sup> pectorale*

first dorsal fin
*première nageoire<sup>F</sup> dorsale*

carina
*carène<sup>F</sup>*

second dorsal fin
*seconde nageoire<sup>F</sup> dorsale*

caudal fin
*nageoire<sup>F</sup> caudale*

pelvic fin
*nageoire<sup>F</sup> pelvienne*

anal fin
*nageoire<sup>F</sup> anale*

# bony fish

poisson<sup>M</sup> osseux

**morphology of a perch**
*morphologie<sup>F</sup> de la perche<sup>F</sup> ; morphologie<sup>F</sup> de la perchaude<sup>F</sup>*

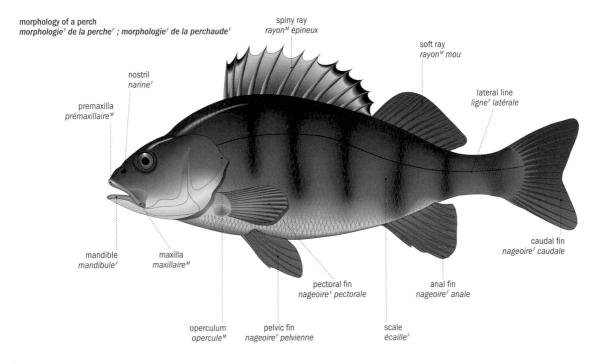

spiny ray
*rayon<sup>M</sup> épineux*

soft ray
*rayon<sup>M</sup> mou*

nostril
*narine<sup>F</sup>*

lateral line
*ligne<sup>F</sup> latérale*

premaxilla
*prémaxillaire<sup>M</sup>*

mandible
*mandibule<sup>F</sup>*

maxilla
*maxillaire<sup>M</sup>*

caudal fin
*nageoire<sup>F</sup> caudale*

pectoral fin
*nageoire<sup>F</sup> pectorale*

anal fin
*nageoire<sup>F</sup> anale*

operculum
*opercule<sup>M</sup>*

pelvic fin
*nageoire<sup>F</sup> pelvienne*

scale
*écaille<sup>F</sup>*

# frog

grenouille<sup>F</sup>

ANIMAL KINGDOM

**morphology of a frog**
*morphologie<sup>F</sup> de la grenouille<sup>F</sup>*

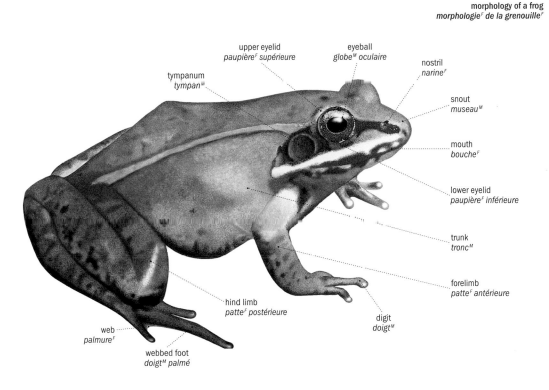

upper eyelid
*paupière<sup>F</sup> supérieure*

eyeball
*globe<sup>M</sup> oculaire*

nostril
*narine<sup>F</sup>*

tympanum
*tympan<sup>M</sup>*

snout
*museau<sup>M</sup>*

mouth
*bouche<sup>F</sup>*

lower eyelid
*paupière<sup>F</sup> inférieure*

trunk
*tronc<sup>M</sup>*

forelimb
*patte<sup>F</sup> antérieure*

hind limb
*patte<sup>F</sup> postérieure*

digit
*doigt<sup>M</sup>*

web
*palmure<sup>F</sup>*

webbed foot
*doigt<sup>M</sup> palmé*

# examples of amphibians

exemples<sup>M</sup> d'amphibiens<sup>M</sup>

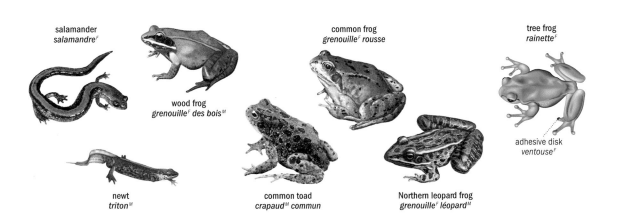

salamander
*salamandre<sup>F</sup>*

wood frog
*grenouille<sup>F</sup> des bois<sup>M</sup>*

common frog
*grenouille<sup>F</sup> rousse*

tree frog
*rainette<sup>F</sup>*

adhesive disk
*ventouse<sup>F</sup>*

newt
*triton<sup>M</sup>*

common toad
*crapaud<sup>M</sup> commun*

Northern leopard frog
*grenouille<sup>F</sup> léopard<sup>M</sup>*

ANIMAL KINGDOM

# snake
serpent<sup>M</sup>

**morphology of a venomous snake: head**
*morphologie<sup>F</sup> du serpent<sup>M</sup> venimeux : tête<sup>F</sup>*

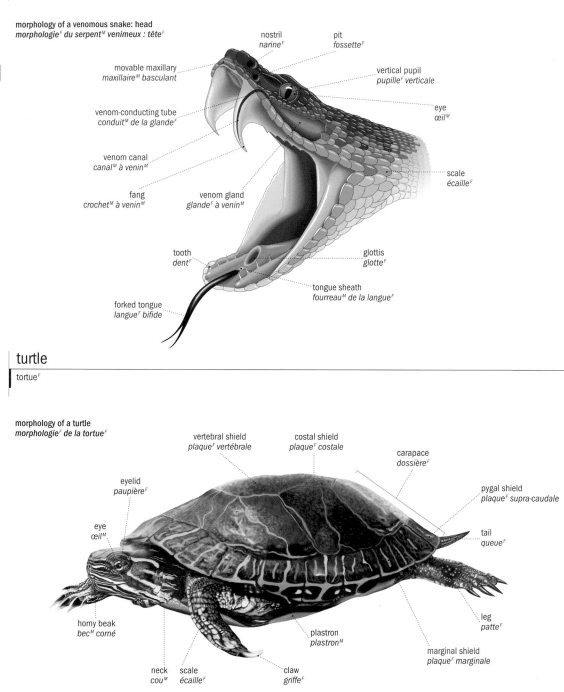

nostril
*narine<sup>F</sup>*

pit
*fossette<sup>F</sup>*

movable maxillary
*maxillaire<sup>M</sup> basculant*

vertical pupil
*pupille<sup>F</sup> verticale*

venom-conducting tube
*conduit<sup>M</sup> de la glande<sup>F</sup>*

eye
*œil<sup>M</sup>*

venom canal
*canal<sup>M</sup> à venin<sup>M</sup>*

scale
*écaille<sup>F</sup>*

fang
*crochet<sup>M</sup> à venin<sup>M</sup>*

venom gland
*glande<sup>F</sup> à venin<sup>M</sup>*

tooth
*dent<sup>F</sup>*

glottis
*glotte<sup>F</sup>*

forked tongue
*langue<sup>F</sup> bifide*

tongue sheath
*fourreau<sup>M</sup> de la langue<sup>F</sup>*

# turtle
tortue<sup>F</sup>

**morphology of a turtle**
*morphologie<sup>F</sup> de la tortue<sup>F</sup>*

vertebral shield
*plaque<sup>F</sup> vertébrale*

costal shield
*plaque<sup>F</sup> costale*

carapace
*dossière<sup>F</sup>*

eyelid
*paupière<sup>F</sup>*

pygal shield
*plaque<sup>F</sup> supra-caudale*

eye
*œil<sup>M</sup>*

tail
*queue<sup>F</sup>*

horny beak
*bec<sup>M</sup> corné*

leg
*patte<sup>F</sup>*

plastron
*plastron<sup>M</sup>*

marginal shield
*plaque<sup>F</sup> marginale*

neck
*cou<sup>M</sup>*

scale
*écaille<sup>F</sup>*

claw
*griffe<sup>F</sup>*

# examples of reptiles
exemples<sup>M</sup> de reptiles<sup>M</sup>

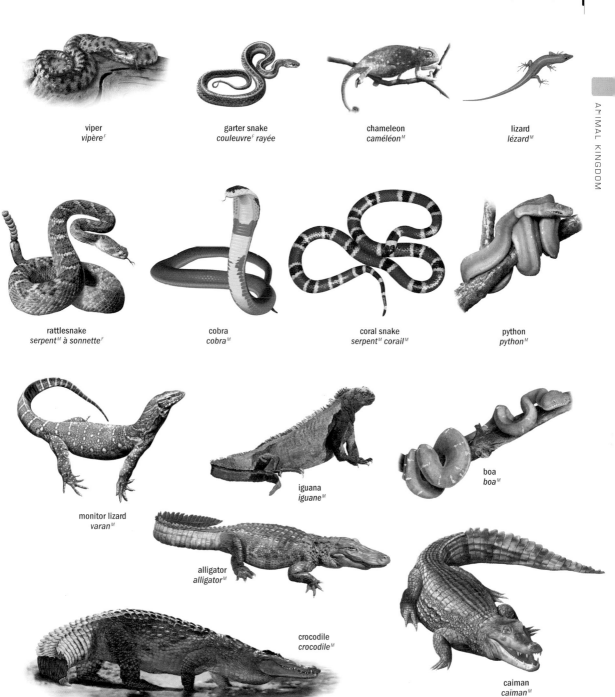

viper
*vipère*<sup>F</sup>

garter snake
*couleuvre*<sup>F</sup> *rayée*

chameleon
*caméléon*<sup>M</sup>

lizard
*lézard*<sup>M</sup>

rattlesnake
*serpent*<sup>M</sup> *à sonnette*<sup>F</sup>

cobra
*cobra*<sup>M</sup>

coral snake
*serpent*<sup>M</sup> *corail*<sup>M</sup>

python
*python*<sup>M</sup>

monitor lizard
*varan*<sup>M</sup>

iguana
*iguane*<sup>M</sup>

boa
*boa*<sup>M</sup>

alligator
*alligator*<sup>M</sup>

crocodile
*crocodile*<sup>M</sup>

caiman
*caïman*<sup>M</sup>

# bird

oiseau^M

**morphology of a bird**
*morphologie^F de l'oiseau^M*

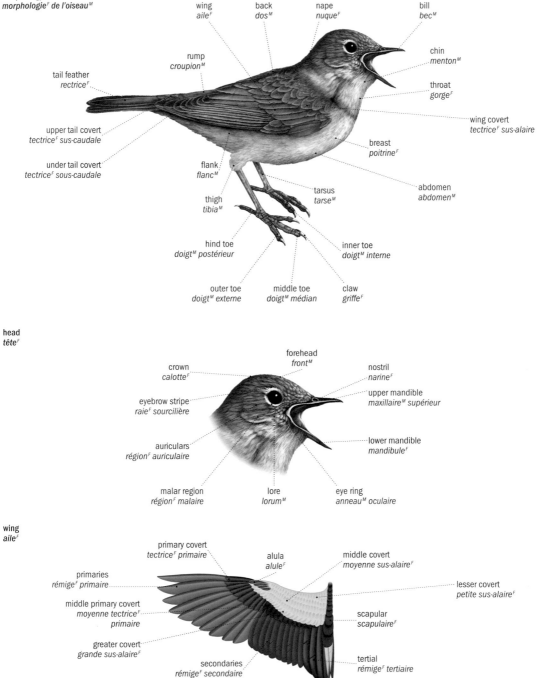

wing
*aile^F*

back
*dos^M*

nape
*nuque^F*

bill
*bec^M*

rump
*croupion^M*

chin
*menton^M*

tail feather
*rectrice^F*

throat
*gorge^F*

wing covert
*tectrice^F sus-alaire*

upper tail covert
*tectrice^F sus-caudale*

breast
*poitrine^F*

under tail covert
*tectrice^F sous-caudale*

flank
*flanc^M*

abdomen
*abdomen^M*

tarsus
*tarse^M*

thigh
*tibia^M*

hind toe
*doigt^M postérieur*

inner toe
*doigt^M interne*

outer toe
*doigt^M externe*

middle toe
*doigt^M médian*

claw
*griffe^F*

**head**
*tête^F*

forehead
*front^M*

crown
*calotte^F*

nostril
*narine^F*

eyebrow stripe
*raie^F sourcilière*

upper mandible
*maxillaire^M supérieur*

auriculars
*région^F auriculaire*

lower mandible
*mandibule^F*

malar region
*région^F malaire*

lore
*lorum^M*

eye ring
*anneau^M oculaire*

**wing**
*aile^F*

primary covert
*tectrice^F primaire*

alula
*alule^F*

middle covert
*moyenne sus-alaire^F*

primaries
*rémige^F primaire*

lesser covert
*petite sus-alaire^F*

middle primary covert
*moyenne tectrice^F primaire*

scapular
*scapulaire^F*

greater covert
*grande sus-alaire^F*

secondaries
*rémige^F secondaire*

tertial
*rémige^F tertiaire*

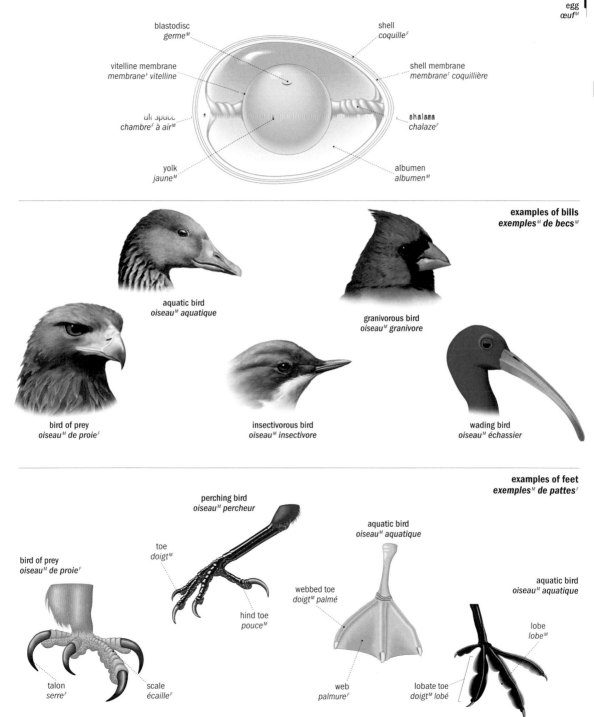

egg
*œuf*ᴹ

blastodisc
*germe*ᴹ

shell
*coquille*ᶠ

vitelline membrane
*membrane*ᴵ *vitelline*

shell membrane
*membrane*ᶠ *coquillière*

air space
*chambre*ᶠ *à air*ᴹ

chalaza
*chalaze*ᶠ

yolk
*jaune*ᴹ

albumen
*albumen*ᴹ

examples of bills
*exemples*ᴹ *de becs*ᴹ

aquatic bird
*oiseau*ᴹ *aquatique*

granivorous bird
*oiseau*ᴹ *granivore*

bird of prey
*oiseau*ᴹ *de proie*ᶠ

insectivorous bird
*oiseau*ᴹ *insectivore*

wading bird
*oiseau*ᴹ *échassier*

examples of feet
*exemples*ᴹ *de pattes*ᶠ

perching bird
*oiseau*ᴹ *percheur*

aquatic bird
*oiseau*ᴹ *aquatique*

bird of prey
*oiseau*ᴹ *de proie*ᶠ

toe
*doigt*ᴹ

aquatic bird
*oiseau*ᴹ *aquatique*

webbed toe
*doigt*ᴹ *palmé*

hind toe
*pouce*ᴹ

lobe
*lobe*ᴹ

talon
*serre*ᶠ

scale
*écaille*ᶠ

web
*palmure*ᶠ

lobate toe
*doigt*ᴹ *lobé*

# examples of birds

exemples<sup>M</sup> d'oiseaux<sup>M</sup>

hummingbird
*colibri*<sup>M</sup>

European robin
*rouge-gorge*<sup>M</sup>

finch
*pinson*<sup>M</sup>

kingfisher
*martin-pêcheur*<sup>M</sup>

nightingale
*rossignol*<sup>M</sup>

sparrow
*moineau*<sup>M</sup>

swallow
*hirondelle*<sup>F</sup>

starling
*étourneau*<sup>M</sup>

jay
*geai*<sup>M</sup>

cardinal
*cardinal*<sup>M</sup>

swift
*martinet*<sup>M</sup>

partridge
*perdrix*<sup>F</sup>

condor
*condor*<sup>M</sup>

raven
*corbeau*<sup>M</sup>

toucan
*toucan*<sup>M</sup>

vulture
*vautour*<sup>M</sup>

macaw
*ara*<sup>M</sup>

woodpecker
*pic*<sup>M</sup>

penguin
*manchot*<sup>M</sup>

albatross
*albatros*<sup>M</sup>

heron
*héron*<sup>M</sup>

pelican
*pélican*<sup>M</sup>

stork
*cigogne*<sup>F</sup>

pheasant
*faisan*<sup>M</sup>

great horned owl
*grand duc*<sup>M</sup> *d'Amérique*<sup>F</sup>

falcon
*faucon*<sup>M</sup>

quail
*caille*<sup>F</sup>

eagle
*aigle*<sup>M</sup>

hen
*poule*<sup>F</sup>

duck
*canard*<sup>M</sup>

pigeon
*pigeon*<sup>M</sup>

turkey
*dindon*<sup>M</sup>

guinea fowl
*pintade*<sup>F</sup>

goose
*oie*<sup>F</sup>

rooster
*coq*<sup>M</sup>

ostrich
*autruche*<sup>F</sup>

peacock
*paon*<sup>M</sup>

flamingo
*flamant*<sup>M</sup>

# rodent

rongeur<sup>M</sup>

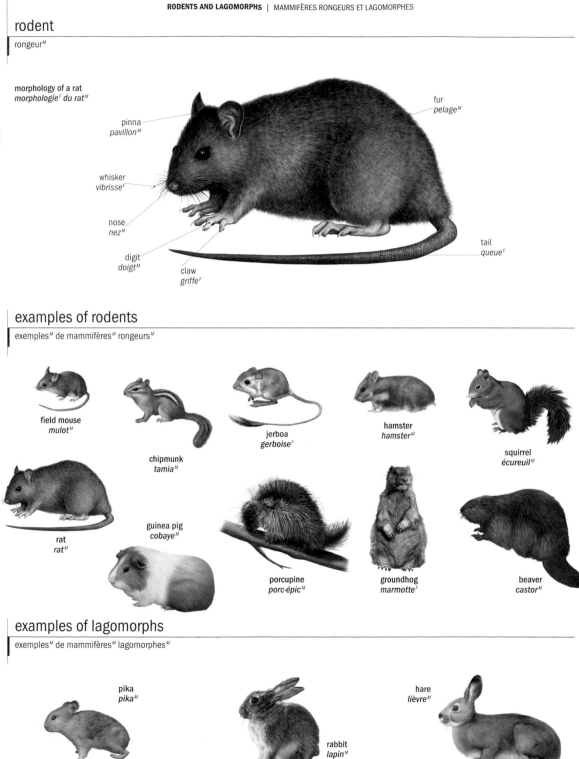

**morphology of a rat**
*morphologie<sup>F</sup> du rat<sup>M</sup>*

pinna
*pavillon<sup>M</sup>*

whisker
*vibrisse<sup>F</sup>*

nose
*nez<sup>M</sup>*

digit
*doigt<sup>M</sup>*

claw
*griffe<sup>F</sup>*

fur
*pelage<sup>M</sup>*

tail
*queue<sup>F</sup>*

# examples of rodents

exemples<sup>M</sup> de mammifères<sup>M</sup> rongeurs<sup>M</sup>

field mouse
*mulot<sup>M</sup>*

chipmunk
*tamia<sup>M</sup>*

jerboa
*gerboise<sup>F</sup>*

hamster
*hamster<sup>M</sup>*

squirrel
*écureuil<sup>M</sup>*

rat
*rat<sup>M</sup>*

guinea pig
*cobaye<sup>M</sup>*

porcupine
*porc-épic<sup>M</sup>*

groundhog
*marmotte<sup>F</sup>*

beaver
*castor<sup>M</sup>*

# examples of lagomorphs

exemples<sup>M</sup> de mammifères<sup>M</sup> lagomorphes<sup>M</sup>

pika
*pika<sup>M</sup>*

rabbit
*lapin<sup>M</sup>*

hare
*lièvre<sup>M</sup>*

# horse

cheval<sup>M</sup>

ANIMAL KINGDOM

**morphology of a horse**
*morphologie<sup>F</sup> du cheval<sup>M</sup>*

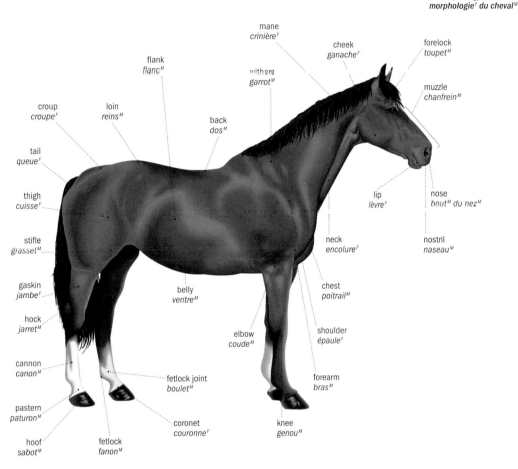

mane
crinière<sup>F</sup>

cheek
ganache<sup>F</sup>

forelock
toupet<sup>M</sup>

flank
flanc<sup>M</sup>

withers
garrot<sup>M</sup>

muzzle
chanfrein<sup>M</sup>

croup
croupe<sup>F</sup>

loin
reins<sup>M</sup>

back
dos<sup>M</sup>

tail
queue<sup>F</sup>

lip
lèvre<sup>F</sup>

nose
bout<sup>M</sup> du nez<sup>M</sup>

thigh
cuisse<sup>F</sup>

neck
encolure<sup>F</sup>

nostril
naseau<sup>M</sup>

stifle
grasset<sup>M</sup>

chest
poitrail<sup>M</sup>

gaskin
jambe<sup>F</sup>

belly
ventre<sup>M</sup>

hock
jarret<sup>M</sup>

elbow
coude<sup>M</sup>

shoulder
épaule<sup>F</sup>

cannon
canon<sup>M</sup>

fetlock joint
boulet<sup>M</sup>

forearm
bras<sup>M</sup>

pastern
paturon<sup>M</sup>

coronet
couronne<sup>F</sup>

knee
genou<sup>M</sup>

hoof
sabot<sup>M</sup>

fetlock
fanon<sup>M</sup>

**gaits**
*allures<sup>F</sup>*

walk
pas<sup>M</sup>

pace
amble<sup>M</sup>

trot
trot<sup>M</sup>

gallop
galop<sup>M</sup>

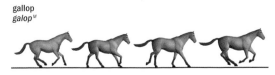

# examples of ungulate mammals

exemples<sup>M</sup> de mammifères<sup>M</sup> ongulés

ANIMAL KINGDOM

peccary
*pécari*<sup>M</sup>

wild boar
*sanglier*<sup>M</sup>

pig
*porc*<sup>M</sup>

goat
*chèvre*<sup>F</sup>

antelope
*antilope*<sup>F</sup>

sheep
*mouton*<sup>M</sup>

calf
*veau*<sup>M</sup>

white-tailed deer
*cerf*<sup>M</sup> *de Virginie ; chevreuil*<sup>M</sup>

mouflon
*mouflon*<sup>M</sup>

caribou
*renne*<sup>M</sup> *; caribou*<sup>M</sup>

wapiti (elk)
*cerf*<sup>M</sup> *du Canada ;*
*wapiti*<sup>M</sup>

okapi
*okapi*<sup>M</sup>

ass
*âne*<sup>M</sup>

mule
*mulet*<sup>M</sup>

cow
*vache*<sup>F</sup>

zebra
*zèbre*<sup>M</sup>

llama
*lama*<sup>M</sup>

bison
*bison*<sup>M</sup>

buffalo
*buffle*<sup>M</sup>

ox
*bœuf*[M]

yak
*yack*[M]

horse
*cheval*[M]

moose
*élan*[M] *; original*[M]

bactrian camel
*chameau*[M]

dromedary camel
*dromadaire*[M]

rhinoceros
*rhinocéros*[M]

hippopotamus
*hippopotame*[M]

giraffe
*girafe*[F]

elephant
*éléphant*[M]

ANIMAL KINGDOM

# dog
chien<sup>M</sup>

**morphology of a dog**
*morphologie<sup>F</sup> du chien<sup>M</sup>*

stop
*stop<sup>M</sup>*

muzzle
*museau<sup>M</sup>*

cheek
*joue<sup>F</sup>*

flews
*babines<sup>F</sup>*

withers
*garrot<sup>M</sup>*

back
*dos<sup>M</sup>*

thigh
*cuisse<sup>F</sup>*

shoulder
*épaule<sup>F</sup>*

elbow
*coude<sup>M</sup>*

hock
*jarret<sup>M</sup>*

tail
*queue<sup>F</sup>*

forearm
*avant-bras<sup>M</sup>*

knee
*genou<sup>M</sup>*

wrist
*poignet<sup>M</sup>*

toe
*orteil<sup>M</sup>*

# examples of dog breeds
races<sup>F</sup> de chiens<sup>M</sup>

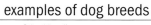

bulldog
*bouledogue<sup>M</sup>*

collie
*colley<sup>M</sup>*

Dalmatian
*dalmatien<sup>M</sup>*

poodle
*caniche<sup>M</sup>*

schnauzer
*schnauzer<sup>M</sup>*

Great Dane
*danois<sup>M</sup>*

German shepherd
*berger<sup>M</sup> allemand*

Saint Bernard
*saint-bernard<sup>M</sup>*

# cat
chat<sup>M</sup>

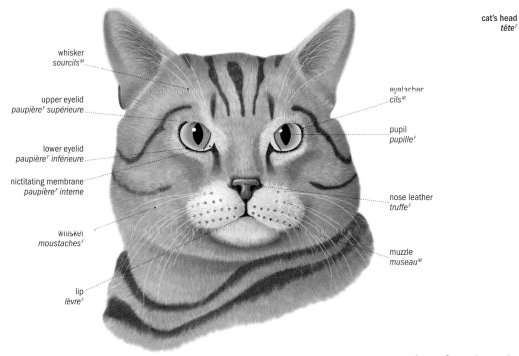

cat's head
tête<sup>F</sup>

whisker
sourcils<sup>M</sup>

upper eyelid
paupière<sup>F</sup> supérieure

lower eyelid
paupière<sup>F</sup> inférieure

nictitating membrane
paupière<sup>F</sup> interne

whisker
moustaches<sup>F</sup>

lip
lèvre<sup>F</sup>

eyelashes
cils<sup>M</sup>

pupil
pupille<sup>F</sup>

nose leather
truffe<sup>F</sup>

muzzle
museau<sup>M</sup>

ANIMAL KINGDOM

## examples of cat breeds
races<sup>F</sup> de chats<sup>M</sup>

Siamese
siamois<sup>M</sup>

Abyssinian
abyssin<sup>M</sup>

Persian
persan<sup>M</sup>

Maine coon
Maine coon<sup>M</sup>

Manx
chat<sup>M</sup> de l'île<sup>F</sup> de Man

# examples of carnivorous mammals

exemples<sup>M</sup> de mammifères<sup>M</sup> carnivores

ANIMAL KINGDOM

weasel
*belette*<sup>F</sup>

mink
*vison*<sup>M</sup>

stone marten
*fouine*<sup>F</sup>

marten
*martre*<sup>F</sup>

fox
*renard*<sup>M</sup>

raccoon
*raton*<sup>M</sup> *laveur*

fennec
*fennec*<sup>M</sup>

river otter
*loutre*<sup>F</sup> *de rivière*<sup>F</sup>

mongoose
*mangouste*<sup>F</sup>

badger
*blaireau*<sup>M</sup>

skunk
*moufette*<sup>F</sup>

hyena
*hyène*<sup>F</sup>

lynx
*lynx*<sup>M</sup>

wolf
*loup*<sup>M</sup>

cougar
*puma*<sup>M</sup>

examples of carnivorous mammals

cheetah
guépard<sup>M</sup>

leopard
léopard<sup>M</sup>

lion
lion<sup>M</sup>

jaguar
jaguar<sup>M</sup>

tiger
tigre<sup>M</sup>

polar bear
ours<sup>M</sup> polaire

black bear
ours<sup>M</sup> noir

# dolphin

dauphin<sup>M</sup>

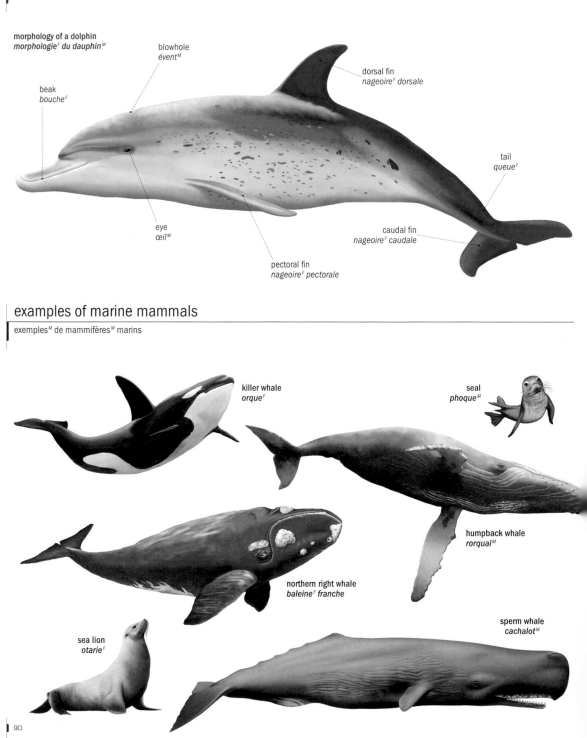

**morphology of a dolphin**
*morphologie<sup>F</sup> du dauphin<sup>M</sup>*

blowhole
*évent<sup>M</sup>*

dorsal fin
*nageoire<sup>F</sup> dorsale*

beak
*bouche<sup>F</sup>*

tail
*queue<sup>F</sup>*

eye
*œil<sup>M</sup>*

caudal fin
*nageoire<sup>F</sup> caudale*

pectoral fin
*nageoire<sup>F</sup> pectorale*

# examples of marine mammals

exemples<sup>M</sup> de mammifères<sup>M</sup> marins

killer whale
*orque<sup>F</sup>*

seal
*phoque<sup>M</sup>*

humpback whale
*rorqual<sup>M</sup>*

northern right whale
*baleine<sup>F</sup> franche*

sperm whale
*cachalot<sup>M</sup>*

sea lion
*otarie<sup>F</sup>*

# gorilla
*gorille*$^M$

## morphology of a gorilla
*morphologie*$^F$ *du gorille*$^M$

face
*face*$^F$

arm
*bras*$^M$

fur
*pelage*$^M$

hand
*main*$^F$

prehensile digit
*doigt*$^M$ *préhensile*

leg
*jambe*$^F$

opposable thumb
*pouce*$^M$ *opposable*

foot
*pied*$^M$

# examples of primates
*exemples*$^M$ *de mammifères*$^M$ *primates*

tamarin
*tamarin*$^M$

baboon
*babouin*$^M$

macaque
*macaque*$^M$

marmoset
*ouistiti*$^M$

orangutan
*orang-outan*$^M$

chimpanzee
*chimpanzé*$^M$

lemur
*lémurien*$^M$

gibbon
*gibbon*$^M$

# man

homme<sup>M</sup>

anterior view
*face<sup>F</sup> antérieure*

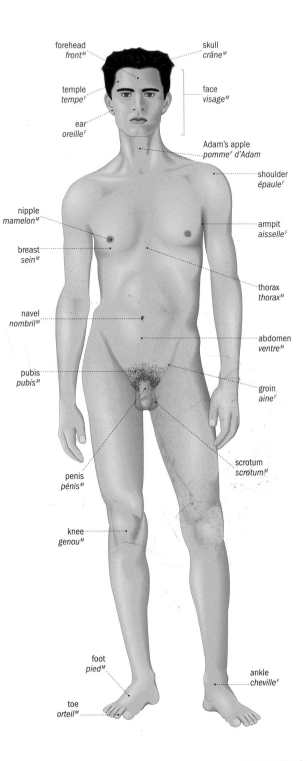

forehead
*front<sup>M</sup>*

skull
*crâne<sup>M</sup>*

temple
*tempe<sup>F</sup>*

face
*visage<sup>M</sup>*

ear
*oreille<sup>F</sup>*

Adam's apple
*pomme<sup>F</sup> d'Adam*

shoulder
*épaule<sup>F</sup>*

nipple
*mamelon<sup>M</sup>*

armpit
*aisselle<sup>F</sup>*

breast
*sein<sup>M</sup>*

thorax
*thorax<sup>M</sup>*

navel
*nombril<sup>M</sup>*

abdomen
*ventre<sup>M</sup>*

pubis
*pubis<sup>M</sup>*

groin
*aine<sup>F</sup>*

scrotum
*scrotum<sup>M</sup>*

penis
*pénis<sup>M</sup>*

knee
*genou<sup>M</sup>*

foot
*pied<sup>M</sup>*

ankle
*cheville<sup>F</sup>*

toe
*orteil<sup>M</sup>*

man

posterior view
*face*<sup>F</sup> *postérieure*

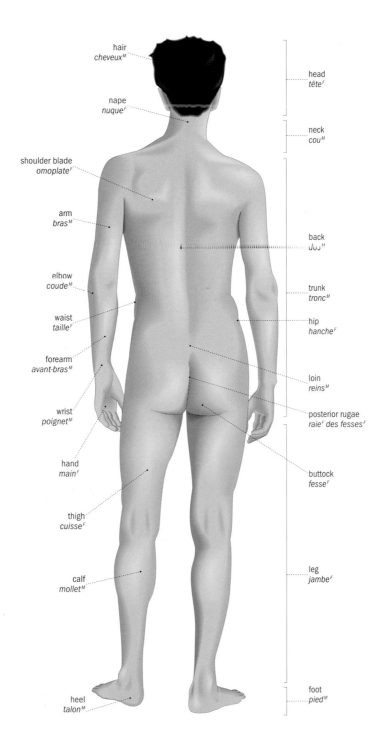

hair
*cheveux*<sup>M</sup>

nape
*nuque*<sup>F</sup>

shoulder blade
*omoplate*<sup>F</sup>

arm
*bras*<sup>M</sup>

elbow
*coude*<sup>M</sup>

waist
*taille*<sup>F</sup>

forearm
*avant-bras*<sup>M</sup>

wrist
*poignet*<sup>M</sup>

hand
*main*<sup>F</sup>

thigh
*cuisse*<sup>F</sup>

calf
*mollet*<sup>M</sup>

heel
*talon*<sup>M</sup>

head
*tête*<sup>F</sup>

neck
*cou*<sup>M</sup>

back
*dos*<sup>M</sup>

trunk
*tronc*<sup>M</sup>

hip
*hanche*<sup>F</sup>

loin
*reins*<sup>M</sup>

posterior rugae
*raie*<sup>F</sup> *des fesses*<sup>F</sup>

buttock
*fesse*<sup>F</sup>

leg
*jambe*<sup>F</sup>

foot
*pied*<sup>M</sup>

# woman

femme<sup>F</sup>

**anterior view**
*face<sup>F</sup> antérieure*

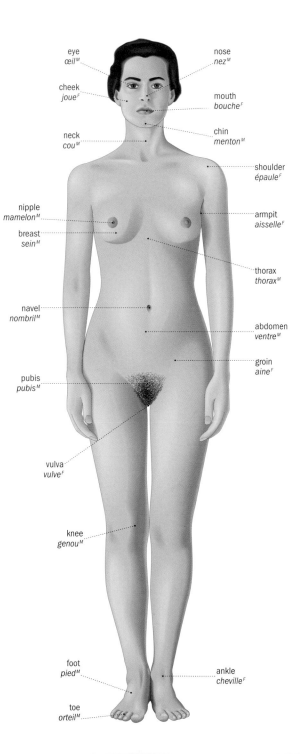

eye
œil<sup>M</sup>

nose
nez<sup>M</sup>

cheek
joue<sup>F</sup>

mouth
bouche<sup>F</sup>

neck
cou<sup>M</sup>

chin
menton<sup>M</sup>

shoulder
épaule<sup>F</sup>

nipple
mamelon<sup>M</sup>

armpit
aisselle<sup>F</sup>

breast
sein<sup>M</sup>

thorax
thorax<sup>M</sup>

navel
nombril<sup>M</sup>

abdomen
ventre<sup>M</sup>

groin
aine<sup>F</sup>

pubis
pubis<sup>M</sup>

vulva
vulve<sup>F</sup>

knee
genou<sup>M</sup>

foot
pied<sup>M</sup>

ankle
cheville<sup>F</sup>

toe
orteil<sup>M</sup>

HUMAN BEING

posterior view
*face<sup>F</sup> postérieure*

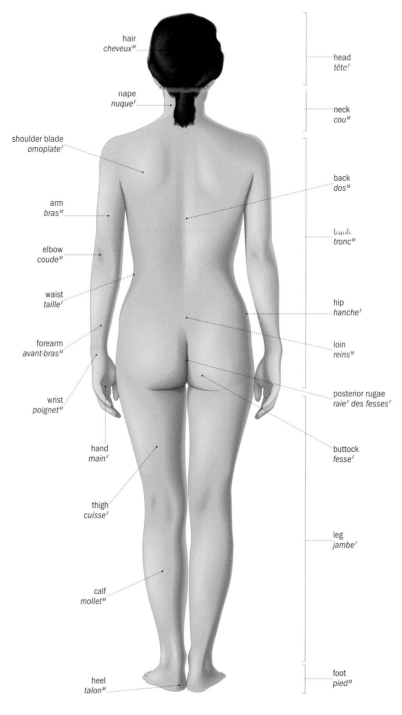

hair
*cheveux<sup>M</sup>*

head
*tête<sup>F</sup>*

nape
*nuque<sup>F</sup>*

neck
*cou<sup>M</sup>*

shoulder blade
*omoplate<sup>F</sup>*

back
*dos<sup>M</sup>*

arm
*bras<sup>M</sup>*

trunk
*tronc<sup>M</sup>*

elbow
*coude<sup>M</sup>*

waist
*taille<sup>F</sup>*

hip
*hanche<sup>F</sup>*

forearm
*avant-bras<sup>M</sup>*

loin
*reins<sup>M</sup>*

wrist
*poignet<sup>M</sup>*

posterior rugae
*raie<sup>F</sup> des fesses<sup>F</sup>*

hand
*main<sup>F</sup>*

buttock
*fesse<sup>F</sup>*

thigh
*cuisse<sup>F</sup>*

leg
*jambe<sup>F</sup>*

calf
*mollet<sup>M</sup>*

heel
*talon<sup>M</sup>*

foot
*pied<sup>M</sup>*

# muscles

muscles<sup>M</sup>

**anterior view**
*face<sup>F</sup> antérieure*

orbicularis oculi
*orbiculaire<sup>M</sup> des
paupières<sup>F</sup>*

masseter
*masséter<sup>M</sup>*

deltoid
*deltoïde<sup>M</sup>*

external oblique
*grand oblique<sup>M</sup> de
l'abdomen<sup>M</sup>*

rectus abdominis
*grand droit<sup>M</sup> de
l'abdomen<sup>M</sup>*

brachioradialis
*huméro-stylo-radial<sup>M</sup>*

tensor fasciae latae
*tenseur<sup>M</sup> du fascia lata<sup>M</sup>*

adductor longus
*moyen adducteur<sup>M</sup>*

sartorius
*couturier<sup>M</sup>*

rectus femoris
*droit<sup>M</sup> antérieur de la cuisse<sup>F</sup>*

vastus medialis
*vaste<sup>M</sup> interne du membre<sup>M</sup>
inférieur*

peroneus longus
*long péronier<sup>M</sup> latéral*

tibialis anterior
*jambier<sup>M</sup> antérieur*

extensor digitorum brevis
*pédieux<sup>M</sup>*

frontalis
*frontal<sup>M</sup>*

sternomastoid
*sterno-cléido-mastoïdien<sup>M</sup>*

trapezius
*trapèze<sup>M</sup>*

pectoralis major
*grand pectoral<sup>M</sup>*

biceps brachii
*biceps<sup>M</sup> brachial*

brachialis
*brachial<sup>M</sup> antérieur*

pronator teres
*rond pronateur<sup>M</sup>*

palmaris longus
*grand palmaire<sup>M</sup>*

flexor carpi ulnaris
*cubital<sup>M</sup> antérieur*

palmaris brevis
*petit palmaire<sup>M</sup>*

vastus lateralis
*vaste<sup>M</sup> externe du membre<sup>M</sup>
inférieur*

gastrocnemius
*jumeau<sup>M</sup>*

soleus
*soléaire<sup>M</sup>*

extensor digitorum longus
*extenseur<sup>M</sup> commun des orteils<sup>M</sup>*

interosseus plantaris
*interosseux<sup>M</sup>*

muscles

posterior view
*face*[F] *postérieure*

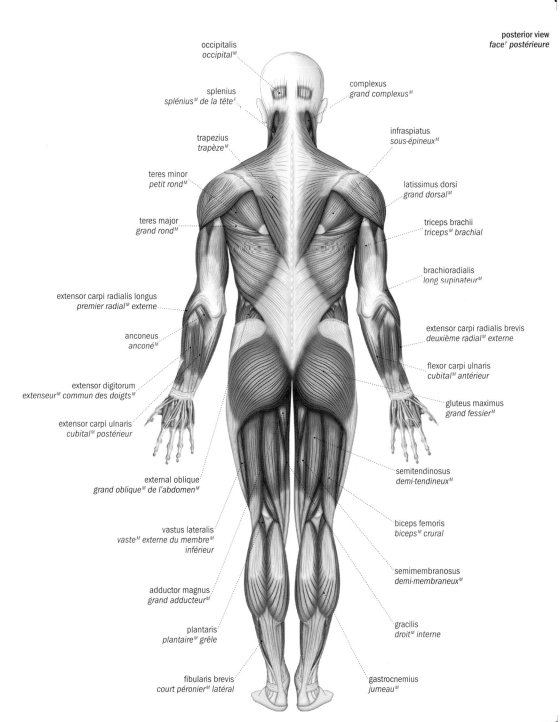

occipitalis
*occipital*[M]

splenius
*splénius*[M] *de la tête*[F]

trapezius
*trapèze*[M]

teres minor
*petit rond*[M]

teres major
*grand rond*[M]

extensor carpi radialis longus
*premier radial*[M] *externe*

anconeus
*anconé*[M]

extensor digitorum
*extenseur*[M] *commun des doigts*[M]

extensor carpi ulnaris
*cubital*[M] *postérieur*

external oblique
*grand oblique*[M] *de l'abdomen*[M]

vastus lateralis
*vaste*[M] *externe du membre*[M]
*inférieur*

adductor magnus
*grand adducteur*[M]

plantaris
*plantaire*[M] *grêle*

fibularis brevis
*court péronier*[M] *latéral*

complexus
*grand complexus*[M]

infraspiatus
*sous-épineux*[M]

latissimus dorsi
*grand dorsal*[M]

triceps brachii
*triceps*[M] *brachial*

brachioradialis
*long supinateur*[M]

extensor carpi radialis brevis
*deuxième radial*[M] *externe*

flexor carpi ulnaris
*cubital*[M] *antérieur*

gluteus maximus
*grand fessier*[M]

semitendinosus
*demi-tendineux*[M]

biceps femoris
*biceps*[M] *crural*

semimembranosus
*demi-membraneux*[M]

gracilis
*droit*[M] *interne*

gastrocnemius
*jumeau*[M]

# skeleton

squelette^M

**anterior view**
*vue^F antérieure*

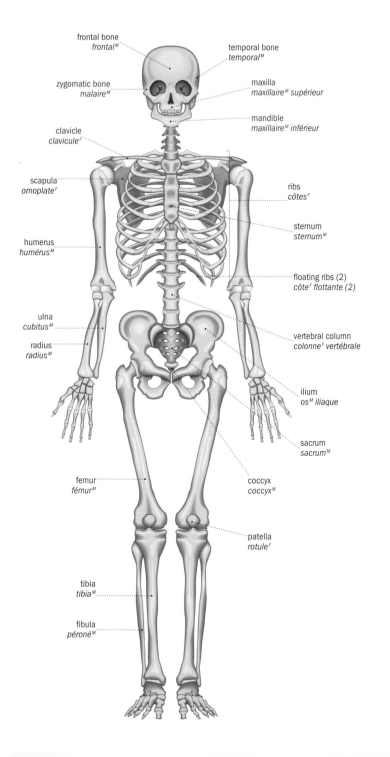

frontal bone
*frontal^M*

temporal bone
*temporal^M*

zygomatic bone
*malaire^M*

maxilla
*maxillaire^M supérieur*

mandible
*maxillaire^M inférieur*

clavicle
*clavicule^F*

scapula
*omoplate^F*

ribs
*côtes^F*

sternum
*sternum^M*

humerus
*humérus^M*

floating ribs (2)
*côte^F flottante (2)*

ulna
*cubitus^M*

radius
*radius^M*

vertebral column
*colonne^F vertébrale*

ilium
*os^M iliaque*

sacrum
*sacrum^M*

femur
*fémur^M*

coccyx
*coccyx^M*

patella
*rotule^F*

tibia
*tibia^M*

fibula
*péroné^M*

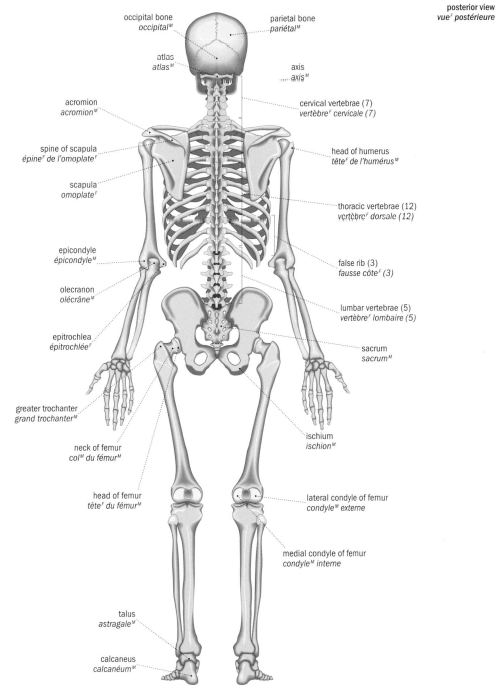

posterior view
*vue^F postérieure*

occipital bone
*occipital^M*

parietal bone
*pariétal^M*

atlas
*atlas^M*

axis
*axis^M*

acromion
*acromion^M*

cervical vertebrae (7)
*vertèbre^F cervicale (7)*

spine of scapula
*épine^F de l'omoplate^F*

head of humerus
*tête^F de l'humérus^M*

scapula
*omoplate^F*

thoracic vertebrae (12)
*vertèbre^F dorsale (12)*

epicondyle
*épicondyle^M*

false rib (3)
*fausse côte^F (3)*

olecranon
*olécrâne^M*

lumbar vertebrae (5)
*vertèbre^F lombaire (5)*

epitrochlea
*épitrochlée^F*

sacrum
*sacrum^M*

greater trochanter
*grand trochanter^M*

ischium
*ischion^M*

neck of femur
*col^M du fémur^M*

head of femur
*tête^F du fémur^M*

lateral condyle of femur
*condyle^M externe*

medial condyle of femur
*condyle^M interne*

talus
*astragale^M*

calcaneus
*calcanéum^M*

HUMAN BEING

skeleton

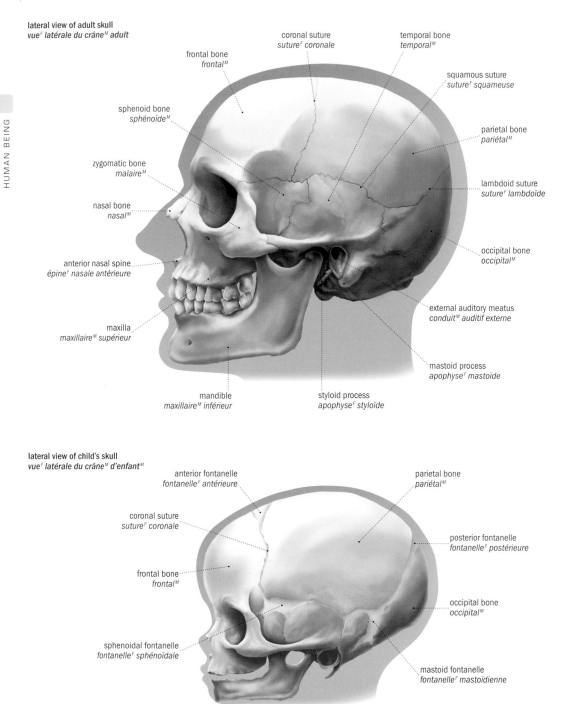

lateral view of adult skull
*vue*F *latérale du crâne*M *adult*

coronal suture
*suture*F *coronale*

temporal bone
*temporal*M

frontal bone
*frontal*M

squamous suture
*suture*F *squameuse*

sphenoid bone
*sphénoïde*M

parietal bone
*pariétal*M

zygomatic bone
*malaire*M

lambdoid suture
*suture*F *lambdoïde*

nasal bone
*nasal*M

anterior nasal spine
*épine*F *nasale antérieure*

occipital bone
*occipital*M

external auditory meatus
*conduit*M *auditif externe*

maxilla
*maxillaire*M *supérieur*

mastoid process
*apophyse*F *mastoïde*

mandible
*maxillaire*M *inférieur*

styloid process
*apophyse*F *styloïde*

lateral view of child's skull
*vue*F *latérale du crâne*M *d'enfant*M

anterior fontanelle
*fontanelle*F *antérieure*

parietal bone
*pariétal*M

coronal suture
*suture*F *coronale*

posterior fontanelle
*fontanelle*F *postérieure*

frontal bone
*frontal*M

occipital bone
*occipital*M

sphenoidal fontanelle
*fontanelle*F *sphénoïdale*

mastoid fontanelle
*fontanelle*F *mastoïdienne*

# teeth
dents<sup>F</sup>

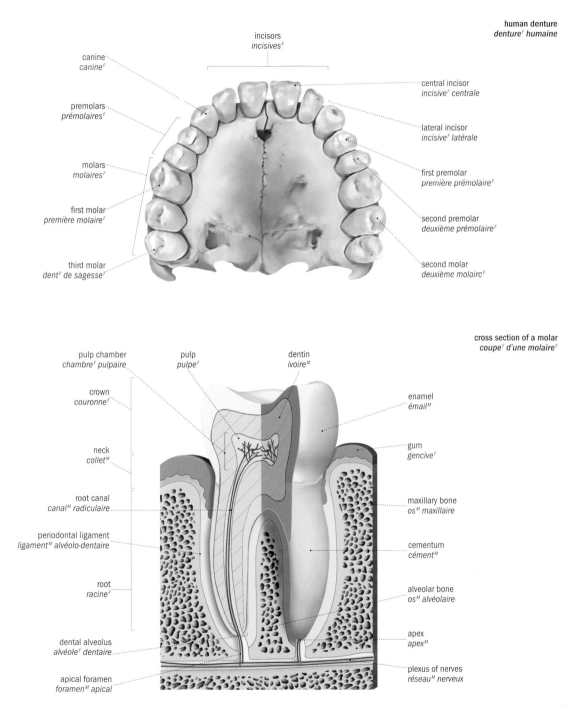

human denture
denture<sup>F</sup> humaine

incisors
incisives<sup>F</sup>

canine
canine<sup>F</sup>

premolars
prémolaires<sup>F</sup>

molars
molaires<sup>F</sup>

first molar
première molaire<sup>F</sup>

third molar
dent<sup>F</sup> de sagesse<sup>F</sup>

central incisor
incisive<sup>F</sup> centrale

lateral incisor
incisive<sup>F</sup> latérale

first premolar
première prémolaire<sup>F</sup>

second premolar
deuxième prémolaire<sup>F</sup>

second molar
deuxième molairc<sup>F</sup>

cross section of a molar
coupe<sup>F</sup> d'une molaire<sup>F</sup>

pulp chamber
chambre<sup>F</sup> pulpaire

pulp
pulpe<sup>F</sup>

dentin
ivoire<sup>M</sup>

crown
couronne<sup>F</sup>

neck
collet<sup>M</sup>

root canal
canal<sup>M</sup> radiculaire

periodontal ligament
ligament<sup>M</sup> alvéolo-dentaire

root
racine<sup>F</sup>

dental alveolus
alvéole<sup>F</sup> dentaire

apical foramen
foramen<sup>M</sup> apical

enamel
émail<sup>M</sup>

gum
gencive<sup>F</sup>

maxillary bone
os<sup>M</sup> maxillaire

cementum
cément<sup>M</sup>

alveolar bone
os<sup>M</sup> alvéolaire

apex
apex<sup>M</sup>

plexus of nerves
réseau<sup>M</sup> nerveux

# blood circulation

circulation<sup>F</sup> sanguine

**principal veins and arteries**
*principales veines<sup>F</sup> et artères<sup>F</sup>*

common carotid artery
*artère<sup>F</sup> carotide primitive*

subclavian artery
*artère<sup>F</sup> sous-clavière*

axillary artery
*artère<sup>F</sup> axillaire*

superior vena cava
*veine<sup>F</sup> cave supérieure*

brachial artery
*artère<sup>F</sup> brachiale*

pulmonary vein
*veine<sup>F</sup> pulmonaire*

inferior vena cava
*veine<sup>F</sup> cave inférieure*

superior mesenteric vein
*veine<sup>F</sup> mésentérique supérieure*

abdominal aorta
*aorte<sup>F</sup> abdominale*

common iliac artery
*artère<sup>F</sup> iliaque commune*

internal iliac artery
*artère<sup>F</sup> iliaque interne*

femoral artery
*artère<sup>F</sup> fémorale*

anterior tibial artery
*artère<sup>F</sup> tibiale antérieure*

dorsalis pedis artery
*artère<sup>F</sup> dorsale du pied<sup>M</sup>*

arch of foot artery
*artère<sup>F</sup> arquée*

external jugular vein
*veine<sup>F</sup> jugulaire externe*

internal jugular vein
*veine<sup>F</sup> jugulaire interne*

subclavian vein
*veine<sup>F</sup> sous-clavière*

axillary vein
*veine<sup>F</sup> axillaire*

arch of aorta
*arc<sup>M</sup> de l'aorte<sup>F</sup>*

pulmonary artery
*artère<sup>F</sup> pulmonaire*

cephalic vein
*veine<sup>F</sup> céphalique*

basilic vein
*veine<sup>F</sup> basilique*

renal vein
*veine<sup>F</sup> rénale*

renal artery
*artère<sup>F</sup> rénale*

superior mesenteric artery
*artère<sup>F</sup> mésentérique supérieure*

femoral vein
*veine<sup>F</sup> fémorale*

great saphenous vein
*veine<sup>F</sup> saphène interne*

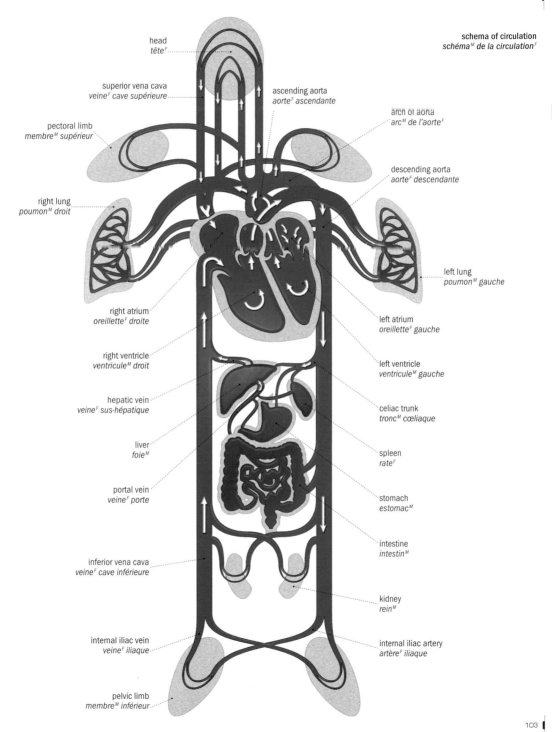

**schema of circulation**
*schema<sup>M</sup> de la circulation<sup>F</sup>*

head
*tête<sup>F</sup>*

superior vena cava
*veine<sup>F</sup> cave supérieure*

ascending aorta
*aorte<sup>F</sup> ascendante*

arch of aorta
*arc<sup>M</sup> de l'aorte<sup>F</sup>*

pectoral limb
*membre<sup>M</sup> supérieur*

descending aorta
*aorte<sup>F</sup> descendante*

right lung
*poumon<sup>M</sup> droit*

left lung
*poumon<sup>M</sup> gauche*

right atrium
*oreillette<sup>F</sup> droite*

left atrium
*oreillette<sup>F</sup> gauche*

right ventricle
*ventricule<sup>M</sup> droit*

left ventricle
*ventricule<sup>M</sup> gauche*

hepatic vein
*veine<sup>F</sup> sus-hépatique*

celiac trunk
*tronc<sup>M</sup> cœliaque*

liver
*foie<sup>M</sup>*

spleen
*rate<sup>F</sup>*

portal vein
*veine<sup>F</sup> porte*

stomach
*estomac<sup>M</sup>*

intestine
*intestin<sup>M</sup>*

inferior vena cava
*veine<sup>F</sup> cave inférieure*

kidney
*rein<sup>M</sup>*

internal iliac vein
*veine<sup>F</sup> iliaque*

internal iliac artery
*artère<sup>F</sup> iliaque*

pelvic limb
*membre<sup>M</sup> inférieur*

# blood circulation

**composition of the blood**
*composition<sup>F</sup> du sang<sup>M</sup>*

**heart**
*cœur<sup>M</sup>*

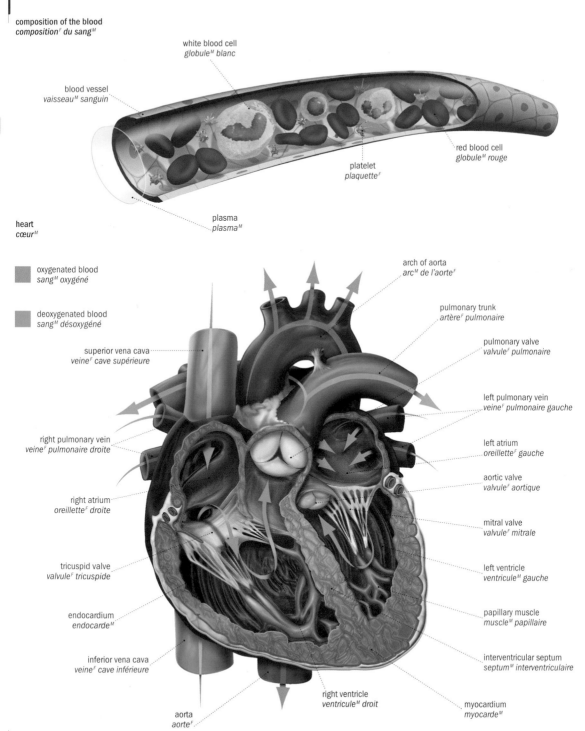

white blood cell
*globule<sup>M</sup> blanc*

blood vessel
*vaisseau<sup>M</sup> sanguin*

red blood cell
*globule<sup>M</sup> rouge*

platelet
*plaquette<sup>F</sup>*

plasma
*plasma<sup>M</sup>*

oxygenated blood
*sang<sup>M</sup> oxygéné*

deoxygenated blood
*sang<sup>M</sup> désoxygéné*

arch of aorta
*arc<sup>M</sup> de l'aorte<sup>F</sup>*

pulmonary trunk
*artère<sup>F</sup> pulmonaire*

pulmonary valve
*valvule<sup>F</sup> pulmonaire*

superior vena cava
*veine<sup>F</sup> cave supérieure*

left pulmonary vein
*veine<sup>F</sup> pulmonaire gauche*

right pulmonary vein
*veine<sup>F</sup> pulmonaire droite*

left atrium
*oreillette<sup>F</sup> gauche*

aortic valve
*valvule<sup>F</sup> aortique*

right atrium
*oreillette<sup>F</sup> droite*

mitral valve
*valvule<sup>F</sup> mitrale*

tricuspid valve
*valvule<sup>F</sup> tricuspide*

left ventricle
*ventricule<sup>M</sup> gauche*

papillary muscle
*muscle<sup>M</sup> papillaire*

endocardium
*endocarde<sup>M</sup>*

inferior vena cava
*veine<sup>F</sup> cave inférieure*

interventricular septum
*septum<sup>M</sup> interventriculaire*

right ventricle
*ventricule<sup>M</sup> droit*

myocardium
*myocarde<sup>M</sup>*

aorta
*aorte<sup>F</sup>*

# respiratory system

appareil<sup>M</sup> respiratoire

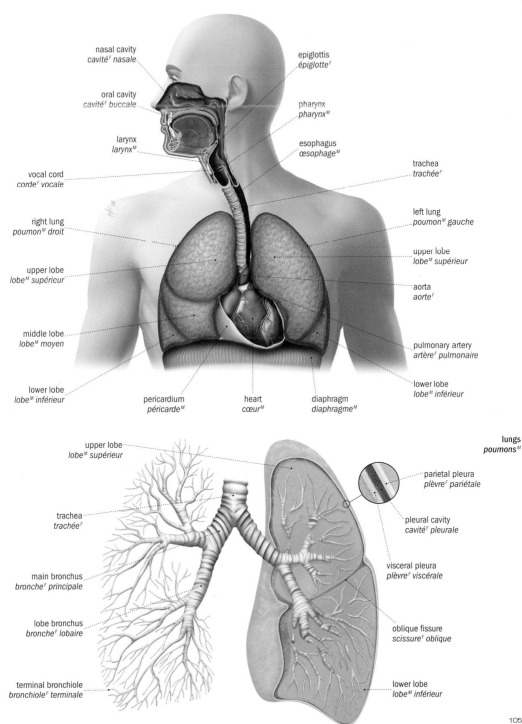

nasal cavity
cavité<sup>F</sup> nasale

epiglottis
épiglotte<sup>F</sup>

oral cavity
cavité<sup>F</sup> buccale

pharynx
pharynx<sup>M</sup>

larynx
larynx<sup>M</sup>

esophagus
œsophage<sup>M</sup>

trachea
trachée<sup>F</sup>

vocal cord
corde<sup>F</sup> vocale

right lung
poumon<sup>M</sup> droit

left lung
poumon<sup>M</sup> gauche

upper lobe
lobe<sup>M</sup> supérieur

upper lobe
lobe<sup>M</sup> supérieur

aorta
aorte<sup>F</sup>

middle lobe
lobe<sup>M</sup> moyen

pulmonary artery
artère<sup>F</sup> pulmonaire

lower lobe
lobe<sup>M</sup> inférieur

lower lobe
lobe<sup>M</sup> inférieur

pericardium
péricarde<sup>M</sup>

heart
cœur<sup>M</sup>

diaphragm
diaphragme<sup>M</sup>

lungs
poumons<sup>M</sup>

upper lobe
lobe<sup>M</sup> supérieur

parietal pleura
plèvre<sup>F</sup> pariétale

trachea
trachée<sup>F</sup>

pleural cavity
cavité<sup>F</sup> pleurale

visceral pleura
plèvre<sup>F</sup> viscérale

main bronchus
bronche<sup>F</sup> principale

lobe bronchus
bronche<sup>F</sup> lobaire

oblique fissure
scissure<sup>F</sup> oblique

terminal bronchiole
bronchiole<sup>F</sup> terminale

lower lobe
lobe<sup>M</sup> inférieur

# digestive system

appareil<sup>M</sup> digestif

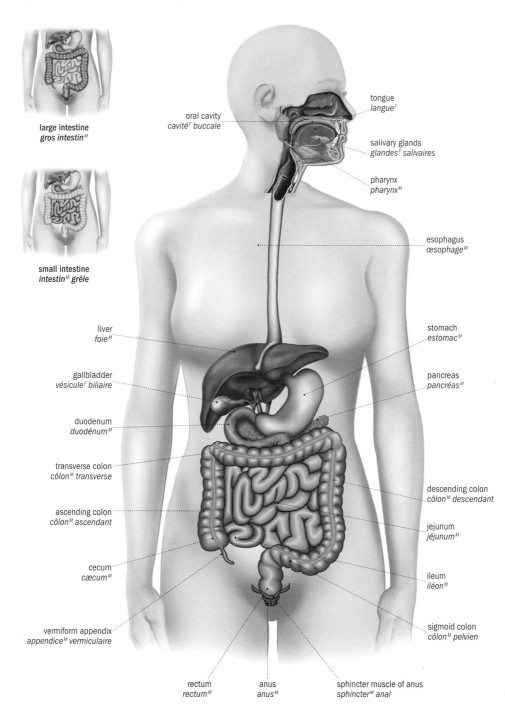

**large intestine**
*gros intestin<sup>M</sup>*

**small intestine**
*intestin<sup>M</sup> grêle*

oral cavity
*cavité<sup>F</sup> buccale*

tongue
*langue<sup>F</sup>*

salivary glands
*glandes<sup>F</sup> salivaires*

pharynx
*pharynx<sup>M</sup>*

esophagus
*œsophage<sup>M</sup>*

liver
*foie<sup>M</sup>*

stomach
*estomac<sup>M</sup>*

gallbladder
*vésicule<sup>F</sup> biliaire*

pancreas
*pancréas<sup>M</sup>*

duodenum
*duodénum<sup>M</sup>*

transverse colon
*côlon<sup>M</sup> transverse*

descending colon
*côlon<sup>M</sup> descendant*

ascending colon
*côlon<sup>M</sup> ascendant*

jejunum
*jéjunum<sup>M</sup>*

cecum
*cæcum<sup>M</sup>*

ileum
*iléon<sup>M</sup>*

vermiform appendix
*appendice<sup>M</sup> vermiculaire*

sigmoid colon
*côlon<sup>M</sup> pelvien*

rectum
*rectum<sup>M</sup>*

anus
*anus<sup>M</sup>*

sphincter muscle of anus
*sphincter<sup>M</sup> anal*

HUMAN BEING

# urinary system

appareil<sup>M</sup> urinaire

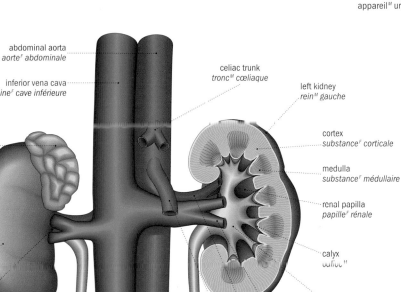

abdominal aorta
*aorte<sup>F</sup> abdominale*

inferior vena cava
*veine<sup>F</sup> cave inférieure*

celiac trunk
*tronc<sup>M</sup> cœliaque*

left kidney
*rein<sup>M</sup> gauche*

cortex
*substance<sup>F</sup> corticale*

medulla
*substance<sup>F</sup> médullaire*

renal papilla
*papille<sup>F</sup> rénale*

suprarenal gland
*glande<sup>F</sup> surrénale*

calyx
*calice<sup>M</sup>*

right kidney
*rein<sup>M</sup> droit*

renal pelvis
*bassinet<sup>M</sup>*

renal hilus
*hile<sup>M</sup> du rein<sup>M</sup>*

renal vein
*veine<sup>F</sup> rénale*

inferior mesenteric artery
*artère<sup>F</sup> mésentérique
inférieure*

renal artery
*artère<sup>F</sup> rénale*

ureter
*uretère<sup>M</sup>*

superior mesenteric artery
*artère<sup>F</sup> mésentérique
supérieure*

common iliac artery
*artère<sup>F</sup> iliaque commune*

common iliac vein
*veine<sup>F</sup> iliaque commune*

internal iliac artery
*artère<sup>F</sup> iliaque interne*

urinary bladder
*vessie<sup>F</sup>*

urethra
*urètre<sup>M</sup>*

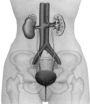

# nervous system

système<sup>M</sup> nerveux

**peripheral nervous system**
*système<sup>M</sup> nerveux périphérique*

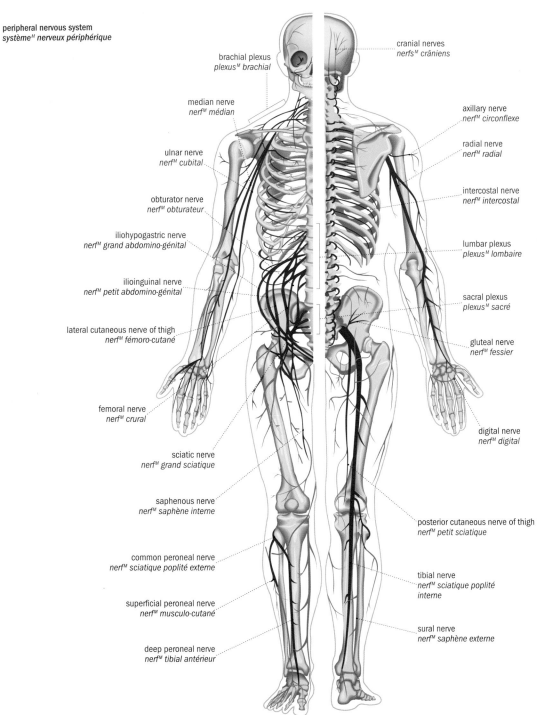

brachial plexus
*plexus<sup>M</sup> brachial*

cranial nerves
*nerfs<sup>M</sup> crâniens*

median nerve
*nerf<sup>M</sup> médian*

axillary nerve
*nerf<sup>M</sup> circonflexe*

ulnar nerve
*nerf<sup>M</sup> cubital*

radial nerve
*nerf<sup>M</sup> radial*

obturator nerve
*nerf<sup>M</sup> obturateur*

intercostal nerve
*nerf<sup>M</sup> intercostal*

iliohypogastric nerve
*nerf<sup>M</sup> grand abdomino-génital*

lumbar plexus
*plexus<sup>M</sup> lombaire*

ilioinguinal nerve
*nerf<sup>M</sup> petit abdomino-génital*

sacral plexus
*plexus<sup>M</sup> sacré*

lateral cutaneous nerve of thigh
*nerf<sup>M</sup> fémoro-cutané*

gluteal nerve
*nerf<sup>M</sup> fessier*

femoral nerve
*nerf<sup>M</sup> crural*

digital nerve
*nerf<sup>M</sup> digital*

sciatic nerve
*nerf<sup>M</sup> grand sciatique*

saphenous nerve
*nerf<sup>M</sup> saphène interne*

posterior cutaneous nerve of thigh
*nerf<sup>M</sup> petit sciatique*

common peroneal nerve
*nerf<sup>M</sup> sciatique poplité externe*

tibial nerve
*nerf<sup>M</sup> sciatique poplité interne*

superficial peroneal nerve
*nerf<sup>M</sup> musculo-cutané*

deep peroneal nerve
*nerf<sup>M</sup> tibial antérieur*

sural nerve
*nerf<sup>M</sup> saphène externe*

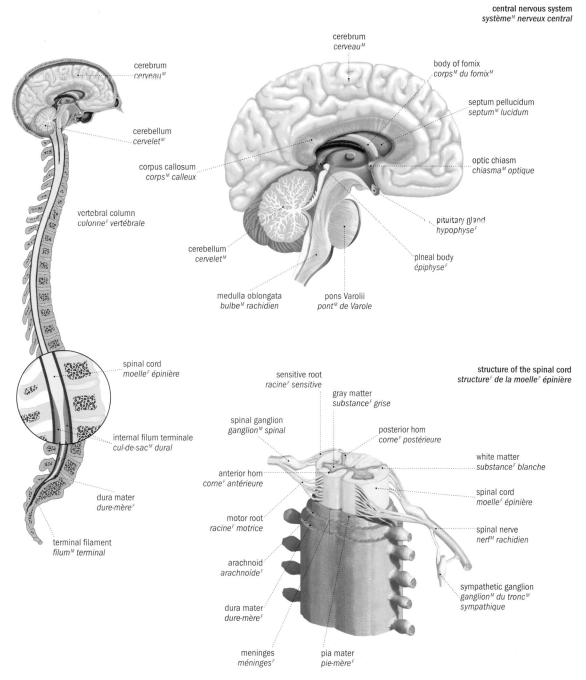

**central nervous system**
*système<sup>M</sup> nerveux central*

cerebrum
*cerveau<sup>M</sup>*

cerebrum
*cerveau<sup>M</sup>*

body of fornix
*corps<sup>M</sup> du fornix<sup>M</sup>*

cerebellum
*cervelet<sup>M</sup>*

septum pellucidum
*septum<sup>M</sup> lucidum*

corpus callosum
*corps<sup>M</sup> calleux*

optic chiasm
*chiasma<sup>M</sup> optique*

vertebral column
*colonne<sup>F</sup> vertébrale*

pituitary gland
*hypophyse<sup>F</sup>*

cerebellum
*cervelet<sup>M</sup>*

pineal body
*épiphyse<sup>F</sup>*

medulla oblongata
*bulbe<sup>M</sup> rachidien*

pons Varolii
*pont<sup>M</sup> de Varole*

spinal cord
*moelle<sup>F</sup> épinière*

**structure of the spinal cord**
*structure<sup>F</sup> de la moelle<sup>F</sup> épinière*

sensitive root
*racine<sup>F</sup> sensitive*

gray matter
*substance<sup>F</sup> grise*

spinal ganglion
*ganglion<sup>M</sup> spinal*

posterior horn
*corne<sup>F</sup> postérieure*

internal filum terminale
*cul-de-sac<sup>M</sup> dural*

white matter
*substance<sup>F</sup> blanche*

anterior horn
*corne<sup>F</sup> antérieure*

spinal cord
*moelle<sup>F</sup> épinière*

motor root
*racine<sup>F</sup> motrice*

spinal nerve
*nerf<sup>M</sup> rachidien*

dura mater
*dure-mère<sup>F</sup>*

arachnoid
*arachnoïde<sup>F</sup>*

sympathetic ganglion
*ganglion<sup>M</sup> du tronc<sup>M</sup>
sympathique*

terminal filament
*filum<sup>M</sup> terminal*

dura mater
*dure-mère<sup>F</sup>*

meninges
*méninges<sup>F</sup>*

pia mater
*pie-mère<sup>F</sup>*

nervous system

**chain of neurons**
*chaîne<sup>F</sup> de neurones<sup>M</sup>*

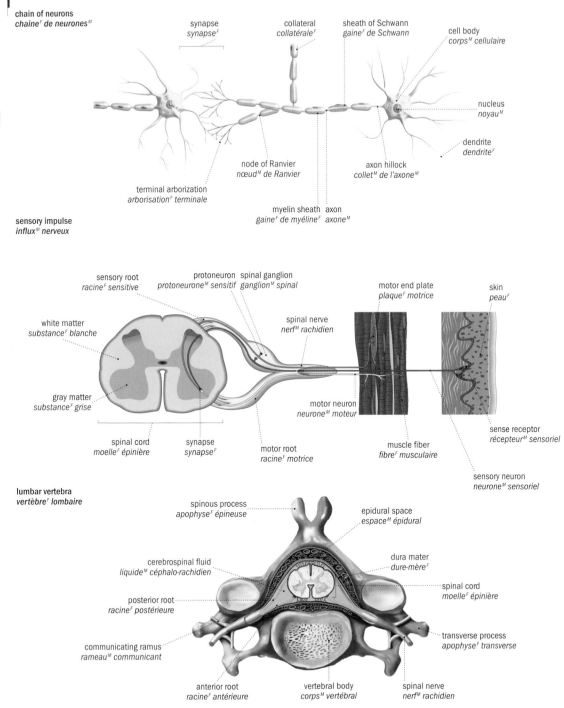

synapse
*synapse<sup>F</sup>*

collateral
*collatérale<sup>F</sup>*

sheath of Schwann
*gaine<sup>F</sup> de Schwann*

cell body
*corps<sup>M</sup> cellulaire*

nucleus
*noyau<sup>M</sup>*

dendrite
*dendrite<sup>F</sup>*

node of Ranvier
*nœud<sup>M</sup> de Ranvier*

axon hillock
*collet<sup>M</sup> de l'axone<sup>M</sup>*

terminal arborization
*arborisation<sup>F</sup> terminale*

myelin sheath
*gaine<sup>F</sup> de myéline<sup>F</sup>*

axon
*axone<sup>M</sup>*

**sensory impulse**
*influx<sup>M</sup> nerveux*

sensory root
*racine<sup>F</sup> sensitive*

protoneuron
*protoneurone<sup>M</sup> sensitif*

spinal ganglion
*ganglion<sup>M</sup> spinal*

motor end plate
*plaque<sup>F</sup> motrice*

skin
*peau<sup>F</sup>*

white matter
*substance<sup>F</sup> blanche*

spinal nerve
*nerf<sup>M</sup> rachidien*

gray matter
*substance<sup>F</sup> grise*

motor neuron
*neurone<sup>M</sup> moteur*

sense receptor
*récepteur<sup>M</sup> sensoriel*

spinal cord
*moelle<sup>F</sup> épinière*

synapse
*synapse<sup>F</sup>*

motor root
*racine<sup>F</sup> motrice*

muscle fiber
*fibre<sup>F</sup> musculaire*

sensory neuron
*neurone<sup>M</sup> sensoriel*

**lumbar vertebra**
*vertèbre<sup>F</sup> lombaire*

spinous process
*apophyse<sup>F</sup> épineuse*

epidural space
*espace<sup>M</sup> épidural*

cerebrospinal fluid
*liquide<sup>M</sup> céphalo-rachidien*

dura mater
*dure-mère<sup>F</sup>*

posterior root
*racine<sup>F</sup> postérieure*

spinal cord
*moelle<sup>F</sup> épinière*

communicating ramus
*rameau<sup>M</sup> communicant*

transverse process
*apophyse<sup>F</sup> transverse*

anterior root
*racine<sup>F</sup> antérieure*

vertebral body
*corps<sup>M</sup> vertébral*

spinal nerve
*nerf<sup>M</sup> rachidien*

# male reproductive organs
organes<sup>M</sup> génitaux masculins

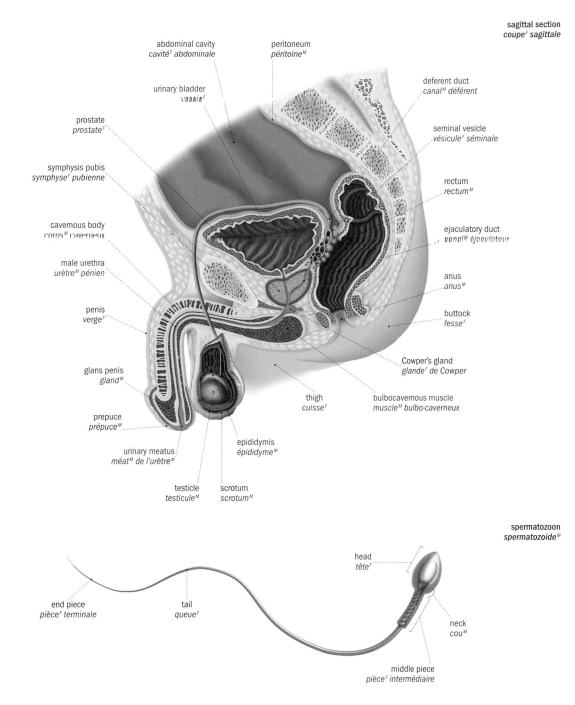

sagittal section
coupe<sup>F</sup> sagittale

HUMAN BEING

abdominal cavity
cavité<sup>F</sup> abdominale

peritoneum
péritoine<sup>M</sup>

urinary bladder
vessie<sup>F</sup>

prostate
prostate<sup>F</sup>

symphysis pubis
symphyse<sup>F</sup> pubienne

cavernous body
corps<sup>M</sup> caverneux

male urethra
urètre<sup>M</sup> pénien

penis
verge<sup>F</sup>

glans penis
gland<sup>M</sup>

prepuce
prépuce<sup>M</sup>

urinary meatus
méat<sup>M</sup> de l'urètre<sup>M</sup>

testicle
testicule<sup>M</sup>

scrotum
scrotum<sup>M</sup>

epididymis
épididyme<sup>M</sup>

thigh
cuisse<sup>F</sup>

deferent duct
canal<sup>M</sup> déférent

seminal vesicle
vésicule<sup>F</sup> séminale

rectum
rectum<sup>M</sup>

ejaculatory duct
canal<sup>M</sup> éjaculateur

anus
anus<sup>M</sup>

buttock
fesse<sup>F</sup>

Cowper's gland
glande<sup>F</sup> de Cowper

bulbocavernous muscle
muscle<sup>M</sup> bulbo-caverneux

spermatozoon
spermatozoïde<sup>M</sup>

head
tête<sup>F</sup>

neck
cou<sup>M</sup>

end piece
pièce<sup>F</sup> terminale

tail
queue<sup>F</sup>

middle piece
pièce<sup>F</sup> intermédiaire

# female reproductive organs

organes<sup>M</sup> génitaux féminins

**sagittal section**
*coupe<sup>F</sup> sagittale*

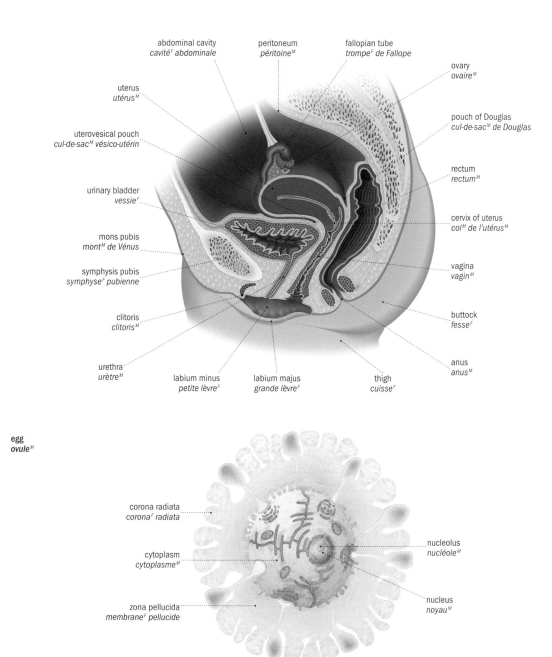

abdominal cavity
*cavité<sup>F</sup> abdominale*

peritoneum
*péritoine<sup>M</sup>*

fallopian tube
*trompe<sup>F</sup> de Fallope*

ovary
*ovaire<sup>M</sup>*

uterus
*utérus<sup>M</sup>*

pouch of Douglas
*cul-de-sac<sup>M</sup> de Douglas*

uterovesical pouch
*cul-de-sac<sup>M</sup> vésico-utérin*

rectum
*rectum<sup>M</sup>*

urinary bladder
*vessie<sup>F</sup>*

cervix of uterus
*col<sup>M</sup> de l'utérus<sup>M</sup>*

mons pubis
*mont<sup>M</sup> de Vénus*

vagina
*vagin<sup>M</sup>*

symphysis pubis
*symphyse<sup>F</sup> pubienne*

buttock
*fesse<sup>F</sup>*

clitoris
*clitoris<sup>M</sup>*

anus
*anus<sup>M</sup>*

urethra
*urètre<sup>M</sup>*

labium minus
*petite lèvre<sup>F</sup>*

labium majus
*grande lèvre<sup>F</sup>*

thigh
*cuisse<sup>F</sup>*

**egg**
*ovule<sup>M</sup>*

corona radiata
*corona<sup>F</sup> radiata*

nucleolus
*nucléole<sup>M</sup>*

cytoplasm
*cytoplasme<sup>M</sup>*

zona pellucida
*membrane<sup>F</sup> pellucide*

nucleus
*noyau<sup>M</sup>*

HUMAN BEING

posterior view
*vue<sup>F</sup> postérieure*

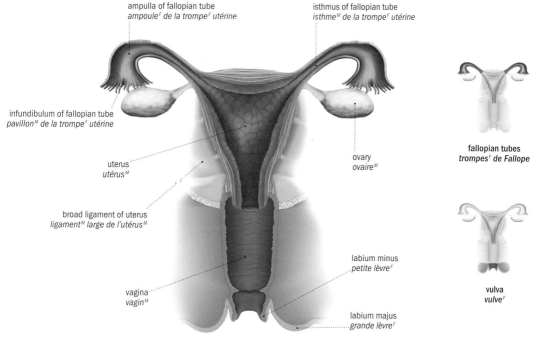

ampulla of fallopian tube
*ampoule<sup>F</sup> de la trompe<sup>F</sup> utérine*

isthmus of fallopian tube
*isthme<sup>M</sup> de la trompe<sup>F</sup> utérine*

infundibulum of fallopian tube
*pavillon<sup>M</sup> de la trompe<sup>F</sup> utérine*

ovary
*ovaire<sup>M</sup>*

uterus
*utérus<sup>M</sup>*

broad ligament of uterus
*ligament<sup>M</sup> large de l'utérus<sup>M</sup>*

labium minus
*petite lèvre<sup>F</sup>*

vagina
*vagin<sup>M</sup>*

labium majus
*grande lèvre<sup>F</sup>*

fallopian tubes
*trompes<sup>F</sup> de Fallope*

vulva
*vulve<sup>F</sup>*

**breast**

*sein<sup>M</sup>*

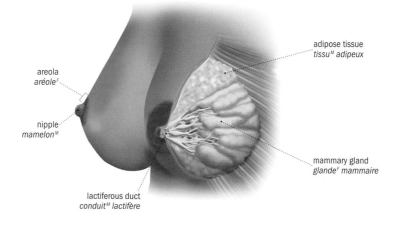

areola
*aréole<sup>F</sup>*

nipple
*mamelon<sup>M</sup>*

lactiferous duct
*conduit<sup>M</sup> lactifère*

adipose tissue
*tissu<sup>M</sup> adipeux*

mammary gland
*glande<sup>F</sup> mammaire*

# touch

toucher<sup>M</sup>

skin
peau<sup>F</sup>

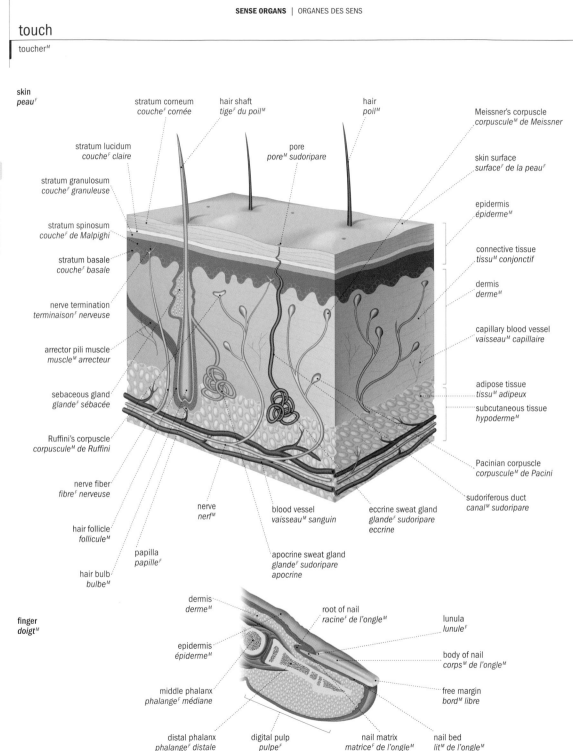

stratum corneum
couche<sup>F</sup> cornée

hair shaft
tige<sup>F</sup> du poil<sup>M</sup>

hair
poil<sup>M</sup>

Meissner's corpuscle
corpuscule<sup>M</sup> de Meissner

stratum lucidum
couche<sup>F</sup> claire

pore
pore<sup>M</sup> sudoripare

skin surface
surface<sup>F</sup> de la peau<sup>F</sup>

stratum granulosum
couche<sup>F</sup> granuleuse

epidermis
épiderme<sup>M</sup>

stratum spinosum
couche<sup>F</sup> de Malpighi

connective tissue
tissu<sup>M</sup> conjonctif

stratum basale
couche<sup>F</sup> basale

dermis
derme<sup>M</sup>

nerve termination
terminaison<sup>F</sup> nerveuse

capillary blood vessel
vaisseau<sup>M</sup> capillaire

arrector pili muscle
muscle<sup>M</sup> arrecteur

adipose tissue
tissu<sup>M</sup> adipeux

sebaceous gland
glande<sup>F</sup> sébacée

subcutaneous tissue
hypoderme<sup>M</sup>

Ruffini's corpuscle
corpuscule<sup>M</sup> de Ruffini

Pacinian corpuscle
corpuscule<sup>M</sup> de Pacini

nerve fiber
fibre<sup>F</sup> nerveuse

sudoriferous duct
canal<sup>M</sup> sudoripare

nerve
nerf<sup>M</sup>

blood vessel
vaisseau<sup>M</sup> sanguin

eccrine sweat gland
glande<sup>F</sup> sudoripare
eccrine

hair follicle
follicule<sup>M</sup>

papilla
papille<sup>F</sup>

apocrine sweat gland
glande<sup>F</sup> sudoripare
apocrine

hair bulb
bulbe<sup>M</sup>

finger
doigt<sup>M</sup>

dermis
derme<sup>M</sup>

root of nail
racine<sup>F</sup> de l'ongle<sup>M</sup>

lunula
lunule<sup>F</sup>

epidermis
épiderme<sup>M</sup>

body of nail
corps<sup>M</sup> de l'ongle<sup>M</sup>

middle phalanx
phalange<sup>F</sup> médiane

free margin
bord<sup>M</sup> libre

distal phalanx
phalange<sup>F</sup> distale

digital pulp
pulpe<sup>F</sup>

nail matrix
matrice<sup>F</sup> de l'ongle<sup>M</sup>

nail bed
lit<sup>M</sup> de l'ongle<sup>M</sup>

touch

**hand**
*main*<sup>F</sup>

HUMAN BEING

palm
*paume*<sup>F</sup>

back
*dos*<sup>M</sup>

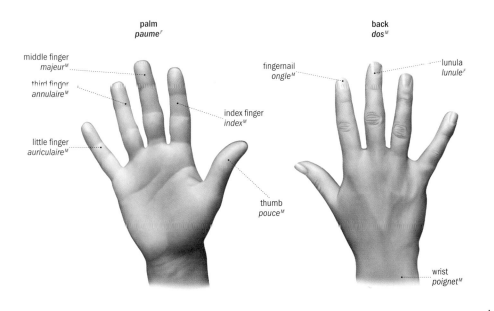

middle finger
*majeur*<sup>M</sup>

third finger
*annulaire*<sup>M</sup>

little finger
*auriculaire*<sup>M</sup>

index finger
*index*<sup>M</sup>

thumb
*pouce*<sup>M</sup>

fingernail
*ongle*<sup>M</sup>

lunula
*lunule*<sup>F</sup>

wrist
*poignet*<sup>M</sup>

hearing
*ouïe*<sup>F</sup>

auricle
*pavillon*<sup>M</sup>

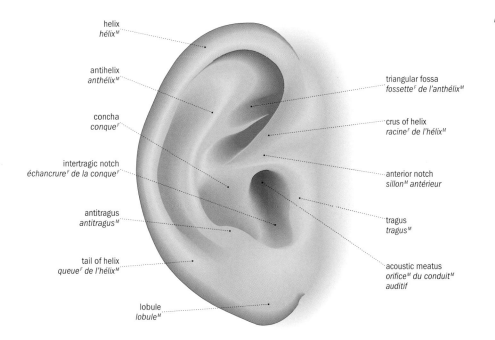

helix
*hélix*<sup>M</sup>

antihelix
*anthélix*<sup>M</sup>

concha
*conque*<sup>F</sup>

intertragic notch
*échancrure*<sup>F</sup> *de la conque*<sup>F</sup>

antitragus
*antitragus*<sup>M</sup>

tail of helix
*queue*<sup>F</sup> *de l'hélix*<sup>M</sup>

lobule
*lobule*<sup>M</sup>

triangular fossa
*fossette*<sup>F</sup> *de l'anthélix*<sup>M</sup>

crus of helix
*racine*<sup>F</sup> *de l'hélix*<sup>M</sup>

anterior notch
*sillon*<sup>M</sup> *antérieur*

tragus
*tragus*<sup>M</sup>

acoustic meatus
*orifice*<sup>M</sup> *du conduit*<sup>M</sup>
*auditif*

## hearing

**HUMAN BEING**

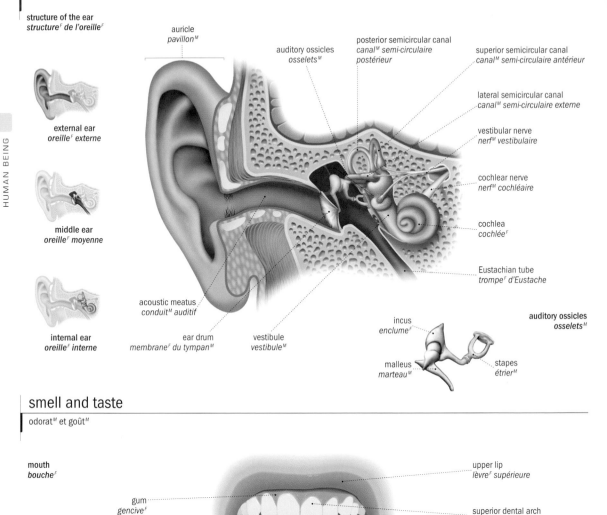

structure of the ear
*structure<sup>F</sup> de l'oreille<sup>F</sup>*

auricle
*pavillon<sup>M</sup>*

external ear
*oreille<sup>F</sup> externe*

middle ear
*oreille<sup>F</sup> moyenne*

internal ear
*oreille<sup>F</sup> interne*

auditory ossicles
*osselets<sup>M</sup>*

posterior semicircular canal
*canal<sup>M</sup> semi-circulaire postérieur*

superior semicircular canal
*canal<sup>M</sup> semi-circulaire antérieur*

lateral semicircular canal
*canal<sup>M</sup> semi-circulaire externe*

vestibular nerve
*nerf<sup>M</sup> vestibulaire*

cochlear nerve
*nerf<sup>M</sup> cochléaire*

cochlea
*cochlée<sup>F</sup>*

Eustachian tube
*trompe<sup>F</sup> d'Eustache*

acoustic meatus
*conduit<sup>M</sup> auditif*

ear drum
*membrane<sup>F</sup> du tympan<sup>M</sup>*

vestibule
*vestibule<sup>M</sup>*

incus
*enclume<sup>F</sup>*

auditory ossicles
*osselets<sup>M</sup>*

malleus
*marteau<sup>M</sup>*

stapes
*étrier<sup>M</sup>*

## smell and taste

*odorat<sup>M</sup> et goût<sup>M</sup>*

mouth
*bouche<sup>F</sup>*

gum
*gencive<sup>F</sup>*

hard palate
*voûte<sup>F</sup> du palais<sup>M</sup>*

soft palate
*voile<sup>M</sup> du palais<sup>M</sup>*

palatoglossal arch
*pilier<sup>M</sup> du voile<sup>M</sup>*

tonsil
*amygdale<sup>F</sup>*

uvula
*luette<sup>F</sup>*

inferior dental arch
*arcade<sup>F</sup> dentaire inférieure*

upper lip
*lèvre<sup>F</sup> supérieure*

superior dental arch
*arcade<sup>F</sup> dentaire supérieure*

isthmus of fauces
*isthme<sup>M</sup> du gosier<sup>M</sup>*

commissure of lips of mouth
*commissure<sup>F</sup> labiale*

tongue
*langue<sup>F</sup>*

lower lip
*lèvre<sup>F</sup> inférieure*

smell and taste

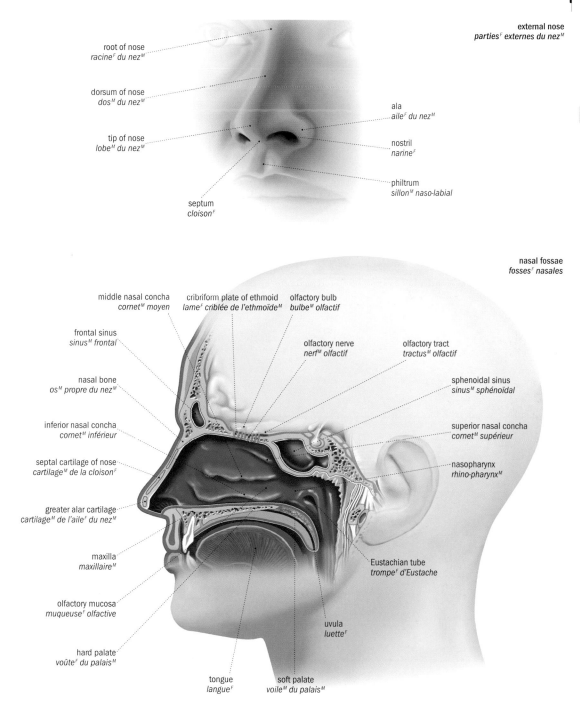

external nose
parties<sup>F</sup> externes du nez<sup>M</sup>

root of nose
racine<sup>F</sup> du nez<sup>M</sup>

dorsum of nose
dos<sup>M</sup> du nez<sup>M</sup>

ala
aile<sup>F</sup> du nez<sup>M</sup>

tip of nose
lobe<sup>M</sup> du nez<sup>M</sup>

nostril
narine<sup>F</sup>

philtrum
sillon<sup>M</sup> naso-labial

septum
cloison<sup>F</sup>

nasal fossae
fosses<sup>F</sup> nasales

middle nasal concha
cornet<sup>M</sup> moyen

cribriform plate of ethmoid
lame<sup>F</sup> criblée de l'ethmoïde<sup>M</sup>

olfactory bulb
bulbe<sup>M</sup> olfactif

frontal sinus
sinus<sup>M</sup> frontal

olfactory nerve
nerf<sup>M</sup> olfactif

olfactory tract
tractus<sup>M</sup> olfactif

nasal bone
os<sup>M</sup> propre du nez<sup>M</sup>

sphenoidal sinus
sinus<sup>M</sup> sphénoïdal

inferior nasal concha
cornet<sup>M</sup> inférieur

superior nasal concha
cornet<sup>M</sup> supérieur

septal cartilage of nose
cartilage<sup>M</sup> de la cloison<sup>F</sup>

nasopharynx
rhino-pharynx<sup>M</sup>

greater alar cartilage
cartilage<sup>M</sup> de l'aile<sup>F</sup> du nez<sup>M</sup>

maxilla
maxillaire<sup>M</sup>

Eustachian tube
trompe<sup>F</sup> d'Eustache

olfactory mucosa
muqueuse<sup>F</sup> olfactive

uvula
luette<sup>F</sup>

hard palate
voûte<sup>F</sup> du palais<sup>M</sup>

tongue
langue<sup>F</sup>

soft palate
voile<sup>M</sup> du palais<sup>M</sup>

smell and taste

dorsum of tongue
*dos*^M *de la langue*^F

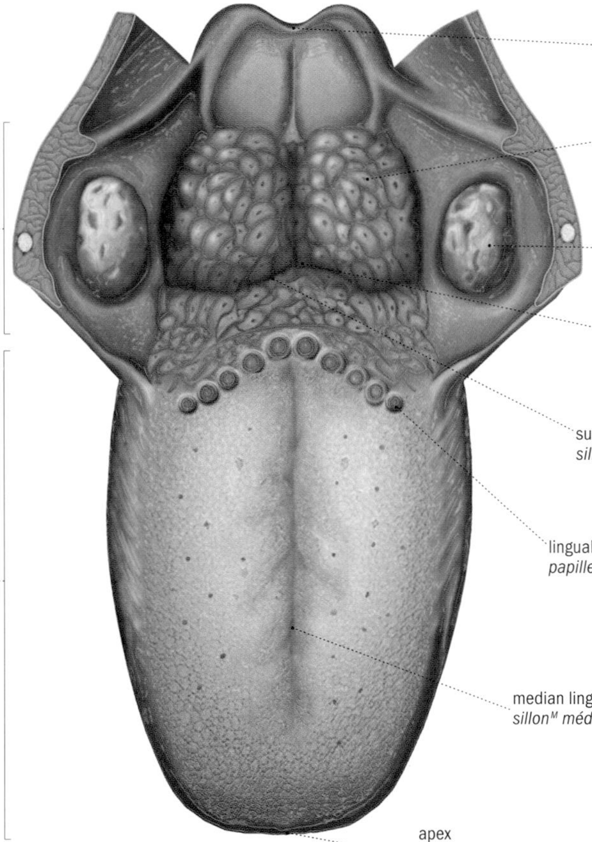

epiglottis
*épiglotte*^F

lingual tonsil
*amygdale*^F *linguale*

root
*base*^F

palatine tonsil
*amygdale*^F *palatine*

foramen cecum
*foramen*^M *cæcum*^M

sulcus terminalis
*sillon*^M *terminal*

lingual papilla
*papille*^F *linguale*

body
*corps*^M

median lingual sulcus
*sillon*^M *médian*

apex
*apex*^M

taste receptors
*récepteurs*^M *du goût*^M

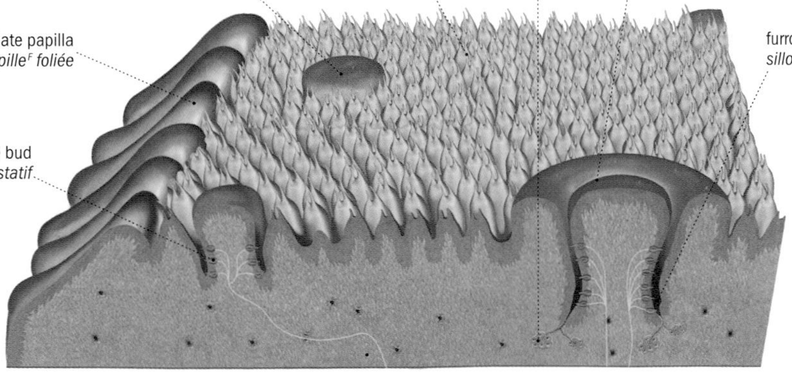

fungiform papilla
*papille*^F *fongiforme*

filiform papilla
*papille*^F *filiforme*

salivary gland
*glande*^F *salivaire*

circumvallate papilla
*papille*^F *caliciforme*

foliate papilla
*papille*^F *foliée*

furrow
*sillon*^M

taste bud
*bourgeon*^M *gustatif*

# sight
*vue*[F]

**eye**
*œil*[M]

**eyeball**
*globe*[M] *oculaire*

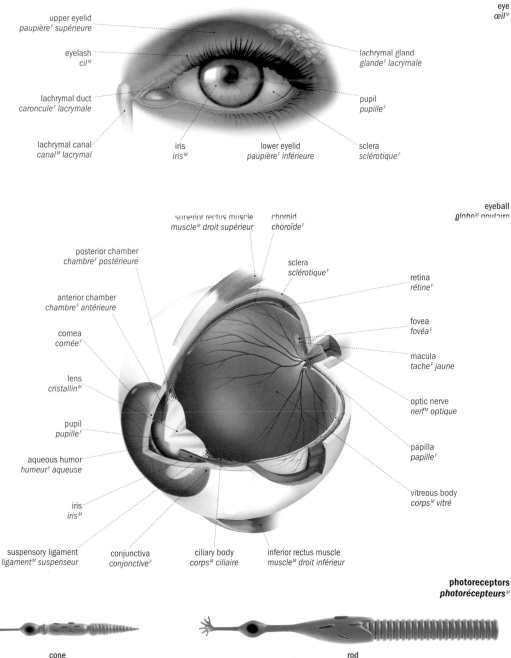

upper eyelid
*paupière*[F] *supérieure*

eyelash
*cil*[M]

lachrymal duct
*caroncule*[F] *lacrymale*

lachrymal canal
*canal*[M] *lacrymal*

lachrymal gland
*glande*[F] *lacrymale*

pupil
*pupille*[F]

iris
*iris*[M]

lower eyelid
*paupière*[F] *inférieure*

sclera
*sclérotique*[F]

superior rectus muscle
*muscle*[M] *droit supérieur*

choroid
*choroïde*[F]

posterior chamber
*chambre*[F] *postérieure*

sclera
*sclérotique*[F]

retina
*rétine*[F]

anterior chamber
*chambre*[F] *antérieure*

fovea
*fovéa*[F]

cornea
*cornée*[F]

macula
*tache*[F] *jaune*

lens
*cristallin*[M]

optic nerve
*nerf*[M] *optique*

pupil
*pupille*[F]

papilla
*papille*[F]

aqueous humor
*humeur*[F] *aqueuse*

vitreous body
*corps*[M] *vitré*

iris
*iris*[M]

suspensory ligament
*ligament*[M] *suspenseur*

conjunctiva
*conjonctive*[F]

ciliary body
*corps*[M] *ciliaire*

inferior rectus muscle
*muscle*[M] *droit inférieur*

**photoreceptors**
*photorécepteurs*[M]

cone
*cône*[M]

rod
*bâtonnet*[M]

# supermarket

supermarché<sup>M</sup>

self-service meat counter
comptoir<sup>M</sup> des viandes<sup>F</sup> libre-
service

butcher's counter
boucherie<sup>F</sup>

delicatessen
épicerie<sup>F</sup> fine

packaging products
produits<sup>M</sup> d'emballage<sup>M</sup>

cold storage chamber
chambre<sup>F</sup> froide

dairy products
produits<sup>M</sup> laitiers

dairy products receiving area
aire<sup>F</sup> de réception<sup>F</sup> des produits<sup>M</sup>
laitiers

receiving area
aire<sup>F</sup> de réception<sup>F</sup>

household products
produits<sup>M</sup> d'entretien<sup>M</sup>

aisle
allée<sup>F</sup>

drinks
boissons<sup>F</sup>

display preparation area
aire<sup>F</sup> de préparation<sup>F</sup> de l'étalage<sup>M</sup>

beer and wine
bière<sup>F</sup> et vin<sup>M</sup>

reach-in freezer
armoire<sup>F</sup> réfrigérée

fruits and vegetables
fruits<sup>M</sup> et légumes<sup>M</sup>

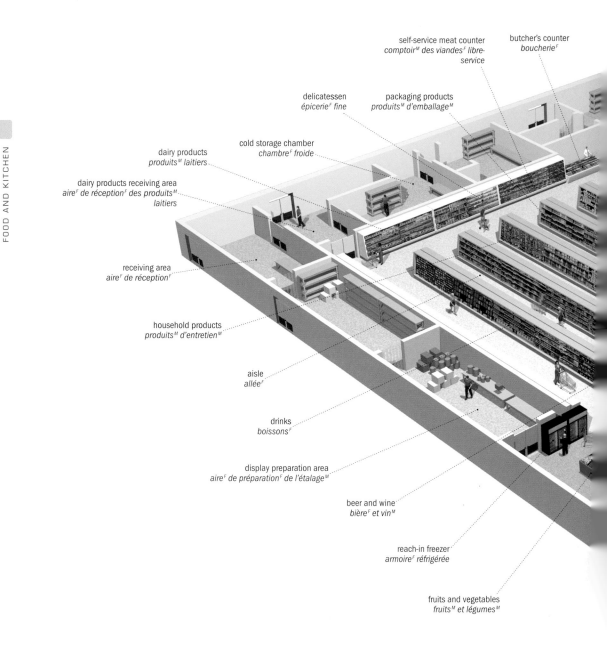

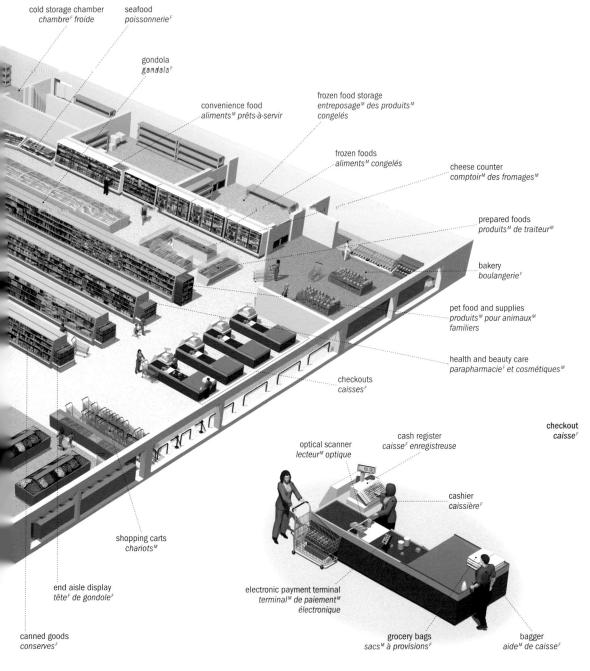

cold storage chamber
*chambre*F *froide*

seafood
*poissonnerie*F

gondola
*gondola*F

convenience food
*aliments*M *prêts-à-servir*

frozen food storage
*entreposage*M *des produits*M
*congelés*

frozen foods
*aliments*M *congelés*

cheese counter
*comptoir*M *des fromages*M

prepared foods
*produits*M *de traiteur*M

bakery
*boulangerie*F

pet food and supplies
*produits*M *pour animaux*M
*familiers*

health and beauty care
*parapharmacie*F *et cosmétiques*M

checkouts
*caisses*F

checkout
*caisse*F

cash register
*caisse*F *enregistreuse*

optical scanner
*lecteur*M *optique*

cashier
*caissière*F

shopping carts
*chariots*M

end aisle display
*tête*F *de gondole*F

electronic payment terminal
*terminal*M *de paiement*M
*électronique*

canned goods
*conserves*F

grocery bags
*sacs*M *à provisions*F

bagger
*aide*M *de caisse*F

FOOD AND KITCHEN

# farmstead
ferme<sup>F</sup>

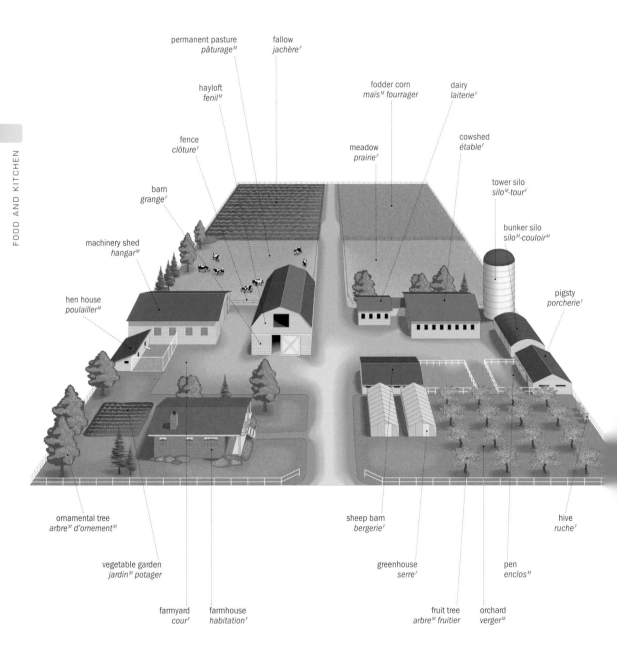

permanent pasture
*pâturage*<sup>M</sup>

fallow
*jachère*<sup>F</sup>

hayloft
*fenil*<sup>M</sup>

fodder corn
*maïs*<sup>M</sup> *fourrager*

dairy
*laiterie*<sup>F</sup>

fence
*clôture*<sup>F</sup>

meadow
*prairie*<sup>F</sup>

cowshed
*étable*<sup>F</sup>

barn
*grange*<sup>F</sup>

tower silo
*silo*<sup>M</sup>*-tour*<sup>F</sup>

bunker silo
*silo*<sup>M</sup>*-couloir*<sup>M</sup>

machinery shed
*hangar*<sup>M</sup>

pigsty
*porcherie*<sup>F</sup>

hen house
*poulailler*<sup>M</sup>

ornamental tree
*arbre*<sup>M</sup> *d'ornement*<sup>M</sup>

sheep barn
*bergerie*<sup>F</sup>

hive
*ruche*<sup>F</sup>

vegetable garden
*jardin*<sup>M</sup> *potager*

greenhouse
*serre*<sup>F</sup>

pen
*enclos*<sup>M</sup>

farmyard
*cour*<sup>F</sup>

farmhouse
*habitation*<sup>F</sup>

fruit tree
*arbre*<sup>M</sup> *fruitier*

orchard
*verger*<sup>M</sup>

# mushrooms
champignons[M]

truffle
*truffe*[F]

wood ear
*oreille-de-Judas*[F]

royal agaric
*oronge*[F] *vraie*

delicious lactarius
*lactaire*[M] *délicieux*

enoki
*collybie*[F] *à pied*[M] *velouté*

oyster
*pleurote*[M] *en forme*[F] *d'huitre*[F]

cultivated mushrooms
*champignon*[M] *de couche*[F]

green russula
*russule*[F] *verdoyante*

morels
*morille*[F]

edible boletus
*cèpe*[M]

shitake
*shiitake*[M]

chanterelles
*chanterelle*[F] *commune*

# seaweed
algues[F]

arame
*aramé*[M]

wakame
*wakamé*[M]

kombu
*kombu*[M]

spirulina
*spiruline*[F]

Irish moss
*mousse*[F] *d'Irlande*[F]

hijiki
*hijiki*[M]

sea lettuce
*laitue*[F] *de mer*[F]

agar-agar
*agar-agar*[M]

nori
*nori*[M]

dulse
*rhodyménie*[M] *palmé*

# vegetables

légumes<sup>M</sup>

légumes *M*

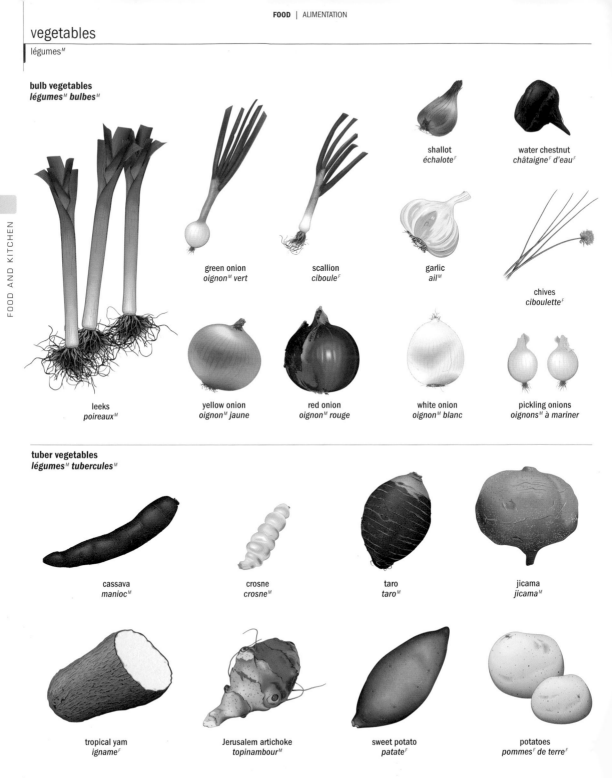

## bulb vegetables
*légumes<sup>M</sup> bulbes<sup>M</sup>*

shallot
*échalote<sup>F</sup>*

water chestnut
*châtaigne<sup>F</sup> d'eau<sup>F</sup>*

green onion
*oignon<sup>M</sup> vert*

scallion
*ciboule<sup>F</sup>*

garlic
*ail<sup>M</sup>*

chives
*ciboulette<sup>F</sup>*

leeks
*poireaux<sup>M</sup>*

yellow onion
*oignon<sup>M</sup> jaune*

red onion
*oignon<sup>M</sup> rouge*

white onion
*oignon<sup>M</sup> blanc*

pickling onions
*oignons<sup>M</sup> à mariner*

## tuber vegetables
*légumes<sup>M</sup> tubercules<sup>M</sup>*

cassava
*manioc<sup>M</sup>*

crosne
*crosne<sup>M</sup>*

taro
*taro<sup>M</sup>*

jicama
*jicama<sup>M</sup>*

tropical yam
*igname<sup>F</sup>*

Jerusalem artichoke
*topinambour<sup>M</sup>*

sweet potato
*patate<sup>F</sup>*

potatoes
*pommes<sup>F</sup> de terre<sup>F</sup>*

FOOD AND KITCHEN

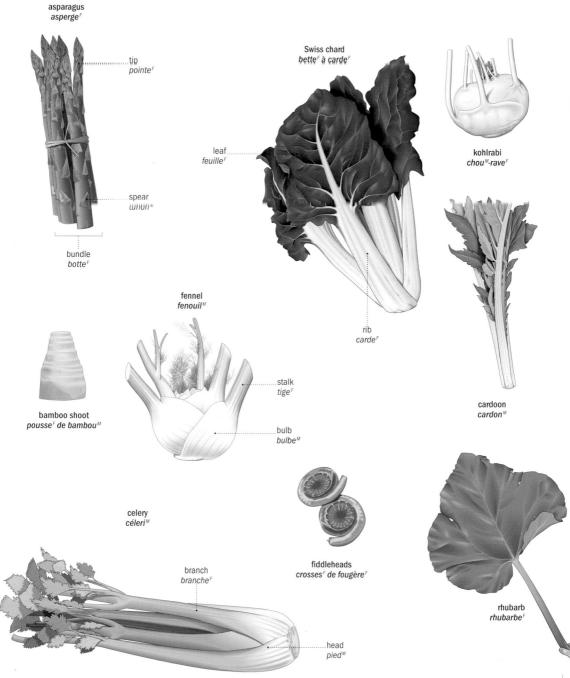

**stalk vegetables**
*légumes*<sup>M</sup> *tiges*<sup>F</sup>

asparagus
*asperge*<sup>F</sup>

tip
*pointe*<sup>F</sup>

spear
*turion*<sup>M</sup>

bundle
*botte*<sup>F</sup>

Swiss chard
*bette*<sup>F</sup> *à carde*<sup>F</sup>

leaf
*feuille*<sup>F</sup>

kohlrabi
*chou*<sup>M</sup>-*rave*<sup>F</sup>

rib
*carde*<sup>F</sup>

fennel
*fenouil*<sup>M</sup>

stalk
*tige*<sup>F</sup>

bulb
*bulbe*<sup>M</sup>

bamboo shoot
*pousse*<sup>F</sup> *de bambou*<sup>M</sup>

cardoon
*cardon*<sup>M</sup>

celery
*céleri*<sup>M</sup>

branch
*branche*<sup>F</sup>

fiddleheads
*crosses*<sup>F</sup> *de fougère*<sup>F</sup>

rhubarb
*rhubarbe*<sup>F</sup>

head
*pied*<sup>M</sup>

vegetables

**leaf vegetables**
*légumes*<sup>M</sup> *feuilles*<sup>F</sup>

leaf lettuce
*laitue*<sup>F</sup> *frisée*

romaine lettuce
*romaine*<sup>F</sup>

celtuce
*laitue*<sup>F</sup> *asperge*<sup>F</sup>

sea kale
*chou*<sup>M</sup> *marin*

collards
*chou*<sup>M</sup> *cavalier*<sup>M</sup>

escarole
*scarole*<sup>F</sup>

butter lettuce
*laitue*<sup>F</sup> *pommée*

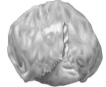

iceberg lettuce
*laitue*<sup>F</sup> *iceberg*<sup>M</sup>

radicchio
*chicorée*<sup>F</sup> *de Trévise*

ornamental kale
*chou*<sup>M</sup> *laitue*<sup>F</sup>

curly kale
*chou*<sup>M</sup> *frisé*

grape leaves
*feuille*<sup>F</sup> *de vigne*<sup>F</sup>

brussels sprouts
*choux*<sup>M</sup> *de Bruxelles*

red cabbage
*chou*<sup>M</sup> *pommé rouge*

white cabbage
*chou*<sup>M</sup> *pommé blanc*

savoy cabbage
*chou*<sup>M</sup> *de Milan*

green cabbage
*chou*<sup>M</sup> *pommé vert*

pe-tsai
*pe-tsaï*<sup>M</sup>

bok choy
*pak-choï*<sup>M</sup>

purslane
*pourpier*$^M$

nettle
*ortie*$^F$

watercress
*cresson*$^M$ *de fontaine*$^F$

dandelion
*pissenlit*$^M$

corn salad
*mâche*$^F$

arugula
*roquette*$^F$

spinach
*épinard*$^M$

garden cress
*cresson*$^M$ *alénois*

garden sorrel
*oseille*$^F$

curly endive
*chicorée*$^F$ *frisée*

Belgian endive
*endive*$^F$

---

**inflorescent vegetables**
*légumes*$^M$ **fleurs**$^F$

cauliflower
*chou*$^M$-*fleur*$^F$

broccoli
*brocoli*$^M$

Gai-lohn
*Gai lon*$^M$

broccoli rabe
*brocoli*$^M$ *italien*

artichoke
*artichaut*$^M$

vegetables

FOOD AND KITCHEN

**fruit vegetables**
*légumes*<sup>M</sup> *fruits*<sup>M</sup>

avocado
*avocat*<sup>M</sup>

tomato
*tomate*<sup>F</sup>

currant tomatoes
*tomates*<sup>F</sup> *en grappe*<sup>F</sup>

tomatillos
*tomatilles*<sup>F</sup>

olives
*olives*<sup>F</sup>

yellow sweet pepper
*poivron*<sup>M</sup> *jaune*

green sweet pepper
*poivron*<sup>M</sup> *vert*

red sweet pepper
*poivron*<sup>M</sup> *rouge*

hot pepper
*piment*<sup>M</sup>

okra
*gombo*<sup>M</sup>

gherkin
*cornichon*<sup>M</sup>

cucumber
*concombre*<sup>M</sup>

seedless cucumber
*concombre*<sup>M</sup> *sans pépins*<sup>M</sup>

wax gourd (winter melon)
*melon*<sup>M</sup> *d'hiver*<sup>M</sup> *chinois*

eggplant
*aubergine*<sup>F</sup>

summer squash
*courge*<sup>F</sup>

zucchini
*courgette*<sup>F</sup>

bitter melon
*margose*<sup>F</sup>

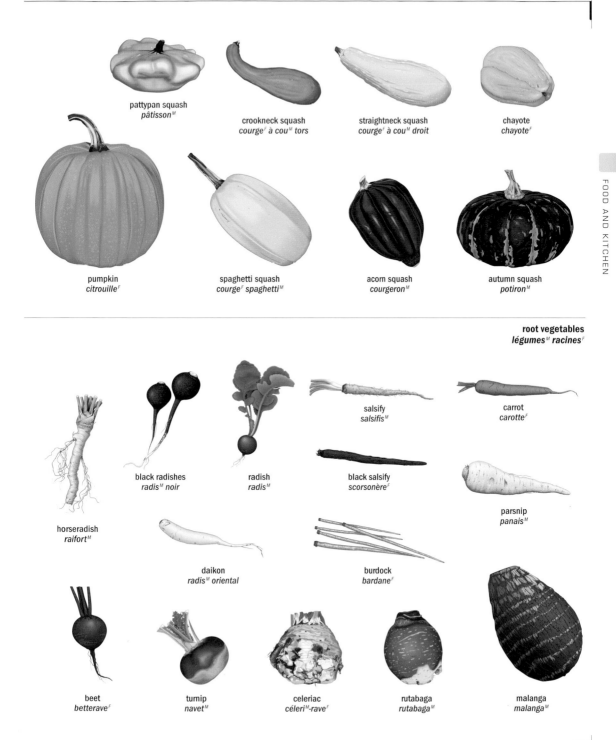

pattypan squash
*pâtisson*<sup>M</sup>

crookneck squash
*courge*<sup>F</sup> *à cou*<sup>M</sup> *tors*

straightneck squash
*courge*<sup>F</sup> *à cou*<sup>M</sup> *droit*

chayote
*chayote*<sup>F</sup>

pumpkin
*citrouille*<sup>F</sup>

spaghetti squash
*courge*<sup>F</sup> *spaghetti*<sup>M</sup>

acorn squash
*courgeron*<sup>M</sup>

autumn squash
*potiron*<sup>M</sup>

**root vegetables**
*légumes*<sup>M</sup> *racines*<sup>F</sup>

salsify
*salsifis*<sup>M</sup>

carrot
*carotte*<sup>F</sup>

black radishes
*radis*<sup>M</sup> *noir*

radish
*radis*<sup>M</sup>

black salsify
*scorsonère*<sup>F</sup>

parsnip
*panais*<sup>M</sup>

horseradish
*raifort*<sup>M</sup>

daikon
*radis*<sup>M</sup> *oriental*

burdock
*bardane*<sup>F</sup>

beet
*betterave*<sup>F</sup>

turnip
*navet*<sup>M</sup>

celeriac
*céleri*<sup>M</sup>*-rave*<sup>F</sup>

rutabaga
*rutabaga*<sup>M</sup>

malanga
*malanga*<sup>M</sup>

# legumes

légumineuses[F]

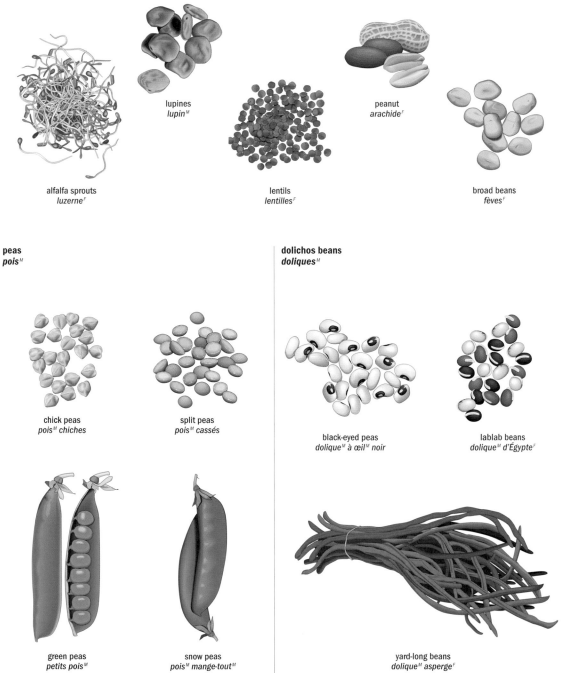

lupines
*lupin*[M]

peanut
*arachide*[F]

alfalfa sprouts
*luzerne*[F]

lentils
*lentilles*[F]

broad beans
*fèves*[F]

**peas**
***pois***[M]

**dolichos beans**
***doliques***[M]

chick peas
*pois*[M] *chiches*

split peas
*pois*[M] *cassés*

black-eyed peas
*dolique*[M] *à œil*[M] *noir*

lablab beans
*dolique*[M] *d'Égypte*[F]

green peas
*petits pois*[M]

snow peas
*pois*[M] *mange-tout*[M]

yard-long beans
*dolique*[M] *asperge*[F]

FOOD AND KITCHEN

**beans**
*haricots*<sup>M</sup>

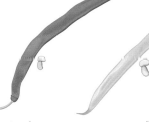

green bean
*haricot*<sup>M</sup> *vert*

wax bean
*haricot*<sup>M</sup> *jaune*

romano beans
*haricots*<sup>M</sup> *romains*

adzuki beans
*haricots*<sup>M</sup> *adzuki*

scarlet runner beans
*haricots*<sup>M</sup> *d'Espagne*<sup>F</sup>

mung beans
*haricots*<sup>M</sup> *mungo*

lima beans
*haricots*<sup>M</sup> *de Lima*

pinto beans
*haricots*<sup>M</sup> *pinto*

red kidney beans
*haricots*<sup>M</sup> *rouge*

black gram beans
*haricots*<sup>M</sup> *mungo à grain*<sup>M</sup>
*noir*

black beans
*haricots*<sup>M</sup> *noir*

soybeans
*graine*<sup>F</sup> *de soja*<sup>M</sup> *; graine*<sup>F</sup> *de soya*<sup>M</sup>

soybean sprouts
*germes*<sup>M</sup> *de soja*<sup>M</sup> *; germes*<sup>M</sup> *de soya*<sup>M</sup>

flageolets
*flageolets*<sup>M</sup>

# fruits

fruits<sup>M</sup>

## berries
*baies*<sup>F</sup>

currants
*groseilles*<sup>F</sup> *à grappes*<sup>F</sup> *; gadelle*<sup>F</sup>

black currants
*cassis*<sup>M</sup>

gooseberries
*groseilles*<sup>F</sup> *à maquereau*<sup>M</sup>

grapes
*raisins*<sup>M</sup>

blueberries
*bleuets*<sup>M</sup>

bilberries
*myrtilles*<sup>F</sup>

red whortleberries
*airelles*<sup>F</sup>

alkekengi
*alkékenge*<sup>M</sup>

cranberries
*canneberges*<sup>F</sup> *; atoca*<sup>M</sup>

raspberries
*framboises*<sup>F</sup>

blackberries
*mûres*<sup>F</sup>

strawberries
*fraises*<sup>F</sup>

## stone fruits
*fruits*<sup>M</sup> *à noyau*<sup>M</sup>

plums
*prunes*<sup>F</sup>

peach
*pêche*<sup>F</sup>

nectarine
*nectarine*<sup>F</sup>

apricot
*abricot*<sup>M</sup>

cherries
*cerises*<sup>F</sup>

dates
*dattes*<sup>F</sup>

**dry fruits**
*fruits*<sup>M</sup> *secs*

macadamia nuts
*noix*<sup>F</sup> *de macadamia*<sup>M</sup>

ginkgo nuts
*noix*<sup>F</sup> *de ginkgo*<sup>M</sup>

pistachio nuts
*pistaches*<sup>F</sup>

pine nuts
*pignons*<sup>M</sup>

cola nuts
*noix*<sup>F</sup> *de cola*<sup>M</sup>

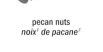

pecan nuts
*noix*<sup>F</sup> *de pacane*<sup>F</sup>

cashews
*noix*<sup>F</sup> *de cajou*<sup>M</sup>

almonds
*amandes*<sup>F</sup>

hazelnuts
*noisettes*<sup>F</sup>

walnut
*noix*<sup>F</sup>

coconut
*noix*<sup>F</sup> *de coco*<sup>M</sup>

chestnuts
*marrons*<sup>M</sup>

beechnut
*faîne*<sup>F</sup>

Brazil nuts
*noix*<sup>F</sup> *du Brésil*<sup>M</sup>

**pome fruits**
*fruits*<sup>M</sup> *à pépins*<sup>M</sup>

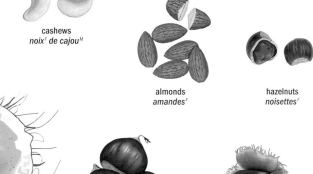

pear
*poire*<sup>F</sup>

quince
*coing*<sup>M</sup>

apple
*pomme*<sup>F</sup>

Japanese plums
*nèfles*<sup>F</sup> *du Japon*<sup>M</sup>

fruits

### citrus fruits
### *agrumes*<sup>M</sup>

lemon
*citron*<sup>M</sup>

kumquat
*kumquat*<sup>M</sup>

lime
*lime*<sup>F</sup>

orange
*orange*<sup>F</sup>

mandarin
*mandarine*<sup>F</sup>

bergamot
*bergamote*<sup>F</sup>

grapefruit
*pomelo*<sup>M</sup>

pomelo
*pamplemousse*<sup>M</sup>

citron
*cédrat*<sup>M</sup>

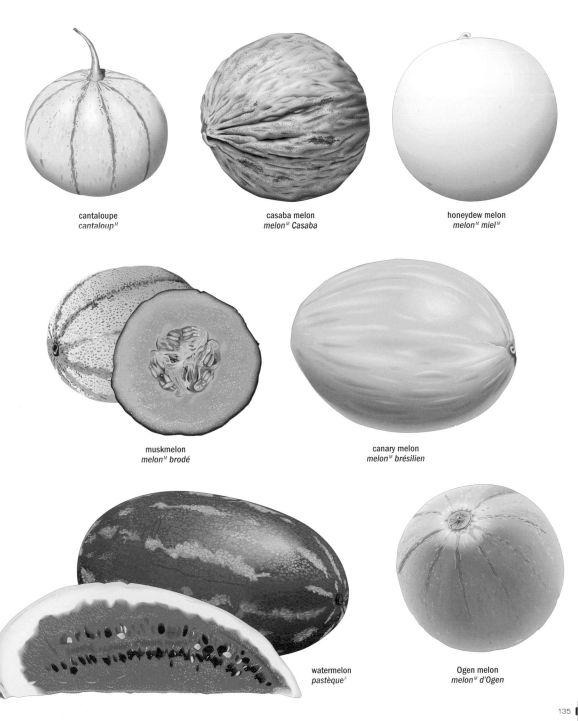

cantaloupe
*cantaloup*<sup>M</sup>

casaba melon
*melon*<sup>M</sup> *Casaba*

honeydew melon
*melon*<sup>M</sup> *miel*<sup>M</sup>

muskmelon
*melon*<sup>M</sup> *brodé*

canary melon
*melon*<sup>M</sup> *brésilien*

watermelon
*pastèque*<sup>F</sup>

Ogen melon
*melon*<sup>M</sup> *d'Ogen*

FOOD AND KITCHEN

fruits

## tropical fruits
*fruits^M tropicaux*

plantain
*banane^F plantain^M*

banana
*banane^F*

longan
*longane^M*

tamarillo
*tamarillo^M*

passion fruit
*fruit^M de la Passion^F*

horned melon
*melon^M à cornes^F*

mangosteen
*mangoustan^M*

kiwi
*kiwi^M*

pomegranate
*grenade^F*

cherimoya
*chérimole^F*

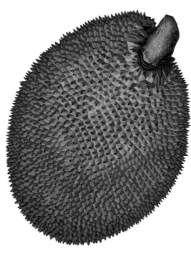

jackfruit
*jaque^M*

pineapple
*ananas^M*

jaboticabas
*jaboticaba*M

litchi
*litchi*M

fig
*figue*F

Chinese dates
*jujube*M

sapodilla
*sapotille*F

guava
*goyave*F

rambutan
*rambutan*M

Japanese persimmon
*kaki*M

prickly pear
*figue*F *de Barbarie*

carambola
*carambole*F

Asian pear
*pomme*F*-poire*F

mango
*mangue*F

durian
*durian*M

papaya
*papaye*F

pepino
*pepino*M

feijoa
*feijoa*M

# spices

*épices*[F]

juniper berries
*baies*[F] *de genièvre*[M]

cloves
*clou*[M] *de girofle*[M]

allspice
*piment*[M] *de la Jamaïque*[F]

white mustard
*moutarde*[F] *blanche*

black mustard
*moutarde*[F] *noire*

black pepper
*poivre*[M] *noir*

white pepper
*poivre*[M] *blanc*

pink pepper
*poivre*[M] *rose*

green pepper
*poivre*[M] *vert*

nutmeg
*noix*[F] *de muscade*[F]

caraway
*carvi*[M]

cardamom
*cardamome*[F]

cinnamon
*cannelle*[F]

saffron
*safran*[M]

cumin
*cumin*[M]

curry
*curry*[M]

turmeric
*curcuma*[M]

fenugreek
*fenugrec*[M]

jalapeño chile
*piment*<sup>M</sup> *Jalapeño*

bird's eye chile
*piment*<sup>M</sup> *oiseau*<sup>M</sup>

crushed chiles
*piments*<sup>M</sup> *broyés*

dried chiles
*piments*<sup>M</sup> *séchés*

cayenne pepper
*piment*<sup>M</sup> *de Cayenne*

paprika
*paprika*<sup>M</sup>

ajowan
*ajowan*<sup>M</sup>

asafetida
*asa-fœtida*<sup>F</sup>

garam masala
*garam masala*<sup>M</sup>

cajun spice seasoning
*mélange*<sup>M</sup> *d'épices*<sup>F</sup> *cajun*

marinade spices
*épices*<sup>F</sup> *à marinade*<sup>F</sup>

five spice powder
*cinq-épices*<sup>M</sup> *chinois*

chili powder
*assaisonnement*<sup>M</sup> *au chili*<sup>M</sup>

ground pepper
*poivre*<sup>M</sup> *moulu*

ras el hanout
*ras-el-hanout*<sup>M</sup>

sumac
*sumac*<sup>M</sup>

poppy seeds
*graines*<sup>F</sup> *de pavot*<sup>M</sup>

ginger
*gingembre*<sup>M</sup>

# condiments

condiments<sup>M</sup>

Tabasco® sauce
*sauce<sup>F</sup> Tabasco*®

Worcestershire sauce
*sauce<sup>F</sup> Worcestershire*

tamarind paste
*pâte<sup>F</sup> de tamarin<sup>M</sup>*

vanilla extract
*extrait<sup>M</sup> de vanille<sup>F</sup>*

tomato paste
*concentré<sup>M</sup> de tomate<sup>F</sup>*

tomato sauce
*coulis<sup>M</sup> de tomate<sup>F</sup>*

hummus
*hoummos<sup>M</sup>*

tahini
*tahini<sup>M</sup>*

hoisin sauce
*sauce<sup>F</sup> hoisin*

soy sauce
*sauce<sup>F</sup> soja<sup>M</sup> ; sauce<sup>F</sup> soya<sup>M</sup>*

powdered mustard
*moutarde<sup>F</sup> en poudre<sup>F</sup>*

wholegrain mustard
*moutarde<sup>F</sup> à l'ancienne<sup>F</sup>*

Dijon mustard
*moutarde<sup>F</sup> de Dijon*

German mustard
*moutarde<sup>F</sup> allemande*

English mustard
*moutarde<sup>F</sup> anglaise*

American mustard
*moutarde<sup>F</sup> américaine*

plum sauce
*sauce<sup>F</sup> aux prunes<sup>F</sup>*

mango chutney
*chutney<sup>M</sup> à la mangue<sup>F</sup>*

harissa
*harissa<sup>F</sup>*

sambal oelek
*sambal oelek<sup>M</sup>*

ketchup
*ketchup<sup>M</sup>*

wasabi
*wasabi<sup>M</sup>*

table salt
*sel<sup>M</sup> fin*

coarse salt
*gros sel<sup>M</sup>*

sea salt
*sel<sup>M</sup> marin*

balsamic vinegar
*vinaigre<sup>M</sup> balsamique*

rice vinegar
*vinaigre<sup>M</sup> de riz<sup>M</sup>*

apple cider vinegar
*vinaigre<sup>M</sup> de cidre<sup>M</sup>*

malt vinegar
*vinaigre<sup>M</sup> de malt<sup>M</sup>*

wine vinegar
*vinaigre<sup>M</sup> de vin<sup>M</sup>*

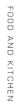

# herbs
fines herbes<sup>F</sup>

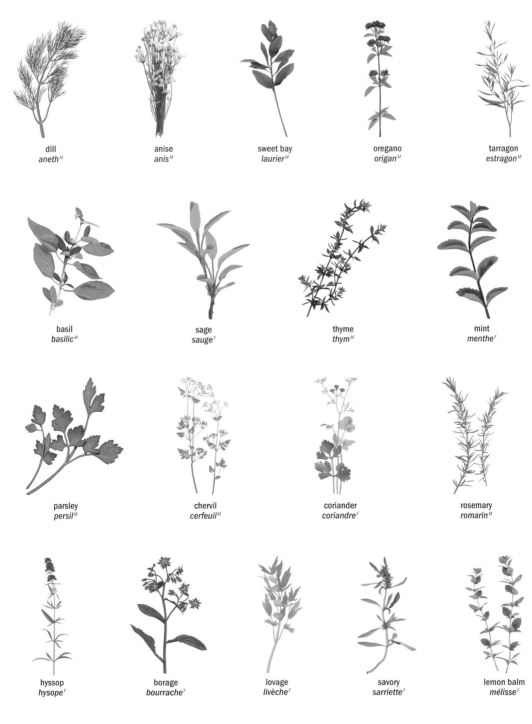

dill
*aneth*<sup>M</sup>

anise
*anis*<sup>M</sup>

sweet bay
*laurier*<sup>M</sup>

oregano
*origan*<sup>M</sup>

tarragon
*estragon*<sup>M</sup>

basil
*basilic*<sup>M</sup>

sage
*sauge*<sup>F</sup>

thyme
*thym*<sup>M</sup>

mint
*menthe*<sup>F</sup>

parsley
*persil*<sup>M</sup>

chervil
*cerfeuil*<sup>M</sup>

coriander
*coriandre*<sup>F</sup>

rosemary
*romarin*<sup>M</sup>

hyssop
*hysope*<sup>F</sup>

borage
*bourrache*<sup>F</sup>

lovage
*livèche*<sup>F</sup>

savory
*sarriette*<sup>F</sup>

lemon balm
*mélisse*<sup>F</sup>

FOOD AND KITCHEN

# cereal

*céréales*<sup>F</sup>

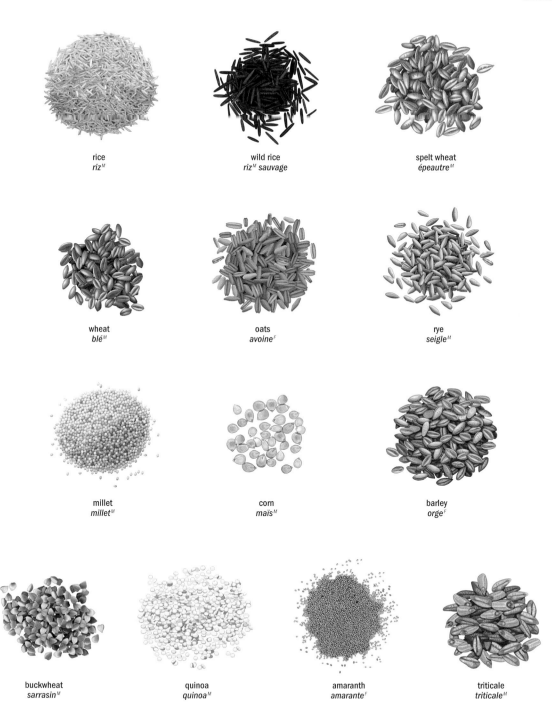

rice
*riz*<sup>M</sup>

wild rice
*riz*<sup>M</sup> *sauvage*

spelt wheat
*épeautre*<sup>M</sup>

wheat
*blé*<sup>M</sup>

oats
*avoine*<sup>F</sup>

rye
*seigle*<sup>M</sup>

millet
*millet*<sup>M</sup>

corn
*maïs*<sup>M</sup>

barley
*orge*<sup>F</sup>

buckwheat
*sarrasin*<sup>M</sup>

quinoa
*quinoa*<sup>M</sup>

amaranth
*amarante*<sup>F</sup>

triticale
*triticale*<sup>M</sup>

# cereal products

produits<sup>M</sup> céréaliers

## flour and semolina
*farine<sup>F</sup> et semoule<sup>F</sup>*

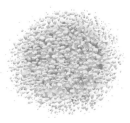

semolina
*semoule<sup>F</sup>*

whole-wheat flour
*farine<sup>F</sup> de blé<sup>M</sup> complet ; farine<sup>F</sup> de blé<sup>M</sup> entier*

couscous
*couscous<sup>M</sup>*

all-purpose flour
*farine<sup>F</sup> tout usage<sup>M</sup>*

unbleached flour
*farine<sup>F</sup> non blanchie*

oat flour
*farine<sup>F</sup> d'avoine<sup>F</sup>*

corn flour
*farine<sup>F</sup> de maïs<sup>M</sup>*

## bread
*pain<sup>M</sup>*

croissant
*croissant<sup>M</sup>*

black rye bread
*pain<sup>M</sup> de seigle<sup>M</sup> noir*

bagel
*bagel<sup>M</sup>*

Greek bread
*pain<sup>M</sup> grec*

baguette
*baguette<sup>F</sup> parisienne*

ear loaf
*baguette<sup>F</sup> épi<sup>M</sup>*

French bread
*pain<sup>M</sup> parisien*

FOOD AND KITCHEN

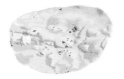

chapati
*pain*<sup>M</sup> *chapati indien*

tortillas
*tortillas*<sup>F</sup>

pita bread
*pain*<sup>M</sup> *pita*

naan
*pain*<sup>M</sup> *naan indien*

cracked rye bread
*cracker*<sup>M</sup> *de seigle*<sup>M</sup>

phyllo dough
*pâte*<sup>F</sup> *phyllo*<sup>F</sup>

unleavened bread
*pain*<sup>M</sup> *azyme*

Danish rye bread
*pain*<sup>M</sup> *de seigle*<sup>M</sup> *danois*

white bread
*pain*<sup>M</sup> *blanc*

multigrain bread
*pain*<sup>M</sup> *multicéréales*

Scandinavian cracked bread
*cracker*<sup>M</sup> *scandinave*

challah
*pain*<sup>M</sup> *tchallah juif*

American corn bread
*pain*<sup>M</sup> *de maïs*<sup>M</sup> *américain*

German rye bread
*pain*<sup>M</sup> *de seigle*<sup>M</sup> *allemand*

Russian pumpernickel
*pain*<sup>M</sup> *noir russe*

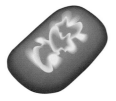

farmhouse bread
*pain*<sup>M</sup> *de campagne*<sup>F</sup>

wholemeal bread
*pain*<sup>M</sup> *complet*

Irish soda bread
*pain*<sup>M</sup> *irlandais*

English loaf
*pain*<sup>M</sup> *de mie*<sup>F</sup>

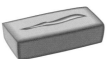

cereal products

## pasta
### *pâtes<sup>F</sup> alimentaires*

rigatoni
*rigatoni<sup>M</sup>*

rotini
*rotini<sup>M</sup>*

conchiglie
*conchiglie<sup>F</sup>*

fusilli
*fusilli<sup>M</sup>*

spaghetti
*spaghetti<sup>M</sup>*

ditali
*ditali<sup>M</sup>*

gnocchi
*gnocchi<sup>M</sup>*

tortellini
*tortellini<sup>M</sup>*

elbows
*coudes<sup>M</sup>*

penne
*penne<sup>M</sup>*

cannelloni
*cannelloni<sup>M</sup>*

spaghettini
*spaghettini<sup>M</sup>*

lasagna
*lasagne<sup>F</sup>*

ravioli
*ravioli<sup>M</sup>*

spinach tagliatelle
*tagliatelle<sup>M</sup> aux épinards<sup>M</sup>*

fettucine
*fettucine<sup>M</sup>*

**Asian noodles**
*nouilles<sup>F</sup> asiatiques*

soba noodles
*nouilles<sup>F</sup> soba*

somen noodles
*nouilles<sup>F</sup> somen*

udon noodles
*nouilles<sup>F</sup> udon*

rice paper
*galettes<sup>F</sup> de riz<sup>M</sup>*

rice noodles
*nouilles<sup>F</sup> de riz<sup>M</sup>*

bean thread cellophane noodles
*nouilles<sup>F</sup> de haricots<sup>M</sup> mungo*

egg noodles
*nouilles<sup>F</sup> aux œufs<sup>M</sup>*

rice vermicelli
*vermicelles<sup>M</sup> de riz<sup>M</sup>*

won ton skins
*pâtes<sup>F</sup> won-ton*

**rice**
*riz<sup>M</sup>*

white rice
*riz<sup>M</sup> blanc*

brown rice
*riz<sup>M</sup> complet*

parboiled rice
*riz<sup>M</sup> étuvé*

basmati rice
*riz<sup>M</sup> basmati*

FOOD AND KITCHEN

# coffee and infusions

café<sup>M</sup> et infusions<sup>F</sup>

**coffee**
*café*<sup>M</sup>

**herbal teas**
*tisanes*<sup>F</sup>

green coffee beans
*grains*<sup>M</sup> *de café*<sup>M</sup> *verts*

roasted coffee beans
*grains*<sup>M</sup> *de café*<sup>M</sup> *torréfiés*

linden
*tilleul*<sup>M</sup>

chamomile
*camomille*<sup>F</sup>

verbena
*verveine*<sup>F</sup>

**tea**
*thé*<sup>M</sup>

green tea
*thé*<sup>M</sup> *vert*

black tea
*thé*<sup>M</sup> *noir*

oolong tea
*thé*<sup>M</sup> *oolong*

tea bag
*thé*<sup>M</sup> *en sachet*<sup>M</sup>

# chocolate

chocolat<sup>M</sup>

dark chocolate
*chocolat*<sup>M</sup> *noir*

milk chocolate
*chocolat*<sup>M</sup> *au lait*<sup>M</sup>

cocoa
*cacao*<sup>M</sup>

white chocolate
*chocolat*<sup>M</sup> *blanc*

FOOD AND KITCHEN

# sugar

granulated sugar
*sucre<sup>M</sup> granulé*

powdered sugar
*sucre<sup>M</sup> glace<sup>F</sup>*

brown sugar
*cassonade<sup>F</sup>*

rock candy
*sucre<sup>M</sup> candi*

molasses
*mélasse<sup>F</sup>*

corn syrup
*sirop<sup>M</sup> de maïs<sup>M</sup>*

maple syrup
*sirop<sup>M</sup> d'érable<sup>M</sup>*

honey
*miel<sup>M</sup>*

FOOD AND KITCHEN

# fats and oils
huiles<sup>F</sup> et matières<sup>F</sup> grasses

corn oil
*huile<sup>F</sup> de maïs<sup>M</sup>*

olive oil
*huile<sup>F</sup> d'olive<sup>F</sup>*

sunflower-seed oil
*huile<sup>F</sup> de tournesol<sup>M</sup>*

peanut oil
*huile<sup>F</sup> d'arachide<sup>F</sup>*

sesame oil
*huile<sup>F</sup> de sésame<sup>M</sup>*

shortening
*saindoux<sup>M</sup>*

lard
*lard<sup>M</sup>*

margarine
*margarine<sup>F</sup>*

# dairy products

produits<sup>M</sup> laitiers

yogurt
*yaourt<sup>M</sup> ; yogourt<sup>M</sup>*

ghee
*ghee<sup>M</sup>*

butter
*beurre<sup>M</sup>*

## cream
*crème<sup>F</sup>*

whipping cream
*crème<sup>F</sup> épaisse ; crème<sup>F</sup> à fouetter*

sour cream
*crème<sup>F</sup> aigre ; crème<sup>F</sup> sure*

## milk
*lait<sup>M</sup>*

homogenized milk
*lait<sup>M</sup> homogénéisé*

goat's milk
*lait<sup>M</sup> de chèvre<sup>F</sup>*

evaporated milk
*lait<sup>M</sup> concentré*

buttermilk
*babeurre<sup>M</sup>*

powdered milk
*lait<sup>M</sup> en poudre<sup>F</sup>*

## fresh cheeses
*fromages<sup>M</sup> frais*

cottage cheese
*cottage<sup>M</sup>*

mozzarella
*mozzarella<sup>F</sup>*

ricotta
*ricotta<sup>F</sup>*

cream cheese
*fromage<sup>M</sup> à la crème<sup>F</sup>*

## goat's-milk cheeses
*fromages<sup>M</sup> de chèvre<sup>F</sup>*

chèvre cheese
*chèvre<sup>M</sup> frais*

Crottin de Chavignol
*crottin<sup>M</sup> de Chavignol*

dairy products

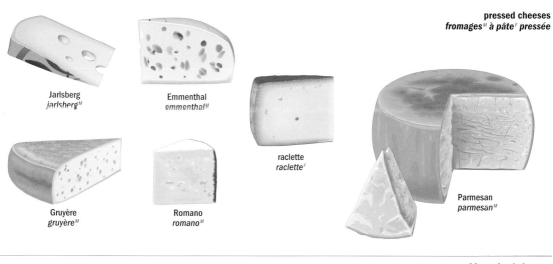

**pressed cheeses**
*fromages*<sup>M</sup> *à pâte*<sup>F</sup> *pressée*

Jarlsberg
*jarlsberg*<sup>M</sup>

Emmenthal
*emmenthal*<sup>M</sup>

raclette
*raclette*<sup>F</sup>

Parmesan
*parmesan*<sup>M</sup>

Gruyère
*gruyère*<sup>M</sup>

Romano
*romano*<sup>M</sup>

**blue-veined cheeses**
*fromages*<sup>M</sup> *à pâte*<sup>F</sup> *persillée*

Roquefort
*roquefort*<sup>M</sup>

Stilton
*stilton*<sup>M</sup>

Gorgonzola
*gorgonzola*<sup>M</sup>

Danish Blue
*bleu*<sup>M</sup> *danois*

**soft cheeses**
*fromages*<sup>M</sup> *à pâte*<sup>F</sup> *molle*

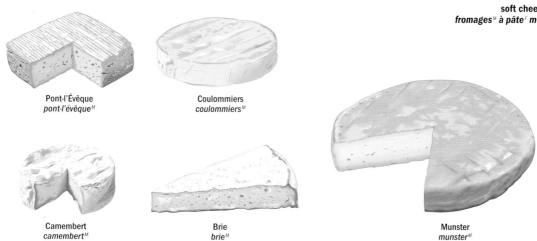

Pont-l'Évêque
*pont-l'évêque*<sup>M</sup>

Coulommiers
*coulommiers*<sup>M</sup>

Camembert
*camembert*<sup>M</sup>

Brie
*brie*<sup>M</sup>

Munster
*munster*<sup>M</sup>

# meat
viande<sup>F</sup>

## cuts of beef
*découpes<sup>F</sup> de bœuf<sup>M</sup>*

steak
*bifteck<sup>M</sup>*

beef cubes
*cubes<sup>M</sup> de bœuf<sup>M</sup>*

ground beef
*bœuf<sup>M</sup> haché*

shank
*jarret<sup>M</sup>*

tenderloin roast
*filet<sup>M</sup> de bœuf<sup>M</sup>*

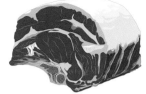

rib roast
*rôti<sup>M</sup> de côtes<sup>F</sup>*

back ribs
*côtes<sup>F</sup> levées de dos<sup>M</sup>*

## cuts of veal
*découpes<sup>F</sup> de veau<sup>M</sup>*

veal cubes
*cubes<sup>M</sup> de veau<sup>M</sup>*

ground veal
*veau<sup>M</sup> haché*

shank
*jarret<sup>M</sup>*

roast
*rôti<sup>M</sup>*

steak
*bifteck<sup>M</sup>*

chop
*côte<sup>F</sup>*

**cuts of lamb**
*découpes*F *d'agneau*M

chop
*côte*F

ground lamb
*agneau*M *haché*

lamb cubes
*cubes*M *d'agneau*M

roast
*rôti*M

shank
*jarret*M

**cuts of pork**
*découpes*F *de porc*M

spareribs
*travers*M ; *côtes*F *levées*

ground pork
*porc*M *haché*

hock
*jarret*M

loin chop
*côtelette*F

smoked ham
*jambon*M *fumé*

roast
*rôti*M

# organ meat

abats<sup>M</sup>

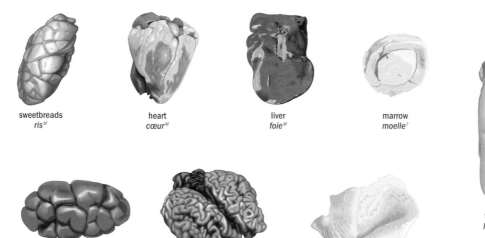

**sweetbreads**
*ris*<sup>M</sup>

**heart**
*cœur*<sup>M</sup>

**liver**
*foie*<sup>M</sup>

**marrow**
*moelle*<sup>F</sup>

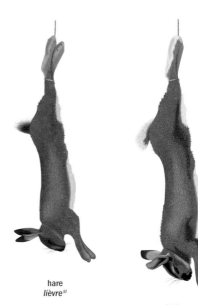

**tongue**
*langue*<sup>F</sup>

**kidney**
*rognons*<sup>M</sup>

**brains**
*cervelle*<sup>F</sup>

**tripe**
*tripes*<sup>F</sup>

# game

gibier<sup>M</sup>

**quail**
*caille*<sup>F</sup>

**pigeon**
*pigeon*<sup>M</sup>

**guinea fowl**
*pintade*<sup>F</sup>

**pheasant**
*faisan*<sup>M</sup>

**hare**
*lièvre*<sup>M</sup>

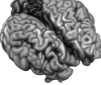

**rabbit**
*lapin*<sup>M</sup>

# poultry

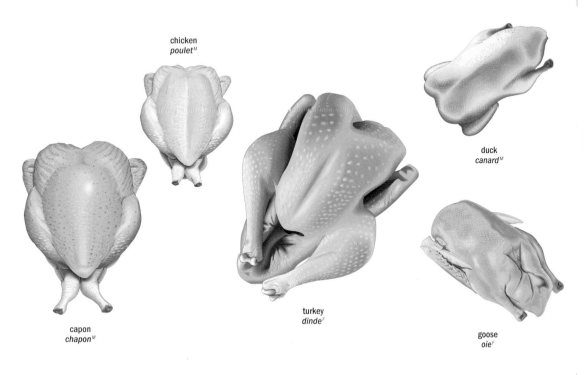

chicken
*poulet*<sup>M</sup>

duck
*canard*<sup>M</sup>

capon
*chapon*<sup>M</sup>

turkey
*dinde*<sup>F</sup>

goose
*oie*<sup>F</sup>

# eggs

quail egg
*œuf*<sup>M</sup> *de caille*<sup>F</sup>

pheasant egg
*œuf*<sup>M</sup> *de faisane*<sup>F</sup>

goose egg
*œuf*<sup>M</sup> *d'oie*<sup>F</sup>

ostrich egg
*œuf*<sup>M</sup> *d'autruche*<sup>F</sup>

duck egg
*œuf*<sup>M</sup> *de cane*<sup>F</sup>

hen egg
*œuf*<sup>M</sup> *de poule*<sup>F</sup>

# delicatessen

charcuterie<sup>F</sup>

rillettes
*rillettes*<sup>F</sup>

foie gras
*foie*<sup>M</sup> *gras*

prosciutto
*prosciutto*<sup>M</sup>

kielbasa sausage
*saucisson*<sup>M</sup> *kielbasa*

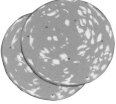

mortadella
*mortadelle*<sup>F</sup>

blood sausage
*boudin*<sup>M</sup>

chorizo
*chorizo*<sup>M</sup>

pepperoni
*pepperoni*<sup>M</sup>

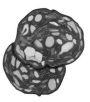

Genoa salami
*salami*<sup>M</sup> *de Gênes*

German salami
*salami*<sup>M</sup> *allemand*

Toulouse sausages
*saucisse*<sup>F</sup> *de Toulouse*

merguez sausages
*merguez*<sup>F</sup>

andouillette
*andouillette*<sup>F</sup>

chipolata sausage
*chipolata*<sup>F</sup>

frankfurters
*saucisse*<sup>F</sup> *de Francfort*

pancetta
*pancetta*<sup>F</sup>

cooked ham
*jambon*<sup>M</sup> *cuit*

American bacon
*bacon*<sup>M</sup> *américain*

Canadian bacon
*bacon*<sup>M</sup> *canadien*

# mollusks
mollusques<sup>M</sup>

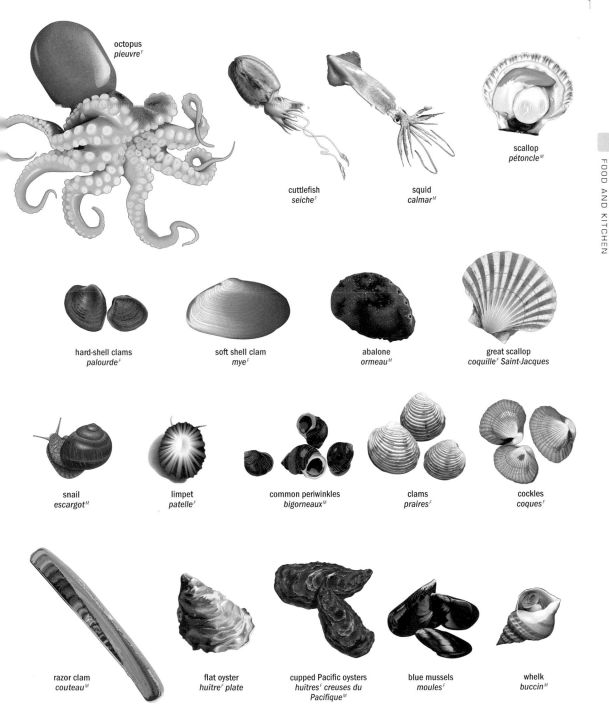

octopus
*pieuvre*<sup>F</sup>

cuttlefish
*seiche*<sup>F</sup>

squid
*calmar*<sup>M</sup>

scallop
*pétoncle*<sup>M</sup>

hard-shell clams
*palourde*<sup>F</sup>

soft shell clam
*mye*<sup>F</sup>

abalone
*ormeau*<sup>M</sup>

great scallop
*coquille*<sup>F</sup> *Saint-Jacques*

snail
*escargot*<sup>M</sup>

limpet
*patelle*<sup>F</sup>

common periwinkles
*bigorneaux*<sup>M</sup>

clams
*praires*<sup>F</sup>

cockles
*coques*<sup>F</sup>

razor clam
*couteau*<sup>M</sup>

flat oyster
*huître*<sup>F</sup> *plate*

cupped Pacific oysters
*huitres*<sup>F</sup> *creuses du Pacifique*<sup>M</sup>

blue mussels
*moules*<sup>F</sup>

whelk
*buccin*<sup>M</sup>

# crustaceans

crustacés*M*

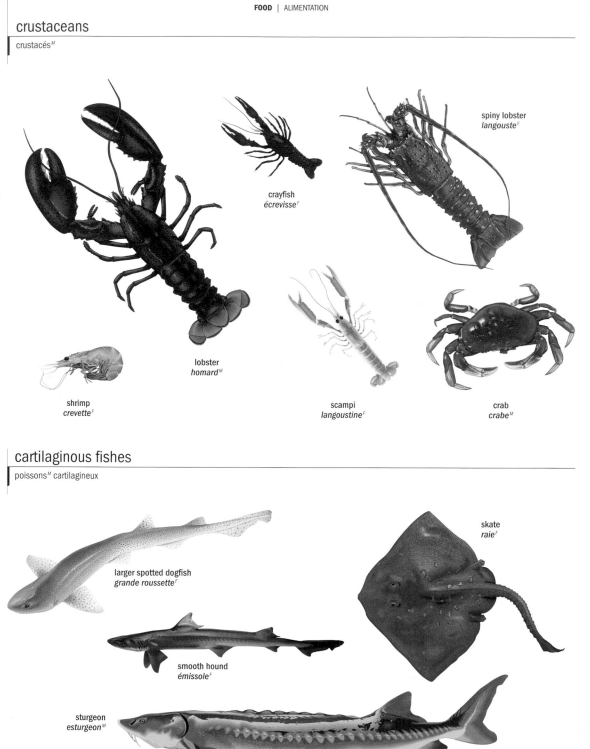

spiny lobster
*langouste*F

crayfish
*écrevisse*F

lobster
*homard*M

shrimp
*crevette*F

scampi
*langoustine*F

crab
*crabe*M

# cartilaginous fishes

poissons*M* cartilagineux

skate
*raie*F

larger spotted dogfish
*grande roussette*F

smooth hound
*émissole*F

sturgeon
*esturgeon*M

# bony fishes

poissons^M osseux

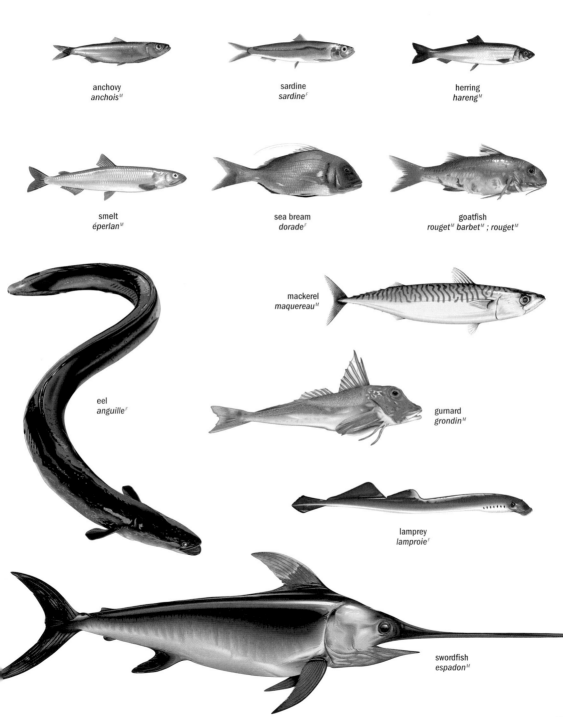

anchovy
*anchois*^M

sardine
*sardine*^F

herring
*hareng*^M

smelt
*éperlan*^M

sea bream
*dorade*^F

goatfish
*rouget*^M *barbet*^M ; *rouget*^M

mackerel
*maquereau*^M

eel
*anguille*^F

gurnard
*grondin*^M

lamprey
*lamproie*^F

swordfish
*espadon*^M

FOOD AND KITCHEN

bony fishes

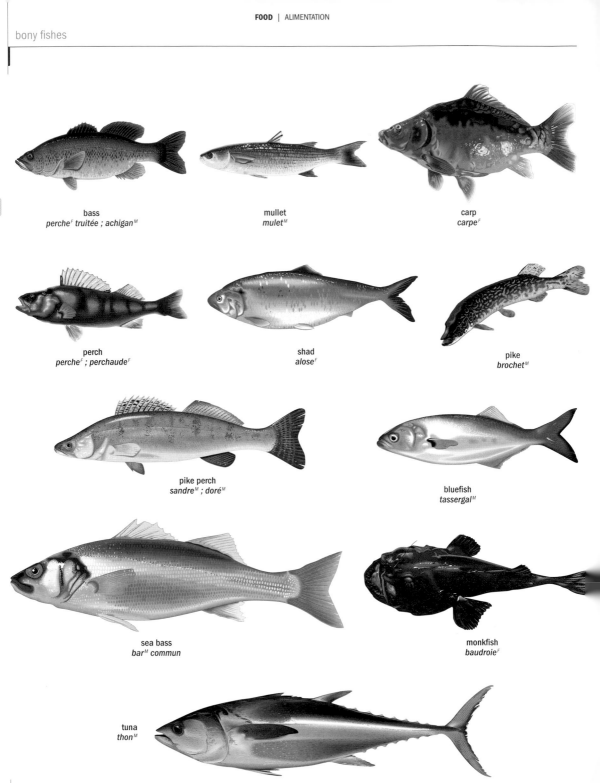

bass
*perche*F *truitée ; achigan*M

mullet
*mulet*M

carp
*carpe*F

perch
*perche*F *; perchaude*F

shad
*alose*F

pike
*brochet*M

pike perch
*sandre*M *; doré*M

bluefish
*tassergal*M

sea bass
*bar*M *commun*

monkfish
*baudroie*F

tuna
*thon*M

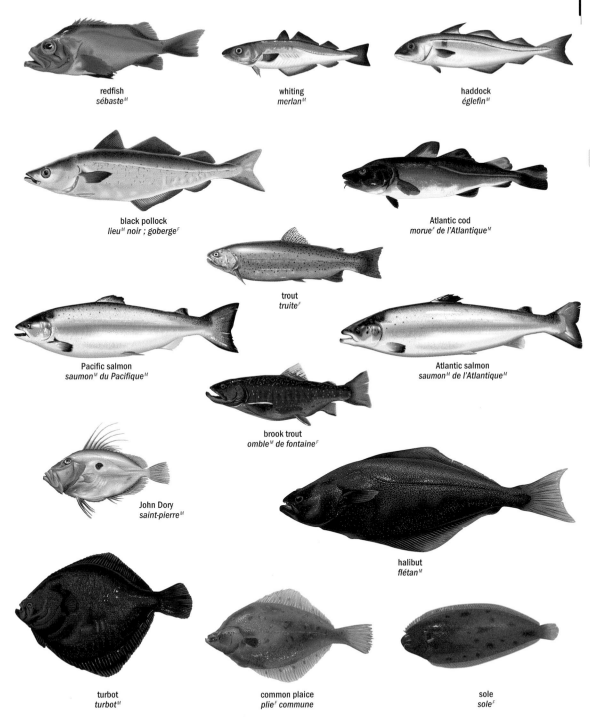

redfish
*sébaste*<sup>M</sup>

whiting
*merlan*<sup>M</sup>

haddock
*églefin*<sup>M</sup>

black pollock
*lieu*<sup>M</sup> *noir ; goberge*<sup>F</sup>

Atlantic cod
*morue*<sup>F</sup> *de l'Atlantique*<sup>M</sup>

trout
*truite*<sup>F</sup>

Pacific salmon
*saumon*<sup>M</sup> *du Pacifique*<sup>M</sup>

Atlantic salmon
*saumon*<sup>M</sup> *de l'Atlantique*<sup>M</sup>

brook trout
*omble*<sup>M</sup> *de fontaine*<sup>F</sup>

John Dory
*saint-pierre*<sup>M</sup>

halibut
*flétan*<sup>M</sup>

turbot
*turbot*<sup>M</sup>

common plaice
*plie*<sup>F</sup> *commune*

sole
*sole*<sup>F</sup>

# packaging

emballage<sup>M</sup>

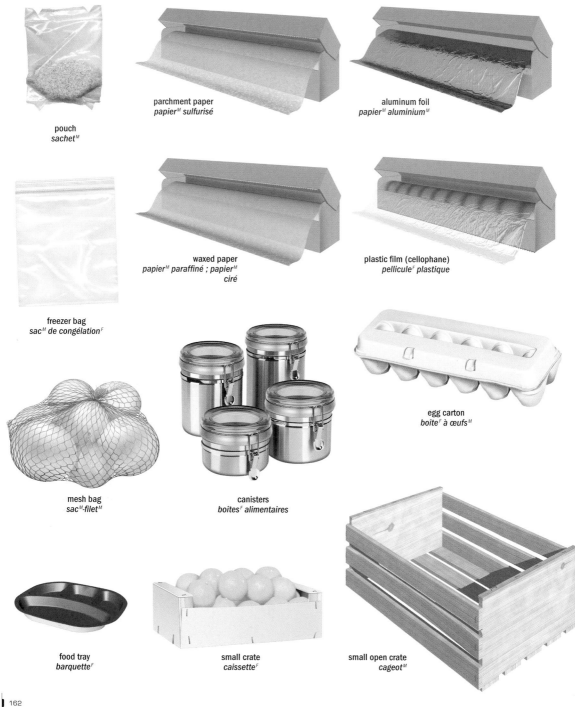

pouch
*sachet*<sup>M</sup>

parchment paper
*papier*<sup>M</sup> *sulfurisé*

aluminum foil
*papier*<sup>M</sup> *aluminium*<sup>M</sup>

freezer bag
*sac*<sup>M</sup> *de congélation*<sup>F</sup>

waxed paper
*papier*<sup>M</sup> *paraffiné ; papier*<sup>M</sup>
*ciré*

plastic film (cellophane)
*pellicule*<sup>F</sup> *plastique*

mesh bag
*sac*<sup>M</sup>*-filet*<sup>M</sup>

canisters
*boîtes*<sup>F</sup> *alimentaires*

egg carton
*boîte*<sup>F</sup> *à œufs*<sup>M</sup>

food tray
*barquette*<sup>F</sup>

small crate
*caissette*<sup>F</sup>

small open crate
*cageot*<sup>M</sup>

packaging

screw cap
*capsule^F à vis^F*

glass bottle
*bouteille^F en verre^M*

food can
*boîte^F de conserve^F*

pull tab
*onglet^M*

beverage can
*cannette^F*

multipack
*pack^M*

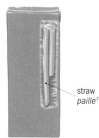

straw
*paille^F*

drink box
*briquette^F*

package
*paquet^M*

heat-sealed film
*opercule^M thermoscellé*

cup
*pot^M*

tube
*tube^M*

gabletop
*pignon^M*

milk/cream cup
*godet^M de lait^M/crème^F*

brick carton
*brique^F*

butter cup
*godet^M de beurre^M*

cheese box
*boîte^F à fromage^M*

small carton
*berlingot^M*

carton
*carton^M*

# kitchen
cuisine<sup>F</sup>

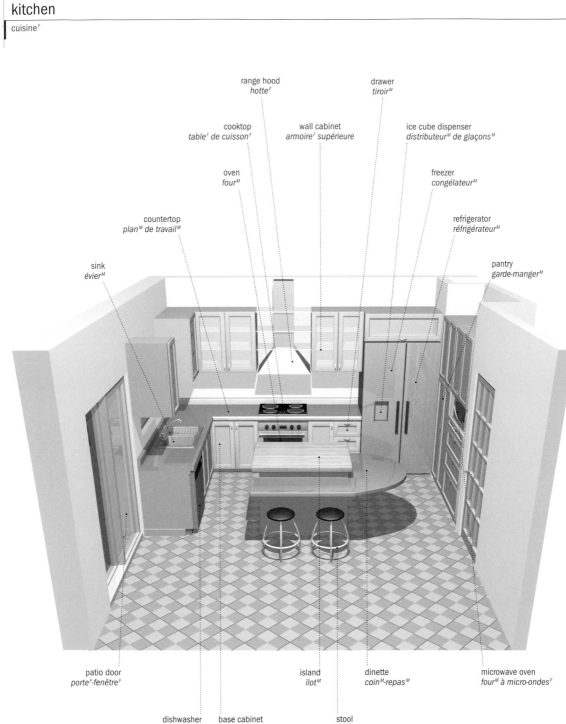

range hood
hotte<sup>F</sup>

drawer
tiroir<sup>M</sup>

cooktop
table<sup>F</sup> de cuisson<sup>F</sup>

wall cabinet
armoire<sup>F</sup> supérieure

ice cube dispenser
distributeur<sup>M</sup> de glaçons<sup>M</sup>

oven
four<sup>M</sup>

freezer
congélateur<sup>M</sup>

countertop
plan<sup>M</sup> de travail<sup>M</sup>

refrigerator
réfrigérateur<sup>M</sup>

sink
évier<sup>M</sup>

pantry
garde-manger<sup>M</sup>

patio door
porte<sup>F</sup>-fenêtre<sup>F</sup>

island
îlot<sup>M</sup>

dinette
coin<sup>M</sup>-repas<sup>M</sup>

microwave oven
four<sup>M</sup> à micro-ondes<sup>F</sup>

dishwasher
lave-vaisselle<sup>M</sup>

base cabinet
armoire<sup>F</sup> inférieure

stool
tabouret<sup>M</sup>

# glassware
verres<sup>M</sup>

liqueur glass
*verre<sup>M</sup> à liqueur<sup>F</sup>*

port glass
*verre<sup>M</sup> à porto<sup>M</sup>*

sparkling wine glass
*coupe<sup>F</sup> à mousseux<sup>M</sup>*

brandy snifter
*verre<sup>M</sup> à cognac<sup>M</sup>*

Alsace glass
*verre<sup>M</sup> à vin<sup>M</sup> d'Alsace<sup>F</sup>*

burgundy glass
*verre<sup>M</sup> à bourgogne<sup>M</sup>*

bordeaux glass
*verre<sup>M</sup> à bordeaux<sup>M</sup>*

white wine glass
*verre<sup>M</sup> à vin<sup>M</sup> blanc*

water goblet
*verre<sup>M</sup> à eau<sup>F</sup>*

cocktail glass
*verre<sup>M</sup> à cocktail<sup>M</sup>*

highball glass
*verre<sup>M</sup> à gin<sup>M</sup>*

old-fashioned glass
*verre<sup>M</sup> à whisky<sup>M</sup>*

beer mug
*chope<sup>F</sup> à bière<sup>F</sup>*

champagne flute
*flûte<sup>F</sup> à champagne<sup>M</sup>*

small decanter
*carafon<sup>M</sup>*

decanter
*carafe<sup>F</sup>*

# dinnerware

vaisselle<sup>F</sup>

demitasse
*tasse*<sup>F</sup> *à café*<sup>M</sup>

cup
*tasse*<sup>F</sup> *à thé*<sup>M</sup>

coffee mug
*chope*<sup>F</sup> *à café*<sup>M</sup>

creamer
*crémier*<sup>M</sup>

sugar bowl
*sucrier*<sup>M</sup>

salt shaker
*salière*<sup>F</sup>

pepper shaker
*poivrière*<sup>F</sup>

gravy boat
*saucière*<sup>F</sup>

butter dish
*beurrier*<sup>M</sup>

ramekin
*ramequin*<sup>M</sup>

soup bowl
*bol*<sup>M</sup>

rim soup bowl
*assiette*<sup>F</sup> *creuse*

dinner plate
*assiette*<sup>F</sup> *plate*

salad plate
*assiette*<sup>F</sup> *à salade*<sup>F</sup>

bread and butter plate
*assiette*<sup>F</sup> *à dessert*<sup>M</sup>

teapot
*théière*<sup>F</sup>

platter
*plat*<sup>M</sup> *ovale*

vegetable bowl
*légumier*<sup>M</sup>

fish platter
*plat*<sup>M</sup> *à poisson*<sup>M</sup>

hors d'oeuvre dish
*ravier*<sup>M</sup>

water pitcher
*pichet*<sup>M</sup>

salad bowl
*saladier*<sup>M</sup>

salad dish
*bol*<sup>M</sup> *à salade*<sup>F</sup>

soup tureen
*soupière*<sup>F</sup>

FOOD AND KITCHEN

# silverware

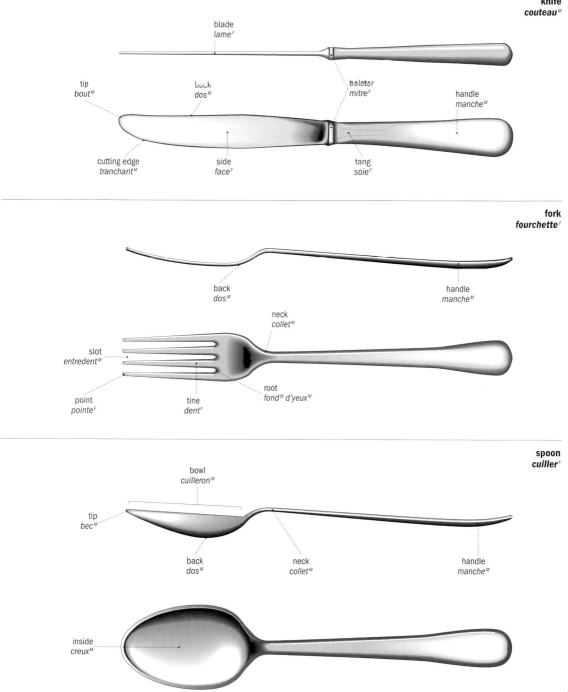

**knife**
*couteau*<sup>M</sup>

blade
*lame*<sup>F</sup>

tip
*bout*<sup>M</sup>

back
*dos*<sup>M</sup>

bolster
*mitre*<sup>F</sup>

handle
*manche*<sup>M</sup>

cutting edge
*tranchant*<sup>M</sup>

side
*face*<sup>F</sup>

tang
*soie*<sup>F</sup>

**fork**
*fourchette*<sup>F</sup>

back
*dos*<sup>M</sup>

handle
*manche*<sup>M</sup>

neck
*collet*<sup>M</sup>

slot
*entredent*<sup>M</sup>

root
*fond*<sup>M</sup> *d'yeux*<sup>M</sup>

point
*pointe*<sup>F</sup>

tine
*dent*<sup>F</sup>

**spoon**
*cuiller*<sup>F</sup>

bowl
*cuilleron*<sup>M</sup>

tip
*bec*<sup>M</sup>

back
*dos*<sup>M</sup>

neck
*collet*<sup>M</sup>

handle
*manche*<sup>M</sup>

inside
*creux*<sup>M</sup>

FOOD AND KITCHEN

FOOD AND KITCHEN

## silverware

### examples of forks
*exemples*M *de fourchettes*F

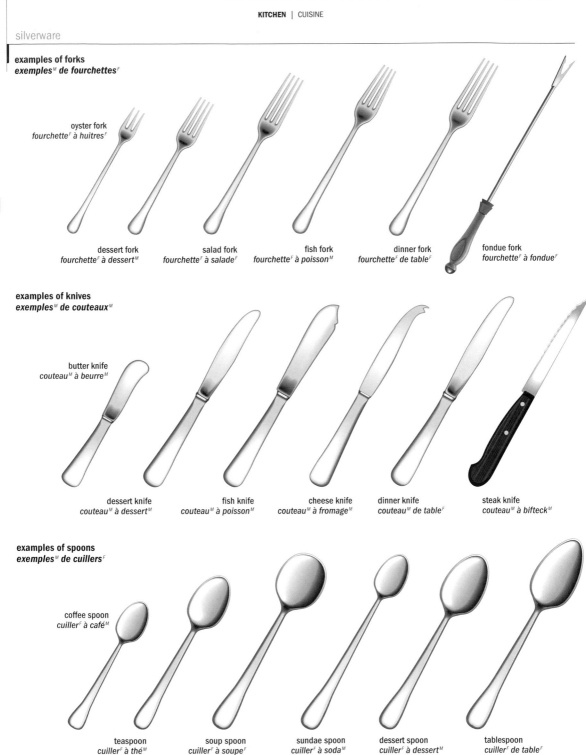

oyster fork
*fourchette*F *à huîtres*F

dessert fork
*fourchette*F *à dessert*M

salad fork
*fourchette*F *à salade*F

fish fork
*fourchette*F *à poisson*M

dinner fork
*fourchette*F *de table*F

fondue fork
*fourchette*F *à fondue*F

### examples of knives
*exemples*M *de couteaux*M

butter knife
*couteau*M *à beurre*M

dessert knife
*couteau*M *à dessert*M

fish knife
*couteau*M *à poisson*M

cheese knife
*couteau*M *à fromage*M

dinner knife
*couteau*M *de table*F

steak knife
*couteau*M *à bifteck*M

### examples of spoons
*exemples*M *de cuillers*F

coffee spoon
*cuiller*F *à café*M

teaspoon
*cuiller*F *à thé*M

soup spoon
*cuiller*F *à soupe*F

sundae spoon
*cuiller*F *à soda*M

dessert spoon
*cuiller*F *à dessert*M

tablespoon
*cuiller*F *de table*F

# kitchen utensils
*ustensiles*<sup>M</sup> *de cuisine*<sup>F</sup>

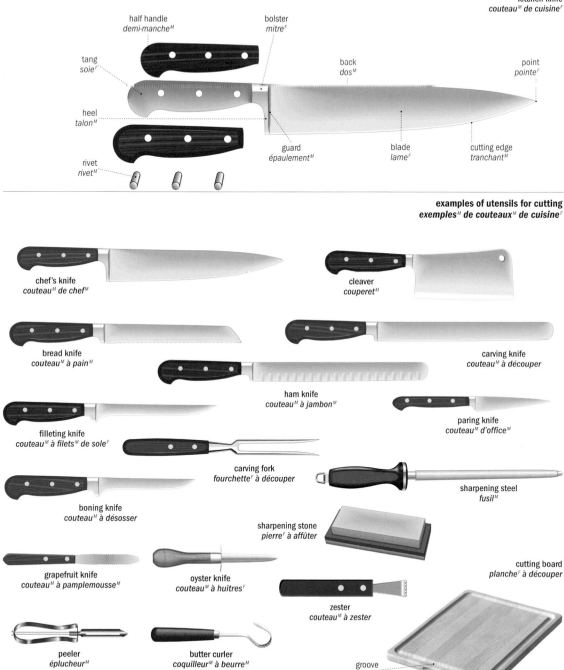

kitchen knife
*couteau*<sup>M</sup> *de cuisine*<sup>F</sup>

half handle
*demi-manche*<sup>M</sup>

bolster
*mitre*<sup>F</sup>

tang
*soie*<sup>F</sup>

back
*dos*<sup>M</sup>

point
*pointe*<sup>F</sup>

heel
*talon*<sup>M</sup>

guard
*épaulement*<sup>M</sup>

blade
*lame*<sup>F</sup>

cutting edge
*tranchant*<sup>M</sup>

rivet
*rivet*<sup>M</sup>

**examples of utensils for cutting**
*exemples*<sup>M</sup> *de couteaux*<sup>M</sup> *de cuisine*<sup>F</sup>

chef's knife
*couteau*<sup>M</sup> *de chef*<sup>M</sup>

cleaver
*couperet*<sup>M</sup>

bread knife
*couteau*<sup>M</sup> *à pain*<sup>M</sup>

carving knife
*couteau*<sup>M</sup> *à découper*

ham knife
*couteau*<sup>M</sup> *à jambon*<sup>M</sup>

filleting knife
*couteau*<sup>M</sup> *à filets*<sup>M</sup> *de sole*<sup>F</sup>

paring knife
*couteau*<sup>M</sup> *d'office*<sup>M</sup>

carving fork
*fourchette*<sup>F</sup> *à découper*

sharpening steel
*fusil*<sup>M</sup>

boning knife
*couteau*<sup>M</sup> *à désosser*

sharpening stone
*pierre*<sup>F</sup> *à affûter*

grapefruit knife
*couteau*<sup>M</sup> *à pamplemousse*<sup>M</sup>

oyster knife
*couteau*<sup>M</sup> *à huîtres*<sup>F</sup>

cutting board
*planche*<sup>F</sup> *à découper*

zester
*couteau*<sup>M</sup> *à zester*

peeler
*éplucheur*<sup>M</sup>

butter curler
*coquilleur*<sup>M</sup> *à beurre*<sup>M</sup>

groove
*rainure*<sup>F</sup>

# kitchen utensils

**for opening**
*pour ouvrir*

can opener
*ouvre-boîtes*$^M$

bottle opener
*décapsuleur*$^M$

waiter's corkscrew
*tire-bouchon*$^M$ *de sommelier*$^M$

lever corkscrew
*tire-bouchon*$^M$ *à levier*$^M$

**for grinding and grating**
*pour broyer et râper*

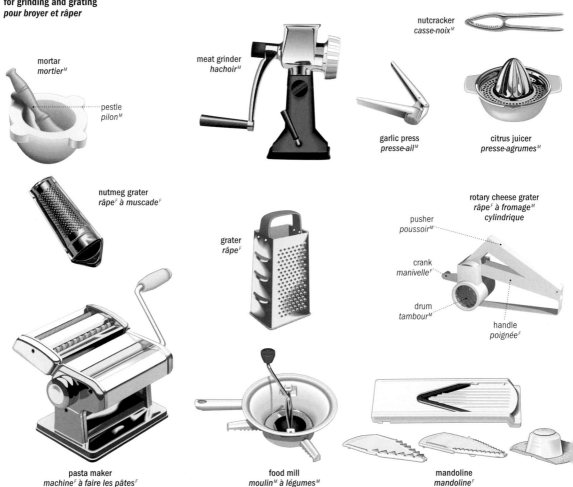

nutcracker
*casse-noix*$^M$

mortar
*mortier*$^M$

meat grinder
*hachoir*$^M$

pestle
*pilon*$^M$

garlic press
*presse-ail*$^M$

citrus juicer
*presse-agrumes*$^M$

nutmeg grater
*râpe*$^F$ *à muscade*$^F$

rotary cheese grater
*râpe*$^F$ *à fromage*$^M$
*cylindrique*

pusher
*poussoir*$^M$

grater
*râpe*$^F$

crank
*manivelle*$^F$

drum
*tambour*$^M$

handle
*poignée*$^F$

pasta maker
*machine*$^F$ *à faire les pâtes*$^F$

food mill
*moulin*$^M$ *à légumes*$^M$

mandoline
*mandoline*$^F$

for measuring
*pour mesurer*

measuring spoons
*cuillers<sup>F</sup> doseuses*

measuring cups
*mesures<sup>F</sup>*

candy thermometer
*thermomètre<sup>M</sup> à sucre<sup>M</sup>*

instant-read thermometer
*thermomètre<sup>M</sup> à mesure<sup>F</sup> instantanée*

measuring cup
*tasse<sup>F</sup> à mesurer*

meat thermometer
*thermomètre<sup>M</sup> à viande<sup>F</sup>*

oven thermometer
*thermomètre<sup>M</sup> de four<sup>M</sup>*

measuring beaker
*verre<sup>M</sup> à mesurer*

kitchen timer
*minuteur<sup>M</sup>*

egg timer
*sablier<sup>M</sup>*

kitchen scale
*balance<sup>F</sup> de cuisine<sup>F</sup>*

for straining and draining
*pour passer et égoutter*

mesh strainer
*passoire<sup>F</sup> fine*

muslin
*mousseline<sup>F</sup>*

chinois
*chinois<sup>M</sup>*

funnel
*entonnoir<sup>M</sup>*

colander
*passoire<sup>F</sup>*

fry basket
*panier<sup>M</sup> à friture<sup>F</sup>*

sieve
*tamis<sup>M</sup>*

salad spinner
*essoreuse<sup>F</sup> à salade<sup>F</sup>*

kitchen utensils

**baking utensils**
*pour la pâtisserie*<sup>F</sup>

icing syringe
*piston*<sup>M</sup> *à décorer*

pastry cutting wheel
*roulette*<sup>F</sup> *de pâtissier*<sup>M</sup>

pastry brush
*pinceau*<sup>M</sup> *à pâtisserie*<sup>F</sup>

egg beater
*batteur*<sup>M</sup> *à œufs*<sup>M</sup>

whisk
*fouet*<sup>M</sup>

sifter
*tamis*<sup>M</sup> *à farine*<sup>F</sup>

cookie cutters
*emporte-pièces*<sup>M</sup>

dredger
*saupoudreuse*<sup>F</sup>

pastry blender
*mélangeur*<sup>M</sup> *à pâtisserie*<sup>F</sup>

pastry bag and nozzles
*poche*<sup>F</sup> *à douilles*<sup>F</sup>

mixing bowls
*bols*<sup>M</sup> *à mélanger*

rolling pin
*rouleau*<sup>M</sup> *à pâtisserie*<sup>F</sup>

baking sheet
*plaque*<sup>F</sup> *à pâtisserie*<sup>F</sup>

muffin pan
*moule*<sup>M</sup> *à muffins*<sup>M</sup>

soufflé dish
*moule*<sup>M</sup> *à soufflé*<sup>M</sup>

charlotte mold
*moule*<sup>M</sup> *à charlotte*<sup>F</sup>

spring-form pan
*moule*<sup>M</sup> *à fond*<sup>M</sup> *amovible*

pie pan
*moule*<sup>M</sup> *à tarte*<sup>F</sup>

quiche plate
*moule*<sup>M</sup> *à quiche*<sup>F</sup>

cake pan
*moule*<sup>M</sup> *à gâteau*<sup>M</sup>

FOOD AND KITCHEN

**set of utensils**
*jeu*$^M$ *d'ustensiles*$^M$

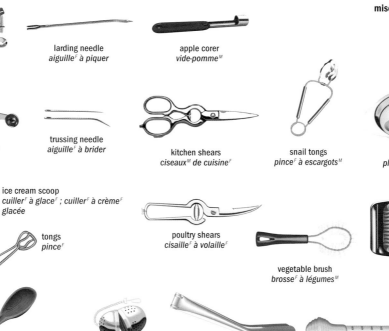

skimmer
*écumoire*$^F$

draining spoon
*cuiller*$^F$ *à égoutter*

spatula
*spatule*$^F$

turner
*pelle*$^F$

ladle
*louche*$^F$

potato masher
*pilon*$^M$

FOOD AND KITCHEN

**miscellaneous utensils**
*ustensiles*$^M$ *divers*

stoner
*dénoyauteur*$^M$

larding needle
*aiguille*$^F$ *à piquer*

apple corer
*vide-pomme*$^M$

melon baller
*cuiller*$^F$ *parisienne*

trussing needle
*aiguille*$^F$ *à brider*

kitchen shears
*ciseaux*$^M$ *de cuisine*$^F$

snail tongs
*pince*$^F$ *à escargots*$^M$

snail dish
*plat*$^M$ *à escargots*$^M$

ice cream scoop
*cuiller*$^F$ *à glace*$^F$ ; *cuiller*$^F$ *à crème*$^F$
*glacée*

tongs
*pince*$^F$

poultry shears
*cisaille*$^F$ *à volaille*$^F$

vegetable brush
*brosse*$^F$ *à légumes*$^M$

egg slicer
*coupe-œuf*$^M$

tasting spoon
*cuiller*$^F$ *à goûter*

tea ball
*boule*$^F$ *à thé*$^M$

spaghetti tongs
*pince*$^F$ *à spaghettis*$^M$

baster
*poire*$^F$ *à jus*$^M$

# cooking utensils

batterie*F* de cuisine*F*

wok set
wok*M*

lid
couvercle*M*

rack
grille*F*

wok
wok*M*

burner ring
collier*M*

tagine
tajine*M*

fish poacher
poissonnière*F*

rack
grille*F*

lid
couvercle*M*

fondue set
service*M* à fondue*F*

fondue pot
caquelon*M*

stand
support*M*

burner
réchaud*M*

terrine
terrine*F*

dripping pan
lèchefrite*F*

roasting pans
plats*M* à rôtir

pressure cooker
autocuiseur*M*

pressure regulator
régulateur*M* de pression*F*

safety valve
soupape*F*

Dutch oven
*faitout*M

stock pot
*marmite*F

couscous kettle
*couscoussier*M

frying pan
*poêle*F *à frire*

steamer
*cuit-vapeur*M

egg poacher
*pocheuse*F

sauté pan
*sauteuse*F

small saucepan
*poêlon*M

diable
*diable*M

crêpe pan
*poêle*F *à crêpes*F

steamer basket
*panier*M *cuit-vapeur*M

double boiler
*bain-marie*M

saucepan
*casserole*F

# domestic appliances

appareils<sup>M</sup> électroménagers

## for mixing and blending
### pour mélanger et battre

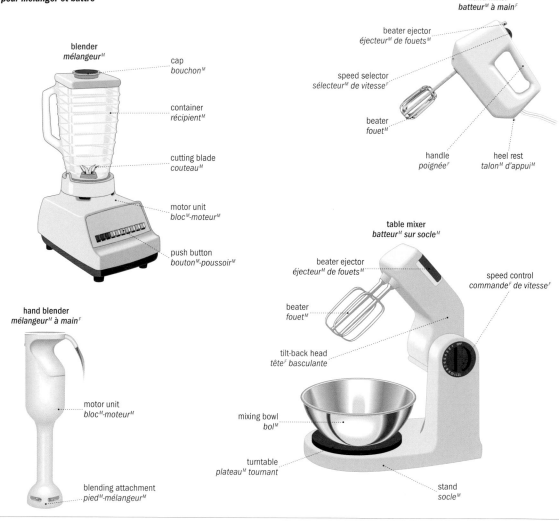

**hand mixer**
*batteur<sup>M</sup> à main<sup>F</sup>*

beater ejector
*éjecteur<sup>M</sup> de fouets<sup>M</sup>*

speed selector
*sélecteur<sup>M</sup> de vitesse<sup>F</sup>*

beater
*fouet<sup>M</sup>*

handle
*poignée<sup>F</sup>*

heel rest
*talon<sup>M</sup> d'appui<sup>M</sup>*

blender
*mélangeur<sup>M</sup>*

cap
*bouchon<sup>M</sup>*

container
*récipient<sup>M</sup>*

cutting blade
*couteau<sup>M</sup>*

motor unit
*bloc<sup>M</sup>-moteur<sup>M</sup>*

push button
*bouton<sup>M</sup>-poussoir<sup>M</sup>*

**table mixer**
*batteur<sup>M</sup> sur socle<sup>M</sup>*

beater ejector
*éjecteur<sup>M</sup> de fouets<sup>M</sup>*

speed control
*commande<sup>F</sup> de vitesse<sup>F</sup>*

beater
*fouet<sup>M</sup>*

tilt-back head
*tête<sup>F</sup> basculante*

**hand blender**
*mélangeur<sup>M</sup> à main<sup>F</sup>*

motor unit
*bloc<sup>M</sup>-moteur<sup>M</sup>*

mixing bowl
*bol<sup>M</sup>*

turntable
*plateau<sup>M</sup> tournant*

blending attachment
*pied<sup>M</sup>-mélangeur<sup>M</sup>*

stand
*socle<sup>M</sup>*

## beaters
### fouets<sup>M</sup>

four blade beater
*fouet<sup>M</sup> quatre pales<sup>F</sup>*

spiral beater
*fouet<sup>M</sup> en spirale<sup>F</sup>*

wire beater
*fouet<sup>M</sup> à fil<sup>M</sup>*

dough hook
*crochet<sup>M</sup> pétrisseur*

FOOD AND KITCHEN

domestic appliances

FOOD AND KITCHEN

**food processor**
*robot<sup>M</sup> de cuisine<sup>F</sup>*

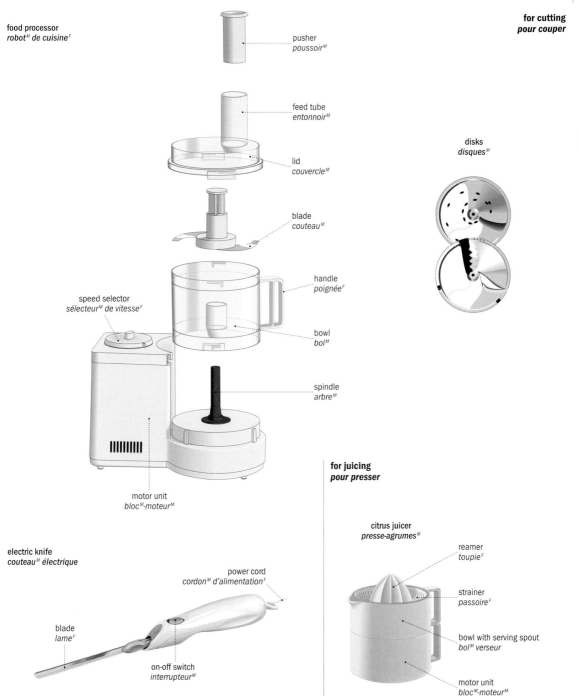

pusher
*poussoir<sup>M</sup>*

feed tube
*entonnoir<sup>M</sup>*

lid
*couvercle<sup>M</sup>*

blade
*couteau<sup>M</sup>*

handle
*poignée<sup>F</sup>*

speed selector
*sélecteur<sup>M</sup> de vitesse<sup>F</sup>*

bowl
*bol<sup>M</sup>*

spindle
*arbre<sup>M</sup>*

motor unit
*bloc<sup>M</sup>-moteur<sup>M</sup>*

**for cutting**
*pour couper*

disks
*disques<sup>M</sup>*

**for juicing**
*pour presser*

**citrus juicer**
*presse-agrumes<sup>M</sup>*

reamer
*toupie<sup>F</sup>*

strainer
*passoire<sup>F</sup>*

bowl with serving spout
*bol<sup>M</sup> verseur*

motor unit
*bloc<sup>M</sup>-moteur<sup>M</sup>*

**electric knife**
*couteau<sup>M</sup> électrique*

power cord
*cordon<sup>M</sup> d'alimentation<sup>F</sup>*

blade
*lame<sup>F</sup>*

on-off switch
*interrupteur<sup>M</sup>*

domestic appliances

**for cooking**
*pour cuire*

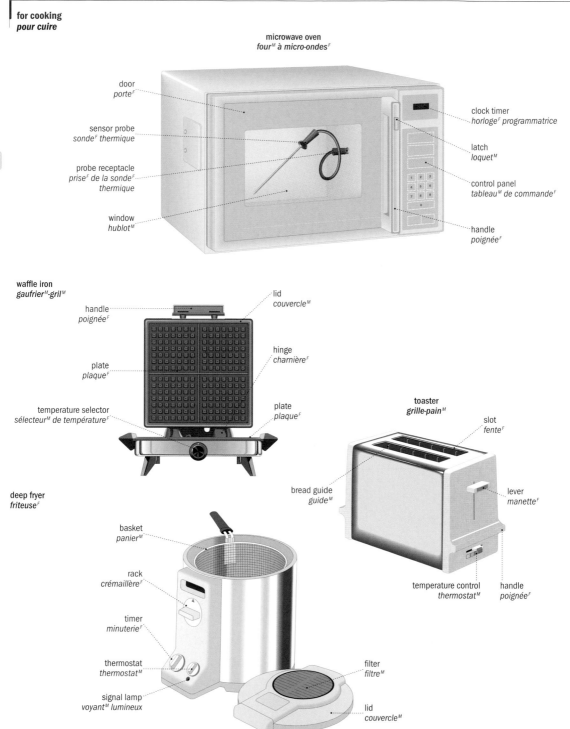

microwave oven
*four^M à micro-ondes^F*

door
*porte^F*

sensor probe
*sonde^F thermique*

probe receptacle
*prise^F de la sonde^F thermique*

window
*hublot^M*

clock timer
*horloge^F programmatrice*

latch
*loquet^M*

control panel
*tableau^M de commande^F*

handle
*poignée^F*

**waffle iron**
*gaufrier^M-gril^M*

handle
*poignée^F*

lid
*couvercle^M*

hinge
*charnière^F*

plate
*plaque^F*

temperature selector
*sélecteur^M de température^F*

plate
*plaque^F*

**toaster**
*grille-pain^M*

slot
*fente^F*

bread guide
*guide^M*

lever
*manette^F*

**deep fryer**
*friteuse^F*

basket
*panier^M*

rack
*crémaillère^F*

timer
*minuterie^F*

thermostat
*thermostat^M*

signal lamp
*voyant^M lumineux*

temperature control
*thermostat^M*

handle
*poignée^F*

filter
*filtre^M*

lid
*couvercle^M*

FOOD AND KITCHEN

**raclette with grill**
*raclette<sup>F</sup>-gril<sup>M</sup>*

dish
*poêlon<sup>M</sup>*

cooking plate
*surface<sup>F</sup> de cuisson<sup>F</sup>*

base
*socle<sup>M</sup>*

**electric steamer**
*cuit-vapeur<sup>M</sup> électrique*

cooking dishes
*bols<sup>M</sup> de cuisson<sup>F</sup>*

water level indicator
*indicateur<sup>M</sup> de niveau<sup>M</sup> d'eau<sup>F</sup>*

signal lamp
*voyant<sup>M</sup> lumineux*

timer
*minuterie<sup>F</sup>*

**indoor electric grill**
*gril<sup>M</sup> barbecue<sup>M</sup>*

insulated handle
*poignée<sup>F</sup> isolante*

drip pan
*bac<sup>M</sup> ramasse-jus<sup>M</sup>*

cooking surface
*surface<sup>F</sup> de cuisson<sup>F</sup>*

adjustable thermostat
*thermostat<sup>M</sup> réglable*

**bread machine**
*robot<sup>M</sup> boulanger<sup>M</sup>*

lid
*couvercle<sup>M</sup>*

control panel
*tableau<sup>M</sup> de commande<sup>F</sup>*

window
*hublot<sup>M</sup>*

loaf pan
*moule<sup>M</sup> à pain<sup>M</sup>*

**electric griddle**
*gril<sup>M</sup> électrique*

cooking surface
*surface<sup>F</sup> de cuisson<sup>F</sup>*

handle
*poignée<sup>F</sup>*

detachable control
*commande<sup>F</sup> amovible*

grease well
*collecteur<sup>M</sup> de graisse<sup>F</sup>*

# miscellaneous domestic appliances

appareils*M* électroménagers divers

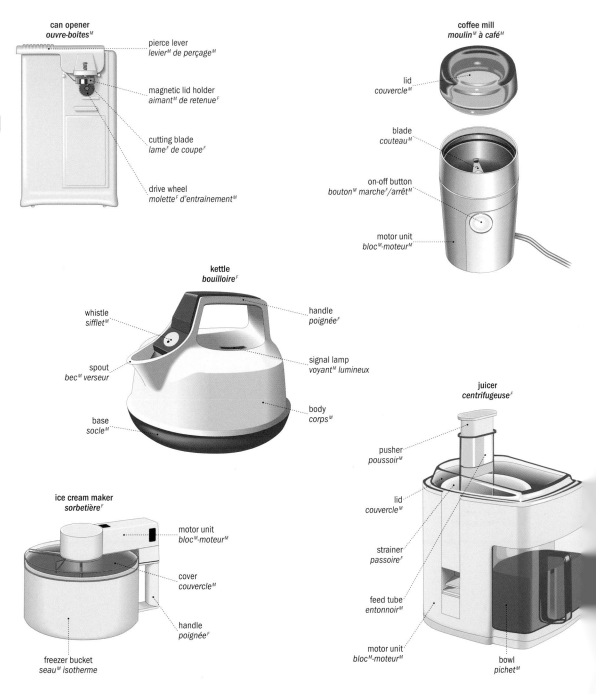

**can opener**
*ouvre-boîtes*M

pierce lever
*levier*M *de perçage*M

magnetic lid holder
*aimant*M *de retenue*F

cutting blade
*lame*F *de coupe*F

drive wheel
*molette*F *d'entrainement*M

**coffee mill**
*moulin*M *à café*M

lid
*couvercle*M

blade
*couteau*M

on-off button
*bouton*M *marche*F/*arrêt*M

motor unit
*bloc*M-*moteur*M

**kettle**
*bouilloire*F

whistle
*sifflet*M

handle
*poignée*F

spout
*bec*M *verseur*

signal lamp
*voyant*M *lumineux*

base
*socle*M

body
*corps*M

**juicer**
*centrifugeuse*F

pusher
*poussoir*M

**ice cream maker**
*sorbetière*F

motor unit
*bloc*M-*moteur*M

lid
*couvercle*M

cover
*couvercle*M

strainer
*passoire*F

handle
*poignée*F

feed tube
*entonnoir*M

freezer bucket
*seau*M *isotherme*

motor unit
*bloc*M-*moteur*M

bowl
*pichet*M

FOOD AND KITCHEN

# coffee makers
cafetières<sup>F</sup>

**automatic drip coffee maker**
*cafetière<sup>F</sup> filtre<sup>M</sup>*

reservoir
*réservoir<sup>M</sup>*

lid
*couvercle<sup>M</sup>*

water level
*niveau<sup>M</sup> d'eau<sup>F</sup>*

basket
*panier<sup>M</sup>*

signal lamp
*voyant<sup>M</sup> lumineux*

carafe
*verseuse<sup>F</sup>*

on-off switch
*interrupteur<sup>M</sup>*

warming plate
*plaque<sup>F</sup> chauffante*

**Neapolitan coffee maker**
*cafetière<sup>F</sup> napolitaine*

**espresso machine**
*machine<sup>F</sup> à espresso<sup>M</sup>*

on-off switch
*interrupteur<sup>M</sup>*

steam control knob
*manette<sup>F</sup> vapeur<sup>F</sup>*

tamper
*presse-café<sup>M</sup>*

filter holder
*porte-filtre<sup>M</sup>*

drip tray
*cuvette<sup>F</sup> ramasse-gouttes<sup>M</sup>*

steam nozzle
*buse<sup>F</sup> vapeur<sup>F</sup>*

water tank
*réservoir<sup>M</sup> d'eau<sup>F</sup>*

**vacuum coffee maker**
*cafetière<sup>F</sup> à infusion<sup>F</sup>*

upper bowl
*tulipe<sup>F</sup>*

stem
*tige<sup>F</sup>*

lower bowl
*ballon<sup>M</sup>*

**French press**
*cafetière<sup>F</sup> à piston<sup>M</sup>*

**espresso maker**
*cafetière<sup>F</sup> espresso<sup>M</sup>*

**percolator**
*percolateur<sup>M</sup>*

spout
*bec<sup>M</sup> verseur*

signal light
*voyant<sup>M</sup> lumineux*

FOOD AND KITCHEN

# exterior of a house

extérieur<sup>M</sup> d'une maison<sup>F</sup>

HOUSE

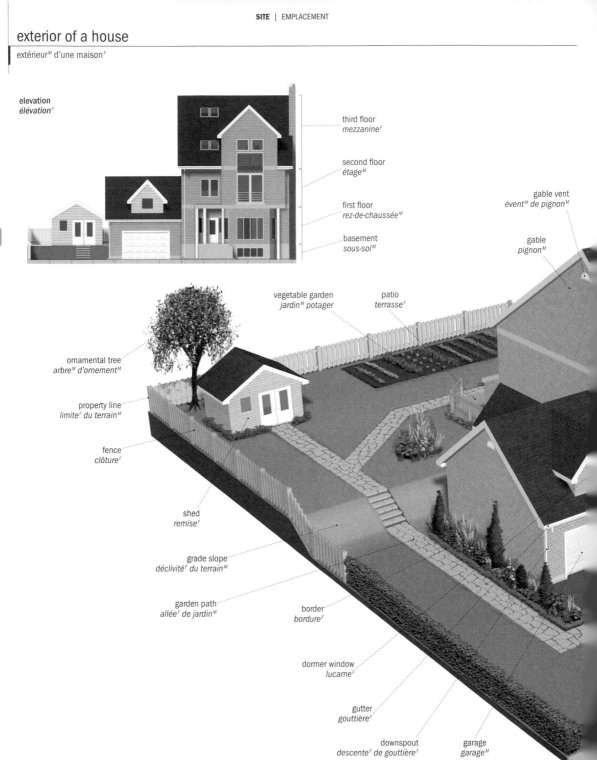

elevation
élévation<sup>F</sup>

third floor
mezzanine<sup>F</sup>

second floor
étage<sup>M</sup>

first floor
rez-de-chaussée<sup>M</sup>

basement
sous-sol<sup>M</sup>

gable vent
évent<sup>M</sup> de pignon<sup>M</sup>

gable
pignon<sup>M</sup>

vegetable garden
jardin<sup>M</sup> potager

patio
terrasse<sup>F</sup>

ornamental tree
arbre<sup>M</sup> d'ornement<sup>M</sup>

property line
limite<sup>F</sup> du terrain<sup>M</sup>

fence
clôture<sup>F</sup>

shed
remise<sup>F</sup>

grade slope
déclivité<sup>F</sup> du terrain<sup>M</sup>

garden path
allée<sup>F</sup> de jardin<sup>M</sup>

border
bordure<sup>F</sup>

dormer window
lucarne<sup>F</sup>

gutter
gouttière<sup>F</sup>

downspout
descente<sup>F</sup> de gouttière<sup>F</sup>

garage
garage<sup>M</sup>

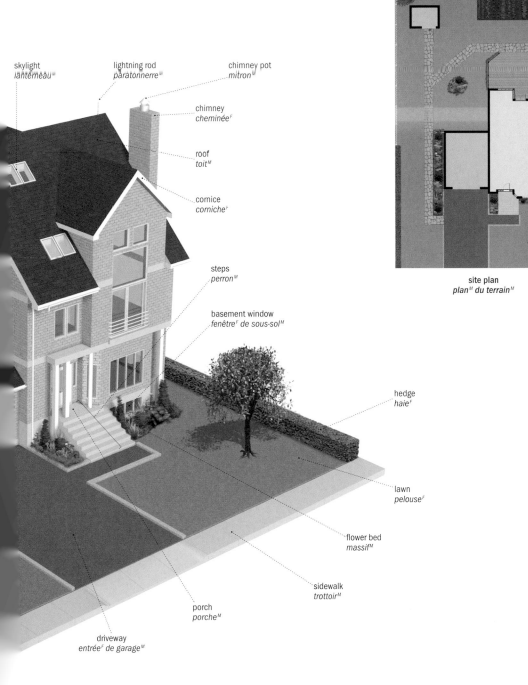

HOUSE

skylight
*lanterneau* M

lightning rod
*paratonnerre* M

chimney pot
*mitron* M

chimney
*cheminée* F

roof
*toit* M

cornice
*corniche* F

steps
*perron* M

basement window
*fenêtre* F *de sous-sol* M

hedge
*haie* F

lawn
*pelouse* F

flower bed
*massif* M

sidewalk
*trottoir* M

porch
*porche* M

driveway
*entrée* F *de garage* M

site plan
*plan* M *du terrain* M

# pool

piscine<sup>F</sup>

**aboveground swimming pool**
*piscine<sup>F</sup> hors sol<sup>M</sup>*

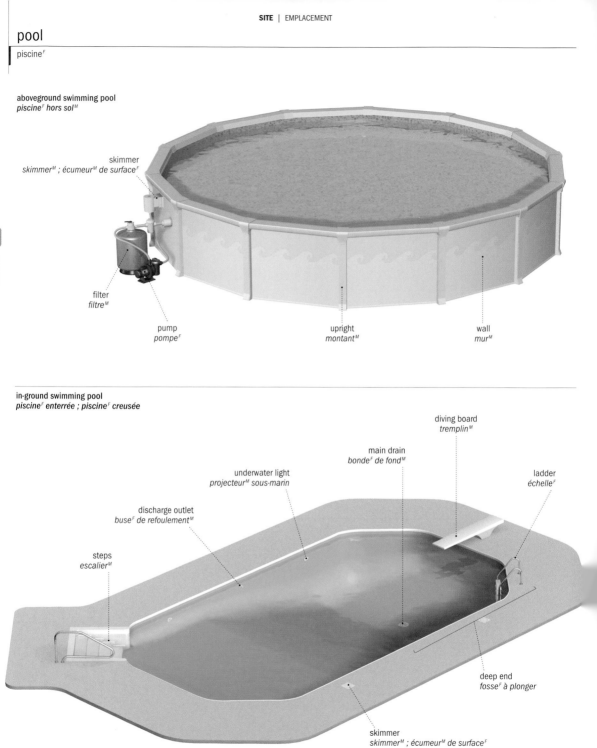

skimmer
*skimmer<sup>M</sup> ; écumeur<sup>M</sup> de surface<sup>F</sup>*

filter
*filtre<sup>M</sup>*

pump
*pompe<sup>F</sup>*

upright
*montant<sup>M</sup>*

wall
*mur<sup>M</sup>*

**in-ground swimming pool**
*piscine<sup>F</sup> enterrée ; piscine<sup>F</sup> creusée*

diving board
*tremplin<sup>M</sup>*

main drain
*bonde<sup>F</sup> de fond<sup>M</sup>*

underwater light
*projecteur<sup>M</sup> sous-marin*

ladder
*échelle<sup>F</sup>*

discharge outlet
*buse<sup>F</sup> de refoulement<sup>M</sup>*

steps
*escalier<sup>M</sup>*

deep end
*fosse<sup>F</sup> à plonger*

skimmer
*skimmer<sup>M</sup> ; écumeur<sup>M</sup> de surface<sup>F</sup>*

# exterior door

porte <sup>F</sup> extérieure

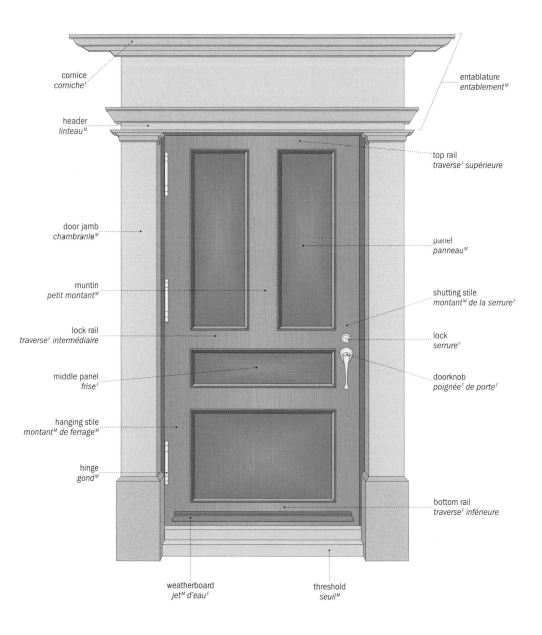

cornice
corniche <sup>F</sup>

entablature
entablement <sup>M</sup>

header
linteau <sup>M</sup>

top rail
traverse <sup>F</sup> supérieure

door jamb
chambranle <sup>M</sup>

panel
panneau <sup>M</sup>

muntin
petit montant <sup>M</sup>

shutting stile
montant <sup>M</sup> de la serrure <sup>F</sup>

lock rail
traverse <sup>F</sup> intermédiaire

lock
serrure <sup>F</sup>

middle panel
frise <sup>F</sup>

doorknob
poignée <sup>F</sup> de porte <sup>F</sup>

hanging stile
montant <sup>M</sup> de ferrage <sup>M</sup>

hinge
gond <sup>M</sup>

bottom rail
traverse <sup>F</sup> inférieure

weatherboard
jet <sup>M</sup> d'eau <sup>F</sup>

threshold
seuil <sup>M</sup>

# lock
serrure<sup>F</sup>

# window
fenêtre<sup>F</sup>

HOUSE

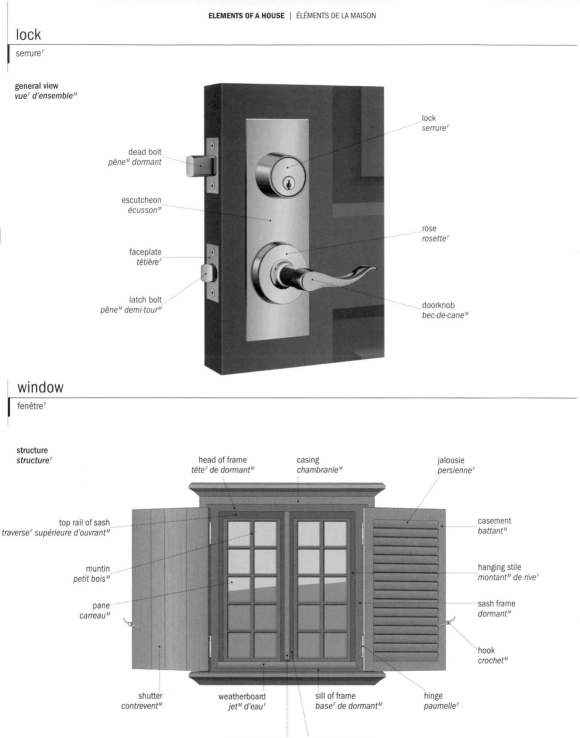

**general view**
*vue<sup>F</sup> d'ensemble<sup>M</sup>*

lock
serrure<sup>F</sup>

dead bolt
pêne<sup>M</sup> dormant

escutcheon
écusson<sup>M</sup>

rose
rosette<sup>F</sup>

faceplate
têtière<sup>F</sup>

latch bolt
pêne<sup>M</sup> demi-tour<sup>M</sup>

doorknob
bec-de-cane<sup>M</sup>

**structure**
*structure<sup>F</sup>*

head of frame
tête<sup>F</sup> de dormant<sup>M</sup>

casing
chambranle<sup>M</sup>

jalousie
persienne<sup>F</sup>

top rail of sash
traverse<sup>F</sup> supérieure d'ouvrant<sup>M</sup>

casement
battant<sup>M</sup>

muntin
petit bois<sup>M</sup>

hanging stile
montant<sup>M</sup> de rive<sup>F</sup>

pane
carreau<sup>M</sup>

sash frame
dormant<sup>M</sup>

hook
crochet<sup>M</sup>

shutter
contrevent<sup>M</sup>

weatherboard
jet<sup>M</sup> d'eau<sup>F</sup>

sill of frame
base<sup>F</sup> de dormant<sup>M</sup>

hinge
paumelle<sup>F</sup>

stile tongue of sash
montant<sup>M</sup> mouton<sup>M</sup>

stile groove of sash
montant<sup>M</sup> embrevé

# frame

charpente<sup>F</sup>

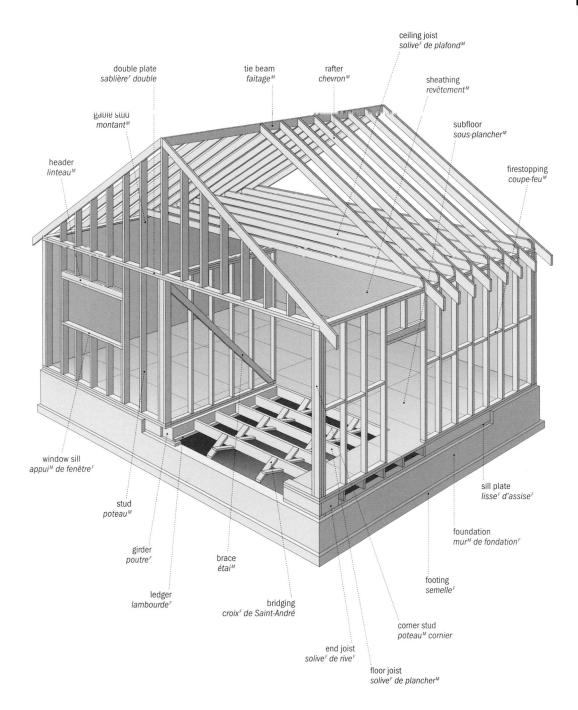

ceiling joist
solive<sup>F</sup> de plafond<sup>M</sup>

double plate
sablière<sup>F</sup> double

tie beam
faitage<sup>M</sup>

rafter
chevron<sup>M</sup>

sheathing
revêtement<sup>M</sup>

gable stud
montant<sup>M</sup>

subfloor
sous-plancher<sup>M</sup>

header
linteau<sup>M</sup>

firestopping
coupe-feu<sup>M</sup>

window sill
appui<sup>M</sup> de fenêtre<sup>F</sup>

stud
poteau<sup>M</sup>

sill plate
lisse<sup>F</sup> d'assise<sup>F</sup>

girder
poutre<sup>F</sup>

brace
étai<sup>M</sup>

foundation
mur<sup>M</sup> de fondation<sup>F</sup>

ledger
lambourde<sup>F</sup>

bridging
croix<sup>F</sup> de Saint-André

footing
semelle<sup>F</sup>

corner stud
poteau<sup>M</sup> cornier

end joist
solive<sup>F</sup> de rive<sup>F</sup>

floor joist
solive<sup>F</sup> de plancher<sup>M</sup>

# main rooms

principales pièces<sup>F</sup> d'une maison<sup>F</sup>

**first floor**
*rez-de-chaussée<sup>M</sup>*

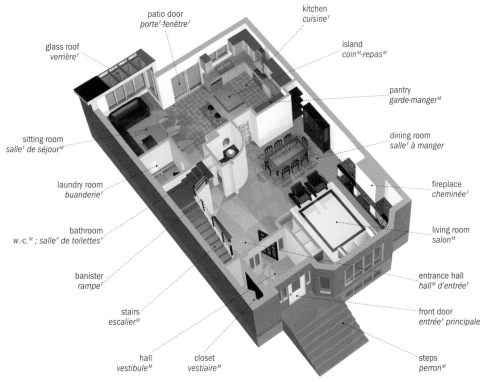

patio door
*porte<sup>F</sup>-fenêtre<sup>F</sup>*

kitchen
*cuisine<sup>F</sup>*

glass roof
*verrière<sup>F</sup>*

island
*coin<sup>M</sup>-repas<sup>M</sup>*

pantry
*garde-manger<sup>M</sup>*

sitting room
*salle<sup>F</sup> de séjour<sup>M</sup>*

dining room
*salle<sup>F</sup> à manger*

laundry room
*buanderie<sup>F</sup>*

fireplace
*cheminée<sup>F</sup>*

bathroom
*w.-c.<sup>M</sup> ; salle<sup>F</sup> de toilettes<sup>F</sup>*

living room
*salon<sup>M</sup>*

banister
*rampe<sup>F</sup>*

entrance hall
*hall<sup>M</sup> d'entrée<sup>F</sup>*

stairs
*escalier<sup>M</sup>*

front door
*entrée<sup>F</sup> principale*

hall
*vestibule<sup>M</sup>*

closet
*vestiaire<sup>M</sup>*

steps
*perron<sup>M</sup>*

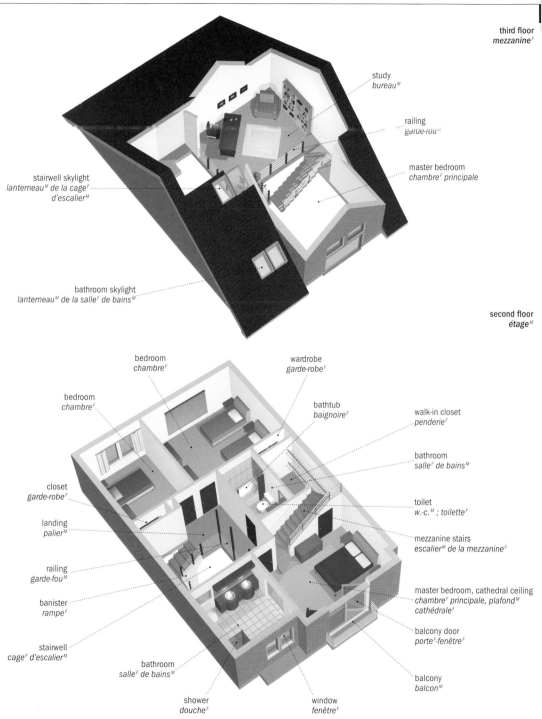

third floor
*mezzanine*<sup>F</sup>

study
*bureau*<sup>M</sup>

railing
*garde-fou*<sup>M</sup>

master bedroom
*chambre*<sup>F</sup> *principale*

stairwell skylight
*lanterneau*<sup>M</sup> *de la cage*<sup>F</sup>
*d'escalier*<sup>M</sup>

bathroom skylight
*lanterneau*<sup>M</sup> *de la salle*<sup>F</sup> *de bains*<sup>M</sup>

second floor
*étage*<sup>M</sup>

bedroom
*chambre*<sup>F</sup>

wardrobe
*garde-robe*<sup>F</sup>

bedroom
*chambre*<sup>F</sup>

bathtub
*baignoire*<sup>F</sup>

walk-in closet
*penderie*<sup>F</sup>

bathroom
*salle*<sup>F</sup> *de bains*<sup>M</sup>

closet
*garde-robe*<sup>F</sup>

toilet
*w.-c.*<sup>M</sup> ; *toilette*<sup>F</sup>

landing
*palier*<sup>M</sup>

mezzanine stairs
*escalier*<sup>M</sup> *de la mezzanine*<sup>F</sup>

railing
*garde-fou*<sup>M</sup>

master bedroom, cathedral ceiling
*chambre*<sup>F</sup> *principale, plafond*<sup>M</sup>
*cathédrale*<sup>F</sup>

banister
*rampe*<sup>F</sup>

balcony door
*porte*<sup>F</sup>-*fenêtre*<sup>F</sup>

stairwell
*cage*<sup>F</sup> *d'escalier*<sup>M</sup>

bathroom
*salle*<sup>F</sup> *de bains*<sup>M</sup>

balcony
*balcon*<sup>M</sup>

shower
*douche*<sup>F</sup>

window
*fenêtre*<sup>F</sup>

# wood flooring
parquet<sup>M</sup>

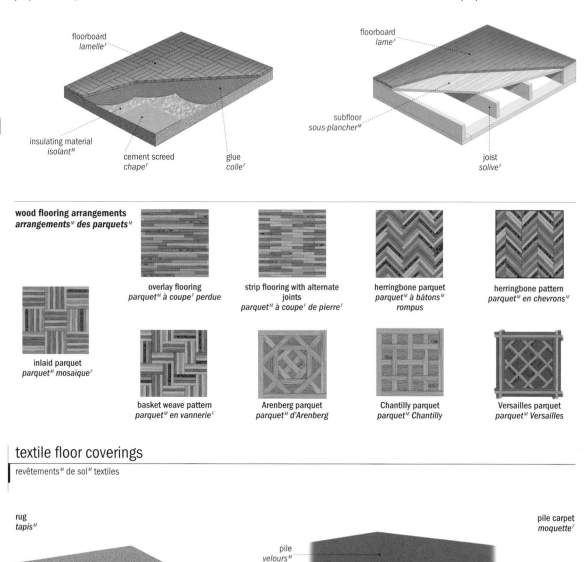

**wood flooring on cement screed**
*parquet<sup>M</sup> sur chape<sup>F</sup> de ciment<sup>M</sup>*

floorboard
*lamelle<sup>F</sup>*

insulating material
*isolant<sup>M</sup>*

cement screed
*chape<sup>F</sup>*

glue
*colle<sup>F</sup>*

**wood flooring on wooden structure**
*parquet<sup>M</sup> sur ossature<sup>F</sup> de bois<sup>M</sup>*

floorboard
*lame<sup>F</sup>*

subfloor
*sous-plancher<sup>M</sup>*

joist
*solive<sup>F</sup>*

**wood flooring arrangements**
*arrangements<sup>M</sup> des parquets<sup>M</sup>*

overlay flooring
*parquet<sup>M</sup> à coupe<sup>F</sup> perdue*

strip flooring with alternate joints
*parquet<sup>M</sup> à coupe<sup>F</sup> de pierre<sup>F</sup>*

herringbone parquet
*parquet<sup>M</sup> à bâtons<sup>M</sup> rompus*

herringbone pattern
*parquet<sup>M</sup> en chevrons<sup>M</sup>*

inlaid parquet
*parquet<sup>M</sup> mosaïque<sup>F</sup>*

basket weave pattern
*parquet<sup>M</sup> en vannerie<sup>F</sup>*

Arenberg parquet
*parquet<sup>M</sup> d'Arenberg*

Chantilly parquet
*parquet<sup>M</sup> Chantilly*

Versailles parquet
*parquet<sup>M</sup> Versailles*

# textile floor coverings
revêtements<sup>M</sup> de sol<sup>M</sup> textiles

rug
*tapis<sup>M</sup>*

pile carpet
*moquette<sup>F</sup>*

pile
*velours<sup>M</sup>*

underlay
*sous-couche<sup>F</sup>*

tackless strip
*bande<sup>F</sup> d'ancrage<sup>M</sup>*

HOUSE

## stairs
escalier^M

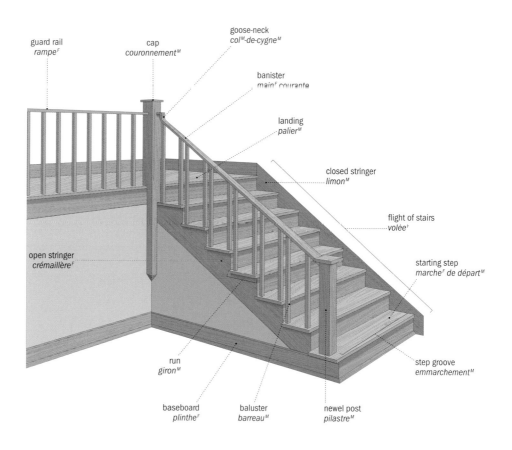

guard rail
rampe^F

cap
couronnement^M

goose-neck
col^M-de-cygne^M

banister
main^F courante

landing
palier^M

closed stringer
limon^M

flight of stairs
volée^F

open stringer
crémaillère^F

starting step
marche^F de départ^M

step groove
emmarchement^M

run
giron^M

baseboard
plinthe^F

baluster
barreau^M

newel post
pilastre^M

## step
marche^F

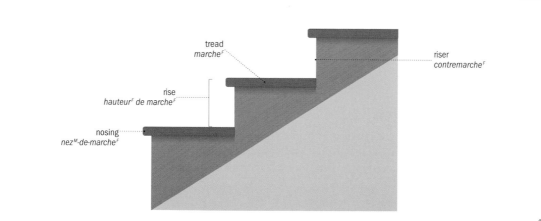

tread
marche^F

riser
contremarche^F

rise
hauteur^F de marche^F

nosing
nez^M-de-marche^F

# wood burning

chauffage<sup>M</sup> au bois<sup>M</sup>

HOUSE

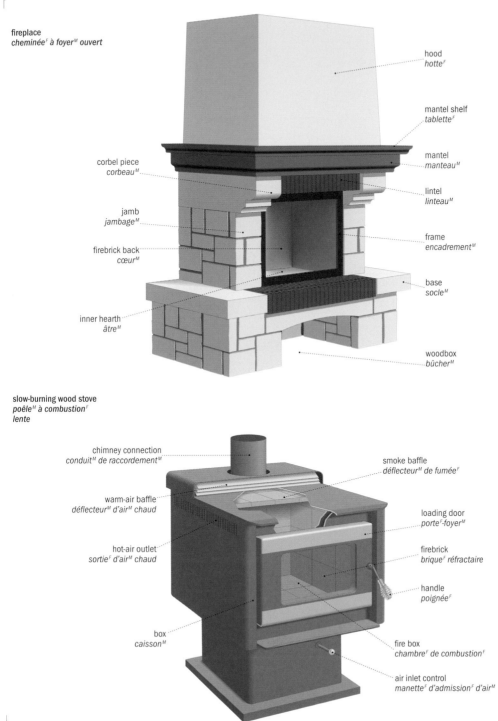

**fireplace**
*cheminée<sup>F</sup> à foyer<sup>M</sup> ouvert*

hood
*hotte<sup>F</sup>*

mantel shelf
*tablette<sup>F</sup>*

corbel piece
*corbeau<sup>M</sup>*

mantel
*manteau<sup>M</sup>*

lintel
*linteau<sup>M</sup>*

jamb
*jambage<sup>M</sup>*

frame
*encadrement<sup>M</sup>*

firebrick back
*cœur<sup>M</sup>*

base
*socle<sup>M</sup>*

inner hearth
*âtre<sup>M</sup>*

woodbox
*bûcher<sup>M</sup>*

**slow-burning wood stove**
*poêle<sup>M</sup> à combustion<sup>F</sup>*
*lente*

chimney connection
*conduit<sup>M</sup> de raccordement<sup>M</sup>*

smoke baffle
*déflecteur<sup>M</sup> de fumée<sup>F</sup>*

warm-air baffle
*déflecteur<sup>M</sup> d'air<sup>M</sup> chaud*

loading door
*porte<sup>F</sup>-foyer<sup>M</sup>*

hot-air outlet
*sortie<sup>F</sup> d'air<sup>M</sup> chaud*

firebrick
*brique<sup>F</sup> réfractaire*

handle
*poignée<sup>F</sup>*

box
*caisson<sup>M</sup>*

fire box
*chambre<sup>F</sup> de combustion<sup>F</sup>*

air inlet control
*manette<sup>F</sup> d'admission<sup>F</sup> d'air<sup>M</sup>*

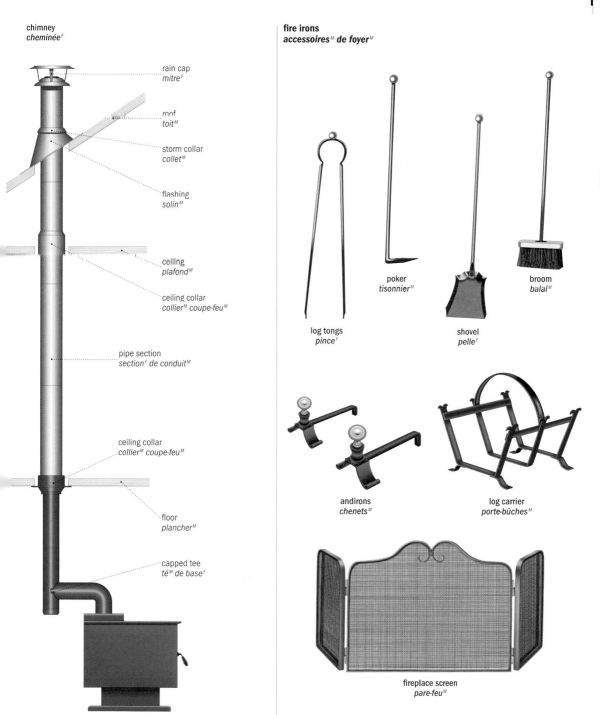

chimney
*cheminée*<sup>F</sup>

rain cap
*mitre*<sup>F</sup>

roof
*toit*<sup>M</sup>

storm collar
*collet*<sup>M</sup>

flashing
*solin*<sup>M</sup>

ceiling
*plafond*<sup>M</sup>

ceiling collar
*collier*<sup>M</sup> *coupe-feu*<sup>M</sup>

pipe section
*section*<sup>F</sup> *de conduit*<sup>M</sup>

ceiling collar
*collier*<sup>M</sup> *coupe-feu*<sup>M</sup>

floor
*plancher*<sup>M</sup>

capped tee
*té*<sup>M</sup> *de base*<sup>F</sup>

fire irons
*accessoires*<sup>M</sup> *de foyer*<sup>M</sup>

poker
*tisonnier*<sup>M</sup>

broom
*balai*<sup>M</sup>

log tongs
*pince*<sup>F</sup>

shovel
*pelle*<sup>F</sup>

andirons
*chenets*<sup>M</sup>

log carrier
*porte-bûches*<sup>M</sup>

fireplace screen
*pare-feu*<sup>M</sup>

# plumbing system
circuit<sup>M</sup> de plomberie<sup>F</sup>

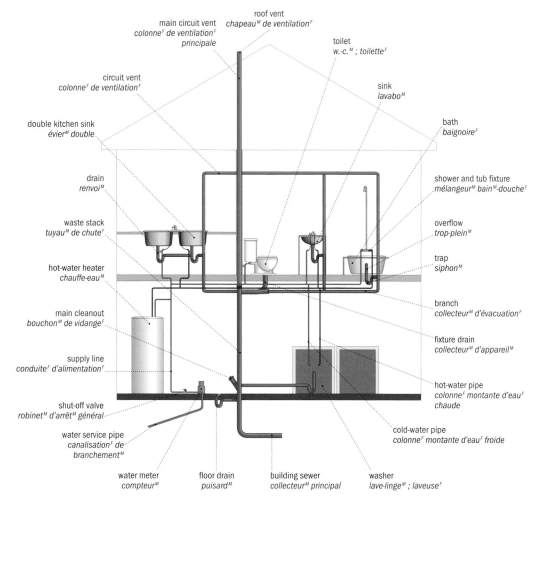

roof vent
chapeau<sup>M</sup> de ventilation<sup>F</sup>

main circuit vent
colonne<sup>F</sup> de ventilation<sup>F</sup>
principale

toilet
w.-c.<sup>M</sup> ; toilette<sup>F</sup>

circuit vent
colonne<sup>F</sup> de ventilation<sup>F</sup>

sink
lavabo<sup>M</sup>

double kitchen sink
évier<sup>M</sup> double

bath
baignoire<sup>F</sup>

drain
renvoi<sup>M</sup>

shower and tub fixture
mélangeur<sup>M</sup> bain<sup>M</sup>-douche<sup>F</sup>

waste stack
tuyau<sup>M</sup> de chute<sup>F</sup>

overflow
trop-plein<sup>M</sup>

hot-water heater
chauffe-eau<sup>M</sup>

trap
siphon<sup>M</sup>

branch
collecteur<sup>M</sup> d'évacuation<sup>F</sup>

main cleanout
bouchon<sup>M</sup> de vidange<sup>F</sup>

fixture drain
collecteur<sup>M</sup> d'appareil<sup>M</sup>

supply line
conduite<sup>F</sup> d'alimentation<sup>F</sup>

hot-water pipe
colonne<sup>F</sup> montante d'eau<sup>F</sup>
chaude

shut-off valve
robinet<sup>M</sup> d'arrêt<sup>M</sup> général

cold-water pipe
colonne<sup>F</sup> montante d'eau<sup>F</sup> froide

water service pipe
canalisation<sup>F</sup> de
branchement<sup>M</sup>

water meter
compteur<sup>M</sup>

floor drain
puisard<sup>M</sup>

building sewer
collecteur<sup>M</sup> principal

washer
lave-linge<sup>M</sup> ; laveuse<sup>F</sup>

ventilating circuit
circuit<sup>M</sup> de ventilation<sup>F</sup>

draining circuit
circuit<sup>M</sup> d'évacuation<sup>F</sup>

cold-water circuit
circuit<sup>M</sup> d'eau<sup>F</sup> froide

hot-water circuit
circuit<sup>M</sup> d'eau<sup>F</sup> chaude

# bathroom

salle<sup>F</sup> de bains<sup>M</sup>

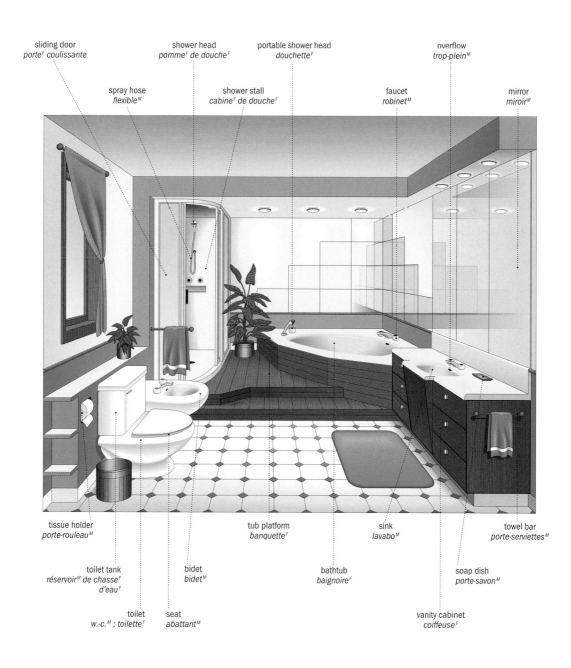

sliding door
porte<sup>F</sup> coulissante

shower head
pomme<sup>F</sup> de douche<sup>F</sup>

portable shower head
douchette<sup>F</sup>

overflow
trop-plein<sup>M</sup>

spray hose
flexible<sup>M</sup>

shower stall
cabine<sup>F</sup> de douche<sup>F</sup>

faucet
robinet<sup>M</sup>

mirror
miroir<sup>M</sup>

tissue holder
porte-rouleau<sup>M</sup>

tub platform
banquette<sup>F</sup>

sink
lavabo<sup>M</sup>

towel bar
porte-serviettes<sup>M</sup>

toilet tank
réservoir<sup>M</sup> de chasse<sup>F</sup>
d'eau<sup>F</sup>

bidet
bidet<sup>M</sup>

bathtub
baignoire<sup>F</sup>

soap dish
porte-savon<sup>M</sup>

toilet
w.-c.<sup>M</sup> ; toilette<sup>F</sup>

seat
abattant<sup>M</sup>

vanity cabinet
coiffeuse<sup>F</sup>

# toilet

w.-c.ᴹ ; toilette ᶠ

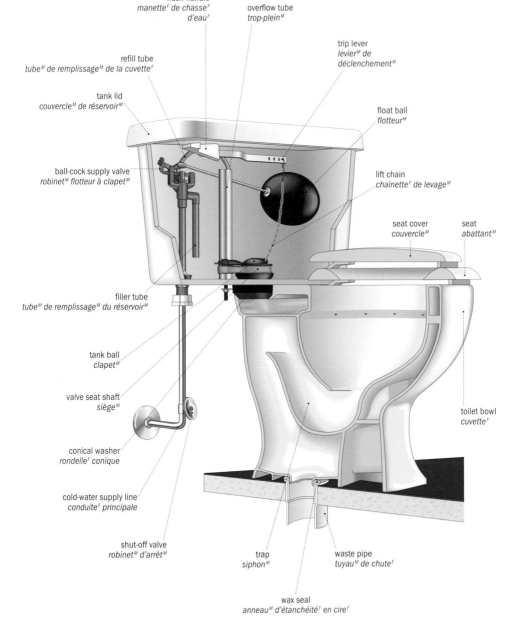

flush handle
manette ᶠ de chasse ᶠ
d'eau ᶠ

overflow tube
trop-plein ᴹ

trip lever
levier ᴹ de
déclenchement ᴹ

refill tube
tube ᴹ de remplissage ᴹ de la cuvette ᶠ

tank lid
couvercle ᴹ de réservoir ᴹ

float ball
flotteur ᴹ

ball-cock supply valve
robinet ᴹ flotteur à clapet ᴹ

lift chain
chainette ᶠ de levage ᴹ

seat cover
couvercle ᴹ

seat
abattant ᴹ

filler tube
tube ᴹ de remplissage ᴹ du réservoir ᴹ

tank ball
clapet ᴹ

valve seat shaft
siège ᴹ

toilet bowl
cuvette ᶠ

conical washer
rondelle ᶠ conique

cold-water supply line
conduite ᶠ principale

shut-off valve
robinet ᴹ d'arrêt ᴹ

trap
siphon ᴹ

waste pipe
tuyau ᴹ de chute ᶠ

wax seal
anneau ᴹ d'étanchéité ᶠ en cire ᶠ

# examples of branching

exemples<sup>M</sup> de branchement<sup>M</sup>

**garbage disposal sink**
*évier<sup>M</sup>-broyeur<sup>M</sup>*

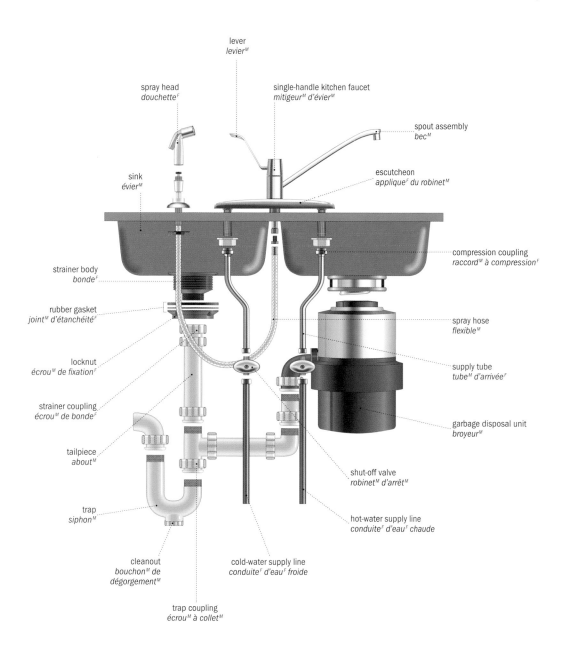

lever
*levier<sup>M</sup>*

spray head
*douchette<sup>F</sup>*

single-handle kitchen faucet
*mitigeur<sup>M</sup> d'évier<sup>M</sup>*

spout assembly
*bec<sup>M</sup>*

sink
*évier<sup>M</sup>*

escutcheon
*applique<sup>F</sup> du robinet<sup>M</sup>*

compression coupling
*raccord<sup>M</sup> à compression<sup>F</sup>*

strainer body
*bonde<sup>F</sup>*

rubber gasket
*joint<sup>M</sup> d'étanchéité<sup>F</sup>*

spray hose
*flexible<sup>M</sup>*

locknut
*écrou<sup>M</sup> de fixation<sup>F</sup>*

supply tube
*tube<sup>M</sup> d'arrivée<sup>F</sup>*

strainer coupling
*écrou<sup>M</sup> de bonde<sup>F</sup>*

garbage disposal unit
*broyeur<sup>M</sup>*

tailpiece
*about<sup>M</sup>*

shut-off valve
*robinet<sup>M</sup> d'arrêt<sup>M</sup>*

trap
*siphon<sup>M</sup>*

hot-water supply line
*conduite<sup>F</sup> d'eau<sup>F</sup> chaude*

cleanout
*bouchon<sup>M</sup> de dégorgement<sup>M</sup>*

cold-water supply line
*conduite<sup>F</sup> d'eau<sup>F</sup> froide*

trap coupling
*écrou<sup>M</sup> à collet<sup>M</sup>*

# network connection

branchement<sup>M</sup> au réseau<sup>M</sup>

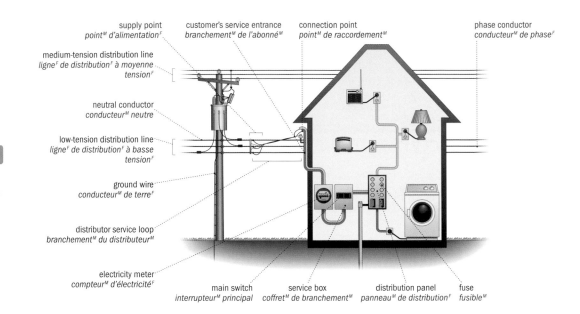

supply point
point<sup>M</sup> d'alimentation<sup>F</sup>

customer's service entrance
branchement<sup>M</sup> de l'abonné<sup>M</sup>

connection point
point<sup>M</sup> de raccordement<sup>M</sup>

phase conductor
conducteur<sup>M</sup> de phase<sup>F</sup>

medium-tension distribution line
ligne<sup>F</sup> de distribution<sup>F</sup> à moyenne
tension<sup>F</sup>

neutral conductor
conducteur<sup>M</sup> neutre

low-tension distribution line
ligne<sup>F</sup> de distribution<sup>F</sup> à basse
tension<sup>F</sup>

ground wire
conducteur<sup>M</sup> de terre<sup>F</sup>

distributor service loop
branchement<sup>M</sup> du distributeur<sup>M</sup>

electricity meter
compteur<sup>M</sup> d'électricité<sup>F</sup>

main switch
interrupteur<sup>M</sup> principal

service box
coffret<sup>M</sup> de branchement<sup>M</sup>

distribution panel
panneau<sup>M</sup> de distribution<sup>F</sup>

fuse
fusible<sup>M</sup>

HOUSE

# contact devices

dispositifs<sup>M</sup> de contact<sup>M</sup>

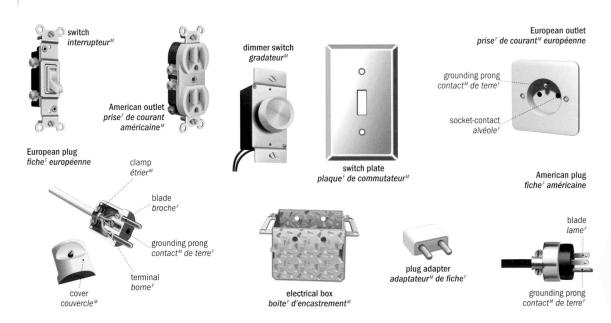

switch
interrupteur<sup>M</sup>

American outlet
prise<sup>F</sup> de courant
américaine<sup>M</sup>

dimmer switch
gradateur<sup>M</sup>

European outlet
prise<sup>F</sup> de courant<sup>M</sup> européenne

grounding prong
contact<sup>M</sup> de terre<sup>F</sup>

socket-contact
alvéole<sup>F</sup>

European plug
fiche<sup>F</sup> européenne

clamp
étrier<sup>M</sup>

blade
broche<sup>F</sup>

grounding prong
contact<sup>M</sup> de terre<sup>F</sup>

terminal
borne<sup>F</sup>

cover
couvercle<sup>M</sup>

switch plate
plaque<sup>F</sup> de commutateur<sup>M</sup>

electrical box
boîte<sup>F</sup> d'encastrement<sup>M</sup>

plug adapter
adaptateur<sup>M</sup> de fiche<sup>F</sup>

American plug
fiche<sup>F</sup> américaine

blade
lame<sup>F</sup>

grounding prong
contact<sup>M</sup> de terre<sup>F</sup>

# lighting
*éclairage<sup>M</sup>*

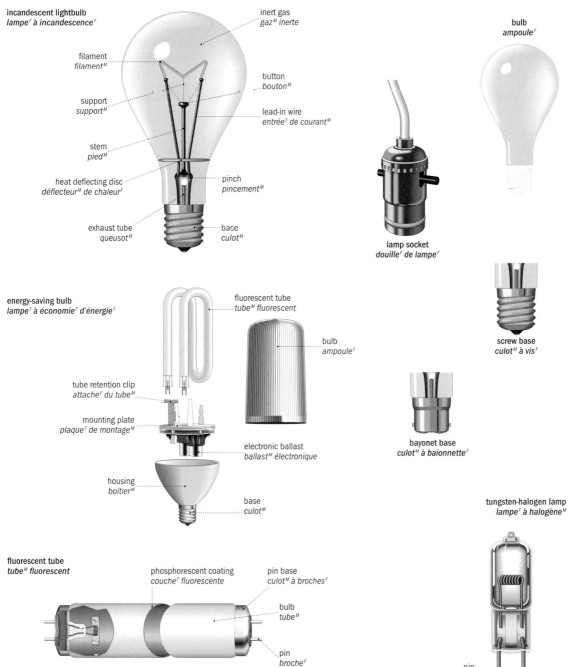

**incandescent lightbulb**
*lampe<sup>F</sup> à incandescence<sup>F</sup>*

inert gas
*gaz<sup>M</sup> inerte*

filament
*filament<sup>M</sup>*

button
*bouton<sup>M</sup>*

support
*support<sup>M</sup>*

lead-in wire
*entrée<sup>F</sup> de courant<sup>M</sup>*

stem
*pied<sup>M</sup>*

heat deflecting disc
*déflecteur<sup>M</sup> de chaleur<sup>F</sup>*

pinch
*pincement<sup>M</sup>*

exhaust tube
*queusot<sup>M</sup>*

base
*culot<sup>M</sup>*

bulb
*ampoule<sup>F</sup>*

lamp socket
*douille<sup>F</sup> de lampe<sup>F</sup>*

**energy-saving bulb**
*lampe<sup>F</sup> à économie<sup>F</sup> d'énergie<sup>F</sup>*

fluorescent tube
*tube<sup>M</sup> fluorescent*

bulb
*ampoule<sup>F</sup>*

tube retention clip
*attache<sup>F</sup> du tube<sup>M</sup>*

mounting plate
*plaque<sup>F</sup> de montage<sup>M</sup>*

electronic ballast
*ballast<sup>M</sup> électronique*

housing
*boîtier<sup>M</sup>*

base
*culot<sup>M</sup>*

screw base
*culot<sup>M</sup> à vis<sup>F</sup>*

bayonet base
*culot<sup>M</sup> à baïonnette<sup>F</sup>*

tungsten-halogen lamp
*lampe<sup>F</sup> à halogène<sup>M</sup>*

**fluorescent tube**
*tube<sup>M</sup> fluorescent*

phosphorescent coating
*couche<sup>F</sup> fluorescente*

pin base
*culot<sup>M</sup> à broches<sup>F</sup>*

bulb
*tube<sup>M</sup>*

pin
*broche<sup>F</sup>*

pin
*broche<sup>F</sup>*

HOUSE

# armchair

fauteuil[M]

HOUSE

**parts**
*parties*[F]

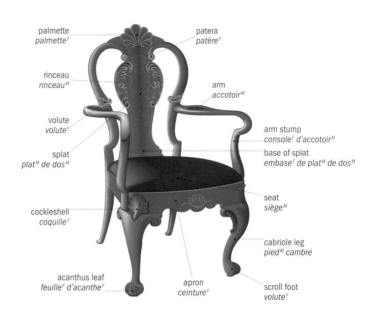

palmette
*palmette*[F]

patera
*patère*[F]

rinceau
*rinceau*[M]

arm
*accotoir*[M]

volute
*volute*[F]

arm stump
*console*[F] *d'accotoir*[M]

splat
*plat*[M] *de dos*[M]

base of splat
*embase*[F] *de plat*[M] *de dos*[M]

cockleshell
*coquille*[F]

seat
*siège*[M]

cabriole leg
*pied*[M] *cambré*

acanthus leaf
*feuille*[F] *d'acanthe*[F]

apron
*ceinture*[F]

scroll foot
*volute*[F]

**examples of armchairs**
*exemples*[M] *de fauteuils*[M]

Wassily chair
*fauteuil*[M] *Wassily*

director's chair
*fauteuil*[M] *metteur*[M] *en scène*[F]

rocking chair
*berceuse*[F]

cabriolet
*cabriolet*[M]

méridienne
*méridienne*[F]

récamier
*récamier*[M]

club chair
*fauteuil*[M] *club*[M]

bergère
*bergère*[F]

sofa
*canapé*[M]

love seat
*causeuse*[F]

chesterfield
*canapé*[M] *capitonné*

# side chair
*chaise*<sup>F</sup>

**parts**
***parties*<sup>F</sup>**

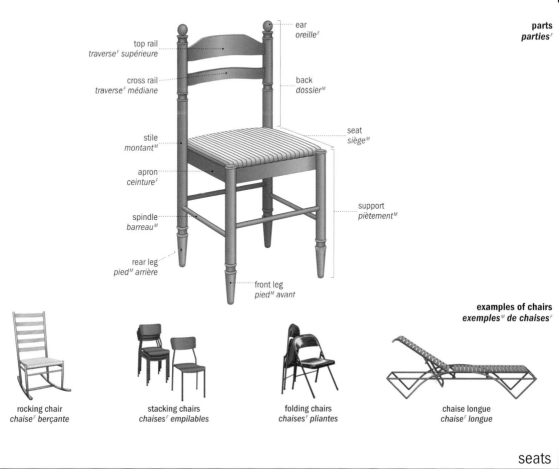

ear
*oreille*<sup>F</sup>

top rail
*traverse*<sup>F</sup> *supérieure*

cross rail
*traverse*<sup>F</sup> *médiane*

back
*dossier*<sup>M</sup>

seat
*siège*<sup>M</sup>

stile
*montant*<sup>M</sup>

apron
*ceinture*<sup>F</sup>

spindle
*barreau*<sup>M</sup>

support
*piètement*<sup>M</sup>

rear leg
*pied*<sup>M</sup> *arrière*

front leg
*pied*<sup>M</sup> *avant*

**examples of chairs**
***exemples*<sup>M</sup> *de chaises*<sup>F</sup>**

rocking chair
*chaise*<sup>F</sup> *berçante*

stacking chairs
*chaises*<sup>F</sup> *empilables*

folding chairs
*chaises*<sup>F</sup> *pliantes*

chaise longue
*chaise*<sup>F</sup> *longue*

HOUSE

# seats
*sièges*<sup>M</sup>

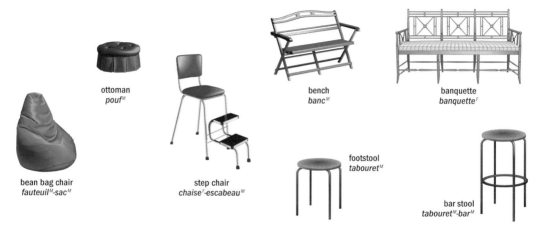

ottoman
*pouf*<sup>M</sup>

bench
*banc*<sup>M</sup>

banquette
*banquette*<sup>F</sup>

bean bag chair
*fauteuil*<sup>M</sup>-*sac*<sup>M</sup>

step chair
*chaise*<sup>F</sup>-*escabeau*<sup>M</sup>

footstool
*tabouret*<sup>M</sup>

bar stool
*tabouret*<sup>M</sup>-*bar*<sup>M</sup>

# table

table<sup>F</sup>

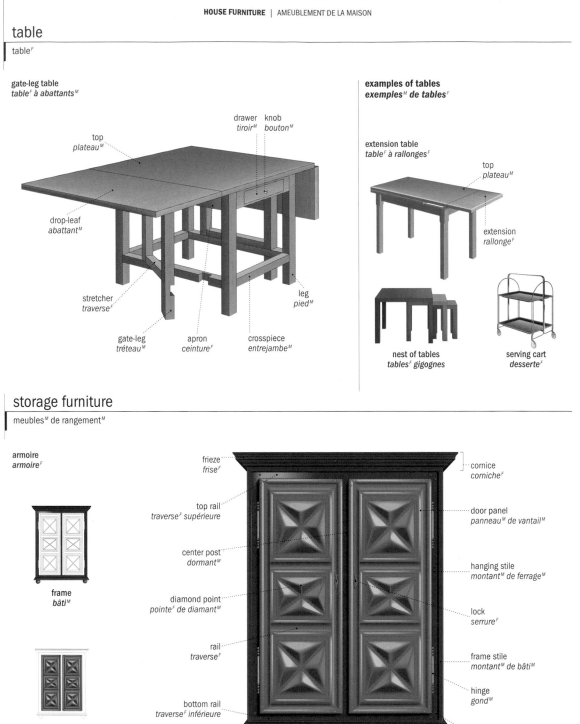

HOUSE

**gate-leg table**
*table<sup>F</sup> à abattants<sup>M</sup>*

drawer
*tiroir<sup>M</sup>*

knob
*bouton<sup>M</sup>*

top
*plateau<sup>M</sup>*

drop-leaf
*abattant<sup>M</sup>*

stretcher
*traverse<sup>F</sup>*

gate-leg
*tréteau<sup>M</sup>*

apron
*ceinture<sup>F</sup>*

crosspiece
*entrejambe<sup>M</sup>*

leg
*pied<sup>M</sup>*

**examples of tables**
*exemples<sup>M</sup> de tables<sup>F</sup>*

extension table
*table<sup>F</sup> à rallonges<sup>F</sup>*

top
*plateau<sup>M</sup>*

extension
*rallonge<sup>F</sup>*

nest of tables
*tables<sup>F</sup> gigognes*

serving cart
*desserte<sup>F</sup>*

# storage furniture

meubles<sup>M</sup> de rangement<sup>M</sup>

armoire
*armoire<sup>F</sup>*

frame
*bâti<sup>M</sup>*

door
*vantail<sup>M</sup>*

frieze
*frise<sup>F</sup>*

top rail
*traverse<sup>F</sup> supérieure*

center post
*dormant<sup>M</sup>*

diamond point
*pointe<sup>F</sup> de diamant<sup>M</sup>*

rail
*traverse<sup>F</sup>*

bottom rail
*traverse<sup>F</sup> inférieure*

foot
*pied<sup>M</sup>*

bracket base
*soubassement<sup>M</sup>*

cornice
*corniche<sup>F</sup>*

door panel
*panneau<sup>M</sup> de vantail<sup>M</sup>*

hanging stile
*montant<sup>M</sup> de ferrage<sup>M</sup>*

lock
*serrure<sup>F</sup>*

frame stile
*montant<sup>M</sup> de bâti<sup>M</sup>*

hinge
*gond<sup>M</sup>*

peg
*cheville<sup>F</sup>*

tray
casier<sup>M</sup>

fall front
abattant<sup>M</sup>

linen chest
coffre<sup>M</sup>

secretary
secrétaire<sup>M</sup>

dresser
commode<sup>F</sup>

closet
penderie<sup>F</sup>

shelf
tablette<sup>F</sup>

wardrobe
armoire<sup>F</sup>-penderie<sup>F</sup>

drawer
tiroir<sup>M</sup>

chiffonier
chiffonnier<sup>M</sup>

display cabinet
vitrine<sup>F</sup>

corner cupboard
encoignure<sup>F</sup>

glass-fronted display cabinet
buffet<sup>M</sup>-vaisselier<sup>M</sup>

buffet
buffet<sup>M</sup>

cocktail cabinet
bar<sup>M</sup>

# bed

lit<sup>M</sup>

HOUSE

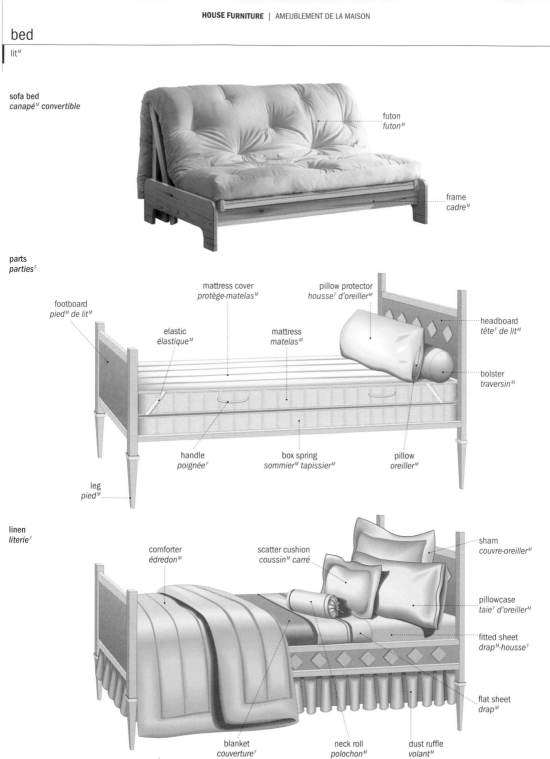

**sofa bed**
*canapé<sup>M</sup> convertible*

futon
*futon<sup>M</sup>*

frame
*cadre<sup>M</sup>*

**parts**
*parties<sup>F</sup>*

mattress cover
*protège-matelas<sup>M</sup>*

pillow protector
*housse<sup>F</sup> d'oreiller<sup>M</sup>*

footboard
*pied<sup>M</sup> de lit<sup>M</sup>*

elastic
*élastique<sup>M</sup>*

mattress
*matelas<sup>M</sup>*

headboard
*tête<sup>F</sup> de lit<sup>M</sup>*

bolster
*traversin<sup>M</sup>*

handle
*poignée<sup>F</sup>*

box spring
*sommier<sup>M</sup> tapissier<sup>M</sup>*

pillow
*oreiller<sup>M</sup>*

leg
*pied<sup>M</sup>*

**linen**
*literie<sup>F</sup>*

comforter
*édredon<sup>M</sup>*

scatter cushion
*coussin<sup>M</sup> carré*

sham
*couvre-oreiller<sup>M</sup>*

pillowcase
*taie<sup>F</sup> d'oreiller<sup>M</sup>*

fitted sheet
*drap<sup>M</sup>-housse<sup>F</sup>*

flat sheet
*drap<sup>M</sup>*

blanket
*couverture<sup>F</sup>*

neck roll
*polochon<sup>M</sup>*

dust ruffle
*volant<sup>M</sup>*

# children's furniture

meubles<sup>M</sup> d'enfants<sup>M</sup>

**playpen**
*lit<sup>M</sup> pliant*

changing table
*plan<sup>M</sup> à langer*

top rail
*bordure<sup>F</sup>*

mesh
*filet<sup>M</sup>*

mattress
*matelas<sup>M</sup>*

armrest
*accoudoir<sup>M</sup>*

**booster seat**
*rehausseur<sup>M</sup>*

back
*dossier<sup>M</sup>*

seat
*siège<sup>M</sup>*

**changing table**
*table<sup>F</sup> à langer*

HOUSE

**high chair**
*chaise<sup>F</sup> haute*

back
*dossier<sup>M</sup>*

tray
*plateau<sup>M</sup>*

waist belt
*ceinture<sup>F</sup> ventrale*

footrest
*repose-pieds<sup>M</sup>*

leg
*pied<sup>M</sup>*

**crib**
*lit<sup>M</sup> à barreaux<sup>M</sup>*

headboard
*tête<sup>F</sup> de lit<sup>M</sup>*

barrier
*barrière<sup>F</sup>*

slat
*barreau<sup>M</sup>*

caster
*roulette<sup>F</sup>*

drawer
*tiroir<sup>M</sup>*

mattress
*matelas<sup>M</sup>*

# lights

luminaires<sup>M</sup>

clamp spotlight
spot<sup>M</sup> à pince<sup>F</sup>

ceiling fixture
plafonnier<sup>M</sup>

hanging pendant
suspension<sup>F</sup>

halogen desk lamp
lampe<sup>F</sup> de bureau<sup>M</sup>
halogène

arm
bras<sup>M</sup>

base
socle<sup>M</sup>

adjustable lamp
lampe<sup>F</sup> d'architecte<sup>M</sup>

on-off switch
interrupteur<sup>M</sup>

arm
bras<sup>M</sup>

shade
abat-jour<sup>M</sup>

reading lamp
lampe<sup>F</sup> liseuse

spring
ressort<sup>M</sup>

adjustable clamp
support<sup>M</sup> de fixation<sup>F</sup>

shade
abat-jour<sup>M</sup>

stand
pied<sup>M</sup>

base
socle<sup>M</sup>

floor lamp
lampadaire<sup>M</sup>

table lamp
lampe<sup>F</sup> de table<sup>F</sup>

desk lamp
lampe<sup>F</sup> de bureau<sup>M</sup>

chandelier
*lustre*$^M$

bobeche
*coupelle*$^F$

crystal drop
*pendeloque*$^F$

crystal button
*pampille*$^F$

column
*fût*$^M$

track lighting
*rail*$^M$ *d'éclairage*$^M$

bar frame
*gouttière*$^F$

transformer
*transformateur*$^M$

contact lever
*manette*$^F$ *de contact*$^M$

spot
*spot*$^M$

wall lantern
*lanterne*$^F$ *murale*

wall sconce
*applique*$^F$

swivel wall lamp
*applique*$^F$ *orientable*

strip lights
*rampe*$^F$ *d'éclairage*$^M$

post lantern
*lanterne*$^F$ *de pied*$^M$

# domestic appliances

appareils<sup>M</sup> électroménagers

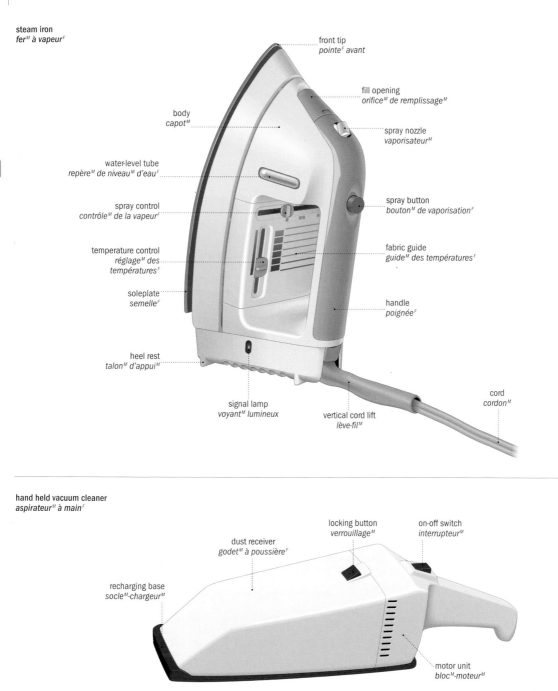

**steam iron**
*fer<sup>M</sup> à vapeur<sup>F</sup>*

front tip
*pointe<sup>F</sup> avant*

fill opening
*orifice<sup>M</sup> de remplissage<sup>M</sup>*

body
*capot<sup>M</sup>*

spray nozzle
*vaporisateur<sup>M</sup>*

water-level tube
*repère<sup>M</sup> de niveau<sup>M</sup> d'eau<sup>F</sup>*

spray control
*contrôle<sup>M</sup> de la vapeur<sup>F</sup>*

spray button
*bouton<sup>M</sup> de vaporisation<sup>F</sup>*

temperature control
*réglage<sup>M</sup> des
températures<sup>F</sup>*

fabric guide
*guide<sup>M</sup> des températures<sup>F</sup>*

soleplate
*semelle<sup>F</sup>*

handle
*poignée<sup>F</sup>*

heel rest
*talon<sup>M</sup> d'appui<sup>M</sup>*

cord
*cordon<sup>M</sup>*

signal lamp
*voyant<sup>M</sup> lumineux*

vertical cord lift
*lève-fil<sup>M</sup>*

**hand held vacuum cleaner**
*aspirateur<sup>M</sup> à main<sup>F</sup>*

locking button
*verrouillage<sup>M</sup>*

on-off switch
*interrupteur<sup>M</sup>*

dust receiver
*godet<sup>M</sup> à poussière<sup>F</sup>*

recharging base
*socle<sup>M</sup>-chargeur<sup>M</sup>*

motor unit
*bloc<sup>M</sup>-moteur<sup>M</sup>*

HOUSE

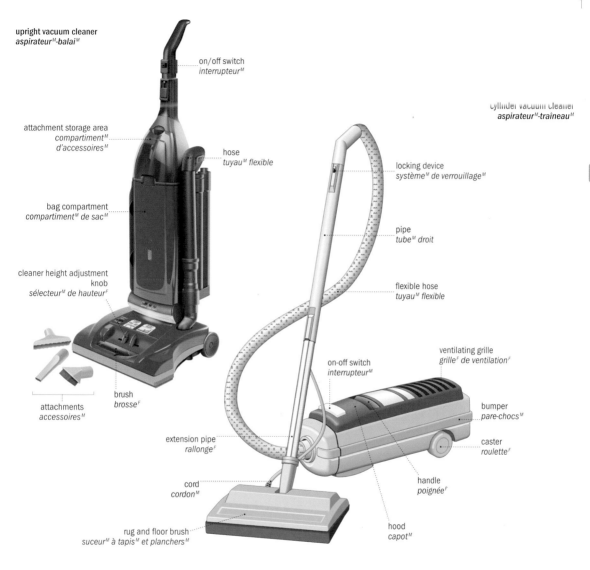

upright vacuum cleaner
*aspirateur*M*-balai*M

on/off switch
*interrupteur*M

cyllnder vacuum cleaner
*aspirateur*M*-traineau*M

attachment storage area
*compartiment*M
*d'accessoires*M

hose
*tuyau*M *flexible*

locking device
*système*M *de verrouillage*M

bag compartment
*compartiment*M *de sac*M

pipe
*tube*M *droit*

cleaner height adjustment
knob
*sélecteur*M *de hauteur*F

flexible hose
*tuyau*M *flexible*

ventilating grille
*grille*F *de ventilation*F

on-off switch
*interrupteur*M

bumper
*pare-chocs*M

attachments
*accessoires*M

brush
*brosse*F

extension pipe
*rallonge*F

caster
*roulette*F

cord
*cordon*M

handle
*poignée*F

rug and floor brush
*suceur*M *à tapis*M *et planchers*M

hood
*capot*M

vacuum cleaner attachments
*accessoires*M

upholstery nozzle
*suceur*M *triangulaire à tissus*M

dusting brush
*brosse*F *à épousseter*

crevice tool
*suceur*M *plat*

floor brush
*brosse*F *à planchers*M

## domestic appliances

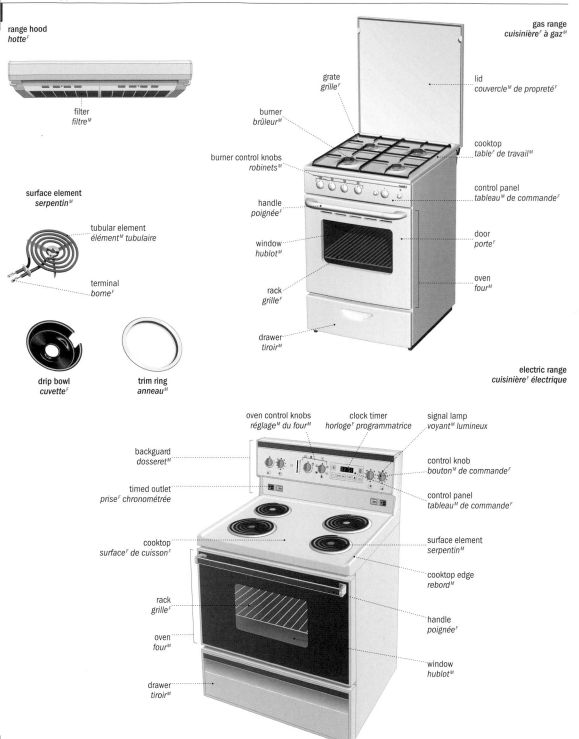

**range hood**
*hotte*[F]

**filter**
*filtre*[M]

**gas range**
*cuisinière*[F] *à gaz*[M]

**grate**
*grille*[F]

**lid**
*couvercle*[M] *de propreté*[F]

**burner**
*brûleur*[M]

**cooktop**
*table*[F] *de travail*[M]

**burner control knobs**
*robinets*[M]

**control panel**
*tableau*[M] *de commande*[F]

**surface element**
*serpentin*[M]

**handle**
*poignée*[F]

**tubular element**
*élément*[M] *tubulaire*

**door**
*porte*[F]

**window**
*hublot*[M]

**terminal**
*borne*[F]

**oven**
*four*[M]

**rack**
*grille*[F]

**drip bowl**
*cuvette*[F]

**trim ring**
*anneau*[M]

**drawer**
*tiroir*[M]

**electric range**
*cuisinière*[F] *électrique*

**oven control knobs**
*réglage*[M] *du four*[M]

**clock timer**
*horloge*[F] *programmatrice*

**signal lamp**
*voyant*[M] *lumineux*

**backguard**
*dosseret*[M]

**control knob**
*bouton*[M] *de commande*[F]

**timed outlet**
*prise*[F] *chronométrée*

**control panel**
*tableau*[M] *de commande*[F]

**cooktop**
*surface*[F] *de cuisson*[F]

**surface element**
*serpentin*[M]

**cooktop edge**
*rebord*[M]

**rack**
*grille*[F]

**handle**
*poignée*[F]

**oven**
*four*[M]

**window**
*hublot*[M]

**drawer**
*tiroir*[M]

HOUSE

HOUSE

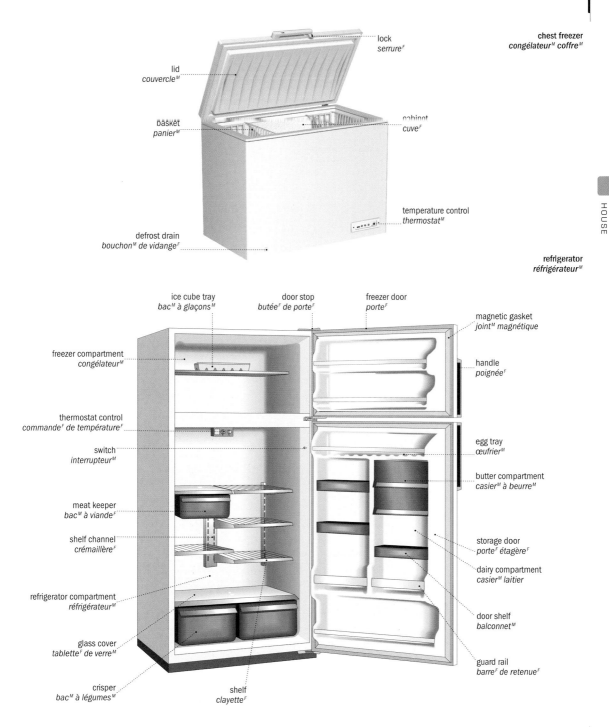

**chest freezer**
*congélateur*$^M$ *coffre*$^M$

lock
*serrure*$^F$

lid
*couvercle*$^M$

basket
*panier*$^M$

cabinet
*cuve*$^F$

temperature control
*thermostat*$^M$

defrost drain
*bouchon*$^M$ *de vidange*$^F$

**refrigerator**
*réfrigérateur*$^M$

ice cube tray
*bac*$^M$ *à glaçons*$^M$

door stop
*butée*$^F$ *de porte*$^F$

freezer door
*porte*$^F$

magnetic gasket
*joint*$^M$ *magnétique*

freezer compartment
*congélateur*$^M$

handle
*poignée*$^F$

thermostat control
*commande*$^F$ *de température*$^F$

egg tray
*œufrier*$^M$

switch
*interrupteur*$^M$

butter compartment
*casier*$^M$ *à beurre*$^M$

meat keeper
*bac*$^M$ *à viande*$^F$

shelf channel
*crémaillère*$^F$

storage door
*porte*$^F$ *étagère*$^F$

dairy compartment
*casier*$^M$ *laitier*

refrigerator compartment
*réfrigérateur*$^M$

door shelf
*balconnet*$^M$

glass cover
*tablette*$^F$ *de verre*$^M$

guard rail
*barre*$^F$ *de retenue*$^F$

crisper
*bac*$^M$ *à légumes*$^M$

shelf
*clayette*$^F$

HOUSE

**washer**
*lave-linge*ᴹ *; laveuse*ᶠ

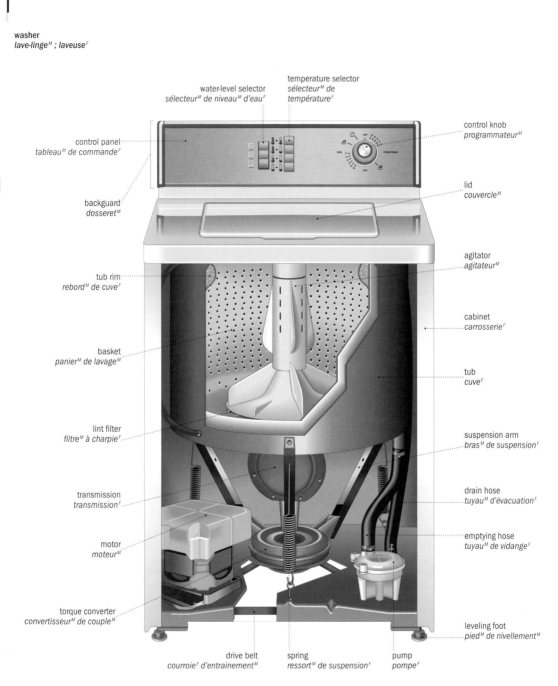

temperature selector
*sélecteur*ᴹ *de*
*température*ᶠ

water-level selector
*sélecteur*ᴹ *de niveau*ᴹ *d'eau*ᶠ

control knob
*programmateur*ᴹ

control panel
*tableau*ᴹ *de commande*ᶠ

backguard
*dosseret*ᴹ

lid
*couvercle*ᴹ

tub rim
*rebord*ᴹ *de cuve*ᶠ

agitator
*agitateur*ᴹ

cabinet
*carrosserie*ᶠ

basket
*panier*ᴹ *de lavage*ᴹ

tub
*cuve*ᶠ

lint filter
*filtre*ᴹ *à charpie*ᶠ

suspension arm
*bras*ᴹ *de suspension*ᶠ

transmission
*transmission*ᶠ

drain hose
*tuyau*ᴹ *d'évacuation*ᶠ

motor
*moteur*ᴹ

emptying hose
*tuyau*ᴹ *de vidange*ᶠ

torque converter
*convertisseur*ᴹ *de couple*ᴹ

leveling foot
*pied*ᴹ *de nivellement*ᴹ

drive belt
*courroie*ᶠ *d'entraînement*ᴹ

spring
*ressort*ᴹ *de suspension*ᶠ

pump
*pompe*ᶠ

dryer
*sèche-linge$^M$ électrique ; sécheuse$^F$*

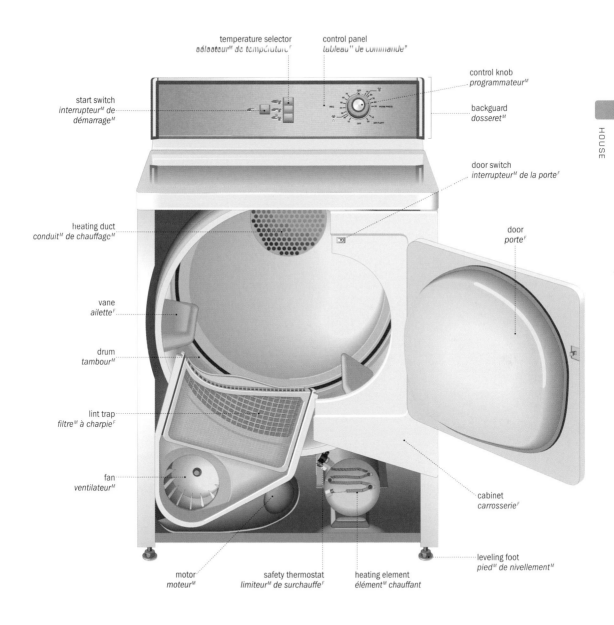

temperature selector
*sélecteur$^M$ de température$^F$*

control panel
*tableau$^M$ de commande$^M$*

control knob
*programmateur$^M$*

start switch
*interrupteur$^M$ de démarrage$^M$*

backguard
*dosseret$^M$*

door switch
*interrupteur$^M$ de la porte$^F$*

heating duct
*conduit$^M$ de chauffage$^M$*

door
*porte$^F$*

vane
*ailette$^F$*

drum
*tambour$^M$*

lint trap
*filtre$^M$ à charpie$^F$*

fan
*ventilateur$^M$*

cabinet
*carrosserie$^F$*

leveling foot
*pied$^M$ de nivellement$^M$*

motor
*moteur$^M$*

safety thermostat
*limiteur$^M$ de surchauffe$^F$*

heating element
*élément$^M$ chauffant*

## domestic appliances

**control panel: dishwasher**
*tableau^M de commande^F*

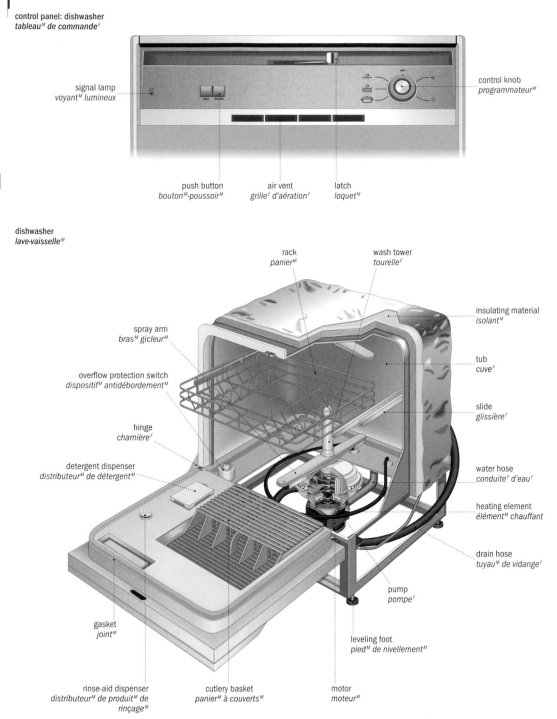

signal lamp
*voyant^M lumineux*

control knob
*programmateur^M*

push button
*bouton^M-poussoir^M*

air vent
*grille^F d'aération^F*

latch
*loquet^M*

**dishwasher**
*lave-vaisselle^M*

rack
*panier^M*

wash tower
*tourelle^F*

insulating material
*isolant^M*

spray arm
*bras^M gicleur^M*

tub
*cuve^F*

overflow protection switch
*dispositif^M antidébordement^M*

slide
*glissière^F*

hinge
*charnière^F*

detergent dispenser
*distributeur^M de détergent^M*

water hose
*conduite^F d'eau^F*

heating element
*élément^M chauffant*

drain hose
*tuyau^M de vidange^F*

pump
*pompe^F*

gasket
*joint^M*

leveling foot
*pied^M de nivellement^M*

rinse-aid dispenser
*distributeur^M de produit^M de rinçage^M*

cutlery basket
*panier^M à couverts^M*

motor
*moteur^M*

HOUSE

# household equipment
## articles<sup>M</sup> ménagers

tea towel
*torchon*<sup>M</sup>

dustpan
*pelle*<sup>F</sup> *à poussière*<sup>F</sup> ; *porte-poussière*<sup>M</sup>

broom
*balai*<sup>M</sup>

mop
*balai*<sup>M</sup> *à franges*<sup>F</sup> ;
*vadrouille*<sup>F</sup>

scouring pad
*éponge*<sup>F</sup> *à récurer*

handle
*manche*<sup>M</sup>

brush
*brosse*<sup>F</sup>

block
*monture*<sup>F</sup>

fibers
*fibres*<sup>F</sup>

garbage can
*poubelle*<sup>F</sup>

lid
*couvercle*<sup>M</sup>

fibers
*fibres*<sup>F</sup>

handle
*poignée*<sup>F</sup>

pail
*seau*<sup>M</sup>

pouring spout
*bec*<sup>M</sup> *verseur*

handle
*anse*<sup>F</sup>

HOUSE

# plumbing tools

plomberie<sup>F</sup> : outils<sup>M</sup>

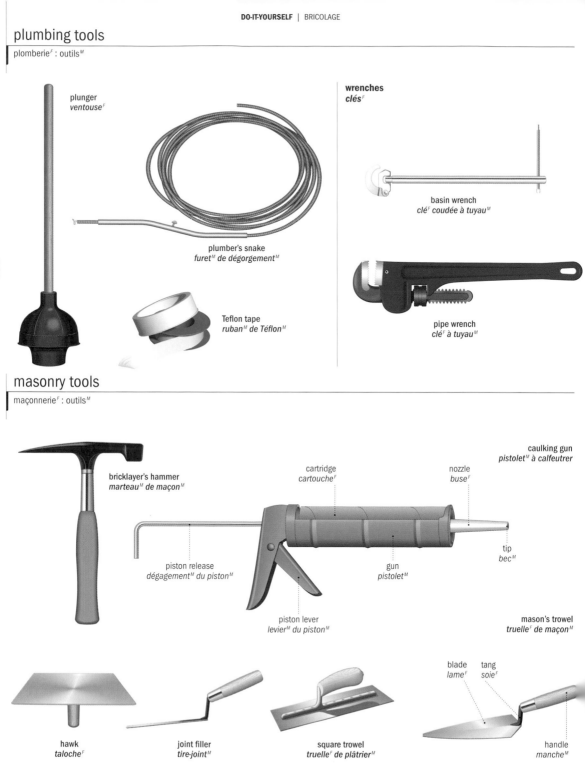

plunger
*ventouse*<sup>F</sup>

plumber's snake
*furet*<sup>M</sup> *de dégorgement*<sup>M</sup>

Teflon tape
*ruban*<sup>M</sup> *de Téflon*<sup>M</sup>

**wrenches**
***clés***<sup>F</sup>

basin wrench
*clé*<sup>F</sup> *coudée à tuyau*<sup>M</sup>

pipe wrench
*clé*<sup>F</sup> *à tuyau*<sup>M</sup>

# masonry tools

maçonnerie<sup>F</sup> : outils<sup>M</sup>

bricklayer's hammer
*marteau*<sup>M</sup> *de maçon*<sup>M</sup>

caulking gun
*pistolet*<sup>M</sup> *à calfeutrer*

cartridge
*cartouche*<sup>F</sup>

nozzle
*buse*<sup>F</sup>

piston release
*dégagement*<sup>M</sup> *du piston*<sup>M</sup>

gun
*pistolet*<sup>M</sup>

tip
*bec*<sup>M</sup>

piston lever
*levier*<sup>M</sup> *du piston*<sup>M</sup>

mason's trowel
*truelle*<sup>F</sup> *de maçon*<sup>M</sup>

blade
*lame*<sup>F</sup>

tang
*soie*<sup>F</sup>

hawk
*taloche*<sup>F</sup>

joint filler
*tire-joint*<sup>M</sup>

square trowel
*truelle*<sup>F</sup> *de plâtrier*<sup>M</sup>

handle
*manche*<sup>M</sup>

# electricity tools
*électricité^F : outils^M*

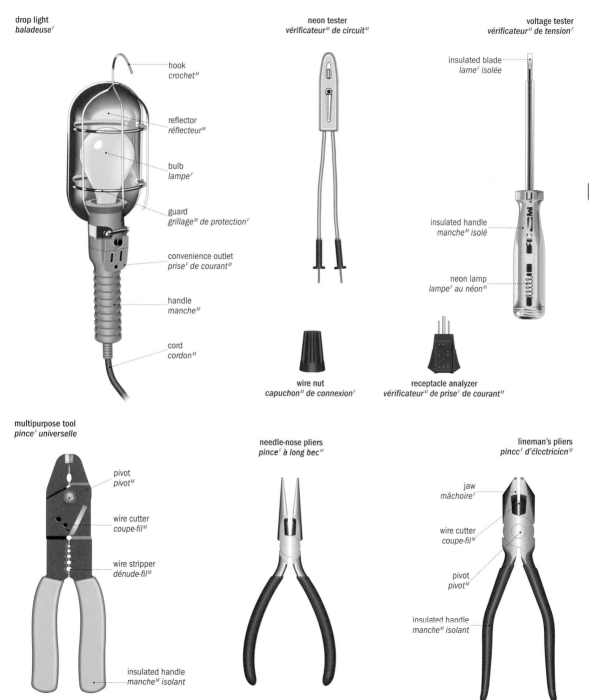

**drop light**
*baladeuse^F*

hook
*crochet^M*

reflector
*réflecteur^M*

bulb
*lampe^F*

guard
*grillage^M de protection^F*

convenience outlet
*prise^F de courant^M*

handle
*manche^M*

cord
*cordon^M*

**neon tester**
*vérificateur^M de circuit^M*

wire nut
*capuchon^M de connexion^F*

receptacle analyzer
*vérificateur^M de prise^F de courant^M*

**voltage tester**
*vérificateur^M de tension^F*

insulated blade
*lame^F isolée*

insulated handle
*manche^M isolé*

neon lamp
*lampe^F au néon^M*

**multipurpose tool**
*pince^F universelle*

pivot
*pivot^M*

wire cutter
*coupe-fil^M*

wire stripper
*dénude-fil^M*

insulated handle
*manche^M isolant*

**needle-nose pliers**
*pince^F à long bec^M*

**lineman's pliers**
*pince^F d'électricien^M*

jaw
*mâchoire^F*

wire cutter
*coupe-fil^M*

pivot
*pivot^M*

insulated handle
*manche^M isolant*

DO-IT-YOURSELF AND GARDENING

217

# soldering and welding tools

soudage<sup>M</sup> : outils<sup>M</sup>

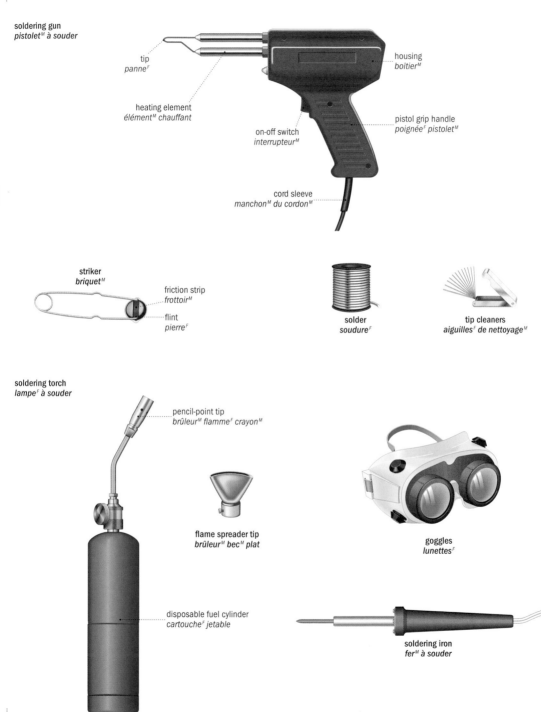

**soldering gun**
*pistolet<sup>M</sup> à souder*

tip
*panne<sup>F</sup>*

housing
*boitier<sup>M</sup>*

heating element
*élément<sup>M</sup> chauffant*

pistol grip handle
*poignée<sup>F</sup> pistolet<sup>M</sup>*

on-off switch
*interrupteur<sup>M</sup>*

cord sleeve
*manchon<sup>M</sup> du cordon<sup>M</sup>*

**striker**
*briquet<sup>M</sup>*

friction strip
*frottoir<sup>M</sup>*

flint
*pierre<sup>F</sup>*

solder
*soudure<sup>F</sup>*

tip cleaners
*aiguilles<sup>F</sup> de nettoyage<sup>M</sup>*

**soldering torch**
*lampe<sup>F</sup> à souder*

pencil-point tip
*brûleur<sup>M</sup> flamme<sup>F</sup> crayon<sup>M</sup>*

flame spreader tip
*brûleur<sup>M</sup> bec<sup>M</sup> plat*

goggles
*lunettes<sup>F</sup>*

disposable fuel cylinder
*cartouche<sup>F</sup> jetable*

soldering iron
*fer<sup>M</sup> à souder*

# painting

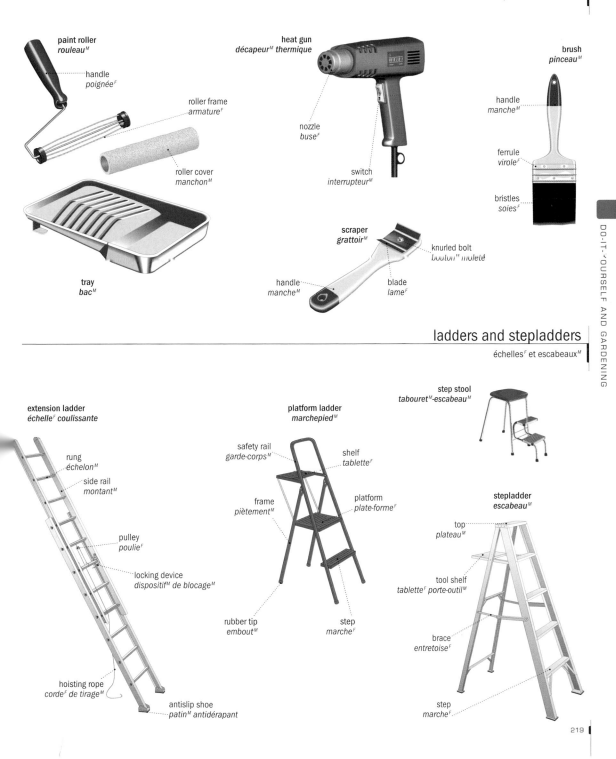

**paint roller**
*rouleau<sup>M</sup>*

handle
*poignée<sup>F</sup>*

roller frame
*armature<sup>F</sup>*

roller cover
*manchon<sup>M</sup>*

tray
*bac<sup>M</sup>*

**heat gun**
*décapeur<sup>M</sup> thermique*

nozzle
*buse<sup>F</sup>*

switch
*interrupteur<sup>M</sup>*

**scraper**
*grattoir<sup>M</sup>*

handle
*manche<sup>M</sup>*

knurled bolt
*bouton<sup>M</sup> moleté*

blade
*lame<sup>F</sup>*

**brush**
*pinceau<sup>M</sup>*

handle
*manche<sup>M</sup>*

ferrule
*virole<sup>F</sup>*

bristles
*soies<sup>F</sup>*

# ladders and stepladders

**extension ladder**
*échelle<sup>F</sup> coulissante*

rung
*échelon<sup>M</sup>*

side rail
*montant<sup>M</sup>*

pulley
*poulie<sup>F</sup>*

locking device
*dispositif<sup>M</sup> de blocage<sup>M</sup>*

hoisting rope
*corde<sup>F</sup> de tirage<sup>M</sup>*

antislip shoe
*patin<sup>M</sup> antidérapant*

**platform ladder**
*marchepied<sup>M</sup>*

safety rail
*garde-corps<sup>M</sup>*

shelf
*tablette<sup>F</sup>*

frame
*piètement<sup>M</sup>*

platform
*plate-forme<sup>F</sup>*

rubber tip
*embout<sup>M</sup>*

step
*marche<sup>F</sup>*

**step stool**
*tabouret<sup>M</sup>-escabeau<sup>M</sup>*

**stepladder**
*escabeau<sup>M</sup>*

top
*plateau<sup>M</sup>*

tool shelf
*tablette<sup>F</sup> porte-outil<sup>M</sup>*

brace
*entretoise<sup>F</sup>*

step
*marche<sup>F</sup>*

DO-IT-YOURSELF AND GARDENING

# carpentry: nailing tools
menuiserie<sup>F</sup> : outils<sup>M</sup> pour clouer

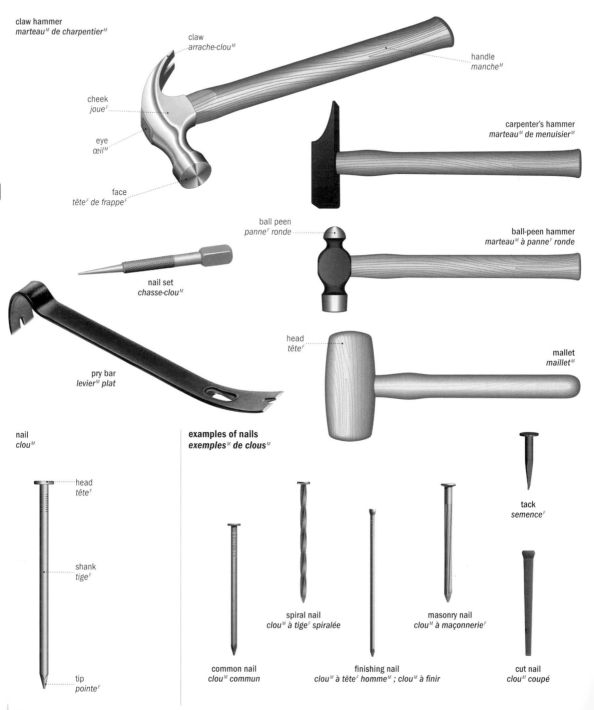

claw hammer
marteau<sup>M</sup> de charpentier<sup>M</sup>

claw
arrache-clou<sup>M</sup>

handle
manche<sup>M</sup>

cheek
joue<sup>F</sup>

carpenter's hammer
marteau<sup>M</sup> de menuisier<sup>M</sup>

eye
œil<sup>M</sup>

face
tête<sup>F</sup> de frappe<sup>F</sup>

ball peen
panne<sup>F</sup> ronde

ball-peen hammer
marteau<sup>M</sup> à panne<sup>F</sup> ronde

nail set
chasse-clou<sup>M</sup>

head
tête<sup>F</sup>

mallet
maillet<sup>M</sup>

pry bar
levier<sup>M</sup> plat

nail
clou<sup>M</sup>

examples of nails
exemples<sup>M</sup> de clous<sup>M</sup>

head
tête<sup>F</sup>

tack
semence<sup>F</sup>

shank
tige<sup>F</sup>

spiral nail
clou<sup>M</sup> à tige<sup>F</sup> spiralée

masonry nail
clou<sup>M</sup> à maçonnerie<sup>F</sup>

tip
pointe<sup>F</sup>

common nail
clou<sup>M</sup> commun

finishing nail
clou<sup>M</sup> à tête<sup>F</sup> homme<sup>M</sup> ; clou<sup>M</sup> à finir

cut nail
clou<sup>M</sup> coupé

# carpentry: screw-driving tools

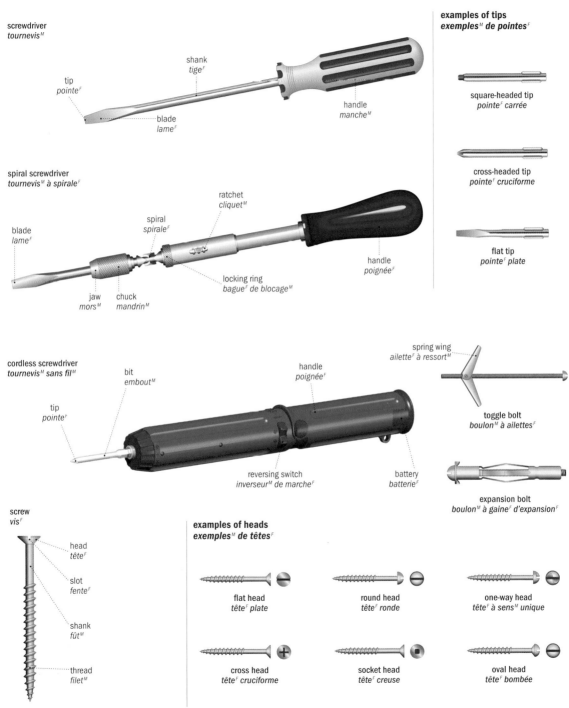

**screwdriver**
*tournevis<sup>M</sup>*

tip
*pointe<sup>F</sup>*

shank
*tige<sup>F</sup>*

blade
*lame<sup>F</sup>*

handle
*manche<sup>M</sup>*

**spiral screwdriver**
*tournevis<sup>M</sup> à spirale<sup>F</sup>*

blade
*lame<sup>F</sup>*

spiral
*spirale<sup>F</sup>*

ratchet
*cliquet<sup>M</sup>*

handle
*poignée<sup>F</sup>*

locking ring
*bague<sup>F</sup> de blocage<sup>M</sup>*

jaw
*mors<sup>M</sup>*

chuck
*mandrin<sup>M</sup>*

**cordless screwdriver**
*tournevis<sup>M</sup> sans fil<sup>M</sup>*

bit
*embout<sup>M</sup>*

handle
*poignée<sup>F</sup>*

tip
*pointe<sup>+</sup>*

reversing switch
*inverseur<sup>M</sup> de marche<sup>F</sup>*

battery
*batterie<sup>F</sup>*

**examples of tips**
*exemples<sup>M</sup> de pointes<sup>F</sup>*

square-headed tip
*pointe<sup>F</sup> carrée*

cross-headed tip
*pointe<sup>F</sup> cruciforme*

flat tip
*pointe<sup>F</sup> plate*

spring wing
*ailette<sup>F</sup> à ressort<sup>M</sup>*

toggle bolt
*boulon<sup>M</sup> à ailettes<sup>F</sup>*

expansion bolt
*boulon<sup>M</sup> à gaine<sup>F</sup> d'expansion<sup>F</sup>*

**screw**
*vis<sup>F</sup>*

head
*tête<sup>F</sup>*

slot
*fente<sup>F</sup>*

shank
*fût<sup>M</sup>*

thread
*filet<sup>M</sup>*

**examples of heads**
*exemples<sup>M</sup> de têtes<sup>F</sup>*

flat head
*tête<sup>F</sup> plate*

round head
*tête<sup>F</sup> ronde*

one-way head
*tête<sup>F</sup> à sens<sup>M</sup> unique*

cross head
*tête<sup>F</sup> cruciforme*

socket head
*tête<sup>F</sup> creuse*

oval head
*tête<sup>F</sup> bombée*

# carpentry: gripping and tightening tools
menuiserie<sup>F</sup> : outils<sup>M</sup> pour serrer

DO-IT-YOURSELF AND GARDENING

**pliers**
*pinces<sup>F</sup>*

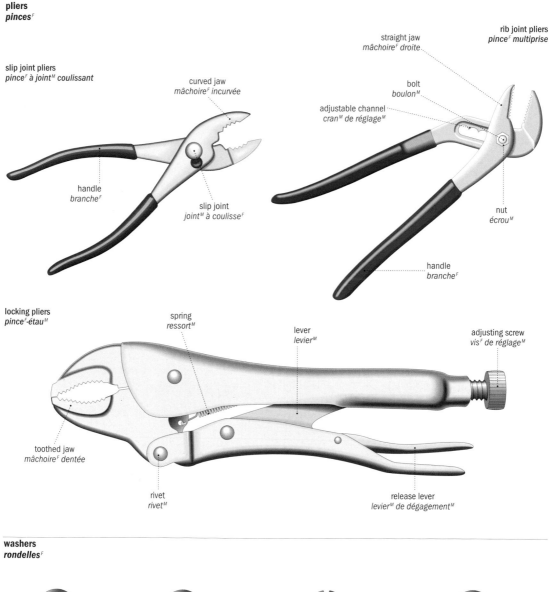

**slip joint pliers**
*pince<sup>F</sup> à joint<sup>M</sup> coulissant*

straight jaw
*mâchoire<sup>F</sup> droite*

**rib joint pliers**
*pince<sup>F</sup> multiprise*

curved jaw
*mâchoire<sup>F</sup> incurvée*

bolt
*boulon<sup>M</sup>*

adjustable channel
*cran<sup>M</sup> de réglage<sup>M</sup>*

handle
*branche<sup>F</sup>*

slip joint
*joint<sup>M</sup> à coulisse<sup>F</sup>*

nut
*écrou<sup>M</sup>*

handle
*branche<sup>F</sup>*

**locking pliers**
*pince<sup>F</sup>-étau<sup>M</sup>*

spring
*ressort<sup>M</sup>*

lever
*levier<sup>M</sup>*

adjusting screw
*vis<sup>F</sup> de réglage<sup>M</sup>*

toothed jaw
*mâchoire<sup>F</sup> dentée*

rivet
*rivet<sup>M</sup>*

release lever
*levier<sup>M</sup> de dégagement<sup>M</sup>*

**washers**
*rondelles<sup>F</sup>*

flat washer
*rondelle<sup>F</sup> plate*

lock washer
*rondelle<sup>F</sup> à ressort<sup>M</sup>*

external tooth lock washer
*rondelle<sup>F</sup> à denture<sup>F</sup> extérieure*

internal tooth lock washer
*rondelle<sup>F</sup> à denture<sup>F</sup> intérieure*

**wrenches**
*clés*F

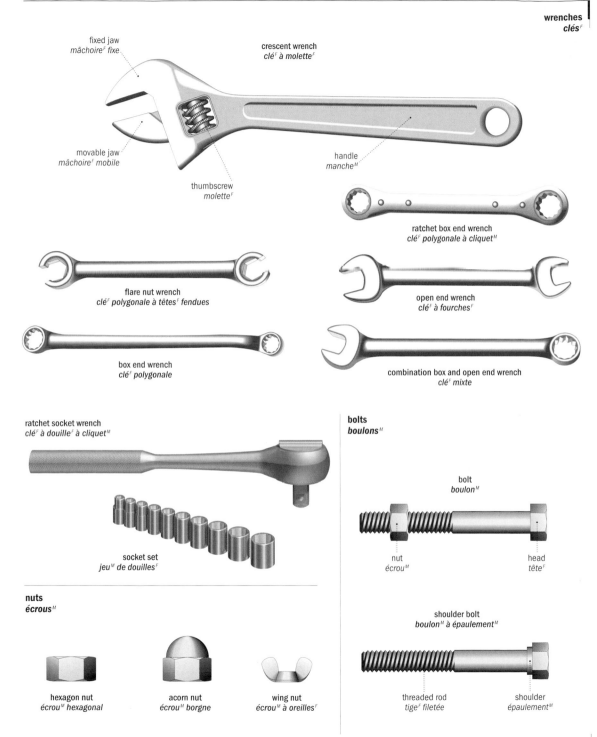

fixed jaw
*mâchoire*F *fixe*

crescent wrench
*clé*F *à molette*F

movable jaw
*mâchoire*F *mobile*

handle
*manche*M

thumbscrew
*molette*F

ratchet box end wrench
*clé*F *polygonale à cliquet*M

flare nut wrench
*clé*F *polygonale à têtes*F *fendues*

open end wrench
*clé*F *à fourches*F

box end wrench
*clé*F *polygonale*

combination box and open end wrench
*clé*F *mixte*

ratchet socket wrench
*clé*F *à douille*F *à cliquet*M

bolts
*boulons*M

socket set
*jeu*M *de douilles*F

bolt
*boulon*M

nut
*écrou*M

head
*tête*F

nuts
*écrous*M

shoulder bolt
*boulon*M *à épaulement*M

hexagon nut
*écrou*M *hexagonal*

acorn nut
*écrou*M *borgne*

wing nut
*écrou*M *à oreilles*F

threaded rod
*tige*F *filetée*

shoulder
*épaulement*M

DO-IT-YOURSELF AND GARDENING

carpentry: gripping and tightening tools

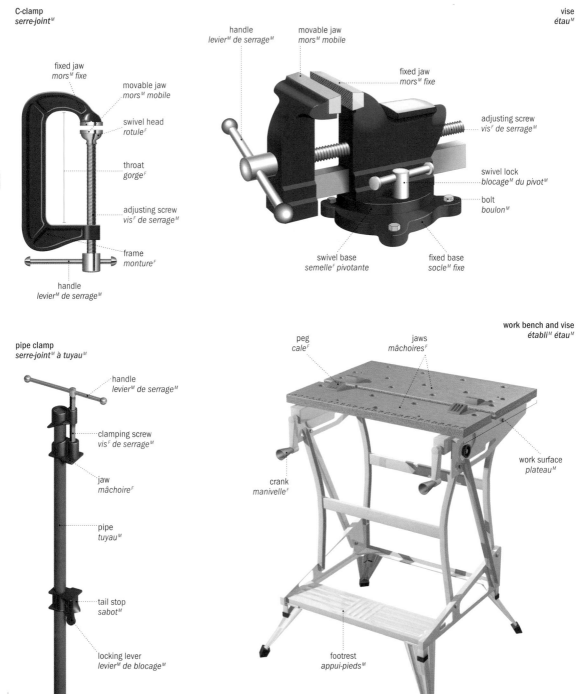

C-clamp
*serre-joint*<sup>M</sup>

vise
*étau*<sup>M</sup>

fixed jaw
*mors*<sup>M</sup> *fixe*

movable jaw
*mors*<sup>M</sup> *mobile*

swivel head
*rotule*<sup>F</sup>

throat
*gorge*<sup>F</sup>

adjusting screw
*vis*<sup>F</sup> *de serrage*<sup>M</sup>

frame
*monture*<sup>F</sup>

handle
*levier*<sup>M</sup> *de serrage*<sup>M</sup>

handle
*levier*<sup>M</sup> *de serrage*<sup>M</sup>

movable jaw
*mors*<sup>M</sup> *mobile*

fixed jaw
*mors*<sup>M</sup> *fixe*

adjusting screw
*vis*<sup>F</sup> *de serrage*<sup>M</sup>

swivel lock
*blocage*<sup>M</sup> *du pivot*<sup>M</sup>

bolt
*boulon*<sup>M</sup>

swivel base
*semelle*<sup>F</sup> *pivotante*

fixed base
*socle*<sup>M</sup> *fixe*

pipe clamp
*serre-joint*<sup>M</sup> *à tuyau*<sup>M</sup>

handle
*levier*<sup>M</sup> *de serrage*<sup>M</sup>

clamping screw
*vis*<sup>F</sup> *de serrage*<sup>M</sup>

jaw
*mâchoire*<sup>F</sup>

pipe
*tuyau*<sup>M</sup>

tail stop
*sabot*<sup>M</sup>

locking lever
*levier*<sup>M</sup> *de blocage*<sup>M</sup>

work bench and vise
*établi*<sup>M</sup> *étau*<sup>M</sup>

peg
*cale*<sup>F</sup>

jaws
*mâchoires*<sup>F</sup>

work surface
*plateau*<sup>M</sup>

crank
*manivelle*<sup>F</sup>

footrest
*appui-pieds*<sup>M</sup>

# carpentry: measuring and marking tools

menuiserie*F* : instruments*M* de traçage*M* et de mesure*F*

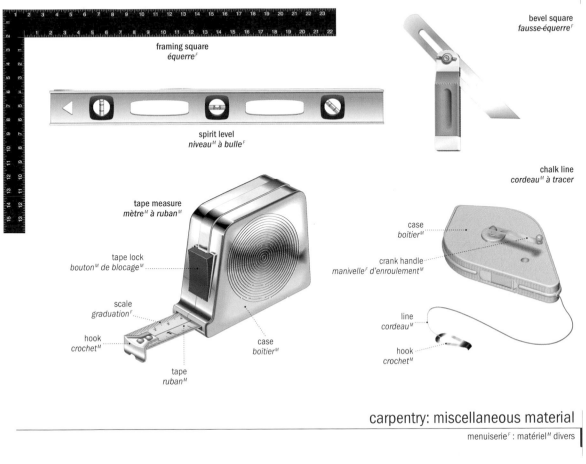

framing square
équerre*F*

bevel square
fausse-équerre*F*

spirit level
niveau*M* à bulle*F*

chalk line
cordeau*M* à tracer

tape measure
mètre*M* à ruban*M*

case
boîtier*M*

tape lock
bouton*M* de blocage*M*

crank handle
manivelle*F* d'enroulement*M*

scale
graduation*F*

line
cordeau*M*

hook
crochet*M*

case
boîtier*M*

hook
crochet*M*

tape
ruban*M*

# carpentry: miscellaneous material

menuiserie*F* : matériel*M* divers

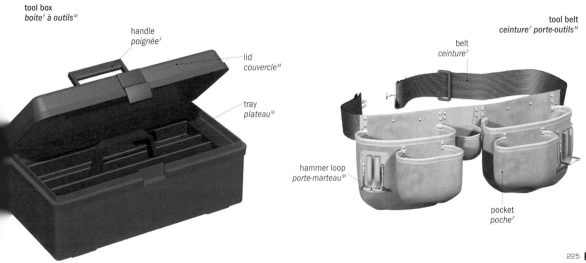

tool box
boîte*F* à outils*M*

handle
poignée*F*

lid
couvercle*M*

tray
plateau*M*

tool belt
ceinture*F* porte-outils*M*

belt
ceinture*F*

hammer loop
porte-marteau*M*

pocket
poche*F*

# carpentry: sawing tools

menuiserie<sup>F</sup> : outils<sup>M</sup> pour scier

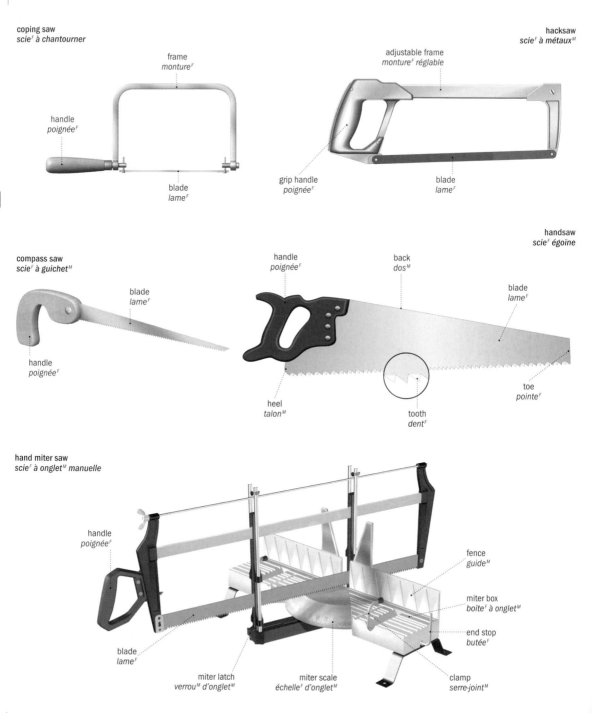

coping saw
*scie<sup>F</sup> à chantourner*

frame
*monture<sup>F</sup>*

handle
*poignée<sup>F</sup>*

blade
*lame<sup>F</sup>*

hacksaw
*scie<sup>F</sup> à métaux<sup>M</sup>*

adjustable frame
*monture<sup>F</sup> réglable*

grip handle
*poignée<sup>F</sup>*

blade
*lame<sup>F</sup>*

compass saw
*scie<sup>F</sup> à guichet<sup>M</sup>*

blade
*lame<sup>F</sup>*

handle
*poignée<sup>F</sup>*

handsaw
*scie<sup>F</sup> égoïne*

handle
*poignée<sup>F</sup>*

back
*dos<sup>M</sup>*

blade
*lame<sup>F</sup>*

heel
*talon<sup>M</sup>*

tooth
*dent<sup>F</sup>*

toe
*pointe<sup>F</sup>*

hand miter saw
*scie<sup>F</sup> à onglet<sup>M</sup> manuelle*

handle
*poignée<sup>F</sup>*

blade
*lame<sup>F</sup>*

miter latch
*verrou<sup>M</sup> d'onglet<sup>M</sup>*

miter scale
*échelle<sup>F</sup> d'onglet<sup>M</sup>*

fence
*guide<sup>M</sup>*

miter box
*boîte<sup>F</sup> à onglet<sup>M</sup>*

end stop
*butée<sup>F</sup>*

clamp
*serre-joint<sup>M</sup>*

DO-IT-YOURSELF AND GARDENING

carpentry: sawing tools

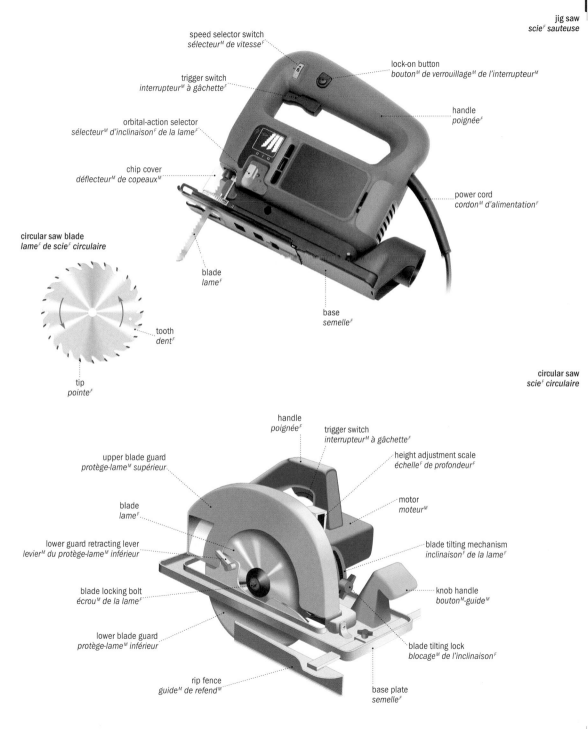

jig saw
*scie^F sauteuse*

speed selector switch
*sélecteur^M de vitesse^F*

lock-on button
*bouton^M de verrouillage^M de l'interrupteur^M*

trigger switch
*interrupteur^M à gâchette^F*

handle
*poignée^F*

orbital-action selector
*sélecteur^M d'inclinaison^F de la lame^F*

chip cover
*déflecteur^M de copeaux^M*

power cord
*cordon^M d'alimentation^F*

circular saw blade
*lame^F de scie^F circulaire*

blade
*lame^F*

base
*semelle^F*

tooth
*dent^F*

circular saw
*scie^F circulaire*

tip
*pointe^F*

handle
*poignée^F*

trigger switch
*interrupteur^M à gâchette^F*

height adjustment scale
*échelle^F de profondeur^F*

upper blade guard
*protège-lame^M supérieur*

motor
*moteur^M*

blade
*lame^F*

blade tilting mechanism
*inclinaison^F de la lame^F*

lower guard retracting lever
*levier^M du protège-lame^M inférieur*

blade locking bolt
*écrou^M de la lame^F*

knob handle
*bouton^M-guide^M*

lower blade guard
*protège-lame^M inférieur*

blade tilting lock
*blocage^M de l'inclinaison^F*

rip fence
*guide^M de refend^M*

base plate
*semelle^F*

DO-IT-YOURSELF AND GARDENING

# carpentry: drilling tools

menuiserie<sup>F</sup> : outils<sup>M</sup> pour percer

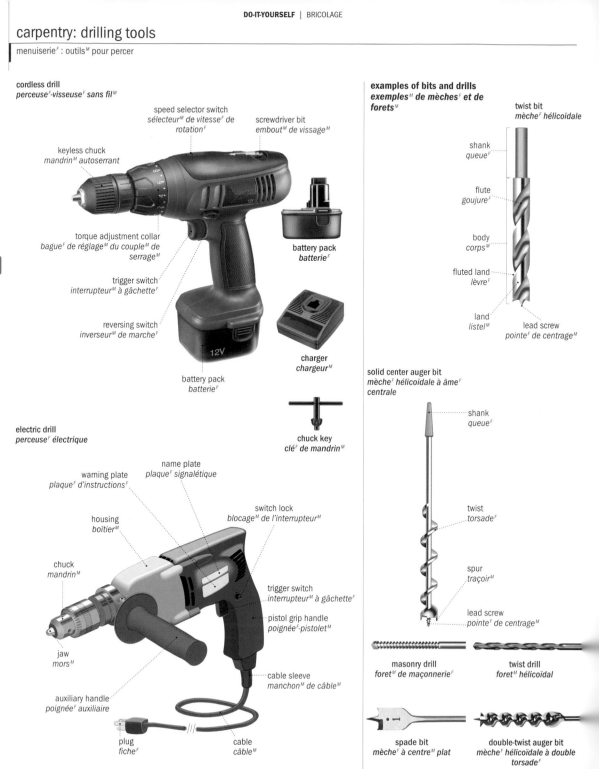

cordless drill
*perceuse<sup>F</sup>-visseuse<sup>F</sup> sans fil<sup>M</sup>*

speed selector switch
*sélecteur<sup>M</sup> de vitesse<sup>F</sup> de rotation<sup>F</sup>*

screwdriver bit
*embout<sup>M</sup> de vissage<sup>M</sup>*

keyless chuck
*mandrin<sup>M</sup> autoserrant*

torque adjustment collar
*bague<sup>F</sup> de réglage<sup>M</sup> du couple<sup>M</sup> de serrage<sup>M</sup>*

battery pack
*batterie<sup>F</sup>*

trigger switch
*interrupteur<sup>M</sup> à gâchette<sup>F</sup>*

reversing switch
*inverseur<sup>M</sup> de marche<sup>F</sup>*

charger
*chargeur<sup>M</sup>*

battery pack
*batterie<sup>F</sup>*

electric drill
*perceuse<sup>F</sup> électrique*

chuck key
*clé<sup>F</sup> de mandrin<sup>M</sup>*

warning plate
*plaque<sup>F</sup> d'instructions<sup>F</sup>*

name plate
*plaque<sup>F</sup> signalétique*

switch lock
*blocage<sup>M</sup> de l'interrupteur<sup>M</sup>*

housing
*boîtier<sup>M</sup>*

chuck
*mandrin<sup>M</sup>*

trigger switch
*interrupteur<sup>M</sup> à gâchette<sup>F</sup>*

pistol grip handle
*poignée<sup>F</sup>-pistolet<sup>M</sup>*

jaw
*mors<sup>M</sup>*

cable sleeve
*manchon<sup>M</sup> de câble<sup>M</sup>*

auxiliary handle
*poignée<sup>F</sup> auxiliaire*

plug
*fiche<sup>F</sup>*

cable
*câble<sup>M</sup>*

examples of bits and drills
*exemples<sup>M</sup> de mèches<sup>F</sup> et de forets<sup>M</sup>*

twist bit
*mèche<sup>F</sup> hélicoïdale*

shank
*queue<sup>F</sup>*

flute
*goujure<sup>F</sup>*

body
*corps<sup>M</sup>*

fluted land
*lèvre<sup>F</sup>*

land
*listel<sup>M</sup>*

lead screw
*pointe<sup>F</sup> de centrage<sup>M</sup>*

solid center auger bit
*mèche<sup>F</sup> hélicoïdale à âme<sup>F</sup> centrale*

shank
*queue<sup>F</sup>*

twist
*torsade<sup>F</sup>*

spur
*traçoir<sup>M</sup>*

lead screw
*pointe<sup>F</sup> de centrage<sup>M</sup>*

masonry drill
*foret<sup>M</sup> de maçonnerie<sup>F</sup>*

twist drill
*foret<sup>M</sup> hélicoïdal*

spade bit
*mèche<sup>F</sup> à centre<sup>M</sup> plat*

double-twist auger bit
*mèche<sup>F</sup> hélicoïdale à double torsade<sup>F</sup>*

# carpentry: shaping tools
menuiserie<sup>F</sup> : outils<sup>M</sup> pour façonner

plane
rabot<sup>M</sup>

lateral-adjustment lever
levier<sup>M</sup> de réglage<sup>M</sup> latéral

wedge lever
levier<sup>M</sup> du bloc<sup>M</sup>

handle
poignée<sup>F</sup>

lever cap
bloc<sup>M</sup> d'arrêt<sup>M</sup>

depth-of-cut adjustment knob
molette<sup>F</sup> de réglage<sup>M</sup> de la saillie<sup>F</sup>

knob
pommeau<sup>M</sup>

heel
talon<sup>M</sup>

toe
nez<sup>M</sup>

sole
semelle<sup>F</sup>

frog-adjustment screw
réglage<sup>M</sup> de l'angle<sup>M</sup>

blade
fer<sup>M</sup>

cap iron
contre-fer<sup>M</sup>

random orbit sander
ponceuse<sup>F</sup> excentrique

lock-on button
bouton<sup>M</sup> de blocage<sup>M</sup>

power cord
cordon<sup>M</sup> d'alimentation<sup>F</sup>

motor
moteur<sup>M</sup>

router
défonceuse<sup>F</sup> ; toupie<sup>F</sup>

housing
boîtier<sup>M</sup>

handle
poignée<sup>F</sup>

head
tête<sup>F</sup>

switch
interrupteur<sup>M</sup>

cord sleeve
manchon<sup>M</sup> du cordon<sup>M</sup>

depth adjustment
réglage<sup>M</sup> de profondeur<sup>F</sup>

dust canister
boîte<sup>F</sup> à poussière<sup>F</sup>

guide handle
poignée<sup>F</sup> de guidage<sup>M</sup>

sanding disc
disque<sup>M</sup> abrasif

trigger switch
interrupteur<sup>M</sup> à gâchette<sup>F</sup>

collet
collet<sup>M</sup>

sanding pad
plateau<sup>M</sup> de ponçage<sup>M</sup>

sand paper
papier<sup>M</sup> de verre<sup>M</sup>

base
base<sup>F</sup>

tool holder
porte-outil<sup>M</sup>

file
lime<sup>F</sup>

wood chisel
ciseau<sup>M</sup> à bois<sup>M</sup>

DO-IT-YOURSELF AND GARDENING

# pleasure garden

jardin<sup>M</sup> d'agrément<sup>M</sup>

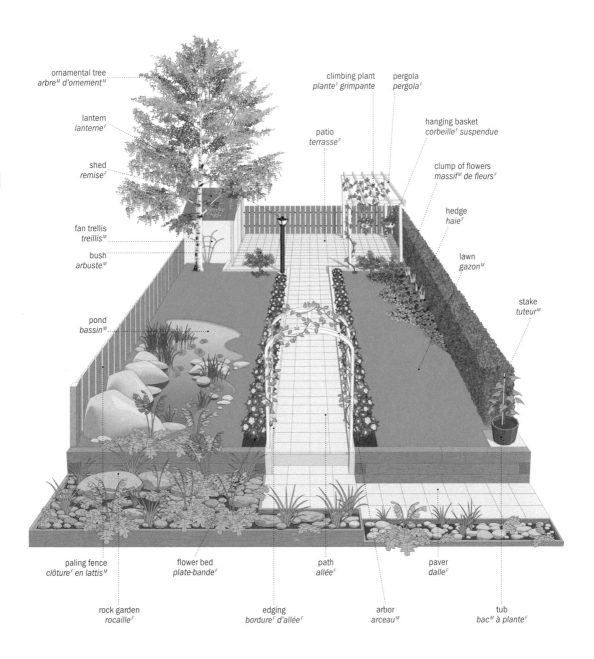

ornamental tree
arbre<sup>M</sup> d'ornement<sup>M</sup>

lantern
lanterne<sup>F</sup>

shed
remise<sup>F</sup>

fan trellis
treillis<sup>M</sup>

bush
arbuste<sup>M</sup>

pond
bassin<sup>M</sup>

climbing plant
plante<sup>F</sup> grimpante

pergola
pergola<sup>F</sup>

patio
terrasse<sup>F</sup>

hanging basket
corbeille<sup>F</sup> suspendue

clump of flowers
massif<sup>M</sup> de fleurs<sup>F</sup>

hedge
haie<sup>F</sup>

lawn
gazon<sup>M</sup>

stake
tuteur<sup>M</sup>

paling fence
clôture<sup>F</sup> en lattis<sup>M</sup>

flower bed
plate-bande<sup>F</sup>

path
allée<sup>F</sup>

paver
dalle<sup>F</sup>

rock garden
rocaille<sup>F</sup>

edging
bordure<sup>F</sup> d'allée<sup>F</sup>

arbor
arceau<sup>M</sup>

tub
bac<sup>M</sup> à plante<sup>F</sup>

# miscellaneous equipment

équipement*M* divers

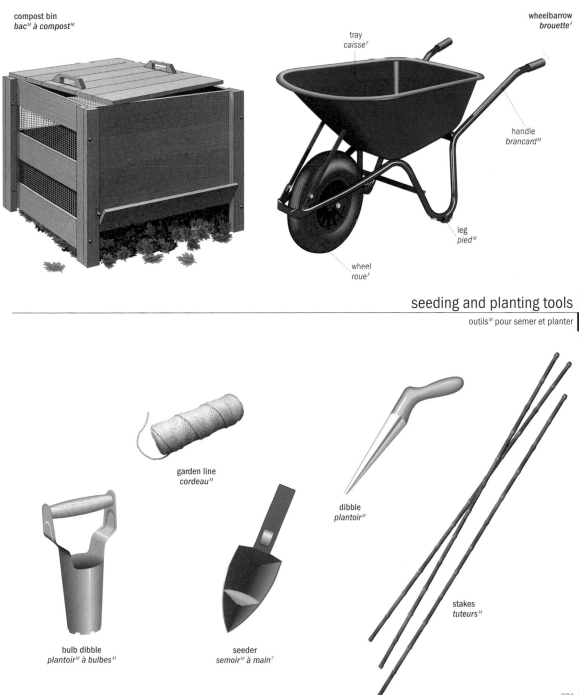

compost bin
*bac*M *à compost*M

tray
*caisse*F

wheelbarrow
*brouette*F

handle
*brancard*M

leg
*pied*M

wheel
*roue*F

# seeding and planting tools

outils*M* pour semer et planter

garden line
*cordeau*M

dibble
*plantoir*M

bulb dibble
*plantoir*M *à bulbes*M

seeder
*semoir*M *à main*F

stakes
*tuteurs*M

# hand tools

jeu<sup>M</sup> de petits outils<sup>M</sup>

small hand cultivator
*griffe<sup>F</sup> à fleurs<sup>F</sup>*

trowel
*transplantoir<sup>M</sup>*

weeder
*tire-racine<sup>M</sup>*

gardening gloves
*gants<sup>M</sup> de jardinage<sup>M</sup>*

hand fork
*fourche<sup>F</sup> à fleurs<sup>F</sup>*

# tools for loosening the earth

outils$^M$ pour remuer la terre$^F$

weeding hoe
*sarcloir*$^M$

hoe-fork
*serfouette*$^F$

draw hoe
*binette*$^F$

scuffle hoe
*ratissoire*$^F$

spade
*bêche*$^F$

shovel
*pelle*$^F$

garden fork
*fourche*$^F$ *à bêcher*

rake
*râteau*$^M$

hoe
*houe*$^F$

pick
*pioche*$^F$

lawn edger
*coupe-bordures*$^M$

DO-IT-YOURSELF AND GARDENING

# pruning and cutting tools

outils<sup>M</sup> pour couper

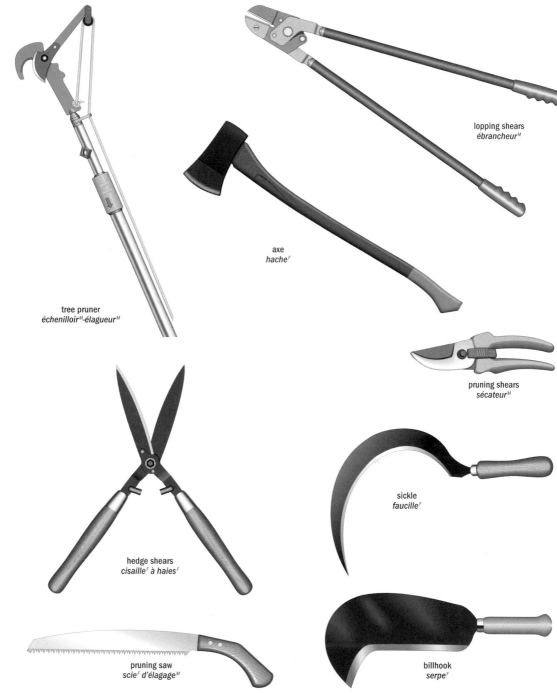

lopping shears
*ébrancheur<sup>M</sup>*

axe
*hache<sup>F</sup>*

tree pruner
*échenilloir<sup>M</sup>-élagueur<sup>M</sup>*

pruning shears
*sécateur<sup>M</sup>*

sickle
*faucille<sup>F</sup>*

hedge shears
*cisaille<sup>F</sup> à haies<sup>F</sup>*

pruning saw
*scie<sup>F</sup> d'élagage<sup>M</sup>*

billhook
*serpe<sup>F</sup>*

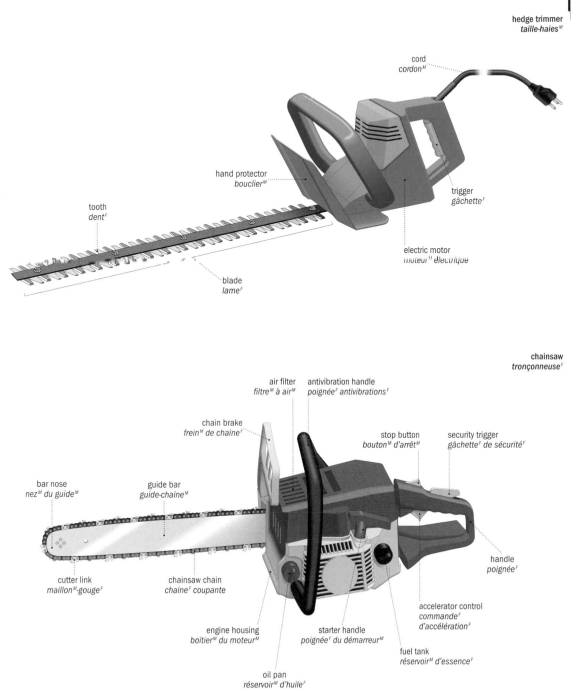

hedge trimmer
*taille-haies*<sup>M</sup>

cord
*cordon*<sup>M</sup>

hand protector
*bouclier*<sup>M</sup>

trigger
*gâchette*<sup>F</sup>

tooth
*dent*<sup>F</sup>

electric motor
*moteur*<sup>M</sup> *électrique*

blade
*lame*<sup>F</sup>

chainsaw
*tronçonneuse*<sup>F</sup>

air filter
*filtre*<sup>M</sup> *à air*<sup>M</sup>

antivibration handle
*poignée*<sup>F</sup> *antivibrations*<sup>F</sup>

chain brake
*frein*<sup>M</sup> *de chaîne*<sup>F</sup>

stop button
*bouton*<sup>M</sup> *d'arrêt*<sup>M</sup>

security trigger
*gâchette*<sup>F</sup> *de sécurité*<sup>F</sup>

bar nose
*nez*<sup>M</sup> *du guide*<sup>M</sup>

guide bar
*guide-chaîne*<sup>M</sup>

handle
*poignée*<sup>F</sup>

cutter link
*maillon*<sup>M</sup>-*gouge*<sup>F</sup>

chainsaw chain
*chaîne*<sup>F</sup> *coupante*

accelerator control
*commande*<sup>F</sup>
*d'accélération*<sup>F</sup>

engine housing
*boîtier*<sup>M</sup> *du moteur*<sup>M</sup>

starter handle
*poignée*<sup>F</sup> *du démarreur*<sup>M</sup>

fuel tank
*réservoir*<sup>M</sup> *d'essence*<sup>F</sup>

oil pan
*réservoir*<sup>M</sup> *d'huile*<sup>F</sup>

DO-IT YOURSELF AND GARDENING

# watering tools
outils<sup>M</sup> pour arroser

sprayer
*vaporisateur*<sup>M</sup>

spray nozzle
*pistolet*<sup>M</sup> *arrosoir*<sup>M</sup>

pistol nozzle
*pistolet*<sup>M</sup> *d'arrosage*<sup>M</sup>

sprinkler hose
*tuyau*<sup>M</sup> *perforé*

tank sprayer
*pulvérisateur*<sup>M</sup>

watering can
*arrosoir*<sup>M</sup>

handle
*anse*<sup>F</sup>

rose
*pomme*<sup>F</sup>

metal arm
*balancier*<sup>M</sup>

diffuser pin
*brise-jet*<sup>M</sup>

impulse sprinkler
*arroseur*<sup>M</sup> *canon*<sup>M</sup>

nozzle
*buse*<sup>F</sup>

deflector
*déflecteur*<sup>M</sup>

hose connector
*raccord*<sup>M</sup> *de tuyau*<sup>M</sup>

trip lever
*bague*<sup>F</sup> *de réglage*<sup>M</sup>

sled
*traîneau*<sup>M</sup>

hose trolley
*dévidoir*<sup>M</sup> *sur roues*<sup>F</sup>

reel
*dévidoir*<sup>M</sup>

garden hose
*tuyau*<sup>M</sup> *d'arrosage*<sup>M</sup>

tap connector
*raccord*<sup>M</sup> *de robinet*<sup>M</sup>

trolley crank
*manivelle*<sup>F</sup>

hose nozzle
*lance*<sup>F</sup> *d'arrosage*<sup>M</sup>

oscillating sprinkler
*arroseur*<sup>M</sup> *oscillant*

revolving sprinkler
*arroseur*<sup>M</sup> *rotatif*

arm
*bras*<sup>M</sup>

# lawn care

soins<sup>M</sup> de la pelouse<sup>F</sup>

edger
*taille-bordures*<sup>M</sup>

cord
*cordon*<sup>M</sup>

electric motor
*moteur*<sup>M</sup> *électrique*

security casing
*carter*<sup>M</sup> *de sécurité*<sup>F</sup>

nylon thread
*fil*<sup>M</sup> *de nylon*<sup>M</sup>

lawn aerator
*aérateur*<sup>M</sup> *à gazon*<sup>M</sup>

lawn rake
*balai*<sup>M</sup> *à feuilles*<sup>F</sup>

power mower
*tondeuse*<sup>F</sup> *à moteur*<sup>M</sup>

handle
*guidon*<sup>M</sup>

safety handle
*poignée*<sup>F</sup> *de sécurité*<sup>F</sup>

speed control
*sélecteur*<sup>M</sup> *de régime*<sup>M</sup>

ignition key
*clé*<sup>F</sup> *de contact*<sup>M</sup>

grassbox
*bac*<sup>M</sup> *de ramassage*<sup>M</sup>

starter
*démarreur*<sup>M</sup> *manuel*

filler cap
*bouchon*<sup>M</sup> *de remplissage*<sup>M</sup>

motor
*moteur*<sup>M</sup>

accelerator cable
*câble*<sup>M</sup> *d'accélération*<sup>F</sup>

deflector
*déflecteur*<sup>M</sup>

spark plug
*bougie*<sup>F</sup>

casing
*carter*<sup>M</sup>

DO-IT YOURSELF AND GARDENING

# headgear

coiffure<sup>F</sup>

CLOTHING

**men's headgear**
***coiffures<sup>F</sup> d'homme<sup>M</sup>***

felt hat
*chapeau<sup>M</sup> de feutre<sup>M</sup>*

hatband
*bourdalou<sup>M</sup>*

binding
*galon<sup>M</sup>*

crown
*calotte<sup>F</sup>*

brim
*bord<sup>M</sup>*

bow
*nœud<sup>M</sup> plat*

boater
*canotier<sup>M</sup>*

skullcap
*calotte<sup>F</sup>*

derby
*melon<sup>M</sup>*

garrison cap
*calot<sup>M</sup>*

top hat
*haut-de-forme<sup>M</sup>*

shapka
*chapka<sup>M</sup>*

hunting cap
*casquette<sup>F</sup> norvégienne*

ear flap
*cache-oreilles<sup>M</sup> abattant*

cap
*casquette<sup>F</sup>*

panama
*panama<sup>M</sup>*

peak
*visière<sup>F</sup>*

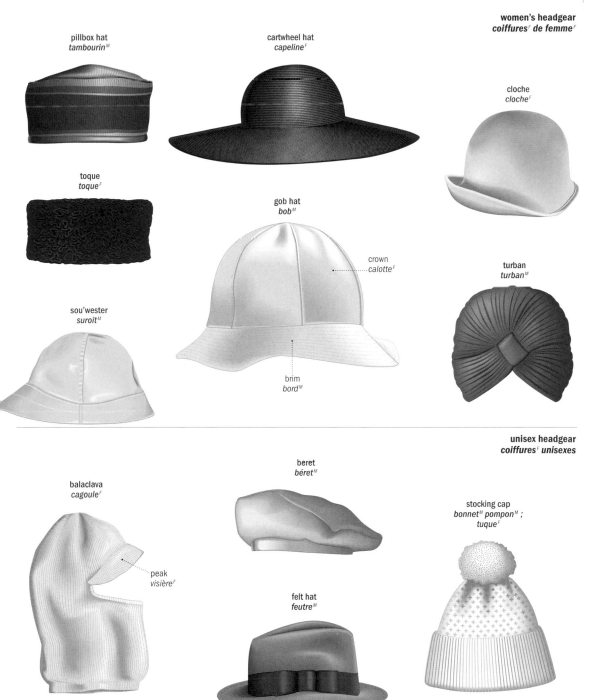

**women's headgear**
*coiffures<sup>F</sup> de femme<sup>F</sup>*

pillbox hat
*tambourin<sup>M</sup>*

cartwheel hat
*capeline<sup>F</sup>*

cloche
*cloche<sup>F</sup>*

toque
*toque<sup>F</sup>*

gob hat
*bob<sup>M</sup>*

crown
*calotte<sup>F</sup>*

turban
*turban<sup>M</sup>*

sou'wester
*suroît<sup>M</sup>*

brim
*bord<sup>M</sup>*

CLOTHING

**unisex headgear**
*coiffures<sup>F</sup> unisexes*

beret
*béret<sup>M</sup>*

balaclava
*cagoule<sup>F</sup>*

stocking cap
*bonnet<sup>M</sup> pompon<sup>M</sup> ;*
*tuque<sup>F</sup>*

peak
*visière<sup>F</sup>*

felt hat
*feutre<sup>M</sup>*

# shoes

chaussures<sup>F</sup>

**men's shoes**
*chaussures<sup>F</sup> d'homme<sup>M</sup>*

parts of a shoe
*parties<sup>F</sup> d'une chaussure<sup>F</sup>*

lining
*doublure<sup>F</sup>*

cuff
*revers<sup>M</sup>*

heel grip
*glissoir<sup>M</sup>*

quarter
*quartier<sup>M</sup>*

outside counter
*talonnette<sup>F</sup> de dessus<sup>M</sup>*

heel
*talon<sup>M</sup>*

top lift
*bonbout<sup>M</sup>*

waist
*cambrure<sup>F</sup>*

nose of the quarter
*aile<sup>F</sup> de quartier<sup>M</sup>*

tag
*ferret<sup>M</sup>*

eyelet tab
*garant<sup>M</sup>*

eyelet
*œillet<sup>M</sup>*

tongue
*languette<sup>F</sup>*

shoelace
*lacet<sup>M</sup>*

vamp
*claque<sup>F</sup>*

stitch
*surpiqûre<sup>F</sup>*

punch hole
*perforation<sup>F</sup>*

perforated toe cap
*bout<sup>M</sup> fleuri*

outsole
*semelle<sup>F</sup> d'usure<sup>F</sup>*

welt
*trépointe<sup>F</sup>*

heavy duty boot
*brodequin<sup>M</sup> de travail<sup>M</sup>*

chukka
*chukka<sup>M</sup>*

rubber
*claque<sup>F</sup>*

bootee
*bottillon<sup>M</sup>*

oxford shoe
*richelieu<sup>M</sup>*

blucher oxford
*derby<sup>M</sup>*

CLOTHING

**women's shoes**
*chaussures* F *de femme* F

ballerina slipper
*ballerine* F

sandal
*sandale* F

sling back shoe
*escarpin* M-*sandale* F

pump
*escarpin* M

one-bar shoe
*Charles IX* M

T-strap shoe
*salomé* M

thigh-boot
*cuissarde* F

boot
*botte* F

casual shoe
*trotteur* M

ankle boot
*bottine* F

**unisex shoes**
*chaussures<sup>F</sup> unisexes*

mule
*mule<sup>F</sup>*

espadrille
*espadrille<sup>F</sup>*

tennis shoe
*tennis<sup>M</sup>*

loafer
*loafer<sup>M</sup> ; flâneur<sup>M</sup>*

sandal
*nu-pied<sup>M</sup>*

moccasin
*mocassin<sup>M</sup>*

thong
*tong<sup>M</sup>*

clog
*socque<sup>M</sup>*

sandal
*sandalette<sup>F</sup>*

hiking boot
*brodequin<sup>M</sup> de randonnée<sup>F</sup>*

**men's gloves**
*gants<sup>M</sup> d'homme<sup>M</sup>*

back of a glove
*dos<sup>M</sup> d'un gant<sup>M</sup>*

palm of a glove
*paume<sup>F</sup> d'un gant<sup>M</sup>*

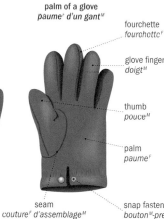

opening
*fenêtre<sup>F</sup>*

perforation
*perforation<sup>F</sup>*

fourchette
*fourchette<sup>F</sup>*

glove finger
*doigt<sup>M</sup>*

thumb
*pouce<sup>M</sup>*

palm
*paume<sup>F</sup>*

stitching
*baguette<sup>F</sup>*

seam
*couture<sup>F</sup> d'assemblage<sup>M</sup>*

snap fastener
*bouton<sup>M</sup>-pression<sup>F</sup>*

driving glove
*gant<sup>M</sup> de conduite<sup>F</sup>*

mitten
*moufle<sup>F</sup> ; mitaine<sup>F</sup>*

CLOTHING

**women's gloves**
*gants<sup>M</sup> de femme<sup>F</sup>*

short glove
*gant<sup>M</sup> court*

gauntlet
*gant<sup>M</sup> à crispin<sup>M</sup>*

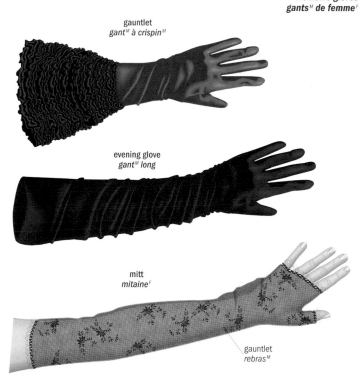

evening glove
*gant<sup>M</sup> long*

mitt
*mitaine<sup>F</sup>*

wrist-length glove
*gant<sup>M</sup> saxe*

gauntlet
*rebras<sup>M</sup>*

## jackets
**veston<sup>M</sup> et veste<sup>F</sup>**

**double-breasted jacket**
**veston<sup>M</sup> croisé**

collar
col<sup>M</sup>

peaked lapel
revers<sup>M</sup> à cran<sup>M</sup> aigu

lining
doublure<sup>F</sup>

breast welt pocket
pochette<sup>F</sup>

sleeve
manche<sup>F</sup>

flap
rabat<sup>M</sup>

outside ticket pocket
poche<sup>F</sup>-ticket<sup>M</sup>

patch pocket
poche<sup>F</sup> plaquée

side back vent
fente<sup>F</sup> latérale

**vest**
**gilet<sup>M</sup>**

V-neck
encolure<sup>F</sup> en V

lining
doublure<sup>F</sup>

welt
patte<sup>F</sup>

front
devant<sup>M</sup>

seam
découpe<sup>F</sup>

welt pocket
poche<sup>F</sup> gilet<sup>M</sup>

adjustable waist tab
tirant<sup>M</sup> de réglage<sup>M</sup>

**single-breasted jacket**
**veste<sup>F</sup> droite**

lapel
revers<sup>M</sup>

notch
cran<sup>M</sup>

front
devant<sup>M</sup>

lining
doublure<sup>F</sup>

pocket handkerchief
pochette<sup>F</sup>

back
dos<sup>M</sup>

sleeve
manche<sup>F</sup>

flap pocket
poche<sup>F</sup> tiroir<sup>M</sup>

center back vent
fente<sup>F</sup> médiane

**shirt**
*chemise*<sup>F</sup>

yoke
*empiècement*<sup>M</sup>

collar
*col*<sup>M</sup>

collar point
*pointe*<sup>F</sup> *de col*<sup>M</sup>

set-in sleeve
*manche*<sup>F</sup> *montée*

breast pocket
*poche*<sup>F</sup> *poitrine*<sup>F</sup>

front
*devant*<sup>M</sup>

buttoned placket
*patte*<sup>F</sup> *de boutonnage*<sup>M</sup>

button
*bouton*<sup>M</sup>

pointed tab end
*patte*<sup>F</sup> *capucin*<sup>M</sup>

cuff
*poignet*<sup>M</sup>

shirttail
*pan*<sup>M</sup>

CLOTHING

collar stay
*baleine*<sup>F</sup> *de col*<sup>M</sup>

buttondown collar
*col*<sup>M</sup> *pointes*<sup>F</sup> *boutonnées*

ascot tie
*lavallière*<sup>F</sup>

bow tie
*nœud*<sup>M</sup> *papillon*<sup>M</sup>

spread collar
*col*<sup>M</sup> *italien*

**necktie**
*cravate*<sup>F</sup>

front apron
*pan*<sup>M</sup> *avant*

neck end
*tour*<sup>M</sup> *de cou*<sup>M</sup>

rear apron
*pan*<sup>M</sup> *arrière*

lining
*doublure*<sup>F</sup>

loop
*passant*<sup>M</sup>

slip-stitched seam
*couture*<sup>F</sup> *médiane*

**pants**
*pantalon*<sup>M</sup>

belt loop
*passant*<sup>M</sup>

waistband
*ceinture*<sup>F</sup> *montée*

front top pocket
*poche*<sup>F</sup> *cavalière*

knife pleat
*pli*<sup>M</sup> *plat*

waistband extension
*patte*<sup>F</sup> *boutonnée*

fly
*braguette*<sup>F</sup>

crease
*pli*<sup>M</sup>

cuff
*revers*<sup>M</sup>

back pocket
*poche*<sup>F</sup>-*revolver*<sup>M</sup>

suspender clip
*pince*<sup>F</sup>

suspenders
*bretelles*<sup>F</sup>

elastic webbing
*bande*<sup>F</sup> *élastique*

adjustment slide
*coulisse*<sup>F</sup>

leather end
*patte*<sup>F</sup>

button loop
*boutonnière*<sup>F</sup>

**belt**
*ceinture*<sup>F</sup>

top stitching
*surpiqûre*<sup>F</sup>

panel
*croûte*<sup>F</sup> *de cuir*<sup>M</sup>

tip
*capucin*<sup>M</sup>

punch hole
*cran*<sup>M</sup>

belt loop
*passant*<sup>M</sup>

tongue
*ardillon*<sup>M</sup>

buckle
*boucle*<sup>F</sup>

CLOTHING

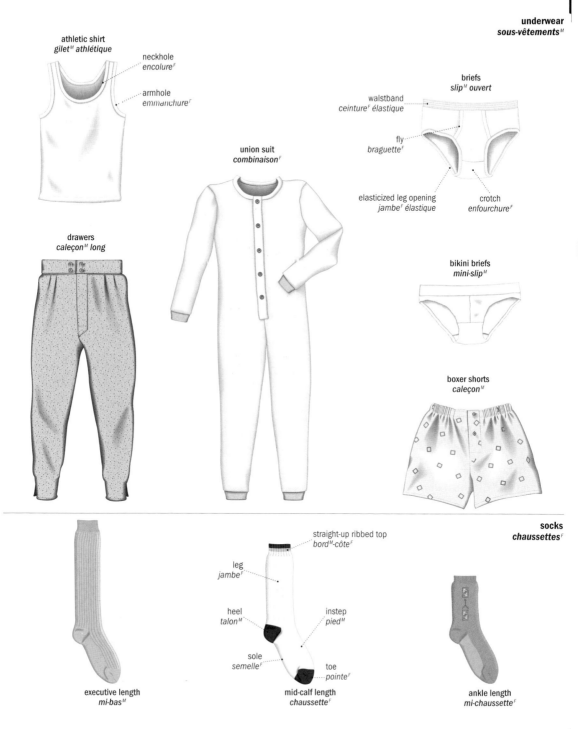

**underwear**
*sous-vêtements* M

athletic shirt
*gilet* M *athlétique*

neckhole
*encolure* F

armhole
*emmanchure* F

briefs
*slip* M *ouvert*

waistband
*ceinture* F *élastique*

fly
*braguette* F

union suit
*combinaison* F

elasticized leg opening
*jambe* F *élastique*

crotch
*enfourchure* F

drawers
*caleçon* M *long*

bikini briefs
*mini-slip* M

boxer shorts
*caleçon* M

**socks**
*chaussettes* F

straight-up ribbed top
*bord* M *-côte* F

leg
*jambe* F

heel
*talon* M

instep
*pied* M

sole
*semelle* F

toe
*pointe* F

executive length
*mi-bas* M

mid-calf length
*chaussette* F

ankle length
*mi-chaussette* F

**coats**
*manteaux<sup>M</sup> et blousons<sup>M</sup>*

raincoat
*imperméable<sup>M</sup>*

overcoat
*pardessus<sup>M</sup>*

collar
*col<sup>M</sup>*

raglan sleeve
*manche<sup>F</sup> raglan*

notched lapel
*revers<sup>M</sup> cranté*

tab
*patte<sup>F</sup>*

broad-welt side pocket
*poche<sup>F</sup> raglan*

buttonhole
*boutonnière<sup>F</sup>*

side panel
*pan<sup>M</sup>*

notched lapel
*revers<sup>M</sup> cranté*

breast pocket
*poche<sup>F</sup> poitrine<sup>F</sup>*

breast dart
*pince<sup>F</sup> de taille<sup>F</sup>*

flap pocket
*poche<sup>F</sup> à rabat<sup>M</sup>*

trench coat
*trench<sup>M</sup>*

three-quarter coat
*paletot<sup>M</sup>*

two-way collar
*col<sup>M</sup> transformable*

epaulet
*patte<sup>F</sup> d'épaule<sup>F</sup>*

raglan sleeve
*manche<sup>F</sup> raglan*

gun flap
*bavolet<sup>M</sup>*

sleeve strap loop
*passant<sup>M</sup>*

double-breasted buttoning
*double boutonnage<sup>M</sup>*

belt
*ceinture<sup>F</sup>*

belt loop
*passant<sup>M</sup>*

frame
*boucle<sup>F</sup> de ceinture<sup>F</sup>*

sleeve strap
*patte<sup>F</sup> de serrage<sup>M</sup>*

broad-welt side pocket
*poche<sup>F</sup> raglan*

parka
*parka*F ; *parka*M

snap-fastening tab
*patte*F *à boutons*M-*pression*F

zipper
*fermeture*F *à glissière*F

sheepskin jacket
*canadienne*F

duffle coat
*duffle-coat*M ; *corvette*F

hood
*capuchon*M

yoke
*empiècement*M

frog
*brandebourg*M

patch pocket
*poche*F *plaquée*

toggle fastening
*bûchette*F

jacket
*blouson*M *court*

snap fastener
*bouton*M-*pression*F

windbreaker
*blouson*M *long*

waistband
*ceinture*F *montée*

hand-warmer pocket
*poche*F *repose-bras*M

elastic waistband
*ceinture*F *élastique*

drawstring
*cordon*M *coulissant*

CLOTHING

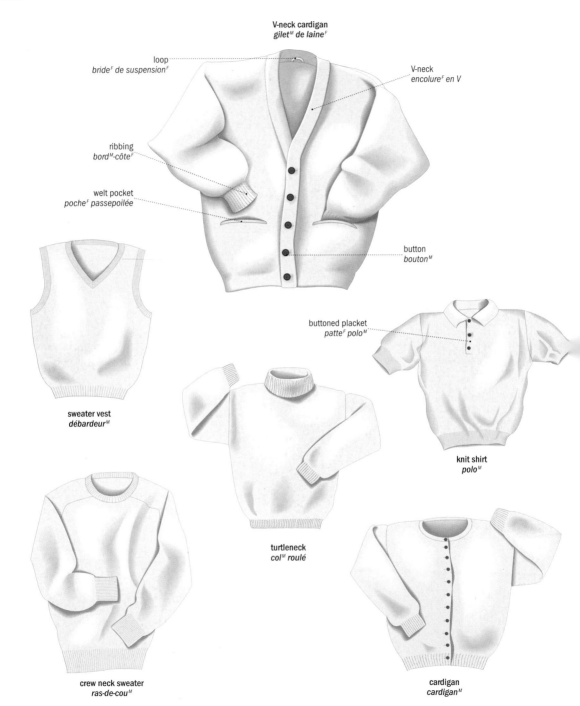

**V-neck cardigan**
*gilet<sup>M</sup> de laine<sup>F</sup>*

loop
*bride<sup>F</sup> de suspension<sup>F</sup>*

V-neck
*encolure<sup>F</sup> en V*

ribbing
*bord<sup>M</sup>-côte<sup>F</sup>*

welt pocket
*poche<sup>F</sup> passepoilée*

button
*bouton<sup>M</sup>*

buttoned placket
*patte<sup>F</sup> polo<sup>M</sup>*

**sweater vest**
*débardeur<sup>M</sup>*

**knit shirt**
*polo<sup>M</sup>*

**turtleneck**
*col<sup>M</sup> roulé*

**crew neck sweater**
*ras-de-cou<sup>M</sup>*

**cardigan**
*cardigan<sup>M</sup>*

suit
tailleur^M

jacket
veste^F

skirt
jupe^F

raglan
raglan^M

raglan sleeve
manche^F raglan

fly front closing
boutonnage^M sous patte^F

broad welt side pocket
poche^F raglan

coats
manteaux^M

top coat
redingote^F

pelerine
pèlerine^F

pelerine
pèlerine^F

seam pocket
poche^F prise dans une couture^F

cape
cape^F

arm slit
passe-bras^M

pea jacket
caban^M

tailored collar
col^M tailleur^M

hand-warmer pocket
poche^F repose-bras^M

mock pocket
fausse poche^F

overcoat
manteau^M

car coat
paletot^M

jacket
veste^F

poncho
poncho^M

CLOTHING

## examples of dresses
*exemples<sup>M</sup> de robes<sup>F</sup>*

coat dress
*robe<sup>F</sup>-manteau<sup>M</sup>*

polo dress
*robe<sup>F</sup>-polo<sup>M</sup>*

sheath dress
*robe<sup>F</sup> fourreau<sup>M</sup>*

princess-seamed dress
*robe<sup>F</sup> princesse<sup>F</sup>*

housedress
*robe<sup>F</sup> de maison<sup>F</sup>*

shirtwaist dress
*robe<sup>F</sup> chemisier<sup>M</sup>*

drop-waist dress
*robe<sup>F</sup> taille<sup>F</sup> basse*

trapeze dress
*robe<sup>F</sup> trapèze<sup>M</sup>*

sundress
*robe<sup>F</sup> bain<sup>M</sup>-de-soleil<sup>M</sup>*

wraparound dress
*robe<sup>F</sup> enveloppe<sup>F</sup>*

tunic dress
*robe<sup>F</sup> tunique<sup>F</sup>*

jumper
*chasuble<sup>F</sup>*

**examples of skirts**
*exemples<sup>M</sup> de jupes<sup>F</sup>*

gored skirt
*jupe<sup>F</sup> à lés<sup>M</sup>*

kilt
*kilt<sup>M</sup>*

sarong
*paréo<sup>M</sup>*

wraparound skirt
*jupe<sup>F</sup> portefeuille<sup>M</sup>*

sheath skirt
*jupe<sup>F</sup> fourreau<sup>M</sup>*

ruffled skirt
*jupe<sup>F</sup> à volants<sup>M</sup> étagés*

straight skirt
*jupe<sup>F</sup> droite*

yoked skirt
*jupe<sup>F</sup> à empiècement<sup>M</sup>*

gathered skirt
*jupe<sup>F</sup> froncée*

culottes
*jupe<sup>F</sup>-culotte<sup>F</sup>*

**examples of pleats**
*exemples<sup>M</sup> de plis<sup>M</sup>*

inverted pleat
*pli<sup>M</sup> creux*

kick pleat
*pli<sup>M</sup> d'aisance<sup>F</sup>*

accordion pleat
*plissé<sup>M</sup> accordéon<sup>M</sup>*

top-stitched pleat
*pli<sup>M</sup> surpiqué*

knife pleat
*pli<sup>M</sup> plat*

CLOTHING

## examples of pants
### *exemples<sup>M</sup> de pantalons<sup>M</sup>*

shorts
*short<sup>M</sup>*

Bermuda shorts
*bermuda<sup>M</sup>*

knickers
*knicker<sup>M</sup>*

pedal pushers
*corsaire<sup>M</sup>*

jeans
*jean<sup>M</sup>*

ski pants
*fuseau<sup>M</sup>*

footstrap
*sous-pied<sup>M</sup>*

jumpsuit
*combinaison<sup>F</sup>-pantalon<sup>M</sup>*

overalls
*salopette<sup>F</sup>*

bell bottoms
*pantalon<sup>M</sup> pattes<sup>F</sup> d'éléphant<sup>M</sup>*

## jackets, vest and sweaters
### *vestes<sup>F</sup> et pulls<sup>M</sup>*

bolero
*boléro<sup>M</sup>*

spencer
*spencer<sup>M</sup>*

blazer
*blazer<sup>M</sup>*

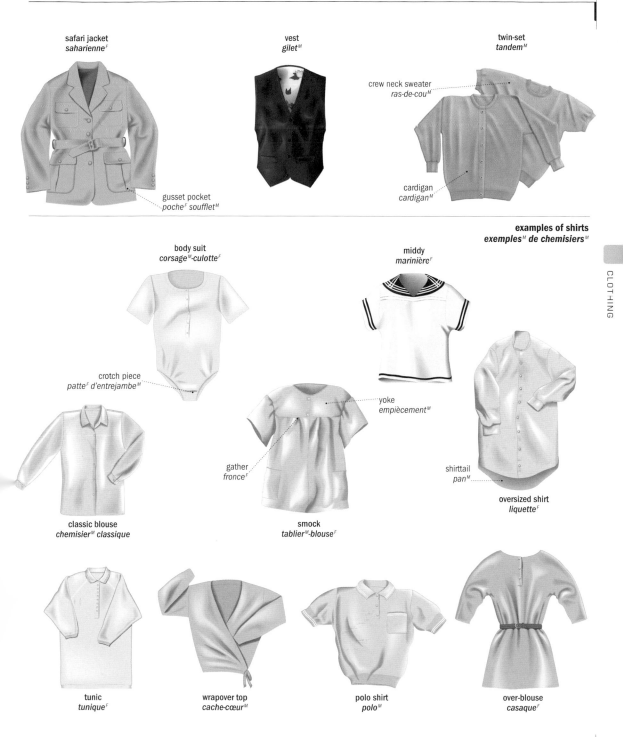

safari jacket
*saharienne*<sup>F</sup>

vest
*gilet*<sup>M</sup>

twin-set
*tandem*<sup>M</sup>

crew neck sweater
*ras-de-cou*<sup>M</sup>

cardigan
*cardigan*<sup>M</sup>

gusset pocket
*poche*<sup>F</sup> *soufflet*<sup>M</sup>

**examples of shirts**
*exemples*<sup>M</sup> *de chemisiers*<sup>M</sup>

CLOTHING

body suit
*corsage*<sup>M</sup>*-culotte*<sup>F</sup>

middy
*marinière*<sup>F</sup>

crotch piece
*patte*<sup>F</sup> *d'entrejambe*<sup>M</sup>

yoke
*empiècement*<sup>M</sup>

gather
*fronce*<sup>F</sup>

shirttail
*pan*<sup>M</sup>

oversized shirt
*liquette*<sup>F</sup>

classic blouse
*chemisier*<sup>M</sup> *classique*

smock
*tablier*<sup>M</sup>*-blouse*<sup>F</sup>

tunic
*tunique*<sup>F</sup>

wrapover top
*cache-cœur*<sup>M</sup>

polo shirt
*polo*<sup>M</sup>

over-blouse
*casaque*<sup>F</sup>

**nightwear**
*vêtements*<sup>M</sup> *de nuit*<sup>F</sup>

kimono
*kimono*<sup>M</sup>

nightgown
*chemise*<sup>F</sup> *de nuit*<sup>F</sup>

baby doll
*nuisette*<sup>F</sup>

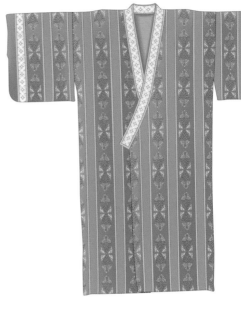

pajamas
*pyjama*<sup>M</sup>

negligee
*déshabillé*<sup>M</sup>

bathrobe
*peignoir*<sup>M</sup>

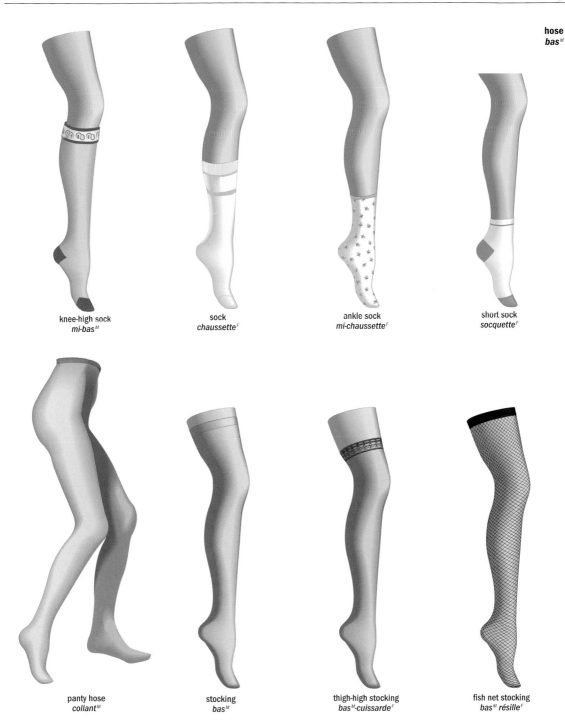

knee-high sock
*mi-bas*<sup>M</sup>

sock
*chaussette*<sup>F</sup>

ankle sock
*mi-chaussette*<sup>F</sup>

short sock
*socquette*<sup>F</sup>

panty hose
*collant*<sup>M</sup>

stocking
*bas*<sup>M</sup>

thigh-high stocking
*bas*<sup>M</sup>-*cuissarde*<sup>F</sup>

fish net stocking
*bas*<sup>M</sup> *résille*<sup>F</sup>

CLOTHING

**underwear**
*sous-vêtements*<sup>M</sup>

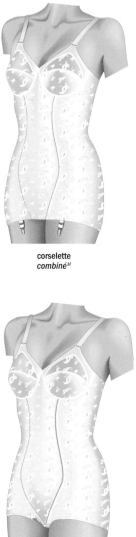

corselette
*combiné*<sup>M</sup>

camisole
*caraco*<sup>M</sup> ; *camisole*<sup>F</sup>

teddy
*teddy*<sup>M</sup> ; *combinaison*<sup>F</sup>-
*culotte*<sup>F</sup>

body suit
*body*<sup>M</sup> ; *combiné-slip*<sup>M</sup>

panty corselette
*combiné*<sup>M</sup>-*culotte*<sup>F</sup>

half-slip
*jupon*<sup>M</sup>

princess seams
*découpe*<sup>F</sup> *princesse*<sup>F</sup>

foundation slip
*fond*<sup>M</sup> *de robe*<sup>F</sup>

slip
*combinaison*<sup>F</sup>-*jupon*<sup>M</sup>

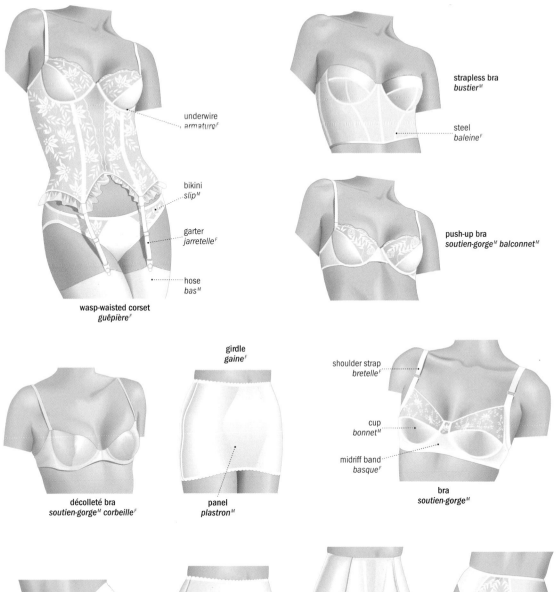

underwire
*armature*[F]

strapless bra
*bustier*[M]

steel
*baleine*[F]

bikini
*slip*[M]

push-up bra
*soutien-gorge*[M] *balconnet*[M]

garter
*jarretelle*[F]

hose
*bas*[M]

**wasp-waisted corset**
*guêpière*[F]

girdle
*gaine*[F]

shoulder strap
*bretelle*[F]

cup
*bonnet*[M]

midriff band
*basque*[F]

**décolleté bra**
*soutien-gorge*[M] *corbeille*[F]

**panel**
*plastron*[M]

**bra**
*soutien-gorge*[M]

**briefs**
*culotte*[F]

**panty girdle**
*gaine*[F]-*culotte*[F]

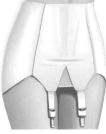

**corset**
*corset*[M]

**garter belt**
*porte-jarretelles*[M]

CLOTHING

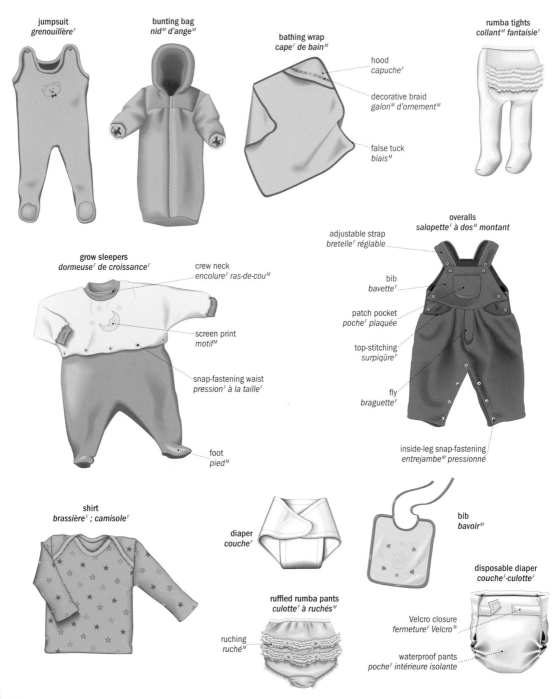

jumpsuit
grenouillère<sup>F</sup>

bunting bag
nid<sup>M</sup> d'ange<sup>M</sup>

bathing wrap
cape<sup>F</sup> de bain<sup>M</sup>

hood
capuche<sup>F</sup>

decorative braid
galon<sup>M</sup> d'ornement<sup>M</sup>

false tuck
biais<sup>M</sup>

rumba tights
collant<sup>M</sup> fantaisie<sup>F</sup>

overalls
salopette<sup>F</sup> à dos<sup>M</sup> montant

adjustable strap
bretelle<sup>F</sup> réglable

grow sleepers
dormeuse<sup>F</sup> de croissance<sup>F</sup>

crew neck
encolure<sup>F</sup> ras-de-cou<sup>M</sup>

bib
bavette<sup>F</sup>

patch pocket
poche<sup>F</sup> plaquée

screen print
motif<sup>M</sup>

top-stitching
surpiqûre<sup>F</sup>

snap-fastening waist
pression<sup>F</sup> à la taille<sup>F</sup>

fly
braguette<sup>F</sup>

foot
pied<sup>M</sup>

inside-leg snap-fastening
entrejambe<sup>M</sup> pressionné

shirt
brassière<sup>F</sup> ; camisole<sup>F</sup>

diaper
couche<sup>F</sup>

bib
bavoir<sup>M</sup>

disposable diaper
couche<sup>F</sup>-culotte<sup>F</sup>

ruffled rumba pants
culotte<sup>F</sup> à ruchés<sup>M</sup>

Velcro closure
fermeture<sup>F</sup> Velcro<sup>®</sup>

ruching
ruché<sup>M</sup>

waterproof pants
poche<sup>F</sup> intérieure isolante

**blanket sleepers**
*dormeuse*F*-couverture*F

ribbing
*bord*M*-côte*F

snap-fastening front
*pression*F *devant*

zipper
*fermeture*F *à glissière*F

vinyl grip sole
*semelle*F *antidérapante*

**sleepers**
*combinaison*F *de nuit*F *;*
*dormeuse*F

raglan sleeve
*manche*F *raglan*

ribbing
*bord*M*-côte*F

screen print
*motif*M

inside-leg snap-fastening
*entrejambe*M *pressionné*

# children's clothing
*vêtements*M *d'enfant*M

CLOTHING

**overalls**
*salopette*F *à bretelles*F *croisées*

button strap
*bretelle*F *boutonnée*

bib
*bavette*F

**snowsuit**
*esquimau*M

drawstring hood
*capuche*F *coulissée*

fly front closing
*fermeture*F *sous patte*F

**pajama**
*polojama*M

**T-shirt dress**
*robe*F *tee-shirt*M

**rompers**
*barboteuse*F

**training set**
*tenue*F *d'exercice*M

tank top
*débardeur*M

shorts
*short*M

**jumpsuit**
*combinaison*F

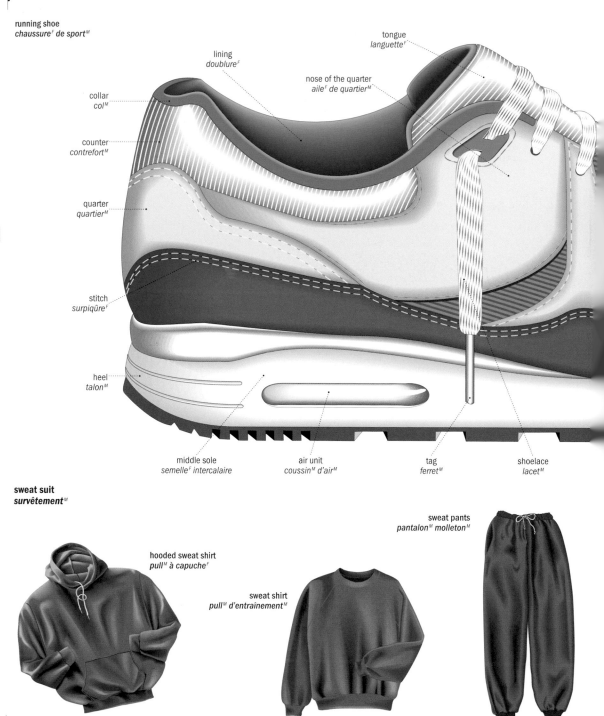

## running shoe
*chaussure<sup>F</sup> de sport<sup>M</sup>*

tongue
*languette<sup>F</sup>*

lining
*doublure<sup>F</sup>*

nose of the quarter
*aile<sup>F</sup> de quartier<sup>M</sup>*

collar
*col<sup>M</sup>*

counter
*contrefort<sup>M</sup>*

quarter
*quartier<sup>M</sup>*

stitch
*surpiqûre<sup>F</sup>*

heel
*talon<sup>M</sup>*

middle sole
*semelle<sup>F</sup> intercalaire*

air unit
*coussin<sup>M</sup> d'air<sup>M</sup>*

tag
*ferret<sup>M</sup>*

shoelace
*lacet<sup>M</sup>*

## sweat suit
*survêtement<sup>M</sup>*

sweat pants
*pantalon<sup>M</sup> molleton<sup>M</sup>*

hooded sweat shirt
*pull<sup>M</sup> à capuche<sup>F</sup>*

sweat shirt
*pull<sup>M</sup> d'entraînement<sup>M</sup>*

CLOTHING

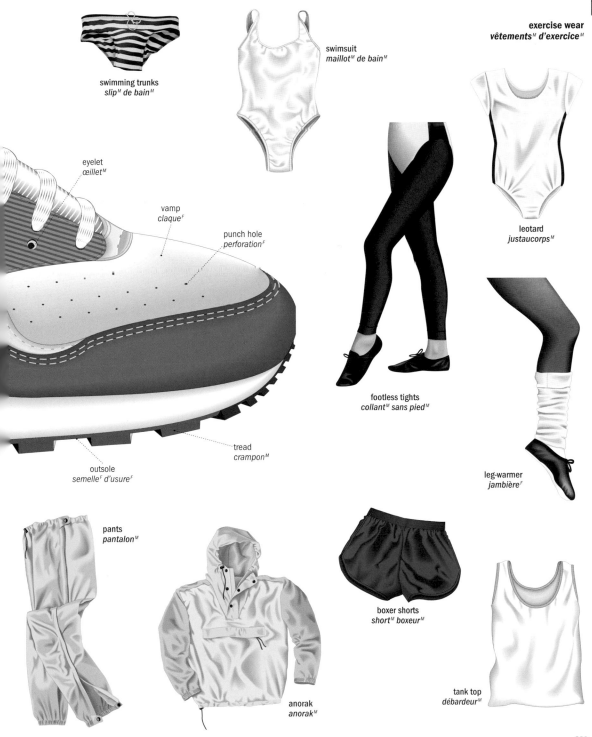

swimming trunks
*slip*<sup>M</sup> *de bain*<sup>M</sup>

swimsuit
*maillot*<sup>M</sup> *de bain*<sup>M</sup>

**exercise wear**
***vêtements*<sup>M</sup> *d'exercice*<sup>M</sup>**

eyelet
*œillet*<sup>M</sup>

vamp
*claque*<sup>F</sup>

punch hole
*perforation*<sup>F</sup>

leotard
*justaucorps*<sup>M</sup>

CLOTHING

footless tights
*collant*<sup>M</sup> *sans pied*<sup>M</sup>

tread
*crampon*<sup>M</sup>

outsole
*semelle*<sup>F</sup> *d'usure*<sup>F</sup>

leg-warmer
*jambière*<sup>F</sup>

pants
*pantalon*<sup>M</sup>

boxer shorts
*short*<sup>M</sup> *boxeur*<sup>M</sup>

anorak
*anorak*<sup>M</sup>

tank top
*débardeur*<sup>M</sup>

# jewelry
*bijouterie*<sup>F</sup>

## earrings
*boucles*<sup>F</sup> *d'oreille*<sup>F</sup>

clip earrings
*boucles*<sup>F</sup> *d'oreille*<sup>F</sup> *à pince*<sup>F</sup>

screw earring
*boucles*<sup>F</sup> *d'oreille*<sup>F</sup> *à vis*<sup>F</sup>

pierced earrings
*boucles*<sup>F</sup> *d'oreille*<sup>F</sup> *à tige*<sup>F</sup>

drop earrings
*pendants*<sup>M</sup> *d'oreille*<sup>F</sup>

hoop earrings
*anneaux*<sup>M</sup>

## necklaces
*colliers*<sup>M</sup>

matinee-length necklace
*collier*<sup>M</sup> *de perles*<sup>F</sup>, *longueur*<sup>F</sup> *matinée*<sup>F</sup>

velvet-band choker
*collier*<sup>M</sup>-*de-chien*<sup>M</sup>

pendant
*pendentif*<sup>M</sup>

rope necklace
*sautoir*<sup>M</sup>

opera-length necklace
*sautoir*<sup>M</sup>, *longueur*<sup>F</sup> *opéra*<sup>M</sup>

bib necklace
*collier*<sup>M</sup> *de soirée*<sup>F</sup>

choker
*ras-de-cou*<sup>M</sup>

locket
*médaillon*<sup>M</sup>

## bracelets
*bracelets*<sup>M</sup>

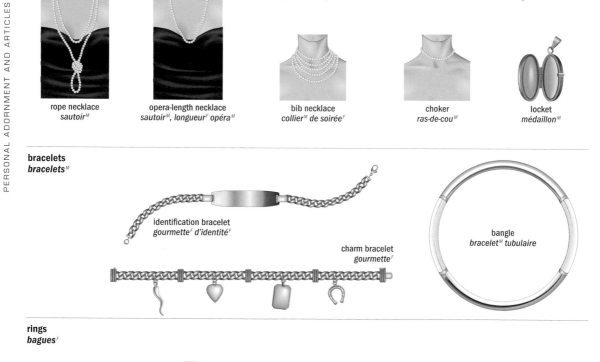

identification bracelet
*gourmette*<sup>F</sup> *d'identité*<sup>F</sup>

charm bracelet
*gourmette*<sup>F</sup>

bangle
*bracelet*<sup>M</sup> *tubulaire*

## rings
*bagues*<sup>F</sup>

band ring
*jonc*<sup>M</sup>

signet ring
*chevalière*<sup>F</sup>

solitaire ring
*bague*<sup>F</sup> *solitaire*<sup>M</sup>

engagement ring
*bague*<sup>F</sup> *de fiançailles*<sup>F</sup>

wedding ring
*alliance*<sup>F</sup>

# nail care
manucure[F]

manicure set
*trousse[F] de manucure[F]*

cuticle pusher
*repousse-chair[M]*

cuticle trimmer
*coupe-cuticules[M]*

nail shaper
*gratte-ongles[M]*

nail file
*lime[F] à ongles[M]*

nail scissors
*ciseaux[M] à ongles[M]*

cuticle nippers
*pince[F] à cuticules[F]*

eyebrow tweezers
*pince[F] à épiler*

case
*étui[M]*

zipper
*fermeture[F] à glissière[F]*

cuticle scissors
*ciseaux[M] à cuticules[F]*

strap
*bride[F]*

nail enamel
*vernis[M] à ongles[M]*

safety scissors
*ciseaux[M] de sûreté[F]*

nail buffer
*polissoir[M] d'ongles[M]*

nail clippers
*coupe-ongles[M]*

lever
*levier[M]*

nail cleaner
*cure-ongles[M]*

chamois leather
*peau[F] de chamois[M]*

jaw
*mors[M]*

folding nail file
*lime[F]*

nail whitener pencil
*crayon[M] blanchisseur d'ongles[M]*

emery boards
*limes[F]-émeri[M]*

toenail scissors
*ciseaux[M] de pédicure[F]*

PERSONAL ADORNMENT AND ARTICLES

# makeup

maquillage*M*

### facial makeup
*maquillage*<sup>M</sup>

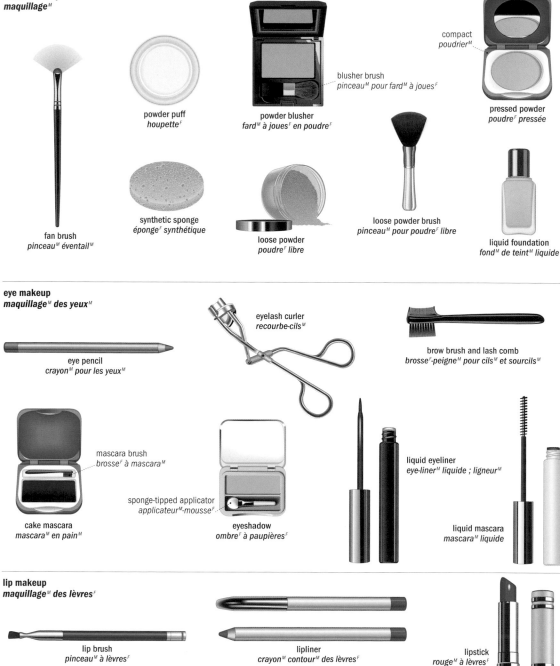

fan brush
*pinceau*<sup>M</sup> *éventail*<sup>M</sup>

powder puff
*houpette*<sup>F</sup>

synthetic sponge
*éponge*<sup>F</sup> *synthétique*

powder blusher
*fard*<sup>M</sup> *à joues*<sup>F</sup> *en poudre*<sup>F</sup>

blusher brush
*pinceau*<sup>M</sup> *pour fard*<sup>M</sup> *à joues*<sup>F</sup>

loose powder
*poudre*<sup>F</sup> *libre*

loose powder brush
*pinceau*<sup>M</sup> *pour poudre*<sup>F</sup> *libre*

compact
*poudrier*<sup>M</sup>

pressed powder
*poudre*<sup>F</sup> *pressée*

liquid foundation
*fond*<sup>M</sup> *de teint*<sup>M</sup> *liquide*

### eye makeup
*maquillage*<sup>M</sup> *des yeux*<sup>M</sup>

eye pencil
*crayon*<sup>M</sup> *pour les yeux*<sup>M</sup>

eyelash curler
*recourbe-cils*<sup>M</sup>

brow brush and lash comb
*brosse*<sup>F</sup>-*peigne*<sup>M</sup> *pour cils*<sup>M</sup> *et sourcils*<sup>M</sup>

mascara brush
*brosse*<sup>F</sup> *à mascara*<sup>M</sup>

sponge-tipped applicator
*applicateur*<sup>M</sup>-*mousse*<sup>F</sup>

cake mascara
*mascara*<sup>M</sup> *en pain*<sup>M</sup>

eyeshadow
*ombre*<sup>F</sup> *à paupières*<sup>F</sup>

liquid eyeliner
*eye-liner*<sup>M</sup> *liquide ; ligneur*<sup>M</sup>

liquid mascara
*mascara*<sup>M</sup> *liquide*

### lip makeup
*maquillage*<sup>M</sup> *des lèvres*<sup>F</sup>

lip brush
*pinceau*<sup>M</sup> *à lèvres*<sup>F</sup>

lipliner
*crayon*<sup>M</sup> *contour*<sup>M</sup> *des lèvres*<sup>F</sup>

lipstick
*rouge*<sup>M</sup> *à lèvres*<sup>F</sup>

PERSONAL ADORNMENT AND ARTICLES

# body care
soins<sup>M</sup> du corps<sup>M</sup>

stopper
bouchon<sup>M</sup>

bottle
flacon<sup>M</sup>

eau de parfum
eau<sup>F</sup> de parfum<sup>M</sup>

toilet soap
savon<sup>M</sup> de toilette<sup>F</sup>

hair conditioner
revitalisant<sup>M</sup> capillaire

shampoo
shampooing<sup>M</sup>

haircolor
colorant<sup>M</sup> capillaire

deodorant
déodorant<sup>M</sup>

eau de toilette
eau<sup>F</sup> de toilette<sup>F</sup>

bubble bath
bain<sup>M</sup> moussant

washcloth
gant<sup>M</sup> de toilette<sup>F</sup>

washcloth
débarbouillette<sup>F</sup>

massage glove
gant<sup>M</sup> de crin<sup>M</sup>

vegetable sponge
éponge<sup>F</sup> végétale

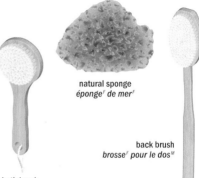

natural sponge
éponge<sup>F</sup> de mer<sup>F</sup>

back brush
brosse<sup>F</sup> pour le dos<sup>M</sup>

bath sheet
drap<sup>M</sup> de bain<sup>M</sup>

bath towel
serviette<sup>F</sup> de toilette<sup>F</sup>

bath brush
brosse<sup>F</sup> pour le bain<sup>M</sup>

# hairdressing

coiffure<sup>F</sup>

## hairbrushes
*brosses<sup>F</sup> à cheveux<sup>M</sup>*

flat-back brush
*brosse<sup>F</sup> pneumatique*

round brush
*brosse<sup>F</sup> ronde*

quill brush
*brosse<sup>F</sup> anglaise*

vent brush
*brosse<sup>F</sup>-araignée<sup>F</sup>*

## combs
*peignes<sup>M</sup>*

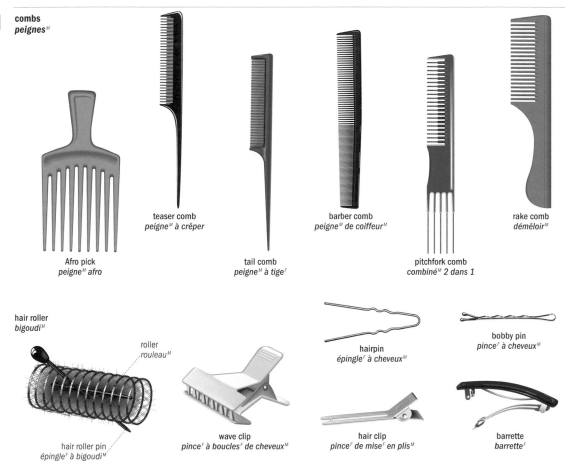

teaser comb
*peigne<sup>M</sup> à crêper*

barber comb
*peigne<sup>M</sup> de coiffeur<sup>M</sup>*

rake comb
*démêloir<sup>M</sup>*

Afro pick
*peigne<sup>M</sup> afro*

tail comb
*peigne<sup>M</sup> à tige<sup>F</sup>*

pitchfork comb
*combiné<sup>M</sup> 2 dans 1*

hair roller
*bigoudi<sup>M</sup>*

roller
*rouleau<sup>M</sup>*

hairpin
*épingle<sup>F</sup> à cheveux<sup>M</sup>*

bobby pin
*pince<sup>F</sup> à cheveux<sup>M</sup>*

hair roller pin
*épingle<sup>F</sup> à bigoudi<sup>M</sup>*

wave clip
*pince<sup>F</sup> à boucles<sup>F</sup> de cheveux<sup>M</sup>*

hair clip
*pince<sup>F</sup> de mise<sup>F</sup> en plis<sup>M</sup>*

barrette
*barrette<sup>F</sup>*

hairdressing

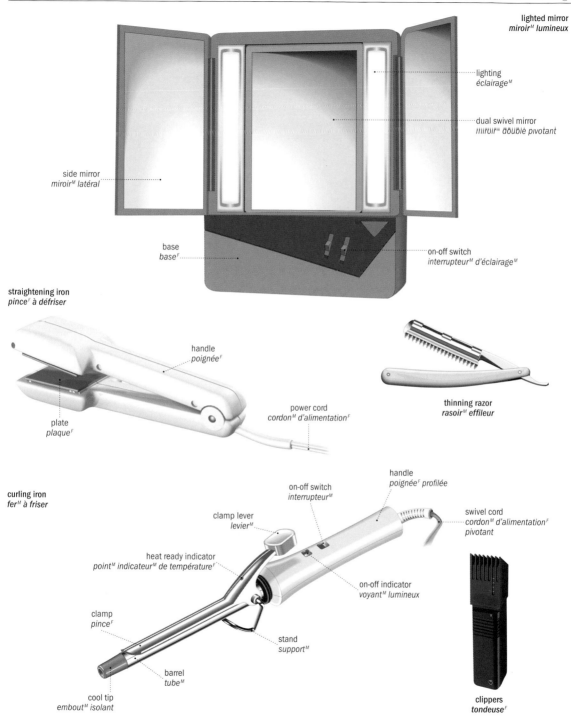

lighted mirror
*miroir^M lumineux*

lighting
*éclairage^M*

dual swivel mirror
*miroir^M double pivotant*

side mirror
*miroir^M latéral*

base
*base^F*

on-off switch
*interrupteur^M d'éclairage^M*

straightening iron
*pince^F à défriser*

handle
*poignée^F*

power cord
*cordon^M d'alimentation^F*

plate
*plaque^F*

thinning razor
*rasoir^M effileur*

curling iron
*fer^M à friser*

handle
*poignée^F profilée*

on-off switch
*interrupteur^M*

swivel cord
*cordon^M d'alimentation^F*
*pivotant*

clamp lever
*levier^M*

heat ready indicator
*point^M indicateur^M de température^F*

on-off indicator
*voyant^M lumineux*

clamp
*pince^F*

stand
*support^M*

barrel
*tube^M*

cool tip
*embout^M isolant*

clippers
*tondeuse^F*

PERSONAL ADORNMENT AND ARTICLES

**haircutting scissors**
*ciseaux*<sup>M</sup> *de coiffeur*<sup>M</sup>

ringhandle
*anneau*<sup>M</sup>

pivot
*pivot*<sup>M</sup>

cutting edge
*tranchant*<sup>M</sup>

blade
*lame*<sup>F</sup>

blade close stop
*amortisseur*<sup>M</sup>

shank
*branche*<sup>F</sup>

**notched single-edged thinning scissors**
*ciseaux*<sup>M</sup> *sculpteurs*

**notched double-edged thinning scissors**
*ciseaux*<sup>M</sup> *à effiler*

notched edge
*lame*<sup>F</sup> *dentée*

blade
*lame*<sup>F</sup> *droite*

tooth
*dent*<sup>F</sup>

**hair dryer**
*sèche-cheveux*<sup>M</sup>

fan housing
*boîtier*<sup>M</sup> *du ventilateur*<sup>M</sup>

barrel
*corps*<sup>M</sup>

air-inlet grille
*grille*<sup>F</sup> *d'aspiration*<sup>F</sup>

air-outlet grille
*grille*<sup>F</sup> *de sortie*<sup>F</sup> *d'air*<sup>M</sup>

speed selector switch
*sélecteur*<sup>M</sup> *de vitesse*<sup>F</sup>

on-off switch
*interrupteur*<sup>M</sup>

heat selector switch
*sélecteur*<sup>M</sup> *de température*<sup>F</sup>

hang-up ring
*anneau*<sup>M</sup> *de suspension*<sup>F</sup>

air concentrator
*buse*<sup>F</sup>

handle
*poignée*<sup>F</sup>

power supply cord
*cordon*<sup>M</sup> *d'alimentation*<sup>F</sup>

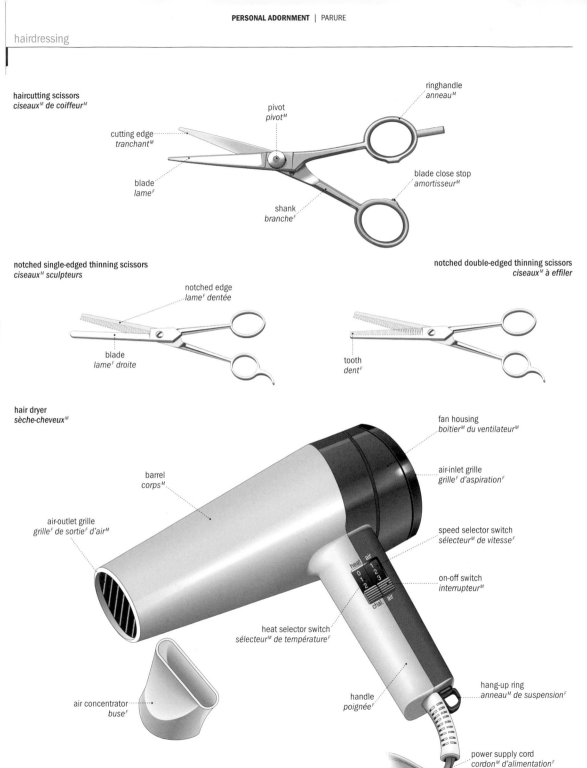

# shaving

rasage<sup>M</sup>

electric razor
rasoir<sup>M</sup> électrique

floating head
tête<sup>F</sup> flottante

trimmer
tondeuse<sup>F</sup>

screen
grille<sup>F</sup>

closeness setting
sélecteur<sup>M</sup> de coupe<sup>F</sup>

cleaning brush
brosse<sup>F</sup> de nettoyage<sup>M</sup>

housing
boitier<sup>M</sup>

charge indicator
indicateur<sup>M</sup> de charge<sup>F</sup>

charging light
voyant<sup>M</sup> de charge<sup>F</sup>

shaving foam
mousse<sup>F</sup> à raser

power cord
cordon<sup>M</sup> d'alimentation<sup>F</sup>

on-off switch
interrupteur<sup>M</sup>

charging plug
prise<sup>F</sup> de charge<sup>F</sup>

shaving brush
blaireau<sup>M</sup>

plug adapter
adaptateur<sup>M</sup> de fiche<sup>F</sup>

straight razor
rasoir<sup>M</sup> à manche<sup>M</sup>

blade
lame<sup>F</sup>

bristle
soie<sup>F</sup>

aftershave
après-rasage<sup>M</sup>

handle
manche<sup>M</sup>

pivot
pivot<sup>M</sup>

double-edged razor
rasoir<sup>M</sup> à double
tranchant<sup>M</sup>

disposable razor
rasoir<sup>M</sup> jetable

blade injector
distributeur<sup>M</sup> de lames<sup>F</sup>

head
tête<sup>F</sup>

collar
anneau<sup>M</sup>

shaving mug
bol<sup>M</sup> à raser

double-edged blade
lame<sup>F</sup> à double tranchant<sup>M</sup>

handle
manche<sup>M</sup>

PERSONAL ADORNMENT AND ARTICLES

# dental care

hygiène<sup>F</sup> dentaire

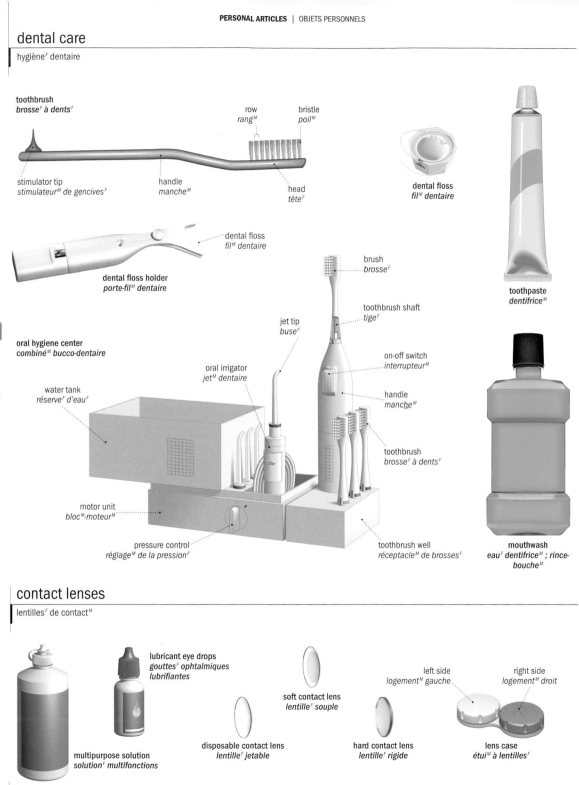

**toothbrush**
*brosse<sup>F</sup> à dents<sup>F</sup>*

row
*rang<sup>M</sup>*

bristle
*poil<sup>M</sup>*

stimulator tip
*stimulateur<sup>M</sup> de gencives<sup>F</sup>*

handle
*manche<sup>M</sup>*

head
*tête<sup>F</sup>*

dental floss
*fil<sup>M</sup> dentaire*

**dental floss**
*fil<sup>M</sup> dentaire*

**dental floss holder**
*porte-fil<sup>M</sup> dentaire*

brush
*brosse<sup>F</sup>*

toothbrush shaft
*tige<sup>F</sup>*

jet tip
*buse<sup>F</sup>*

on-off switch
*interrupteur<sup>M</sup>*

**oral hygiene center**
*combiné<sup>M</sup> bucco-dentaire*

oral irrigator
*jet<sup>M</sup> dentaire*

handle
*manche<sup>M</sup>*

water tank
*réserve<sup>F</sup> d'eau<sup>F</sup>*

toothbrush
*brosse<sup>F</sup> à dents<sup>F</sup>*

motor unit
*bloc<sup>M</sup>-moteur<sup>M</sup>*

pressure control
*réglage<sup>M</sup> de la pression<sup>F</sup>*

toothbrush well
*réceptacle<sup>M</sup> de brosses<sup>F</sup>*

**toothpaste**
*dentifrice<sup>M</sup>*

**mouthwash**
*eau<sup>F</sup> dentifrice<sup>M</sup> ; rince-bouche<sup>M</sup>*

# contact lenses

lentilles<sup>F</sup> de contact<sup>M</sup>

lubricant eye drops
*gouttes<sup>F</sup> ophtalmiques lubrifiantes*

left side
*logement<sup>M</sup> gauche*

right side
*logement<sup>M</sup> droit*

soft contact lens
*lentille<sup>F</sup> souple*

**multipurpose solution**
*solution<sup>F</sup> multifonctions*

disposable contact lens
*lentille<sup>F</sup> jetable*

hard contact lens
*lentille<sup>F</sup> rigide*

**lens case**
*étui<sup>M</sup> à lentilles<sup>F</sup>*

PERSONAL ADORNMENT AND ARTICLES

# eyeglasses

lunettes[F]

## eyeglasses parts
*parties[F] des lunettes[F]*

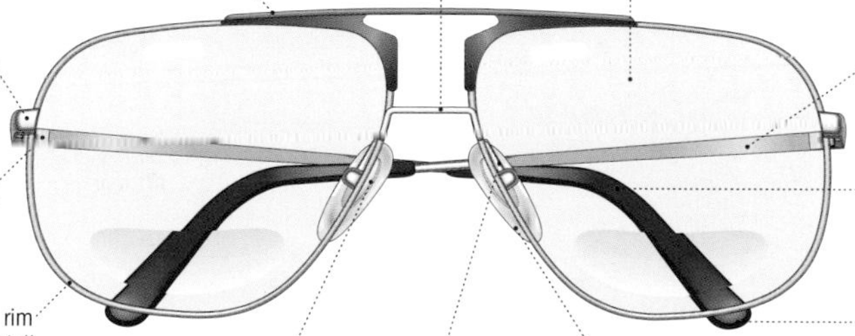

bar
*barre[F]*

bridge
*pont[M]*

glass lens
*verre[M]*

endpiece
*tenon[M]*

tcmple
*branche[F]*

butt-strap
*talon[M]*

bend
*coude[M]*

rim
*cercle[M]*

earpiece
*cambre[F]*

pad plate
*support[M] de plaquette[F]*

pad arm
*bras[M] de plaquette[F]*

nose pad
*plaquette[F]*

## examples of eyeglasses
*exemples[M] de lunettes[F]*

opera glasses
*lorgnette[F]*

sunglasses
*lunettes[F] de soleil[M]*

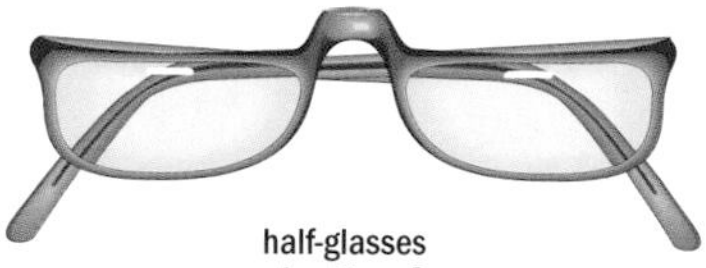

half-glasses
*demi-lune[F]*

# umbrellas and stick

parapluies[M] et canne[F]

umbrellas
*parapluies[M]*

umbrella stand
*porte-parapluies[M]*

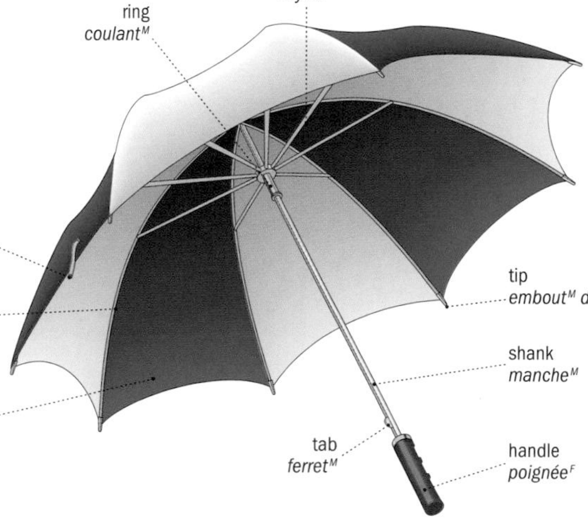

spreader
*rayon[M]*

ring
*coulant[M]*

tie
*attache[F]*

tip
*embout[M] de baleine[F]*

rib
*baleine[F]*

shank
*manche[M]*

walking stick
*canne[F]*

canopy
*toile[F]*

tab
*ferret[M]*

handle
*poignée[F]*

# leather goods

articles*M* de maroquinerie*F*

**attaché case**
*mallette*F *porte-documents*M

clasp
*fermoir*M

divider
*séparation*F*-classeur*M

expandable file pouch
*classeur*M *à soufflets*M

pocket
*pochette*F

pen holder
*porte-stylo*M

hinge
*charnière*F

lining
*doublure*F

frame
*cadre*M

handle
*poignée*F

combination lock
*serrure*F *à combinaison*F

**bottom-fold portfolio**
*porte-documents*M *à soufflet*M

**briefcase**
*serviette*F

retractable handle
*poignée*F *rentrante*

exterior pocket
*poche*F *extérieure*

tab
*patte*F

key lock
*serrure*F *à clé*F

gusset
*soufflet*M

**checkbook/secretary clutch**
*portefeuille*M *chéquier*M

**card case**
*porte-cartes*M

trimming
*grébiche*F

card case
*porte-cartes*M

bill compartment
*poche*F *américaine*

windows
*feuillets*M

calculator
*calculette*F

pen holder
*porte-stylo*M

tab
*patte*F

hidden pocket
*poche*F *secrète*

checkbook
*chéquier*M

slot
*fente*F

window
*volet*M *transparent*

leather goods

wallet
*portefeuille* <sup>M</sup>

coin purse
*porte-monnaie* <sup>M</sup>

key case
*porte-clés* <sup>M</sup>

purse
*bourse* <sup>F</sup> *à monnaie* <sup>F</sup>

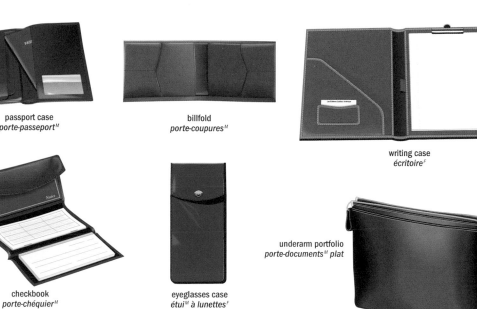

passport case
*porte-passeport* <sup>M</sup>

billfold
*porte-coupures* <sup>M</sup>

writing case
*écritoire* <sup>F</sup>

underarm portfolio
*porte-documents* <sup>M</sup> *plat*

checkbook
*porte-chéquier* <sup>M</sup>

eyeglasses case
*étui* <sup>M</sup> *à lunettes* <sup>F</sup>

PERSONAL ADORNMENT AND ARTICLES

# handbags

sacs <sup>M</sup> à main <sup>F</sup>

drawstring bag
*sac* <sup>M</sup> *seau* <sup>M</sup>

satchel bag
*sac* <sup>M</sup> *cartable* <sup>M</sup>

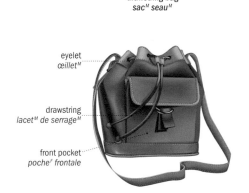

eyelet
*œillet* <sup>M</sup>

drawstring
*lacet* <sup>M</sup> *de serrage* <sup>M</sup>

front pocket
*poche* <sup>F</sup> *frontale*

handle
*poignée* <sup>F</sup>

flap
*rabat* <sup>M</sup>

clasp
*fermoir* <sup>M</sup>

lock
*serrure* <sup>F</sup>

## handbags

**box bag**
*sac*$^M$ *boîte*$^F$

**drawstring bag**
*balluchon*$^M$

shoulder bag
*sac*$^M$ *à bandoulière*$^F$

buckle
*boucle*$^F$

shoulder strap
*bandoulière*$^F$

**muff**
*manchon*$^M$

**hobo bag**
*sac*$^M$ *besace*$^F$

**accordion bag**
*sac*$^M$ *accordéon*$^M$

gusset
*soufflet*$^M$

**tote bag**
*sac*$^M$ *fourre-tout*$^M$

**men's bag**
*pochette*$^F$ *d'homme*$^M$

**sea bag**
*sac*$^M$ *marin*$^M$

**duffel bag**
*sac*$^M$ *polochon*$^M$

**carrier bag**
*sac*$^M$ *à provisions*$^F$

**shopping bag**
*cabas*$^M$

## luggage

bagages$^M$

**utility case**
*trousse*$^F$ *de toilette*$^F$

**carry-on bag**
*sac*$^M$ *de vol*$^M$

handle
*poignée*$^F$

**tote bag**
*sac*$^M$ *fourre-tout*$^M$

exterior pocket
*poche*$^F$ *extérieure*

shoulder strap
*bandoulière*$^F$

luggage

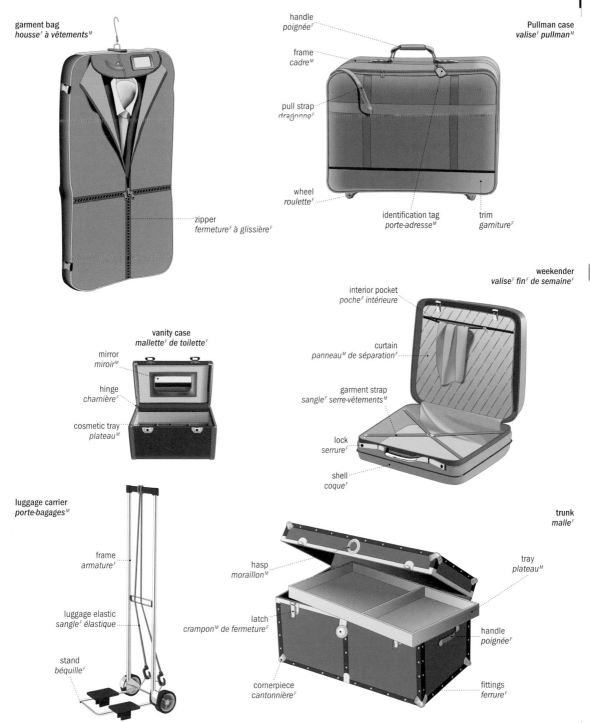

garment bag
housse<sup>F</sup> à vêtements<sup>M</sup>

handle
poignée<sup>F</sup>

Pullman case
valise<sup>F</sup> pullman<sup>M</sup>

frame
cadre<sup>M</sup>

pull strap
dragonne<sup>F</sup>

zipper
fermeture<sup>F</sup> à glissière<sup>F</sup>

wheel
roulette<sup>F</sup>

identification tag
porte-adresse<sup>M</sup>

trim
garniture<sup>F</sup>

weekender
valise<sup>F</sup> fin<sup>F</sup> de semaine<sup>F</sup>

interior pocket
poche<sup>F</sup> intérieure

vanity case
mallette<sup>F</sup> de toilette<sup>F</sup>

curtain
panneau<sup>M</sup> de séparation<sup>F</sup>

mirror
miroir<sup>M</sup>

hinge
charnière<sup>F</sup>

garment strap
sangle<sup>F</sup> serre-vêtements<sup>M</sup>

cosmetic tray
plateau<sup>M</sup>

lock
serrure<sup>F</sup>

shell
coque<sup>F</sup>

luggage carrier
porte-bagages<sup>M</sup>

trunk
malle<sup>F</sup>

frame
armature<sup>F</sup>

hasp
moraillon<sup>M</sup>

tray
plateau<sup>M</sup>

luggage elastic
sangle<sup>F</sup> élastique

latch
crampon<sup>M</sup> de fermeture<sup>F</sup>

handle
poignée<sup>F</sup>

stand
béquille<sup>F</sup>

cornerpiece
cantonnière<sup>F</sup>

fittings
ferrure<sup>F</sup>

PERSONAL ADORNMENT AND ARTICLES

# pyramid
pyramide[F]

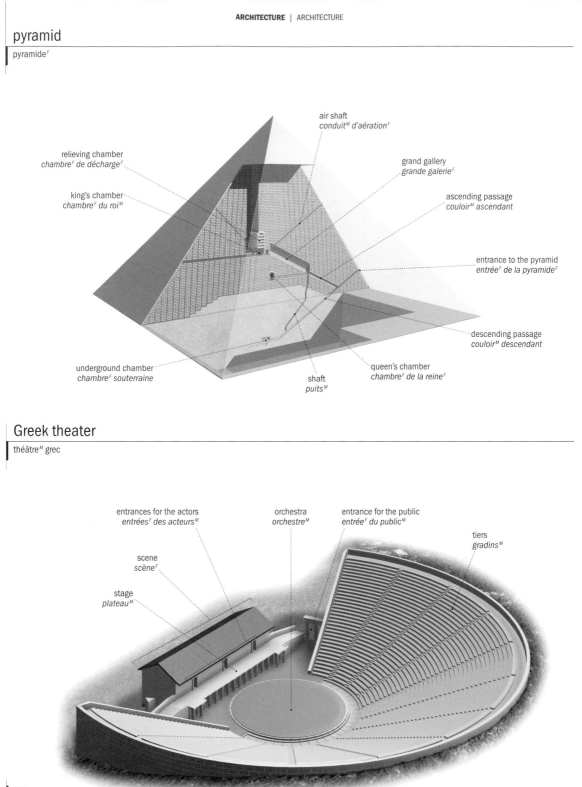

air shaft
conduit[M] d'aération[F]

relieving chamber
chambre[F] de décharge[F]

grand gallery
grande galerie[F]

king's chamber
chambre[F] du roi[M]

ascending passage
couloir[M] ascendant

entrance to the pyramid
entrée[F] de la pyramide[F]

descending passage
couloir[M] descendant

underground chamber
chambre[F] souterraine

shaft
puits[M]

queen's chamber
chambre[F] de la reine[F]

# Greek theater
théâtre[M] grec

entrances for the actors
entrées[F] des acteurs[M]

orchestra
orchestre[M]

entrance for the public
entrée[F] du public[M]

tiers
gradins[M]

scene
scène[F]

stage
plateau[M]

# Greek temple

temple<sup>M</sup> grec

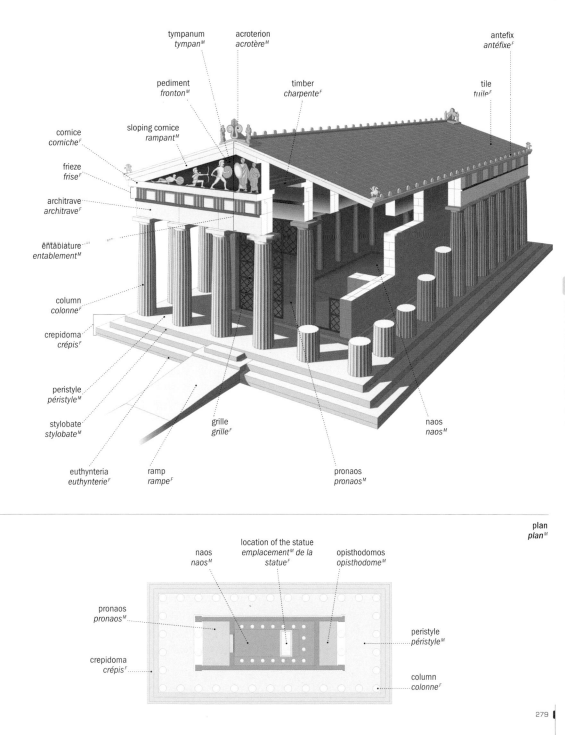

tympanum
tympan<sup>M</sup>

acroterion
acrotère<sup>M</sup>

antefix
antéfixe<sup>F</sup>

pediment
fronton<sup>M</sup>

timber
charpente<sup>F</sup>

tile
tuile<sup>F</sup>

cornice
corniche<sup>F</sup>

sloping cornice
rampant<sup>M</sup>

frieze
frise<sup>F</sup>

architrave
architrave<sup>F</sup>

entablature
entablement<sup>M</sup>

column
colonne<sup>F</sup>

crepidoma
crépis<sup>F</sup>

peristyle
péristyle<sup>M</sup>

stylobate
stylobate<sup>M</sup>

grille
grille<sup>F</sup>

naos
naos<sup>M</sup>

euthynteria
euthynterie<sup>F</sup>

ramp
rampe<sup>F</sup>

pronaos
pronaos<sup>M</sup>

plan
plan<sup>M</sup>

naos
naos<sup>M</sup>

location of the statue
emplacement<sup>M</sup> de la
statue<sup>F</sup>

opisthodomos
opisthodome<sup>M</sup>

pronaos
pronaos<sup>M</sup>

peristyle
péristyle<sup>M</sup>

crepidoma
crépis<sup>F</sup>

column
colonne<sup>F</sup>

ARTS AND ARCHITECTURE

279

# Roman house

maison<sup>F</sup> romaine

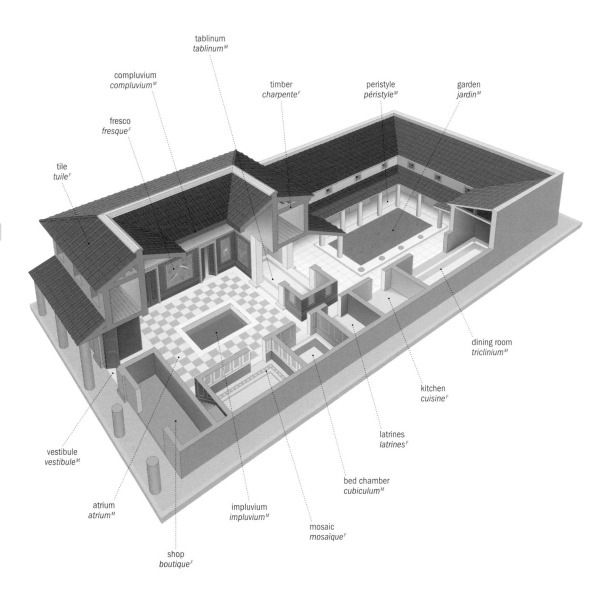

tablinum
*tablinum*<sup>M</sup>

compluvium
*compluvium*<sup>M</sup>

timber
*charpente*<sup>F</sup>

peristyle
*péristyle*<sup>M</sup>

garden
*jardin*<sup>M</sup>

fresco
*fresque*<sup>F</sup>

tile
*tuile*<sup>F</sup>

dining room
*triclinium*<sup>M</sup>

kitchen
*cuisine*<sup>F</sup>

latrines
*latrines*<sup>F</sup>

vestibule
*vestibule*<sup>M</sup>

bed chamber
*cubiculum*<sup>M</sup>

atrium
*atrium*<sup>M</sup>

impluvium
*impluvium*<sup>M</sup>

mosaic
*mosaïque*<sup>F</sup>

shop
*boutique*<sup>F</sup>

# Roman amphitheater
*amphithéâtre*<sup>M</sup> romain

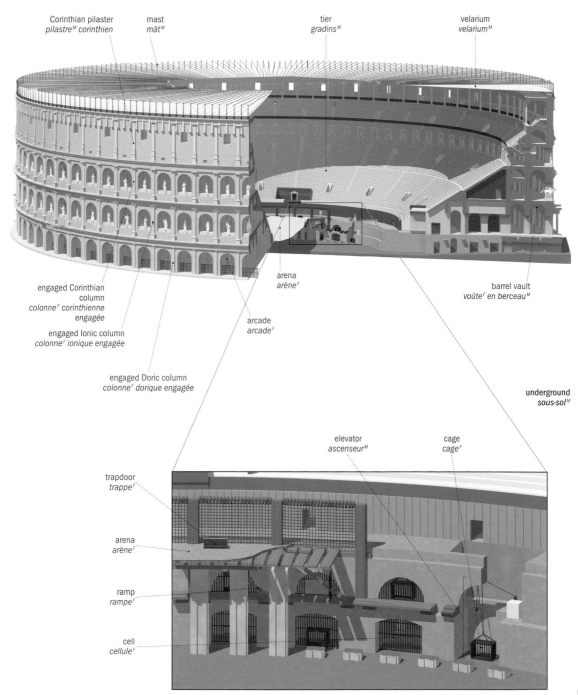

Corinthian pilaster
*pilastre*<sup>M</sup> *corinthien*

mast
*mât*<sup>M</sup>

tier
*gradins*<sup>M</sup>

velarium
*velarium*<sup>M</sup>

engaged Corinthian
column
*colonne*<sup>F</sup> *corinthienne
engagée*

engaged Ionic column
*colonne*<sup>F</sup> *ionique engagée*

engaged Doric column
*colonne*<sup>F</sup> *dorique engagée*

arena
*arène*<sup>F</sup>

arcade
*arcade*<sup>F</sup>

barrel vault
*voûte*<sup>F</sup> *en berceau*<sup>M</sup>

underground
*sous-sol*<sup>M</sup>

elevator
*ascenseur*<sup>M</sup>

cage
*cage*<sup>F</sup>

trapdoor
*trappe*<sup>F</sup>

arena
*arène*<sup>F</sup>

ramp
*rampe*<sup>F</sup>

cell
*cellule*<sup>F</sup>

# castle

château<sup>M</sup> fort

châteauᴹ fort

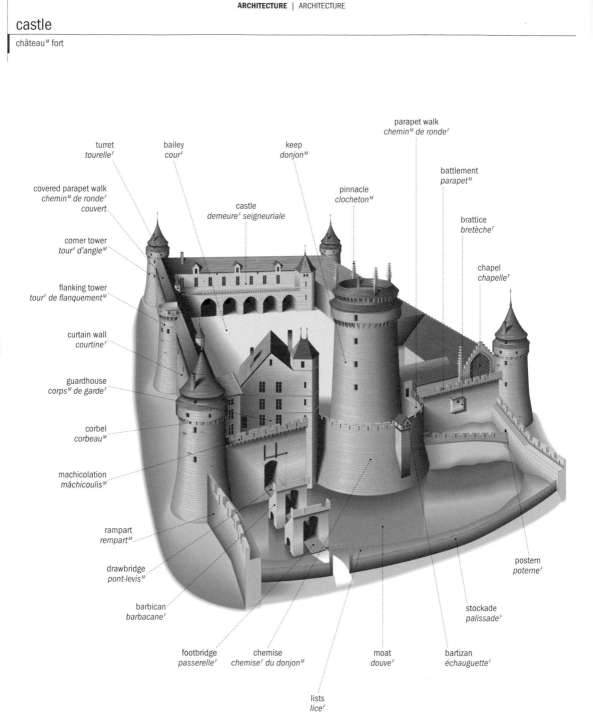

parapet walk
*chemin<sup>M</sup> de ronde<sup>F</sup>*

turret
*tourelle<sup>F</sup>*

bailey
*cour<sup>F</sup>*

keep
*donjon<sup>M</sup>*

battlement
*parapet<sup>M</sup>*

covered parapet walk
*chemin<sup>M</sup> de ronde<sup>F</sup>
couvert*

pinnacle
*clocheton<sup>M</sup>*

castle
*demeure<sup>F</sup> seigneuriale*

brattice
*bretèche<sup>F</sup>*

corner tower
*tour<sup>F</sup> d'angle<sup>M</sup>*

chapel
*chapelle<sup>F</sup>*

flanking tower
*tour<sup>F</sup> de flanquement<sup>M</sup>*

curtain wall
*courtine<sup>F</sup>*

guardhouse
*corps<sup>M</sup> de garde<sup>F</sup>*

corbel
*corbeau<sup>M</sup>*

machicolation
*mâchicoulis<sup>M</sup>*

rampart
*rempart<sup>M</sup>*

postern
*poterne<sup>F</sup>*

drawbridge
*pont-levis<sup>M</sup>*

barbican
*barbacane<sup>F</sup>*

stockade
*palissade<sup>F</sup>*

footbridge
*passerelle<sup>F</sup>*

chemise
*chemise<sup>F</sup> du donjon<sup>M</sup>*

moat
*douve<sup>F</sup>*

bartizan
*échauguette<sup>F</sup>*

lists
*lice<sup>F</sup>*

# pagoda

pagode<sup>F</sup>

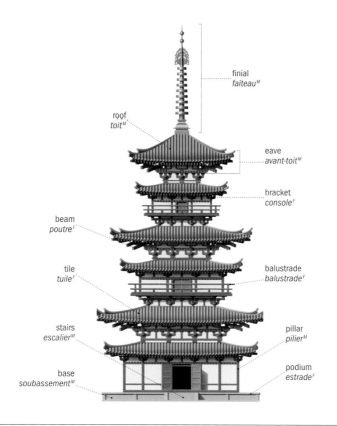

finial
faiteau<sup>M</sup>

roof
toit<sup>M</sup>

eave
avant-toit<sup>M</sup>

bracket
console<sup>F</sup>

beam
poutre<sup>F</sup>

tile
tuile<sup>F</sup>

balustrade
balustrade<sup>F</sup>

stairs
escalier<sup>M</sup>

pillar
pilier<sup>M</sup>

base
soubassement<sup>M</sup>

podium
estrade<sup>F</sup>

# Aztec temple

temple<sup>M</sup> aztèque

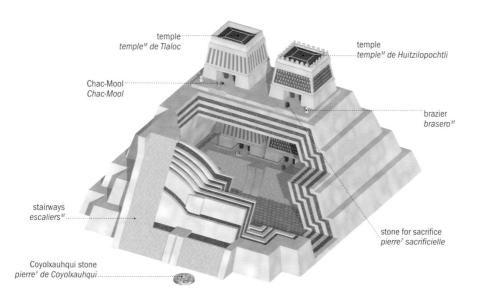

temple
temple<sup>M</sup> de Tlaloc

temple
temple<sup>M</sup> de Huitzilopochtli

Chac-Mool
Chac-Mool

brazier
brasero<sup>M</sup>

stairways
escaliers<sup>M</sup>

stone for sacrifice
pierre<sup>F</sup> sacrificielle

Coyolxauhqui stone
pierre<sup>F</sup> de Coyolxauhqui

ARTS AND ARCHITECTURE

283

# cathedral

cathédrale<sup>F</sup>

**Gothic cathedral**
*cathédrale<sup>F</sup> gothique*

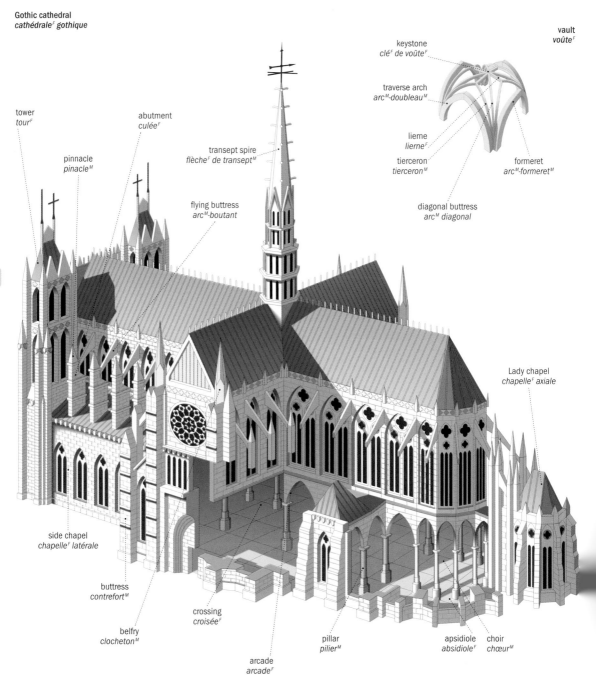

vault
*voûte<sup>F</sup>*

keystone
*clé<sup>F</sup> de voûte<sup>F</sup>*

traverse arch
*arc<sup>M</sup>-doubleau<sup>M</sup>*

lierne
*lierne<sup>F</sup>*

tierceron
*tierceron<sup>M</sup>*

formeret
*arc<sup>M</sup>-formeret<sup>M</sup>*

diagonal buttress
*arc<sup>M</sup> diagonal*

tower
*tour<sup>F</sup>*

abutment
*culée<sup>F</sup>*

transept spire
*flèche<sup>F</sup> de transept<sup>M</sup>*

pinnacle
*pinacle<sup>M</sup>*

flying buttress
*arc<sup>M</sup>-boutant*

Lady chapel
*chapelle<sup>F</sup> axiale*

side chapel
*chapelle<sup>F</sup> latérale*

buttress
*contrefort<sup>M</sup>*

crossing
*croisée<sup>F</sup>*

belfry
*clocheton<sup>M</sup>*

arcade
*arcade<sup>F</sup>*

pillar
*pilier<sup>M</sup>*

apsidiole
*absidiole<sup>F</sup>*

choir
*chœur<sup>M</sup>*

cathedral

façade
*façade*<sup>F</sup>

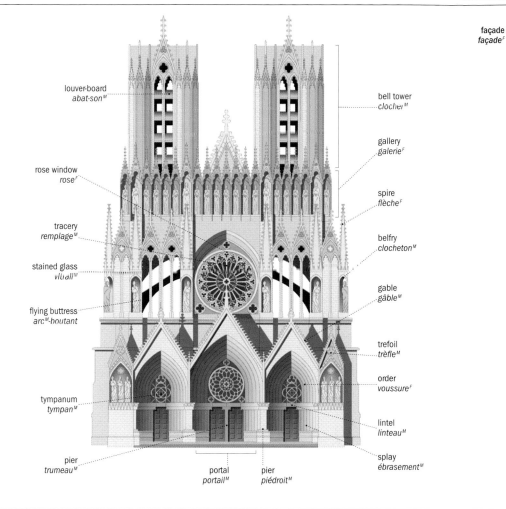

louver-board
*abat-son*<sup>M</sup>

bell tower
*clocher*<sup>M</sup>

gallery
*galerie*<sup>F</sup>

rose window
*rose*<sup>F</sup>

spire
*flèche*<sup>F</sup>

tracery
*remplage*<sup>M</sup>

belfry
*clocheton*<sup>M</sup>

stained glass
*vitrail*<sup>M</sup>

flying buttress
*arc*<sup>M</sup>-*boutant*

gable
*gâble*<sup>M</sup>

trefoil
*trèfle*<sup>M</sup>

order
*voussure*<sup>F</sup>

tympanum
*tympan*<sup>M</sup>

lintel
*linteau*<sup>M</sup>

pier
*trumeau*<sup>M</sup>

portal
*portail*<sup>M</sup>

pier
*piédroit*<sup>M</sup>

splay
*ébrasement*<sup>M</sup>

plan
*plan*<sup>M</sup>

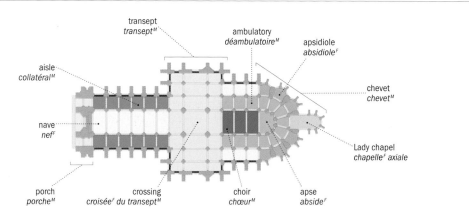

transept
*transept*<sup>M</sup>

ambulatory
*déambulatoire*<sup>M</sup>

apsidiole
*absidiole*<sup>F</sup>

aisle
*collatéral*<sup>M</sup>

chevet
*chevet*<sup>M</sup>

nave
*nef*<sup>F</sup>

Lady chapel
*chapelle*<sup>F</sup> *axiale*

porch
*porche*<sup>M</sup>

crossing
*croisée*<sup>F</sup> *du transept*<sup>M</sup>

choir
*chœur*<sup>M</sup>

apse
*abside*<sup>F</sup>

# elements of architecture
éléments<sup>M</sup> d'architecture<sup>F</sup>

**examples of doors**
*exemples<sup>M</sup> de portes<sup>F</sup>*

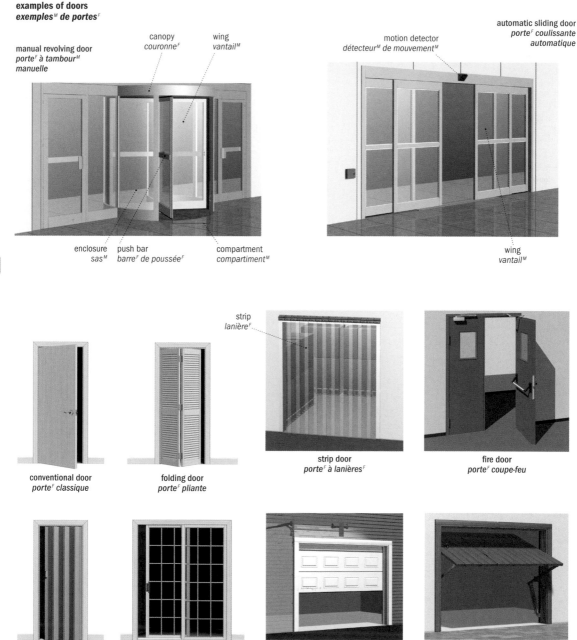

automatic sliding door
*porte<sup>F</sup> coulissante automatique*

canopy
*couronne<sup>F</sup>*

wing
*vantail<sup>M</sup>*

motion detector
*détecteur<sup>M</sup> de mouvement<sup>M</sup>*

manual revolving door
*porte<sup>F</sup> à tambour<sup>M</sup> manuelle*

enclosure
*sas<sup>M</sup>*

push bar
*barre<sup>F</sup> de poussée<sup>F</sup>*

compartment
*compartiment<sup>M</sup>*

wing
*vantail<sup>M</sup>*

strip
*lanière<sup>F</sup>*

conventional door
*porte<sup>F</sup> classique*

folding door
*porte<sup>F</sup> pliante*

strip door
*porte<sup>F</sup> à lanières<sup>F</sup>*

fire door
*porte<sup>F</sup> coupe-feu*

sliding folding door
*porte<sup>F</sup> accordéon<sup>M</sup>*

sliding door
*porte<sup>F</sup> coulissante*

sectional garage door
*porte<sup>F</sup> de garage<sup>M</sup> sectionnelle*

up and over garage door
*porte<sup>F</sup> de garage<sup>M</sup> basculante*

## examples of windows
### *exemples<sup>M</sup> de fenêtres<sup>F</sup>*

sliding folding window
*fenêtre<sup>F</sup> en accordéon<sup>M</sup>*

French window
*fenêtre<sup>F</sup> à la française<sup>F</sup>*

casement window
*fenêtre<sup>F</sup> à l'anglaise<sup>F</sup>*

louvered window
*fenêtre<sup>F</sup> à jalousies<sup>F</sup>*

sliding window
*fenêtre<sup>F</sup> coulissante*

sash window
*fenêtre<sup>F</sup> à guillotine<sup>F</sup>*

horizontal pivoting window
*fenêtre<sup>F</sup> basculante*

vertical pivoting window
*fenêtre<sup>F</sup> pivotante*

# elevator
### *ascenseur<sup>M</sup>*

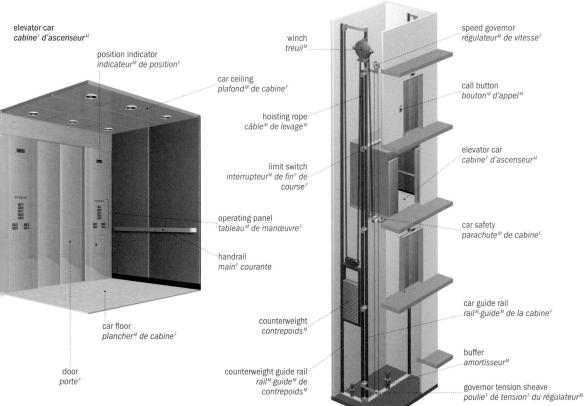

elevator car
*cabine<sup>F</sup> d'ascenseur<sup>M</sup>*

winch
*treuil<sup>M</sup>*

speed governor
*régulateur<sup>M</sup> de vitesse<sup>F</sup>*

position indicator
*indicateur<sup>M</sup> de position<sup>F</sup>*

car ceiling
*plafond<sup>M</sup> de cabine<sup>F</sup>*

call button
*bouton<sup>M</sup> d'appel<sup>M</sup>*

hoisting rope
*câble<sup>M</sup> de levage<sup>M</sup>*

elevator car
*cabine<sup>F</sup> d'ascenseur<sup>M</sup>*

limit switch
*interrupteur<sup>M</sup> de fin<sup>F</sup> de course<sup>F</sup>*

operating panel
*tableau<sup>M</sup> de manœuvre<sup>F</sup>*

car safety
*parachute<sup>M</sup> de cabine<sup>F</sup>*

handrail
*main<sup>F</sup> courante*

car floor
*plancher<sup>M</sup> de cabine<sup>F</sup>*

car guide rail
*rail<sup>M</sup>-guide<sup>M</sup> de la cabine<sup>F</sup>*

counterweight
*contrepoids<sup>M</sup>*

buffer
*amortisseur<sup>M</sup>*

door
*porte<sup>F</sup>*

counterweight guide rail
*rail<sup>M</sup>-guide<sup>M</sup> de contrepoids<sup>M</sup>*

governor tension sheave
*poulie<sup>F</sup> de tension<sup>F</sup> du régulateur<sup>M</sup>*

# traditional houses

maisons<sup>F</sup> traditionnelles

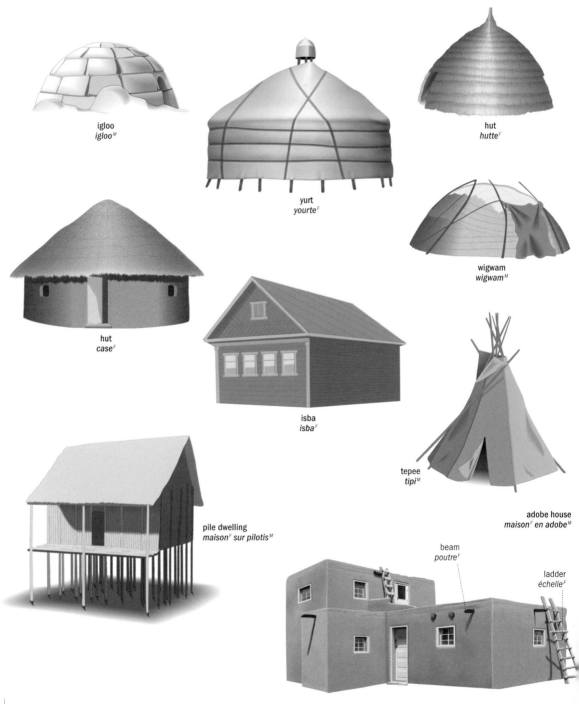

igloo
*igloo*<sup>M</sup>

yurt
*yourte*<sup>F</sup>

hut
*hutte*<sup>F</sup>

hut
*case*<sup>F</sup>

wigwam
*wigwam*<sup>M</sup>

isba
*isba*<sup>F</sup>

tepee
*tipi*<sup>M</sup>

pile dwelling
*maison*<sup>F</sup> *sur pilotis*<sup>M</sup>

adobe house
*maison*<sup>F</sup> *en adobe*<sup>M</sup>

beam
*poutre*<sup>F</sup>

ladder
*échelle*<sup>F</sup>

# city houses
maisons<sup>F</sup> de ville<sup>F</sup>

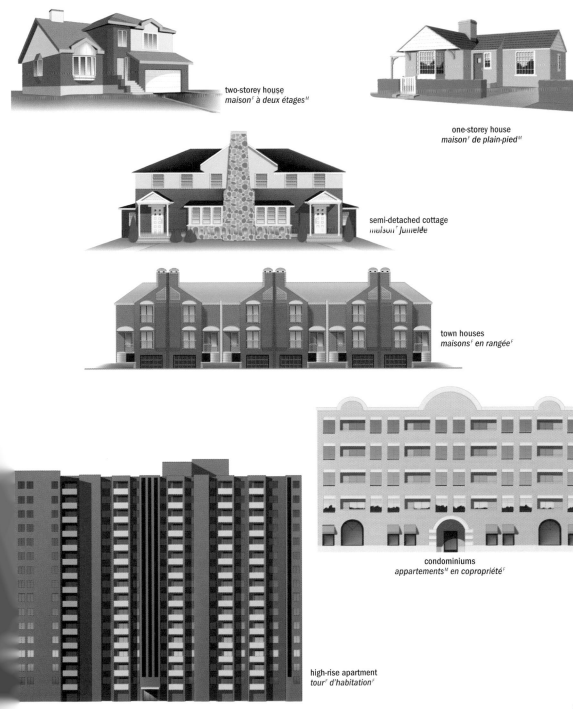

two-storey house
*maison<sup>F</sup> à deux étages<sup>M</sup>*

one-storey house
*maison<sup>F</sup> de plain-pied<sup>M</sup>*

semi-detached cottage
*maison<sup>F</sup> jumelée*

town houses
*maisons<sup>F</sup> en rangée<sup>F</sup>*

condominiums
*appartements<sup>M</sup> en copropriété<sup>F</sup>*

high-rise apartment
*tour<sup>F</sup> d'habitation<sup>F</sup>*

ARTS AND ARCHITECTURE

# sound stage

plateau<sup>M</sup> de tournage<sup>M</sup>

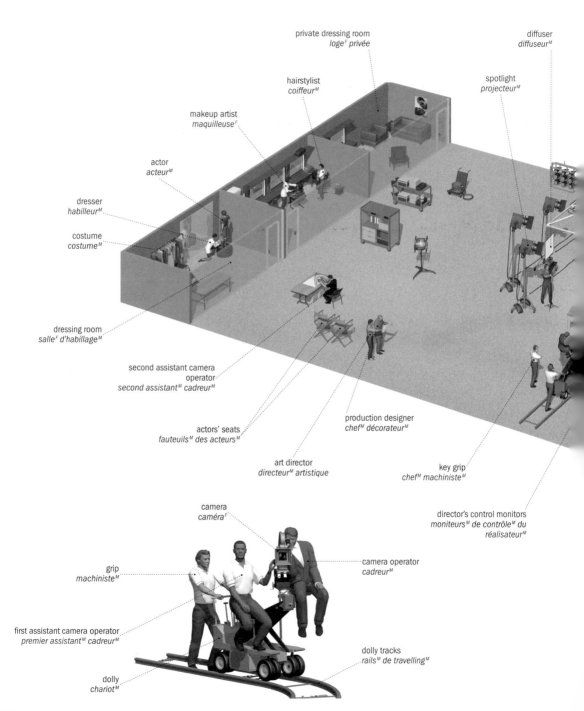

private dressing room
loge<sup>F</sup> privée

diffuser
diffuseur<sup>M</sup>

hairstylist
coiffeur<sup>M</sup>

spotlight
projecteur<sup>M</sup>

makeup artist
maquilleuse<sup>F</sup>

actor
acteur<sup>M</sup>

dresser
habilleur<sup>M</sup>

costume
costume<sup>M</sup>

dressing room
salle<sup>F</sup> d'habillage<sup>M</sup>

second assistant camera
operator
second assistant<sup>M</sup> cadreur<sup>M</sup>

actors' seats
fauteuils<sup>M</sup> des acteurs<sup>M</sup>

art director
directeur<sup>M</sup> artistique

production designer
chef<sup>M</sup> décorateur<sup>M</sup>

key grip
chef<sup>M</sup> machiniste<sup>M</sup>

director's control monitors
moniteurs<sup>M</sup> de contrôle<sup>M</sup> du
réalisateur<sup>M</sup>

camera
caméra<sup>F</sup>

camera operator
cadreur<sup>M</sup>

grip
machiniste<sup>M</sup>

first assistant camera operator
premier assistant<sup>M</sup> cadreur<sup>M</sup>

dolly
chariot<sup>M</sup>

dolly tracks
rails<sup>M</sup> de travelling<sup>M</sup>

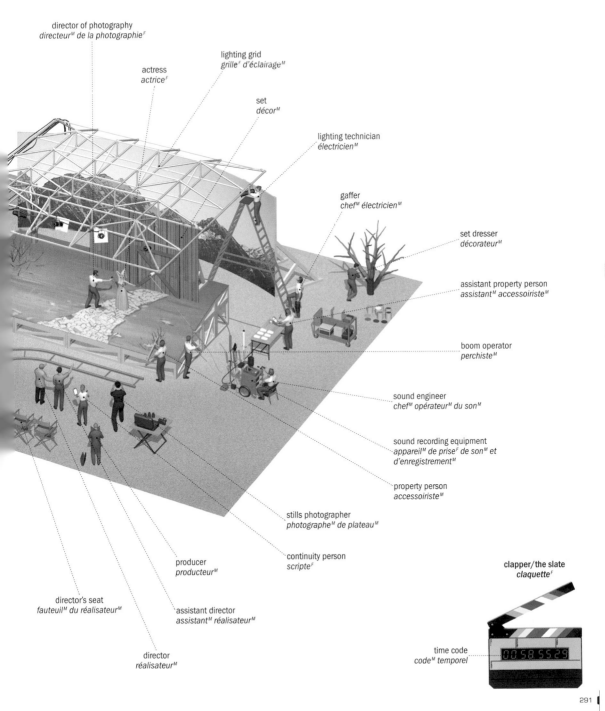

director of photography
*directeur$^M$ de la photographie$^F$*

lighting grid
*grille$^F$ d'éclairage$^M$*

actress
*actrice$^F$*

set
*décor$^M$*

lighting technician
*électricien$^M$*

gaffer
*chef$^M$ électricien$^M$*

set dresser
*décorateur$^M$*

assistant property person
*assistant$^M$ accessoiriste$^M$*

boom operator
*perchiste$^M$*

sound engineer
*chef$^M$ opérateur$^M$ du son$^M$*

sound recording equipment
*appareil$^M$ de prise$^F$ de son$^M$ et d'enregistrement$^M$*

property person
*accessoiriste$^M$*

stills photographer
*photographe$^M$ de plateau$^M$*

continuity person
*scripte$^F$*

producer
*producteur$^M$*

assistant director
*assistant$^M$ réalisateur$^M$*

director's seat
*fauteuil$^M$ du réalisateur$^M$*

director
*réalisateur$^M$*

clapper/the slate
*claquette$^F$*

time code
*code$^M$ temporel*

ARTS AND ARCHITECTURE

# theater

salle<sup>F</sup> de spectacle<sup>M</sup>

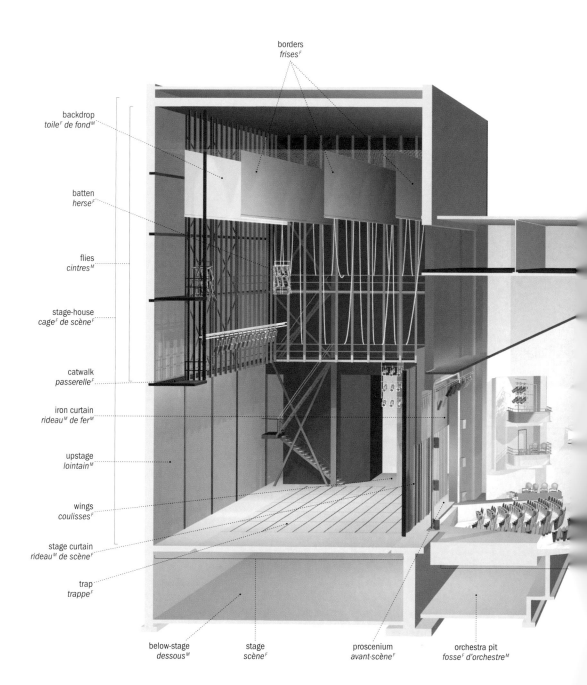

borders
*frises*<sup>F</sup>

backdrop
*toile*<sup>F</sup> *de fond*<sup>M</sup>

batten
*herse*<sup>F</sup>

flies
*cintres*<sup>M</sup>

stage-house
*cage*<sup>F</sup> *de scène*<sup>F</sup>

catwalk
*passerelle*<sup>F</sup>

iron curtain
*rideau*<sup>M</sup> *de fer*<sup>M</sup>

upstage
*lointain*<sup>M</sup>

wings
*coulisses*<sup>F</sup>

stage curtain
*rideau*<sup>M</sup> *de scène*<sup>F</sup>

trap
*trappe*<sup>F</sup>

below-stage
*dessous*<sup>M</sup>

stage
*scène*<sup>F</sup>

proscenium
*avant-scène*<sup>F</sup>

orchestra pit
*fosse*<sup>F</sup> *d'orchestre*<sup>M</sup>

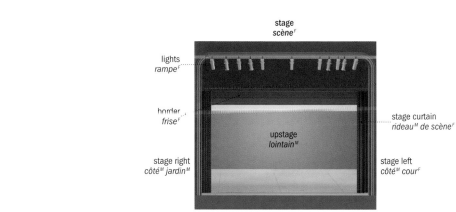

stage
*scène*^F

lights
*rampe*^F

border
*frise*^F

upstage
*lointain*^M

stage curtain
*rideau*^M *de scène*^F

stage right
*côté*^M *jardin*^M

stage left
*côté*^M *cour*^F

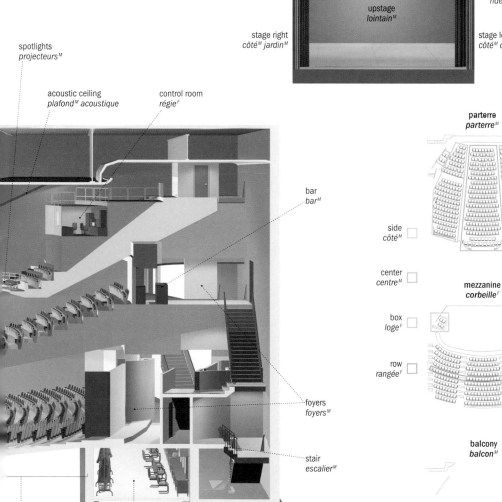

spotlights
*projecteurs*^M

acoustic ceiling
*plafond*^M *acoustique*

control room
*régie*^F

bar
*bar*^M

foyers
*foyers*^M

stair
*escalier*^M

dressing room
*loge*^F *d'artiste*^M

house
*salle*^F

parterre
*parterre*^M

side
*côté*^M

center
*centre*^M

box
*loge*^F

row
*rangée*^F

mezzanine
*corbeille*^F

balcony
*balcon*^M

seat
*fauteuil*^M

ARTS AND ARCHITECTURE

# movie theater
cinéma<sup>M</sup>

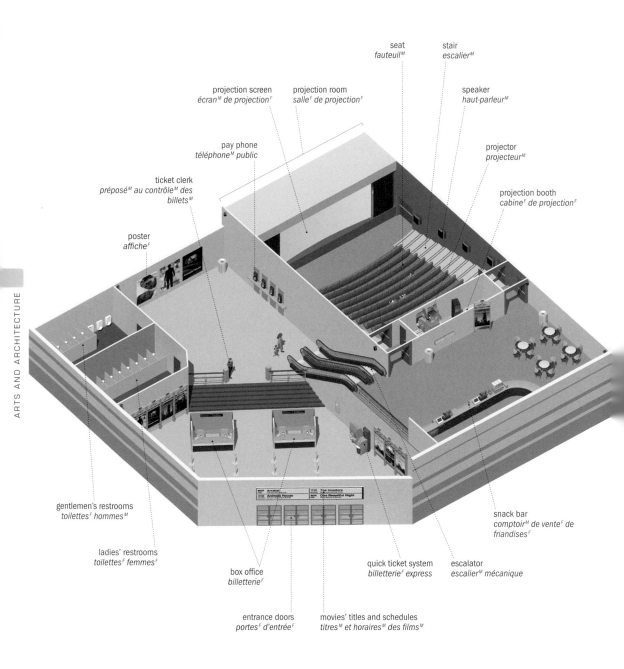

seat
fauteuil<sup>M</sup>

stair
escalier<sup>M</sup>

projection screen
écran<sup>M</sup> de projection<sup>F</sup>

projection room
salle<sup>F</sup> de projection<sup>F</sup>

speaker
haut-parleur<sup>M</sup>

pay phone
téléphone<sup>M</sup> public

projector
projecteur<sup>M</sup>

ticket clerk
préposé<sup>M</sup> au contrôle<sup>M</sup> des
billets<sup>M</sup>

projection booth
cabine<sup>F</sup> de projection<sup>F</sup>

poster
affiche<sup>F</sup>

gentlemen's restrooms
toilettes<sup>F</sup> hommes<sup>M</sup>

snack bar
comptoir<sup>M</sup> de vente<sup>F</sup> de
friandises<sup>F</sup>

ladies' restrooms
toilettes<sup>F</sup> femmes<sup>F</sup>

quick ticket system
billetterie<sup>F</sup> express

escalator
escalier<sup>M</sup> mécanique

box office
billetterie<sup>F</sup>

entrance doors
portes<sup>F</sup> d'entrée<sup>F</sup>

movies' titles and schedules
titres<sup>M</sup> et horaires<sup>M</sup> des films<sup>M</sup>

# symphony orchestra
orchestre<sup>M</sup> symphonique

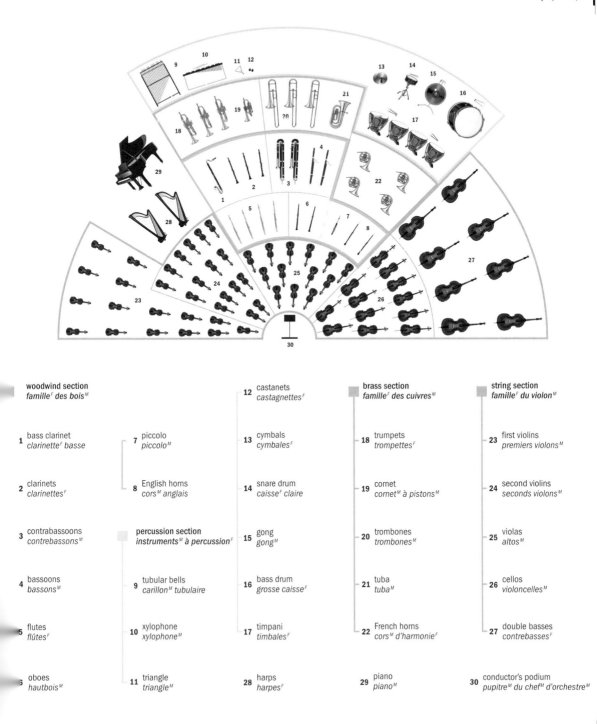

**woodwind section**
*famille<sup>F</sup> des bois<sup>M</sup>*

**1** bass clarinet
*clarinette<sup>F</sup> basse*

**2** clarinets
*clarinettes<sup>F</sup>*

**3** contrabassoons
*contrebassons<sup>M</sup>*

**4** bassoons
*bassons<sup>M</sup>*

**5** flutes
*flûtes<sup>F</sup>*

**6** oboes
*hautbois<sup>M</sup>*

**7** piccolo
*piccolo<sup>M</sup>*

**8** English horns
*cors<sup>M</sup> anglais*

**percussion section**
*instruments<sup>M</sup> à percussion<sup>F</sup>*

**9** tubular bells
*carillon<sup>M</sup> tubulaire*

**10** xylophone
*xylophone<sup>M</sup>*

**11** triangle
*triangle<sup>M</sup>*

**12** castanets
*castagnettes<sup>F</sup>*

**13** cymbals
*cymbales<sup>F</sup>*

**14** snare drum
*caisse<sup>F</sup> claire*

**15** gong
*gong<sup>M</sup>*

**16** bass drum
*grosse caisse<sup>F</sup>*

**17** timpani
*timbales<sup>F</sup>*

**28** harps
*harpes<sup>F</sup>*

**brass section**
*famille<sup>F</sup> des cuivres<sup>M</sup>*

**18** trumpets
*trompettes<sup>F</sup>*

**19** cornet
*cornet<sup>M</sup> à pistons<sup>M</sup>*

**20** trombones
*trombones<sup>M</sup>*

**21** tuba
*tuba<sup>M</sup>*

**22** French horns
*cors<sup>M</sup> d'harmonie<sup>F</sup>*

**29** piano
*piano<sup>M</sup>*

**string section**
*famille<sup>F</sup> du violon<sup>M</sup>*

**23** first violins
*premiers violons<sup>M</sup>*

**24** second violins
*seconds violons<sup>M</sup>*

**25** violas
*altos<sup>M</sup>*

**26** cellos
*violoncelles<sup>M</sup>*

**27** double basses
*contrebasses<sup>F</sup>*

**30** conductor's podium
*pupitre<sup>M</sup> du chef<sup>M</sup> d'orchestre<sup>M</sup>*

# traditional musical instruments

instruments<sup>M</sup> traditionnels

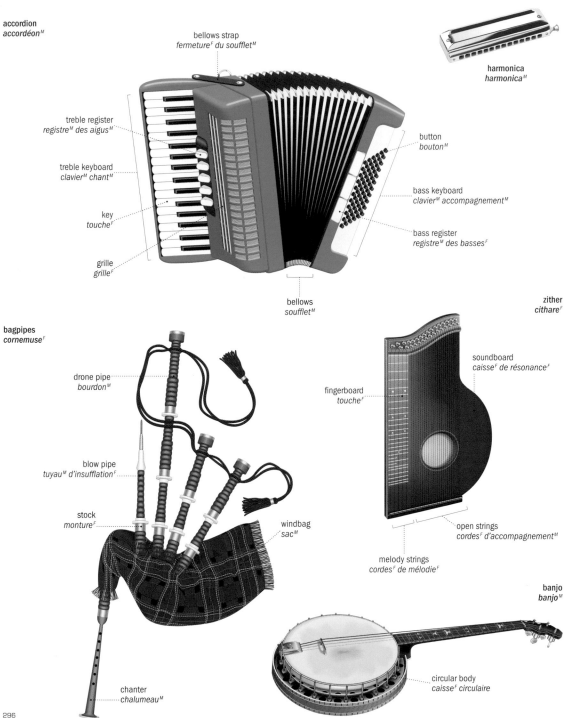

**accordion**
*accordéon<sup>M</sup>*

bellows strap
*fermeture<sup>F</sup> du soufflet<sup>M</sup>*

**harmonica**
*harmonica<sup>M</sup>*

treble register
*registre<sup>M</sup> des aigus<sup>M</sup>*

button
*bouton<sup>M</sup>*

treble keyboard
*clavier<sup>M</sup> chant<sup>M</sup>*

bass keyboard
*clavier<sup>M</sup> accompagnement<sup>M</sup>*

key
*touche<sup>F</sup>*

bass register
*registre<sup>M</sup> des basses<sup>F</sup>*

grille
*grille<sup>F</sup>*

bellows
*soufflet<sup>M</sup>*

**zither**
*cithare<sup>F</sup>*

**bagpipes**
*cornemuse<sup>F</sup>*

drone pipe
*bourdon<sup>M</sup>*

soundboard
*caisse<sup>F</sup> de résonance<sup>F</sup>*

fingerboard
*touche<sup>F</sup>*

blow pipe
*tuyau<sup>M</sup> d'insufflation<sup>F</sup>*

stock
*monture<sup>F</sup>*

windbag
*sac<sup>M</sup>*

open strings
*cordes<sup>F</sup> d'accompagnement<sup>M</sup>*

melody strings
*cordes<sup>F</sup> de mélodie<sup>F</sup>*

**banjo**
*banjo<sup>M</sup>*

circular body
*caisse<sup>F</sup> circulaire*

chanter
*chalumeau<sup>M</sup>*

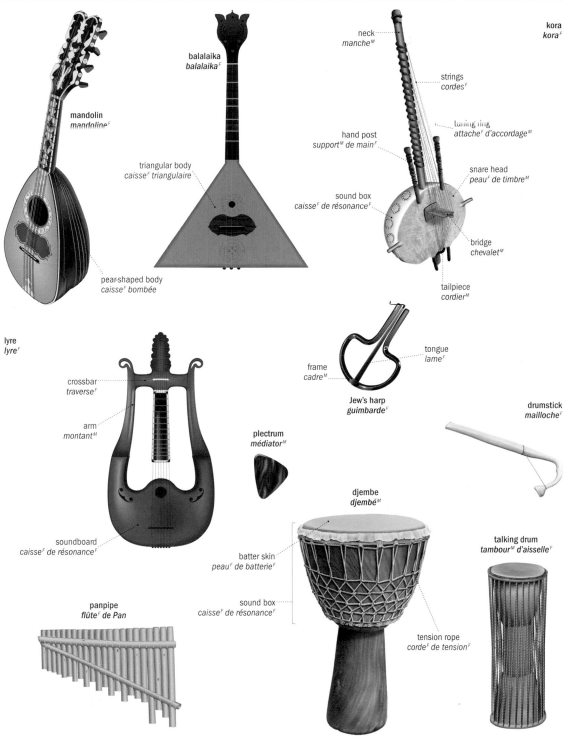

mandolin
*mandoline*<sup>F</sup>

pear-shaped body
*caisse*<sup>F</sup> *bombée*

balalaika
*balalaïka*<sup>F</sup>

triangular body
*caisse*<sup>F</sup> *triangulaire*

hand post
*support*<sup>M</sup> *de main*<sup>F</sup>

sound box
*caisse*<sup>F</sup> *de résonance*<sup>F</sup>

neck
*manche*<sup>M</sup>

kora
*kora*<sup>F</sup>

strings
*cordes*<sup>F</sup>

tuning ring
*attache*<sup>F</sup> *d'accordage*<sup>M</sup>

snare head
*peau*<sup>F</sup> *de timbre*<sup>M</sup>

bridge
*chevalet*<sup>M</sup>

tailpiece
*cordier*<sup>M</sup>

lyre
*lyre*<sup>F</sup>

crossbar
*traverse*<sup>F</sup>

arm
*montant*<sup>M</sup>

soundboard
*caisse*<sup>F</sup> *de résonance*<sup>F</sup>

frame
*cadre*<sup>M</sup>

tongue
*lame*<sup>F</sup>

Jew's harp
*guimbarde*<sup>F</sup>

plectrum
*médiator*<sup>M</sup>

drumstick
*mailloche*<sup>F</sup>

djembe
*djembé*<sup>M</sup>

batter skin
*peau*<sup>F</sup> *de batterie*<sup>F</sup>

sound box
*caisse*<sup>F</sup> *de résonance*<sup>F</sup>

tension rope
*corde*<sup>F</sup> *de tension*<sup>F</sup>

talking drum
*tambour*<sup>M</sup> *d'aisselle*<sup>F</sup>

panpipe
*flûte*<sup>F</sup> *de Pan*

ARTS AND ARCHITECTURE

297

# musical notation

notation<sup>F</sup> musicale

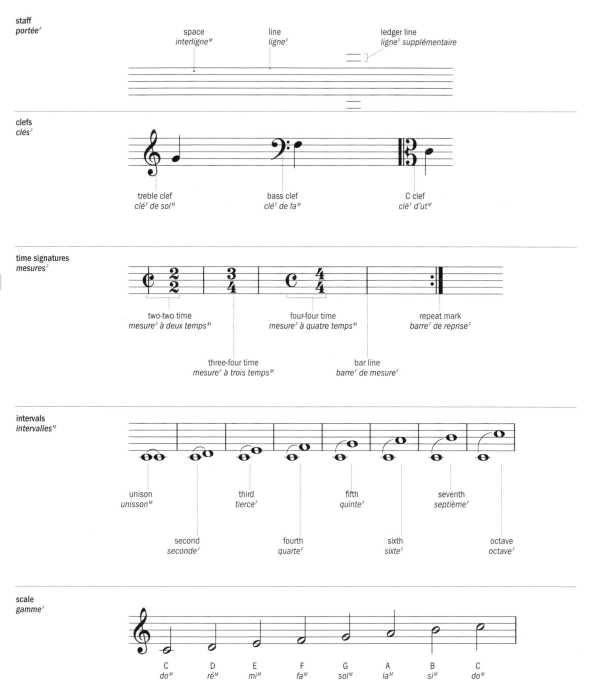

**staff**
*portée<sup>F</sup>*

space
*interligne<sup>M</sup>*

line
*ligne<sup>F</sup>*

ledger line
*ligne<sup>F</sup> supplémentaire*

**clefs**
*clés<sup>F</sup>*

treble clef
*clé<sup>F</sup> de sol<sup>M</sup>*

bass clef
*clé<sup>F</sup> de fa<sup>M</sup>*

C clef
*clé<sup>F</sup> d'ut<sup>M</sup>*

**time signatures**
*mesures<sup>F</sup>*

two-two time
*mesure<sup>F</sup> à deux temps<sup>M</sup>*

three-four time
*mesure<sup>F</sup> à trois temps<sup>M</sup>*

four-four time
*mesure<sup>F</sup> à quatre temps<sup>M</sup>*

bar line
*barre<sup>F</sup> de mesure<sup>F</sup>*

repeat mark
*barre<sup>F</sup> de reprise<sup>F</sup>*

**intervals**
*intervalles<sup>M</sup>*

unison
*unisson<sup>M</sup>*

second
*seconde<sup>F</sup>*

third
*tierce<sup>F</sup>*

fourth
*quarte<sup>F</sup>*

fifth
*quinte<sup>F</sup>*

sixth
*sixte<sup>F</sup>*

seventh
*septième<sup>F</sup>*

octave
*octave<sup>F</sup>*

**scale**
*gamme<sup>F</sup>*

C
*do<sup>M</sup>*

D
*ré<sup>M</sup>*

E
*mi<sup>M</sup>*

F
*fa<sup>M</sup>*

G
*sol<sup>M</sup>*

A
*la<sup>M</sup>*

B
*si<sup>M</sup>*

C
*do<sup>M</sup>*

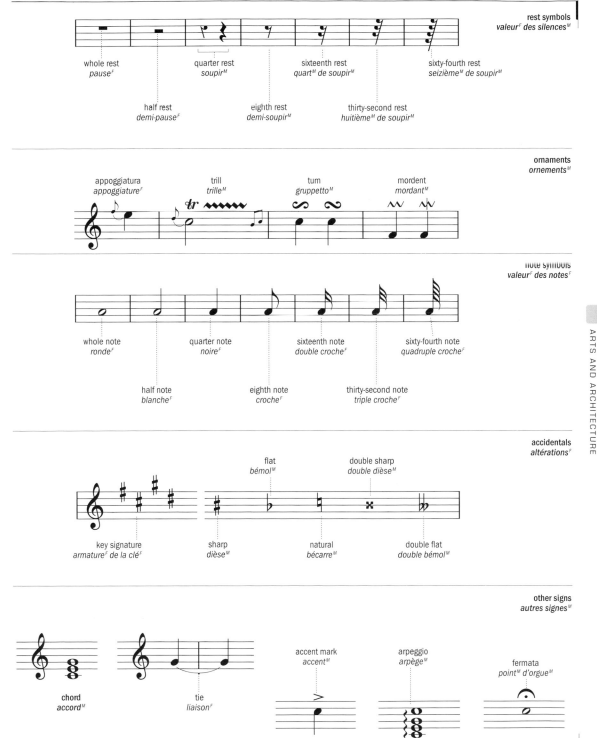

rest symbols
*valeur<sup>F</sup> des silences<sup>M</sup>*

whole rest
*pause<sup>F</sup>*

quarter rest
*soupir<sup>M</sup>*

sixteenth rest
*quart<sup>M</sup> de soupir<sup>M</sup>*

sixty-fourth rest
*seizième<sup>M</sup> de soupir<sup>M</sup>*

half rest
*demi-pause<sup>F</sup>*

eighth rest
*demi-soupir<sup>M</sup>*

thirty-second rest
*huitième<sup>M</sup> de soupir<sup>M</sup>*

ornaments
*ornements<sup>M</sup>*

appoggiatura
*appoggiature<sup>F</sup>*

trill
*trille<sup>M</sup>*

turn
*gruppetto<sup>M</sup>*

mordent
*mordant<sup>M</sup>*

note symbols
*valeur<sup>F</sup> des notes<sup>F</sup>*

whole note
*ronde<sup>F</sup>*

quarter note
*noire<sup>F</sup>*

sixteenth note
*double croche<sup>F</sup>*

sixty-fourth note
*quadruple croche<sup>F</sup>*

half note
*blanche<sup>F</sup>*

eighth note
*croche<sup>F</sup>*

thirty-second note
*triple croche<sup>F</sup>*

accidentals
*altérations<sup>F</sup>*

flat
*bémol<sup>M</sup>*

double sharp
*double dièse<sup>M</sup>*

key signature
*armature<sup>F</sup> de la clé<sup>F</sup>*

sharp
*dièse<sup>M</sup>*

natural
*bécarre<sup>M</sup>*

double flat
*double bémol<sup>M</sup>*

other signs
*autres signes<sup>M</sup>*

accent mark
*accent<sup>M</sup>*

arpeggio
*arpège<sup>M</sup>*

fermata
*point<sup>M</sup> d'orgue<sup>M</sup>*

chord
*accord<sup>M</sup>*

tie
*liaison<sup>F</sup>*

ARTS AND ARCHITECTURE

# examples of instrumental groups

exemples<sup>M</sup> de groupes<sup>M</sup> instrumentaux

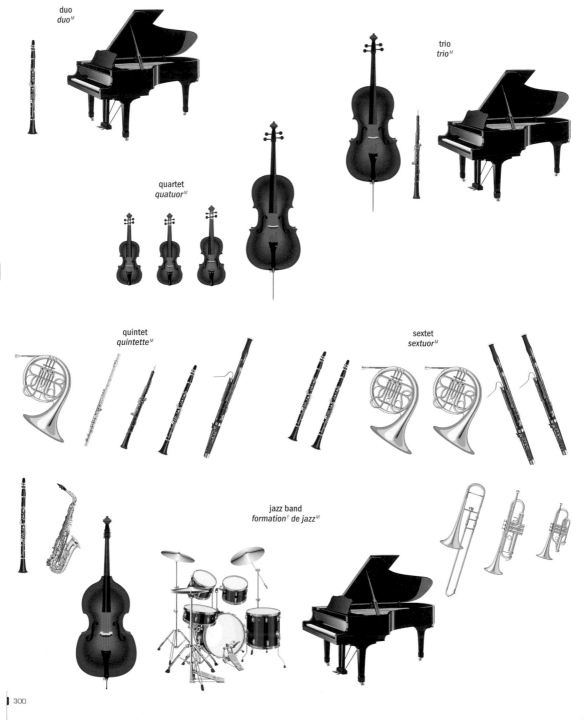

duo
*duo*<sup>M</sup>

trio
*trio*<sup>M</sup>

quartet
*quatuor*<sup>M</sup>

quintet
*quintette*<sup>M</sup>

sextet
*sextuor*<sup>M</sup>

jazz band
*formation*<sup>F</sup> *de jazz*<sup>M</sup>

# stringed instruments
instruments<sup>M</sup> à cordes<sup>F</sup>

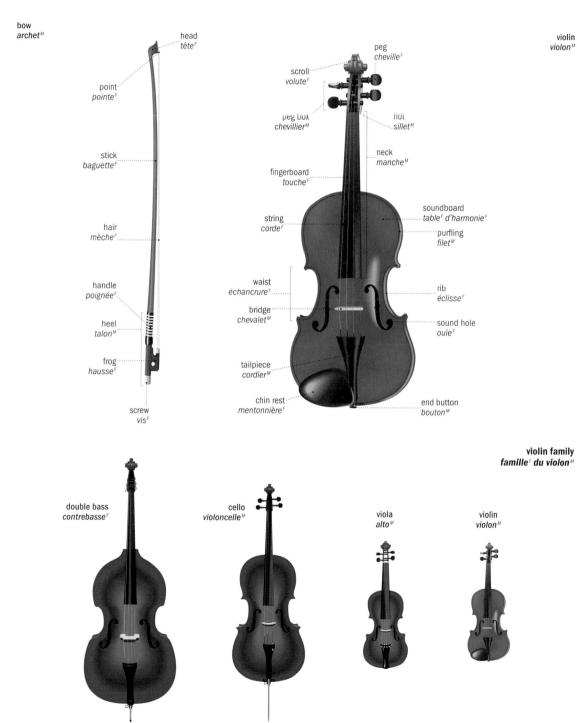

bow
archet<sup>M</sup>

head
tête<sup>F</sup>

point
pointe<sup>F</sup>

stick
baguette<sup>F</sup>

hair
mèche<sup>F</sup>

handle
poignée<sup>F</sup>

heel
talon<sup>M</sup>

frog
hausse<sup>F</sup>

screw
vis<sup>F</sup>

violin
violon<sup>M</sup>

peg
cheville<sup>F</sup>

scroll
volute<sup>F</sup>

peg box
chevillier<sup>M</sup>

nut
sillet<sup>M</sup>

neck
manche<sup>M</sup>

fingerboard
touche<sup>F</sup>

string
corde<sup>F</sup>

soundboard
table<sup>F</sup> d'harmonie<sup>F</sup>

purfling
filet<sup>M</sup>

waist
échancrure<sup>F</sup>

bridge
chevalet<sup>M</sup>

rib
éclisse<sup>F</sup>

sound hole
ouïe<sup>F</sup>

tailpiece
cordier<sup>M</sup>

chin rest
mentonnière<sup>F</sup>

end button
bouton<sup>M</sup>

**violin family**
**famille<sup>F</sup> du violon<sup>M</sup>**

double bass
contrebasse<sup>F</sup>

cello
violoncelle<sup>M</sup>

viola
alto<sup>M</sup>

violin
violon<sup>M</sup>

ARTS AND ARCHITECTURE

## stringed instruments

**harp**
*harpe*[F]

crown ·······
*chapiteau*[M]

tuning peg
*cheville*[F]

neck
*console*[F]

shoulder
*crosse*[F]

string
*corde*[F]

soundboard
*table*[F] *d'harmonie*[F]

pillar
*colonne*[F]

sound box
*caisse*[F] *de résonance*[F]

pedal
*pédale*[F]

pedestal
*cuvette*[F] ·······

foot
*pied*[M]

**acoustic guitar**
*guitare*[F] *acoustique*

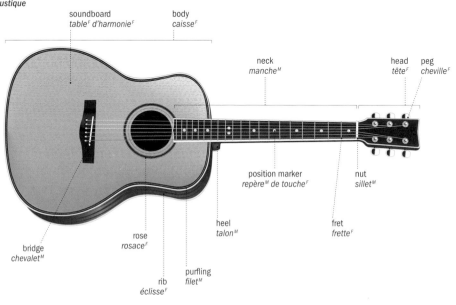

soundboard
*table*[F] *d'harmonie*[F]

body
*caisse*[F]

neck
*manche*[M]

head
*tête*[F]

peg
*cheville*[F]

position marker
*repère*[M] *de touche*[F]

nut
*sillet*[M]

heel
*talon*[M]

fret
*frette*[F]

bridge
*chevalet*[M]

rose
*rosace*[F]

rib
*éclisse*[F]

purfling
*filet*[M]

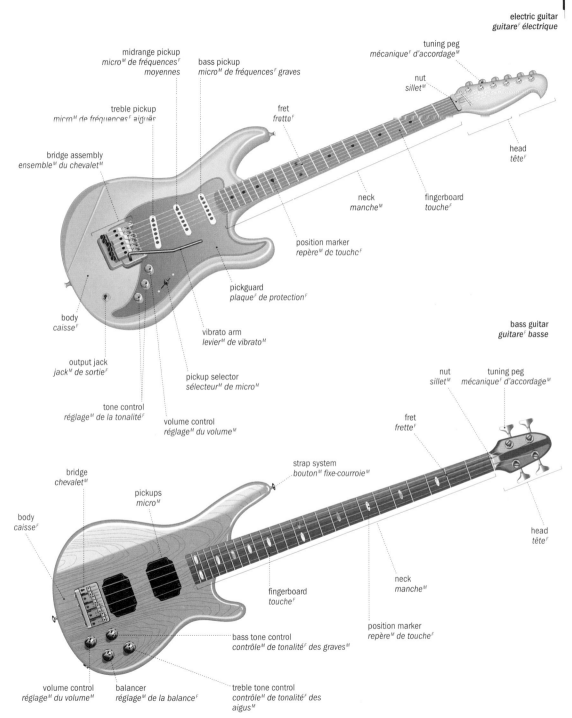

electric guitar
*guitare<sup>F</sup> électrique*

midrange pickup
*micro<sup>M</sup> de fréquences<sup>F</sup>
moyennes*

bass pickup
*micro<sup>M</sup> de fréquences<sup>F</sup> graves*

tuning peg
*mécanique<sup>F</sup> d'accordage<sup>M</sup>*

nut
*sillet<sup>M</sup>*

treble pickup
*micro<sup>M</sup> de fréquences<sup>F</sup> aiguës*

fret
*frette<sup>F</sup>*

head
*tête<sup>F</sup>*

bridge assembly
*ensemble<sup>M</sup> du chevalet<sup>M</sup>*

neck
*manche<sup>M</sup>*

fingerboard
*touche<sup>F</sup>*

position marker
*repère<sup>M</sup> de touche<sup>F</sup>*

pickguard
*plaque<sup>F</sup> de protection<sup>F</sup>*

body
*caisse<sup>F</sup>*

vibrato arm
*levier<sup>M</sup> de vibrato<sup>M</sup>*

bass guitar
*guitare<sup>F</sup> basse*

output jack
*jack<sup>M</sup> de sortie<sup>F</sup>*

pickup selector
*sélecteur<sup>M</sup> de micro<sup>M</sup>*

nut
*sillet<sup>M</sup>*

tuning peg
*mécanique<sup>F</sup> d'accordage<sup>M</sup>*

tone control
*réglage<sup>M</sup> de la tonalité<sup>F</sup>*

volume control
*réglage<sup>M</sup> du volume<sup>M</sup>*

fret
*frette<sup>F</sup>*

head
*tête<sup>F</sup>*

bridge
*chevalet<sup>M</sup>*

strap system
*bouton<sup>M</sup> fixe-courroie<sup>M</sup>*

pickups
*micro<sup>M</sup>*

body
*caisse<sup>F</sup>*

fingerboard
*touche<sup>F</sup>*

neck
*manche<sup>M</sup>*

position marker
*repère<sup>M</sup> de touche<sup>F</sup>*

bass tone control
*contrôle<sup>M</sup> de tonalité<sup>F</sup> des graves<sup>M</sup>*

volume control
*réglage<sup>M</sup> du volume<sup>M</sup>*

balancer
*réglage<sup>M</sup> de la balance<sup>F</sup>*

treble tone control
*contrôle<sup>M</sup> de tonalité<sup>F</sup> des
aigus<sup>M</sup>*

ARTS AND ARCHITECTURE

# keyboard instruments

instruments<sup>M</sup> à clavier<sup>M</sup>

**upright piano**
*piano<sup>M</sup> droit*

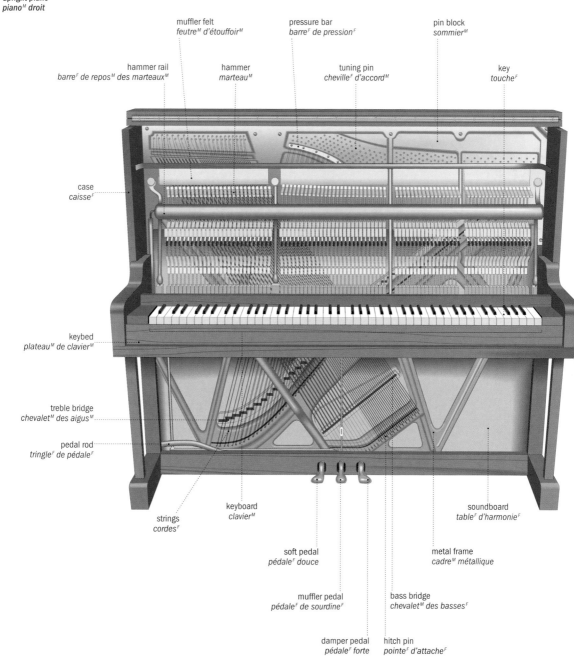

muffler felt
*feutre<sup>M</sup> d'étouffoir<sup>M</sup>*

pressure bar
*barre<sup>F</sup> de pression<sup>F</sup>*

pin block
*sommier<sup>M</sup>*

hammer rail
*barre<sup>F</sup> de repos<sup>M</sup> des marteaux<sup>M</sup>*

hammer
*marteau<sup>M</sup>*

tuning pin
*cheville<sup>F</sup> d'accord<sup>M</sup>*

key
*touche<sup>F</sup>*

case
*caisse<sup>F</sup>*

keybed
*plateau<sup>M</sup> de clavier<sup>M</sup>*

treble bridge
*chevalet<sup>M</sup> des aigus<sup>M</sup>*

pedal rod
*tringle<sup>F</sup> de pédale<sup>F</sup>*

strings
*cordes<sup>F</sup>*

keyboard
*clavier<sup>M</sup>*

soundboard
*table<sup>F</sup> d'harmonie<sup>F</sup>*

soft pedal
*pédale<sup>F</sup> douce*

metal frame
*cadre<sup>M</sup> métallique*

muffler pedal
*pédale<sup>F</sup> de sourdine<sup>F</sup>*

bass bridge
*chevalet<sup>M</sup> des basses<sup>F</sup>*

damper pedal
*pédale<sup>F</sup> forte*

hitch pin
*pointe<sup>F</sup> d'attache<sup>F</sup>*

ARTS AND ARCHITECTURE

organ
orgue<sup>M</sup>

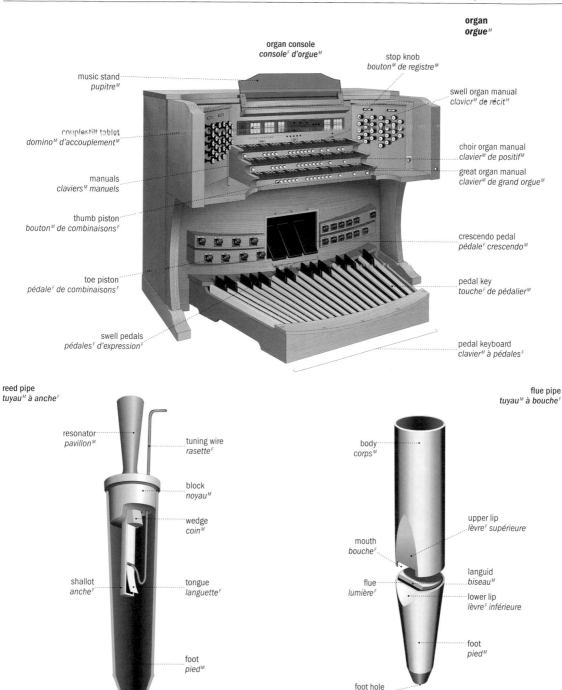

organ console
console<sup>F</sup> d'orgue<sup>M</sup>

stop knob
bouton<sup>M</sup> de registre<sup>M</sup>

music stand
pupitre<sup>M</sup>

swell organ manual
clavier<sup>M</sup> de récit<sup>M</sup>

coupler tilt tablet
domino<sup>M</sup> d'accouplement<sup>M</sup>

choir organ manual
clavier<sup>M</sup> de positif<sup>M</sup>

manuals
claviers<sup>M</sup> manuels

great organ manual
clavier<sup>M</sup> de grand orgue<sup>M</sup>

thumb piston
bouton<sup>M</sup> de combinaisons<sup>F</sup>

crescendo pedal
pédale<sup>F</sup> crescendo<sup>M</sup>

toe piston
pédale<sup>F</sup> de combinaisons<sup>F</sup>

pedal key
touche<sup>F</sup> de pédalier<sup>M</sup>

swell pedals
pédales<sup>F</sup> d'expression<sup>F</sup>

pedal keyboard
clavier<sup>M</sup> à pédales<sup>F</sup>

reed pipe
tuyau<sup>M</sup> à anche<sup>F</sup>

flue pipe
tuyau<sup>M</sup> à bouche<sup>F</sup>

resonator
pavillon<sup>M</sup>

tuning wire
rasette<sup>F</sup>

body
corps<sup>M</sup>

block
noyau<sup>M</sup>

wedge
coin<sup>M</sup>

upper lip
lèvre<sup>F</sup> supérieure

mouth
bouche<sup>F</sup>

shallot
anche<sup>F</sup>

tongue
languette<sup>F</sup>

flue
lumière<sup>F</sup>

languid
biseau<sup>M</sup>

lower lip
lèvre<sup>F</sup> inférieure

foot
pied<sup>M</sup>

foot
pied<sup>M</sup>

foot hole
orifice<sup>M</sup> du pied<sup>M</sup>

foot hole
orifice<sup>M</sup> du pied<sup>M</sup>

ARTS AND ARCHITECTURE

# wind instruments

instruments<sup>M</sup> à vent<sup>M</sup>

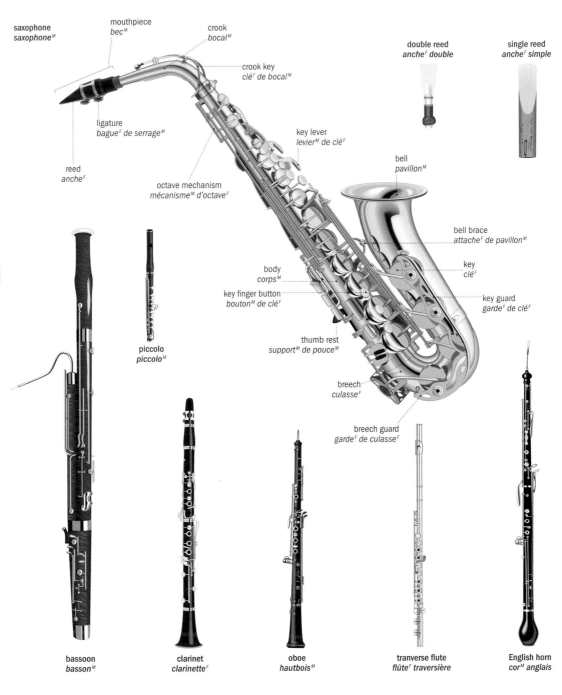

saxophone
saxophone<sup>M</sup>

mouthpiece
bec<sup>M</sup>

crook
bocal<sup>M</sup>

crook key
clé<sup>F</sup> de bocal<sup>M</sup>

ligature
bague<sup>F</sup> de serrage<sup>M</sup>

reed
anche<sup>F</sup>

octave mechanism
mécanisme<sup>M</sup> d'octave<sup>F</sup>

key lever
levier<sup>M</sup> de clé<sup>F</sup>

double reed
anche<sup>F</sup> double

single reed
anche<sup>F</sup> simple

bell
pavillon<sup>M</sup>

bell brace
attache<sup>F</sup> de pavillon<sup>M</sup>

key
clé<sup>F</sup>

key guard
garde<sup>F</sup> de clé<sup>F</sup>

body
corps<sup>M</sup>

key finger button
bouton<sup>M</sup> de clé<sup>F</sup>

thumb rest
support<sup>M</sup> de pouce<sup>M</sup>

breech
culasse<sup>F</sup>

breech guard
garde<sup>F</sup> de culasse<sup>F</sup>

piccolo
piccolo<sup>M</sup>

bassoon
basson<sup>M</sup>

clarinet
clarinette<sup>F</sup>

oboe
hautbois<sup>M</sup>

tranverse flute
flûte<sup>F</sup> traversière

English horn
cor<sup>M</sup> anglais

ARTS AND ARCHITECTURE

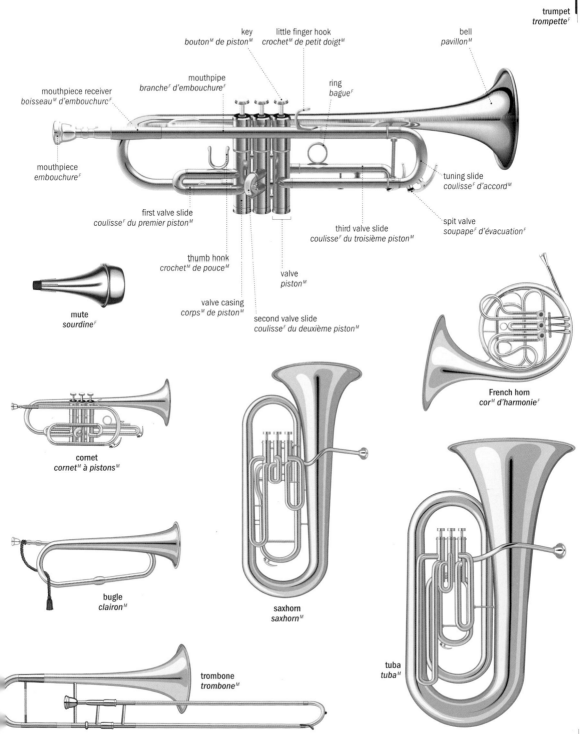

trumpet
*trompette*<sup>F</sup>

key
bouton<sup>M</sup> de piston<sup>M</sup>

little finger hook
crochet<sup>M</sup> de petit doigt<sup>M</sup>

bell
pavillon<sup>M</sup>

mouthpipe
branche<sup>F</sup> d'embouchure<sup>F</sup>

ring
bague<sup>F</sup>

mouthpiece receiver
boisseau<sup>M</sup> d'embouchure<sup>F</sup>

mouthpiece
embouchure<sup>F</sup>

tuning slide
coulisse<sup>F</sup> d'accord<sup>M</sup>

first valve slide
coulisse<sup>F</sup> du premier piston<sup>M</sup>

third valve slide
coulisse<sup>F</sup> du troisième piston<sup>M</sup>

spit valve
soupape<sup>F</sup> d'évacuation<sup>F</sup>

thumb hook
crochet<sup>M</sup> de pouce<sup>M</sup>

valve
piston<sup>M</sup>

mute
sourdine<sup>F</sup>

valve casing
corps<sup>M</sup> de piston<sup>M</sup>

second valve slide
coulisse<sup>F</sup> du deuxième piston<sup>M</sup>

French horn
cor<sup>M</sup> d'harmonie<sup>F</sup>

cornet
cornet<sup>M</sup> à pistons<sup>M</sup>

saxhorn
saxhorn<sup>M</sup>

bugle
clairon<sup>M</sup>

tuba
tuba<sup>M</sup>

trombone
trombone<sup>M</sup>

ARTS AND ARCHITECTURE

# percussion instruments
instruments<sup>M</sup> à percussion<sup>F</sup>

drums
*batterie<sup>F</sup>*

tom-tom
*tam-tam<sup>M</sup>*

cymbal
*cymbale<sup>F</sup> suspendue*

mallet
*mailloche<sup>F</sup>*

high-hat cymbal
*cymbale<sup>F</sup> charleston*

tenor drum
*caisse<sup>F</sup> roulante*

superior cymbal
*cymbale<sup>F</sup> supérieure*

spur
*éperon<sup>M</sup>*

inferior cymbal
*cymbale<sup>F</sup> inférieure*

batter head
*peau<sup>F</sup> de batterie<sup>F</sup>*

pedal
*pédale<sup>F</sup>*

snare drum
*caisse<sup>F</sup> claire*

leg
*pied<sup>M</sup>*

tripod stand
*trépied<sup>M</sup>*

stand
*support<sup>M</sup>*

tension screw
*vis<sup>F</sup> de tension<sup>F</sup>*

bass drum
*grosse caisse<sup>F</sup>*

kettledrum
*timbale<sup>F</sup>*

snare drum
*caisse<sup>F</sup> claire*

metal counterhoop
*cercle<sup>M</sup> de serrage<sup>M</sup>*

batter head
*peau<sup>F</sup> de batterie<sup>F</sup>*

lug
*attache<sup>F</sup>*

tie rod
*tirant<sup>M</sup>*

tuning gauge
*manomètre<sup>M</sup> d'accord<sup>M</sup>*

tension rod
*tringle<sup>F</sup> de tension<sup>F</sup>*

shell
*fût<sup>M</sup>*

snare strainer
*tendeur<sup>M</sup> de timbre<sup>M</sup>*

strut
*châssis<sup>M</sup>*

snare
*cordes<sup>F</sup> de timbre<sup>M</sup>*

tension rod
*tringle<sup>F</sup> de tension<sup>F</sup>*

snare head
*peau<sup>F</sup> de timbre<sup>M</sup>*

caster
*roulette<sup>F</sup>*

foot
*pied<sup>M</sup>*

crown
*couronne<sup>F</sup>*

pedal
*pédale<sup>F</sup>*

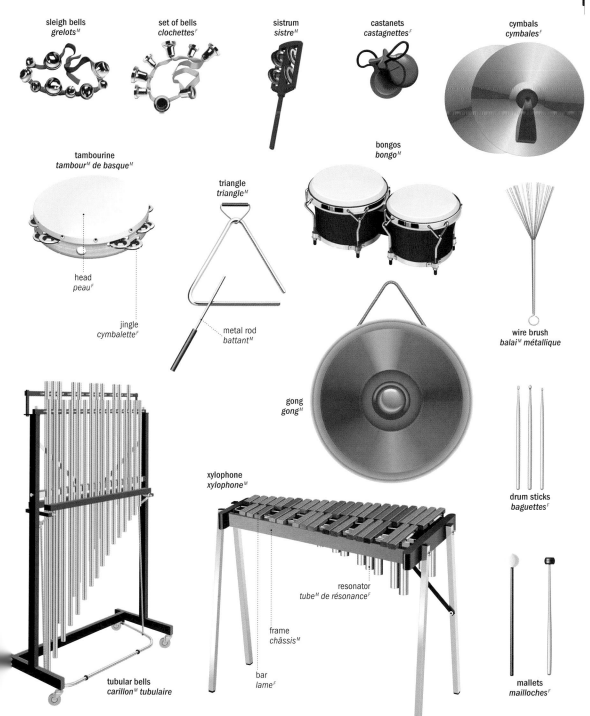

sleigh bells
grelots^M

set of bells
clochettes^F

sistrum
sistre^M

castanets
castagnettes^F

cymbals
cymbales^F

tambourine
tambour^M de basque^M

triangle
triangle^M

bongos
bongo^M

head
peau^F

jingle
cymbalette^F

metal rod
battant^M

gong
gong^M

wire brush
balai^M métallique

drum sticks
baguettes^F

xylophone
xylophone^M

resonator
tube^M de résonance^F

frame
châssis^M

tubular bells
carillon^M tubulaire

bar
lame^F

mallets
mailloches^F

# electronic instruments

instruments*M* électroniques

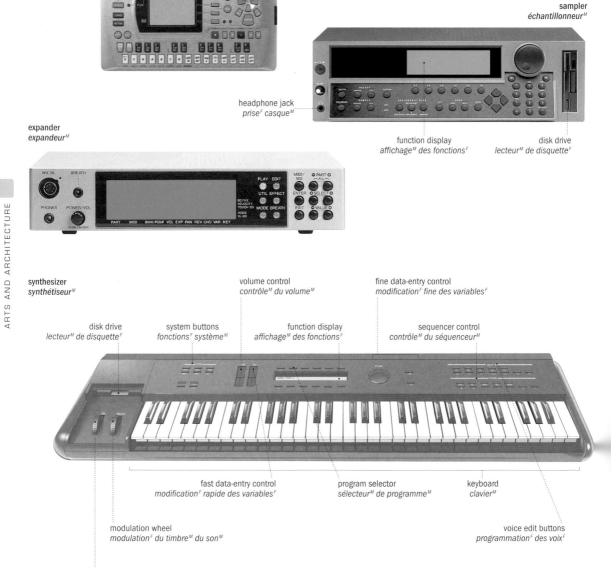

sequencer
*séquenceur*M

sampler
*échantillonneur*M

headphone jack
*prise*F *casque*M

expander
*expandeur*M

function display
*affichage*M *des fonctions*F

disk drive
*lecteur*M *de disquette*F

synthesizer
*synthétiseur*M

volume control
*contrôle*M *du volume*M

fine data-entry control
*modification*F *fine des variables*F

disk drive
*lecteur*M *de disquette*F

system buttons
*fonctions*F *système*M

function display
*affichage*M *des fonctions*F

sequencer control
*contrôle*M *du séquenceur*M

fast data-entry control
*modification*F *rapide des variables*F

program selector
*sélecteur*M *de programme*M

keyboard
*clavier*M

modulation wheel
*modulation*F *du timbre*M *du son*M

voice edit buttons
*programmation*F *des voix*F

pitch wheel
*modulation*F *de la hauteur*F *du son*M

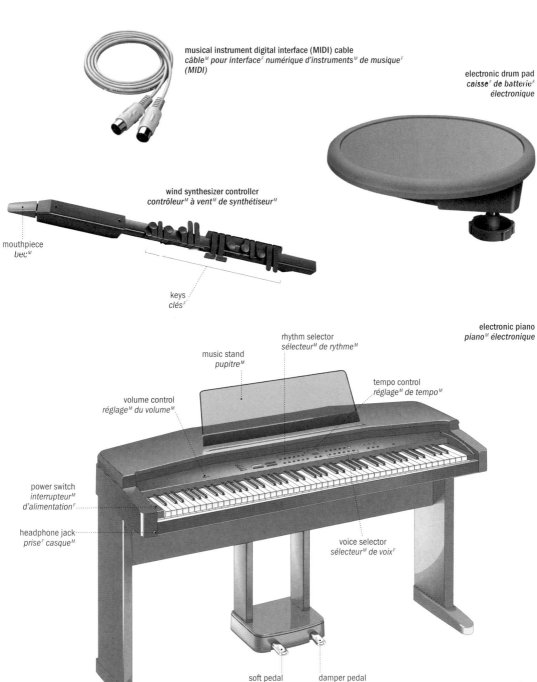

musical instrument digital interface (MIDI) cable
*câble<sup>M</sup> pour interface<sup>F</sup> numérique d'instruments<sup>M</sup> de musique<sup>F</sup> (MIDI)*

electronic drum pad
*caisse<sup>F</sup> de batterie<sup>F</sup> électronique*

wind synthesizer controller
*contrôleur<sup>M</sup> à vent<sup>M</sup> de synthétiseur<sup>M</sup>*

mouthpiece
*bec<sup>M</sup>*

keys
*clés<sup>F</sup>*

electronic piano
*piano<sup>M</sup> électronique*

rhythm selector
*sélecteur<sup>M</sup> de rythme<sup>M</sup>*

music stand
*pupitre<sup>M</sup>*

tempo control
*réglage<sup>M</sup> de tempo<sup>M</sup>*

volume control
*réglage<sup>M</sup> du volume<sup>M</sup>*

power switch
*interrupteur<sup>M</sup> d'alimentation<sup>F</sup>*

headphone jack
*prise<sup>F</sup> casque<sup>M</sup>*

voice selector
*sélecteur<sup>M</sup> de voix<sup>F</sup>*

soft pedal
*pédale<sup>F</sup> douce*

damper pedal
*pédale<sup>F</sup> forte*

# writing instruments

instruments<sup>M</sup> d'écriture<sup>F</sup>

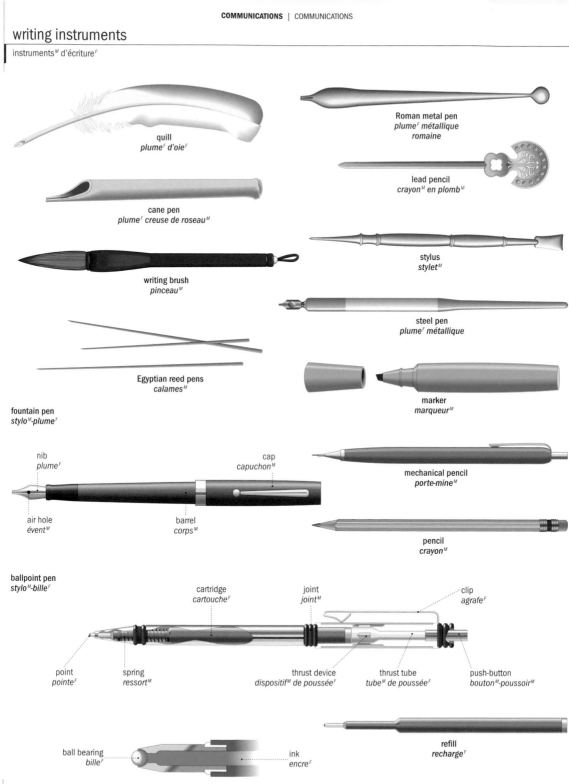

quill
plume<sup>F</sup> d'oie<sup>F</sup>

cane pen
plume<sup>F</sup> creuse de roseau<sup>M</sup>

writing brush
pinceau<sup>M</sup>

Egyptian reed pens
calames<sup>M</sup>

Roman metal pen
plume<sup>F</sup> métallique
romaine

lead pencil
crayon<sup>M</sup> en plomb<sup>M</sup>

stylus
stylet<sup>M</sup>

steel pen
plume<sup>F</sup> métallique

marker
marqueur<sup>M</sup>

**fountain pen**
**stylo<sup>M</sup>-plume<sup>F</sup>**

nib
plume<sup>F</sup>

cap
capuchon<sup>M</sup>

air hole
évent<sup>M</sup>

barrel
corps<sup>M</sup>

mechanical pencil
porte-mine<sup>M</sup>

pencil
crayon<sup>M</sup>

**ballpoint pen**
**stylo<sup>M</sup>-bille<sup>F</sup>**

cartridge
cartouche<sup>F</sup>

joint
joint<sup>M</sup>

clip
agrafe<sup>F</sup>

point
pointe<sup>F</sup>

spring
ressort<sup>M</sup>

thrust device
dispositif<sup>M</sup> de poussée<sup>F</sup>

thrust tube
tube<sup>M</sup> de poussée<sup>F</sup>

push-button
bouton<sup>M</sup>-poussoir<sup>M</sup>

ball bearing
bille<sup>F</sup>

ink
encre<sup>F</sup>

refill
recharge<sup>F</sup>

# newspaper
journal<sup>M</sup>

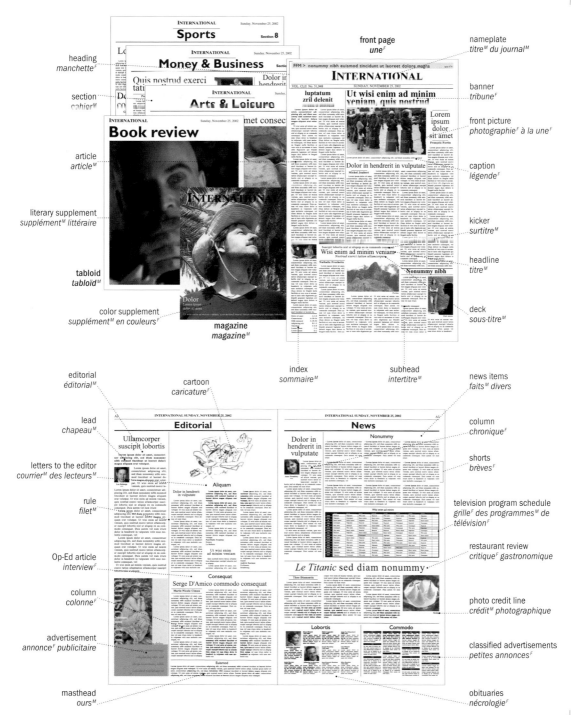

front page
une<sup>F</sup>

nameplate
titre<sup>M</sup> du journal<sup>M</sup>

heading
manchette<sup>F</sup>

section
cahier<sup>M</sup>

banner
tribune<sup>F</sup>

front picture
photographie<sup>F</sup> à la une<sup>F</sup>

caption
légende<sup>F</sup>

article
article<sup>M</sup>

literary supplement
supplément<sup>M</sup> littéraire

kicker
surtitre<sup>M</sup>

headline
titre<sup>M</sup>

tabloid
tabloid<sup>M</sup>

deck
sous-titre<sup>M</sup>

color supplement
supplément<sup>M</sup> en couleurs<sup>F</sup>

magazine
magazine<sup>M</sup>

editorial
éditorial<sup>M</sup>

cartoon
caricature<sup>F</sup>

index
sommaire<sup>M</sup>

subhead
intertitre<sup>M</sup>

news items
faits<sup>M</sup> divers

lead
chapeau<sup>M</sup>

column
chronique<sup>F</sup>

letters to the editor
courrier<sup>M</sup> des lecteurs<sup>M</sup>

shorts
brèves<sup>F</sup>

rule
filet<sup>M</sup>

television program schedule
grille<sup>F</sup> des programmes<sup>M</sup> de télévision<sup>F</sup>

Op-Ed article
interview<sup>F</sup>

restaurant review
critique<sup>F</sup> gastronomique

column
colonne<sup>F</sup>

photo credit line
crédit<sup>M</sup> photographique

advertisement
annonce<sup>F</sup> publicitaire

classified advertisements
petites annonces<sup>F</sup>

masthead
ours<sup>M</sup>

obituaries
nécrologie<sup>F</sup>

# photography

photographie<sup>F</sup>

single-lens reflex (SLR) camera: front view
*appareil<sup>M</sup> à visée<sup>F</sup> reflex mono-objectif<sup>M</sup> : vue<sup>F</sup> avant*

film rewind knob
*rebobinage<sup>M</sup>*

accessory shoe
*griffe<sup>F</sup> porte-accessoires<sup>M</sup>*

exposure adjustment knob
*correction<sup>F</sup> d'exposition<sup>F</sup>*

hot-shoe contact
*contact<sup>M</sup> électrique*

film advance mode
*mode<sup>M</sup> d'entraînement<sup>M</sup> du film<sup>M</sup>*

control panel
*écran<sup>M</sup> de contrôle<sup>M</sup>*

exposure mode
*mode<sup>M</sup> d'exposition<sup>F</sup>*

command control dial
*sélecteur<sup>M</sup> de fonctions<sup>F</sup>*

multiple exposure mode
*surimpression<sup>F</sup>*

on-off switch
*commutateur<sup>M</sup> marche<sup>F</sup>/arrêt<sup>M</sup>*

film speed
*sensibilité<sup>F</sup> du film<sup>M</sup>*

shutter release button
*déclencheur<sup>M</sup>*

self-timer indicator
*témoin<sup>M</sup> du retardateur<sup>M</sup>*

remote control terminal
*prise<sup>F</sup> de télécommande<sup>F</sup>*

camera body
*boîtier<sup>M</sup>*

focus mode selector
*mode<sup>M</sup> de mise<sup>F</sup> au point<sup>M</sup>*

lens release button
*déverrouillage<sup>M</sup> de l'objectif<sup>M</sup>*

objective lens
*objectif<sup>M</sup>*

depth-of-field preview button
*vérification<sup>F</sup> de la profondeur<sup>F</sup> de champ<sup>M</sup>*

## lenses
***objectifs<sup>M</sup>***

## lens accessories
***accessoires<sup>M</sup> de l'objectif<sup>M</sup>***

wide-angle lens
*objectif<sup>M</sup> grand-angulaire*

lens cap
*capuchon<sup>M</sup> d'objectif<sup>M</sup>*

lens hood
*parasoleil<sup>M</sup>*

polarizing filter
*filtre<sup>M</sup> de polarisation<sup>F</sup>*

telephoto lens
*téléobjectif<sup>M</sup>*

zoom lens
*objectif<sup>M</sup> zoom<sup>M</sup>*

macro lens
*objectif<sup>M</sup> macro*

menu button
*touche^F de sélection^F des menus^M*

power switch
*commutateur^M d'alimentation^F*

digital reflex camera: camera back
*appareil^M à visée^F reflex numérique : dos^M*

settings display button
*touche^F d'affichage^M des réglages^M*

viewfinder
*viseur^M*

strap eyelet
*œillet^M d'attache^F*

cover
*couvercle^M*

multi-image jump button
*touche^F de saut^M d'images^F*

video and digital terminals
*prises^F vidéo et numérique*

index/enlarge button
*touche^F d'index^M/agrandissement^M*

compact memory card
*carte^F de mémoire^F*

remote control terminal
*prise^F de télécommande^F*

image review button
*touche^F de visualisation^F des images^F*

liquid crystal display
*écran^M à cristaux^M liquides*

erase button
*touche^F d'effacement^M*

four-way selector
*sélecteur^M quadridirectionnel*

eject button
*bouton^M d'éjection^F*

**still cameras**
***appareils^M photographiques***

**Polaroid® camera**
*Polaroid®^M*

**medium-format SLR (6 x 6)**
*appareil^M reflex 6 X 6 mono-objectif^M*

rangefinder
*appareil^M à télémètre^M couplé*

**digital camera**
*appareil^M numérique*

**disposable camera**
*appareil^M jetable*

**view camera**
*chambre^F photographique*

COMMUNICATIONS AND OFFICE AUTOMATION

# broadcast satellite communication

télédiffusion<sup>F</sup> par satellite<sup>M</sup>

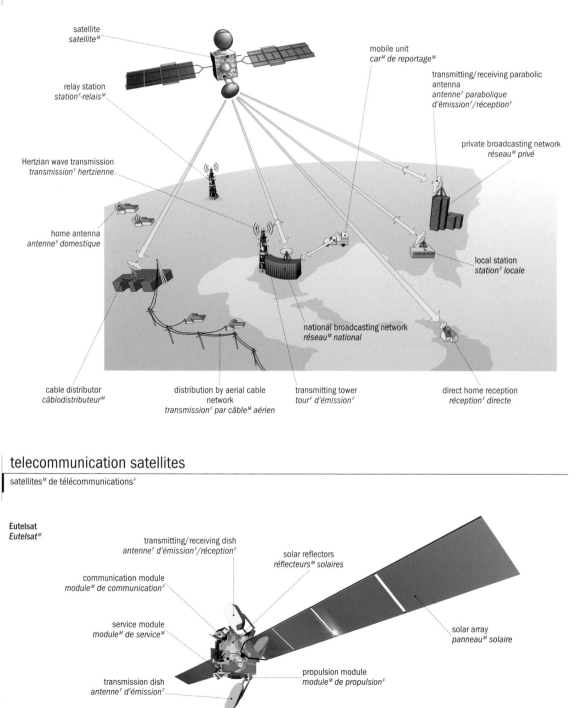

satellite
satellite<sup>M</sup>

mobile unit
car<sup>M</sup> de reportage<sup>M</sup>

transmitting/receiving parabolic antenna
antenne<sup>F</sup> parabolique
d'émission<sup>F</sup>/réception<sup>F</sup>

relay station
station<sup>F</sup>-relais<sup>M</sup>

private broadcasting network
réseau<sup>M</sup> privé

Hertzian wave transmission
transmission<sup>F</sup> hertzienne

home antenna
antenne<sup>F</sup> domestique

local station
station<sup>F</sup> locale

cable distributor
câblodistributeur<sup>M</sup>

distribution by aerial cable network
transmission<sup>F</sup> par câble<sup>M</sup> aérien

transmitting tower
tour<sup>F</sup> d'émission<sup>F</sup>

national broadcasting network
réseau<sup>M</sup> national

direct home reception
réception<sup>F</sup> directe

# telecommunication satellites

satellites<sup>M</sup> de télécommunications<sup>F</sup>

**Eutelsat**
*Eutelsat<sup>M</sup>*

transmitting/receiving dish
antenne<sup>F</sup> d'émission<sup>F</sup>/réception<sup>F</sup>

solar reflectors
réflecteurs<sup>M</sup> solaires

communication module
module<sup>M</sup> de communication<sup>F</sup>

service module
module<sup>M</sup> de service<sup>M</sup>

solar array
panneau<sup>M</sup> solaire

transmission dish
antenne<sup>F</sup> d'émission<sup>F</sup>

propulsion module
module<sup>M</sup> de propulsion<sup>F</sup>

# telecommunications by satellite

télécommunications<sup>F</sup> par satellite<sup>M</sup>

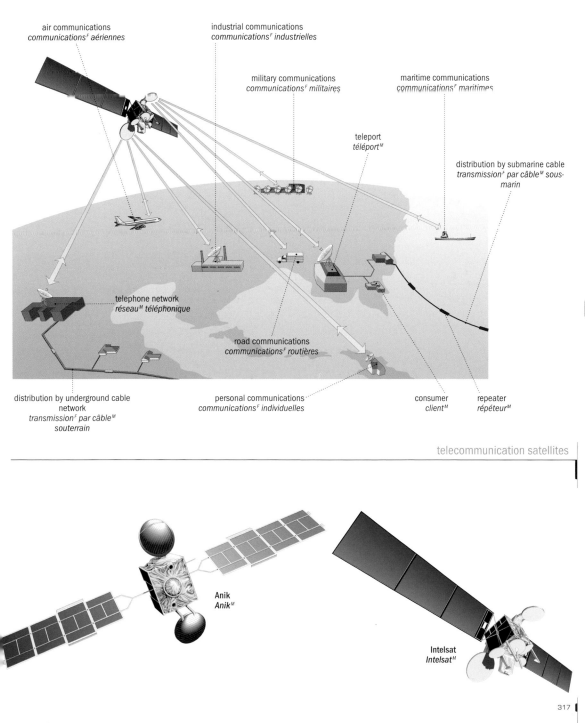

air communications
communications<sup>F</sup> aériennes

industrial communications
communications<sup>F</sup> industrielles

military communications
communications<sup>F</sup> militaires

maritime communications
communications<sup>F</sup> maritimes

teleport
téléport<sup>M</sup>

distribution by submarine cable
transmission<sup>F</sup> par câble<sup>M</sup> sous-
marin

telephone network
réseau<sup>M</sup> téléphonique

road communications
communications<sup>F</sup> routières

distribution by underground cable
network
transmission<sup>F</sup> par câble<sup>M</sup>
souterrain

personal communications
communications<sup>F</sup> individuelles

consumer
client<sup>M</sup>

repeater
répéteur<sup>M</sup>

## telecommunication satellites

Anik
Anik<sup>M</sup>

Intelsat
Intelsat<sup>M</sup>

# television

télévision<sup>F</sup>

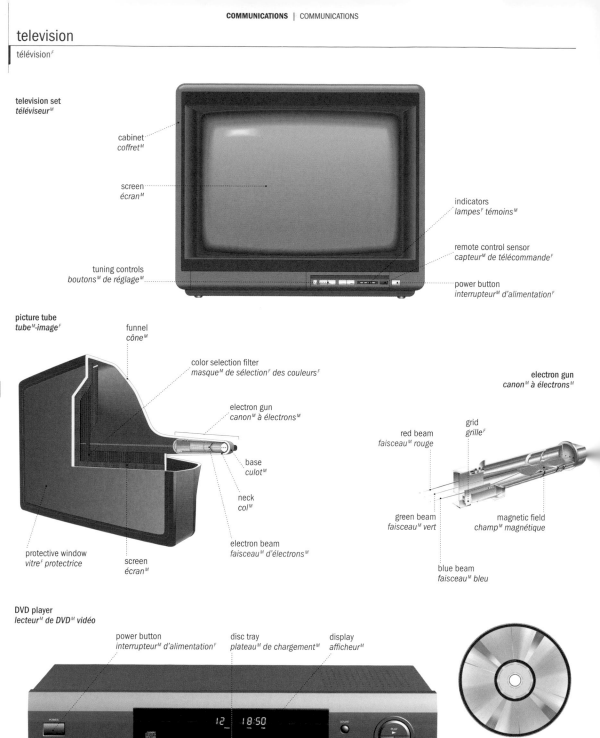

television set
téléviseur<sup>M</sup>

cabinet
coffret<sup>M</sup>

screen
écran<sup>M</sup>

indicators
lampes<sup>F</sup> témoins<sup>M</sup>

remote control sensor
capteur<sup>M</sup> de télécommande<sup>F</sup>

tuning controls
boutons<sup>M</sup> de réglage<sup>M</sup>

power button
interrupteur<sup>M</sup> d'alimentation<sup>F</sup>

picture tube
tube<sup>M</sup>-image<sup>F</sup>

funnel
cône<sup>M</sup>

color selection filter
masque<sup>M</sup> de sélection<sup>F</sup> des couleurs<sup>F</sup>

electron gun
canon<sup>M</sup> à électrons<sup>M</sup>

base
culot<sup>M</sup>

neck
col<sup>M</sup>

protective window
vitre<sup>F</sup> protectrice

screen
écran<sup>M</sup>

electron beam
faisceau<sup>M</sup> d'électrons<sup>M</sup>

electron gun
canon<sup>M</sup> à électrons<sup>M</sup>

grid
grille<sup>F</sup>

red beam
faisceau<sup>M</sup> rouge

green beam
faisceau<sup>M</sup> vert

magnetic field
champ<sup>M</sup> magnétique

blue beam
faisceau<sup>M</sup> bleu

DVD player
lecteur<sup>M</sup> de DVD<sup>M</sup> vidéo

power button
interrupteur<sup>M</sup> d'alimentation<sup>F</sup>

disc tray
plateau<sup>M</sup> de chargement<sup>M</sup>

display
afficheur<sup>M</sup>

digital versatile disc (DVD)
disque<sup>M</sup> numérique
polyvalent (DVD)

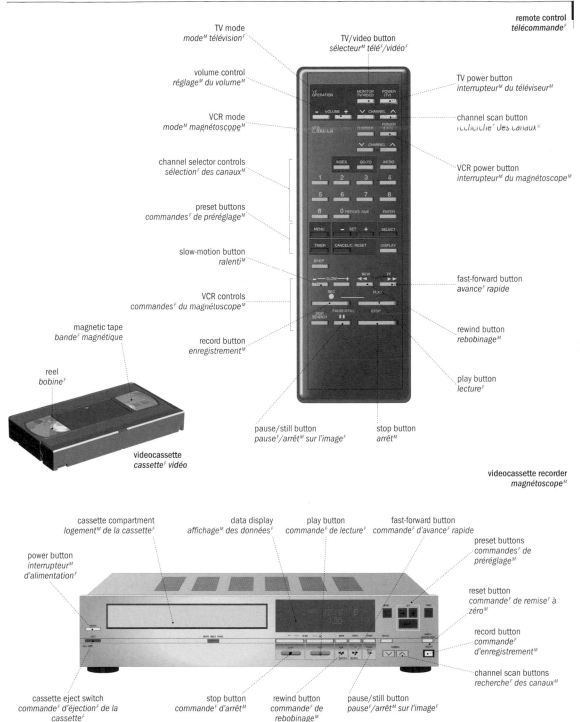

remote control
*télécommande*<sup>F</sup>

TV mode
*mode*<sup>M</sup> *télévision*<sup>F</sup>

TV/video button
*sélecteur*<sup>M</sup> *télé*<sup>F</sup>/*vidéo*<sup>F</sup>

volume control
*réglage*<sup>M</sup> *du volume*<sup>M</sup>

TV power button
*interrupteur*<sup>M</sup> *du téléviseur*<sup>M</sup>

VCR mode
*mode*<sup>M</sup> *magnétoscope*<sup>M</sup>

channel scan button
*recherche*<sup>F</sup> *des canaux*<sup>M</sup>

channel selector controls
*sélection*<sup>F</sup> *des canaux*<sup>M</sup>

VCR power button
*interrupteur*<sup>M</sup> *du magnétoscope*<sup>M</sup>

preset buttons
*commandes*<sup>F</sup> *de préréglage*<sup>M</sup>

slow-motion button
*ralenti*<sup>M</sup>

VCR controls
*commandes*<sup>F</sup> *du magnétoscope*<sup>M</sup>

fast-forward button
*avance*<sup>F</sup> *rapide*

magnetic tape
*bande*<sup>F</sup> *magnétique*

record button
*enregistrement*<sup>M</sup>

reel
*bobine*<sup>F</sup>

rewind button
*rebobinage*<sup>M</sup>

play button
*lecture*<sup>F</sup>

pause/still button
*pause*<sup>F</sup>/*arrêt*<sup>M</sup> *sur l'image*<sup>F</sup>

stop button
*arrêt*<sup>M</sup>

videocassette
*cassette*<sup>F</sup> *vidéo*

videocassette recorder
*magnétoscope*<sup>M</sup>

cassette compartment
*logement*<sup>M</sup> *de la cassette*<sup>F</sup>

data display
*affichage*<sup>M</sup> *des données*<sup>F</sup>

play button
*commande*<sup>F</sup> *de lecture*<sup>F</sup>

fast-forward button
*commande*<sup>F</sup> *d'avance*<sup>F</sup> *rapide*

preset buttons
*commandes*<sup>F</sup> *de
préréglage*<sup>M</sup>

power button
*interrupteur*<sup>M</sup>
*d'alimentation*<sup>F</sup>

reset button
*commande*<sup>F</sup> *de remise*<sup>F</sup> *à
zéro*<sup>M</sup>

record button
*commande*<sup>F</sup>
*d'enregistrement*<sup>M</sup>

channel scan buttons
*recherche*<sup>F</sup> *des canaux*<sup>M</sup>

cassette eject switch
*commande*<sup>F</sup> *d'éjection*<sup>F</sup> *de la
cassette*<sup>F</sup>

stop button
*commande*<sup>F</sup> *d'arrêt*<sup>M</sup>

rewind button
*commande*<sup>F</sup> *de
rebobinage*<sup>M</sup>

pause/still button
*pause*<sup>F</sup>/*arrêt*<sup>M</sup> *sur l'image*<sup>F</sup>

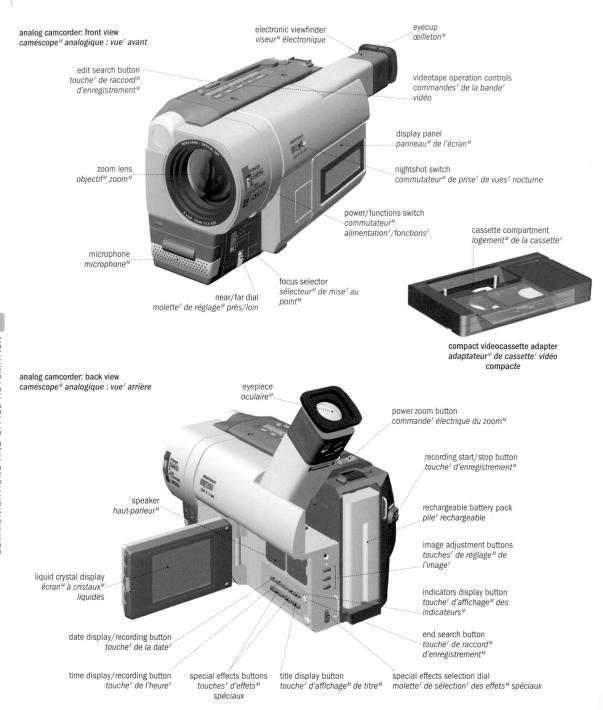

analog camcorder: front view
caméscope<sup>M</sup> analogique : vue<sup>F</sup> avant

electronic viewfinder
viseur<sup>M</sup> électronique

eyecup
œilleton<sup>M</sup>

edit search button
touche<sup>F</sup> de raccord<sup>M</sup>
d'enregistrement<sup>M</sup>

videotape operation controls
commandes<sup>F</sup> de la bande<sup>F</sup>
vidéo

display panel
panneau<sup>M</sup> de l'écran<sup>M</sup>

zoom lens
objectif<sup>M</sup> zoom<sup>M</sup>

nightshot switch
commutateur<sup>M</sup> de prise<sup>F</sup> de vues<sup>F</sup> nocturne

power/functions switch
commutateur<sup>M</sup>
alimentation<sup>F</sup>/fonctions<sup>F</sup>

cassette compartment
logement<sup>M</sup> de la cassette<sup>F</sup>

microphone
microphone<sup>M</sup>

focus selector
sélecteur<sup>M</sup> de mise<sup>F</sup> au
point<sup>M</sup>

near/far dial
molette<sup>F</sup> de réglage<sup>M</sup> près/loin

compact videocassette adapter
adaptateur<sup>M</sup> de cassette<sup>F</sup> vidéo
compacte

analog camcorder: back view
caméscope<sup>M</sup> analogique : vue<sup>F</sup> arrière

eyepiece
oculaire<sup>M</sup>

power zoom button
commande<sup>F</sup> électrique du zoom<sup>M</sup>

recording start/stop button
touche<sup>F</sup> d'enregistrement<sup>M</sup>

speaker
haut-parleur<sup>M</sup>

rechargeable battery pack
pile<sup>F</sup> rechargeable

image adjustment buttons
touches<sup>F</sup> de réglage<sup>M</sup> de
l'image<sup>F</sup>

liquid crystal display
écran<sup>M</sup> à cristaux<sup>M</sup>
liquides

indicators display button
touche<sup>F</sup> d'affichage<sup>M</sup> des
indicateurs<sup>M</sup>

date display/recording button
touche<sup>F</sup> de la date<sup>F</sup>

end search button
touche<sup>F</sup> de raccord<sup>M</sup>
d'enregistrement<sup>M</sup>

time display/recording button
touche<sup>F</sup> de l'heure<sup>F</sup>

special effects buttons
touches<sup>F</sup> d'effets<sup>M</sup>
spéciaux

title display button
touche<sup>F</sup> d'affichage<sup>M</sup> de titre<sup>M</sup>

special effects selection dial
molette<sup>F</sup> de sélection<sup>F</sup> des effets<sup>M</sup> spéciaux

COMMUNICATIONS AND OFFICE AUTOMATION

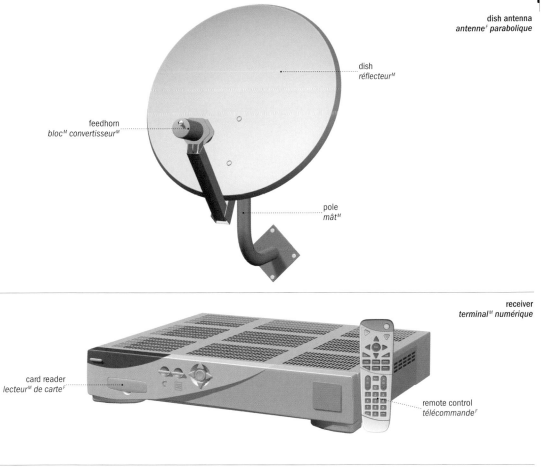

dish antenna
*antenne<sup>F</sup> parabolique*

dish
*réflecteur<sup>M</sup>*

feedhorn
*bloc<sup>M</sup> convertisseur<sup>M</sup>*

pole
*mât<sup>M</sup>*

receiver
*terminal<sup>M</sup> numérique*

card reader
*lecteur<sup>M</sup> de carte<sup>F</sup>*

remote control
*télécommande<sup>F</sup>*

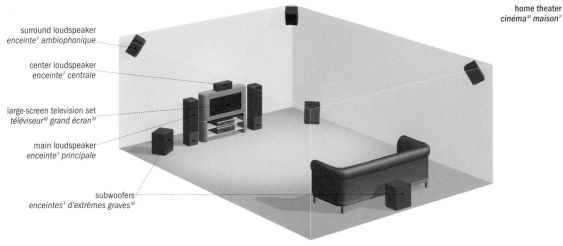

home theater
*cinéma<sup>M</sup> maison<sup>F</sup>*

surround loudspeaker
*enceinte<sup>F</sup> ambiophonique*

center loudspeaker
*enceinte<sup>F</sup> centrale*

large-screen television set
*téléviseur<sup>M</sup> grand écran<sup>M</sup>*

main loudspeaker
*enceinte<sup>F</sup> principale*

subwoofers
*enceintes<sup>F</sup> d'extrêmes graves<sup>M</sup>*

# sound reproducing system

chaine^F stéréo

**ampli-tuner: front view**
*ampli^M-syntoniseur^M : vue^F avant*

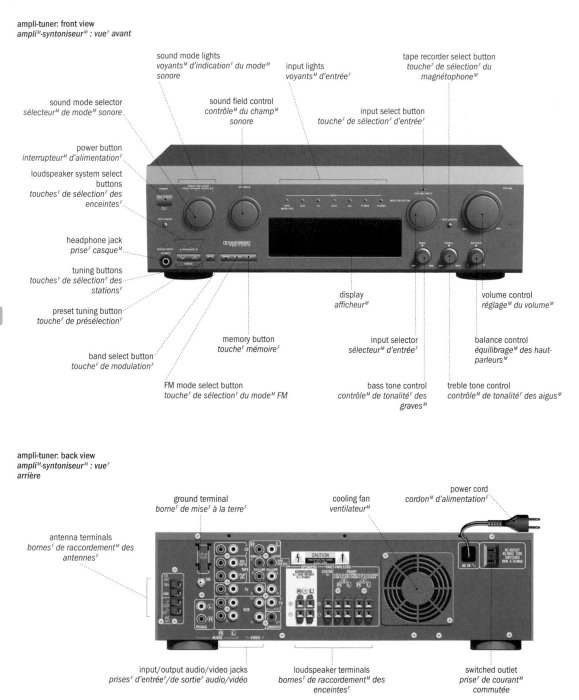

sound mode lights
*voyants^M d'indication^F du mode^M sonore*

input lights
*voyants^M d'entrée^F*

tape recorder select button
*touche^F de sélection^F du magnétophone^M*

sound mode selector
*sélecteur^M de mode^M sonore*

sound field control
*contrôle^M du champ^M sonore*

input select button
*touche^F de sélection^F d'entrée^F*

power button
*interrupteur^M d'alimentation^F*

loudspeaker system select buttons
*touches^F de sélection^F des enceintes^F*

headphone jack
*prise^F casque^M*

tuning buttons
*touches^F de sélection^F des stations^F*

preset tuning button
*touche^F de présélection^F*

band select button
*touche^F de modulation^F*

FM mode select button
*touche^F de sélection^F du mode^M FM*

memory button
*touche^F mémoire^F*

display
*afficheur^M*

input selector
*sélecteur^M d'entrée^F*

bass tone control
*contrôle^M de tonalité^F des graves^M*

treble tone control
*contrôle^M de tonalité^F des aigus^M*

balance control
*équilibrage^M des haut-parleurs^M*

volume control
*réglage^M du volume^M*

**ampli-tuner: back view**
*ampli^M-syntoniseur^M : vue^F arrière*

ground terminal
*borne^F de mise^F à la terre^F*

cooling fan
*ventilateur^M*

power cord
*cordon^M d'alimentation^F*

antenna terminals
*bornes^F de raccordement^M des antennes^F*

input/output audio/video jacks
*prises^F d'entrée^F/de sortie^F audio/vidéo*

loudspeaker terminals
*bornes^F de raccordement^M des enceintes^F*

switched outlet
*prise^F de courant^M commutée*

sound reproducing system

**cassette tape deck**
*platine<sup>F</sup> cassette<sup>F</sup>*

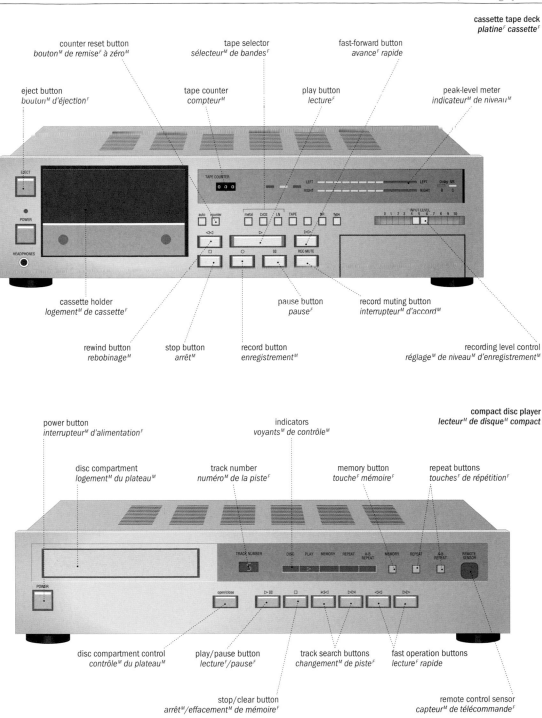

counter reset button
*bouton<sup>M</sup> de remise<sup>F</sup> à zéro<sup>M</sup>*

tape selector
*sélecteur<sup>M</sup> de bandes<sup>F</sup>*

fast-forward button
*avance<sup>F</sup> rapide*

eject button
*bouton<sup>M</sup> d'éjection<sup>F</sup>*

tape counter
*compteur<sup>M</sup>*

play button
*lecture<sup>F</sup>*

peak-level meter
*indicateur<sup>M</sup> de niveau<sup>M</sup>*

cassette holder
*logement<sup>M</sup> de cassette<sup>F</sup>*

pause button
*pause<sup>F</sup>*

record muting button
*interrupteur<sup>M</sup> d'accord<sup>M</sup>*

rewind button
*rebobinage<sup>M</sup>*

stop button
*arrêt<sup>M</sup>*

record button
*enregistrement<sup>M</sup>*

recording level control
*réglage<sup>M</sup> de niveau<sup>M</sup> d'enregistrement<sup>M</sup>*

**compact disc player**
*lecteur<sup>M</sup> de disque<sup>M</sup> compact*

power button
*interrupteur<sup>M</sup> d'alimentation<sup>F</sup>*

indicators
*voyants<sup>M</sup> de contrôle<sup>M</sup>*

disc compartment
*logement<sup>M</sup> du plateau<sup>M</sup>*

track number
*numéro<sup>M</sup> de la piste<sup>F</sup>*

memory button
*touche<sup>F</sup> mémoire<sup>F</sup>*

repeat buttons
*touches<sup>F</sup> de répétition<sup>F</sup>*

disc compartment control
*contrôle<sup>M</sup> du plateau<sup>M</sup>*

play/pause button
*lecture<sup>F</sup>/pause<sup>F</sup>*

track search buttons
*changement<sup>M</sup> de piste<sup>F</sup>*

fast operation buttons
*lecture<sup>F</sup> rapide*

stop/clear button
*arrêt<sup>M</sup>/effacement<sup>M</sup> de mémoire<sup>F</sup>*

remote control sensor
*capteur<sup>M</sup> de télécommande<sup>F</sup>*

COMMUNICATIONS AND OFFICE AUTOMATION

## sound reproducing system

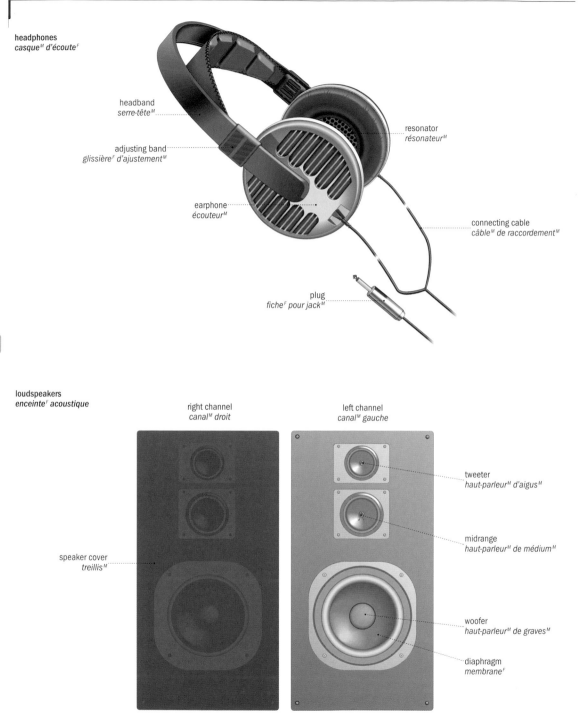

**headphones**
*casque^M d'écoute^F*

headband
*serre-tête^M*

resonator
*résonateur^M*

adjusting band
*glissière^F d'ajustement^M*

earphone
*écouteur^M*

connecting cable
*câble^M de raccordement^M*

plug
*fiche^F pour jack^M*

**loudspeakers**
*enceinte^F acoustique*

right channel
*canal^M droit*

left channel
*canal^M gauche*

tweeter
*haut-parleur^M d'aigus^M*

midrange
*haut-parleur^M de médium^M*

speaker cover
*treillis^M*

woofer
*haut-parleur^M de graves^M*

diaphragm
*membrane^F*

# mini stereo sound system

minichaine<sup>F</sup> stéréo

compact disc player
*lecteur<sup>M</sup> de disque<sup>M</sup> compact*

ampli-tuner
*ampli<sup>M</sup>-syntoniseur<sup>M</sup>*

loudspeaker
*enceinte<sup>F</sup> acoustique*

compact disc recorder
*graveur<sup>M</sup> de disque<sup>M</sup> compact*

dual cassette deck
*double platine<sup>F</sup> cassette<sup>F</sup>*

# portable sound systems

appareils<sup>M</sup> de son<sup>M</sup> portatifs

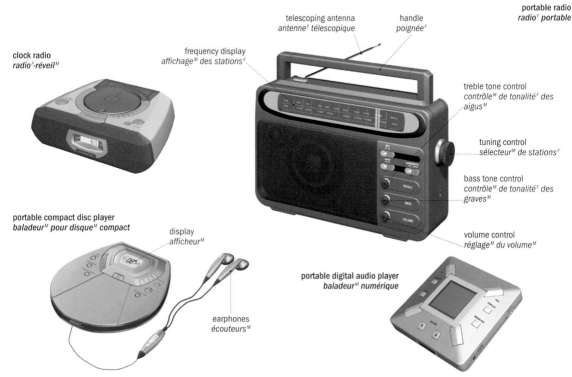

portable radio
*radio<sup>F</sup> portable*

telescoping antenna
*antenne<sup>F</sup> télescopique*

handle
*poignée<sup>F</sup>*

clock radio
*radio<sup>F</sup>-réveil<sup>M</sup>*

frequency display
*affichage<sup>M</sup> des stations<sup>F</sup>*

treble tone control
*contrôle<sup>M</sup> de tonalité<sup>F</sup> des aigus<sup>M</sup>*

tuning control
*sélecteur<sup>M</sup> de stations<sup>F</sup>*

bass tone control
*contrôle<sup>M</sup> de tonalité<sup>F</sup> des graves<sup>M</sup>*

portable compact disc player
*baladeur<sup>M</sup> pour disque<sup>M</sup> compact*

display
*afficheur<sup>M</sup>*

volume control
*réglage<sup>M</sup> du volume<sup>M</sup>*

portable digital audio player
*baladeur<sup>M</sup> numérique*

earphones
*écouteurs<sup>M</sup>*

COMMUNICATIONS AND OFFICE AUTOMATION

## portable sound systems

**personal radio cassette player**
*baladeur*<sup>M</sup>

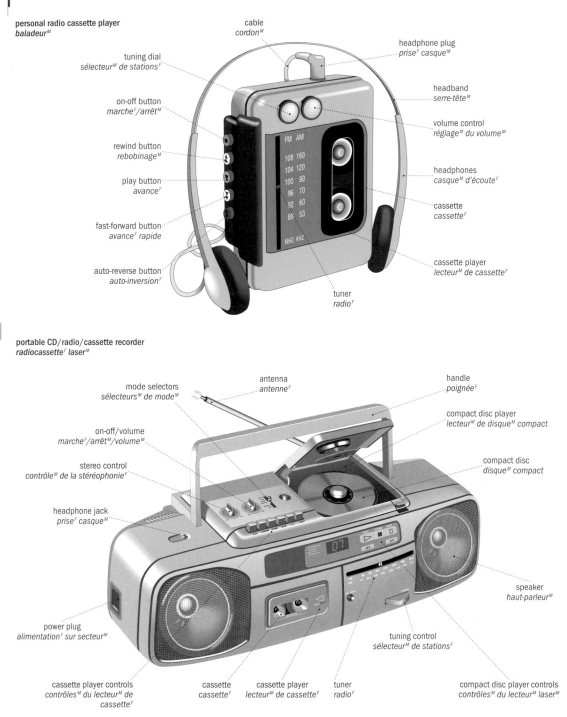

cable
*cordon*<sup>M</sup>

headphone plug
*prise*<sup>F</sup> *casque*<sup>M</sup>

tuning dial
*sélecteur*<sup>M</sup> *de stations*<sup>F</sup>

headband
*serre-tête*<sup>M</sup>

on-off button
*marche*<sup>F</sup>/*arrêt*<sup>M</sup>

volume control
*réglage*<sup>M</sup> *du volume*<sup>M</sup>

rewind button
*rebobinage*<sup>M</sup>

headphones
*casque*<sup>M</sup> *d'écoute*<sup>F</sup>

play button
*avance*<sup>F</sup>

cassette
*cassette*<sup>F</sup>

fast-forward button
*avance*<sup>F</sup> *rapide*

cassette player
*lecteur*<sup>M</sup> *de cassette*<sup>F</sup>

auto-reverse button
*auto-inversion*<sup>F</sup>

tuner
*radio*<sup>F</sup>

**portable CD/radio/cassette recorder**
*radiocassette*<sup>F</sup> *laser*<sup>M</sup>

mode selectors
*sélecteurs*<sup>M</sup> *de mode*<sup>M</sup>

antenna
*antenne*<sup>F</sup>

handle
*poignée*<sup>F</sup>

on-off/volume
*marche*<sup>F</sup>/*arrêt*<sup>M</sup>/*volume*<sup>M</sup>

compact disc player
*lecteur*<sup>M</sup> *de disque*<sup>M</sup> *compact*

stereo control
*contrôle*<sup>M</sup> *de la stéréophonie*<sup>F</sup>

compact disc
*disque*<sup>M</sup> *compact*

headphone jack
*prise*<sup>F</sup> *casque*<sup>M</sup>

speaker
*haut-parleur*<sup>M</sup>

power plug
*alimentation*<sup>F</sup> *sur secteur*<sup>M</sup>

tuning control
*sélecteur*<sup>M</sup> *de stations*<sup>F</sup>

cassette player controls
*contrôles*<sup>M</sup> *du lecteur*<sup>M</sup> *de cassette*<sup>F</sup>

cassette
*cassette*<sup>F</sup>

cassette player
*lecteur*<sup>M</sup> *de cassette*<sup>F</sup>

tuner
*radio*<sup>F</sup>

compact disc player controls
*contrôles*<sup>M</sup> *du lecteur*<sup>M</sup> *laser*<sup>M</sup>

# communication by telephone

communication<sup>F</sup> par téléphone<sup>M</sup>

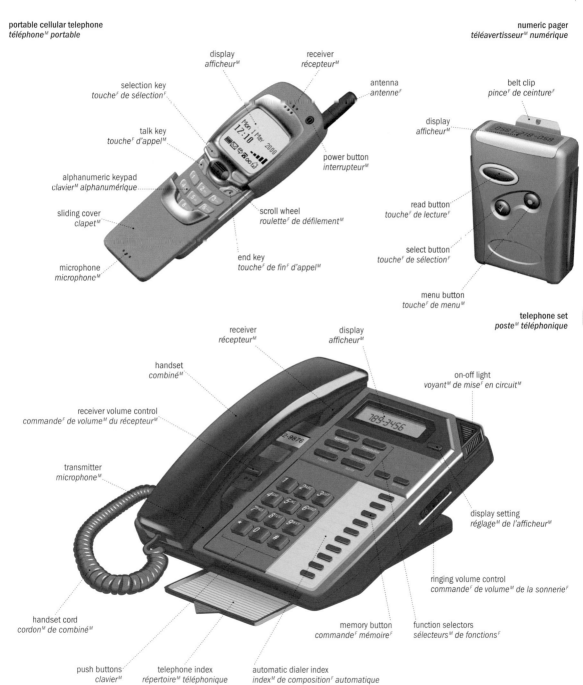

**portable cellular telephone**
*téléphone<sup>M</sup> portable*

**numeric pager**
*téléavertisseur<sup>M</sup> numérique*

display
*afficheur<sup>M</sup>*

receiver
*récepteur<sup>M</sup>*

antenna
*antenne<sup>F</sup>*

belt clip
*pince<sup>F</sup> de ceinture<sup>F</sup>*

selection key
*touche<sup>F</sup> de sélection<sup>F</sup>*

display
*afficheur<sup>M</sup>*

talk key
*touche<sup>F</sup> d'appel<sup>M</sup>*

power button
*interrupteur<sup>M</sup>*

alphanumeric keypad
*clavier<sup>M</sup> alphanumérique*

read button
*touche<sup>F</sup> de lecture<sup>F</sup>*

sliding cover
*clapet<sup>M</sup>*

scroll wheel
*roulette<sup>F</sup> de défilement<sup>M</sup>*

select button
*touche<sup>F</sup> de sélection<sup>F</sup>*

microphone
*microphone<sup>M</sup>*

end key
*touche<sup>F</sup> de fin<sup>F</sup> d'appel<sup>M</sup>*

menu button
*touche<sup>F</sup> de menu<sup>M</sup>*

**telephone set**
*poste<sup>M</sup> téléphonique*

receiver
*récepteur<sup>M</sup>*

display
*afficheur<sup>M</sup>*

handset
*combiné<sup>M</sup>*

on-off light
*voyant<sup>M</sup> de mise<sup>F</sup> en circuit<sup>M</sup>*

receiver volume control
*commande<sup>F</sup> de volume<sup>M</sup> du récepteur<sup>M</sup>*

transmitter
*microphone<sup>M</sup>*

display setting
*réglage<sup>M</sup> de l'afficheur<sup>M</sup>*

ringing volume control
*commande<sup>F</sup> de volume<sup>M</sup> de la sonnerie<sup>F</sup>*

handset cord
*cordon<sup>M</sup> de combiné<sup>M</sup>*

memory button
*commande<sup>F</sup> mémoire<sup>F</sup>*

function selectors
*sélecteurs<sup>M</sup> de fonctions<sup>F</sup>*

push buttons
*clavier<sup>M</sup>*

telephone index
*répertoire<sup>M</sup> téléphonique*

automatic dialer index
*index<sup>M</sup> de composition<sup>F</sup> automatique*

COMMUNICATIONS AND OFFICE AUTOMATION

## communication by telephone

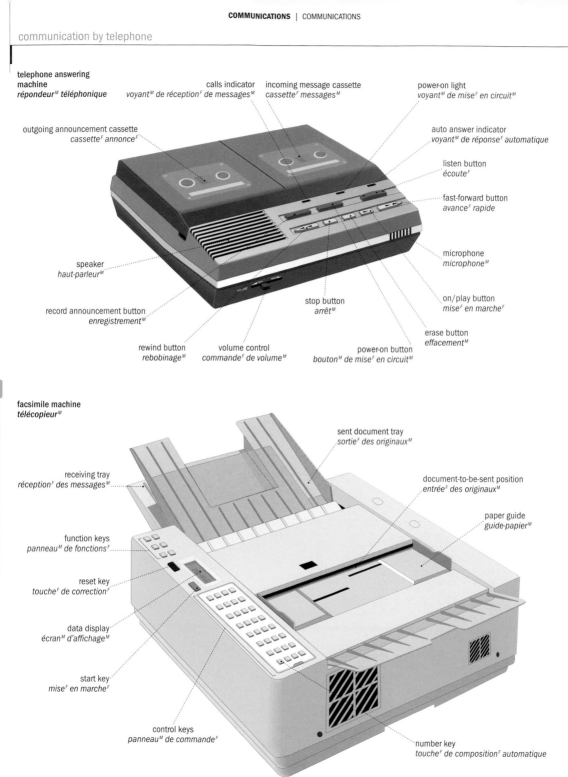

**telephone answering machine**
*répondeur^M téléphonique*

calls indicator
*voyant^M de réception^F de messages^M*

incoming message cassette
*cassette^F messages^M*

power-on light
*voyant^M de mise^F en circuit^M*

outgoing announcement cassette
*cassette^F annonce^F*

auto answer indicator
*voyant^M de réponse^F automatique*

listen button
*écoute^F*

fast-forward button
*avance^F rapide*

microphone
*microphone^M*

speaker
*haut-parleur^M*

record announcement button
*enregistrement^M*

rewind button
*rebobinage^M*

volume control
*commande^F de volume^M*

stop button
*arrêt^M*

power-on button
*bouton^M de mise^F en circuit^M*

on/play button
*mise^F en marche^F*

erase button
*effacement^M*

**facsimile machine**
*télécopieur^M*

sent document tray
*sortie^F des originaux^M*

receiving tray
*réception^F des messages^M*

document-to-be-sent position
*entrée^F des originaux^M*

paper guide
*guide-papier^M*

function keys
*panneau^M de fonctions^F*

reset key
*touche^F de correction^F*

data display
*écran^M d'affichage^M*

start key
*mise^F en marche^F*

control keys
*panneau^M de commande^F*

number key
*touche^F de composition^F automatique*

# personal computer

*micro-ordinateur*[M]

**video monitor**
*écran*[M]

vertical control
*réglage*[M] *vertical*

horizontal control
*réglage*[M] *horizontal*

centering control
*réglage*[M] *de centrage*[M]

contrast control
*réglage*[M] *du contraste*[M]

power indicator
*témoin*[M] *d'alimentation*[F]

power switch
*interrupteur*[M]

brightness control
*réglage*[M] *de la luminosité*[F]

**tower case: back view**
*boîtier*[M] *tour*[F] *: vue*[F] *arrière*

power cable plug
*prise*[F] *d'alimentation*[F]

mouse port
*port*[M] *souris*[F]

power supply fan
*ventilateur*[M] *du bloc*[M]
*d'alimentation*[F]

keyboard port
*port*[M] *clavier*[M]

case fan
*ventilateur*[M] *du boîtier*[M]

earphone jack
*prise*[F] *pour écouteurs*[M]

network port
*port*[M] *réseau*[M]

parallel port
*port*[M] *parallèle*

bay filler panel
*obturateur*[M] *de baie*[F]

USB port
*port*[M] *USB*

audio jack
*prise*[F] *audio*

video port
*port*[M] *vidéo*

game/MIDI port
*port*[M] *jeux*[M]*/MIDI*

internal modem port
*port*[M] *modem*[M] *interne*

serial port
*port*[M] *série*[F]

**tower case: front view**
*boîtier*[M] *tour*[F] *: vue*[F] *avant*

volume control
*réglage*[M] *du volume*[M]

CD/DVD-ROM drive
*lecteur*[M] *de CD/DVD-ROM*[M]

CD/DVD-ROM eject button
*bouton*[M] *d'éjection*[F] *du CD/DVD-*
*ROM*[M]

floppy disk drive
*lecteur*[M] *de disquette*[F]

floppy disk eject button
*bouton*[M] *d'éjection*[F] *de la*
*disquette*[F]

power button
*bouton*[M] *de démarrage*[M]

reset button
*bouton*[M] *de réinitialisation*[F]

COMMUNICATIONS AND OFFICE AUTOMATION

# input devices

*périphériques<sup>M</sup> d'entrée<sup>F</sup>*

**keyboard and pictograms**
*clavier<sup>M</sup> et pictogrammes<sup>M</sup>*

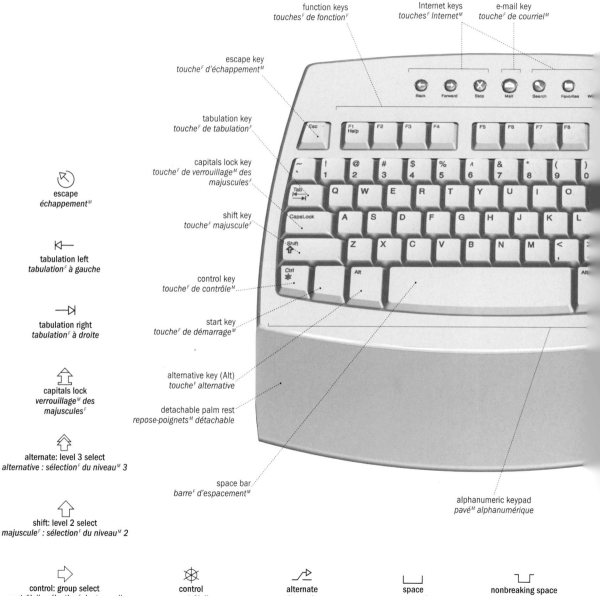

function keys
*touches<sup>F</sup> de fonction<sup>F</sup>*

Internet keys
*touches<sup>F</sup> Internet<sup>M</sup>*

e-mail key
*touche<sup>F</sup> de courriel<sup>M</sup>*

escape key
*touche<sup>F</sup> d'échappement<sup>M</sup>*

tabulation key
*touche<sup>F</sup> de tabulation<sup>F</sup>*

capitals lock key
*touche<sup>F</sup> de verrouillage<sup>M</sup> des majuscules<sup>F</sup>*

shift key
*touche<sup>F</sup> majuscule<sup>F</sup>*

control key
*touche<sup>F</sup> de contrôle<sup>M</sup>*

start key
*touche<sup>F</sup> de démarrage<sup>M</sup>*

alternative key (Alt)
*touche<sup>F</sup> alternative*

detachable palm rest
*repose-poignets<sup>M</sup> détachable*

space bar
*barre<sup>F</sup> d'espacement<sup>M</sup>*

alphanumeric keypad
*pavé<sup>M</sup> alphanumérique*

escape
*échappement<sup>M</sup>*

tabulation left
*tabulation<sup>F</sup> à gauche*

tabulation right
*tabulation<sup>F</sup> à droite*

capitals lock
*verrouillage<sup>M</sup> des majuscules<sup>F</sup>*

alternate: level 3 select
*alternative : sélection<sup>F</sup> du niveau<sup>M</sup> 3*

shift: level 2 select
*majuscule<sup>F</sup> : sélection<sup>F</sup> du niveau<sup>M</sup> 2*

control: group select
*contrôle<sup>M</sup> : sélection<sup>F</sup> de groupe<sup>M</sup>*

control
*contrôle<sup>M</sup>*

alternate
*alternative*

space
*espace<sup>F</sup>*

nonbreaking space
*espace<sup>F</sup> insécable*

COMMUNICATIONS AND OFFICE AUTOMATION

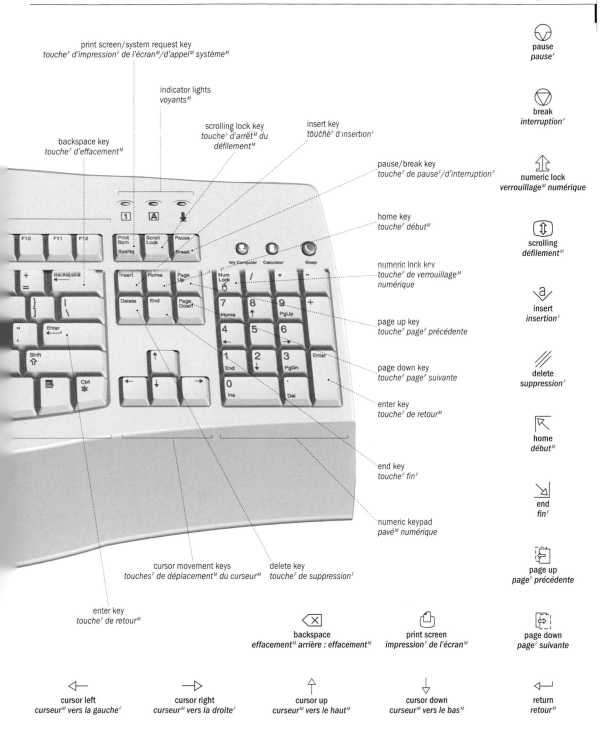

print screen/system request key
*touche[F] d'impression[F] de l'écran[M]/d'appel[M] système[M]*

indicator lights
*voyants[M]*

scrolling lock key
*touche[F] d'arrêt[M] du défilement[M]*

insert key
*touche[F] d'insertion[F]*

backspace key
*touche[F] d'effacement[M]*

pause/break key
*touche[F] de pause[F]/d'interruption[F]*

home key
*touche[F] début[M]*

numeric lock key
*touche[F] de verrouillage[M] numérique*

page up key
*touche[F] page[F] précédente*

page down key
*touche[F] page[F] suivante*

enter key
*touche[F] de retour[M]*

end key
*touche[F] fin[F]*

numeric keypad
*pavé[M] numérique*

cursor movement keys
*touches[F] de déplacement[M] du curseur[M]*

delete key
*touche[F] de suppression[F]*

enter key
*touche[F] de retour[M]*

pause
*pause[F]*

break
*interruption[F]*

numeric lock
*verrouillage[M] numérique*

scrolling
*défilement[M]*

insert
*insertion[F]*

delete
*suppression[F]*

home
*début[M]*

end
*fin[F]*

page up
*page[F] précédente*

page down
*page[F] suivante*

backspace
*effacement[M] arrière : effacement[M]*

print screen
*impression[F] de l'écran[M]*

cursor left
*curseur[M] vers la gauche[F]*

cursor right
*curseur[M] vers la droite[F]*

cursor up
*curseur[M] vers le haut[M]*

cursor down
*curseur[M] vers le bas[M]*

return
*retour[M]*

## input devices

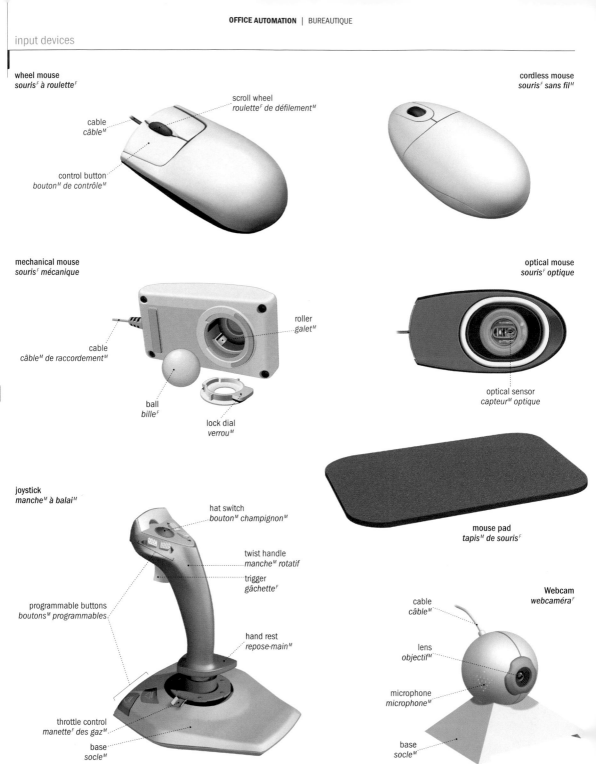

wheel mouse
*souris*[F] *à roulette*[F]

scroll wheel
*roulette*[F] *de défilement*[M]

cable
*câble*[M]

control button
*bouton*[M] *de contrôle*[M]

cordless mouse
*souris*[F] *sans fil*[M]

mechanical mouse
*souris*[F] *mécanique*

cable
*câble*[M] *de raccordement*[M]

roller
*galet*[M]

ball
*bille*[F]

lock dial
*verrou*[M]

optical mouse
*souris*[F] *optique*

optical sensor
*capteur*[M] *optique*

mouse pad
*tapis*[M] *de souris*[F]

joystick
*manche*[M] *à balai*[M]

hat switch
*bouton*[M] *champignon*[M]

twist handle
*manche*[M] *rotatif*

trigger
*gâchette*[F]

programmable buttons
*boutons*[M] *programmables*

hand rest
*repose-main*[M]

throttle control
*manette*[F] *des gaz*[M]

base
*socle*[M]

Webcam
*webcaméra*[F]

cable
*câble*[M]

lens
*objectif*[M]

microphone
*microphone*[M]

base
*socle*[M]

# output devices
*périphériques^M de sortie^F*

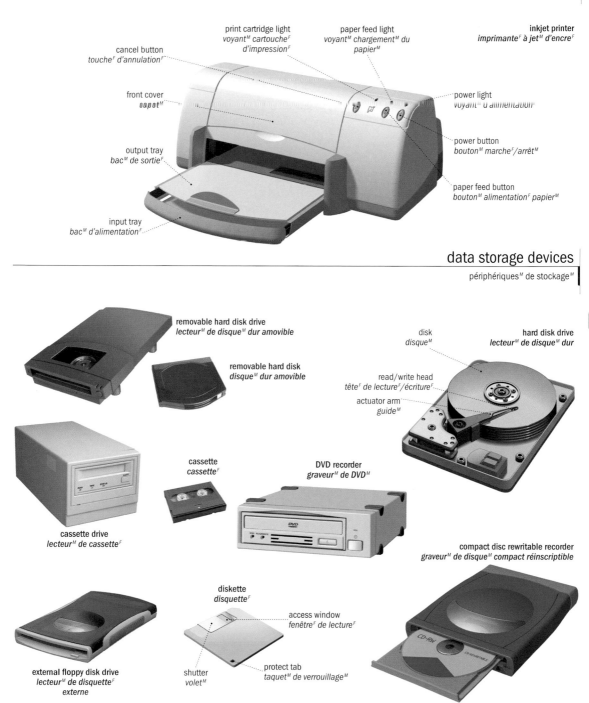

cancel button
*touche^F d'annulation^F*

print cartridge light
*voyant^M cartouche^F
d'impression^F*

paper feed light
*voyant^M chargement^M du
papier^M*

**inkjet printer**
*imprimante^F à jet^M d'encre^F*

front cover
*capot^M*

power light
*voyant^M d'alimentation^F*

output tray
*bac^M de sortie^F*

power button
*bouton^M marche^F/arrêt^M*

paper feed button
*bouton^M alimentation^F papier^M*

input tray
*bac^M d'alimentation^F*

# data storage devices
*périphériques^M de stockage^M*

removable hard disk drive
*lecteur^M de disque^M dur amovible*

disk
*disque^M*

**hard disk drive**
*lecteur^M de disque^M dur*

removable hard disk
*disque^M dur amovible*

read/write head
*tête^F de lecture^F/écriture^F*

actuator arm
*guide^M*

cassette
*cassette^F*

**DVD recorder**
*graveur^M de DVD^M*

**cassette drive**
*lecteur^M de cassette^F*

**compact disc rewritable recorder**
*graveur^M de disque^M compact réinscriptible*

diskette
*disquette^F*

access window
*fenêtre^F de lecture^F*

**external floppy disk drive**
*lecteur^M de disquette^F
externe*

shutter
*volet^M*

protect tab
*taquet^M de verrouillage^M*

# Internet

Internet<sup>M</sup>

**URL (uniform resource locator)**
*adresse<sup>F</sup> URL<sup>F</sup> (localisateur<sup>M</sup> universel de ressources<sup>F</sup>)*

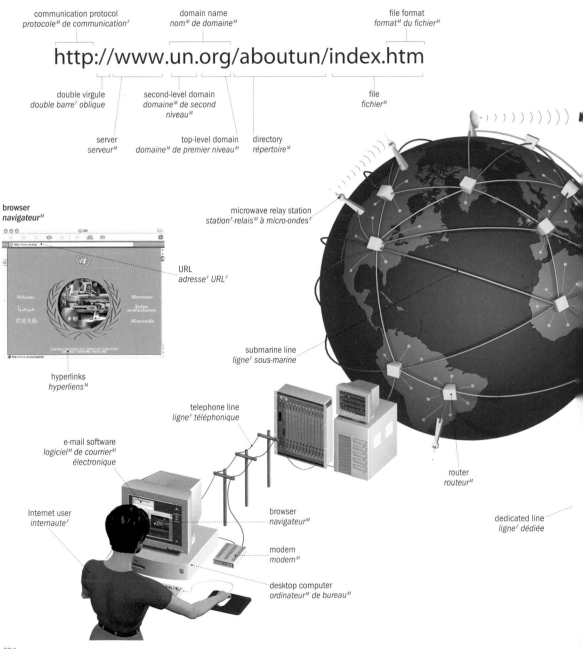

communication protocol
*protocole<sup>M</sup> de communication<sup>F</sup>*

domain name
*nom<sup>M</sup> de domaine<sup>M</sup>*

file format
*format<sup>M</sup> du fichier<sup>M</sup>*

http://www.un.org/aboutun/index.htm

double virgule
*double barre<sup>F</sup> oblique*

second-level domain
*domaine<sup>M</sup> de second niveau<sup>M</sup>*

file
*fichier<sup>M</sup>*

server
*serveur<sup>M</sup>*

top-level domain
*domaine<sup>M</sup> de premier niveau<sup>M</sup>*

directory
*répertoire<sup>M</sup>*

browser
*navigateur<sup>M</sup>*

microwave relay station
*station<sup>F</sup>-relais<sup>M</sup> à micro-ondes<sup>F</sup>*

URL
*adresse<sup>F</sup> URL<sup>F</sup>*

submarine line
*ligne<sup>F</sup> sous-marine*

hyperlinks
*hyperliens<sup>M</sup>*

telephone line
*ligne<sup>F</sup> téléphonique*

e-mail software
*logiciel<sup>M</sup> de courrier<sup>M</sup> électronique*

router
*routeur<sup>M</sup>*

Internet user
*internaute<sup>F</sup>*

browser
*navigateur<sup>M</sup>*

dedicated line
*ligne<sup>F</sup> dédiée*

modem
*modem<sup>M</sup>*

desktop computer
*ordinateur<sup>M</sup> de bureau<sup>M</sup>*

# Internet uses
utilisations<sup>F</sup> d'Internet<sup>M</sup>

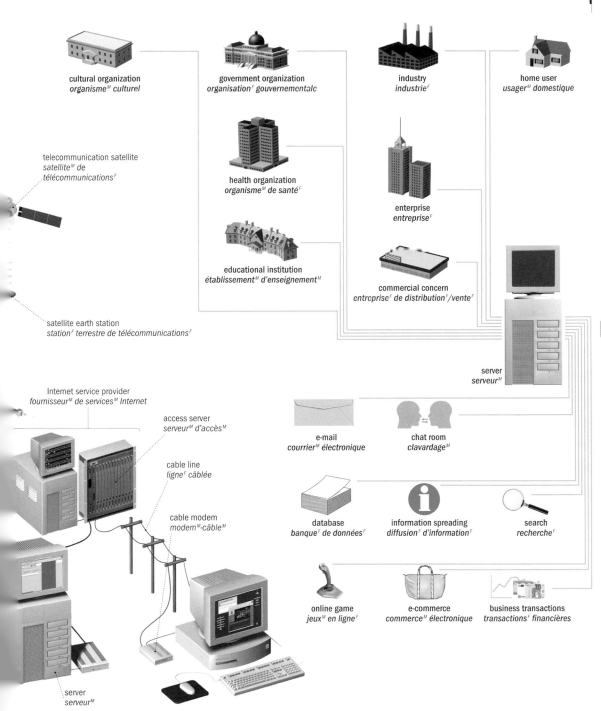

cultural organization
organisme<sup>M</sup> culturel

government organization
organisation<sup>F</sup> gouvernementale

industry
industrie<sup>F</sup>

home user
usager<sup>M</sup> domestique

telecommunication satellite
satellite<sup>M</sup> de
télécommunications<sup>F</sup>

health organization
organisme<sup>M</sup> de santé<sup>F</sup>

enterprise
entreprise<sup>F</sup>

educational institution
établissement<sup>M</sup> d'enseignement<sup>M</sup>

commercial concern
entreprise<sup>F</sup> de distribution<sup>F</sup>/vente<sup>F</sup>

satellite earth station
station<sup>F</sup> terrestre de télécommunications<sup>F</sup>

server
serveur<sup>M</sup>

Internet service provider
fournisseur<sup>M</sup> de services<sup>M</sup> Internet

access server
serveur<sup>M</sup> d'accès<sup>M</sup>

cable line
ligne<sup>F</sup> câblée

cable modem
modem<sup>M</sup>-câble<sup>M</sup>

e-mail
courrier<sup>M</sup> électronique

chat room
clavardage<sup>M</sup>

database
banque<sup>F</sup> de données<sup>F</sup>

information spreading
diffusion<sup>F</sup> d'information<sup>F</sup>

search
recherche<sup>F</sup>

online game
jeux<sup>M</sup> en ligne<sup>F</sup>

e-commerce
commerce<sup>M</sup> électronique

business transactions
transactions<sup>F</sup> financières

server
serveur<sup>M</sup>

COMMUNICATIONS AND OFFICE AUTOMATION

# laptop computer

ordinateur<sup>M</sup> portable

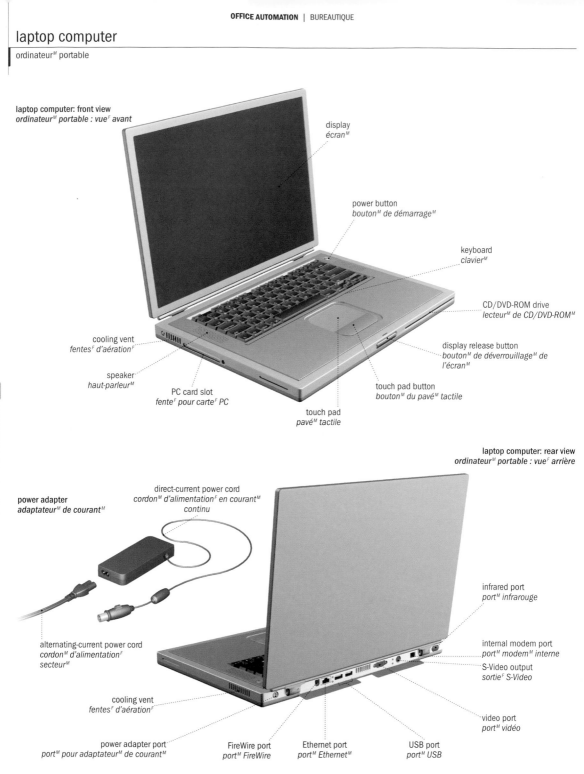

laptop computer: front view
*ordinateur<sup>M</sup> portable : vue<sup>F</sup> avant*

display
*écran<sup>M</sup>*

power button
*bouton<sup>M</sup> de démarrage<sup>M</sup>*

keyboard
*clavier<sup>M</sup>*

CD/DVD-ROM drive
*lecteur<sup>M</sup> de CD/DVD-ROM<sup>M</sup>*

cooling vent
*fentes<sup>F</sup> d'aération<sup>F</sup>*

display release button
*bouton<sup>M</sup> de déverrouillage<sup>M</sup> de l'écran<sup>M</sup>*

speaker
*haut-parleur<sup>M</sup>*

PC card slot
*fente<sup>F</sup> pour carte<sup>F</sup> PC*

touch pad button
*bouton<sup>M</sup> du pavé<sup>M</sup> tactile*

touch pad
*pavé<sup>M</sup> tactile*

laptop computer: rear view
*ordinateur<sup>M</sup> portable : vue<sup>F</sup> arrière*

power adapter
*adaptateur<sup>M</sup> de courant<sup>M</sup>*

direct-current power cord
*cordon<sup>M</sup> d'alimentation<sup>F</sup> en courant<sup>M</sup> continu*

infrared port
*port<sup>M</sup> infrarouge*

internal modem port
*port<sup>M</sup> modem<sup>M</sup> interne*

S-Video output
*sortie<sup>F</sup> S-Video*

alternating-current power cord
*cordon<sup>M</sup> d'alimentation<sup>F</sup> secteur<sup>M</sup>*

cooling vent
*fentes<sup>F</sup> d'aération<sup>F</sup>*

video port
*port<sup>M</sup> vidéo*

power adapter port
*port<sup>M</sup> pour adaptateur<sup>M</sup> de courant<sup>M</sup>*

FireWire port
*port<sup>M</sup> FireWire*

Ethernet port
*port<sup>M</sup> Ethernet<sup>M</sup>*

USB port
*port<sup>M</sup> USB*

# handheld computer/personal digital assistant (PDA)

ordinateur<sup>M</sup> de poche<sup>F</sup>

audio input/output jack
prise<sup>F</sup> d'entrée<sup>F</sup>/sortie<sup>F</sup> audio

microphone
microphone<sup>M</sup>

infrared port
port<sup>M</sup> infrarouge

voice recorder button
bouton<sup>M</sup> d'enregistreur<sup>M</sup> vocal

alarm/charge indicator light
voyant<sup>M</sup> d'alarme<sup>F</sup>/de mise<sup>F</sup> en charge<sup>F</sup>

dial/action button
roulette<sup>F</sup> de commande<sup>F</sup>

touch screen
écran<sup>M</sup> tactile

exit button
bouton<sup>M</sup> de sortie<sup>F</sup>

application launch buttons
boutons<sup>M</sup> de lancement<sup>M</sup> d'applications<sup>F</sup>

sync cable
câble<sup>M</sup> de synchronisation<sup>F</sup>

power and backlight button
bouton<sup>M</sup> de démarrage<sup>M</sup> et de rétroéclairage<sup>M</sup>

power plug
fiche<sup>F</sup> d'alimentation<sup>F</sup>

docking cradle
station<sup>F</sup> d'accueil<sup>M</sup>

stylus
stylet<sup>M</sup>

## stationery

articles<sup>M</sup> de bureau<sup>M</sup>

scientific calculator
calculatrice<sup>F</sup> scientifique

display
affichage<sup>M</sup>

solar cell
alimentation<sup>F</sup> solaire

wallet
étui<sup>M</sup>

pocket calculator
calculette<sup>F</sup>

subtract from memory
soustraction<sup>F</sup> en mémoire<sup>F</sup>

add to memory
addition<sup>F</sup> en mémoire<sup>F</sup>

memory recall
rappel<sup>M</sup> de mémoire<sup>F</sup>

clear key
effacement<sup>M</sup> total

memory cancel
effacement<sup>M</sup> de mémoire<sup>F</sup>

divide key
division<sup>F</sup>

printing calculator
calculatrice<sup>F</sup> à imprimante<sup>F</sup>

number key
touche<sup>F</sup> numérique

clear-entry key
effacement<sup>M</sup> partiel

subtract key
soustraction<sup>F</sup>

square root key
racine<sup>F</sup> carrée

decimal key
touche<sup>F</sup> de décimale<sup>F</sup>

multiply key
multiplication<sup>F</sup>

percent key
pourcentage<sup>M</sup>

add key
addition<sup>F</sup>

equals key
touche<sup>F</sup> de résultat<sup>M</sup>

change-sign key
inverseur<sup>M</sup> de signe<sup>M</sup>

COMMUNICATIONS AND OFFICE AUTOMATION

## stationery

**for time management**
*pour l'emploi*[M] *du temps*[M]

tear-off calendar
*calendrier*[M]*-mémorandum*[M]

calendar pad
*bloc*[M]*-éphéméride*[F]

electronic organizer
*organiseur*[M]

display
*écran*[M]

alphabetical keypad
*pavé*[M] *alphabétique*

numeric keypad
*pavé*[M] *numérique*

appointment book
*agenda*[M]

memo pad
*bloc*[M]*-notes*[F]

**for correspondence**
*pour la*
*correspondance*[F]

rubber stamp
*timbre*[M] *caoutchouc*[M]

numbering machine
*numéroteur*[M]

dater
*timbre*[M] *dateur*

stamp pad
*tampon*[M] *encreur*

desk tray
*boîte*[F] *à courrier*[M]

rotary file
*fichier*[M] *rotatif*

telephone index
*répertoire*[M] *téléphonique*

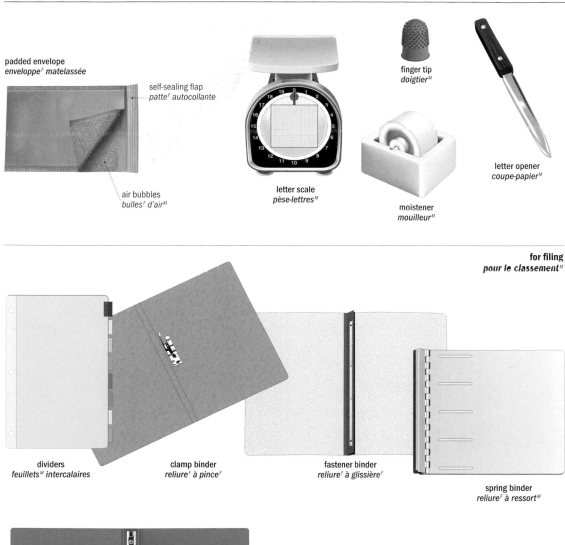

padded envelope
*enveloppe*<sup>F</sup> *matelassée*

self-sealing flap
*patte*<sup>F</sup> *autocollante*

air bubbles
*bulles*<sup>F</sup> *d'air*<sup>M</sup>

letter scale
*pèse-lettres*<sup>M</sup>

finger tip
*doigtier*<sup>M</sup>

moistener
*mouilleur*<sup>M</sup>

letter opener
*coupe-papier*<sup>M</sup>

**for filing**
*pour le classement*<sup>M</sup>

dividers
*feuillets*<sup>M</sup> *intercalaires*

clamp binder
*reliure*<sup>F</sup> *à pince*<sup>F</sup>

fastener binder
*reliure*<sup>F</sup> *à glissière*<sup>F</sup>

spring binder
*reliure*<sup>F</sup> *à ressort*<sup>M</sup>

ring binder
*classeur*<sup>M</sup> *; reliure*<sup>F</sup> *à anneaux*<sup>M</sup>

document folder
*pochette*<sup>F</sup> *d'information*<sup>F</sup>

post binder
*reliure*<sup>F</sup> *à vis*<sup>F</sup>

COMMUNICATIONS AND OFFICE AUTOMATION

## stationery

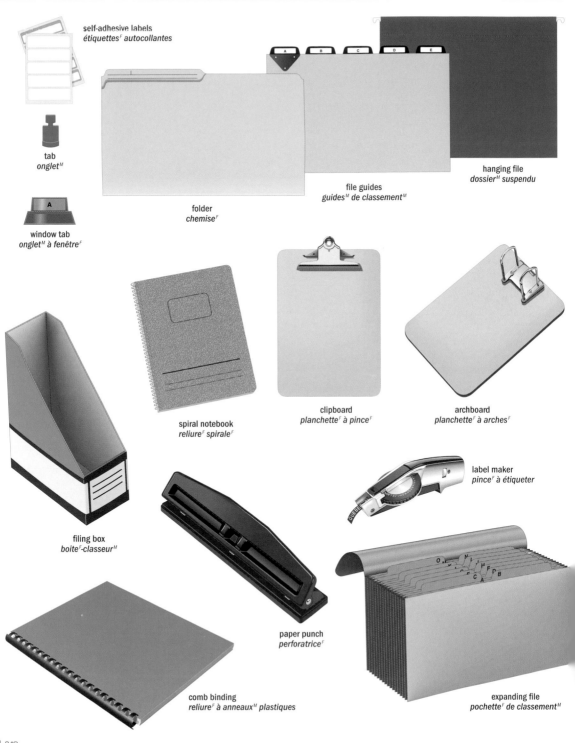

self-adhesive labels
*étiquettes<sup>F</sup> autocollantes*

tab
*onglet<sup>M</sup>*

window tab
*onglet<sup>M</sup> à fenêtre<sup>F</sup>*

folder
*chemise<sup>F</sup>*

file guides
*guides<sup>M</sup> de classement<sup>M</sup>*

hanging file
*dossier<sup>M</sup> suspendu*

filing box
*boîte<sup>F</sup>-classeur<sup>M</sup>*

spiral notebook
*reliure<sup>F</sup> spirale<sup>F</sup>*

clipboard
*planchette<sup>F</sup> à pince<sup>F</sup>*

archboard
*planchette<sup>F</sup> à arches<sup>F</sup>*

label maker
*pince<sup>F</sup> à étiqueter*

comb binding
*reliure<sup>F</sup> à anneaux<sup>M</sup> plastiques*

paper punch
*perforatrice<sup>F</sup>*

expanding file
*pochette<sup>F</sup> de classement<sup>M</sup>*

**miscellaneous articles**
*articles[M] divers*

paper clips
*trombones[M]*

thumb tacks
*punaises[F]*

paper fasteners
*attaches[F] parisiennes*

packing tape dispenser
*dévidoir[M] pistolet[M]*

hub
*moyeu[M]*

tape guide
*guide-bande[M]*

tension-adjusting screw
*vis[F] de réglage[M] de tension[F]*

pencil sharpener
*taille-crayon[M]*

cutting blade
*lame[F]*

eraser
*gomme[F]*

bill-file
*pique-notes[M]*

handle
*poignée[F]*

staple remover
*dégrafeuse[F]*

tape dispenser
*dévidoir[M] de ruban[M] adhésif*

glue stick
*bâtonnet[M] de colle[F]*

stapler
*agrafeuse[F]*

staples
*agrafes[F]*

book ends
*serre-livres[M]*

paper clip holder
*distributeur[M] de trombones[M]*

magnet
*aimant[M]*

pencil sharpener
*taille-crayon[M]*

bulletin board
*tableau[M] d'affichage[M] ; babillard[M]*

cutting head
*tête[F] de coupe[F]*

waste basket
*corbeille[F] à papier[M]*

waste basket
*corbeille[F] à papier[M]*

posting surface
*surface[F] d'affichage[M]*

paper shredder
*destructeur[M] de documents[M] ;
déchiqueteuse[F]*

# road system
système<sup>M</sup> routier

système*<sup>M</sup>* routier

**cross section of a road**
*coupe<sup>F</sup> d'une route<sup>F</sup>*

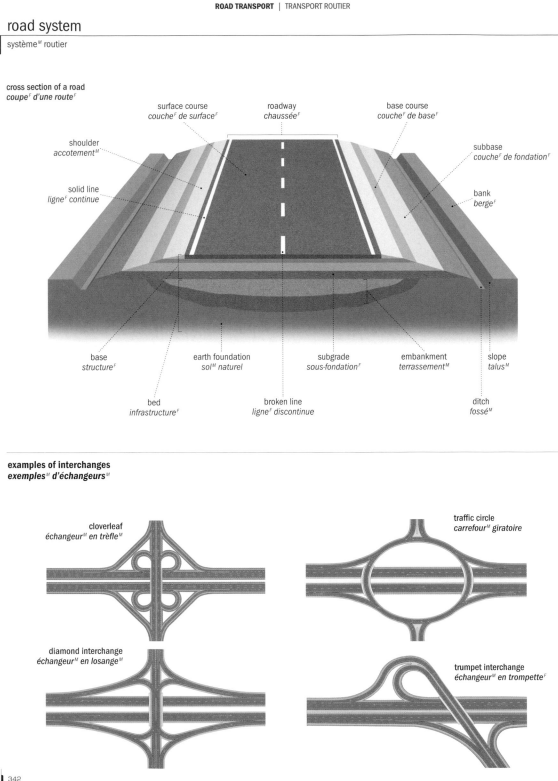

surface course
*couche<sup>F</sup> de surface<sup>F</sup>*

roadway
*chaussée<sup>F</sup>*

base course
*couche<sup>F</sup> de base<sup>F</sup>*

shoulder
*accotement<sup>M</sup>*

subbase
*couche<sup>F</sup> de fondation<sup>F</sup>*

solid line
*ligne<sup>F</sup> continue*

bank
*berge<sup>F</sup>*

base
*structure<sup>F</sup>*

earth foundation
*sol<sup>M</sup> naturel*

subgrade
*sous-fondation<sup>F</sup>*

embankment
*terrassement<sup>M</sup>*

slope
*talus<sup>M</sup>*

bed
*infrastructure<sup>F</sup>*

broken line
*ligne<sup>F</sup> discontinue*

ditch
*fossé<sup>M</sup>*

**examples of interchanges**
*exemples<sup>M</sup> d'échangeurs<sup>M</sup>*

cloverleaf
*échangeur<sup>M</sup> en trèfle<sup>M</sup>*

traffic circle
*carrefour<sup>M</sup> giratoire*

diamond interchange
*échangeur<sup>M</sup> en losange<sup>M</sup>*

trumpet interchange
*échangeur<sup>M</sup> en trompette<sup>F</sup>*

**cloverleaf**
*échangeur^M en trèfle^M*

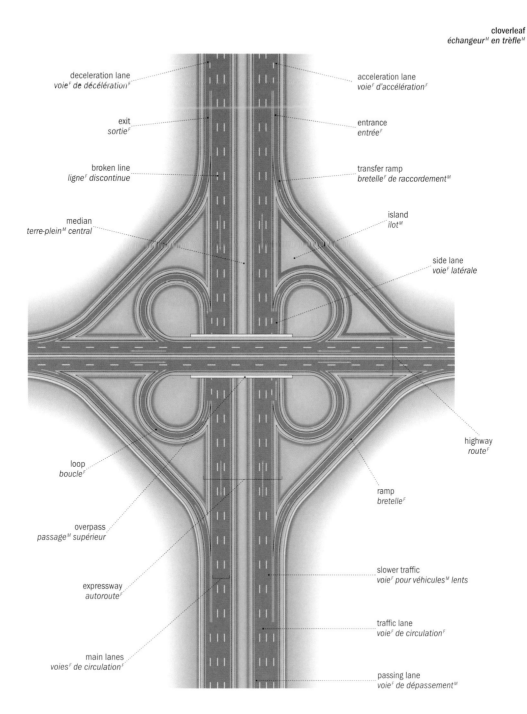

deceleration lane
*voie^F de décélération^F*

acceleration lane
*voie^F d'accélération^F*

exit
*sortie^F*

entrance
*entrée^F*

broken line
*ligne^F discontinue*

transfer ramp
*bretelle^F de raccordement^M*

median
*terre-plein^M central*

island
*îlot^M*

side lane
*voie^F latérale*

loop
*boucle^F*

highway
*route^F*

overpass
*passage^M supérieur*

ramp
*bretelle^F*

expressway
*autoroute^F*

slower traffic
*voie^F pour véhicules^M lents*

traffic lane
*voie^F de circulation^F*

main lanes
*voies^F de circulation^F*

passing lane
*voie^F de dépassement^M*

# fixed bridges

ponts<sup>M</sup> fixes

### beam bridge
*pont<sup>M</sup> à poutre<sup>F</sup>*

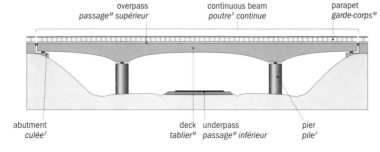

overpass
*passage<sup>M</sup> supérieur*

continuous beam
*poutre<sup>F</sup> continue*

parapet
*garde-corps<sup>M</sup>*

abutment
*culée<sup>F</sup>*

deck
*tablier<sup>M</sup>*

underpass
*passage<sup>M</sup> inférieur*

pier
*pile<sup>F</sup>*

### suspension bridge
*pont<sup>M</sup> suspendu à câble<sup>M</sup>*
*porteur*

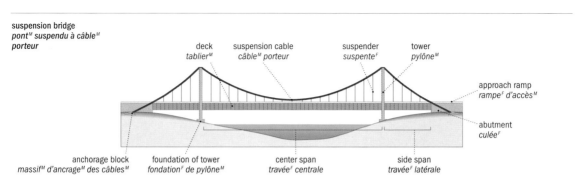

deck
*tablier<sup>M</sup>*

suspension cable
*câble<sup>M</sup> porteur*

suspender
*suspente<sup>F</sup>*

tower
*pylône<sup>M</sup>*

approach ramp
*rampe<sup>F</sup> d'accès<sup>M</sup>*

abutment
*culée<sup>F</sup>*

anchorage block
*massif<sup>M</sup> d'ancrage<sup>M</sup> des câbles<sup>M</sup>*

foundation of tower
*fondation<sup>F</sup> de pylône<sup>M</sup>*

center span
*travée<sup>F</sup> centrale*

side span
*travée<sup>F</sup> latérale*

### cantilever bridge
*pont<sup>M</sup> cantilever*

suspended span
*poutre<sup>F</sup> suspendue*

cantilever span
*poutre<sup>F</sup> cantilever*

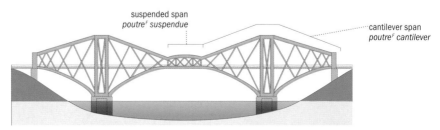

# movable bridges

ponts<sup>M</sup> mobiles

### swing bridge
*pont<sup>M</sup> tournant*

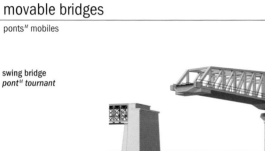

turntable
*plaque<sup>F</sup> tournante*

TRANSPORT AND MACHINERY

## movable bridges

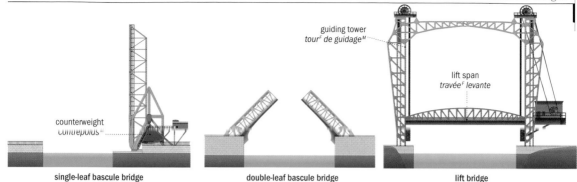

counterweight
*contrepoids* M

single-leaf bascule bridge
*pont* M *basculant à simple volée* F

double-leaf bascule bridge
*pont* M *basculant à double volée* F

guiding tower
*tour* F *de guidage* M

lift span
*travée* F *levante*

lift bridge
*pont* M *levant*

## road tunnel
tunnel M routier

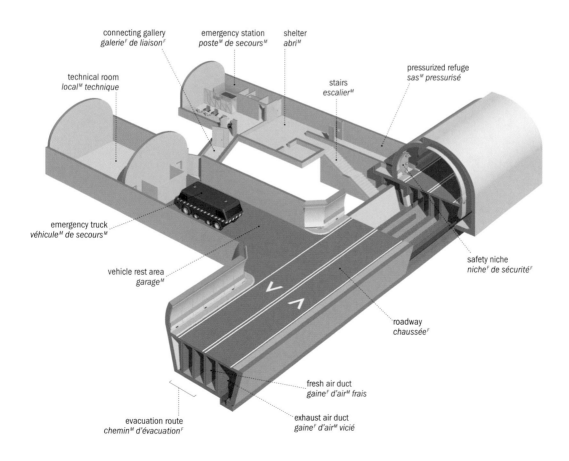

connecting gallery
*galerie* F *de liaison* F

emergency station
*poste* M *de secours* M

shelter
*abri* M

pressurized refuge
*sas* M *pressurisé*

technical room
*local* M *technique*

stairs
*escalier* M

emergency truck
*véhicule* M *de secours* M

vehicle rest area
*garage* M

safety niche
*niche* F *de sécurité* F

roadway
*chaussée* F

fresh air duct
*gaine* F *d'air* M *frais*

evacuation route
*chemin* M *d'évacuation* F

exhaust air duct
*gaine* F *d'air* M *vicié*

TRANSPORT AND MACHINERY

# service station

station<sup>F</sup>-service<sup>M</sup>

**gasoline pump**
*distributeur<sup>M</sup> d'essence<sup>F</sup>*

display
écran<sup>M</sup>

card-reader slot
fente<sup>F</sup> du lecteur<sup>M</sup> de carte<sup>F</sup>

alphanumeric keyboard
clavier<sup>M</sup> alphanumérique

slip presenter
sortie<sup>F</sup> des tickets<sup>M</sup>

type of fuel
type<sup>M</sup> de carburant<sup>M</sup>

operating instructions
mode<sup>M</sup> d'emploi<sup>M</sup>

total sale display
afficheur<sup>M</sup> totaliseur

volume display
afficheur<sup>M</sup> volume<sup>M</sup>

price per gallon/liter
afficheur<sup>M</sup> prix<sup>M</sup>

pump number
numéro<sup>M</sup> de la pompe<sup>F</sup>

pump nozzle
pistolet<sup>M</sup> de distribution<sup>F</sup>

gasoline pump hose
flexible<sup>M</sup> de distribution<sup>F</sup>

**service station**
*station<sup>F</sup>-service<sup>M</sup>*

mechanics
atelier<sup>M</sup> de mécanique<sup>F</sup>

ice dispenser
distributeur<sup>M</sup> de glaçons<sup>M</sup>

car wash
lave-auto<sup>M</sup>

maintenance
service<sup>M</sup> d'entretien<sup>M</sup>

soft-drink dispenser
distributeur<sup>M</sup> de boissons<sup>F</sup>

office
bureau<sup>M</sup>

air pump
borne<sup>F</sup> de gonflage<sup>M</sup>

pump island
aire<sup>F</sup> de ravitaillement<sup>M</sup>

kiosk
kiosque<sup>M</sup>

gasoline pump
distributeur<sup>M</sup> d'essence<sup>F</sup>

# automobile

automobile<sup>F</sup>

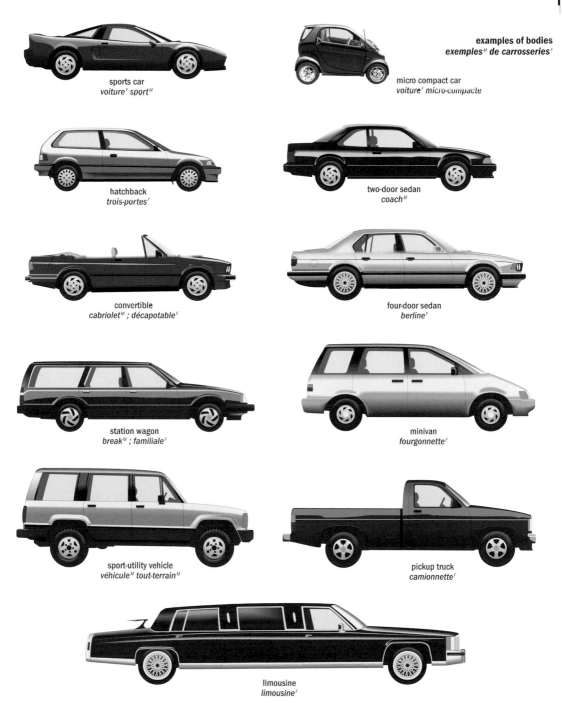

sports car
*voiture<sup>F</sup> sport<sup>M</sup>*

**examples of bodies**
*exemples<sup>M</sup> de carrosseries<sup>F</sup>*

micro compact car
*voiture<sup>F</sup> micro-compacte*

hatchback
*trois-portes<sup>F</sup>*

two-door sedan
*coach<sup>M</sup>*

convertible
*cabriolet<sup>M</sup> ; décapotable<sup>F</sup>*

four-door sedan
*berline<sup>F</sup>*

station wagon
*break<sup>M</sup> ; familiale<sup>F</sup>*

minivan
*fourgonnette<sup>F</sup>*

sport-utility vehicle
*véhicule<sup>M</sup> tout-terrain<sup>M</sup>*

pickup truck
*camionnette<sup>F</sup>*

limousine
*limousine<sup>F</sup>*

TRANSPORT AND MACHINERY

**automobile**

**body**
*carrosserie*<sup>F</sup>

windshield
*pare-brise*<sup>M</sup>

outside mirror
*rétroviseur*<sup>M</sup> *extérieur*

windshield wiper
*essuie-glace*<sup>M</sup>

cowl
*auvent*<sup>M</sup>

washer nozzle
*gicleur*<sup>M</sup> *de lave-glace*<sup>M</sup>

hood
*capot*<sup>M</sup>

grille
*calandre*<sup>F</sup>

bumper molding
*moulure*<sup>F</sup> *de pare-chocs*<sup>M</sup>

headlight
*phare*<sup>M</sup>

front fascia
*carénage*<sup>M</sup> *avant*

fender
*aile*<sup>F</sup>

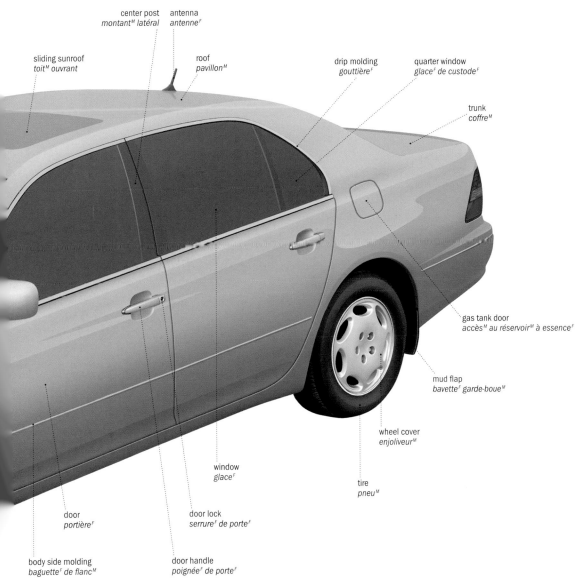

center post
montant<sup>M</sup> latéral

antenna
antenne<sup>F</sup>

sliding sunroof
toit<sup>M</sup> ouvrant

roof
pavillon<sup>M</sup>

drip molding
gouttière<sup>F</sup>

quarter window
glace<sup>F</sup> de custode<sup>F</sup>

trunk
coffre<sup>M</sup>

gas tank door
accès<sup>M</sup> au réservoir<sup>M</sup> à essence<sup>F</sup>

mud flap
bavette<sup>F</sup> garde-boue<sup>M</sup>

wheel cover
enjoliveur<sup>M</sup>

window
glace<sup>F</sup>

tire
pneu<sup>M</sup>

door
portière<sup>F</sup>

door lock
serrure<sup>F</sup> de porte<sup>F</sup>

body side molding
baguette<sup>F</sup> de flanc<sup>M</sup>

door handle
poignée<sup>F</sup> de porte<sup>F</sup>

automobile

automobile systems: main parts
*principaux organes<sup>M</sup> des systèmes<sup>M</sup> automobiles*

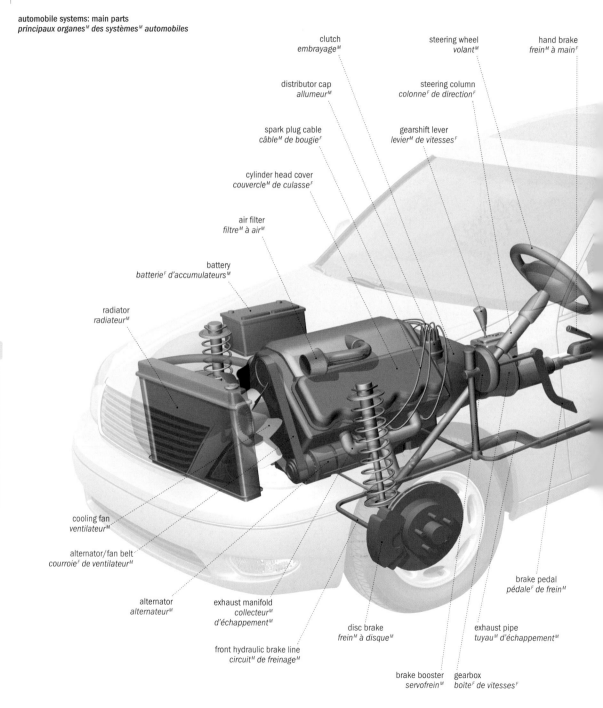

clutch
*embrayage<sup>M</sup>*

steering wheel
*volant<sup>M</sup>*

hand brake
*frein<sup>M</sup> à main<sup>F</sup>*

distributor cap
*allumeur<sup>M</sup>*

steering column
*colonne<sup>F</sup> de direction<sup>F</sup>*

spark plug cable
*câble<sup>M</sup> de bougie<sup>F</sup>*

gearshift lever
*levier<sup>M</sup> de vitesses<sup>F</sup>*

cylinder head cover
*couvercle<sup>M</sup> de culasse<sup>F</sup>*

air filter
*filtre<sup>M</sup> à air<sup>M</sup>*

battery
*batterie<sup>F</sup> d'accumulateurs<sup>M</sup>*

radiator
*radiateur<sup>M</sup>*

cooling fan
*ventilateur<sup>M</sup>*

alternator/fan belt
*courroie<sup>F</sup> de ventilateur<sup>M</sup>*

alternator
*alternateur<sup>M</sup>*

exhaust manifold
*collecteur<sup>M</sup>
d'échappement<sup>M</sup>*

disc brake
*frein<sup>M</sup> à disque<sup>M</sup>*

brake pedal
*pédale<sup>F</sup> de frein<sup>M</sup>*

exhaust pipe
*tuyau<sup>M</sup> d'échappement<sup>M</sup>*

front hydraulic brake line
*circuit<sup>M</sup> de freinage<sup>M</sup>*

brake booster
*servofrein<sup>M</sup>*

gearbox
*boîte<sup>F</sup> de vitesses<sup>F</sup>*

TRANSPORT AND MACHINERY

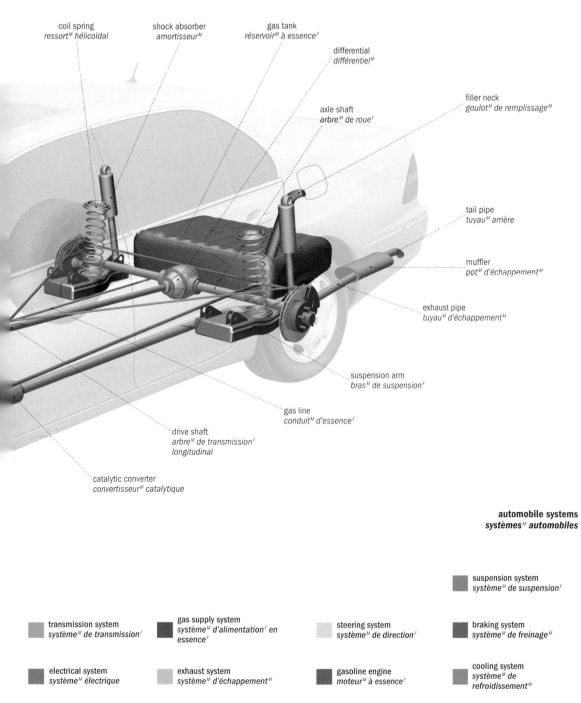

coil spring
ressort<sup>M</sup> hélicoïdal

shock absorber
amortisseur<sup>M</sup>

gas tank
réservoir<sup>M</sup> à essence<sup>F</sup>

differential
différentiel<sup>M</sup>

axle shaft
arbre<sup>M</sup> de roue<sup>F</sup>

filler neck
goulot<sup>M</sup> de remplissage<sup>M</sup>

tail pipe
tuyau<sup>M</sup> arrière

muffler
pot<sup>M</sup> d'échappement<sup>M</sup>

exhaust pipe
tuyau<sup>M</sup> d'échappement<sup>M</sup>

suspension arm
bras<sup>M</sup> de suspension<sup>F</sup>

gas line
conduit<sup>M</sup> d'essence<sup>F</sup>

drive shaft
arbre<sup>M</sup> de transmission<sup>F</sup>
longitudinal

catalytic converter
convertisseur<sup>M</sup> catalytique

**automobile systems**
**systèmes<sup>M</sup> automobiles**

transmission system
système<sup>M</sup> de transmission<sup>F</sup>

gas supply system
système<sup>M</sup> d'alimentation<sup>F</sup> en
essence<sup>F</sup>

steering system
système<sup>M</sup> de direction<sup>F</sup>

suspension system
système<sup>M</sup> de suspension<sup>F</sup>

braking system
système<sup>M</sup> de freinage<sup>M</sup>

electrical system
système<sup>M</sup> électrique

exhaust system
système<sup>M</sup> d'échappement<sup>M</sup>

gasoline engine
moteur<sup>M</sup> à essence<sup>F</sup>

cooling system
système<sup>M</sup> de
refroidissement<sup>M</sup>

TRANSPORT AND MACHINERY

automobile

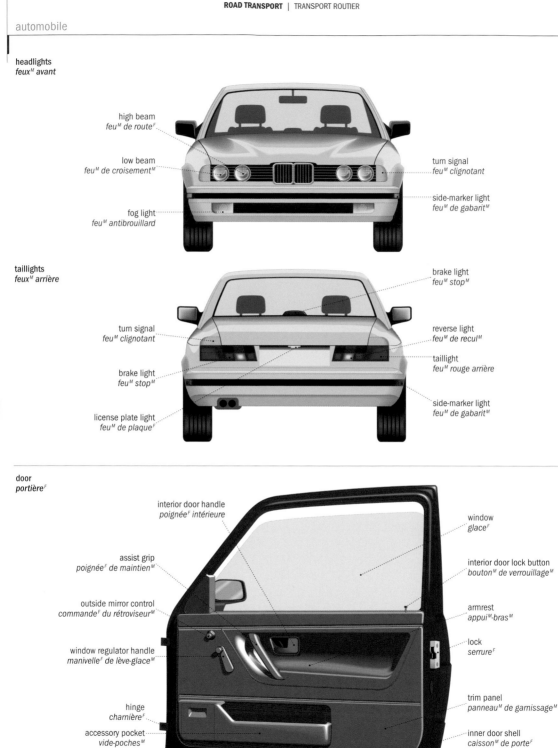

headlights
*feux^M avant*

high beam
*feu^M de route^F*

low beam
*feu^M de croisement^M*

fog light
*feu^M antibrouillard*

turn signal
*feu^M clignotant*

side-marker light
*feu^M de gabarit^M*

taillights
*feux^M arrière*

brake light
*feu^M stop^M*

turn signal
*feu^M clignotant*

reverse light
*feu^M de recul^M*

brake light
*feu^M stop^M*

taillight
*feu^M rouge arrière*

license plate light
*feu^M de plaque^F*

side-marker light
*feu^M de gabarit^M*

door
*portière^F*

interior door handle
*poignée^F intérieure*

window
*glace^F*

assist grip
*poignée^F de maintien^M*

interior door lock button
*bouton^M de verrouillage^M*

outside mirror control
*commande^F du rétroviseur^M*

armrest
*appui^M-bras^M*

window regulator handle
*manivelle^F de lève-glace^M*

lock
*serrure^F*

hinge
*charnière^F*

trim panel
*panneau^M de garnissage^M*

accessory pocket
*vide-poches^M*

inner door shell
*caisson^M de porte^F*

bucket seat: front view
*siège<sup>M</sup>-baquet<sup>M</sup> : vue<sup>F</sup> de face<sup>F</sup>*

bucket seat: side view
*siège<sup>M</sup>-baquet<sup>M</sup> : vue<sup>F</sup> de profil<sup>M</sup>*

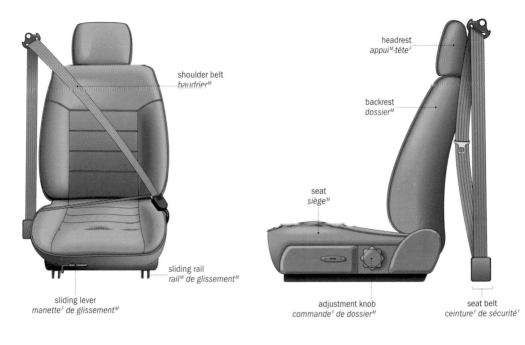

shoulder belt
*baudrier<sup>M</sup>*

headrest
*appui<sup>M</sup>-tête<sup>F</sup>*

backrest
*dossier<sup>M</sup>*

seat
*siège<sup>M</sup>*

sliding rail
*rail<sup>M</sup> de glissement<sup>M</sup>*

sliding lever
*manette<sup>F</sup> de glissement<sup>M</sup>*

adjustment knob
*commande<sup>F</sup> de dossier<sup>M</sup>*

seat belt
*ceinture<sup>F</sup> de sécurité<sup>F</sup>*

rear seat
*banquette<sup>F</sup> arrière*

armrest
*appui<sup>M</sup>-bras<sup>M</sup>*

webbing
*sangle<sup>F</sup>*

buckle
*boucle<sup>F</sup>*

bench seat
*banquette<sup>F</sup>*

TRANSPORT AND MACHINERY

353

automobile

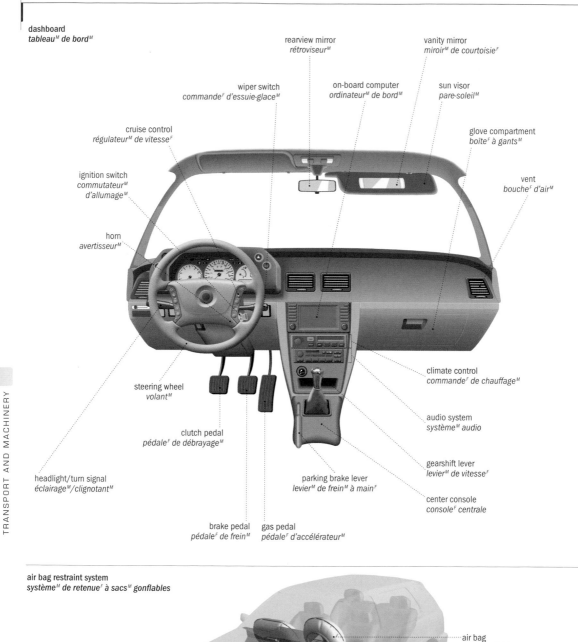

dashboard
*tableau*<sup>M</sup> *de bord*<sup>M</sup>

rearview mirror
*rétroviseur*<sup>M</sup>

vanity mirror
*miroir*<sup>M</sup> *de courtoisie*<sup>F</sup>

wiper switch
*commande*<sup>F</sup> *d'essuie-glace*<sup>M</sup>

on-board computer
*ordinateur*<sup>M</sup> *de bord*<sup>M</sup>

sun visor
*pare-soleil*<sup>M</sup>

cruise control
*régulateur*<sup>M</sup> *de vitesse*<sup>F</sup>

glove compartment
*boîte*<sup>F</sup> *à gants*<sup>M</sup>

ignition switch
*commutateur*<sup>M</sup>
*d'allumage*<sup>M</sup>

vent
*bouche*<sup>F</sup> *d'air*<sup>M</sup>

horn
*avertisseur*<sup>M</sup>

steering wheel
*volant*<sup>M</sup>

climate control
*commande*<sup>F</sup> *de chauffage*<sup>M</sup>

clutch pedal
*pédale*<sup>F</sup> *de débrayage*<sup>M</sup>

audio system
*système*<sup>M</sup> *audio*

headlight/turn signal
*éclairage*<sup>M</sup>/*clignotant*<sup>M</sup>

parking brake lever
*levier*<sup>M</sup> *de frein*<sup>M</sup> *à main*<sup>F</sup>

gearshift lever
*levier*<sup>M</sup> *de vitesse*<sup>F</sup>

center console
*console*<sup>F</sup> *centrale*

brake pedal
*pédale*<sup>F</sup> *de frein*<sup>M</sup>

gas pedal
*pédale*<sup>F</sup> *d'accélérateur*<sup>M</sup>

air bag restraint system
*système*<sup>M</sup> *de retenue*<sup>F</sup> *à sacs*<sup>M</sup> *gonflables*

air bag
*sac*<sup>M</sup> *gonflable*

safing sensor
*détecteur*<sup>M</sup> *de sécurité*<sup>F</sup>

primary crash sensor
*détecteur*<sup>M</sup> *d'impact*<sup>M</sup> *primaire*

electrical cable
*câble*<sup>M</sup> *électrique*

TRANSPORT AND MACHINERY

automobile

instrument panel
*instruments*<sup>M</sup> *de bord*<sup>M</sup>

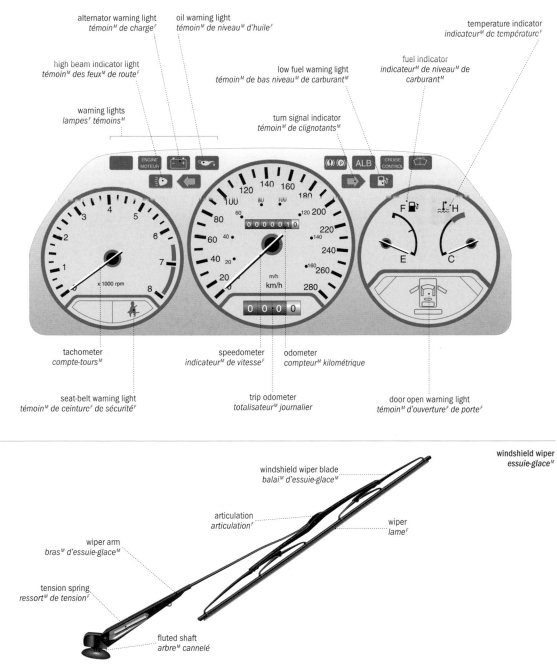

alternator warning light
*témoin*<sup>M</sup> *de charge*<sup>F</sup>

oil warning light
*témoin*<sup>M</sup> *de niveau*<sup>M</sup> *d'huile*<sup>F</sup>

temperature indicator
*indicateur*<sup>M</sup> *de température*<sup>F</sup>

high beam indicator light
*témoin*<sup>M</sup> *des feux*<sup>M</sup> *de route*<sup>F</sup>

low fuel warning light
*témoin*<sup>M</sup> *de bas niveau*<sup>M</sup> *de carburant*<sup>M</sup>

fuel indicator
*indicateur*<sup>M</sup> *de niveau*<sup>M</sup> *de carburant*<sup>M</sup>

warning lights
*lampes*<sup>F</sup> *témoins*<sup>M</sup>

turn signal indicator
*témoin*<sup>M</sup> *de clignotants*<sup>M</sup>

tachometer
*compte-tours*<sup>M</sup>

speedometer
*indicateur*<sup>M</sup> *de vitesse*<sup>F</sup>

odometer
*compteur*<sup>M</sup> *kilométrique*

seat-belt warning light
*témoin*<sup>M</sup> *de ceinture*<sup>F</sup> *de sécurité*<sup>F</sup>

trip odometer
*totalisateur*<sup>M</sup> *journalier*

door open warning light
*témoin*<sup>M</sup> *d'ouverture*<sup>F</sup> *de porte*<sup>F</sup>

windshield wiper
*essuie-glace*<sup>M</sup>

windshield wiper blade
*balai*<sup>M</sup> *d'essuie-glace*<sup>M</sup>

articulation
*articulation*<sup>F</sup>

wiper
*lame*<sup>F</sup>

wiper arm
*bras*<sup>M</sup> *d'essuie-glace*<sup>M</sup>

tension spring
*ressort*<sup>M</sup> *de tension*<sup>F</sup>

fluted shaft
*arbre*<sup>M</sup> *cannelé*

TRANSPORT AND MACHINERY

automobile

**accessories**
*accessoires*<sup>M</sup>

jumper cables
*câbles*<sup>M</sup> *de démarrage*<sup>M</sup>

floor mat
*tapis*<sup>M</sup> *de plancher*<sup>M</sup>

black clamp
*pince*<sup>F</sup> *noire*

roller shade
*store*<sup>M</sup> *à enroulement*<sup>M</sup>
*automatique*

red clamp
*pince*<sup>F</sup> *rouge*

cable
*câble*<sup>M</sup>

snow brush with scraper
*balai*<sup>M</sup> *à neige*<sup>F</sup> *à grattoir*<sup>M</sup>

ball mount
*ferrure*<sup>F</sup> *d'attelage*<sup>M</sup>

four-way lug wrench
*clé*<sup>F</sup> *en croix*<sup>F</sup>

hitch ball
*boule*<sup>F</sup> *d'attelage*<sup>M</sup>

ski rack
*porte-skis*<sup>M</sup>

bike carrier
*porte-vélos*<sup>M</sup>

vehicle jack
*cric*<sup>M</sup>

sun visor
*pare-soleil*<sup>M</sup>

handle
*manivelle*<sup>F</sup>

car cover
*housse*<sup>F</sup> *pour automobile*<sup>F</sup>

child safety seat
*siège*<sup>M</sup> *de sécurité*<sup>F</sup> *pour
enfant*<sup>M</sup>

TRANSPORT AND MACHINERY

# brakes

freins<sup>M</sup>

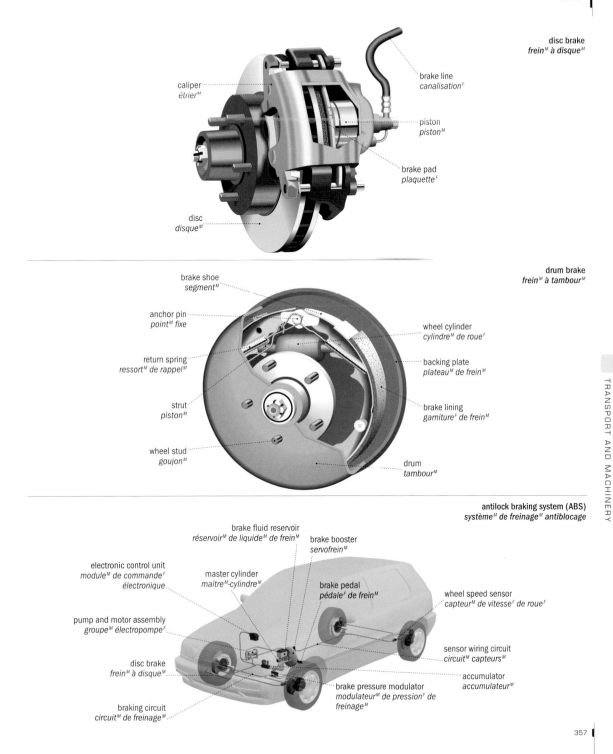

disc brake
*frein<sup>M</sup> à disque<sup>M</sup>*

brake line
*canalisation<sup>F</sup>*

caliper
*étrier<sup>M</sup>*

piston
*piston<sup>M</sup>*

brake pad
*plaquette<sup>F</sup>*

disc
*disque<sup>M</sup>*

drum brake
*frein<sup>M</sup> à tambour<sup>M</sup>*

brake shoe
*segment<sup>M</sup>*

anchor pin
*point<sup>M</sup> fixe*

wheel cylinder
*cylindre<sup>M</sup> de roue<sup>F</sup>*

return spring
*ressort<sup>M</sup> de rappel<sup>M</sup>*

backing plate
*plateau<sup>M</sup> de frein<sup>M</sup>*

strut
*piston<sup>M</sup>*

brake lining
*garniture<sup>F</sup> de frein<sup>M</sup>*

wheel stud
*goujon<sup>M</sup>*

drum
*tambour<sup>M</sup>*

antilock braking system (ABS)
*système<sup>M</sup> de freinage<sup>M</sup> antiblocage*

brake fluid reservoir
*réservoir<sup>M</sup> de liquide<sup>M</sup> de frein<sup>M</sup>*

brake booster
*servofrein<sup>M</sup>*

electronic control unit
*module<sup>M</sup> de commande<sup>F</sup>
électronique*

master cylinder
*maitre<sup>M</sup>-cylindre<sup>M</sup>*

brake pedal
*pédale<sup>F</sup> de frein<sup>M</sup>*

wheel speed sensor
*capteur<sup>M</sup> de vitesse<sup>F</sup> de roue<sup>F</sup>*

pump and motor assembly
*groupe<sup>M</sup> électropompe<sup>F</sup>*

sensor wiring circuit
*circuit<sup>M</sup> capteurs<sup>M</sup>*

disc brake
*frein<sup>M</sup> à disque<sup>M</sup>*

accumulator
*accumulateur<sup>M</sup>*

brake pressure modulator
*modulateur<sup>M</sup> de pression<sup>F</sup> de
freinage<sup>M</sup>*

braking circuit
*circuit<sup>M</sup> de freinage<sup>M</sup>*

TRANSPORT AND MACHINERY

357

# tire

pneu<sup>M</sup>

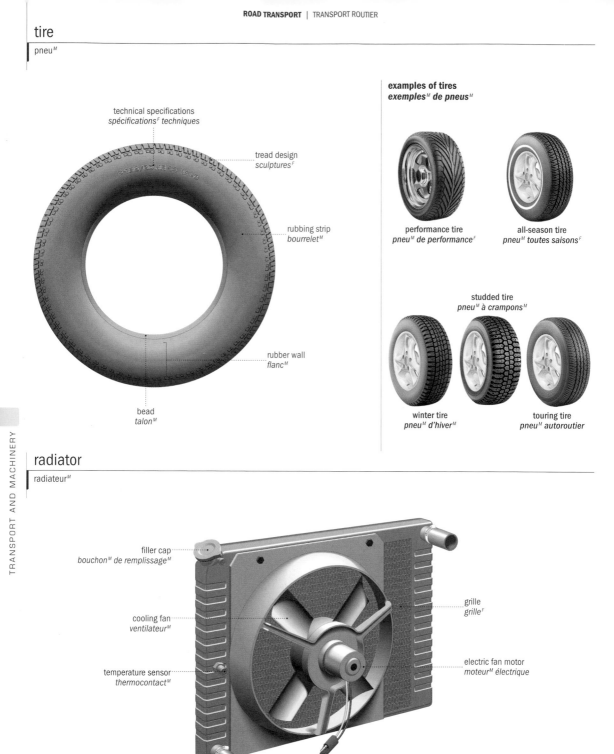

technical specifications
spécifications<sup>F</sup> techniques

tread design
sculptures<sup>F</sup>

rubbing strip
bourrelet<sup>M</sup>

rubber wall
flanc<sup>M</sup>

bead
talon<sup>M</sup>

**examples of tires**
*exemples<sup>M</sup> de pneus<sup>M</sup>*

performance tire
pneu<sup>M</sup> de performance<sup>F</sup>

all-season tire
pneu<sup>M</sup> toutes saisons<sup>F</sup>

studded tire
pneu<sup>M</sup> à crampons<sup>M</sup>

winter tire
pneu<sup>M</sup> d'hiver<sup>M</sup>

touring tire
pneu<sup>M</sup> autoroutier

# radiator

radiateur<sup>M</sup>

filler cap
bouchon<sup>M</sup> de remplissage<sup>M</sup>

cooling fan
ventilateur<sup>M</sup>

temperature sensor
thermocontact<sup>M</sup>

lower radiator hose
durite<sup>F</sup> de radiateur<sup>M</sup>

grille
grille<sup>F</sup>

electric fan motor
moteur<sup>M</sup> électrique

TRANSPORT AND MACHINERY

# spark plug
bougie<sup>F</sup> d'allumage<sup>M</sup>

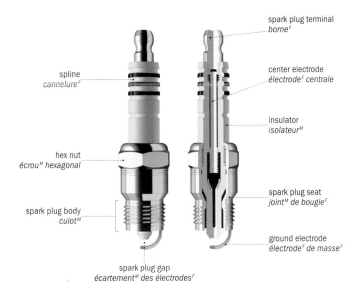

spark plug terminal
*borne*<sup>F</sup>

center electrode
*électrode*<sup>F</sup> *centrale*

insulator
*isolateur*<sup>M</sup>

spline
*cannelure*<sup>F</sup>

hex nut
*écrou*<sup>M</sup> *hexagonal*

spark plug body
*culot*<sup>M</sup>

spark plug seat
*joint*<sup>M</sup> *de bougie*<sup>F</sup>

ground electrode
*électrode*<sup>F</sup> *de masse*<sup>F</sup>

spark plug gap
*écartement*<sup>M</sup> *des électrodes*<sup>F</sup>

# battery
batterie<sup>F</sup> d'accumulateurs<sup>M</sup>

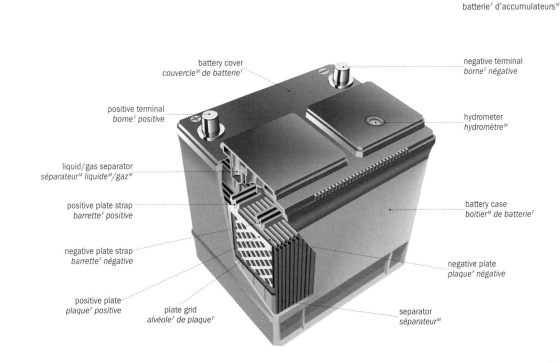

battery cover
*couvercle*<sup>M</sup> *de batterie*<sup>F</sup>

negative terminal
*borne*<sup>F</sup> *négative*

positive terminal
*borne*<sup>F</sup> *positive*

hydrometer
*hydromètre*<sup>M</sup>

liquid/gas separator
*séparateur*<sup>M</sup> *liquide*<sup>M</sup>/*gaz*<sup>M</sup>

positive plate strap
*barrette*<sup>F</sup> *positive*

battery case
*boitier*<sup>M</sup> *de batterie*<sup>F</sup>

negative plate strap
*barrette*<sup>F</sup> *négative*

negative plate
*plaque*<sup>F</sup> *négative*

positive plate
*plaque*<sup>F</sup> *positive*

plate grid
*alvéole*<sup>F</sup> *de plaque*<sup>F</sup>

separator
*séparateur*<sup>M</sup>

# gasoline engine

moteur$^M$ à essence$^F$

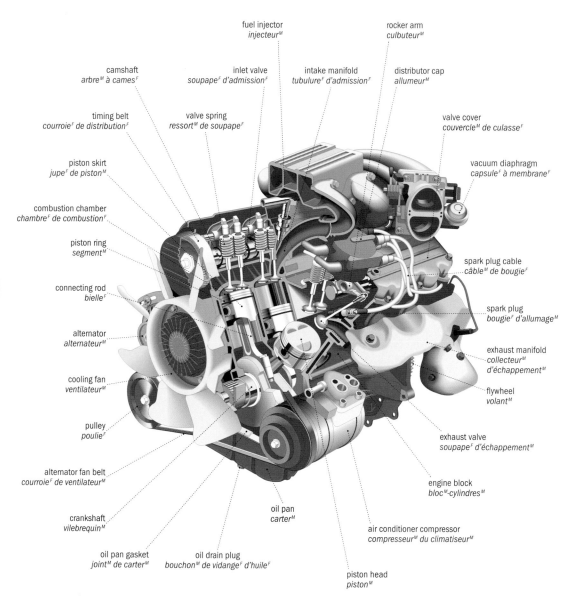

fuel injector
injecteur$^M$

rocker arm
culbuteur$^M$

camshaft
arbre$^M$ à cames$^F$

inlet valve
soupape$^F$ d'admission$^F$

intake manifold
tubulure$^F$ d'admission$^F$

distributor cap
allumeur$^M$

timing belt
courroie$^F$ de distribution$^F$

valve spring
ressort$^M$ de soupape$^F$

valve cover
couvercle$^M$ de culasse$^F$

piston skirt
jupe$^F$ de piston$^M$

vacuum diaphragm
capsule$^F$ à membrane$^F$

combustion chamber
chambre$^F$ de combustion$^F$

piston ring
segment$^M$

spark plug cable
câble$^M$ de bougie$^F$

connecting rod
bielle$^F$

spark plug
bougie$^F$ d'allumage$^M$

alternator
alternateur$^M$

exhaust manifold
collecteur$^M$
d'échappement$^M$

cooling fan
ventilateur$^M$

flywheel
volant$^M$

pulley
poulie$^F$

exhaust valve
soupape$^F$ d'échappement$^M$

alternator fan belt
courroie$^F$ de ventilateur$^M$

engine block
bloc$^M$-cylindres$^M$

crankshaft
vilebrequin$^M$

oil pan
carter$^M$

air conditioner compressor
compresseur$^M$ du climatiseur$^M$

oil pan gasket
joint$^M$ de carter$^M$

oil drain plug
bouchon$^M$ de vidange$^F$ d'huile$^F$

piston head
piston$^M$

# camping trailers

caravane<sup>F</sup>

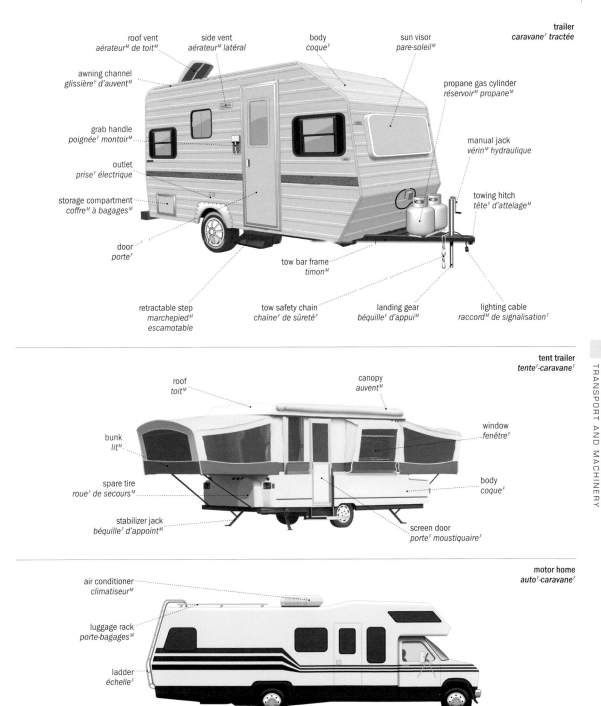

**trailer**
*caravane<sup>F</sup> tractée*

roof vent
*aérateur<sup>M</sup> de toit<sup>M</sup>*

side vent
*aérateur<sup>M</sup> latéral*

body
*coque<sup>F</sup>*

sun visor
*pare-soleil<sup>M</sup>*

awning channel
*glissière<sup>F</sup> d'auvent<sup>M</sup>*

propane gas cylinder
*réservoir<sup>M</sup> propane<sup>M</sup>*

grab handle
*poignée<sup>F</sup> montoir<sup>M</sup>*

manual jack
*vérin<sup>M</sup> hydraulique*

outlet
*prise<sup>F</sup> électrique*

storage compartment
*coffre<sup>M</sup> à bagages<sup>M</sup>*

towing hitch
*tête<sup>F</sup> d'attelage<sup>M</sup>*

door
*porte<sup>F</sup>*

tow bar frame
*timon<sup>M</sup>*

retractable step
*marchepied<sup>M</sup> escamotable*

tow safety chain
*chaine<sup>F</sup> de sûreté<sup>F</sup>*

landing gear
*béquille<sup>F</sup> d'appui<sup>M</sup>*

lighting cable
*raccord<sup>M</sup> de signalisation<sup>F</sup>*

**tent trailer**
*tente<sup>F</sup>-caravane<sup>F</sup>*

roof
*toit<sup>M</sup>*

canopy
*auvent<sup>M</sup>*

window
*fenêtre<sup>F</sup>*

bunk
*lit<sup>M</sup>*

spare tire
*roue<sup>F</sup> de secours<sup>M</sup>*

body
*coque<sup>F</sup>*

stabilizer jack
*béquille<sup>F</sup> d'appoint<sup>M</sup>*

screen door
*porte<sup>F</sup> moustiquaire<sup>F</sup>*

**motor home**
*auto<sup>F</sup>-caravane<sup>F</sup>*

air conditioner
*climatiseur<sup>M</sup>*

luggage rack
*porte-bagages<sup>M</sup>*

ladder
*échelle<sup>F</sup>*

TRANSPORT AND MACHINERY

361

# buses
autobus<sup>M</sup>

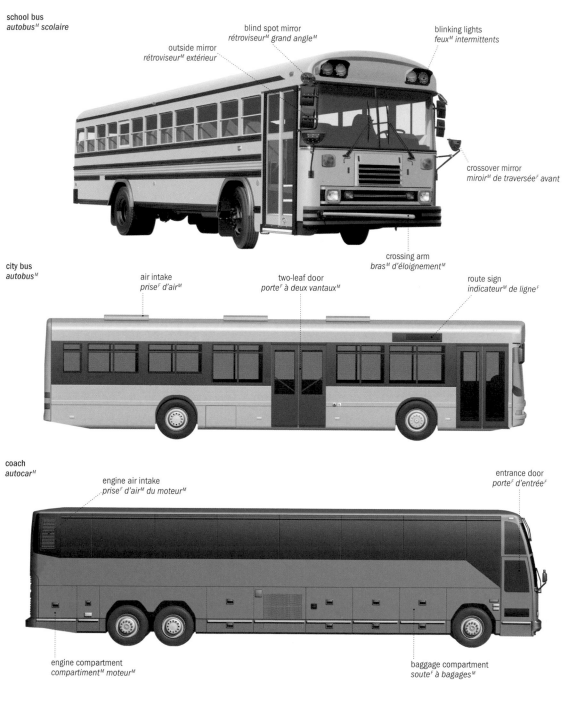

school bus
*autobus<sup>M</sup> scolaire*

outside mirror
*rétroviseur<sup>M</sup> extérieur*

blind spot mirror
*rétroviseur<sup>M</sup> grand angle<sup>M</sup>*

blinking lights
*feux<sup>M</sup> intermittents*

crossover mirror
*miroir<sup>M</sup> de traversée<sup>F</sup> avant*

crossing arm
*bras<sup>M</sup> d'éloignement<sup>M</sup>*

city bus
*autobus<sup>M</sup>*

air intake
*prise<sup>F</sup> d'air<sup>M</sup>*

two-leaf door
*porte<sup>F</sup> à deux vantaux<sup>M</sup>*

route sign
*indicateur<sup>M</sup> de ligne<sup>F</sup>*

coach
*autocar<sup>M</sup>*

engine air intake
*prise<sup>F</sup> d'air<sup>M</sup> du moteur<sup>M</sup>*

entrance door
*porte<sup>F</sup> d'entrée<sup>F</sup>*

engine compartment
*compartiment<sup>M</sup> moteur<sup>M</sup>*

baggage compartment
*soute<sup>F</sup> à bagages<sup>M</sup>*

TRANSPORT AND MACHINERY

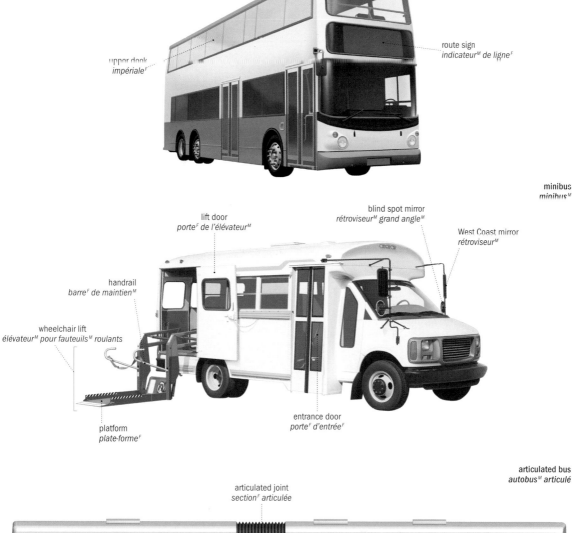

double-decker bus
*autobus*<sup>M</sup> *à impériale*<sup>F</sup>

route sign
*indicateur*<sup>M</sup> *de ligne*<sup>F</sup>

upper deck
*impériale*<sup>F</sup>

minibus
*minibus*<sup>M</sup>

lift door
*porte*<sup>F</sup> *de l'élévateur*<sup>M</sup>

blind spot mirror
*rétroviseur*<sup>M</sup> *grand angle*<sup>M</sup>

West Coast mirror
*rétroviseur*<sup>M</sup>

handrail
*barre*<sup>F</sup> *de maintien*<sup>M</sup>

wheelchair lift
*élévateur*<sup>M</sup> *pour fauteuils*<sup>M</sup> *roulants*

platform
*plate-forme*<sup>F</sup>

entrance door
*porte*<sup>F</sup> *d'entrée*<sup>F</sup>

articulated bus
*autobus*<sup>M</sup> *articulé*

articulated joint
*section*<sup>F</sup> *articulée*

rear rigid section
*tronçon*<sup>M</sup> *rigide arrière*

front rigid section
*tronçon*<sup>M</sup> *rigide avant*

TRANSPORT AND MACHINERY

# trucking
*camionnage*[M]

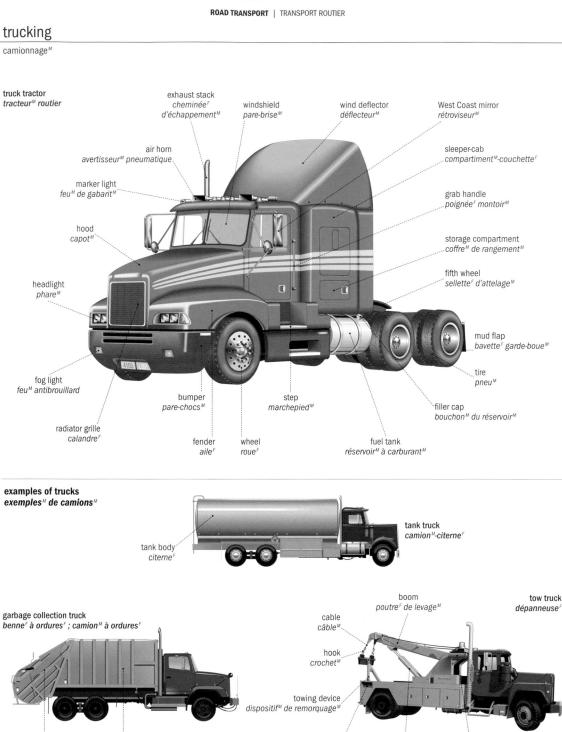

**truck tractor**
*tracteur*[M] *routier*

exhaust stack
*cheminée*[F]
*d'échappement*[M]

windshield
*pare-brise*[M]

wind deflector
*déflecteur*[M]

West Coast mirror
*rétroviseur*[M]

air horn
*avertisseur*[M] *pneumatique*

sleeper-cab
*compartiment*[M]*-couchette*[F]

marker light
*feu*[M] *de gabarit*[M]

grab handle
*poignée*[F] *montoir*[M]

hood
*capot*[M]

storage compartment
*coffre*[M] *de rangement*[M]

headlight
*phare*[M]

fifth wheel
*sellette*[F] *d'attelage*[M]

mud flap
*bavette*[F] *garde-boue*[M]

tire
*pneu*[M]

fog light
*feu*[M] *antibrouillard*

bumper
*pare-chocs*[M]

step
*marchepied*[M]

filler cap
*bouchon*[M] *du réservoir*[M]

radiator grille
*calandre*[F]

fender
*aile*[F]

wheel
*roue*[F]

fuel tank
*réservoir*[M] *à carburant*[M]

**examples of trucks**
*exemples*[M] *de camions*[M]

tank truck
*camion*[M]*-citerne*[F]

tank body
*citerne*[F]

**garbage collection truck**
*benne*[F] *à ordures*[F] ; *camion*[M] *à ordures*[F]

boom
*poutre*[F] *de levage*[M]

tow truck
*dépanneuse*[F]

cable
*câble*[M]

hook
*crochet*[M]

towing device
*dispositif*[M] *de remorquage*[M]

loading hopper
*trémie*[F] *de chargement*[M]

packer body
*benne*[F] *tasseuse*

winch controls
*commandes*[F] *du treuil*[M]

elevating cylinder
*vérin*[M]

winch
*treuil*[M]

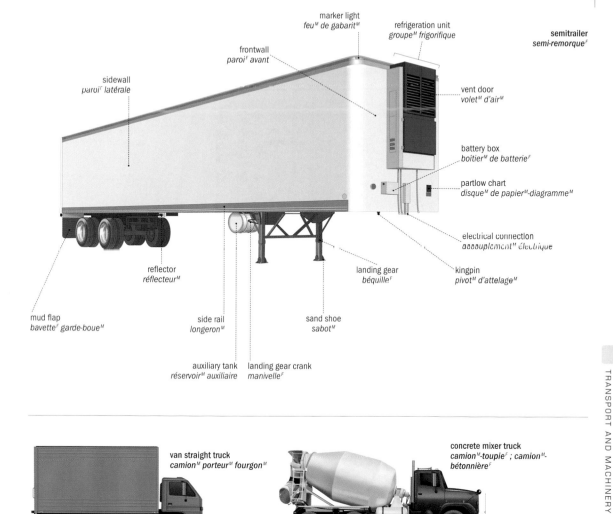

marker light
feu<sup>M</sup> de gabarit<sup>M</sup>

refrigeration unit
groupe<sup>M</sup> frigorifique

semitrailer
semi-remorque<sup>F</sup>

frontwall
paroi<sup>F</sup> avant

sidewall
paroi<sup>F</sup> latérale

vent door
volet<sup>M</sup> d'air<sup>M</sup>

battery box
boîtier<sup>M</sup> de batterie<sup>F</sup>

partlow chart
disque<sup>M</sup> de papier<sup>M</sup>-diagramme<sup>M</sup>

electrical connection
accouplement<sup>M</sup> électrique

kingpin
pivot<sup>M</sup> d'attelage<sup>M</sup>

reflector
réflecteur<sup>M</sup>

landing gear
béquille<sup>F</sup>

mud flap
bavette<sup>F</sup> garde-boue<sup>M</sup>

side rail
longeron<sup>M</sup>

sand shoe
sabot<sup>M</sup>

auxiliary tank
réservoir<sup>M</sup> auxiliaire

landing gear crank
manivelle<sup>F</sup>

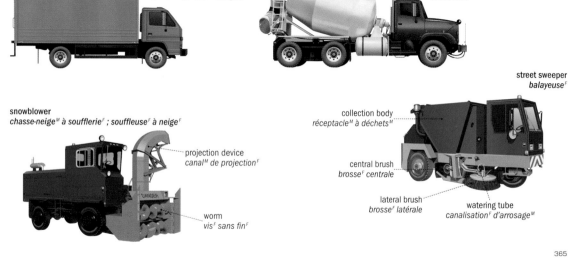

van straight truck
camion<sup>M</sup> porteur<sup>M</sup> fourgon<sup>M</sup>

concrete mixer truck
camion<sup>M</sup>-toupie<sup>F</sup> ; camion<sup>M</sup>-bétonnière<sup>F</sup>

street sweeper
balayeuse<sup>F</sup>

snowblower
chasse-neige<sup>M</sup> à soufflerie<sup>F</sup> ; souffleuse<sup>F</sup> à neige<sup>F</sup>

collection body
réceptacle<sup>M</sup> à déchets<sup>M</sup>

projection device
canal<sup>M</sup> de projection<sup>F</sup>

central brush
brosse<sup>F</sup> centrale

lateral brush
brosse<sup>F</sup> latérale

watering tube
canalisation<sup>F</sup> d'arrosage<sup>M</sup>

worm
vis<sup>F</sup> sans fin<sup>F</sup>

TRANSPORT AND MACHINERY

365

# motorcycle

moto<sup>F</sup>

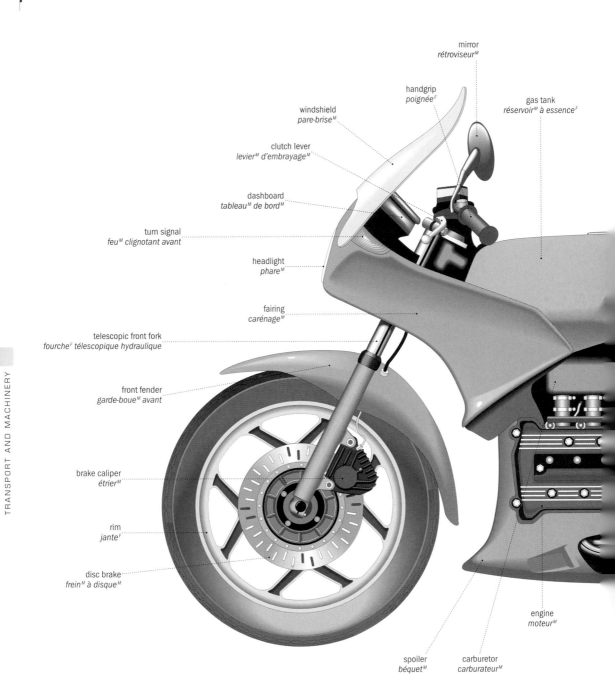

mirror
*rétroviseur*<sup>M</sup>

handgrip
*poignée*<sup>F</sup>

gas tank
*réservoir*<sup>M</sup> *à essence*<sup>F</sup>

windshield
*pare-brise*<sup>M</sup>

clutch lever
*levier*<sup>M</sup> *d'embrayage*<sup>M</sup>

dashboard
*tableau*<sup>M</sup> *de bord*<sup>M</sup>

turn signal
*feu*<sup>M</sup> *clignotant avant*

headlight
*phare*<sup>M</sup>

fairing
*carénage*<sup>M</sup>

telescopic front fork
*fourche*<sup>F</sup> *télescopique hydraulique*

front fender
*garde-boue*<sup>M</sup> *avant*

brake caliper
*étrier*<sup>M</sup>

rim
*jante*<sup>F</sup>

disc brake
*frein*<sup>M</sup> *à disque*<sup>M</sup>

engine
*moteur*<sup>M</sup>

spoiler
*béquet*<sup>M</sup>

carburetor
*carburateur*<sup>M</sup>

motorcycle

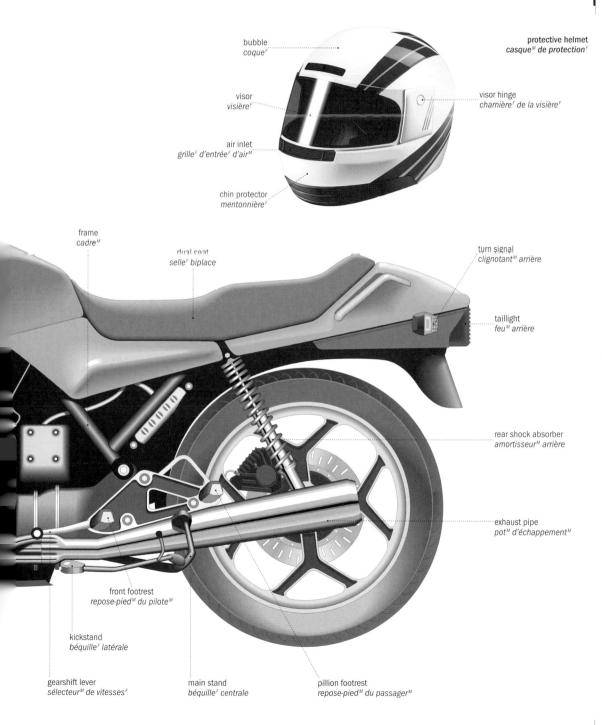

bubble
*coque*<sup>F</sup>

**protective helmet**
*casque*<sup>M</sup> *de protection*<sup>F</sup>

visor
*visière*<sup>F</sup>

visor hinge
*charnière*<sup>F</sup> *de la visière*<sup>F</sup>

air inlet
*grille*<sup>F</sup> *d'entrée*<sup>F</sup> *d'air*<sup>M</sup>

chin protector
*mentonnière*<sup>F</sup>

frame
*cadre*<sup>M</sup>

dual seat
*selle*<sup>F</sup> *biplace*

turn signal
*clignotant*<sup>M</sup> *arrière*

taillight
*feu*<sup>M</sup> *arrière*

rear shock absorber
*amortisseur*<sup>M</sup> *arrière*

exhaust pipe
*pot*<sup>M</sup> *d'échappement*<sup>M</sup>

front footrest
*repose-pied*<sup>M</sup> *du pilote*<sup>M</sup>

kickstand
*béquille*<sup>F</sup> *latérale*

gearshift lever
*sélecteur*<sup>M</sup> *de vitesses*<sup>F</sup>

main stand
*béquille*<sup>F</sup> *centrale*

pillion footrest
*repose-pied*<sup>M</sup> *du passager*<sup>M</sup>

TRANSPORT AND MACHINERY

367

motorcycle

**motorcycle dashboard**
*tableau<sup>M</sup> de bord<sup>M</sup>*

speedometer
*indicateur<sup>M</sup> de vitesse<sup>F</sup>*

tachometer
*tachymètre<sup>M</sup>*

oil pressure warning indicator
*témoin<sup>M</sup> de pression<sup>F</sup> d'huile<sup>F</sup>*

high beam warning indicator
*témoin<sup>M</sup> de phare<sup>M</sup>*

neutral indicator
*témoin<sup>M</sup> de position<sup>F</sup> neutre*

turn signal indicator
*témoin<sup>M</sup> de clignotants<sup>M</sup>*

ignition switch
*démarreur<sup>M</sup> électrique*

**motorcycle: view from above**
*moto<sup>F</sup> : vue<sup>F</sup> en plongée<sup>F</sup>*

headlight
*phare<sup>M</sup>*

turn signal
*feu<sup>M</sup> clignotant avant*

mirror
*rétroviseur<sup>M</sup>*

front brake lever
*levier<sup>M</sup> de frein<sup>M</sup> avant*

clutch lever
*levier<sup>M</sup> d'embrayage<sup>M</sup>*

twist grip throttle
*poignée<sup>F</sup> des gaz<sup>M</sup>*

dip switch
*inverseur<sup>M</sup> route<sup>F</sup>-croisement<sup>M</sup>*

emergency switch
*coupe-circuit<sup>M</sup> d'urgence<sup>F</sup>*

horn
*avertisseur<sup>M</sup>*

starter button
*bouton<sup>M</sup> de démarreur<sup>M</sup>*

gas tank cap
*bouchon<sup>M</sup> de remplissage<sup>M</sup>*

clutch housing
*carter<sup>M</sup> d'embrayage<sup>M</sup>*

gear shift
*sélecteur<sup>M</sup> de vitesses<sup>F</sup>*

rear brake pedal
*pédale<sup>F</sup> de frein<sup>M</sup> arrière*

front footrest
*repose-pied<sup>M</sup> du pilote<sup>M</sup>*

pillion footrest
*repose-pied<sup>M</sup> du passager<sup>M</sup>*

exhaust pipe
*pot<sup>M</sup> d'échappement<sup>M</sup>*

turn signal
*feu<sup>M</sup> clignotant arrière*

taillight
*feu<sup>M</sup> arrière*

TRANSPORT AND MACHINERY

motorcycle

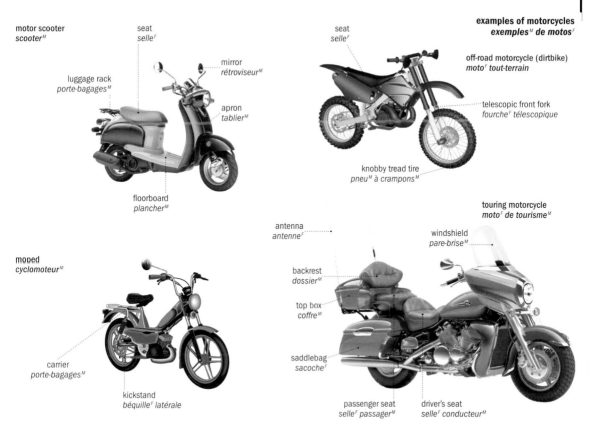

**motor scooter**
*scooter*M

seat
*selle*F

mirror
*rétroviseur*M

luggage rack
*porte-bagages*M

apron
*tablier*M

floorboard
*plancher*M

seat
*selle*F

**examples of motorcycles**
*exemples*M *de motos*F

**off-road motorcycle (dirtbike)**
*moto*F *tout-terrain*

telescopic front fork
*fourche*F *télescopique*

knobby tread tire
*pneu*M *à crampons*M

**moped**
*cyclomoteur*M

carrier
*porte-bagages*M

kickstand
*béquille*F *latérale*

**touring motorcycle**
*moto*F *de tourisme*M

antenna
*antenne*F

windshield
*pare-brise*M

backrest
*dossier*M

top box
*coffre*M

saddlebag
*sacoche*F

passenger seat
*selle*F *passager*M

driver's seat
*selle*F *conducteur*M

## 4 X 4 all-terrain vehicle

quad M

rear cargo rack
*porte-bagages*M *arrière*

seat
*selle*F

gas tank
*réservoir*M *à essence*F

handgrip
*poignée*F

rear fender
*garde-boue*M *arrière*

bumper
*pare-chocs*M

muffler
*pot*M *d'échappement*M

front shock absorber
*amortisseur*M *avant*

gearshift lever
*sélecteur*M *de vitesses*F

TRANSPORT AND MACHINERY

# bicycle

bicyclette<sup>F</sup>

parts of a bicycle
*parties<sup>F</sup> d'une bicyclette<sup>F</sup>*

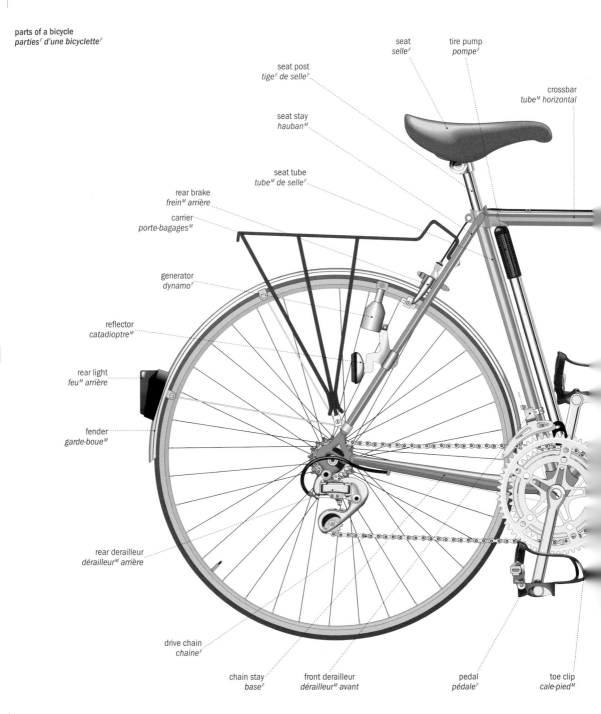

seat
*selle<sup>F</sup>*

tire pump
*pompe<sup>F</sup>*

seat post
*tige<sup>F</sup> de selle<sup>F</sup>*

crossbar
*tube<sup>M</sup> horizontal*

seat stay
*hauban<sup>M</sup>*

seat tube
*tube<sup>M</sup> de selle<sup>F</sup>*

rear brake
*frein<sup>M</sup> arrière*

carrier
*porte-bagages<sup>M</sup>*

generator
*dynamo<sup>F</sup>*

reflector
*catadioptre<sup>M</sup>*

rear light
*feu<sup>M</sup> arrière*

fender
*garde-boue<sup>M</sup>*

rear derailleur
*dérailleur<sup>M</sup> arrière*

drive chain
*chaîne<sup>F</sup>*

chain stay
*base<sup>F</sup>*

front derailleur
*dérailleur<sup>M</sup> avant*

pedal
*pédale<sup>F</sup>*

toe clip
*cale-pied<sup>M</sup>*

TRANSPORT AND MACHINERY

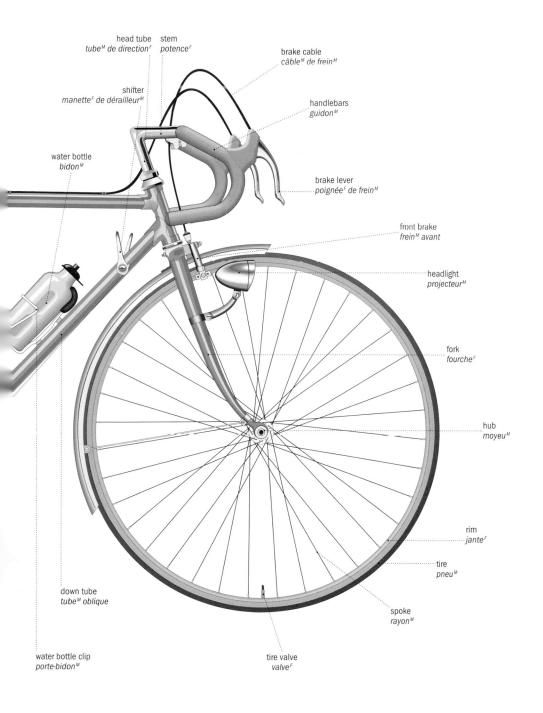

head tube
tube$^M$ de direction$^F$

stem
potence$^F$

brake cable
câble$^M$ de frein$^M$

shifter
manette$^F$ de dérailleur$^M$

handlebars
guidon$^M$

water bottle
bidon$^M$

brake lever
poignée$^F$ de frein$^M$

front brake
frein$^M$ avant

headlight
projecteur$^M$

fork
fourche$^F$

hub
moyeu$^M$

rim
jante$^F$

tire
pneu$^M$

down tube
tube$^M$ oblique

spoke
rayon$^M$

water bottle clip
porte-bidon$^M$

tire valve
valve$^F$

TRANSPORT AND MACHINERY

bicycle

**power train**
*mécanisme<sup>M</sup> de propulsion<sup>F</sup>*

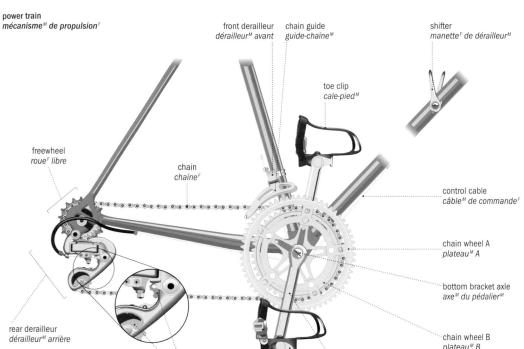

front derailleur
*dérailleur<sup>M</sup> avant*

chain guide
*guide-chaîne<sup>M</sup>*

shifter
*manette<sup>F</sup> de dérailleur<sup>M</sup>*

toe clip
*cale-pied<sup>M</sup>*

freewheel
*roue<sup>F</sup> libre*

chain
*chaîne<sup>F</sup>*

control cable
*câble<sup>M</sup> de commande<sup>F</sup>*

chain wheel A
*plateau<sup>M</sup> A*

bottom bracket axle
*axe<sup>M</sup> du pédalier<sup>M</sup>*

rear derailleur
*dérailleur<sup>M</sup> arrière*

chain wheel B
*plateau<sup>M</sup> B*

jockey rollers
*galets<sup>M</sup> tendeurs*

pedal
*pédale<sup>F</sup>*

crank
*manivelle<sup>F</sup>*

**accessories**
*accessoires<sup>M</sup>*

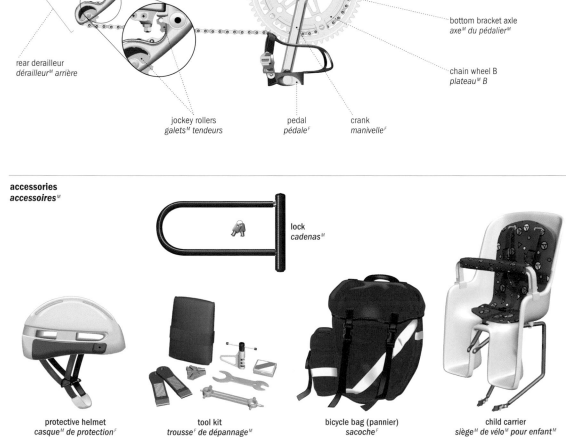

lock
*cadenas<sup>M</sup>*

protective helmet
*casque<sup>M</sup> de protection<sup>F</sup>*

tool kit
*trousse<sup>F</sup> de dépannage<sup>M</sup>*

bicycle bag (pannier)
*sacoche<sup>F</sup>*

child carrier
*siège<sup>M</sup> de vélo<sup>M</sup> pour enfant<sup>M</sup>*

TRANSPORT AND MACHINERY

examples of bicycles
*exemples*<sup>M</sup> *de bicyclettes*<sup>F</sup>

child's tricycle
*tricycle*<sup>M</sup> *d'enfant*<sup>M</sup>

BMX bike
*vélo*<sup>M</sup> *cross*<sup>M</sup>

Dutch bicycle
*bicyclette*<sup>F</sup> *hollandaise*

mountain bike
*bicyclette*<sup>F</sup> *tout-terrain*

city bicycle
*bicyclette*<sup>F</sup> *de ville*<sup>F</sup>

road bicycle
*bicyclette*<sup>F</sup> *de course*<sup>F</sup>

touring bicycle
*bicyclette*<sup>F</sup> *de tourisme*<sup>M</sup>

tandem bicycle
*tandem*<sup>M</sup>

TRANSPORT AND MACHINERY

# passenger station

gare<sup>F</sup> de voyageurs<sup>M</sup>

office
locaux<sup>M</sup> administratifs

indicator board
panneau<sup>M</sup> indicateur

baggage cart
chariot<sup>M</sup> à bagages<sup>M</sup>

baggage lockers
consigne<sup>F</sup> automatique

glassed roof
verrière<sup>F</sup>

metal structure
structure<sup>F</sup> métallique

platform number
numéro<sup>M</sup> de quai<sup>M</sup>

platform edge
bordure<sup>F</sup> de quai<sup>M</sup>

ticket collector
contrôleur<sup>M</sup>

passenger train
train<sup>M</sup>

booking hall
salle<sup>F</sup> des pas<sup>M</sup> perdus

departure time indicator
affichage<sup>M</sup> de l'heure<sup>F</sup> de
départ<sup>M</sup>

track
voie<sup>F</sup> ferrée

baggage room
enregistrement<sup>M</sup> des bagages<sup>M</sup>

passenger platform
quai<sup>M</sup> de gare<sup>F</sup>

schedules
tableau<sup>M</sup> horaire

platform entrance
accès<sup>M</sup> aux quais<sup>M</sup>

parcels office
service<sup>M</sup> de colis<sup>M</sup>

destination
destination<sup>F</sup>

# railroad station
gare<sup>F</sup>

passenger station
gare<sup>F</sup> de voyageurs<sup>M</sup>

station platform
quai<sup>M</sup>

commuter train
train<sup>M</sup> de banlieue<sup>F</sup>

main line
grandes lignes<sup>F</sup>

suburban commuter railroad
voie<sup>F</sup> de banlieue<sup>F</sup>

subsidiary track
voie<sup>F</sup> de service<sup>M</sup>

bumper
butoir<sup>M</sup>

level crossing
passage<sup>M</sup> à niveau<sup>M</sup>

parking
parking<sup>M</sup> ; stationnement<sup>M</sup>

platform shelter
abri<sup>M</sup>

footbridge
passerelle<sup>F</sup>

signal
sémaphore<sup>M</sup>

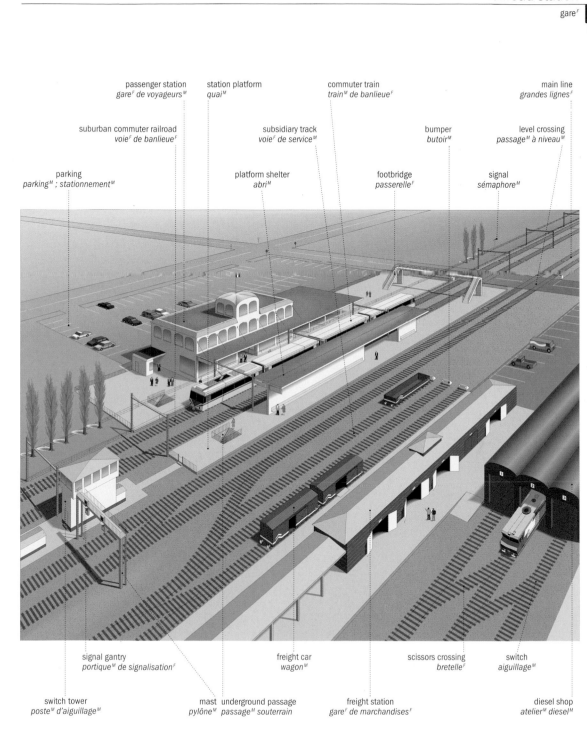

signal gantry
portique<sup>M</sup> de signalisation<sup>F</sup>

freight car
wagon<sup>M</sup>

scissors crossing
bretelle<sup>F</sup>

switch
aiguillage<sup>M</sup>

switch tower
poste<sup>M</sup> d'aiguillage<sup>M</sup>

mast
pylône<sup>M</sup>

underground passage
passage<sup>M</sup> souterrain

freight station
gare<sup>F</sup> de marchandises<sup>F</sup>

diesel shop
atelier<sup>M</sup> diesel<sup>M</sup>

TRANSPORT AND MACHINERY

# high-speed train

train$^M$ à grande vitesse$^F$ (T.G.V.)

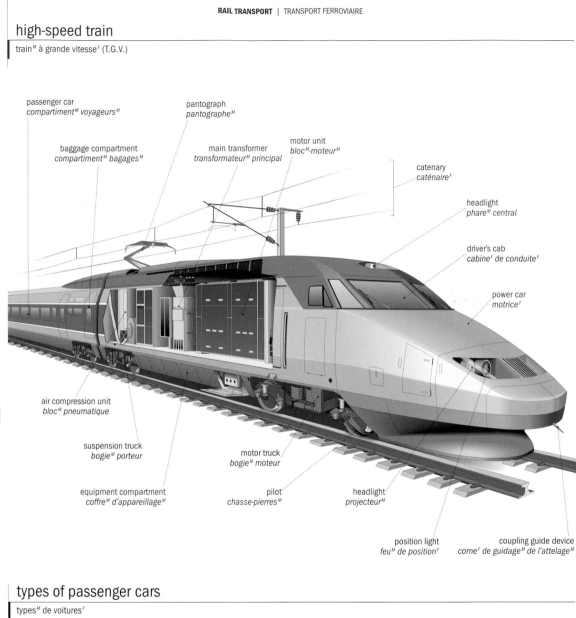

passenger car
compartiment$^M$ voyageurs$^M$

pantograph
pantographe$^M$

baggage compartment
compartiment$^M$ bagages$^M$

main transformer
transformateur$^M$ principal

motor unit
bloc$^M$-moteur$^M$

catenary
caténaire$^F$

headlight
phare$^M$ central

driver's cab
cabine$^F$ de conduite$^F$

power car
motrice$^F$

air compression unit
bloc$^M$ pneumatique

suspension truck
bogie$^M$ porteur

motor truck
bogie$^M$ moteur

equipment compartment
coffre$^M$ d'appareillage$^M$

pilot
chasse-pierres$^M$

headlight
projecteur$^M$

position light
feu$^M$ de position$^F$

coupling guide device
corne$^F$ de guidage$^M$ de l'attelage$^M$

# types of passenger cars

types$^M$ de voitures$^F$

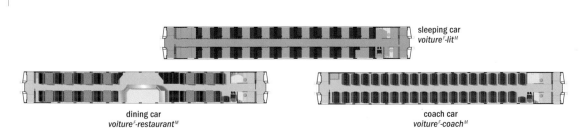

sleeping car
voiture$^F$-lit$^M$

dining car
voiture$^F$-restaurant$^M$

coach car
voiture$^F$-coach$^M$

# diesel-electric locomotive

locomotive<sup>F</sup> diesel-électrique

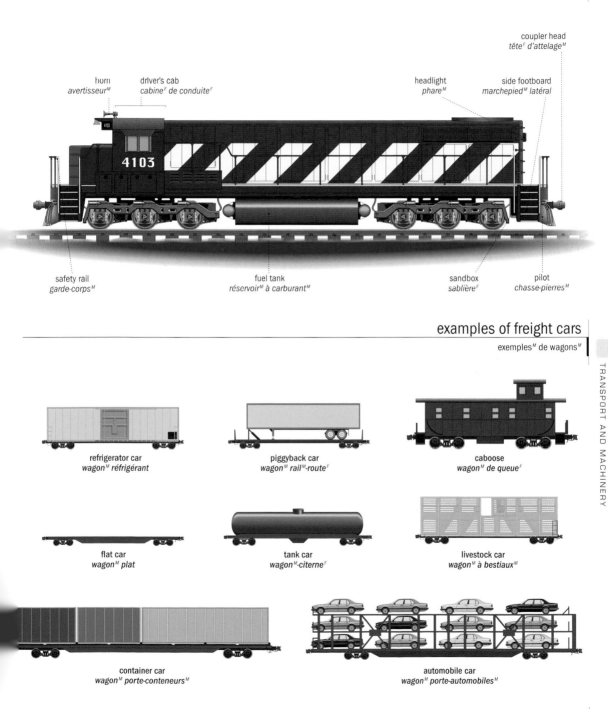

coupler head
tête<sup>F</sup> d'attelage<sup>M</sup>

horn
avertisseur<sup>M</sup>

driver's cab
cabine<sup>F</sup> de conduite<sup>F</sup>

headlight
phare<sup>M</sup>

side footboard
marchepied<sup>M</sup> latéral

4103

safety rail
garde-corps<sup>M</sup>

fuel tank
réservoir<sup>M</sup> à carburant<sup>M</sup>

sandbox
sablière<sup>F</sup>

pilot
chasse-pierres<sup>M</sup>

# examples of freight cars

exemples<sup>M</sup> de wagons<sup>M</sup>

refrigerator car
wagon<sup>M</sup> réfrigérant

piggyback car
wagon<sup>M</sup> rail<sup>M</sup>-route<sup>F</sup>

caboose
wagon<sup>M</sup> de queue<sup>F</sup>

flat car
wagon<sup>M</sup> plat

tank car
wagon<sup>M</sup>-citerne<sup>F</sup>

livestock car
wagon<sup>M</sup> à bestiaux<sup>M</sup>

container car
wagon<sup>M</sup> porte-conteneurs<sup>M</sup>

automobile car
wagon<sup>M</sup> porte-automobiles<sup>M</sup>

TRANSPORT AND MACHINERY

# subway
chemin<sup>M</sup> de fer<sup>M</sup> métropolitain

**subway station**
*station<sup>F</sup> de métro<sup>M</sup>*

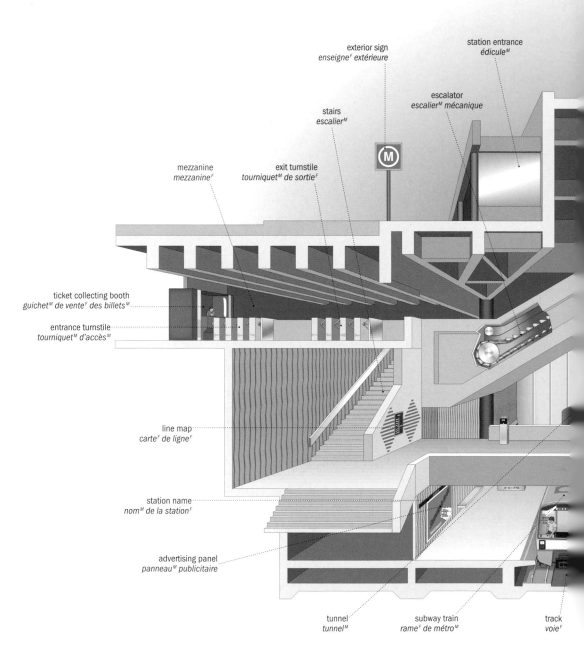

exterior sign
*enseigne<sup>F</sup> extérieure*

station entrance
*édicule<sup>M</sup>*

escalator
*escalier<sup>M</sup> mécanique*

stairs
*escalier<sup>M</sup>*

mezzanine
*mezzanine<sup>F</sup>*

exit turnstile
*tourniquet<sup>M</sup> de sortie<sup>F</sup>*

ticket collecting booth
*guichet<sup>M</sup> de vente<sup>F</sup> des billets<sup>M</sup>*

entrance turnstile
*tourniquet<sup>M</sup> d'accès<sup>M</sup>*

line map
*carte<sup>F</sup> de ligne<sup>F</sup>*

station name
*nom<sup>M</sup> de la station<sup>F</sup>*

advertising panel
*panneau<sup>M</sup> publicitaire*

tunnel
*tunnel<sup>M</sup>*

subway train
*rame<sup>F</sup> de métro<sup>M</sup>*

track
*voie<sup>F</sup>*

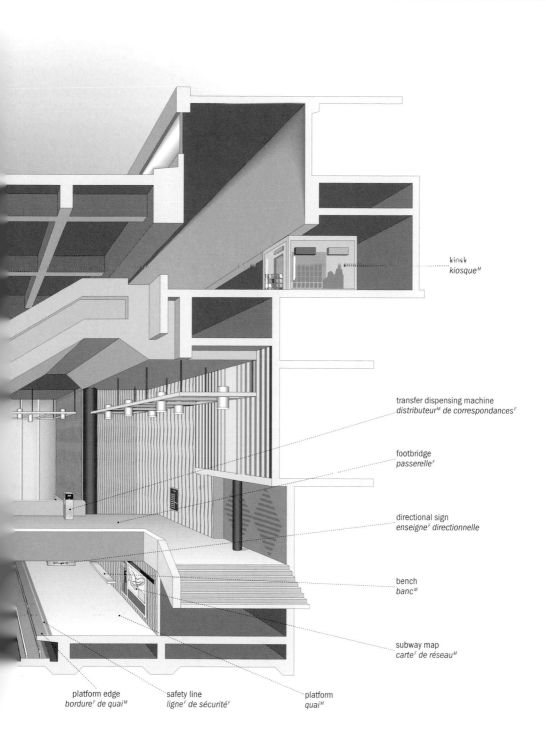

kiosk
*kiosque*<sup>M</sup>

transfer dispensing machine
*distributeur*<sup>M</sup> *de correspondances*<sup>F</sup>

footbridge
*passerelle*<sup>F</sup>

directional sign
*enseigne*<sup>F</sup> *directionnelle*

bench
*banc*<sup>M</sup>

subway map
*carte*<sup>F</sup> *de réseau*<sup>M</sup>

platform edge
*bordure*<sup>F</sup> *de quai*<sup>M</sup>

safety line
*ligne*<sup>F</sup> *de sécurité*<sup>F</sup>

platform
*quai*<sup>M</sup>

TRANSPORT AND MACHINERY

TRANSPORT AND MACHINERY

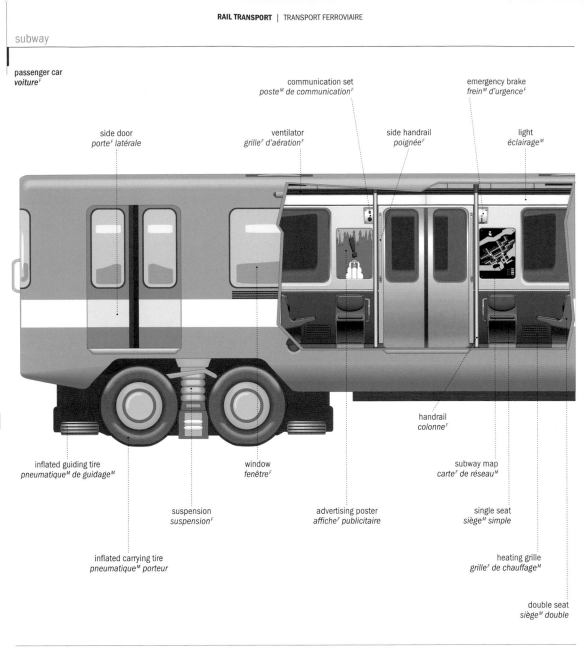

passenger car
*voiture*F

communication set
*poste*M *de communication*F

emergency brake
*frein*M *d'urgence*F

side door
*porte*F *latérale*

ventilator
*grille*F *d'aération*F

side handrail
*poignée*F

light
*éclairage*M

handrail
*colonne*F

inflated guiding tire
*pneumatique*M *de guidage*M

window
*fenêtre*F

subway map
*carte*F *de réseau*M

suspension
*suspension*F

advertising poster
*affiche*F *publicitaire*

single seat
*siège*M *simple*

inflated carrying tire
*pneumatique*M *porteur*

heating grille
*grille*F *de chauffage*M

double seat
*siège*M *double*

subway train
*rame*F *de métro*M

motor car
*motrice*F

trailer car
*remorque*F

motor car
*motrice*F

# harbor
port<sup>M</sup> maritime

canal lock
écluse<sup>F</sup>

container-loading bridge
portique<sup>M</sup> de chargement<sup>M</sup> de
conteneurs<sup>M</sup>

oil terminal
terminal<sup>M</sup> pétrolier

dry dock
bassin<sup>M</sup> de radoub<sup>M</sup>

transit shed
hangar<sup>M</sup> de transit<sup>M</sup>

tanker
pétrolier<sup>M</sup>

quayside crane
grue<sup>F</sup> à flèche<sup>F</sup>

bulk terminal
terminal<sup>M</sup> de vrac<sup>M</sup>

cold shed
entrepôt<sup>M</sup> frigorifique

ferryboat
transbordeur<sup>M</sup>

gate
porte<sup>F</sup>

quay
quai<sup>M</sup>

lighthouse
phare<sup>M</sup>

passenger terminal
gare<sup>F</sup> maritime

bridge
portique<sup>M</sup>

customs house
bureau<sup>M</sup> des douanes<sup>F</sup>

dock
bassin<sup>M</sup>

quay ramp
rampe<sup>F</sup> de quai<sup>M</sup>

parking lot
parking<sup>M</sup> ; stationnement<sup>M</sup>

floating crane
grue<sup>F</sup> sur ponton<sup>M</sup>

container terminal
terminal<sup>M</sup> à conteneurs<sup>M</sup>

office building
bâtiment<sup>M</sup> administratif

grain terminal
terminal<sup>M</sup> à céréales<sup>F</sup>

container ship
navire<sup>M</sup> porte-conteneurs<sup>M</sup>

quayside railway
voie<sup>F</sup> ferrée bord<sup>M</sup> à quai<sup>M</sup>

road transport
transport<sup>M</sup> routier

silos
silos<sup>M</sup>

# examples of boats and ships

exemples<sup>M</sup> de bateaux<sup>M</sup> et d'embarcations<sup>F</sup>

**drill ship**
*navire<sup>M</sup> de forage<sup>M</sup>*

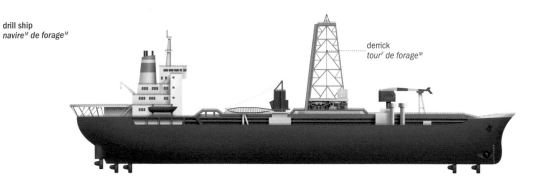

derrick
*tour<sup>F</sup> de forage<sup>M</sup>*

**bulk carrier**
*vraquier<sup>M</sup>*

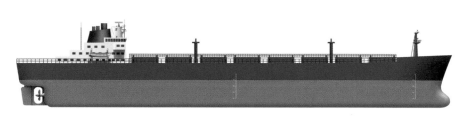

**container ship**
*navire<sup>M</sup> porte-conteneurs<sup>M</sup>*

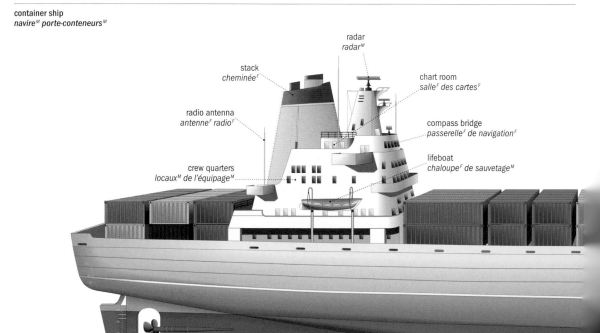

radar
*radar<sup>M</sup>*

stack
*cheminée<sup>F</sup>*

chart room
*salle<sup>F</sup> des cartes<sup>F</sup>*

radio antenna
*antenne<sup>F</sup> radio<sup>F</sup>*

compass bridge
*passerelle<sup>F</sup> de navigation<sup>F</sup>*

crew quarters
*locaux<sup>M</sup> de l'équipage<sup>M</sup>*

lifeboat
*chaloupe<sup>F</sup> de sauvetage<sup>M</sup>*

examples of boats and ships

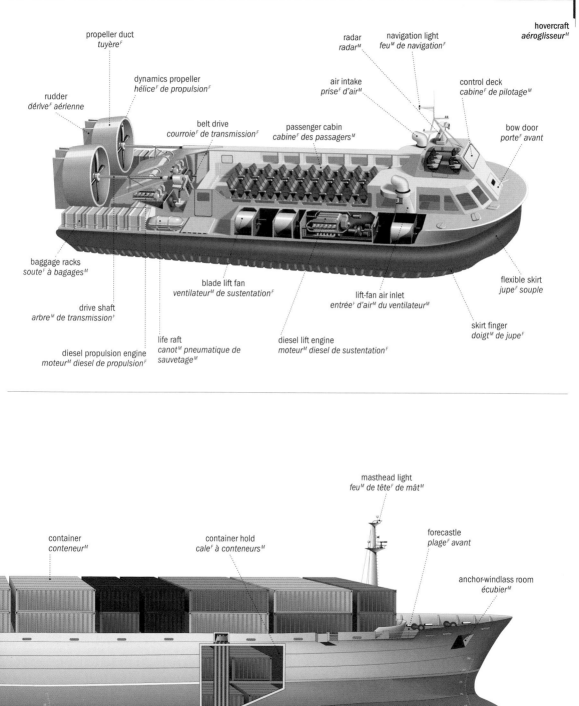

**hovercraft**
*aéroglisseur*<sup>M</sup>

propeller duct
*tuyère*<sup>F</sup>

dynamics propeller
*hélice*<sup>F</sup> *de propulsion*<sup>F</sup>

rudder
*dérive*<sup>F</sup> *aérienne*

belt drive
*courroie*<sup>F</sup> *de transmission*<sup>F</sup>

passenger cabin
*cabine*<sup>F</sup> *des passagers*<sup>M</sup>

radar
*radar*<sup>M</sup>

navigation light
*feu*<sup>M</sup> *de navigation*<sup>F</sup>

air intake
*prise*<sup>F</sup> *d'air*<sup>M</sup>

control deck
*cabine*<sup>F</sup> *de pilotage*<sup>M</sup>

bow door
*porte*<sup>F</sup> *avant*

baggage racks
*soute*<sup>F</sup> *à bagages*<sup>M</sup>

drive shaft
*arbre*<sup>M</sup> *de transmission*<sup>F</sup>

diesel propulsion engine
*moteur*<sup>M</sup> *diesel de propulsion*<sup>F</sup>

life raft
*canot*<sup>M</sup> *pneumatique de sauvetage*<sup>M</sup>

blade lift fan
*ventilateur*<sup>M</sup> *de sustentation*<sup>F</sup>

diesel lift engine
*moteur*<sup>M</sup> *diesel de sustentation*<sup>F</sup>

lift-fan air inlet
*entrée*<sup>F</sup> *d'air*<sup>M</sup> *du ventilateur*<sup>M</sup>

flexible skirt
*jupe*<sup>F</sup> *souple*

skirt finger
*doigt*<sup>M</sup> *de jupe*<sup>F</sup>

masthead light
*feu*<sup>M</sup> *de tête*<sup>F</sup> *de mât*<sup>M</sup>

container
*conteneur*<sup>M</sup>

container hold
*cale*<sup>F</sup> *à conteneurs*<sup>M</sup>

forecastle
*plage*<sup>F</sup> *avant*

anchor-windlass room
*écubier*<sup>M</sup>

TRANSPORT AND MACHINERY

examples of boats and ships

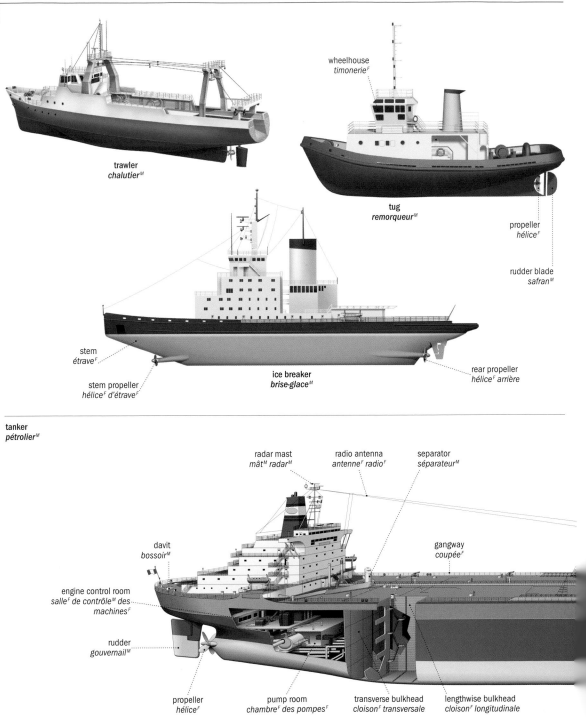

trawler
*chalutier*<sup>M</sup>

wheelhouse
*timonerie*<sup>F</sup>

tug
*remorqueur*<sup>M</sup>

propeller
*hélice*<sup>F</sup>

rudder blade
*safran*<sup>M</sup>

stem
*étrave*<sup>F</sup>

stem propeller
*hélice*<sup>F</sup> *d'étrave*<sup>F</sup>

ice breaker
*brise-glace*<sup>M</sup>

rear propeller
*hélice*<sup>F</sup> *arrière*

tanker
*pétrolier*<sup>M</sup>

radar mast
*mât*<sup>M</sup> *radar*<sup>M</sup>

radio antenna
*antenne*<sup>F</sup> *radio*<sup>F</sup>

separator
*séparateur*<sup>M</sup>

davit
*bossoir*<sup>M</sup>

gangway
*coupée*<sup>F</sup>

engine control room
*salle*<sup>F</sup> *de contrôle*<sup>M</sup> *des*
*machines*<sup>F</sup>

rudder
*gouvernail*<sup>M</sup>

propeller
*hélice*<sup>F</sup>

pump room
*chambre*<sup>F</sup> *des pompes*<sup>F</sup>

transverse bulkhead
*cloison*<sup>F</sup> *transversale*

lengthwise bulkhead
*cloison*<sup>F</sup> *longitudinale*

TRANSPORT AND MACHINERY

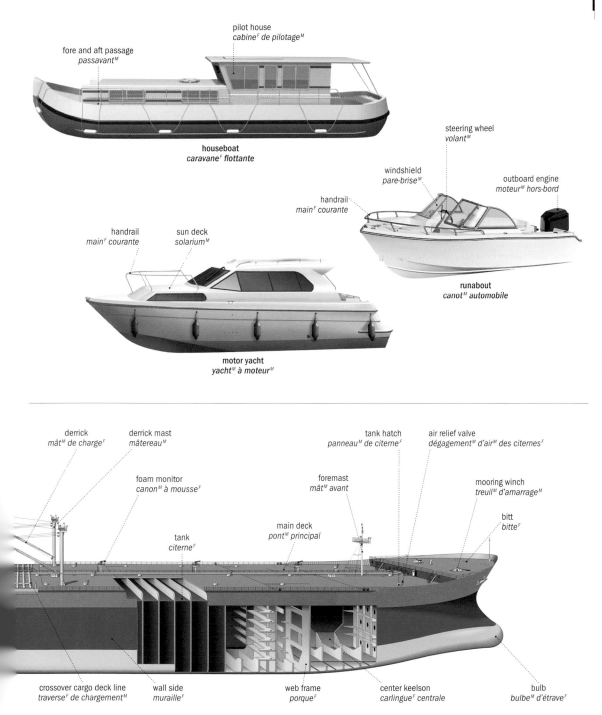

pilot house
*cabine*F *de pilotage*M

fore and aft passage
*passavant*M

houseboat
*caravane*F *flottante*

steering wheel
*volant*M

windshield
*pare-brise*M

outboard engine
*moteur*M *hors-bord*

handrail
*main*F *courante*

handrail
*main*F *courante*

sun deck
*solarium*M

runabout
*canot*M *automobile*

motor yacht
*yacht*M *à moteur*M

derrick
*mât*M *de charge*F

derrick mast
*mâtereau*M

tank hatch
*panneau*M *de citerne*F

air relief valve
*dégagement*M *d'air*M *des citernes*F

foam monitor
*canon*M *à mousse*F

foremast
*mât*M *avant*

mooring winch
*treuil*M *d'amarrage*M

main deck
*pont*M *principal*

bitt
*bitte*F

tank
*citerne*F

crossover cargo deck line
*traverse*F *de chargement*M

wall side
*muraille*F

web frame
*porque*F

center keelson
*carlingue*F *centrale*

bulb
*bulbe*M *d'étrave*F

## examples of boats and ships

**ferry**
*transbordeur*M

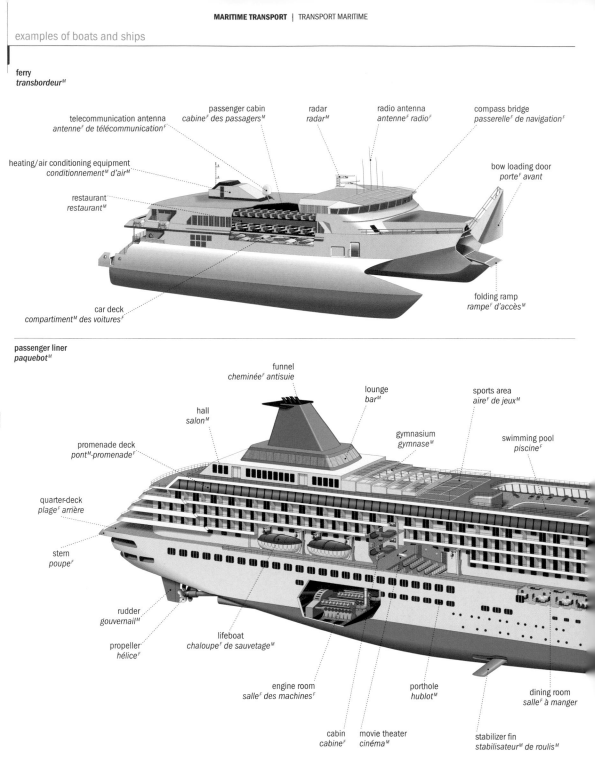

telecommunication antenna
*antenne*F *de télécommunication*F

passenger cabin
*cabine*F *des passagers*M

radar
*radar*M

radio antenna
*antenne*F *radio*F

compass bridge
*passerelle*F *de navigation*F

heating/air conditioning equipment
*conditionnement*M *d'air*M

restaurant
*restaurant*M

bow loading door
*porte*F *avant*

folding ramp
*rampe*F *d'accès*M

car deck
*compartiment*M *des voitures*F

**passenger liner**
*paquebot*M

funnel
*cheminée*F *antisuie*

hall
*salon*M

lounge
*bar*M

sports area
*aire*F *de jeux*M

promenade deck
*pont*M-*promenade*F

gymnasium
*gymnase*M

swimming pool
*piscine*F

quarter-deck
*plage*F *arrière*

stern
*poupe*F

rudder
*gouvernail*M

lifeboat
*chaloupe*F *de sauvetage*M

propeller
*hélice*F

engine room
*salle*F *des machines*F

porthole
*hublot*M

dining room
*salle*F *à manger*

cabin
*cabine*F

movie theater
*cinéma*M

stabilizer fin
*stabilisateur*M *de roulis*M

examples of boats and ships

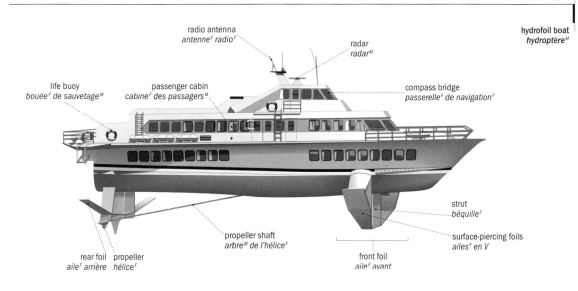

**hydrofoil boat**
*hydroptère*<sup>M</sup>

radio antenna
*antenne*<sup>F</sup> *radio*<sup>F</sup>

radar
*radar*<sup>M</sup>

life buoy
*bouée*<sup>F</sup> *de sauvetage*<sup>M</sup>

passenger cabin
*cabine*<sup>F</sup> *des passagers*<sup>M</sup>

compass bridge
*passerelle*<sup>F</sup> *de navigation*<sup>F</sup>

strut
*béquille*<sup>F</sup>

propeller shaft
*arbre*<sup>M</sup> *de l'hélice*<sup>F</sup>

surface-piercing foils
*ailes*<sup>F</sup> *en V*

rear foil
*aile*<sup>F</sup> *arrière*

propeller
*hélice*<sup>F</sup>

front foil
*aile*<sup>F</sup> *avant*

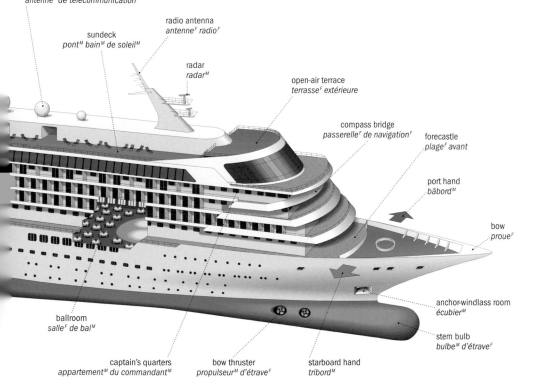

telecommunication antenna
*antenne*<sup>F</sup> *de télécommunication*<sup>F</sup>

sundeck
*pont*<sup>M</sup> *bain*<sup>M</sup> *de soleil*<sup>M</sup>

radio antenna
*antenne*<sup>F</sup> *radio*<sup>F</sup>

radar
*radar*<sup>M</sup>

open-air terrace
*terrasse*<sup>F</sup> *extérieure*

compass bridge
*passerelle*<sup>F</sup> *de navigation*<sup>F</sup>

forecastle
*plage*<sup>F</sup> *avant*

port hand
*bâbord*<sup>M</sup>

bow
*proue*<sup>F</sup>

anchor-windlass room
*écubier*<sup>M</sup>

stem bulb
*bulbe*<sup>M</sup> *d'étrave*<sup>F</sup>

ballroom
*salle*<sup>F</sup> *de bal*<sup>M</sup>

captain's quarters
*appartement*<sup>M</sup> *du commandant*<sup>M</sup>

bow thruster
*propulseur*<sup>M</sup> *d'étrave*<sup>F</sup>

starboard hand
*tribord*<sup>M</sup>

TRANSPORT AND MACHINERY

# airport

aéroport<sup>M</sup>

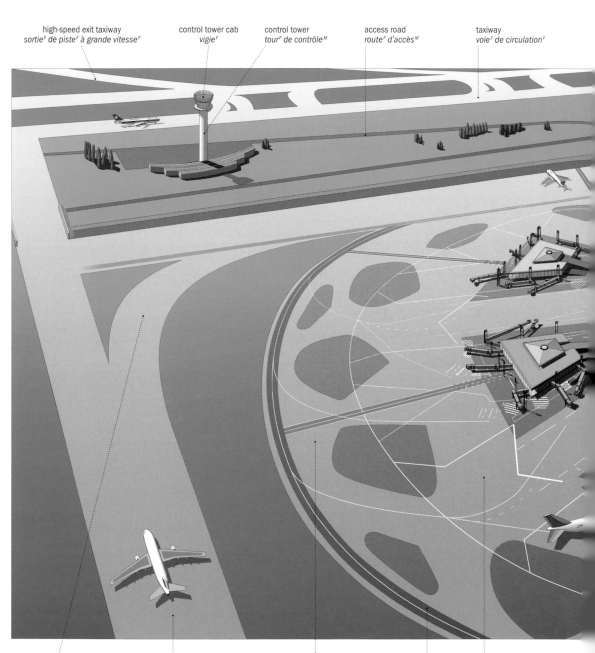

high-speed exit taxiway
*sortie<sup>F</sup> de piste<sup>F</sup> à grande vitesse<sup>F</sup>*

control tower cab
*vigie<sup>F</sup>*

control tower
*tour<sup>F</sup> de contrôle<sup>M</sup>*

access road
*route<sup>F</sup> d'accès<sup>M</sup>*

taxiway
*voie<sup>F</sup> de circulation<sup>F</sup>*

by-pass taxiway
*bretelle<sup>F</sup>*

taxiway
*voie<sup>F</sup> de circulation<sup>F</sup>*

apron
*aire<sup>F</sup> de trafic<sup>M</sup>*

service road
*voie<sup>F</sup> de service<sup>M</sup>*

apron
*aire<sup>F</sup> de manœuvre<sup>F</sup>*

TRANSPORT AND MACHINERY

passenger terminal
*aérogare*F *de passagers*M

maintenance hangar
*hangar*M

parking area
*aire*F *de stationnement*M

telescopic corridor
*passerelle*F *télescopique*

service area
*aire*F *de service*M

boarding walkway
*quai*M *d'embarquement*M

taxiway line
*marques*F *de circulation*F

radial passenger-loading area
*aérogare*F *satellite*M

airport

TRANSPORT AND MACHINERY

**passenger terminal**
*aérogare*F

information counter
*comptoir*M *de renseignements*M

baggage claim area
*zone*F *de retrait*M *des bagages*M

hotel reservation desk
*bureau*M *de réservation*F *de chambres*F *d'hôtel*M

ticket counter
*comptoir*M *de vente*F *des billets*M

lobby
*hall*M *public*

automatically controlled door
*porte*F *automatique*

baggage check-in counter
*comptoir*M *d'enregistrement*M

parking lot
*parc*M *à voitures*F

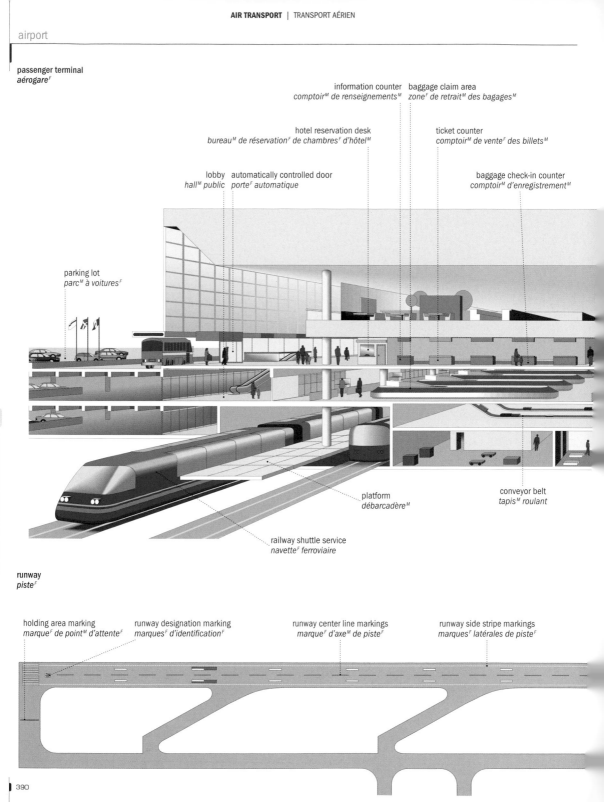

platform
*débarcadère*M

conveyor belt
*tapis*M *roulant*

railway shuttle service
*navette*F *ferroviaire*

**runway**
*piste*F

holding area marking
*marque*F *de point*M *d'attente*F

runway designation marking
*marques*F *d'identification*F

runway center line markings
*marque*F *d'axe*M *de piste*F

runway side stripe markings
*marques*F *latérales de piste*F

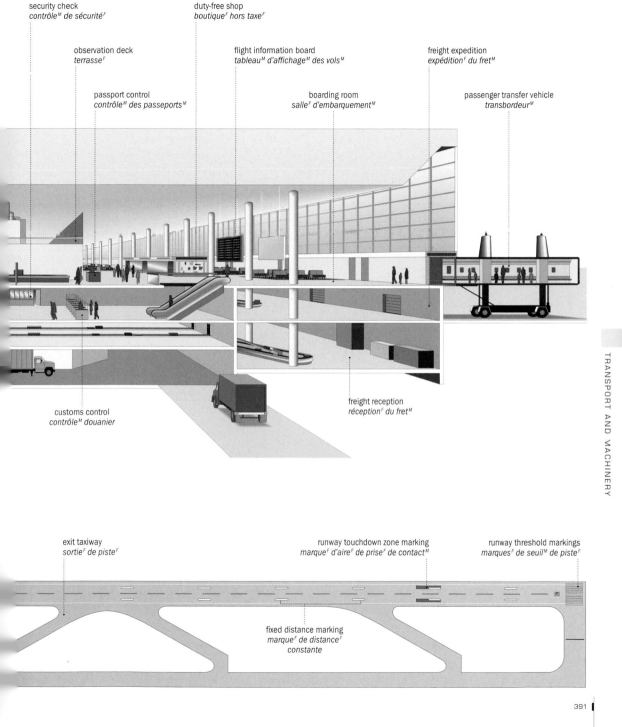

security check
contrôle<sup>M</sup> de sécurité<sup>F</sup>

duty-free shop
boutique<sup>F</sup> hors taxe<sup>F</sup>

observation deck
terrasse<sup>F</sup>

flight information board
tableau<sup>M</sup> d'affichage<sup>M</sup> des vols<sup>M</sup>

freight expedition
expédition<sup>F</sup> du fret<sup>M</sup>

passport control
contrôle<sup>M</sup> des passeports<sup>M</sup>

boarding room
salle<sup>F</sup> d'embarquement<sup>M</sup>

passenger transfer vehicle
transbordeur<sup>M</sup>

customs control
contrôle<sup>M</sup> douanier

freight reception
réception<sup>F</sup> du fret<sup>M</sup>

exit taxiway
sortie<sup>F</sup> de piste<sup>F</sup>

runway touchdown zone marking
marque<sup>F</sup> d'aire<sup>F</sup> de prise<sup>F</sup> de contact<sup>M</sup>

runway threshold markings
marques<sup>F</sup> de seuil<sup>M</sup> de piste<sup>F</sup>

fixed distance marking
marque<sup>F</sup> de distance<sup>F</sup>
constante

TRANSPORT AND MACHINERY

# long-range jet

*avion^M long-courrier^M*

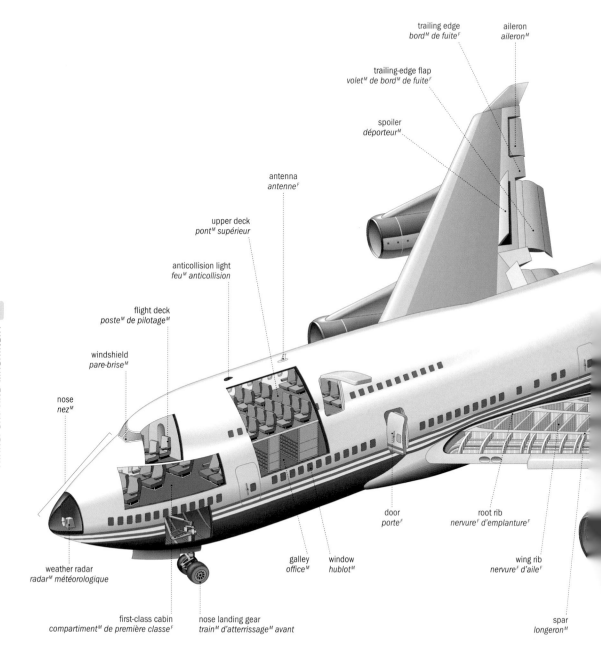

trailing edge
*bord^M de fuite^F*

aileron
*aileron^M*

trailing-edge flap
*volet^M de bord^M de fuite^F*

spoiler
*déporteur^M*

antenna
*antenne^F*

upper deck
*pont^M supérieur*

anticollision light
*feu^M anticollision*

flight deck
*poste^M de pilotage^M*

windshield
*pare-brise^M*

nose
*nez^M*

weather radar
*radar^M météorologique*

first-class cabin
*compartiment^M de première classe^F*

nose landing gear
*train^M d'atterrissage^M avant*

galley
*office^M*

window
*hublot^M*

door
*porte^F*

root rib
*nervure^F d'emplanture^F*

wing rib
*nervure^F d'aile^F*

spar
*longeron^M*

long-range jet

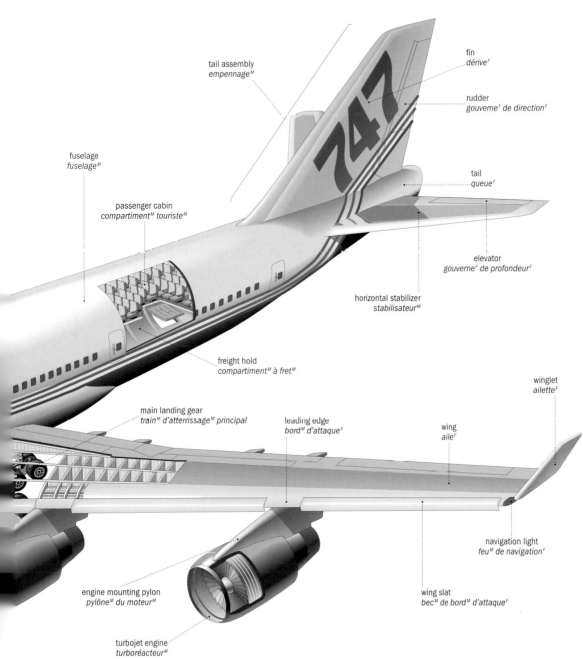

tail assembly
empennage<sup>M</sup>

fin
dérive<sup>F</sup>

rudder
gouverne<sup>F</sup> de direction<sup>F</sup>

fuselage
fuselage<sup>M</sup>

tail
queue<sup>F</sup>

passenger cabin
compartiment<sup>M</sup> touriste<sup>M</sup>

elevator
gouverne<sup>F</sup> de profondeur<sup>F</sup>

horizontal stabilizer
stabilisateur<sup>M</sup>

freight hold
compartiment<sup>M</sup> à fret<sup>M</sup>

winglet
ailette<sup>F</sup>

main landing gear
train<sup>M</sup> d'atterrissage<sup>M</sup> principal

leading edge
bord<sup>M</sup> d'attaque<sup>F</sup>

wing
aile<sup>F</sup>

navigation light
feu<sup>M</sup> de navigation<sup>F</sup>

engine mounting pylon
pylône<sup>M</sup> du moteur<sup>M</sup>

wing slat
bec<sup>M</sup> de bord<sup>M</sup> d'attaque<sup>F</sup>

turbojet engine
turboréacteur<sup>M</sup>

TRANSPORT AND MACHINERY

# examples of airplanes

exemples<sup>M</sup> d'avions<sup>M</sup>

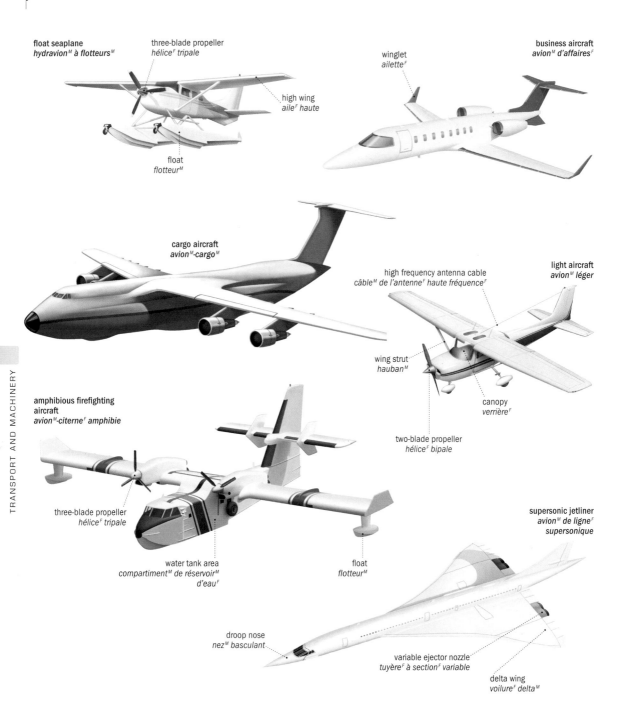

float seaplane
*hydravion<sup>M</sup> à flotteurs<sup>M</sup>*

three-blade propeller
*hélice<sup>F</sup> tripale*

winglet
*ailette<sup>F</sup>*

business aircraft
*avion<sup>M</sup> d'affaires<sup>F</sup>*

high wing
*aile<sup>F</sup> haute*

float
*flotteur<sup>M</sup>*

cargo aircraft
*avion<sup>M</sup>-cargo<sup>M</sup>*

high frequency antenna cable
*câble<sup>M</sup> de l'antenne<sup>F</sup> haute fréquence<sup>F</sup>*

light aircraft
*avion<sup>M</sup> léger*

wing strut
*hauban<sup>M</sup>*

canopy
*verrière<sup>F</sup>*

amphibious firefighting
aircraft
*avion<sup>M</sup>-citerne<sup>F</sup> amphibie*

two-blade propeller
*hélice<sup>F</sup> bipale*

three-blade propeller
*hélice<sup>F</sup> tripale*

supersonic jetliner
*avion<sup>M</sup> de ligne<sup>F</sup>
supersonique*

water tank area
*compartiment<sup>M</sup> de réservoir<sup>M</sup>
d'eau<sup>F</sup>*

float
*flotteur<sup>M</sup>*

droop nose
*nez<sup>M</sup> basculant*

variable ejector nozzle
*tuyère<sup>F</sup> à section<sup>F</sup> variable*

delta wing
*voilure<sup>F</sup> delta<sup>M</sup>*

TRANSPORT AND MACHINERY

# movements of an airplane
mouvements<sup>M</sup> de l'avion<sup>M</sup>

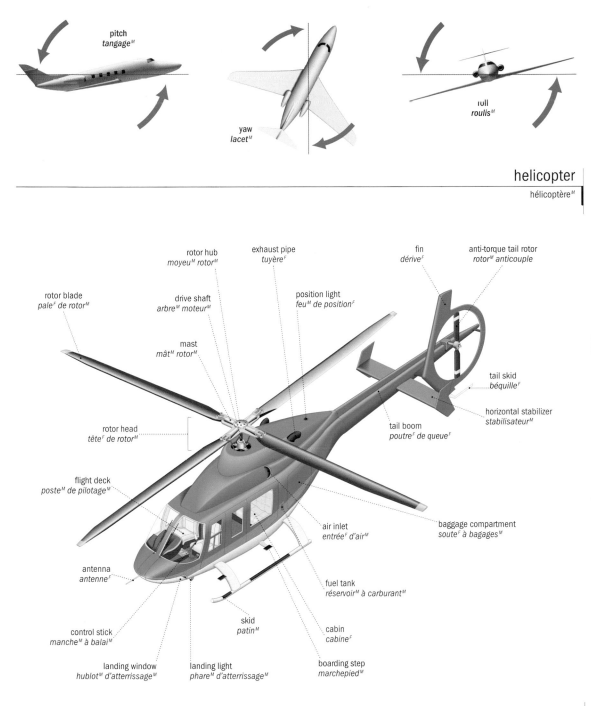

pitch
*tangage<sup>M</sup>*

yaw
*lacet<sup>M</sup>*

roll
*roulis<sup>M</sup>*

# helicopter
hélicoptère<sup>M</sup>

rotor hub
*moyeu<sup>M</sup> rotor<sup>M</sup>*

exhaust pipe
*tuyère<sup>F</sup>*

fin
*dérive<sup>F</sup>*

anti-torque tail rotor
*rotor<sup>M</sup> anticouple*

rotor blade
*pale<sup>F</sup> de rotor<sup>M</sup>*

drive shaft
*arbre<sup>M</sup> moteur<sup>M</sup>*

position light
*feu<sup>M</sup> de position<sup>F</sup>*

mast
*mât<sup>M</sup> rotor<sup>M</sup>*

tail skid
*béquille<sup>F</sup>*

horizontal stabilizer
*stabilisateur<sup>M</sup>*

rotor head
*tête<sup>F</sup> de rotor<sup>M</sup>*

tail boom
*poutre<sup>F</sup> de queue<sup>F</sup>*

flight deck
*poste<sup>M</sup> de pilotage<sup>M</sup>*

air inlet
*entrée<sup>F</sup> d'air<sup>M</sup>*

baggage compartment
*soute<sup>F</sup> à bagages<sup>M</sup>*

antenna
*antenne<sup>F</sup>*

fuel tank
*réservoir<sup>M</sup> à carburant<sup>M</sup>*

control stick
*manche<sup>M</sup> à balai<sup>M</sup>*

skid
*patin<sup>M</sup>*

cabin
*cabine<sup>F</sup>*

landing window
*hublot<sup>M</sup> d'atterrissage<sup>M</sup>*

landing light
*phare<sup>M</sup> d'atterrissage<sup>M</sup>*

boarding step
*marchepied<sup>M</sup>*

TRANSPORT AND MACHINERY

# material handling

manutention<sup>F</sup>

**forklift truck**
*chariot<sup>M</sup> élévateur*

mast
*mât<sup>M</sup>*

crosshead
*tête<sup>F</sup> du vérin<sup>M</sup> de levage<sup>M</sup>*

lifting chain
*chaine<sup>F</sup> de levage<sup>M</sup>*

hydraulic hoses
*système<sup>M</sup> hydraulique*

carriage
*tablier<sup>M</sup>*

fork
*bras<sup>M</sup> de fourche<sup>F</sup>*

forks
*fourches<sup>F</sup>*

overhead guard
*toit<sup>M</sup> de protection<sup>F</sup>*

mast-operating lever
*levier<sup>M</sup> de manœuvre<sup>F</sup> du mât<sup>M</sup>*

engine compartment
*moteur<sup>M</sup>*

frame
*châssis<sup>M</sup>*

hand truck
*diable<sup>M</sup>*

**pallet truck**
*transpalette<sup>F</sup> manuelle*

**wing pallet**
*palette<sup>F</sup> à ailes<sup>F</sup>*

top deckboard
*plancher<sup>M</sup> supérieur*

entry
*entrée<sup>F</sup>*

stringer
*entretoise<sup>F</sup>*

bottom deckboard
*plancher<sup>M</sup> inférieur*

# cranes

grues<sup>F</sup> et portique<sup>M</sup>

**tower crane**
*grue<sup>F</sup> à tour<sup>F</sup>*

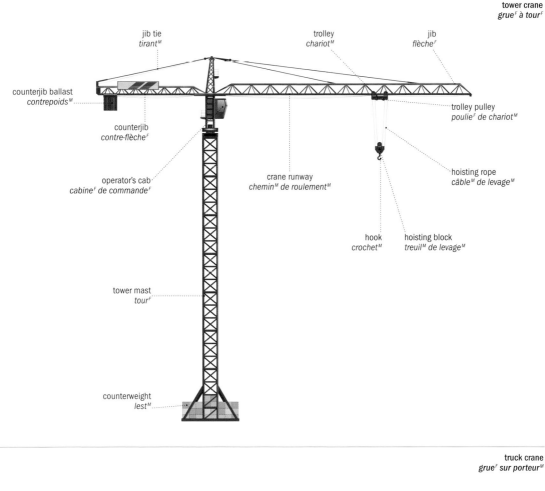

jib tie
*tirant<sup>M</sup>*

trolley
*chariot<sup>M</sup>*

jib
*flèche<sup>F</sup>*

counterjib ballast
*contrepoids<sup>M</sup>*

trolley pulley
*poulie<sup>F</sup> de chariot<sup>M</sup>*

counterjib
*contre-flèche<sup>F</sup>*

operator's cab
*cabine<sup>F</sup> de commande<sup>F</sup>*

crane runway
*chemin<sup>M</sup> de roulement<sup>M</sup>*

hoisting rope
*câble<sup>M</sup> de levage<sup>M</sup>*

hook
*crochet<sup>M</sup>*

hoisting block
*treuil<sup>M</sup> de levage<sup>M</sup>*

tower mast
*tour<sup>F</sup>*

counterweight
*lest<sup>M</sup>*

**truck crane**
*grue<sup>F</sup> sur porteur<sup>M</sup>*

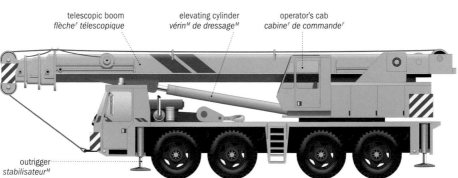

telescopic boom
*flèche<sup>F</sup> télescopique*

elevating cylinder
*vérin<sup>M</sup> de dressage<sup>M</sup>*

operator's cab
*cabine<sup>F</sup> de commande<sup>F</sup>*

outrigger
*stabilisateur<sup>M</sup>*

TRANSPORT AND MACHINERY

# bulldozer

bouteur<sup>M</sup>

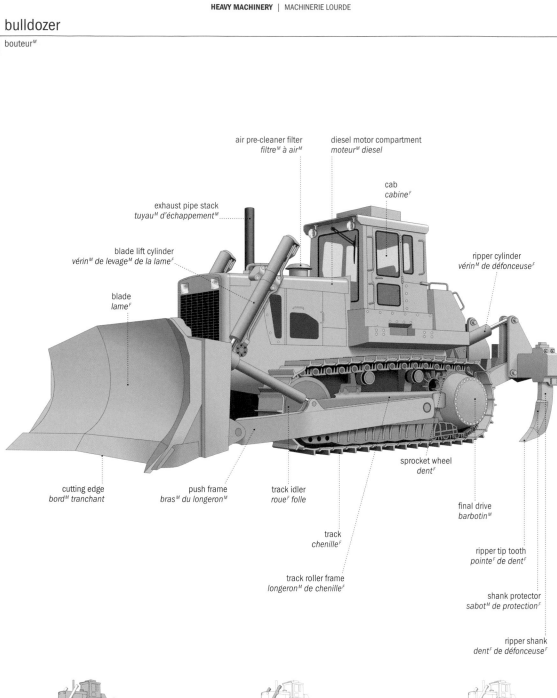

air pre-cleaner filter
filtre<sup>M</sup> à air<sup>M</sup>

diesel motor compartment
moteur<sup>M</sup> diesel

cab
cabine<sup>F</sup>

exhaust pipe stack
tuyau<sup>M</sup> d'échappement<sup>M</sup>

blade lift cylinder
vérin<sup>M</sup> de levage<sup>M</sup> de la lame<sup>F</sup>

ripper cylinder
vérin<sup>M</sup> de défonceuse<sup>F</sup>

blade
lame<sup>F</sup>

cutting edge
bord<sup>M</sup> tranchant

push frame
bras<sup>M</sup> du longeron<sup>M</sup>

track idler
roue<sup>F</sup> folle

sprocket wheel
dent<sup>F</sup>

final drive
barbotin<sup>M</sup>

track
chenille<sup>F</sup>

ripper tip tooth
pointe<sup>F</sup> de dent<sup>F</sup>

track roller frame
longeron<sup>M</sup> de chenille<sup>F</sup>

shank protector
sabot<sup>M</sup> de protection<sup>F</sup>

ripper shank
dent<sup>F</sup> de défonceuse<sup>F</sup>

crawler tractor
tracteur<sup>M</sup> à chenilles<sup>F</sup>

blade
lame<sup>F</sup>

ripper
défonceuse<sup>F</sup>

# wheel loader
*chargeuse<sup>F</sup>-pelleteuse<sup>F</sup>*

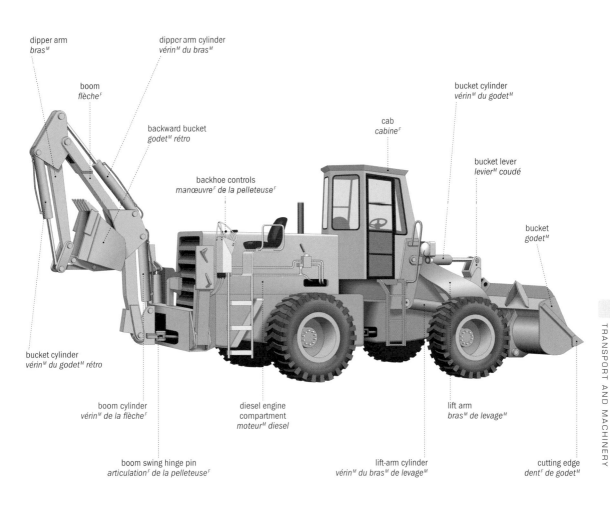

dipper arm
*bras<sup>M</sup>*

dipper arm cylinder
*vérin<sup>M</sup> du bras<sup>M</sup>*

boom
*flèche<sup>F</sup>*

bucket cylinder
*vérin<sup>M</sup> du godet<sup>M</sup>*

backward bucket
*godet<sup>M</sup> rétro*

cab
*cabine<sup>F</sup>*

bucket lever
*levier<sup>M</sup> coudé*

backhoe controls
*manœuvre<sup>F</sup> de la pelleteuse<sup>F</sup>*

bucket
*godet<sup>M</sup>*

bucket cylinder
*vérin<sup>M</sup> du godet<sup>M</sup> rétro*

boom cylinder
*vérin<sup>M</sup> de la flèche<sup>F</sup>*

diesel engine
compartment
*moteur<sup>M</sup> diesel*

lift arm
*bras<sup>M</sup> de levage<sup>M</sup>*

boom swing hinge pin
*articulation<sup>F</sup> de la pelleteuse<sup>F</sup>*

lift-arm cylinder
*vérin<sup>M</sup> du bras<sup>M</sup> de levage<sup>M</sup>*

cutting edge
*dent<sup>F</sup> de godet<sup>M</sup>*

front-end loader
*chargeuse<sup>F</sup> frontale*

wheel tractor
*tracteur<sup>M</sup>*

backhoe
*pelleteuse<sup>F</sup>*

TRANSPORT AND MACHINERY

399

# scraper

décapeuse<sup>F</sup>

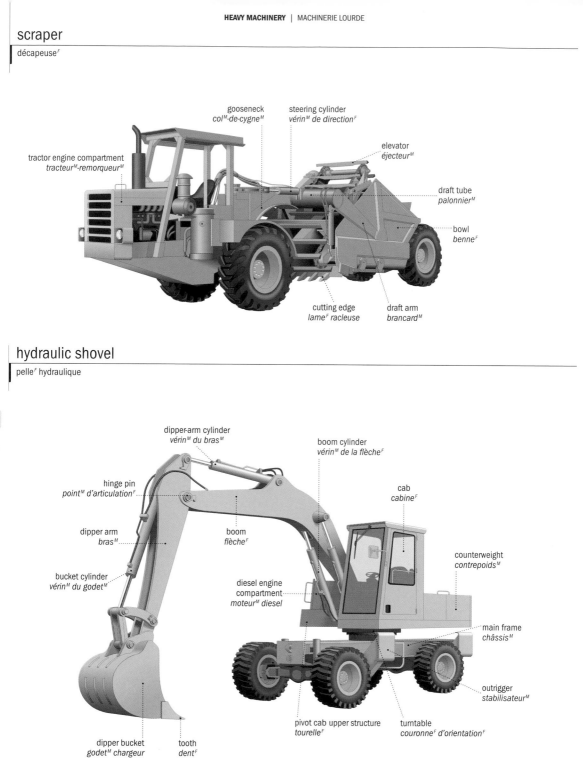

gooseneck
col<sup>M</sup>-de-cygne<sup>M</sup>

steering cylinder
vérin<sup>M</sup> de direction<sup>F</sup>

elevator
éjecteur<sup>M</sup>

tractor engine compartment
tracteur<sup>M</sup>-remorqueur<sup>M</sup>

draft tube
palonnier<sup>M</sup>

bowl
benne<sup>F</sup>

cutting edge
lame<sup>F</sup> racleuse

draft arm
brancard<sup>M</sup>

# hydraulic shovel

pelle<sup>F</sup> hydraulique

dipper-arm cylinder
vérin<sup>M</sup> du bras<sup>M</sup>

boom cylinder
vérin<sup>M</sup> de la flèche<sup>F</sup>

hinge pin
point<sup>M</sup> d'articulation<sup>F</sup>

cab
cabine<sup>F</sup>

dipper arm
bras<sup>M</sup>

boom
flèche<sup>F</sup>

counterweight
contrepoids<sup>M</sup>

bucket cylinder
vérin<sup>M</sup> du godet<sup>M</sup>

diesel engine
compartment
moteur<sup>M</sup> diesel

main frame
châssis<sup>M</sup>

outrigger
stabilisateur<sup>M</sup>

dipper bucket
godet<sup>M</sup> chargeur

tooth
dent<sup>F</sup>

pivot cab upper structure
tourelle<sup>F</sup>

turntable
couronne<sup>F</sup> d'orientation<sup>F</sup>

# grader

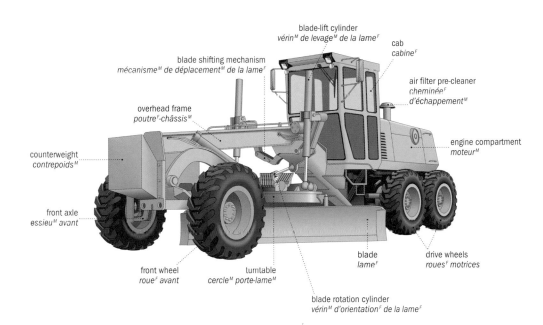

blade-lift cylinder
*vérin<sup>M</sup> de levage<sup>M</sup> de la lame<sup>F</sup>*

cab
*cabine<sup>F</sup>*

blade shifting mechanism
*mécanisme<sup>M</sup> de déplacement<sup>M</sup> de la lame<sup>F</sup>*

air filter pre-cleaner
*cheminée<sup>F</sup>
d'échappement<sup>M</sup>*

overhead frame
*poutre<sup>F</sup>-châssis<sup>M</sup>*

engine compartment
*moteur<sup>M</sup>*

counterweight
*contrepoids<sup>M</sup>*

front axle
*essieu<sup>M</sup> avant*

front wheel
*roue<sup>F</sup> avant*

turntable
*cercle<sup>M</sup> porte-lame<sup>M</sup>*

blade
*lame<sup>F</sup>*

drive wheels
*roues<sup>F</sup> motrices*

blade rotation cylinder
*vérin<sup>M</sup> d'orientation<sup>F</sup> de la lame<sup>F</sup>*

# dump truck

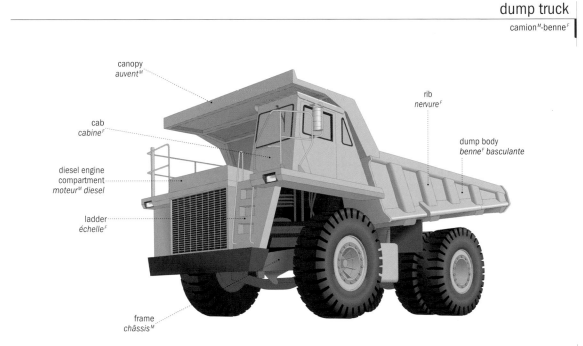

canopy
*auvent<sup>M</sup>*

rib
*nervure<sup>F</sup>*

cab
*cabine<sup>F</sup>*

dump body
*benne<sup>F</sup> basculante*

diesel engine
compartment
*moteur<sup>M</sup> diesel*

ladder
*échelle<sup>F</sup>*

frame
*châssis<sup>M</sup>*

# production of electricity from geothermal energy

production[F] d'électricité[F] par énergie[F] géothermique

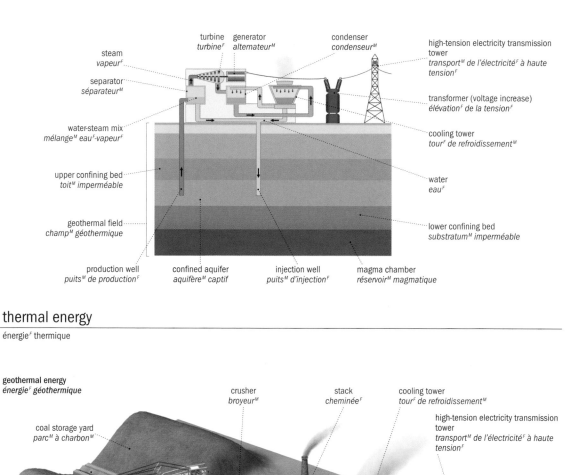

turbine
turbine[F]

generator
alternateur[M]

condenser
condenseur[M]

steam
vapeur[F]

separator
séparateur[M]

high-tension electricity transmission tower
transport[M] de l'électricité[F] à haute tension[F]

transformer (voltage increase)
élévation[F] de la tension[F]

water-steam mix
mélange[M] eau[F]-vapeur[F]

cooling tower
tour[F] de refroidissement[M]

upper confining bed
toit[M] imperméable

water
eau[F]

geothermal field
champ[M] géothermique

lower confining bed
substratum[M] imperméable

production well
puits[M] de production[F]

confined aquifer
aquifère[M] captif

injection well
puits[M] d'injection[F]

magma chamber
réservoir[M] magmatique

# thermal energy

énergie[F] thermique

geothermal energy
énergie[F] géothermique

crusher
broyeur[M]

stack
cheminée[F]

cooling tower
tour[F] de refroidissement[M]

high-tension electricity transmission tower
transport[M] de l'électricité[F] à haute tension[F]

coal storage yard
parc[M] à charbon[M]

transformer (voltage decrease)
abaissement[M] de la tension[F]

conveyor
convoyeur[M]

belt loader
sauterelle[F]

pulverizer
pulvérisateur[M]

transmission to consumers
transport[M] vers les usagers[M]

steam generator
générateur[M] de vapeur[F]

coal-fired thermal power plant
centrale[F] thermique au charbon[M]

condenser
condenseur[M]

turbo-alternator unit
groupe[M] turbo-alternateur[M]

transformer (voltage increase)
élévation[F] de la tension[F]

ENERGY

# oil
*pétrole[M]*

**surface prospecting**
*prospection[F] terrestre*

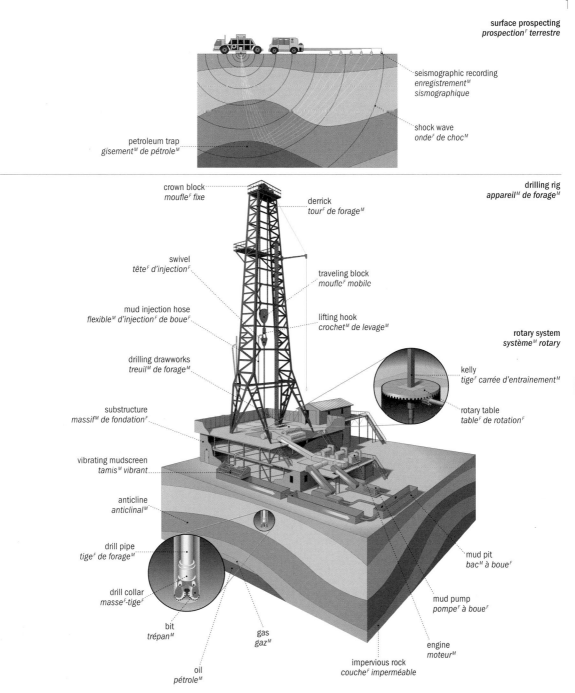

seismographic recording
*enregistrement[M]
sismographique*

shock wave
*onde[F] de choc[M]*

petroleum trap
*gisement[M] de pétrole[M]*

crown block
*moufle[F] fixe*

derrick
*tour[F] de forage[M]*

**drilling rig**
*appareil[M] de forage[M]*

swivel
*tête[F] d'injection[F]*

traveling block
*moufle[F] mobile*

mud injection hose
*flexible[M] d'injection[F] de boue[F]*

lifting hook
*crochet[M] de levage[M]*

**rotary system**
*système[M] rotary*

drilling drawworks
*treuil[M] de forage[M]*

kelly
*tige[F] carrée d'entraînement[M]*

substructure
*massif[M] de fondation[F]*

rotary table
*table[F] de rotation[F]*

vibrating mudscreen
*tamis[M] vibrant*

anticline
*anticlinal[M]*

drill pipe
*tige[F] de forage[M]*

mud pit
*bac[M] à boue[F]*

drill collar
*masse[F]-tige[F]*

mud pump
*pompe[F] à boue[F]*

bit
*trépan[M]*

gas
*gaz[M]*

engine
*moteur[M]*

oil
*pétrole[M]*

impervious rock
*couche[F] imperméable*

ENERGY

**floating-roof tank**
*réservoir<sup>M</sup> à toit<sup>M</sup> flottant*

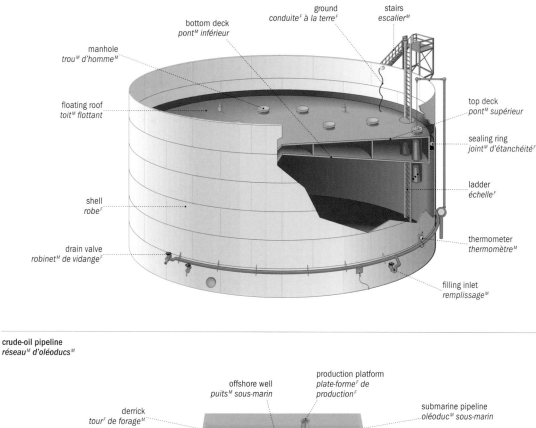

manhole
*trou<sup>M</sup> d'homme<sup>M</sup>*

bottom deck
*pont<sup>M</sup> inférieur*

ground
*conduite<sup>F</sup> à la terre<sup>F</sup>*

stairs
*escalier<sup>M</sup>*

floating roof
*toit<sup>M</sup> flottant*

top deck
*pont<sup>M</sup> supérieur*

sealing ring
*joint<sup>M</sup> d'étanchéité<sup>F</sup>*

ladder
*échelle<sup>F</sup>*

shell
*robe<sup>F</sup>*

thermometer
*thermomètre<sup>M</sup>*

drain valve
*robinet<sup>M</sup> de vidange<sup>F</sup>*

filling inlet
*remplissage<sup>M</sup>*

**crude-oil pipeline**
*réseau<sup>M</sup> d'oléoducs<sup>M</sup>*

offshore well
*puits<sup>M</sup> sous-marin*

production platform
*plate-forme<sup>F</sup> de
production<sup>F</sup>*

derrick
*tour<sup>F</sup> de forage<sup>M</sup>*

submarine pipeline
*oléoduc<sup>M</sup> sous-marin*

pumping station
*station<sup>F</sup> de pompage<sup>M</sup>*

Christmas tree
*arbre<sup>M</sup> de Noël<sup>M</sup>*

buffer tank
*réservoir<sup>M</sup> tampon<sup>M</sup>*

tank farm
*parc<sup>M</sup> de stockage<sup>M</sup>*

central pumping station
*station<sup>F</sup> de pompage<sup>M</sup> principale*

aboveground pipeline
*oléoduc<sup>M</sup> surélevé*

pipeline
*oléoduc<sup>M</sup>*

terminal
*parc<sup>M</sup> de stockage<sup>M</sup>
terminal*

intermediate booster station
*station<sup>F</sup> de pompage<sup>M</sup> intermédiaire*

refinery
*raffinerie<sup>F</sup>*

ENERGY

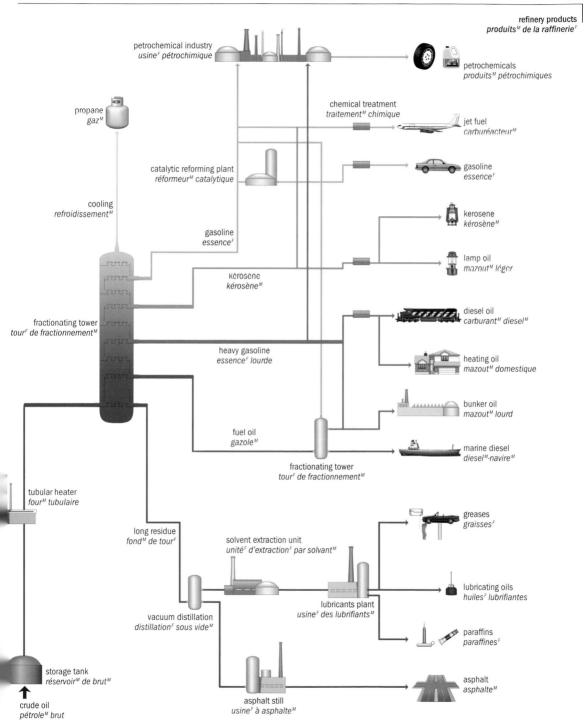

refinery products
*produits*[M] *de la raffinerie*[F]

petrochemical industry
*usine*[F] *pétrochimique*

petrochemicals
*produits*[M] *pétrochimiques*

chemical treatment
*traitement*[M] *chimique*

propane
*gaz*[M]

jet fuel
*carburéacteur*[M]

catalytic reforming plant
*réformeur*[M] *catalytique*

gasoline
*essence*[F]

cooling
*refroidissement*[M]

kerosene
*kérosène*[M]

gasoline
*essence*[F]

lamp oil
*mazout*[M] *léger*

kérosène
*kérosène*[M]

diesel oil
*carburant*[M] *diesel*[M]

fractionating tower
*tour*[F] *de fractionnement*[M]

heavy gasoline
*essence*[F] *lourde*

heating oil
*mazout*[M] *domestique*

bunker oil
*mazout*[M] *lourd*

fuel oil
*gazole*[M]

marine diesel
*diesel*[M]*-navire*[M]

fractionating tower
*tour*[F] *de fractionnement*[M]

tubular heater
*four*[M] *tubulaire*

greases
*graisses*[F]

long residue
*fond*[M] *de tour*[F]

solvent extraction unit
*unité*[F] *d'extraction*[F] *par solvant*[M]

lubricating oils
*huiles*[F] *lubrifiantes*

lubricants plant
*usine*[F] *des lubrifiants*[M]

vacuum distillation
*distillation*[F] *sous vide*[M]

paraffins
*paraffines*[F]

storage tank
*réservoir*[M] *de brut*[M]

asphalt
*asphalte*[M]

crude oil
*pétrole*[M] *brut*

asphalt still
*usine*[F] *à asphalte*[M]

# hydroelectric complex

complexe<sup>M</sup> hydroélectrique

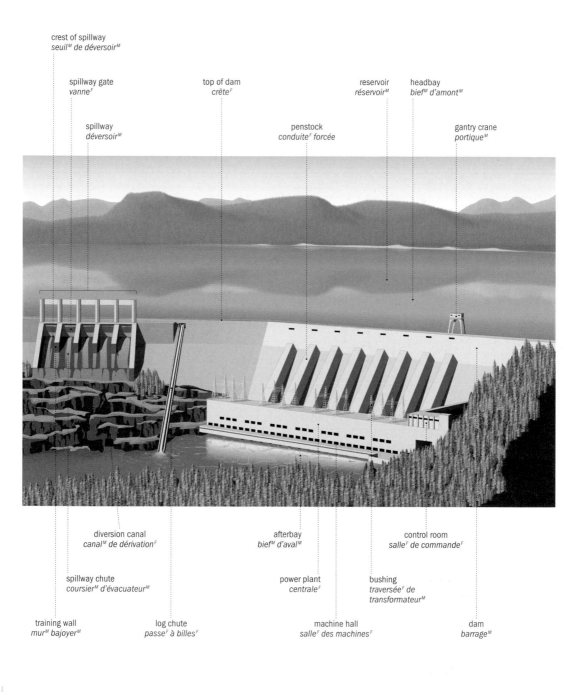

crest of spillway
seuil<sup>M</sup> de déversoir<sup>M</sup>

spillway gate
vanne<sup>F</sup>

top of dam
crête<sup>F</sup>

reservoir
réservoir<sup>M</sup>

headbay
bief<sup>M</sup> d'amont<sup>M</sup>

spillway
déversoir<sup>M</sup>

penstock
conduite<sup>F</sup> forcée

gantry crane
portique<sup>M</sup>

diversion canal
canal<sup>M</sup> de dérivation<sup>F</sup>

afterbay
bief<sup>M</sup> d'aval<sup>M</sup>

control room
salle<sup>F</sup> de commande<sup>F</sup>

spillway chute
coursier<sup>M</sup> d'évacuateur<sup>M</sup>

power plant
centrale<sup>F</sup>

bushing
traversée<sup>F</sup> de
transformateur<sup>M</sup>

training wall
mur<sup>M</sup> bajoyer<sup>M</sup>

log chute
passe<sup>F</sup> à billes<sup>F</sup>

machine hall
salle<sup>F</sup> des machines<sup>F</sup>

dam
barrage<sup>M</sup>

cross section of a hydroelectric power
plant
*coupe[F] d'une centrale[F] hydroélectrique*

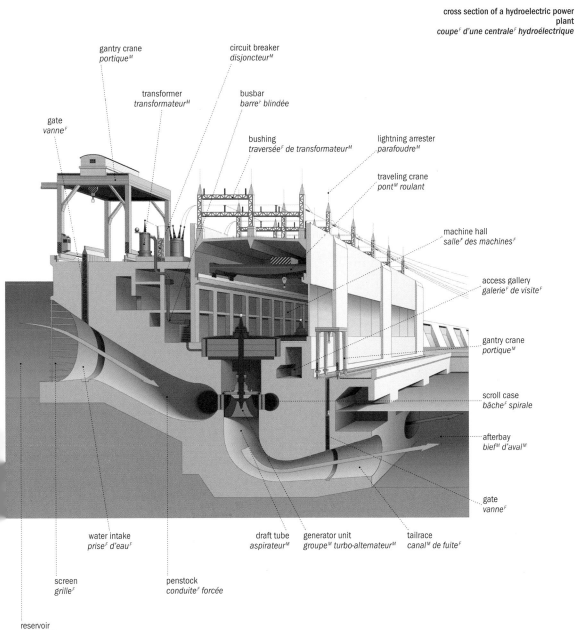

gantry crane
*portique[M]*

circuit breaker
*disjoncteur[M]*

transformer
*transformateur[M]*

busbar
*barre[F] blindée*

gate
*vanne[F]*

bushing
*traversée[F] de transformateur[M]*

lightning arrester
*parafoudre[M]*

traveling crane
*pont[M] roulant*

machine hall
*salle[F] des machines[F]*

access gallery
*galerie[F] de visite[F]*

gantry crane
*portique[M]*

scroll case
*bâche[F] spirale*

afterbay
*bief[M] d'aval[M]*

gate
*vanne[F]*

water intake
*prise[F] d'eau[F]*

draft tube
*aspirateur[M]*

generator unit
*groupe[M] turbo-alternateur[M]*

tailrace
*canal[M] de fuite[F]*

screen
*grille[F]*

penstock
*conduite[F] forcée*

reservoir
*réservoir[M]*

# production of electricity from nuclear energy

production<sup>F</sup> d'électricité<sup>F</sup> par énergie<sup>F</sup> nucléaire

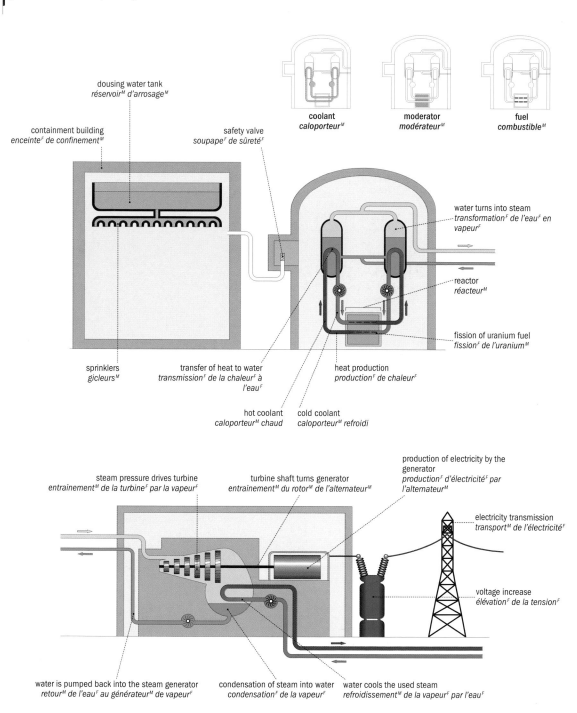

coolant
*caloporteur*<sup>M</sup>

moderator
*modérateur*<sup>M</sup>

fuel
*combustible*<sup>M</sup>

dousing water tank
*réservoir*<sup>M</sup> *d'arrosage*<sup>M</sup>

containment building
*enceinte*<sup>F</sup> *de confinement*<sup>M</sup>

safety valve
*soupape*<sup>F</sup> *de sûreté*<sup>F</sup>

water turns into steam
*transformation*<sup>F</sup> *de l'eau*<sup>F</sup> *en vapeur*<sup>F</sup>

reactor
*réacteur*<sup>M</sup>

fission of uranium fuel
*fission*<sup>F</sup> *de l'uranium*<sup>M</sup>

sprinklers
*gicleurs*<sup>M</sup>

transfer of heat to water
*transmission*<sup>F</sup> *de la chaleur*<sup>F</sup> *à l'eau*<sup>F</sup>

heat production
*production*<sup>F</sup> *de chaleur*<sup>F</sup>

hot coolant
*caloporteur*<sup>M</sup> *chaud*

cold coolant
*caloporteur*<sup>M</sup> *refroidi*

steam pressure drives turbine
*entraînement*<sup>M</sup> *de la turbine*<sup>F</sup> *par la vapeur*<sup>F</sup>

turbine shaft turns generator
*entraînement*<sup>M</sup> *du rotor*<sup>M</sup> *de l'alternateur*<sup>M</sup>

production of electricity by the generator
*production*<sup>F</sup> *d'électricité*<sup>F</sup> *par l'alternateur*<sup>M</sup>

electricity transmission
*transport*<sup>M</sup> *de l'électricité*<sup>F</sup>

voltage increase
*élévation*<sup>F</sup> *de la tension*<sup>F</sup>

water is pumped back into the steam generator
*retour*<sup>M</sup> *de l'eau*<sup>F</sup> *au générateur*<sup>M</sup> *de vapeur*<sup>F</sup>

condensation of steam into water
*condensation*<sup>F</sup> *de la vapeur*<sup>F</sup>

water cools the used steam
*refroidissement*<sup>M</sup> *de la vapeur*<sup>F</sup> *par l'eau*<sup>F</sup>

ENERGY

# fuel bundle

grappe<sup>F</sup> de combustible<sup>M</sup>

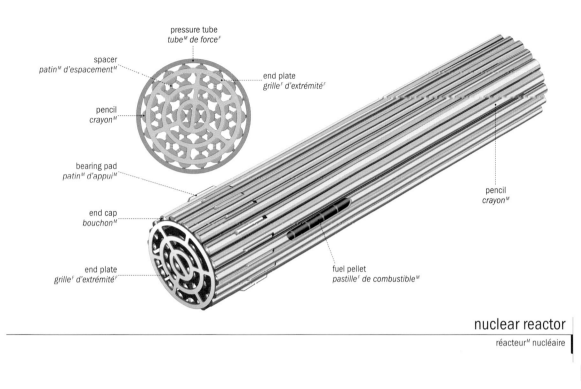

pressure tube
*tube<sup>M</sup> de force<sup>F</sup>*

spacer
*patin<sup>M</sup> d'espacement<sup>M</sup>*

end plate
*grille<sup>F</sup> d'extrémité<sup>F</sup>*

pencil
*crayon<sup>M</sup>*

bearing pad
*patin<sup>M</sup> d'appui<sup>M</sup>*

end cap
*bouchon<sup>M</sup>*

end plate
*grille<sup>F</sup> d'extrémité<sup>F</sup>*

pencil
*crayon<sup>M</sup>*

fuel pellet
*pastille<sup>F</sup> de combustible<sup>M</sup>*

# nuclear reactor

réacteur<sup>M</sup> nucléaire

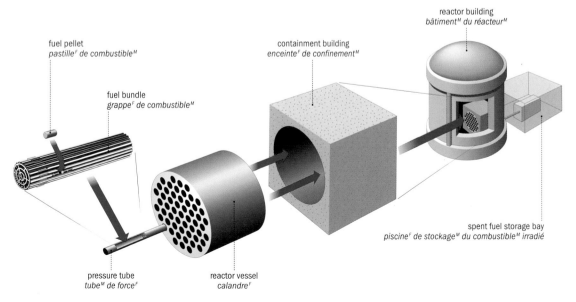

fuel pellet
*pastille<sup>F</sup> de combustible<sup>M</sup>*

fuel bundle
*grappe<sup>F</sup> de combustible<sup>M</sup>*

containment building
*enceinte<sup>F</sup> de confinement<sup>M</sup>*

reactor building
*bâtiment<sup>M</sup> du réacteur<sup>M</sup>*

spent fuel storage bay
*piscine<sup>F</sup> de stockage<sup>M</sup> du combustible<sup>M</sup> irradié*

pressure tube
*tube<sup>M</sup> de force<sup>F</sup>*

reactor vessel
*calandre<sup>F</sup>*

# solar cell

photopile<sup>F</sup>

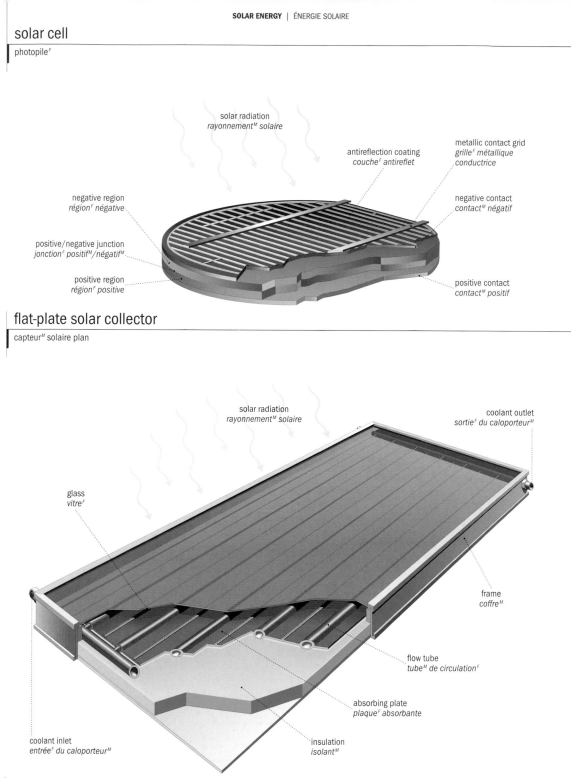

solar radiation
rayonnement<sup>M</sup> solaire

antireflection coating
couche<sup>F</sup> antireflet

metallic contact grid
grille<sup>F</sup> métallique
conductrice

negative region
région<sup>F</sup> négative

negative contact
contact<sup>M</sup> négatif

positive/negative junction
jonction<sup>F</sup> positif<sup>M</sup>/négatif<sup>M</sup>

positive region
région<sup>F</sup> positive

positive contact
contact<sup>M</sup> positif

# flat-plate solar collector

capteur<sup>M</sup> solaire plan

solar radiation
rayonnement<sup>M</sup> solaire

coolant outlet
sortie<sup>F</sup> du caloporteur<sup>M</sup>

glass
vitre<sup>F</sup>

frame
coffre<sup>M</sup>

flow tube
tube<sup>M</sup> de circulation<sup>F</sup>

absorbing plate
plaque<sup>F</sup> absorbante

coolant inlet
entrée<sup>F</sup> du caloporteur<sup>M</sup>

insulation
isolant<sup>M</sup>

ENERGY

# solar-cell system
circuit$^M$ de photopiles$^F$

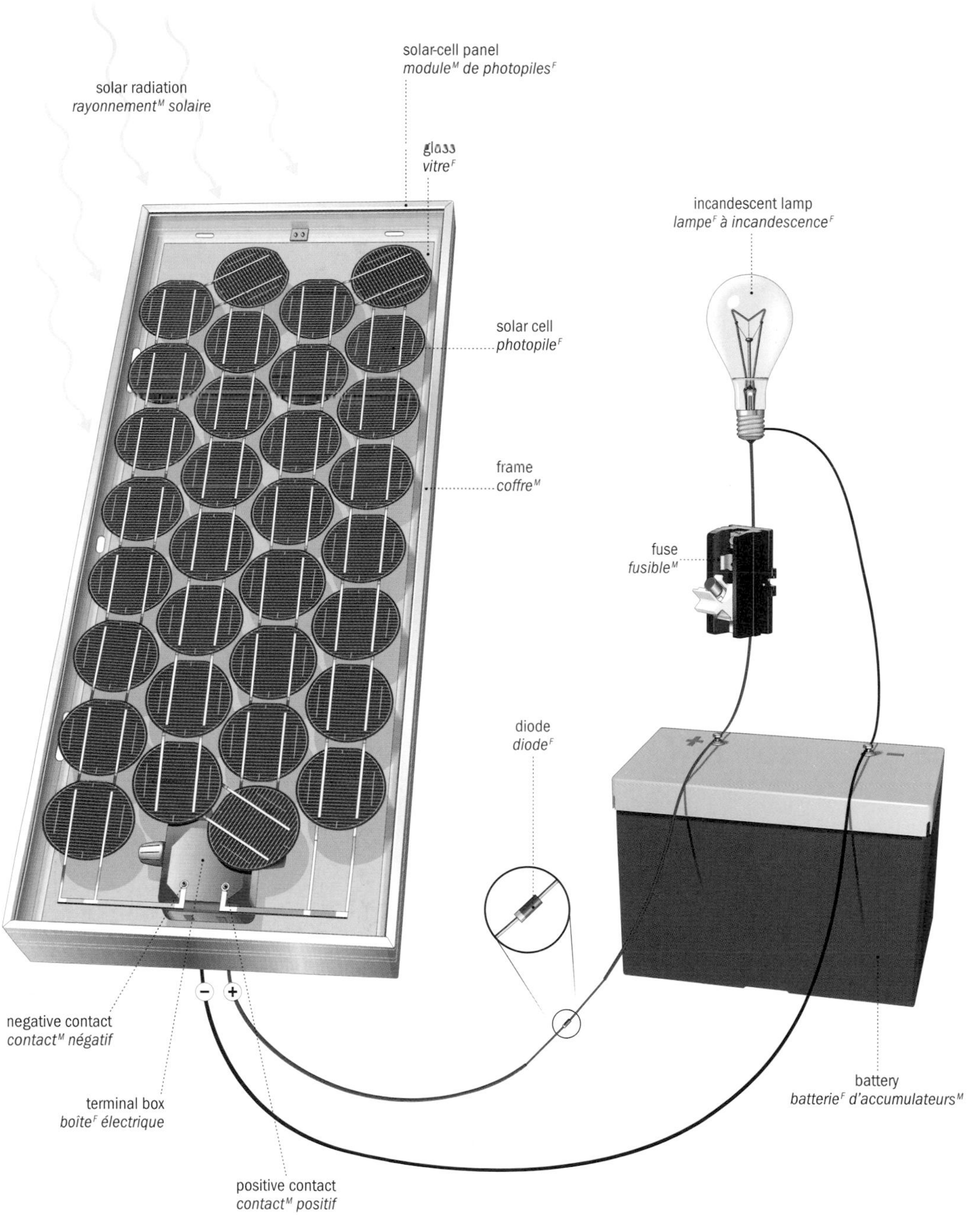

solar radiation
rayonnement$^M$ solaire

solar-cell panel
module$^M$ de photopiles$^F$

glass
vitre$^F$

incandescent lamp
lampe$^F$ à incandescence$^F$

solar cell
photopile$^F$

frame
coffre$^M$

fuse
fusible$^M$

diode
diode$^F$

negative contact
contact$^M$ négatif

battery
batterie$^F$ d'accumulateurs$^M$

terminal box
boîte$^F$ électrique

positive contact
contact$^M$ positif

# windmill

moulin<sup>M</sup> à vent<sup>M</sup>

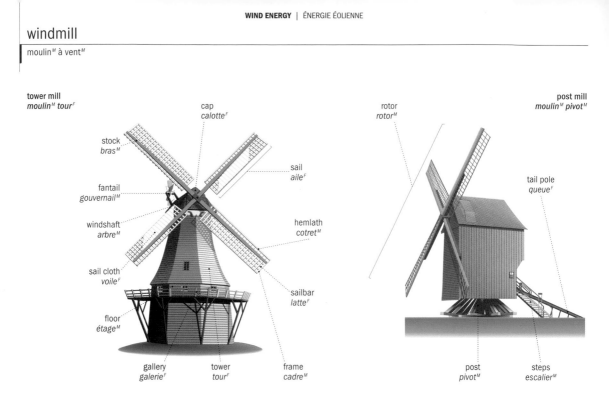

**tower mill**
*moulin<sup>M</sup> tour<sup>F</sup>*

cap
*calotte<sup>F</sup>*

stock
*bras<sup>M</sup>*

fantail
*gouvernail<sup>M</sup>*

windshaft
*arbre<sup>M</sup>*

sail cloth
*voile<sup>F</sup>*

floor
*étage<sup>M</sup>*

gallery
*galerie<sup>F</sup>*

tower
*tour<sup>F</sup>*

frame
*cadre<sup>M</sup>*

sail
*aile<sup>F</sup>*

hemlath
*cotret<sup>M</sup>*

sailbar
*latte<sup>F</sup>*

rotor
*rotor<sup>M</sup>*

**post mill**
*moulin<sup>M</sup> pivot<sup>M</sup>*

tail pole
*queue<sup>F</sup>*

post
*pivot<sup>M</sup>*

steps
*escalier<sup>M</sup>*

# wind turbines and electricity production

éoliennes<sup>F</sup> et production<sup>F</sup> d'électricité<sup>F</sup>

**vertical-axis wind turbine**
*éolienne<sup>F</sup> à axe<sup>M</sup> vertical*

guy wire
*hauban<sup>M</sup>*

strut
*entretoise<sup>F</sup>*

central column
*axe<sup>M</sup> central*

aerodynamic brake
*aérofrein<sup>M</sup>*

rotor
*rotor<sup>M</sup>*

blade
*pale<sup>F</sup>*

base
*socle<sup>M</sup>*

ENERGY

412

horizontal-axis wind turbine
*éolienne^F à axe^M horizontal*

nacelle cross-section
*coupe^F de la nacelle^F*

blade
*pale^F*

anemometer
*anémomètre^M*

wind vane
*girouette^F*

ball bearing
*roulement^M à billes^F*

lightning rod
*paratonnerre^M*

nacelle
*nacelle^F*

alternator
*alternateur^M*

hub
*moyeu^M*

low-speed shaft
*arbre^M lent*

flexible coupling
*accouplement^M flexible*

speed-increasing gearbox
*boite^F d'engrenage^M multiplicateur*

high-speed shaft
*arbre^M rapide*

tower
*tour^F*

production of electricity from wind energy
*production^F d'électricité^F par énergie^F éolienne*

horizontal-axis wind turbine
*éolienne^F à axe^M horizontal*

high-tension electricity transmission
*transport^M de l'électricité^F à haute tension^F*

voltage decrease
*abaissement^M de la tension^F*

transmission to consumers
*transport^M vers les usagers^M*

energy integration to the transmission network
*intégration^F de l'électricité^F au réseau^M de transport^M*

second voltage increase
*seconde élévation^F de la tension^F*

first voltage increase
*première élévation^F de la tension^F*

ENERGY

# matter

matière[F]

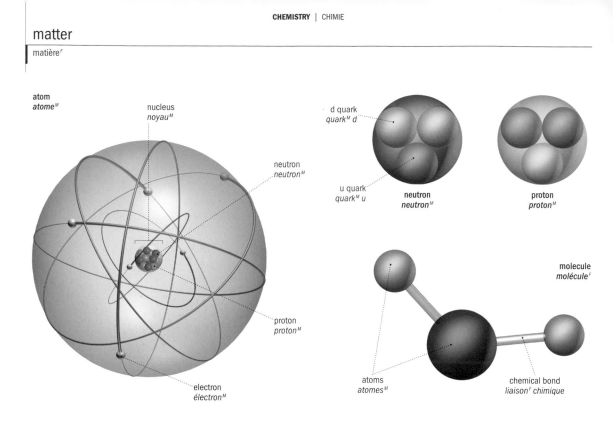

**atom**
*atome*[M]

nucleus
*noyau*[M]

neutron
*neutron*[M]

proton
*proton*[M]

electron
*électron*[M]

d quark
*quark*[M] *d*

u quark
*quark*[M] *u*

**neutron**
*neutron*[M]

**proton**
*proton*[M]

molecule
*molécule*[F]

atoms
*atomes*[M]

chemical bond
*liaison*[F] *chimique*

**states of matter**
*états*[M] *de la matière*[F]

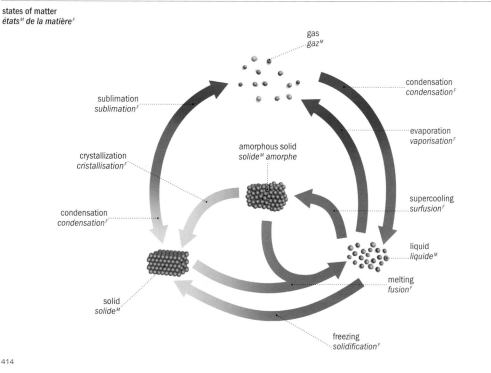

gas
*gaz*[M]

sublimation
*sublimation*[F]

condensation
*condensation*[F]

crystallization
*cristallisation*[F]

amorphous solid
*solide*[M] *amorphe*

evaporation
*vaporisation*[F]

condensation
*condensation*[F]

supercooling
*surfusion*[F]

liquid
*liquide*[M]

melting
*fusion*[F]

solid
*solide*[M]

freezing
*solidification*[F]

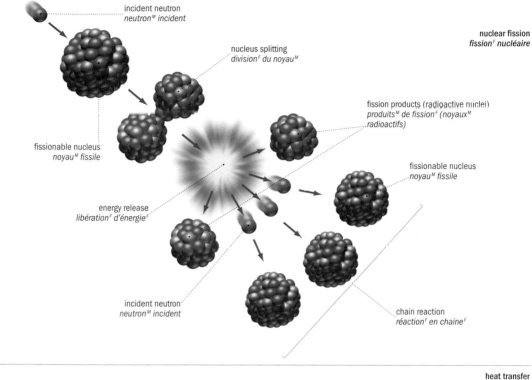

**nuclear fission**
*fission^F nucléaire*

incident neutron
*neutron^M incident*

nucleus splitting
*division^F du noyau^M*

fission products (radioactive nuclei)
*produits^M de fission^F (noyaux^M radioactifs)*

fissionable nucleus
*noyau^M fissile*

fissionable nucleus
*noyau^M fissile*

energy release
*libération^F d'énergie^F*

incident neutron
*neutron^M incident*

chain reaction
*réaction^F en chaine^F*

**heat transfer**
*transfert^M de la chaleur^F*

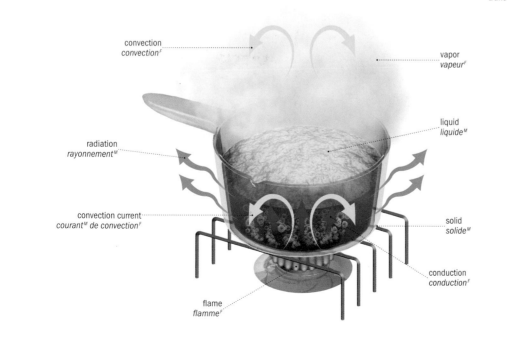

convection
*convection^F*

vapor
*vapeur^F*

radiation
*rayonnement^M*

liquid
*liquide^M*

convection current
*courant^M de convection^F*

solid
*solide^M*

conduction
*conduction^F*

flame
*flamme^F*

# magnetism

magnétisme<sup>M</sup>

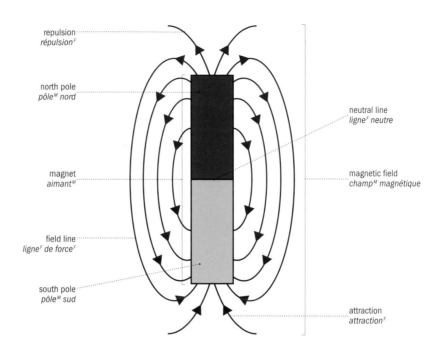

repulsion
répulsion<sup>F</sup>

north pole
pôle<sup>M</sup> nord

neutral line
ligne<sup>F</sup> neutre

magnet
aimant<sup>M</sup>

magnetic field
champ<sup>M</sup> magnétique

field line
ligne<sup>F</sup> de force<sup>F</sup>

south pole
pôle<sup>M</sup> sud

attraction
attraction<sup>F</sup>

# parallel electrical circuit

circuit<sup>M</sup> électrique en parallèle<sup>F</sup>

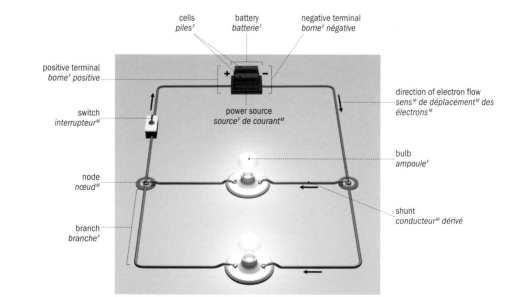

cells
piles<sup>F</sup>

battery
batterie<sup>F</sup>

negative terminal
borne<sup>F</sup> négative

positive terminal
borne<sup>F</sup> positive

direction of electron flow
sens<sup>M</sup> de déplacement<sup>M</sup> des
électrons<sup>M</sup>

switch
interrupteur<sup>M</sup>

power source
source<sup>F</sup> de courant<sup>M</sup>

bulb
ampoule<sup>F</sup>

node
nœud<sup>M</sup>

shunt
conducteur<sup>M</sup> dérivé

branch
branche<sup>F</sup>

# dry cells
piles<sup>F</sup> sèches

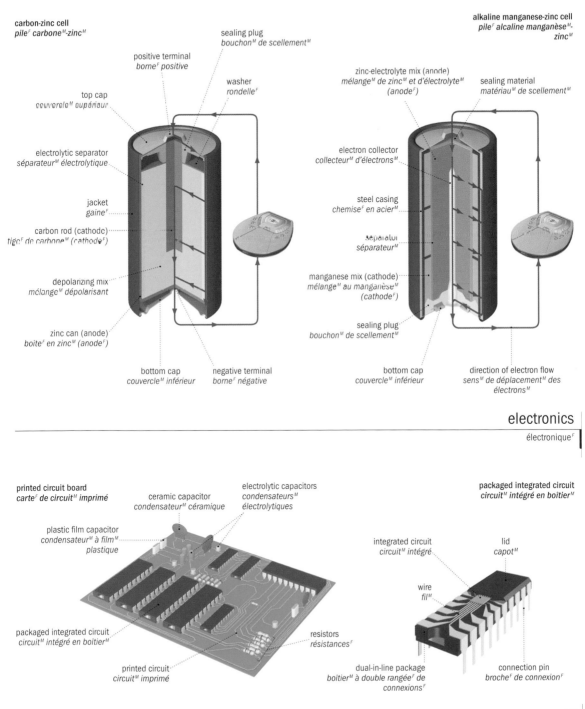

**carbon-zinc cell**
*pile<sup>F</sup> carbone<sup>M</sup>-zinc<sup>M</sup>*

positive terminal
*borne<sup>F</sup> positive*

sealing plug
*bouchon<sup>M</sup> de scellement<sup>M</sup>*

washer
*rondelle<sup>F</sup>*

top cap
*couvercle<sup>M</sup> supérieur*

electrolytic separator
*séparateur<sup>F</sup> électrolytique*

jacket
*gaine<sup>F</sup>*

carbon rod (cathode)
*tige<sup>F</sup> de carbone<sup>M</sup> (cathode<sup>F</sup>)*

depolarizing mix
*mélange<sup>M</sup> dépolarisant*

zinc can (anode)
*boîte<sup>F</sup> en zinc<sup>M</sup> (anode<sup>F</sup>)*

bottom cap
*couvercle<sup>M</sup> inférieur*

negative terminal
*borne<sup>F</sup> négative*

**alkaline manganese-zinc cell**
*pile<sup>F</sup> alcaline manganèse<sup>M</sup>-zinc<sup>M</sup>*

zinc-electrolyte mix (anode)
*mélange<sup>M</sup> de zinc<sup>M</sup> et d'électrolyte<sup>M</sup> (anode<sup>F</sup>)*

sealing material
*matériau<sup>M</sup> de scellement<sup>M</sup>*

electron collector
*collecteur<sup>M</sup> d'électrons<sup>M</sup>*

steel casing
*chemise<sup>F</sup> en acier<sup>M</sup>*

séparateur
*séparateur<sup>M</sup>*

manganese mix (cathode)
*mélange<sup>M</sup> au manganèse<sup>M</sup> (cathode<sup>F</sup>)*

sealing plug
*bouchon<sup>M</sup> de scellement<sup>M</sup>*

bottom cap
*couvercle<sup>M</sup> inférieur*

direction of electron flow
*sens<sup>M</sup> de déplacement<sup>M</sup> des électrons<sup>M</sup>*

# electronics
électronique<sup>F</sup>

SCIENCE

**printed circuit board**
*carte<sup>F</sup> de circuit<sup>M</sup> imprimé*

ceramic capacitor
*condensateur<sup>M</sup> céramique*

electrolytic capacitors
*condensateurs<sup>M</sup> électrolytiques*

plastic film capacitor
*condensateur<sup>M</sup> à film<sup>M</sup> plastique*

packaged integrated circuit
*circuit<sup>M</sup> intégré en boîtier<sup>M</sup>*

printed circuit
*circuit<sup>M</sup> imprimé*

resistors
*résistances<sup>F</sup>*

**packaged integrated circuit**
*circuit<sup>M</sup> intégré en boîtier<sup>M</sup>*

integrated circuit
*circuit<sup>M</sup> intégré*

lid
*capot<sup>M</sup>*

wire
*fil<sup>M</sup>*

dual-in-line package
*boîtier<sup>M</sup> à double rangée<sup>F</sup> de connexions<sup>F</sup>*

connection pin
*broche<sup>F</sup> de connexion<sup>F</sup>*

# electromagnetic spectrum

spectre$^M$ électromagnétique

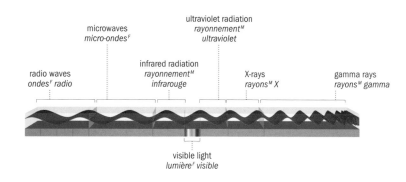

microwaves
micro-ondes$^F$

ultraviolet radiation
rayonnement$^M$
ultraviolet

infrared radiation
rayonnement$^M$
infrarouge

radio waves
ondes$^F$ radio

X-rays
rayons$^M$ X

gamma rays
rayons$^M$ gamma

visible light
lumière$^F$ visible

# wave

onde$^F$

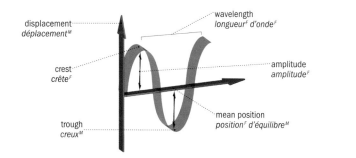

wavelength
longueur$^F$ d'onde$^F$

displacement
déplacement$^M$

crest
crête$^F$

amplitude
amplitude$^F$

trough
creux$^M$

mean position
position$^F$ d'équilibre$^M$

# color synthesis

synthèse$^F$ des couleurs$^F$

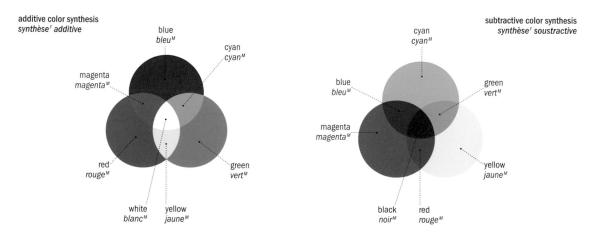

**additive color synthesis**
*synthèse$^F$ additive*

blue
bleu$^M$

cyan
cyan$^M$

magenta
magenta$^M$

red
rouge$^M$

green
vert$^M$

white
blanc$^M$

yellow
jaune$^M$

**subtractive color synthesis**
*synthèse$^F$ soustractive*

cyan
cyan$^M$

blue
bleu$^M$

green
vert$^M$

magenta
magenta$^M$

yellow
jaune$^M$

black
noir$^M$

red
rouge$^M$

# vision
vision<sup>F</sup>

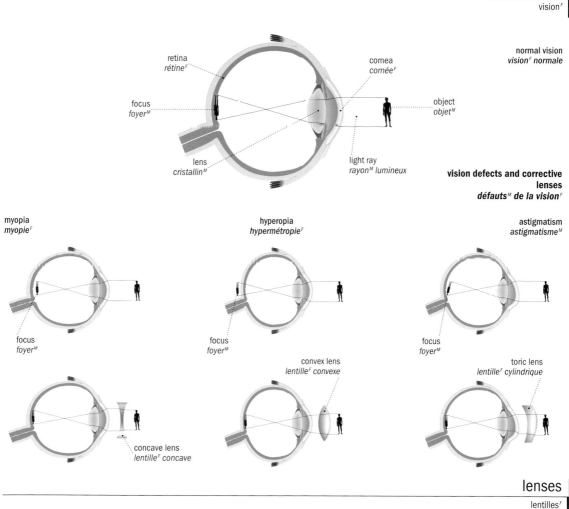

**normal vision**
*vision<sup>F</sup> normale*

retina
*rétine<sup>F</sup>*

cornea
*cornée<sup>F</sup>*

object
*objet<sup>M</sup>*

focus
*foyer<sup>M</sup>*

lens
*cristallin<sup>M</sup>*

light ray
*rayon<sup>M</sup> lumineux*

**vision defects and corrective lenses**
*défauts<sup>M</sup> de la vision<sup>F</sup>*

myopia
*myopie<sup>F</sup>*

hyperopia
*hypermétropie<sup>F</sup>*

astigmatism
*astigmatisme<sup>M</sup>*

focus
*foyer<sup>M</sup>*

focus
*foyer<sup>M</sup>*

focus
*foyer<sup>M</sup>*

convex lens
*lentille<sup>F</sup> convexe*

toric lens
*lentille<sup>F</sup> cylindrique*

concave lens
*lentille<sup>F</sup> concave*

# lenses
lentilles<sup>F</sup>

SCIENCE

**converging lenses**
*lentilles<sup>F</sup> convergentes*

biconvex lens
*lentille<sup>F</sup> biconvexe*

positive meniscus
*ménisque<sup>M</sup> convergent*

convex lens
*lentille<sup>F</sup> convexe*

plano-convex lens
*lentille<sup>F</sup> plan<sup>M</sup>-convexe*

**diverging lenses**
*lentilles<sup>F</sup> divergentes*

plano-concave lens
*lentille<sup>F</sup> plan<sup>M</sup>-concave*

concave lens
*lentille<sup>F</sup> concave*

biconcave lens
*lentille<sup>F</sup> biconcave*

negative meniscus
*ménisque<sup>M</sup> divergent*

# pulsed ruby laser

laser<sup>M</sup> à rubis<sup>M</sup> pulsé

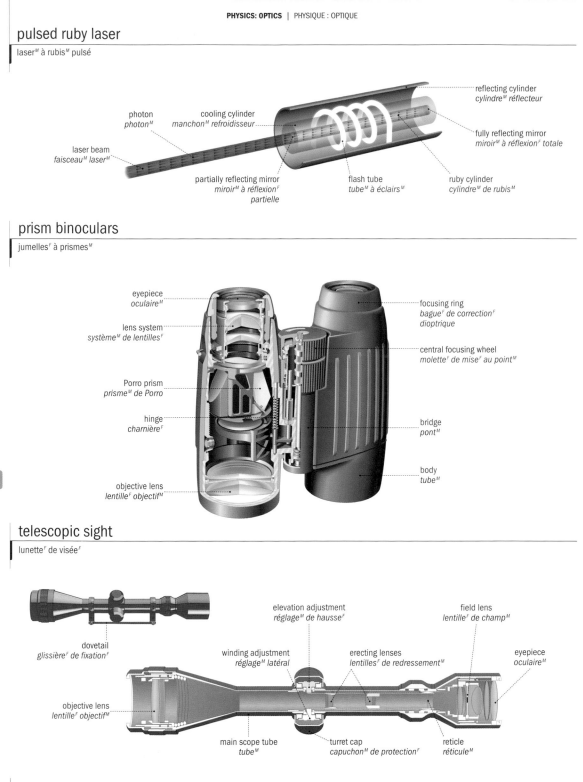

reflecting cylinder
cylindre<sup>M</sup> réflecteur

fully reflecting mirror
miroir<sup>M</sup> à réflexion<sup>F</sup> totale

photon
photon<sup>M</sup>

cooling cylinder
manchon<sup>M</sup> refroidisseur

laser beam
faisceau<sup>M</sup> laser<sup>M</sup>

partially reflecting mirror
miroir<sup>M</sup> à réflexion<sup>F</sup>
partielle

flash tube
tube<sup>M</sup> à éclairs<sup>M</sup>

ruby cylinder
cylindre<sup>M</sup> de rubis<sup>M</sup>

# prism binoculars

jumelles<sup>F</sup> à prismes<sup>M</sup>

eyepiece
oculaire<sup>M</sup>

lens system
système<sup>M</sup> de lentilles<sup>F</sup>

Porro prism
prisme<sup>M</sup> de Porro

hinge
charnière<sup>F</sup>

objective lens
lentille<sup>F</sup> objectif<sup>M</sup>

focusing ring
bague<sup>F</sup> de correction<sup>F</sup>
dioptrique

central focusing wheel
molette<sup>F</sup> de mise<sup>F</sup> au point<sup>M</sup>

bridge
pont<sup>M</sup>

body
tube<sup>M</sup>

# telescopic sight

lunette<sup>F</sup> de visée<sup>F</sup>

elevation adjustment
réglage<sup>M</sup> de hausse<sup>F</sup>

field lens
lentille<sup>F</sup> de champ<sup>M</sup>

dovetail
glissière<sup>F</sup> de fixation<sup>F</sup>

winding adjustment
réglage<sup>M</sup> latéral

erecting lenses
lentilles<sup>F</sup> de redressement<sup>M</sup>

eyepiece
oculaire<sup>M</sup>

objective lens
lentille<sup>F</sup> objectif<sup>M</sup>

main scope tube
tube<sup>M</sup>

turret cap
capuchon<sup>M</sup> de protection<sup>F</sup>

reticle
réticule<sup>M</sup>

SCIENCE

# magnifying glass and microscopes

loupe[F] et microscopes[M]

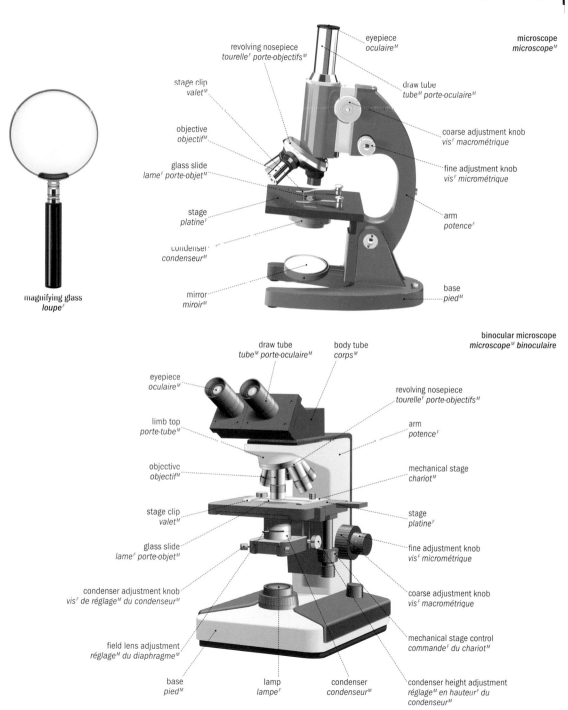

**microscope**
*microscope*[M]

eyepiece
*oculaire*[M]

revolving nosepiece
*tourelle*[F] *porte-objectifs*[M]

draw tube
*tube*[M] *porte-oculaire*[M]

stage clip
*valet*[M]

coarse adjustment knob
*vis*[F] *macrométrique*

objective
*objectif*[M]

fine adjustment knob
*vis*[F] *micrométrique*

glass slide
*lame*[F] *porte-objet*[M]

stage
*platine*[F]

arm
*potence*[F]

condenser
*condenseur*[M]

mirror
*miroir*[M]

base
*pied*[M]

magnifying glass
*loupe*[F]

**binocular microscope**
*microscope*[M] *binoculaire*

draw tube
*tube*[M] *porte-oculaire*[M]

body tube
*corps*[M]

eyepiece
*oculaire*[M]

revolving nosepiece
*tourelle*[F] *porte-objectifs*[M]

limb top
*porte-tube*[M]

arm
*potence*[F]

objective
*objectif*[M]

mechanical stage
*chariot*[M]

stage clip
*valet*[M]

stage
*platine*[F]

glass slide
*lame*[F] *porte-objet*[M]

fine adjustment knob
*vis*[F] *micrométrique*

condenser adjustment knob
*vis*[F] *de réglage*[M] *du condenseur*[M]

coarse adjustment knob
*vis*[F] *macrométrique*

field lens adjustment
*réglage*[M] *du diaphragme*[M]

mechanical stage control
*commande*[F] *du chariot*[M]

base
*pied*[M]

lamp
*lampe*[F]

condenser
*condenseur*[M]

condenser height adjustment
*réglage*[M] *en hauteur*[F] *du condenseur*[M]

SCIENCE

# measurement of weight
mesure<sup>F</sup> de la masse<sup>F</sup>

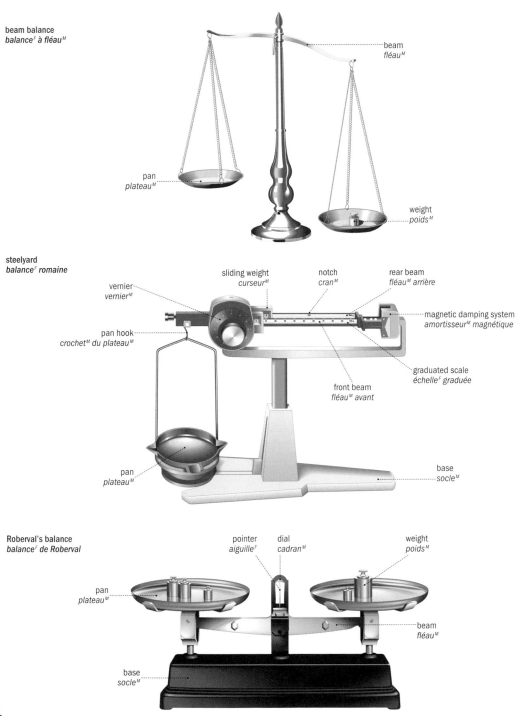

**beam balance**
*balance<sup>F</sup> à fléau<sup>M</sup>*

beam
*fléau<sup>M</sup>*

pan
*plateau<sup>M</sup>*

weight
*poids<sup>M</sup>*

**steelyard**
*balance<sup>F</sup> romaine*

sliding weight
*curseur<sup>M</sup>*

notch
*cran<sup>M</sup>*

rear beam
*fléau<sup>M</sup> arrière*

vernier
*vernier<sup>M</sup>*

magnetic damping system
*amortisseur<sup>M</sup> magnétique*

pan hook
*crochet<sup>M</sup> du plateau<sup>M</sup>*

graduated scale
*échelle<sup>F</sup> graduée*

front beam
*fléau<sup>M</sup> avant*

pan
*plateau<sup>M</sup>*

base
*socle<sup>M</sup>*

**Roberval's balance**
*balance<sup>F</sup> de Roberval*

pointer
*aiguille<sup>F</sup>*

dial
*cadran<sup>M</sup>*

weight
*poids<sup>M</sup>*

pan
*plateau<sup>M</sup>*

beam
*fléau<sup>M</sup>*

base
*socle<sup>M</sup>*

SCIENCE

measurement of weight

spring balance
*peson*<sup>M</sup>

ring
*anneau*<sup>M</sup>

pointer
*index*<sup>M</sup>

graduated scale
*échelle*<sup>F</sup> *graduée*

hook
*crochet*<sup>M</sup>

weight
*poids*<sup>M</sup>

electronic scale
*balance*<sup>F</sup> *électronique*

unit price
*prix*<sup>M</sup> *à l'unité*<sup>F</sup>

display
*afficheur*<sup>M</sup>

total
*prix*<sup>M</sup> *à payer*

platform
*plateau*<sup>M</sup>

POIDS/WEIGHT
PRIX/PRICE/kg
TOTAL

function keys
*touches*<sup>F</sup> *de fonctions*<sup>F</sup>

product code
*code*<sup>M</sup> *des produits*<sup>M</sup>

numeric keyboard
*clavier*<sup>M</sup> *numérique*

printout
*étiquette*<sup>F</sup>

bathroom scale
*pèse-personne*<sup>M</sup>

digital display
*affichage*<sup>M</sup> *numérique*

weighing platform
*plate-forme*<sup>F</sup>

analytical balance
*balance*<sup>F</sup> *de précision*<sup>F</sup>

glass case
*cage*<sup>F</sup> *vitrée*

access door
*porte*<sup>F</sup>

pan
*plateau*<sup>M</sup>

leveling screw
*vis*<sup>F</sup> *calante*

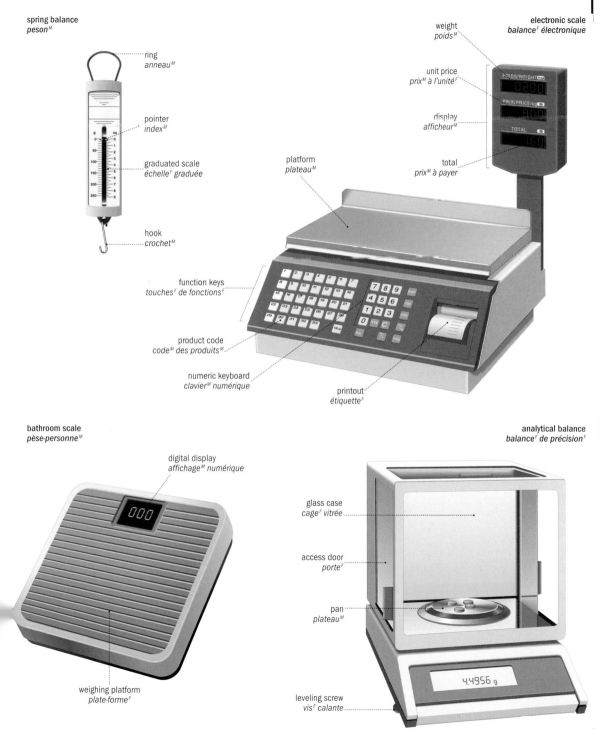

# measurement of temperature

mesure<sup>F</sup> de la température<sup>F</sup>

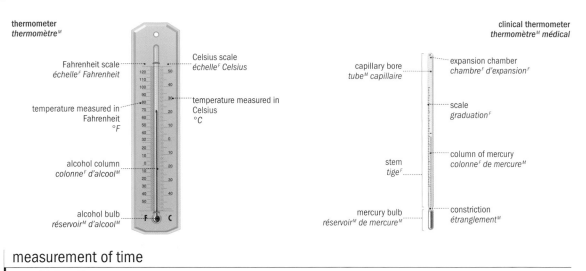

**thermometer**
*thermomètre<sup>M</sup>*

Fahrenheit scale
*échelle<sup>F</sup> Fahrenheit*

Celsius scale
*échelle<sup>F</sup> Celsius*

temperature measured in
Fahrenheit
°F

temperature measured in
Celsius
°C

alcohol column
*colonne<sup>F</sup> d'alcool<sup>M</sup>*

alcohol bulb
*réservoir<sup>M</sup> d'alcool<sup>M</sup>*

**clinical thermometer**
*thermomètre<sup>M</sup> médical*

capillary bore
*tube<sup>M</sup> capillaire*

expansion chamber
*chambre<sup>F</sup> d'expansion<sup>F</sup>*

scale
*graduation<sup>F</sup>*

stem
*tige<sup>F</sup>*

column of mercury
*colonne<sup>F</sup> de mercure<sup>M</sup>*

mercury bulb
*réservoir<sup>M</sup> de mercure<sup>M</sup>*

constriction
*étranglement<sup>M</sup>*

# measurement of time

mesure<sup>F</sup> du temps<sup>M</sup>

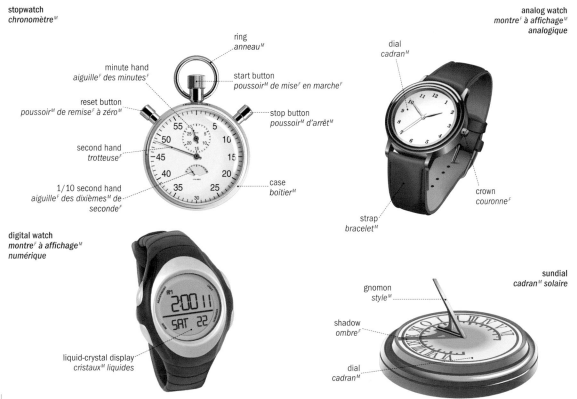

**stopwatch**
*chronomètre<sup>M</sup>*

ring
*anneau<sup>M</sup>*

minute hand
*aiguille<sup>F</sup> des minutes<sup>F</sup>*

start button
*poussoir<sup>M</sup> de mise<sup>F</sup> en marche<sup>F</sup>*

reset button
*poussoir<sup>M</sup> de remise<sup>F</sup> à zéro<sup>M</sup>*

stop button
*poussoir<sup>M</sup> d'arrêt<sup>M</sup>*

second hand
*trotteuse<sup>F</sup>*

1/10 second hand
*aiguille<sup>F</sup> des dixièmes<sup>M</sup> de
seconde<sup>F</sup>*

case
*boîtier<sup>M</sup>*

**analog watch**
*montre<sup>F</sup> à affichage<sup>M</sup>
analogique*

dial
*cadran<sup>M</sup>*

crown
*couronne<sup>F</sup>*

strap
*bracelet<sup>M</sup>*

**digital watch**
*montre<sup>F</sup> à affichage<sup>M</sup>
numérique*

liquid-crystal display
*cristaux<sup>M</sup> liquides*

**sundial**
*cadran<sup>M</sup> solaire*

gnomon
*style<sup>M</sup>*

shadow
*ombre<sup>F</sup>*

dial
*cadran<sup>M</sup>*

SCIENCE

# measurement of length
mesure<sup>F</sup> de la longueur<sup>F</sup>

ruler
*règle<sup>F</sup> graduée*

scales
*graduation<sup>F</sup>*

# measurement of thickness
mesure<sup>F</sup> de l'épaisseur<sup>F</sup>

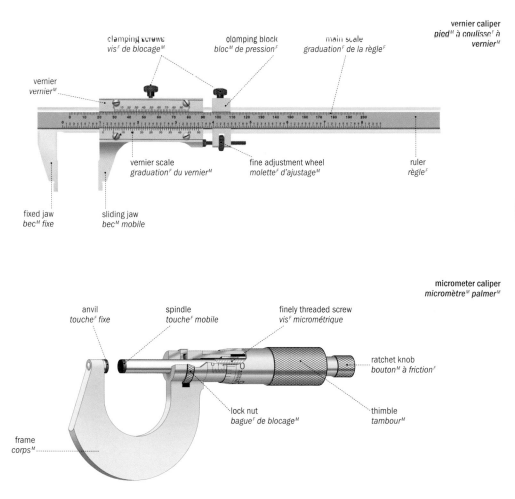

vernier caliper
*pied<sup>M</sup> à coulisse<sup>F</sup> à vernier<sup>M</sup>*

clamping screws
*vis<sup>F</sup> de blocage<sup>M</sup>*

clamping block
*bloc<sup>M</sup> de pression<sup>F</sup>*

main scale
*graduation<sup>F</sup> de la règle<sup>F</sup>*

vernier
*vernier<sup>M</sup>*

vernier scale
*graduation<sup>F</sup> du vernier<sup>M</sup>*

fine adjustment wheel
*molette<sup>F</sup> d'ajustage<sup>M</sup>*

ruler
*règle<sup>F</sup>*

fixed jaw
*bec<sup>M</sup> fixe*

sliding jaw
*bec<sup>M</sup> mobile*

SCIENCE

micrometer caliper
*micromètre<sup>M</sup> palmer<sup>M</sup>*

anvil
*touche<sup>F</sup> fixe*

spindle
*touche<sup>F</sup> mobile*

finely threaded screw
*vis<sup>F</sup> micrométrique*

ratchet knob
*bouton<sup>M</sup> à friction<sup>F</sup>*

lock nut
*bague<sup>F</sup> de blocage<sup>M</sup>*

thimble
*tambour<sup>M</sup>*

frame
*corps<sup>M</sup>*

# international system of units

système<sup>M</sup> international d'unités<sup>F</sup>

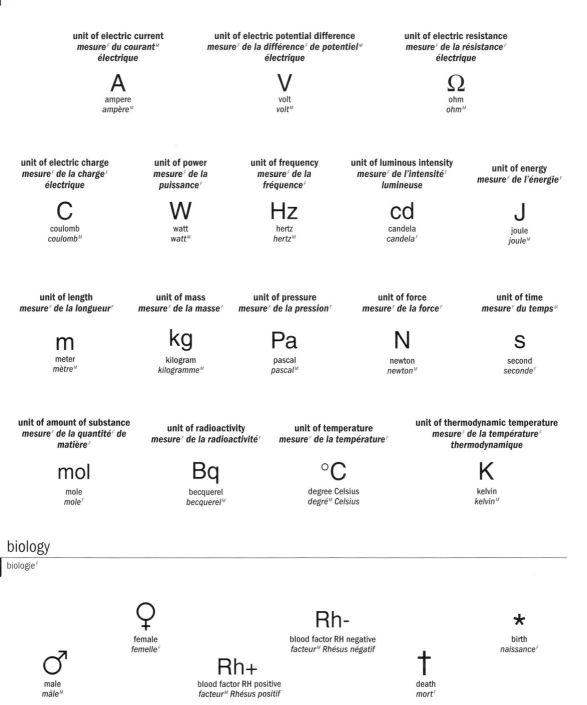

**unit of electric current**
*mesure<sup>F</sup> du courant<sup>M</sup>
électrique*

A

ampere
*ampère<sup>M</sup>*

**unit of electric potential difference**
*mesure<sup>F</sup> de la différence<sup>F</sup> de potentiel<sup>M</sup>
électrique*

V

volt
*volt<sup>M</sup>*

**unit of electric resistance**
*mesure<sup>F</sup> de la résistance<sup>F</sup>
électrique*

Ω

ohm
*ohm<sup>M</sup>*

**unit of electric charge**
*mesure<sup>F</sup> de la charge<sup>F</sup>
électrique*

C

coulomb
*coulomb<sup>M</sup>*

**unit of power**
*mesure<sup>F</sup> de la
puissance<sup>F</sup>*

W

watt
*watt<sup>M</sup>*

**unit of frequency**
*mesure<sup>F</sup> de la
fréquence<sup>F</sup>*

Hz

hertz
*hertz<sup>M</sup>*

**unit of luminous intensity**
*mesure<sup>F</sup> de l'intensité<sup>F</sup>
lumineuse*

cd

candela
*candela<sup>F</sup>*

**unit of energy**
*mesure<sup>F</sup> de l'énergie<sup>F</sup>*

J

joule
*joule<sup>M</sup>*

**unit of length**
*mesure<sup>F</sup> de la longueur<sup>F</sup>*

m

meter
*mètre<sup>M</sup>*

**unit of mass**
*mesure<sup>F</sup> de la masse<sup>F</sup>*

kg

kilogram
*kilogramme<sup>M</sup>*

**unit of pressure**
*mesure<sup>F</sup> de la pression<sup>F</sup>*

Pa

pascal
*pascal<sup>M</sup>*

**unit of force**
*mesure<sup>F</sup> de la force<sup>F</sup>*

N

newton
*newton<sup>M</sup>*

**unit of time**
*mesure<sup>F</sup> du temps<sup>M</sup>*

s

second
*seconde<sup>F</sup>*

**unit of amount of substance**
*mesure<sup>F</sup> de la quantité<sup>F</sup> de
matière<sup>F</sup>*

mol

mole
*mole<sup>F</sup>*

**unit of radioactivity**
*mesure<sup>F</sup> de la radioactivité<sup>F</sup>*

Bq

becquerel
*becquerel<sup>M</sup>*

**unit of temperature**
*mesure<sup>F</sup> de la température<sup>F</sup>*

°C

degree Celsius
*degré<sup>M</sup> Celsius*

**unit of thermodynamic temperature**
*mesure<sup>F</sup> de la température<sup>F</sup>
thermodynamique*

K

kelvin
*kelvin<sup>M</sup>*

# biology

biologie<sup>F</sup>

♀

female
*femelle<sup>F</sup>*

♂

male
*mâle<sup>M</sup>*

Rh+

blood factor RH positive
*facteur<sup>M</sup> Rhésus positif*

Rh-

blood factor RH negative
*facteur<sup>M</sup> Rhésus négatif*

†

death
*mort<sup>F</sup>*

∗

birth
*naissance<sup>F</sup>*

# mathematics
mathématiques[F]

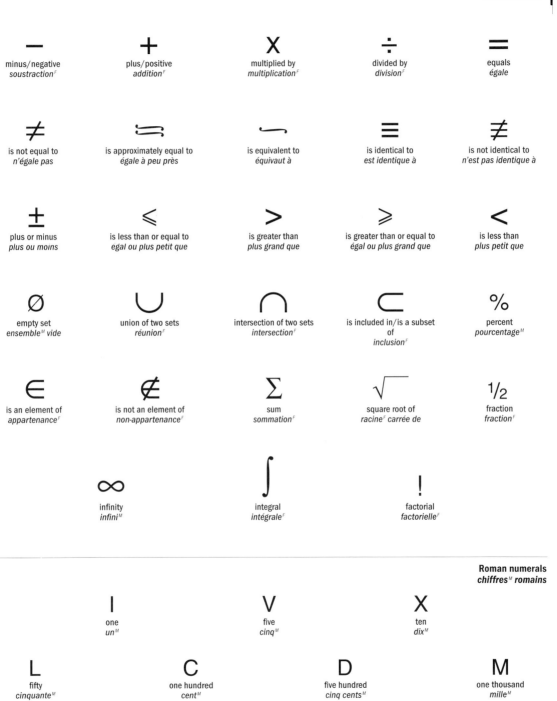

minus/negative
*soustraction*[F]

plus/positive
*addition*[F]

multiplied by
*multiplication*[F]

divided by
*division*[F]

equals
*égale*

is not equal to
*n'égale pas*

is approximately equal to
*égale à peu près*

is equivalent to
*équivaut à*

is identical to
*est identique à*

is not identical to
*n'est pas identique à*

plus or minus
*plus ou moins*

is less than or equal to
*egal ou plus petit que*

is greater than
*plus grand que*

is greater than or equal to
*égal ou plus grand que*

is less than
*plus petit que*

empty set
*ensemble*[M] *vide*

union of two sets
*réunion*[F]

intersection of two sets
*intersection*[F]

is included in/is a subset
of
*inclusion*[F]

percent
*pourcentage*[M]

is an element of
*appartenance*[F]

is not an element of
*non-appartenance*[F]

sum
*sommation*[F]

square root of
*racine*[F] *carrée de*

fraction
*fraction*[F]

infinity
*infini*[M]

integral
*intégrale*[F]

factorial
*factorielle*[F]

**Roman numerals**
***chiffres*[M] *romains***

one
*un*[M]

five
*cinq*[M]

ten
*dix*[M]

fifty
*cinquante*[M]

one hundred
*cent*[M]

five hundred
*cinq cents*[M]

one thousand
*mille*[M]

SCIENCE

# geometry

géométrie[F]

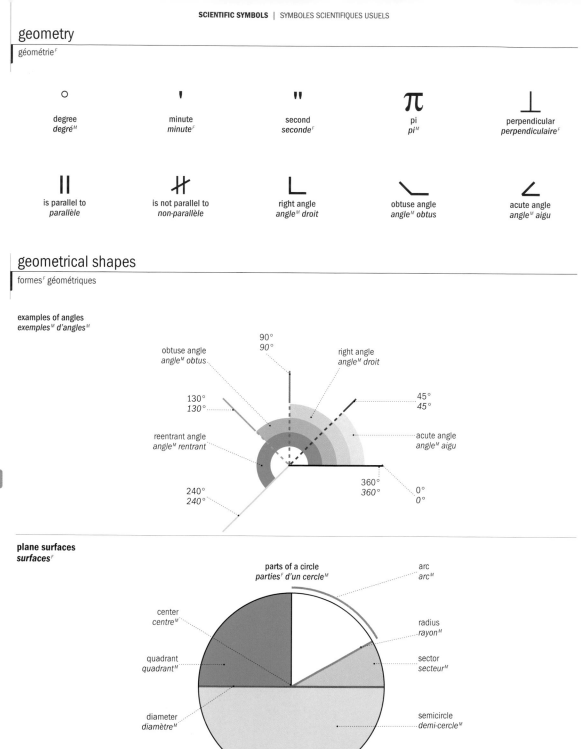

○
degree
degré[M]

'
minute
minute[F]

"
second
seconde[F]

π
pi
pi[M]

⊥
perpendicular
perpendiculaire[F]

‖
is parallel to
parallèle

⫲
is not parallel to
non-parallèle

∟
right angle
angle[M] droit

⦦
obtuse angle
angle[M] obtus

∠
acute angle
angle[M] aigu

# geometrical shapes

formes[F] géométriques

**examples of angles**
exemples[M] d'angles[M]

90°
90°

obtuse angle
angle[M] obtus

right angle
angle[M] droit

130°
130°

45°
45°

reentrant angle
angle[M] rentrant

acute angle
angle[M] aigu

240°
240°

360°
360°

0°
0°

**plane surfaces**
**surfaces[F]**

parts of a circle
parties[F] d'un cercle[M]

arc
arc[M]

center
centre[M]

radius
rayon[M]

quadrant
quadrant[M]

sector
secteur[M]

diameter
diamètre[M]

semicircle
demi-cercle[M]

circumference
circonférence[F]

SCIENCE

**polygons**
*polygones*[M]

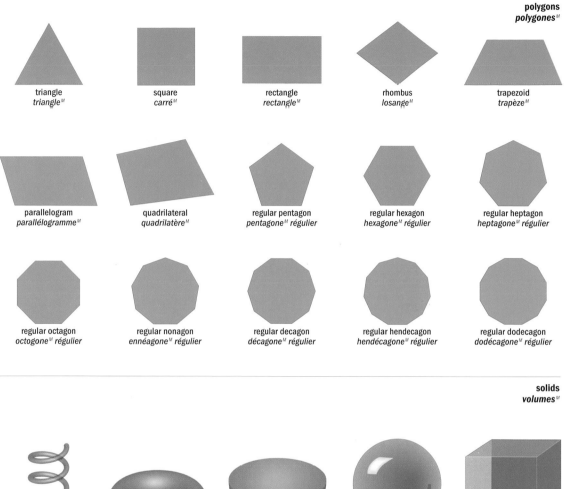

triangle
*triangle*[M]

square
*carré*[M]

rectangle
*rectangle*[M]

rhombus
*losange*[M]

trapezoid
*trapèze*[M]

parallelogram
*parallélogramme*[M]

quadrilateral
*quadrilatère*[M]

regular pentagon
*pentagone*[M] *régulier*

regular hexagon
*hexagone*[M] *régulier*

regular heptagon
*heptagone*[M] *régulier*

regular octagon
*octogone*[M] *régulier*

regular nonagon
*ennéagone*[M] *régulier*

regular decagon
*décagone*[M] *régulier*

regular hendecagon
*hendécagone*[M] *régulier*

regular dodecagon
*dodécagone*[M] *régulier*

**solids**
*volumes*[M]

helix
*hélice*[F]

torus
*tore*[M]

hemisphere
*hémisphère*[M]

sphere
*sphère*[F]

cube
*cube*[M]

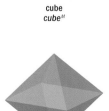

cone
*cône*[M]

pyramid
*pyramide*[F]

cylinder
*cylindre*[M]

parallelepiped
*parallélépipède*[M]

regular octahedron
*octaèdre*[M] *régulier*

# agglomeration

agglomération<sup>F</sup>

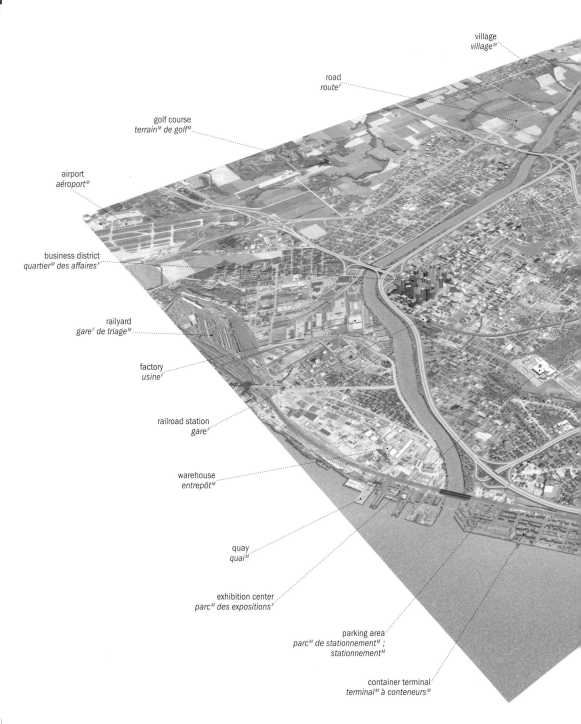

village
village<sup>M</sup>

road
route<sup>F</sup>

golf course
terrain<sup>M</sup> de golf<sup>M</sup>

airport
aéroport<sup>M</sup>

business district
quartier<sup>M</sup> des affaires<sup>F</sup>

railyard
gare<sup>F</sup> de triage<sup>M</sup>

factory
usine<sup>F</sup>

railroad station
gare<sup>F</sup>

warehouse
entrepôt<sup>M</sup>

quay
quai<sup>M</sup>

exhibition center
parc<sup>M</sup> des expositions<sup>F</sup>

parking area
parc<sup>M</sup> de stationnement<sup>M</sup> ;
stationnement<sup>M</sup>

container terminal
terminal<sup>M</sup> à conteneurs<sup>M</sup>

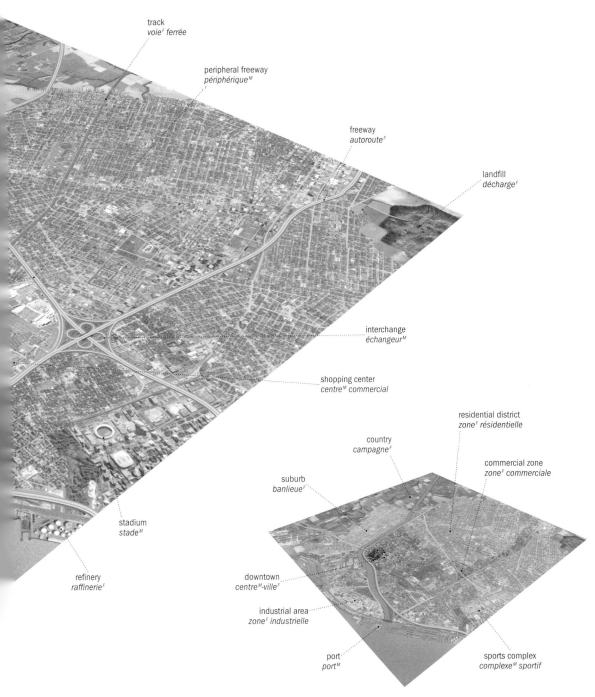

track
*voie*[F] *ferrée*

peripheral freeway
*périphérique*[M]

freeway
*autoroute*[F]

landfill
*décharge*[F]

interchange
*échangeur*[M]

shopping center
*centre*[M] *commercial*

residential district
*zone*[F] *résidentielle*

country
*campagne*[F]

commercial zone
*zone*[F] *commerciale*

suburb
*banlieue*[F]

stadium
*stade*[M]

refinery
*raffinerie*[F]

downtown
*centre*[M]*-ville*[F]

industrial area
*zone*[F] *industrielle*

port
*port*[M]

sports complex
*complexe*[M] *sportif*

SOCIETY

# downtown

centre<sup>M</sup>-ville<sup>F</sup>

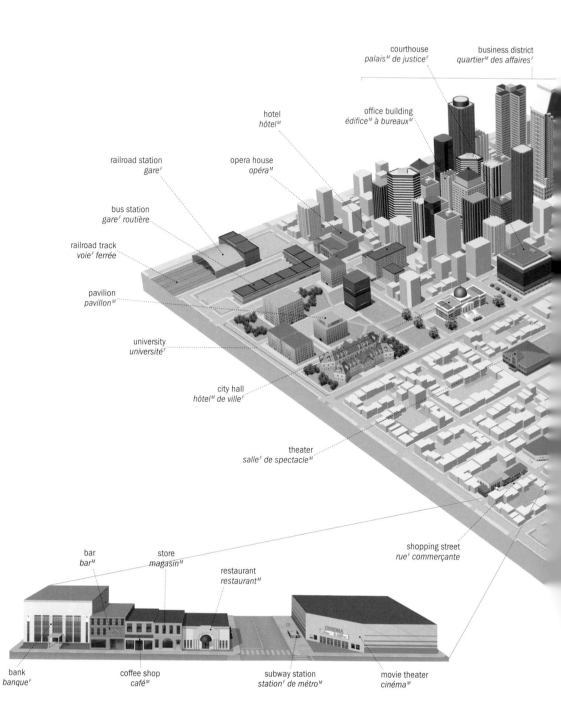

courthouse
palais<sup>M</sup> de justice<sup>F</sup>

business district
quartier<sup>M</sup> des affaires<sup>F</sup>

hotel
hôtel<sup>M</sup>

office building
édifice<sup>M</sup> à bureaux<sup>M</sup>

railroad station
gare<sup>F</sup>

opera house
opéra<sup>M</sup>

bus station
gare<sup>F</sup> routière

railroad track
voie<sup>F</sup> ferrée

pavilion
pavillon<sup>M</sup>

university
université<sup>F</sup>

city hall
hôtel<sup>M</sup> de ville<sup>F</sup>

theater
salle<sup>F</sup> de spectacle<sup>M</sup>

shopping street
rue<sup>F</sup> commerçante

bar
bar<sup>M</sup>

store
magasin<sup>M</sup>

restaurant
restaurant<sup>M</sup>

bank
banque<sup>F</sup>

coffee shop
café<sup>M</sup>

subway station
station<sup>F</sup> de métro<sup>M</sup>

movie theater
cinéma<sup>M</sup>

convention center
*palais*<sup>M</sup> *des congrès*<sup>M</sup>

educational institution
*établissement*<sup>M</sup> *scolaire*

boulevard
*boulevard*<sup>M</sup>

street
*rue*<sup>F</sup>

avenue
*avenue*<sup>F</sup>

fire station
*caserne*<sup>F</sup> *de pompiers*<sup>M</sup>

cemetery
*cimetière*<sup>M</sup>

church
*église*<sup>F</sup>

lane
*ruelle*<sup>F</sup>

apartment building
*immeuble*<sup>M</sup> *résidentiel*

police station
*poste*<sup>M</sup> *de police*<sup>F</sup>

park
*parc*<sup>M</sup>

library
*bibliothèque*<sup>F</sup>

post office
*bureau*<sup>M</sup> *de poste*<sup>F</sup>

service station
*station*<sup>F</sup>*-service*<sup>M</sup>

museum
*musée*<sup>M</sup>

supermarket
*supermarché*<sup>M</sup>

theater
*théâtre*<sup>M</sup>

car dealer
*concessionnaire*<sup>M</sup>
*d'automobiles*<sup>F</sup>

hospital
*hôpital*<sup>M</sup>

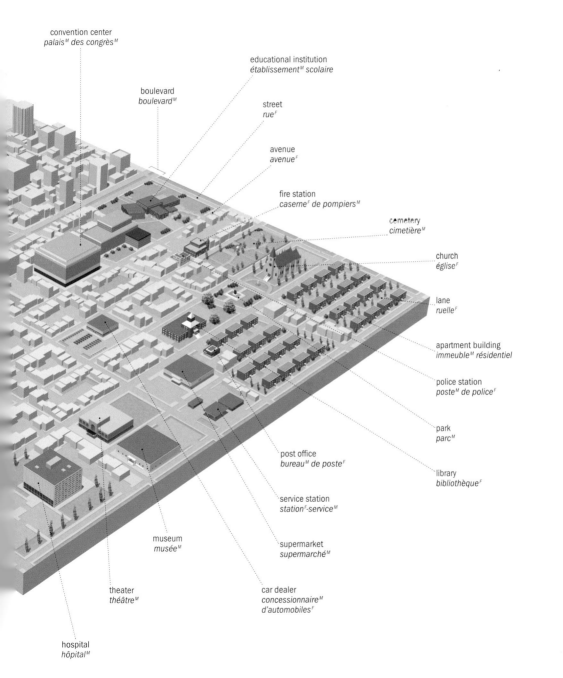

SOCIETY

# cross section of a street

coupe<sup>F</sup> d'une rue<sup>F</sup>

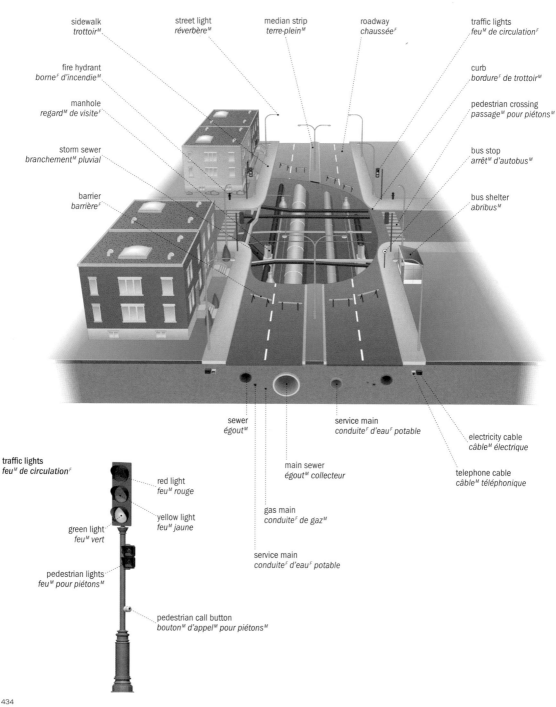

sidewalk
trottoir<sup>M</sup>

street light
réverbère<sup>M</sup>

median strip
terre-plein<sup>M</sup>

roadway
chaussée<sup>F</sup>

traffic lights
feu<sup>M</sup> de circulation<sup>F</sup>

fire hydrant
borne<sup>F</sup> d'incendie<sup>M</sup>

curb
bordure<sup>F</sup> de trottoir<sup>M</sup>

manhole
regard<sup>M</sup> de visite<sup>F</sup>

pedestrian crossing
passage<sup>M</sup> pour piétons<sup>M</sup>

storm sewer
branchement<sup>M</sup> pluvial

bus stop
arrêt<sup>M</sup> d'autobus<sup>M</sup>

barrier
barrière<sup>F</sup>

bus shelter
abribus<sup>M</sup>

sewer
égout<sup>M</sup>

service main
conduite<sup>F</sup> d'eau<sup>F</sup> potable

electricity cable
câble<sup>M</sup> électrique

**traffic lights**
feu<sup>M</sup> de circulation<sup>F</sup>

main sewer
égout<sup>M</sup> collecteur

telephone cable
câble<sup>M</sup> téléphonique

red light
feu<sup>M</sup> rouge

yellow light
feu<sup>M</sup> jaune

gas main
conduite<sup>F</sup> de gaz<sup>M</sup>

green light
feu<sup>M</sup> vert

service main
conduite<sup>F</sup> d'eau<sup>F</sup> potable

pedestrian lights
feu<sup>M</sup> pour piétons<sup>M</sup>

pedestrian call button
bouton<sup>M</sup> d'appel<sup>M</sup> pour piétons<sup>M</sup>

SOCIETY

# office building
*édifice^M à bureaux^M*

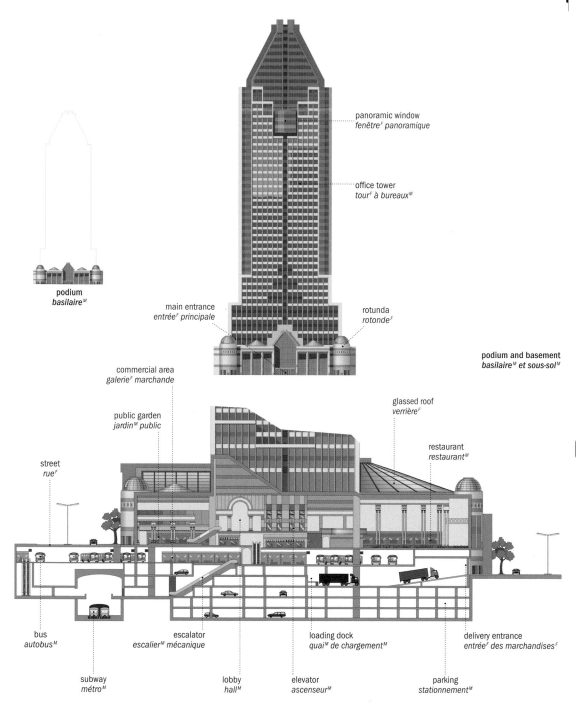

panoramic window
*fenêtre^F panoramique*

office tower
*tour^F à bureaux^M*

main entrance
*entrée^F principale*

rotunda
*rotonde^F*

podium
*basilaire^M*

**podium and basement**
*basilaire^M et sous-sol^M*

commercial area
*galerie^F marchande*

glassed roof
*verrière^F*

public garden
*jardin^M public*

restaurant
*restaurant^M*

street
*rue^F*

bus
*autobus^M*

escalator
*escalier^M mécanique*

loading dock
*quai^M de chargement^M*

delivery entrance
*entrée^F des marchandises^F*

subway
*métro^M*

lobby
*hall^M*

elevator
*ascenseur^M*

parking
*stationnement^M*

SOCIETY

# shopping center

centre<sup>M</sup> commercial

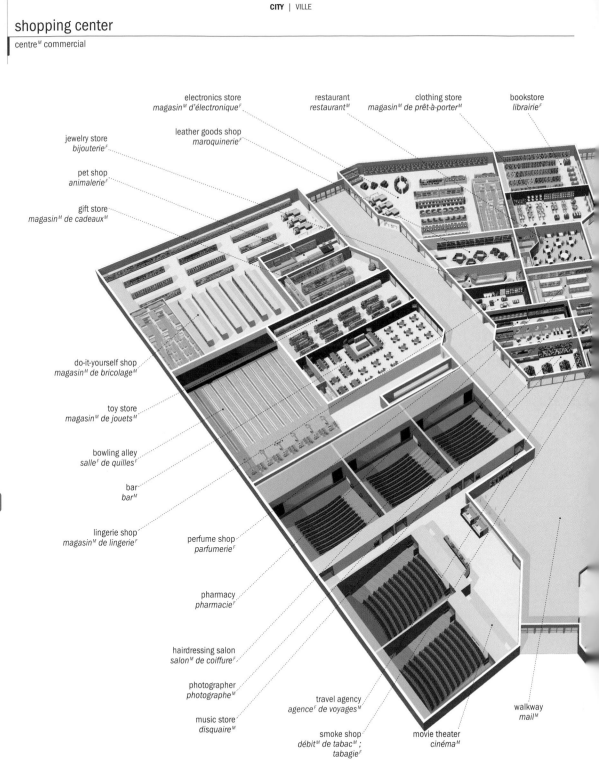

electronics store
magasin<sup>M</sup> d'électronique<sup>F</sup>

restaurant
restaurant<sup>M</sup>

clothing store
magasin<sup>M</sup> de prêt-à-porter<sup>M</sup>

bookstore
librairie<sup>F</sup>

leather goods shop
maroquinerie<sup>F</sup>

jewelry store
bijouterie<sup>F</sup>

pet shop
animalerie<sup>F</sup>

gift store
magasin<sup>M</sup> de cadeaux<sup>M</sup>

do-it-yourself shop
magasin<sup>M</sup> de bricolage<sup>M</sup>

toy store
magasin<sup>M</sup> de jouets<sup>M</sup>

bowling alley
salle<sup>F</sup> de quilles<sup>F</sup>

bar
bar<sup>M</sup>

lingerie shop
magasin<sup>M</sup> de lingerie<sup>F</sup>

perfume shop
parfumerie<sup>F</sup>

pharmacy
pharmacie<sup>F</sup>

hairdressing salon
salon<sup>M</sup> de coiffure<sup>F</sup>

photographer
photographe<sup>M</sup>

music store
disquaire<sup>M</sup>

travel agency
agence<sup>F</sup> de voyages<sup>M</sup>

smoke shop
débit<sup>M</sup> de tabac<sup>M</sup> ;
tabagie<sup>F</sup>

movie theater
cinéma<sup>M</sup>

walkway
mail<sup>M</sup>

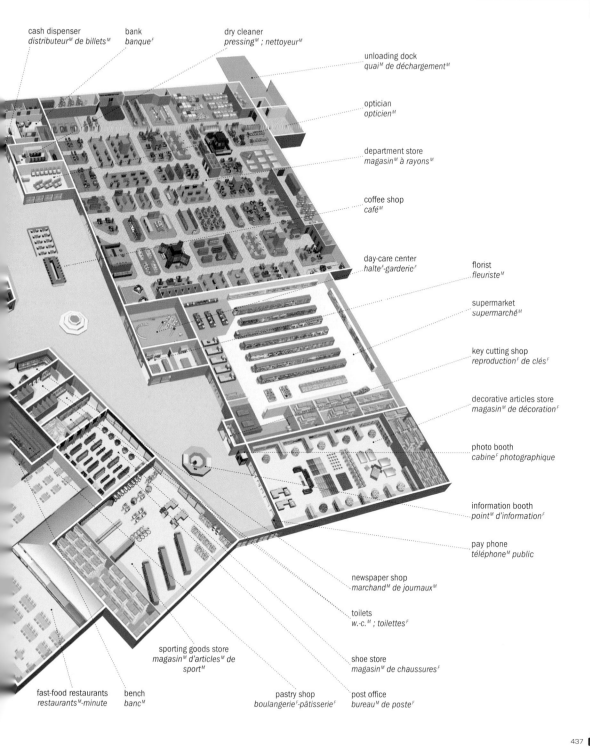

cash dispenser
*distributeur*<sup>M</sup> *de billets*<sup>M</sup>

bank
*banque*<sup>F</sup>

dry cleaner
*pressing*<sup>M</sup> ; *nettoyeur*<sup>M</sup>

unloading dock
*quai*<sup>M</sup> *de déchargement*<sup>M</sup>

optician
*opticien*<sup>M</sup>

department store
*magasin*<sup>M</sup> *à rayons*<sup>M</sup>

coffee shop
*café*<sup>M</sup>

day-care center
*halte*<sup>F</sup>*-garderie*<sup>F</sup>

florist
*fleuriste*<sup>M</sup>

supermarket
*supermarché*<sup>M</sup>

key cutting shop
*reproduction*<sup>F</sup> *de clés*<sup>F</sup>

decorative articles store
*magasin*<sup>M</sup> *de décoration*<sup>F</sup>

photo booth
*cabine*<sup>F</sup> *photographique*

information booth
*point*<sup>M</sup> *d'information*<sup>F</sup>

pay phone
*téléphone*<sup>M</sup> *public*

newspaper shop
*marchand*<sup>M</sup> *de journaux*<sup>M</sup>

toilets
*w.-c.*<sup>M</sup> ; *toilettes*<sup>F</sup>

shoe store
*magasin*<sup>M</sup> *de chaussures*<sup>F</sup>

sporting goods store
*magasin*<sup>M</sup> *d'articles*<sup>M</sup> *de sport*<sup>M</sup>

fast-food restaurants
*restaurants*<sup>M</sup>*-minute*

bench
*banc*<sup>M</sup>

pastry shop
*boulangerie*<sup>F</sup>*-pâtisserie*<sup>F</sup>

post office
*bureau*<sup>M</sup> *de poste*<sup>F</sup>

# restaurant

restaurant<sup>M</sup>

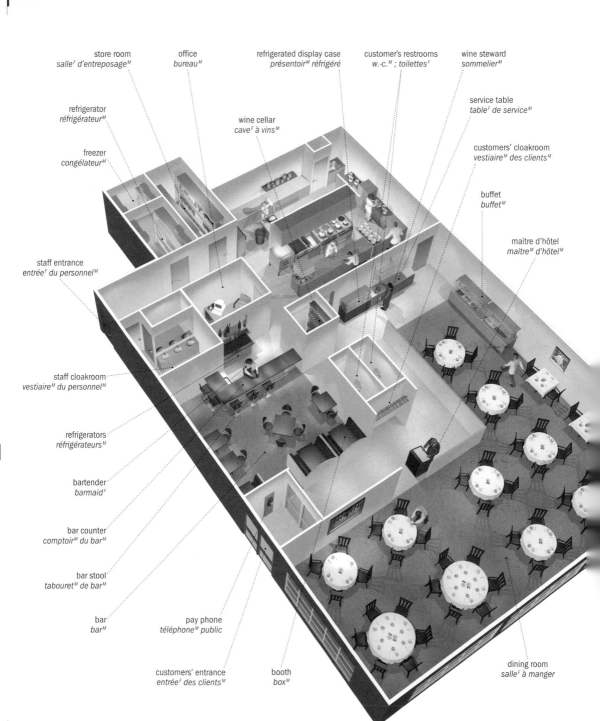

store room
salle<sup>F</sup> d'entreposage<sup>M</sup>

office
bureau<sup>M</sup>

refrigerated display case
présentoir<sup>M</sup> réfrigéré

customer's restrooms
w.-c.<sup>M</sup> ; toilettes<sup>F</sup>

wine steward
sommelier<sup>M</sup>

refrigerator
réfrigérateur<sup>M</sup>

wine cellar
cave<sup>F</sup> à vins<sup>M</sup>

service table
table<sup>F</sup> de service<sup>M</sup>

freezer
congélateur<sup>M</sup>

customers' cloakroom
vestiaire<sup>M</sup> des clients<sup>M</sup>

buffet
buffet<sup>M</sup>

maître d'hôtel
maître<sup>M</sup> d'hôtel<sup>M</sup>

staff entrance
entrée<sup>F</sup> du personnel<sup>M</sup>

staff cloakroom
vestiaire<sup>M</sup> du personnel<sup>M</sup>

refrigerators
réfrigérateurs<sup>M</sup>

bartender
barmaid<sup>F</sup>

bar counter
comptoir<sup>M</sup> du bar<sup>M</sup>

bar stool
tabouret<sup>M</sup> de bar<sup>M</sup>

bar
bar<sup>M</sup>

pay phone
téléphone<sup>M</sup> public

customers' entrance
entrée<sup>F</sup> des clients<sup>M</sup>

booth
box<sup>M</sup>

dining room
salle<sup>F</sup> à manger

# hotel

hôtel<sup>M</sup>

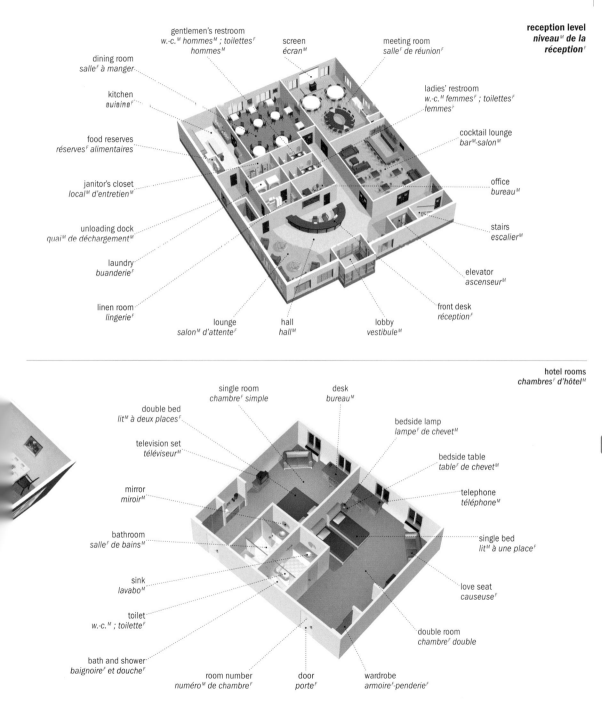

**reception level**
*niveau<sup>M</sup> de la
réception<sup>F</sup>*

gentlemen's restroom
*w.-c.<sup>M</sup> hommes<sup>M</sup> ; toilettes<sup>F</sup>
hommes<sup>M</sup>*

screen
*écran<sup>M</sup>*

meeting room
*salle<sup>F</sup> de réunion<sup>F</sup>*

dining room
*salle<sup>F</sup> à manger*

kitchen
*cuisine<sup>F</sup>*

ladies' restroom
*w.-c.<sup>M</sup> femmes<sup>F</sup> ; toilettes<sup>F</sup>
femmes<sup>F</sup>*

food reserves
*réserves<sup>F</sup> alimentaires*

cocktail lounge
*bar<sup>M</sup>-salon<sup>M</sup>*

janitor's closet
*local<sup>M</sup> d'entretien<sup>M</sup>*

office
*bureau<sup>M</sup>*

unloading dock
*quai<sup>M</sup> de déchargement<sup>M</sup>*

stairs
*escalier<sup>M</sup>*

laundry
*buanderie<sup>F</sup>*

elevator
*ascenseur<sup>M</sup>*

linen room
*lingerie<sup>F</sup>*

front desk
*réception<sup>F</sup>*

lounge
*salon<sup>M</sup> d'attente<sup>F</sup>*

hall
*hall<sup>M</sup>*

lobby
*vestibule<sup>M</sup>*

**hotel rooms**
*chambres<sup>F</sup> d'hôtel<sup>M</sup>*

single room
*chambre<sup>F</sup> simple*

desk
*bureau<sup>M</sup>*

double bed
*lit<sup>M</sup> à deux places<sup>F</sup>*

bedside lamp
*lampe<sup>F</sup> de chevet<sup>M</sup>*

television set
*téléviseur<sup>M</sup>*

bedside table
*table<sup>F</sup> de chevet<sup>M</sup>*

mirror
*miroir<sup>M</sup>*

telephone
*téléphone<sup>M</sup>*

bathroom
*salle<sup>F</sup> de bains<sup>M</sup>*

single bed
*lit<sup>M</sup> à une place<sup>F</sup>*

sink
*lavabo<sup>M</sup>*

love seat
*causeuse<sup>F</sup>*

toilet
*w.-c.<sup>M</sup> ; toilette<sup>F</sup>*

double room
*chambre<sup>F</sup> double*

bath and shower
*baignoire<sup>F</sup> et douche<sup>F</sup>*

room number
*numéro<sup>M</sup> de chambre<sup>F</sup>*

door
*porte<sup>F</sup>*

wardrobe
*armoire<sup>F</sup>-penderie<sup>F</sup>*

SOCIETY

# court

tribunal<sup>M</sup>

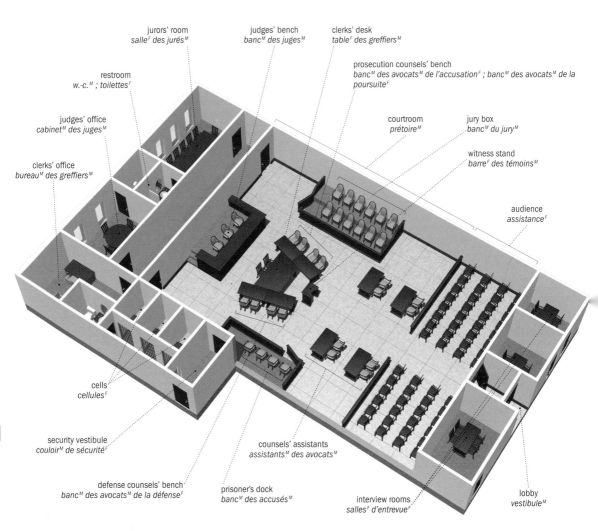

jurors' room
salle<sup>F</sup> des jurés<sup>M</sup>

judges' bench
banc<sup>M</sup> des juges<sup>M</sup>

clerks' desk
table<sup>F</sup> des greffiers<sup>M</sup>

restroom
w.-c.<sup>M</sup> ; toilettes<sup>F</sup>

prosecution counsels' bench
banc<sup>M</sup> des avocats<sup>M</sup> de l'accusation<sup>F</sup> ; banc<sup>M</sup> des avocats<sup>M</sup> de la poursuite<sup>F</sup>

judges' office
cabinet<sup>M</sup> des juges<sup>M</sup>

courtroom
prétoire<sup>M</sup>

jury box
banc<sup>M</sup> du jury<sup>M</sup>

clerks' office
bureau<sup>M</sup> des greffiers<sup>M</sup>

witness stand
barre<sup>F</sup> des témoins<sup>M</sup>

audience
assistance<sup>F</sup>

cells
cellules<sup>F</sup>

security vestibule
couloir<sup>M</sup> de sécurité<sup>F</sup>

counsels' assistants
assistants<sup>M</sup> des avocats<sup>M</sup>

defense counsels' bench
banc<sup>M</sup> des avocats<sup>M</sup> de la défense<sup>F</sup>

prisoner's dock
banc<sup>M</sup> des accusés<sup>M</sup>

interview rooms
salles<sup>F</sup> d'entrevue<sup>F</sup>

lobby
vestibule<sup>M</sup>

# examples of currency abbreviations

exemples<sup>M</sup> d'unités<sup>F</sup> monétaires

cent
cent<sup>M</sup>

euro
euro<sup>M</sup>

peso
peso<sup>M</sup>

pound
livre<sup>F</sup>

dollar
dollar<sup>M</sup>

rupee
roupie<sup>F</sup>

new shekel
nouveau shekel<sup>M</sup>

yen
yen<sup>M</sup>

£

# money and modes of payment

monnaie*F* et modes*M* de paiement*M*

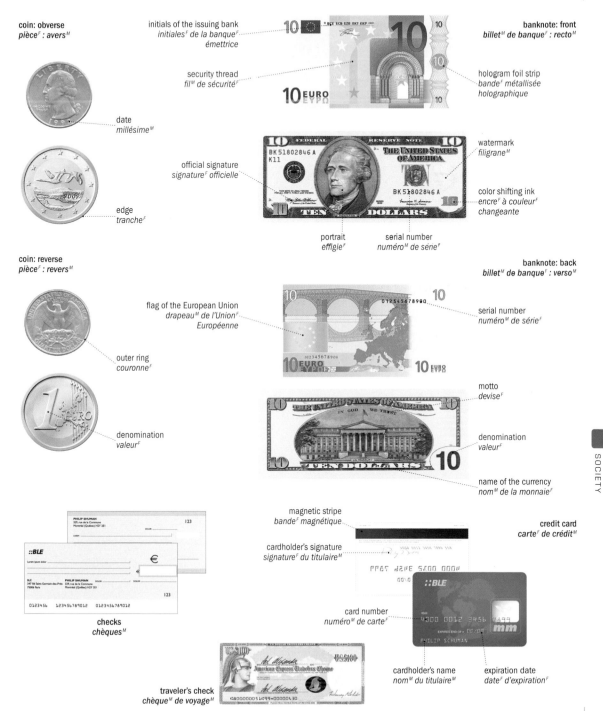

coin: obverse
pièce*F* : avers*M*

initials of the issuing bank
initiales*F* de la banque*F*
émettrice

security thread
fil*M* de sécurité*F*

date
millésime*M*

official signature
signature*F* officielle

edge
tranche*F*

banknote: front
billet*M* de banque*F* : recto*M*

hologram foil strip
bande*F* métallisée
holographique

watermark
filigrane*M*

color shifting ink
encre*F* à couleur*F*
changeante

portrait
effigie*F*

serial number
numéro*M* de série*F*

coin: reverse
pièce*F* : revers*M*

flag of the European Union
drapeau*M* de l'Union*F*
Européenne

outer ring
couronne*F*

denomination
valeur*F*

banknote: back
billet*M* de banque*F* : verso*M*

serial number
numéro*M* de série*F*

motto
devise*F*

denomination
valeur*F*

name of the currency
nom*M* de la monnaie*F*

magnetic stripe
bande*F* magnétique

cardholder's signature
signature*F* du titulaire*M*

credit card
carte*F* de crédit*M*

card number
numéro*M* de carte*F*

checks
chèques*M*

cardholder's name
nom*M* du titulaire*M*

expiration date
date*F* d'expiration*F*

traveler's check
chèque*M* de voyage*M*

SOCIETY

# bank

banque<sup>F</sup>

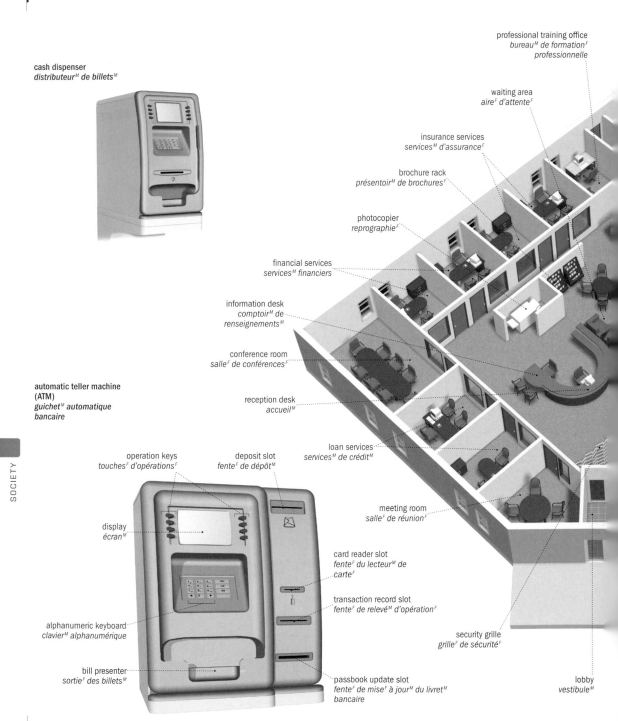

**cash dispenser**
*distributeur<sup>M</sup> de billets<sup>M</sup>*

professional training office
*bureau<sup>M</sup> de formation<sup>F</sup>
professionnelle*

waiting area
*aire<sup>F</sup> d'attente<sup>F</sup>*

insurance services
*services<sup>M</sup> d'assurance<sup>F</sup>*

brochure rack
*présentoir<sup>M</sup> de brochures<sup>F</sup>*

photocopier
*reprographie<sup>F</sup>*

financial services
*services<sup>M</sup> financiers*

information desk
*comptoir<sup>M</sup> de
renseignements<sup>M</sup>*

conference room
*salle<sup>F</sup> de conférences<sup>F</sup>*

**automatic teller machine
(ATM)**
*guichet<sup>M</sup> automatique
bancaire*

reception desk
*accueil<sup>M</sup>*

operation keys
*touches<sup>F</sup> d'opérations<sup>F</sup>*

deposit slot
*fente<sup>F</sup> de dépôt<sup>M</sup>*

loan services
*services<sup>M</sup> de crédit<sup>M</sup>*

display
*écran<sup>M</sup>*

meeting room
*salle<sup>F</sup> de réunion<sup>F</sup>*

card reader slot
*fente<sup>F</sup> du lecteur<sup>M</sup> de
carte<sup>F</sup>*

transaction record slot
*fente<sup>F</sup> de relevé<sup>M</sup> d'opération<sup>F</sup>*

alphanumeric keyboard
*clavier<sup>M</sup> alphanumérique*

security grille
*grille<sup>F</sup> de sécurité<sup>F</sup>*

bill presenter
*sortie<sup>F</sup> des billets<sup>M</sup>*

passbook update slot
*fente<sup>F</sup> de mise<sup>F</sup> à jour<sup>M</sup> du livret<sup>M</sup>
bancaire*

lobby
*vestibule<sup>M</sup>*

SOCIETY

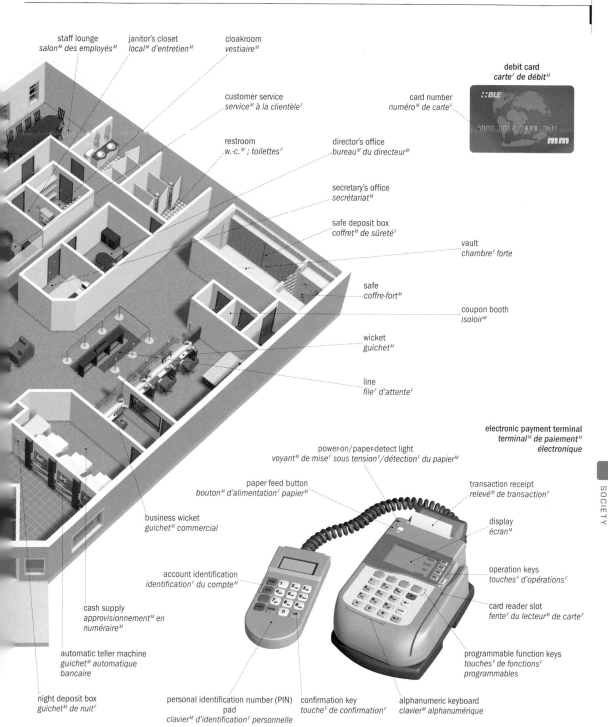

staff lounge
*salon^M des employés^M*

janitor's closet
*local^M d'entretien^M*

cloakroom
*vestiaire^M*

debit card
*carte^F de débit^M*

customer service
*service^M à la clientèle^F*

card number
*numéro^M de carte^F*

restroom
*w.-c.^M ; toilettes^F*

director's office
*bureau^M du directeur^M*

secretary's office
*secrétariat^M*

safe deposit box
*coffret^M de sûreté^F*

vault
*chambre^F forte*

safe
*coffre-fort^M*

coupon booth
*isoloir^M*

wicket
*guichet^M*

line
*file^F d'attente^F*

electronic payment terminal
*terminal^M de paiement^M
électronique*

power-on/paper-detect light
*voyant^M de mise^F sous tension^F/détection^F du papier^M*

paper feed button
*bouton^M d'alimentation^F papier^M*

transaction receipt
*relevé^M de transaction^F*

display
*écran^M*

business wicket
*guichet^M commercial*

account identification
*identification^F du compte^M*

operation keys
*touches^F d'opérations^F*

cash supply
*approvisionnement^M en
numéraire^M*

card reader slot
*fente^F du lecteur^M de carte^F*

automatic teller machine
*guichet^M automatique
bancaire*

programmable function keys
*touches^F de fonctions^F
programmables*

night deposit box
*guichet^M de nuit^F*

personal identification number (PIN)
pad
*clavier^M d'identification^F personnelle*

confirmation key
*touche^F de confirmation^F*

alphanumeric keyboard
*clavier^M alphanumérique*

# school

école[F]

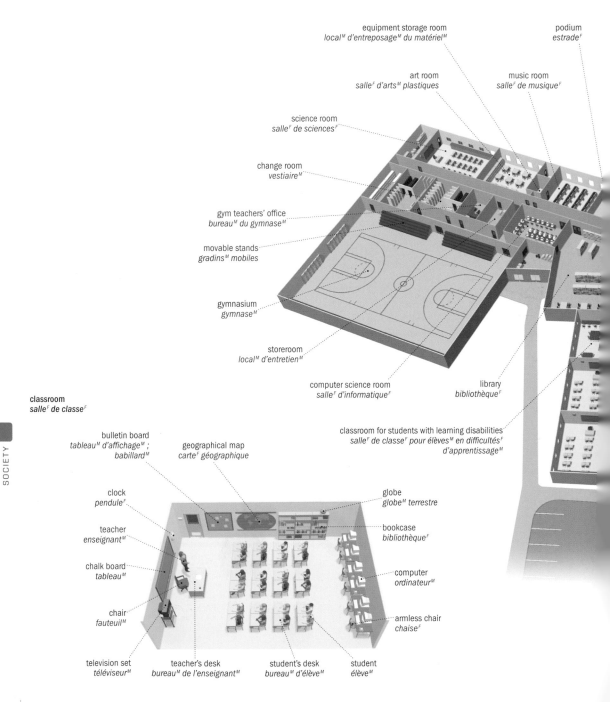

equipment storage room
local[M] d'entreposage[M] du matériel[M]

podium
estrade[F]

art room
salle[F] d'arts[M] plastiques

music room
salle[F] de musique[F]

science room
salle[F] de sciences[F]

change room
vestiaire[M]

gym teachers' office
bureau[M] du gymnase[M]

movable stands
gradins[M] mobiles

gymnasium
gymnase[M]

storeroom
local[M] d'entretien[M]

computer science room
salle[F] d'informatique[F]

library
bibliothèque[F]

classroom for students with learning disabilities
salle[F] de classe[F] pour élèves[M] en difficultés[F]
d'apprentissage[M]

**classroom**
salle[F] de classe[F]

bulletin board
tableau[M] d'affichage[M] ;
babillard[M]

geographical map
carte[F] géographique

clock
pendule[F]

globe
globe[M] terrestre

teacher
enseignant[M]

bookcase
bibliothèque[F]

chalk board
tableau[M]

computer
ordinateur[M]

chair
fauteuil[M]

armless chair
chaise[F]

television set
téléviseur[M]

teacher's desk
bureau[M] de l'enseignant[M]

student's desk
bureau[M] d'élève[M]

student
élève[M]

school

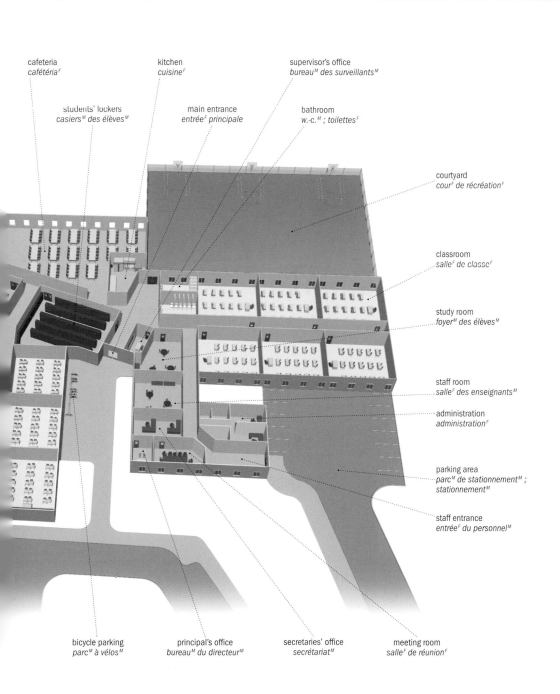

cafeteria
*cafétéria*<sup>F</sup>

kitchen
*cuisine*<sup>F</sup>

supervisor's office
*bureau*<sup>M</sup> *des surveillants*<sup>M</sup>

students' lockers
*casiers*<sup>M</sup> *des élèves*<sup>M</sup>

main entrance
*entrée*<sup>F</sup> *principale*

bathroom
*w.-c.*<sup>M</sup> ; *toilettes*<sup>F</sup>

courtyard
*cour*<sup>F</sup> *de récréation*<sup>F</sup>

classroom
*salle*<sup>F</sup> *de classe*<sup>F</sup>

study room
*foyer*<sup>M</sup> *des élèves*<sup>M</sup>

staff room
*salle*<sup>F</sup> *des enseignants*<sup>M</sup>

administration
*administration*<sup>F</sup>

parking area
*parc*<sup>M</sup> *de stationnement*<sup>M</sup> ;
*stationnement*<sup>M</sup>

staff entrance
*entrée*<sup>F</sup> *du personnel*<sup>M</sup>

bicycle parking
*parc*<sup>M</sup> *à vélos*<sup>M</sup>

principal's office
*bureau*<sup>M</sup> *du directeur*<sup>M</sup>

secretaries' office
*secrétariat*<sup>M</sup>

meeting room
*salle*<sup>F</sup> *de réunion*<sup>F</sup>

SOCIETY

# Catholic church

église[F]

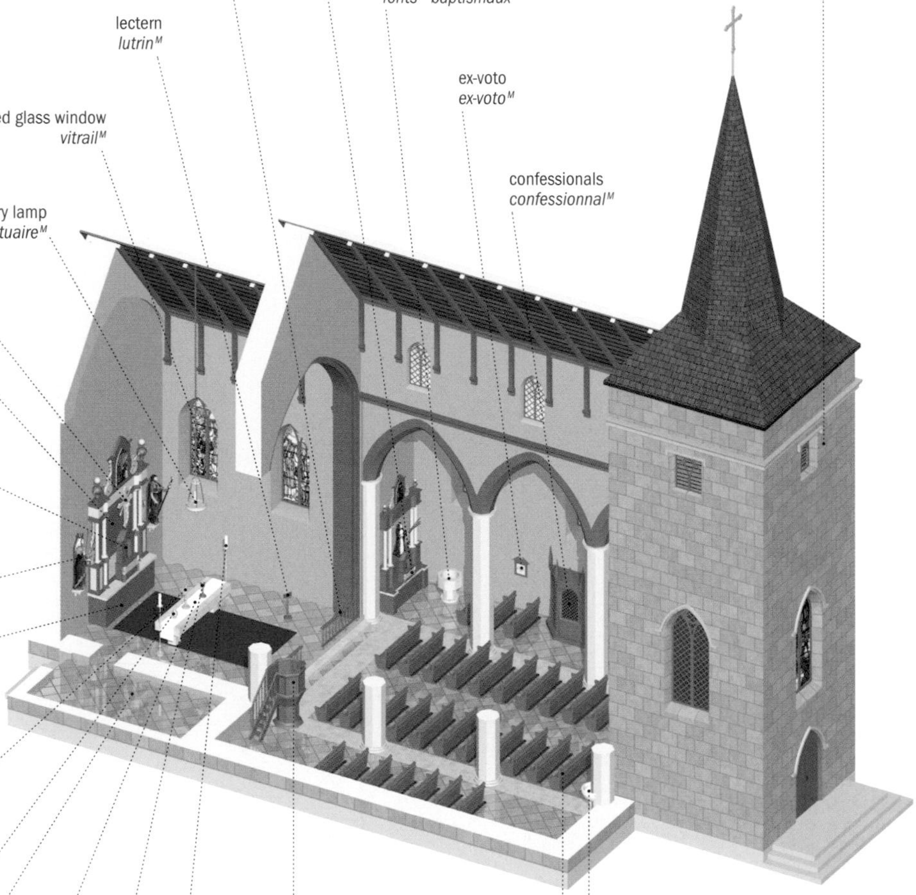

secondary altar
*autel[M] secondaire*

communion rail
*table[F] de communion[F]*

baptismal font
*fonts[M] baptismaux*

bell tower
*clocher[M]*

lectern
*lutrin[M]*

ex-voto
*ex-voto[M]*

stained glass window
*vitrail[M]*

confessionals
*confessionnal[M]*

sanctuary lamp
*lampe[F] de sanctuaire[M]*

crucifix
*crucifix[M]*

altarpiece
*retable[M]*

tabernacle
*tabernacle[M]*

statue
*statue[F]*

frontal
*devant[M] d'autel[M]*

altar cross
*croix[F] d'autel[M]*

censer
*encensoir[M]*

sacristy
*sacristie[F]*

high altar
*maître-autel[M]*

candle
*cierge[M]*

pulpit
*chaire[F]*

holy water font
*bénitier[M]*

pew
*banc[M]*

chalice
*calice[M]*

# synagogue

synagogue<sup>F</sup>

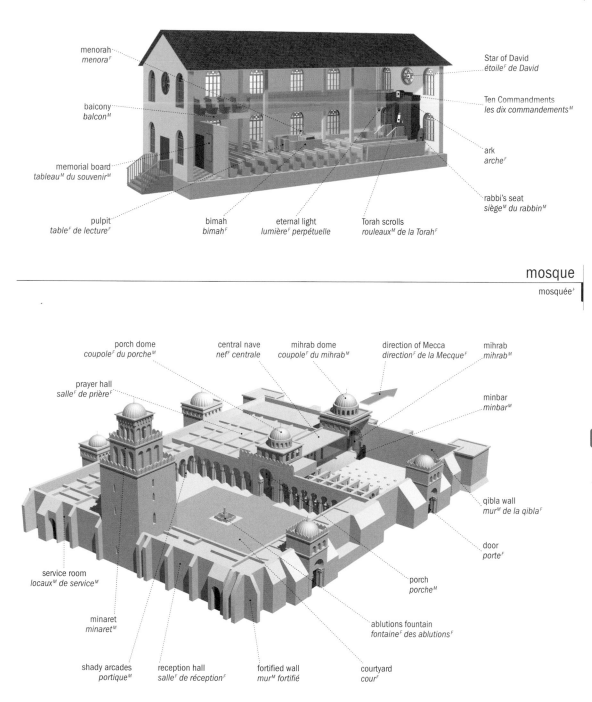

menorah
menora<sup>F</sup>

Star of David
étoile<sup>F</sup> de David

balcony
balcon<sup>M</sup>

Ten Commandments
les dix commandements<sup>M</sup>

memorial board
tableau<sup>M</sup> du souvenir<sup>M</sup>

ark
arche<sup>F</sup>

rabbi's seat
siège<sup>M</sup> du rabbin<sup>M</sup>

pulpit
table<sup>F</sup> de lecture<sup>F</sup>

bimah
bimah<sup>F</sup>

eternal light
lumière<sup>F</sup> perpétuelle

Torah scrolls
rouleaux<sup>M</sup> de la Torah<sup>F</sup>

# mosque

mosquée<sup>F</sup>

porch dome
coupole<sup>F</sup> du porche<sup>M</sup>

central nave
nef<sup>F</sup> centrale

mihrab dome
coupole<sup>F</sup> du mihrab<sup>M</sup>

direction of Mecca
direction<sup>F</sup> de la Mecque<sup>F</sup>

mihrab
mihrab<sup>M</sup>

prayer hall
salle<sup>F</sup> de prière<sup>F</sup>

minbar
minbar<sup>M</sup>

qibla wall
mur<sup>M</sup> de la qibla<sup>F</sup>

door
porte<sup>F</sup>

service room
locaux<sup>M</sup> de service<sup>M</sup>

porch
porche<sup>M</sup>

minaret
minaret<sup>M</sup>

ablutions fountain
fontaine<sup>F</sup> des ablutions<sup>F</sup>

shady arcades
portique<sup>M</sup>

reception hall
salle<sup>F</sup> de réception<sup>F</sup>

fortified wall
mur<sup>M</sup> fortifié

courtyard
cour<sup>F</sup>

SOCIETY

# flags

drapeaux<sup>M</sup>

## Americas
### *Amériques*<sup>F</sup>

1 Canada
*Canada*<sup>M</sup>

2 United States of America
*États-Unis*<sup>M</sup> *d'Amérique*<sup>F</sup>

3 Mexico
*Mexique*<sup>M</sup>

4 Honduras
*Honduras*<sup>M</sup>

5 Guatemala
*Guatemala*<sup>M</sup>

6 Belize
*Belize*<sup>M</sup>

7 El Salvador
*El Salvador*<sup>M</sup>

8 Nicaragua
*Nicaragua*<sup>M</sup>

9 Costa Rica
*Costa Rica*<sup>M</sup>

10 Panama
*Panama*<sup>M</sup>

11 Colombia
*Colombie*<sup>F</sup>

12 Venezuela
*Venezuela*<sup>M</sup>

13 Guyana
*Guyana*<sup>F</sup>

14 Suriname
*Suriname*<sup>M</sup>

15 Ecuador
*Équateur*<sup>M</sup>

16 Peru
*Pérou*<sup>M</sup>

17 Brazil
*Brésil*<sup>M</sup>

18 Bolivia
*Bolivie*<sup>F</sup>

19 Paraguay
*Paraguay*<sup>M</sup>

20 Chile
*Chili*<sup>M</sup>

21 Argentina
*Argentine*<sup>F</sup>

22 Uruguay
*Uruguay*<sup>M</sup>

## Caribbean Islands
### *Antilles*<sup>F</sup>

23 The Bahamas
*Bahamas*<sup>F</sup>

24 Cuba
*Cuba*<sup>F</sup>

25 Jamaica
*Jamaïque*<sup>F</sup>

26 Haiti
*Haïti*<sup>M</sup>

27 Saint Kitts and Nevis
*Saint-Kitts-et-Nevis*[M]

28 Antigua and Barbuda
*Antigua-et-Barbuda*[F]

29 Dominica
*Dominique*[F]

30 Saint Lucia
*Sainte-Lucie*[F]

31 Saint Vincent and the Grenadines
*Saint-Vincent*[M]*-et-les Grenadines*[F]

32 Dominican Republic
*République*[F] *dominicaine*

33 Barbados
*Barbade*[F]

34 Grenada
*Grenade*[F]

35 Trinidad and Tobago
*Trinité-et-Tobago*[F]

**Europe**
*Europe*[F]

36 Andorra
*Andorre*[F]

37 Portugal
*Portugal*[M]

38 Spain
*Espagne*[F]

39 United Kingdom
*Royaume-Uni*[M] *de Grande-Bretagne*[F] *et d'Irlande*[F] *du Nord*[M]

40 France
*France*[F]

41 Ireland
*Irlande*[F]

42 Belgium
*Belgique*[F]

43 Luxembourg
*Luxembourg*[M]

44 Netherlands
*Pays-Bas*[M]

SOCIETY

flags

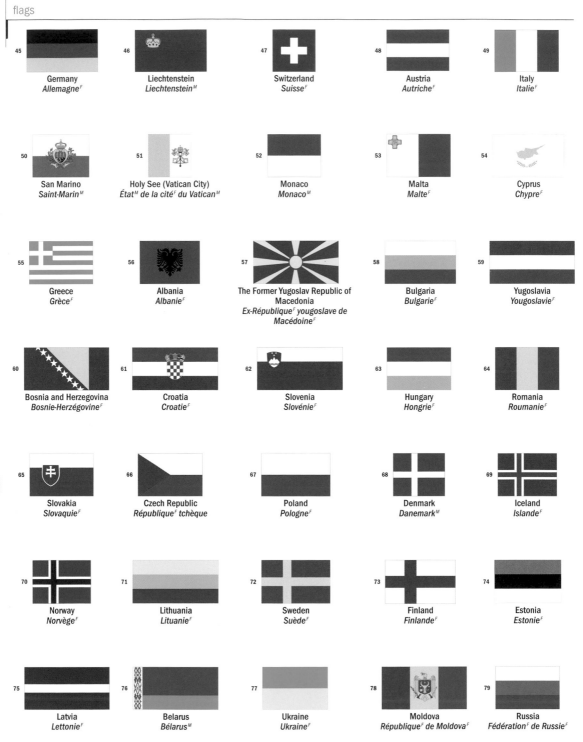

45 Germany
*Allemagne*F

46 Liechtenstein
*Liechtenstein*M

47 Switzerland
*Suisse*F

48 Austria
*Autriche*F

49 Italy
*Italie*F

50 San Marino
*Saint-Marin*M

51 Holy See (Vatican City)
*État*M *de la cité*F *du Vatican*M

52 Monaco
*Monaco*M

53 Malta
*Malte*F

54 Cyprus
*Chypre*F

55 Greece
*Grèce*F

56 Albania
*Albanie*F

57 The Former Yugoslav Republic of
Macedonia
*Ex-République*F *yougoslave de
Macédoine*F

58 Bulgaria
*Bulgarie*F

59 Yugoslavia
*Yougoslavie*F

60 Bosnia and Herzegovina
*Bosnie-Herzégovine*F

61 Croatia
*Croatie*F

62 Slovenia
*Slovénie*F

63 Hungary
*Hongrie*F

64 Romania
*Roumanie*F

65 Slovakia
*Slovaquie*F

66 Czech Republic
*République*F *tchèque*

67 Poland
*Pologne*F

68 Denmark
*Danemark*M

69 Iceland
*Islande*F

70 Norway
*Norvège*F

71 Lithuania
*Lituanie*F

72 Sweden
*Suède*F

73 Finland
*Finlande*F

74 Estonia
*Estonie*F

75 Latvia
*Lettonie*F

76 Belarus
*Bélarus*M

77 Ukraine
*Ukraine*F

78 Moldova
*République*F *de Moldova*F

79 Russia
*Fédération*F *de Russie*F

flags

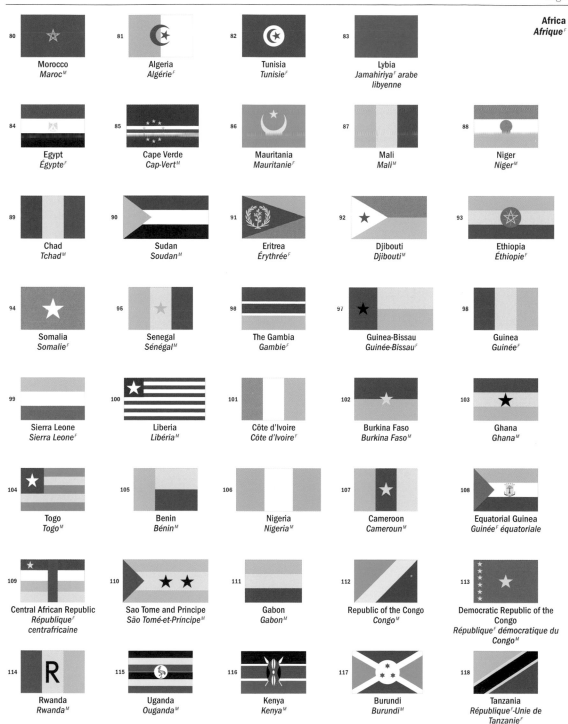

**Africa**
*Afrique*<sup>F</sup>

80 Morocco
*Maroc*<sup>M</sup>

81 Algeria
*Algérie*<sup>F</sup>

82 Tunisia
*Tunisie*<sup>F</sup>

83 Lybia
*Jamahiriya*<sup>F</sup> *arabe libyenne*

84 Egypt
*Égypte*<sup>F</sup>

85 Cape Verde
*Cap-Vert*<sup>M</sup>

86 Mauritania
*Mauritanie*<sup>F</sup>

87 Mali
*Mali*<sup>M</sup>

88 Niger
*Niger*<sup>M</sup>

89 Chad
*Tchad*<sup>M</sup>

90 Sudan
*Soudan*<sup>M</sup>

91 Eritrea
*Érythrée*<sup>F</sup>

92 Djibouti
*Djibouti*<sup>M</sup>

93 Ethiopia
*Éthiopie*<sup>F</sup>

94 Somalia
*Somalie*<sup>F</sup>

95 Senegal
*Sénégal*<sup>M</sup>

96 The Gambia
*Gambie*<sup>F</sup>

97 Guinea-Bissau
*Guinée-Bissau*<sup>F</sup>

98 Guinea
*Guinée*<sup>F</sup>

99 Sierra Leone
*Sierra Leone*<sup>F</sup>

100 Liberia
*Libéria*<sup>M</sup>

101 Côte d'Ivoire
*Côte d'Ivoire*<sup>F</sup>

102 Burkina Faso
*Burkina Faso*<sup>M</sup>

103 Ghana
*Ghana*<sup>M</sup>

104 Togo
*Togo*<sup>M</sup>

105 Benin
*Bénin*<sup>M</sup>

106 Nigeria
*Nigeria*<sup>M</sup>

107 Cameroon
*Cameroun*<sup>M</sup>

108 Equatorial Guinea
*Guinée*<sup>F</sup> *équatoriale*

109 Central African Republic
*République*<sup>F</sup> *centrafricaine*

110 Sao Tome and Principe
*São Tomé-et-Principe*<sup>M</sup>

111 Gabon
*Gabon*<sup>M</sup>

112 Republic of the Congo
*Congo*<sup>M</sup>

113 Democratic Republic of the Congo
*République*<sup>F</sup> *démocratique du Congo*<sup>M</sup>

114 Rwanda
*Rwanda*<sup>M</sup>

115 Uganda
*Ouganda*<sup>M</sup>

116 Kenya
*Kenya*<sup>M</sup>

117 Burundi
*Burundi*<sup>M</sup>

118 Tanzania
*République*<sup>F</sup>*-Unie de Tanzanie*<sup>F</sup>

SOCIETY

451

flags

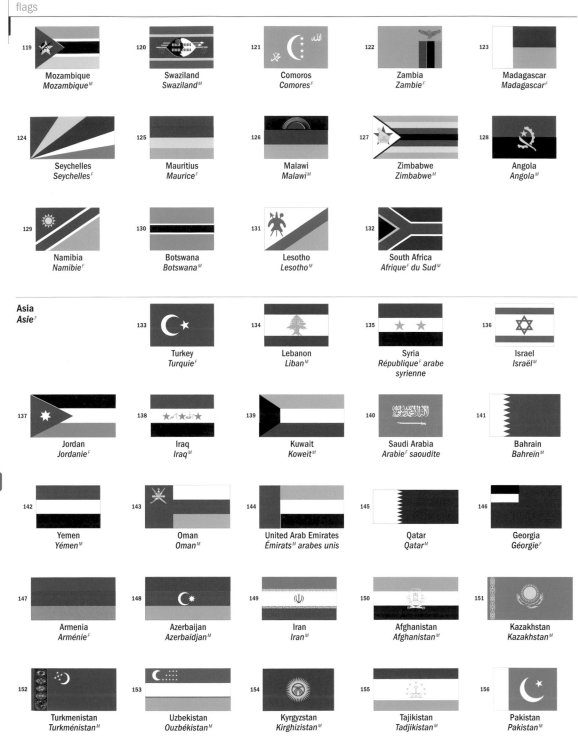

119 Mozambique
*Mozambique* M

120 Swaziland
*Swaziland* M

121 Comoros
*Comores* F

122 Zambia
*Zambie* F

123 Madagascar
*Madagascar* F

124 Seychelles
*Seychelles* F

125 Mauritius
*Maurice* F

126 Malawi
*Malawi* M

127 Zimbabwe
*Zimbabwe* M

128 Angola
*Angola* M

129 Namibia
*Namibie* F

130 Botswana
*Botswana* M

131 Lesotho
*Lesotho* M

132 South Africa
*Afrique* F *du Sud* M

**Asia**
*Asie* F

133 Turkey
*Turquie* F

134 Lebanon
*Liban* M

135 Syria
*République* F *arabe syrienne*

136 Israel
*Israël* M

137 Jordan
*Jordanie* F

138 Iraq
*Iraq* M

139 Kuwait
*Koweït* M

140 Saudi Arabia
*Arabie* F *saoudite*

141 Bahrain
*Bahrein* M

142 Yemen
*Yémen* M

143 Oman
*Oman* M

144 United Arab Emirates
*Émirats* M *arabes unis*

145 Qatar
*Qatar* M

146 Georgia
*Géorgie* F

147 Armenia
*Arménie* F

148 Azerbaijan
*Azerbaïdjan* M

149 Iran
*Iran* M

150 Afghanistan
*Afghanistan* M

151 Kazakhstan
*Kazakhstan* M

152 Turkmenistan
*Turkménistan* M

153 Uzbekistan
*Ouzbékistan* M

154 Kyrgyzstan
*Kirghizistan* M

155 Tajikistan
*Tadjikistan* M

156 Pakistan
*Pakistan* M

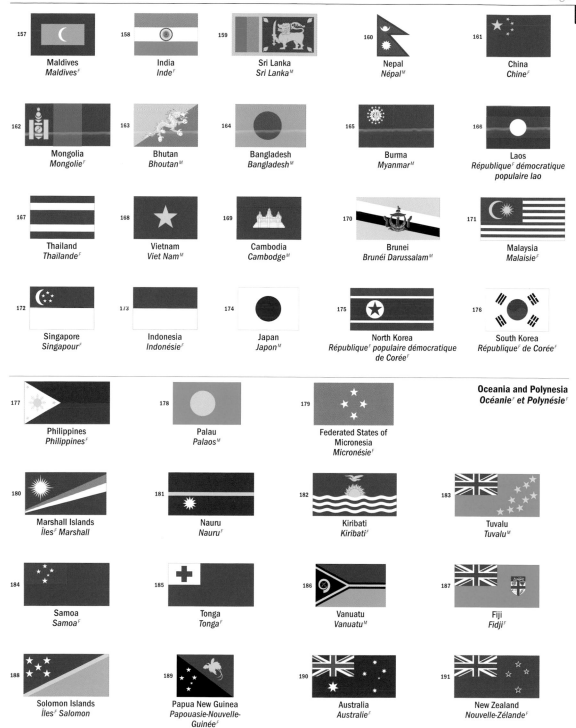

157 Maldives
*Maldives*<sup>F</sup>

158 India
*Inde*<sup>F</sup>

159 Sri Lanka
*Sri Lanka*<sup>M</sup>

160 Nepal
*Népal*<sup>M</sup>

161 China
*Chine*<sup>F</sup>

162 Mongolia
*Mongolie*<sup>F</sup>

163 Bhutan
*Bhoutan*<sup>M</sup>

164 Bangladesh
*Bangladesh*<sup>M</sup>

165 Burma
*Myanmar*<sup>M</sup>

166 Laos
*République*<sup>F</sup> *démocratique populaire lao*

167 Thailand
*Thaïlande*<sup>F</sup>

168 Vietnam
*Viet Nam*<sup>M</sup>

169 Cambodia
*Cambodge*<sup>M</sup>

170 Brunei
*Brunéi Darussalam*<sup>M</sup>

171 Malaysia
*Malaisie*<sup>F</sup>

172 Singapore
*Singapour*<sup>F</sup>

173 Indonesia
*Indonésie*<sup>F</sup>

174 Japan
*Japon*<sup>M</sup>

175 North Korea
*République*<sup>F</sup> *populaire démocratique de Corée*<sup>F</sup>

176 South Korea
*République*<sup>F</sup> *de Corée*<sup>F</sup>

**Oceania and Polynesia**
*Océanie*<sup>F</sup> *et Polynésie*<sup>F</sup>

177 Philippines
*Philippines*<sup>F</sup>

178 Palau
*Palaos*<sup>M</sup>

179 Federated States of Micronesia
*Micronésie*<sup>F</sup>

180 Marshall Islands
*Îles*<sup>F</sup> *Marshall*

181 Nauru
*Nauru*<sup>F</sup>

182 Kiribati
*Kiribati*<sup>F</sup>

183 Tuvalu
*Tuvalu*<sup>M</sup>

184 Samoa
*Samoa*<sup>F</sup>

185 Tonga
*Tonga*<sup>F</sup>

186 Vanuatu
*Vanuatu*<sup>M</sup>

187 Fiji
*Fidji*<sup>F</sup>

188 Solomon Islands
*Îles*<sup>F</sup> *Salomon*

189 Papua New Guinea
*Papouasie-Nouvelle-Guinée*<sup>F</sup>

190 Australia
*Australie*<sup>F</sup>

191 New Zealand
*Nouvelle-Zélande*<sup>F</sup>

SOCIETY

# fire prevention

prévention<sup>F</sup> des incendies<sup>M</sup>

**fire-fighting materials**
*matériel<sup>M</sup> de lutte<sup>F</sup> contre les incendies<sup>M</sup>*

firefighter
*sapeur<sup>M</sup>-pompier<sup>M</sup>*

smoke detector
*détecteur<sup>M</sup> de fumée<sup>F</sup>*

base
*base<sup>F</sup>*

helmet
*casque<sup>M</sup>*

compressed-air cylinder
*bouteille<sup>F</sup> d'air<sup>M</sup> comprimé*

cover
*couvercle<sup>M</sup>*

full face mask
*masque<sup>M</sup> complet*

self-contained breathing apparatus
*appareil<sup>M</sup> de protection<sup>F</sup> respiratoire*

test button
*bouton<sup>M</sup> d'essai<sup>M</sup>*

indicator light
*témoin<sup>M</sup> lumineux*

air-supply tube
*tube<sup>M</sup> d'alimentation<sup>F</sup> en air<sup>M</sup>*

pressure demand regulator
*robinet<sup>M</sup> de réglage<sup>M</sup> de débit<sup>M</sup>*

portable fire extinguisher
*extincteur<sup>M</sup>*

trigger
*gâchette<sup>F</sup>*

pin
*goupille<sup>F</sup>*

hose
*tuyau<sup>M</sup>*

warning device
*avertisseur<sup>M</sup> sonore*

fireproof and waterproof garment
*vêtement<sup>M</sup> ignifuge et hydrofuge*

tank
*réservoir<sup>M</sup>*

pike pole
*gaffe<sup>F</sup>*

hatchet
*hache<sup>F</sup>*

fire hose
*tuyau<sup>M</sup> de refoulement<sup>M</sup>*

fire hydrant
*borne<sup>F</sup> d'incendie<sup>M</sup>*

rubber boot
*botte<sup>F</sup> de caoutchouc<sup>M</sup>*

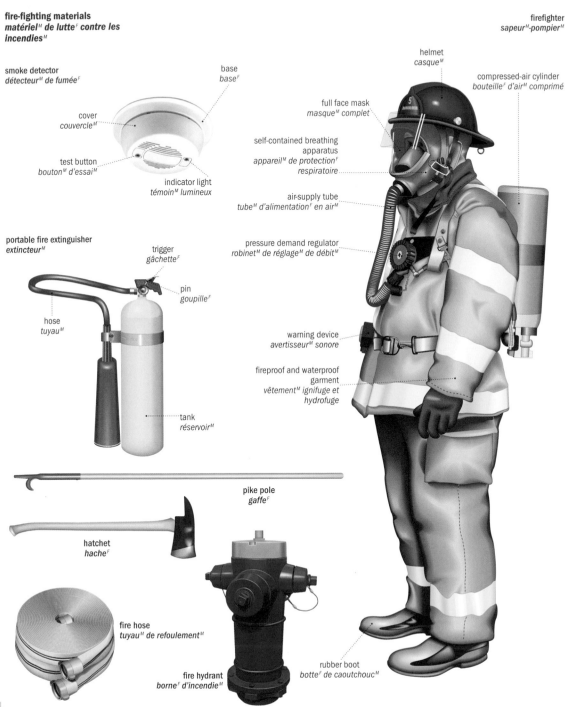

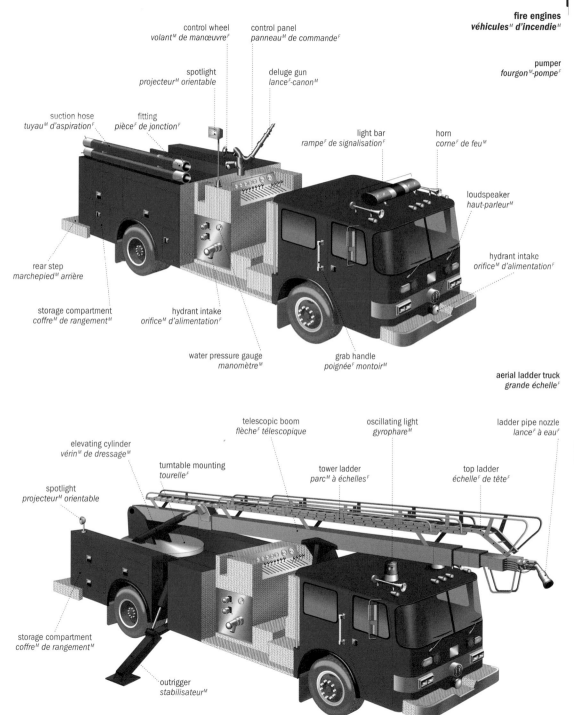

**fire engines**
*véhicules*<sup>M</sup> *d'incendie*<sup>M</sup>

**pumper**
*fourgon*<sup>M</sup>*-pompe*<sup>F</sup>

control wheel
*volant*<sup>M</sup> *de manœuvre*<sup>F</sup>

control panel
*panneau*<sup>M</sup> *de commande*<sup>F</sup>

spotlight
*projecteur*<sup>M</sup> *orientable*

deluge gun
*lance*<sup>F</sup>*-canon*<sup>M</sup>

suction hose
*tuyau*<sup>M</sup> *d'aspiration*<sup>F</sup>

fitting
*pièce*<sup>F</sup> *de jonction*<sup>F</sup>

light bar
*rampe*<sup>F</sup> *de signalisation*<sup>F</sup>

horn
*corne*<sup>F</sup> *de feu*<sup>M</sup>

loudspeaker
*haut-parleur*<sup>M</sup>

hydrant intake
*orifice*<sup>M</sup> *d'alimentation*<sup>F</sup>

rear step
*marchepied*<sup>M</sup> *arrière*

storage compartment
*coffre*<sup>M</sup> *de rangement*<sup>M</sup>

hydrant intake
*orifice*<sup>M</sup> *d'alimentation*<sup>F</sup>

water pressure gauge
*manomètre*<sup>M</sup>

grab handle
*poignée*<sup>F</sup> *montoir*<sup>M</sup>

**aerial ladder truck**
*grande échelle*<sup>F</sup>

elevating cylinder
*vérin*<sup>M</sup> *de dressage*<sup>M</sup>

telescopic boom
*flèche*<sup>F</sup> *télescopique*

oscillating light
*gyrophare*<sup>M</sup>

ladder pipe nozzle
*lance*<sup>F</sup> *à eau*<sup>F</sup>

turntable mounting
*tourelle*<sup>F</sup>

tower ladder
*parc*<sup>M</sup> *à échelles*<sup>F</sup>

top ladder
*échelle*<sup>F</sup> *de tête*<sup>F</sup>

spotlight
*projecteur*<sup>M</sup> *orientable*

storage compartment
*coffre*<sup>M</sup> *de rangement*<sup>M</sup>

outrigger
*stabilisateur*<sup>M</sup>

SOCIETY

# crime prevention

prévention<sup>F</sup> de la criminalité<sup>F</sup>

**police officer**
*agent<sup>M</sup> de police<sup>F</sup>*

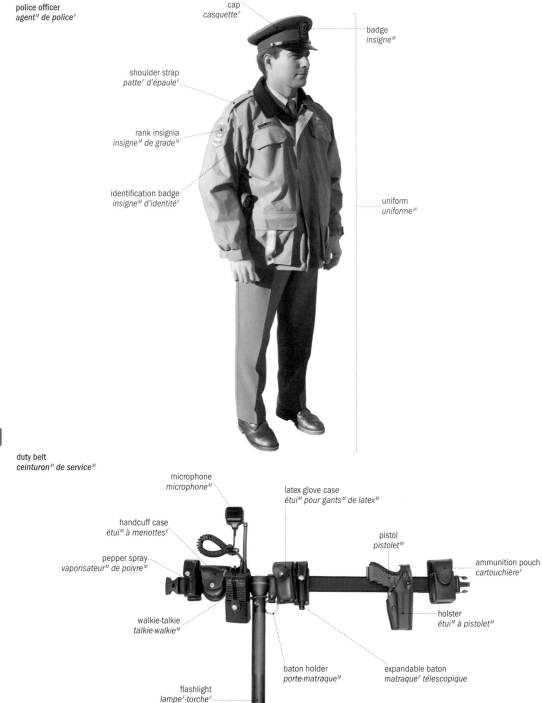

cap
*casquette<sup>F</sup>*

badge
*insigne<sup>M</sup>*

shoulder strap
*patte<sup>F</sup> d'épaule<sup>F</sup>*

rank insignia
*insigne<sup>M</sup> de grade<sup>M</sup>*

identification badge
*insigne<sup>M</sup> d'identité<sup>F</sup>*

uniform
*uniforme<sup>M</sup>*

**duty belt**
*ceinturon<sup>M</sup> de service<sup>M</sup>*

microphone
*microphone<sup>M</sup>*

latex glove case
*étui<sup>M</sup> pour gants<sup>M</sup> de latex<sup>M</sup>*

handcuff case
*étui<sup>M</sup> à menottes<sup>F</sup>*

pistol
*pistolet<sup>M</sup>*

pepper spray
*vaporisateur<sup>M</sup> de poivre<sup>M</sup>*

ammunition pouch
*cartouchière<sup>F</sup>*

walkie-talkie
*talkie-walkie<sup>M</sup>*

holster
*étui<sup>M</sup> à pistolet<sup>M</sup>*

baton holder
*porte-matraque<sup>M</sup>*

expandable baton
*matraque<sup>F</sup> télescopique*

flashlight
*lampe<sup>F</sup>-torche<sup>F</sup>*

dashboard equipment
*équipement^M du tableau^M de
bord^M*

light bar controller
*système^M de contrôle^M de la barre^F de
signalisation^F*

radar transceiver
*émetteur^M-récepteur^M
radar^M*

reading light
*lampe^F de lecture^F*

microphones
*microphones^M*

dashboard computer
*ordinateur^M de bord^M*

computer programs
*programmes^M informatiques*

radar display
*affichage^M radar^M*

radio
*radio^F*

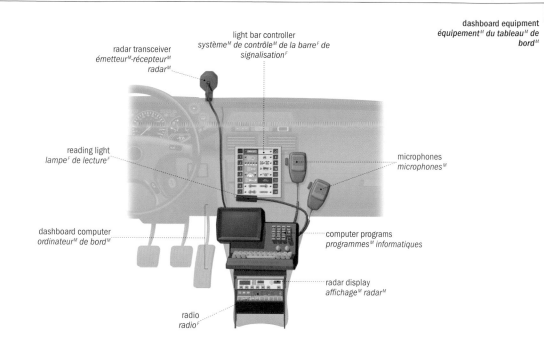

police car
*voiture^F de police^F*

light bar
*rampe^F de signalisation^F*

antenna
*antenne^F*

safety lighting
*éclairage^M de sécurité^F*

fire extinguisher
*extincteur^M*

barrier barricade tape
*ruban^M de bouclage^M*

partition
*cloison^F*

road flare
*fusée^F éclairante*

life buoy
*bouée^F de sauvetage^M*

first aid kit
*trousse^F de secours^M*

used syringe box
*boîte^F pour seringues^F
usagées*

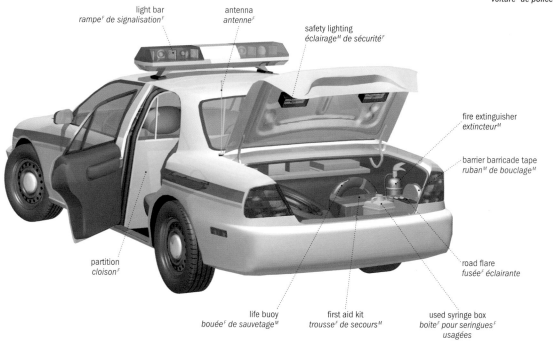

# ear protection

protection<sup>F</sup> de l'ouïe<sup>F</sup>

**safety earmuffs**
*serre-tête<sup>M</sup> antibruit*

headband
*serre-tête<sup>M</sup>*

**earplugs**
*protège-tympan<sup>M</sup>*

foam cushion
*coussinet<sup>M</sup> en mousse<sup>F</sup>*

# eye protection

protection<sup>F</sup> des yeux<sup>M</sup>

**safety glasses**
*lunettes<sup>F</sup> de sécurité<sup>F</sup>*

**safety goggles**
*lunettes<sup>F</sup> de protection<sup>F</sup>*

# head protection

protection<sup>F</sup> de la tête<sup>F</sup>

**hard hat**
*casque<sup>M</sup> de sécurité<sup>F</sup>*

suspension band
*sangle<sup>F</sup> d'amortissement<sup>M</sup>*

headband
*tour<sup>M</sup> de tête<sup>F</sup>*

rib
*nervure<sup>F</sup>*

peak
*visière<sup>F</sup>*

neck strap
*sangle<sup>F</sup> de nuque<sup>F</sup>*

SOCIETY

# respiratory system protection

protection<sup>F</sup> des voies<sup>F</sup> respiratoires

**respirator**
*masque<sup>M</sup> respiratoire*

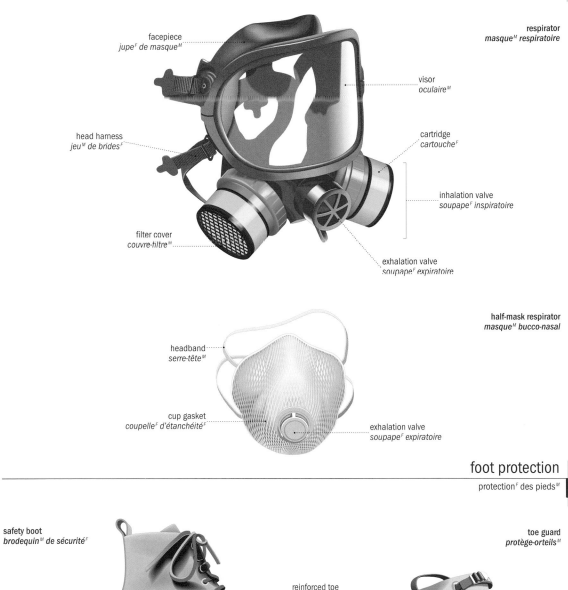

facepiece
*jupe<sup>F</sup> de masque<sup>M</sup>*

visor
*oculaire<sup>M</sup>*

head harness
*jeu<sup>M</sup> de brides<sup>F</sup>*

cartridge
*cartouche<sup>F</sup>*

inhalation valve
*soupape<sup>F</sup> inspiratoire*

filter cover
*couvre-filtre<sup>M</sup>*

exhalation valve
*soupape<sup>F</sup> expiratoire*

**half-mask respirator**
*masque<sup>M</sup> bucco-nasal*

headband
*serre-tête<sup>M</sup>*

cup gasket
*coupelle<sup>F</sup> d'étanchéité<sup>F</sup>*

exhalation valve
*soupape<sup>F</sup> expiratoire*

# foot protection

protection<sup>F</sup> des pieds<sup>M</sup>

SOCIETY

**safety boot**
*brodequin<sup>M</sup> de sécurité<sup>F</sup>*

**toe guard**
*protège-orteils<sup>M</sup>*

reinforced toe
*embout<sup>M</sup> de protection<sup>F</sup>*

# ambulance

ambulance<sup>F</sup>

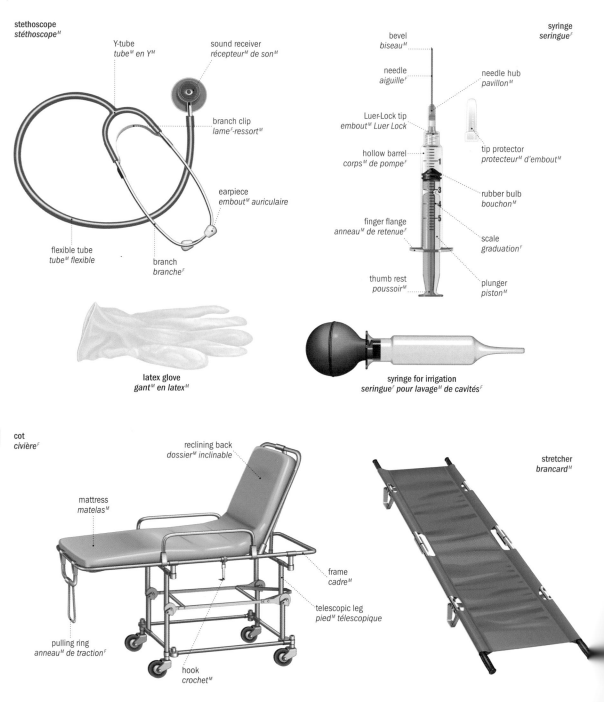

stethoscope
stéthoscope<sup>M</sup>

Y-tube
tube<sup>M</sup> en Y<sup>M</sup>

sound receiver
récepteur<sup>M</sup> de son<sup>M</sup>

branch clip
lame<sup>F</sup>-ressort<sup>M</sup>

earpiece
embout<sup>M</sup> auriculaire

flexible tube
tube<sup>M</sup> flexible

branch
branche<sup>F</sup>

syringe
seringue<sup>F</sup>

bevel
biseau<sup>M</sup>

needle
aiguille<sup>F</sup>

needle hub
pavillon<sup>M</sup>

Luer-Lock tip
embout<sup>M</sup> Luer Lock

tip protector
protecteur<sup>M</sup> d'embout<sup>M</sup>

hollow barrel
corps<sup>M</sup> de pompe<sup>F</sup>

rubber bulb
bouchon<sup>M</sup>

finger flange
anneau<sup>M</sup> de retenue<sup>F</sup>

scale
graduation<sup>F</sup>

thumb rest
poussoir<sup>M</sup>

plunger
piston<sup>M</sup>

latex glove
gant<sup>M</sup> en latex<sup>M</sup>

syringe for irrigation
seringue<sup>F</sup> pour lavage<sup>M</sup> de cavités<sup>F</sup>

cot
civière<sup>F</sup>

reclining back
dossier<sup>M</sup> inclinable

stretcher
brancard<sup>M</sup>

mattress
matelas<sup>M</sup>

frame
cadre<sup>M</sup>

telescopic leg
pied<sup>M</sup> télescopique

pulling ring
anneau<sup>M</sup> de traction<sup>F</sup>

hook
crochet<sup>M</sup>

# first aid kit

trousse<sup>F</sup> de secours<sup>M</sup>

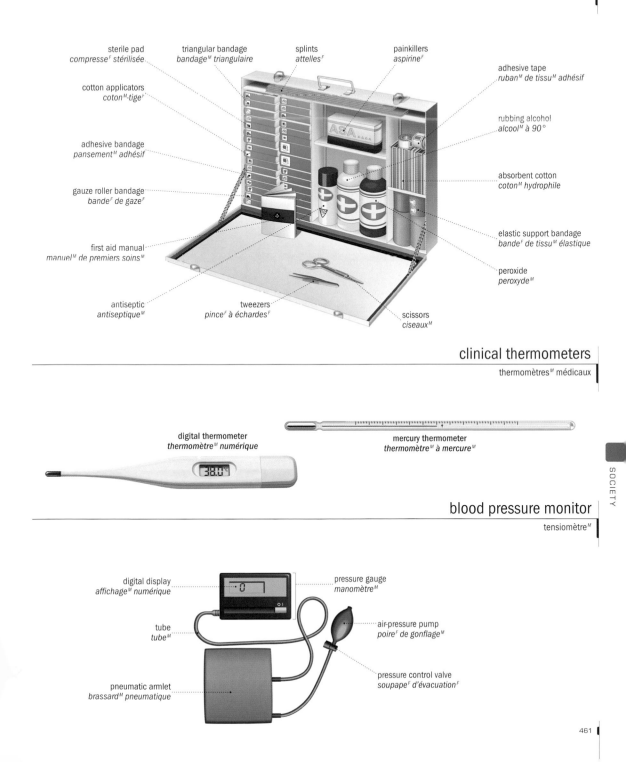

sterile pad
compresse<sup>F</sup> stérilisée

triangular bandage
bandage<sup>M</sup> triangulaire

splints
attelles<sup>F</sup>

painkillers
aspirine<sup>F</sup>

adhesive tape
ruban<sup>M</sup> de tissu<sup>M</sup> adhésif

cotton applicators
coton<sup>M</sup>-tige<sup>+</sup>

rubbing alcohol
alcool<sup>M</sup> à 90°

adhesive bandage
pansement<sup>M</sup> adhésif

absorbent cotton
coton<sup>M</sup> hydrophile

gauze roller bandage
bande<sup>F</sup> de gaze<sup>F</sup>

elastic support bandage
bande<sup>F</sup> de tissu<sup>M</sup> élastique

first aid manual
manuel<sup>M</sup> de premiers soins<sup>M</sup>

peroxide
peroxyde<sup>M</sup>

antiseptic
antiseptique<sup>M</sup>

tweezers
pince<sup>F</sup> à échardes<sup>F</sup>

scissors
ciseaux<sup>M</sup>

# clinical thermometers

thermomètres<sup>M</sup> médicaux

digital thermometer
thermomètre<sup>M</sup> numérique

mercury thermometer
thermomètre<sup>M</sup> à mercure<sup>M</sup>

# blood pressure monitor

tensiomètre<sup>M</sup>

digital display
affichage<sup>M</sup> numérique

pressure gauge
manomètre<sup>M</sup>

tube
tube<sup>M</sup>

air-pressure pump
poire<sup>F</sup> de gonflage<sup>M</sup>

pneumatic armlet
brassard<sup>M</sup> pneumatique

pressure control valve
soupape<sup>F</sup> d'évacuation<sup>F</sup>

SOCIETY

# hospital

hôpital[M]

emergency
urgences[F] ; urgence[F]

soiled utility room
salle[F] de stockage[M] du matériel[M]
souillé

family waiting room
salle[F] d'attente[F] des
familles[F]

clean utility room
salle[F] de stockage[M] du matériel[M]
stérile

observation room
chambre[F] d'observation[F]

nurses' station (major emergency)
poste[M] des infirmières[F] (urgence[F] majeure)

pharmacy
pharmacie[F]

resuscitation room
salle[F] de réanimation[F]

isolation room
chambre[F] d'isolement[M]

psychiatric observation room
chambre[F] d'observation[F]
psychiatrique

psychiatric examination room
examen[M] psychiatrique

mobile X-ray unit
appareil[M] de radiographie[F]
mobile

stretcher area
secteur[M] des civières[F]

ambulance
ambulance[F]

minor surgery room
chirurgie[F] mineure

reception area
aire[F] d'accueil[M]

emergency physician's office
bureau[M] de l'urgentiste[M] ; bureau[M] de
l'urgentologue[M]

ophthalmology and ENT (ear, nose and throat) room
salle<sup>F</sup> d'ophtalmologie<sup>F</sup> et d'oto-rhino-laryngologie<sup>F</sup>

plaster room
salle<sup>F</sup> de plâtre<sup>M</sup>

social worker's office
bureau<sup>M</sup> du travailleur<sup>M</sup>
social

gynecological examination room
salle<sup>F</sup> d'examen<sup>M</sup> gynécologique

examination and treatment room
salle<sup>F</sup> d'examen<sup>M</sup> et de soins<sup>M</sup>

restrooms
w.-c.<sup>M</sup> ; toilettes<sup>F</sup>

beverage dispenser
distributeur<sup>M</sup> de boissons<sup>F</sup>

pay phone
téléphone<sup>M</sup> public

nurses' station (ambulatory emergency)
poste<sup>M</sup> des infirmières<sup>F</sup> (urgence<sup>F</sup> ambulatoire)

waiting room
salle<sup>F</sup> d'attente<sup>F</sup>

security guard's work station
poste<sup>M</sup> de l'agent<sup>M</sup> de sécurité<sup>F</sup>

triage room
salle<sup>F</sup> de triage<sup>M</sup>

information desk
comptoir<sup>M</sup> de renseignements<sup>M</sup>

head nurse's office
bureau<sup>M</sup> de l'infirmière<sup>F</sup> en chef<sup>M</sup>

staff lounge
salon<sup>M</sup> du personnel<sup>M</sup>

## patient room
*chambre<sup>F</sup> d'hôpital<sup>M</sup>*

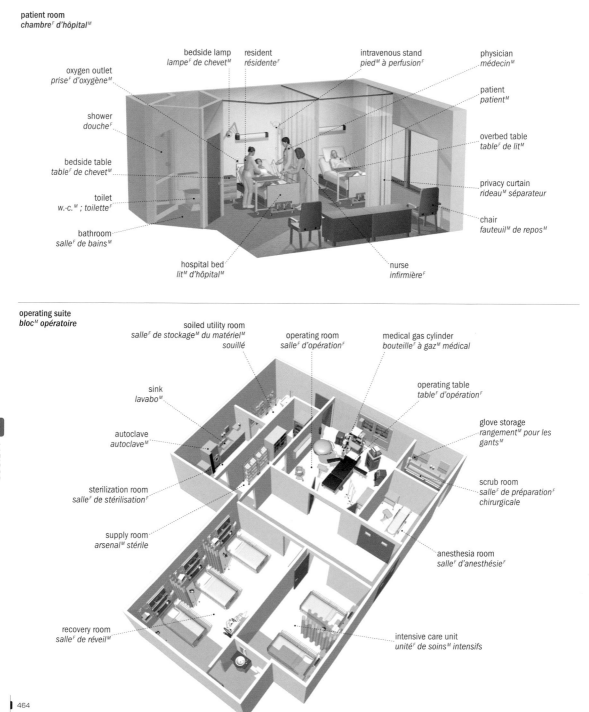

oxygen outlet
*prise<sup>F</sup> d'oxygène<sup>M</sup>*

bedside lamp
*lampe<sup>F</sup> de chevet<sup>M</sup>*

resident
*résidente<sup>F</sup>*

intravenous stand
*pied<sup>M</sup> à perfusion<sup>F</sup>*

physician
*médecin<sup>M</sup>*

shower
*douche<sup>F</sup>*

patient
*patient<sup>M</sup>*

bedside table
*table<sup>F</sup> de chevet<sup>M</sup>*

overbed table
*table<sup>F</sup> de lit<sup>M</sup>*

toilet
*w.-c.<sup>M</sup> ; toilette<sup>F</sup>*

privacy curtain
*rideau<sup>M</sup> séparateur*

bathroom
*salle<sup>F</sup> de bains<sup>M</sup>*

chair
*fauteuil<sup>M</sup> de repos<sup>M</sup>*

hospital bed
*lit<sup>M</sup> d'hôpital<sup>M</sup>*

nurse
*infirmière<sup>F</sup>*

## operating suite
*bloc<sup>M</sup> opératoire*

soiled utility room
*salle<sup>F</sup> de stockage<sup>M</sup> du matériel<sup>M</sup> souillé*

operating room
*salle<sup>F</sup> d'opération<sup>F</sup>*

medical gas cylinder
*bouteille<sup>F</sup> à gaz<sup>M</sup> médical*

sink
*lavabo<sup>M</sup>*

operating table
*table<sup>F</sup> d'opération<sup>F</sup>*

autoclave
*autoclave<sup>M</sup>*

glove storage
*rangement<sup>M</sup> pour les gants<sup>M</sup>*

sterilization room
*salle<sup>F</sup> de stérilisation<sup>F</sup>*

scrub room
*salle<sup>F</sup> de préparation<sup>F</sup> chirurgicale*

supply room
*arsenal<sup>M</sup> stérile*

anesthesia room
*salle<sup>F</sup> d'anesthésie<sup>F</sup>*

recovery room
*salle<sup>F</sup> de réveil<sup>M</sup>*

intensive care unit
*unité<sup>F</sup> de soins<sup>M</sup> intensifs*

ambulatory care unit
*unité<sup>F</sup> de soins<sup>M</sup>
ambulatoires*

specimen collection center waiting room
*salle<sup>F</sup> d'attente<sup>F</sup> du centre<sup>M</sup> de prélèvements<sup>M</sup>*

surgeon's sink
*lavabo<sup>M</sup> du chirurgien<sup>M</sup>*

pathology laboratory
*laboratoire<sup>M</sup> de pathologie<sup>F</sup>*

sterilization room
*salle<sup>F</sup> de stérilisation<sup>F</sup>*

operating room
*salle<sup>F</sup> d'opération<sup>F</sup>*

undressing booth
*cabine<sup>F</sup> de déshabillage<sup>M</sup>*

secondary waiting room
*salle<sup>F</sup> d'attente<sup>F</sup>
secondaire*

observation room
*chambre<sup>F</sup> d'observation<sup>F</sup>*

restrooms
*w.-c.<sup>M</sup> ; toilettes<sup>F</sup>*

social services
*services<sup>M</sup> sociaux*

staff change room
*vestiaire<sup>M</sup> du personnel<sup>M</sup>*

nurses' lounge
*salle<sup>F</sup> de repos<sup>M</sup> des
infirmières<sup>F</sup>*

specimen collection room
*salle<sup>F</sup> de prélèvements<sup>M</sup>*

treatment room
*salle<sup>F</sup> de soins<sup>M</sup>*

main entrance
*entrée<sup>F</sup> principale*

medical equipment storage room
*salle<sup>F</sup> de rangement<sup>M</sup> du matériel<sup>M</sup>
médical*

reception area
*aire<sup>F</sup> d'accueil<sup>M</sup>*

audiometric examination room
*salle<sup>F</sup> d'examen<sup>M</sup> audiométrique*

medical records
*archives<sup>F</sup> médicales*

main waiting room
*salle<sup>F</sup> d'attente<sup>F</sup> principale*

examination room
*salle<sup>F</sup> d'examen<sup>M</sup>*

pharmacy
*pharmacie<sup>F</sup>*

SOCIETY

# walking aids

aides<sup>F</sup> à la marche<sup>F</sup>

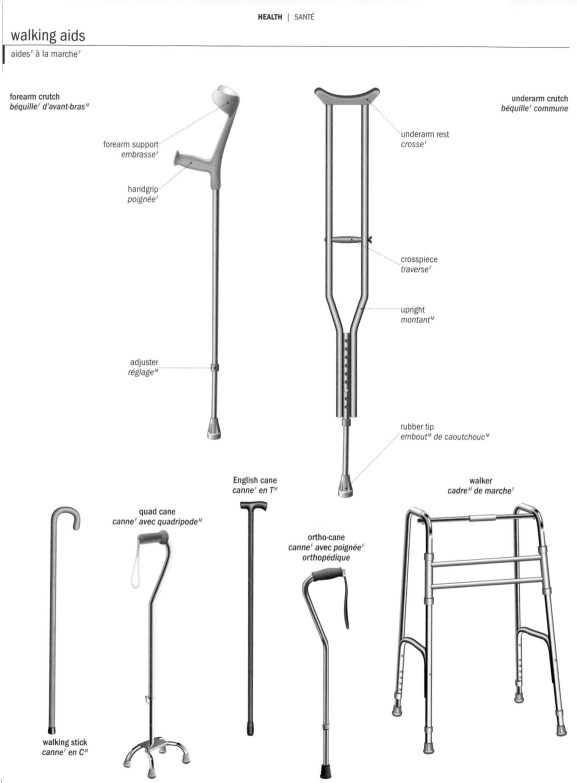

**forearm crutch**
*béquille<sup>F</sup> d'avant-bras<sup>M</sup>*

forearm support
*embrasse<sup>F</sup>*

handgrip
*poignée<sup>F</sup>*

adjuster
*réglage<sup>M</sup>*

**underarm crutch**
*béquille<sup>F</sup> commune*

underarm rest
*crosse<sup>F</sup>*

crosspiece
*traverse<sup>F</sup>*

upright
*montant<sup>M</sup>*

rubber tip
*embout<sup>M</sup> de caoutchouc<sup>M</sup>*

**English cane**
*canne<sup>F</sup> en T<sup>M</sup>*

**quad cane**
*canne<sup>F</sup> avec quadripode<sup>M</sup>*

**ortho-cane**
*canne<sup>F</sup> avec poignée<sup>F</sup>*
*orthopédique*

**walker**
*cadre<sup>M</sup> de marche<sup>F</sup>*

**walking stick**
*canne<sup>F</sup> en C<sup>M</sup>*

# wheelchair

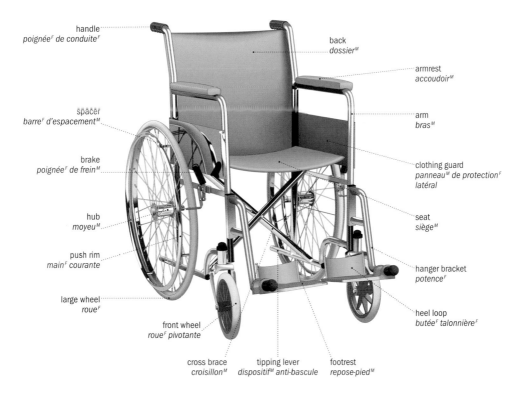

handle
poignée<sup>F</sup> de conduite<sup>F</sup>

back
dossier<sup>M</sup>

armrest
accoudoir<sup>M</sup>

spacer
barre<sup>F</sup> d'espacement<sup>M</sup>

arm
bras<sup>M</sup>

brake
poignée<sup>F</sup> de frein<sup>M</sup>

clothing guard
panneau<sup>M</sup> de protection<sup>F</sup>
latéral

hub
moyeu<sup>M</sup>

seat
siège<sup>M</sup>

push rim
main<sup>F</sup> courante

hanger bracket
potence<sup>F</sup>

large wheel
roue<sup>F</sup>

heel loop
butée<sup>F</sup> talonnière<sup>F</sup>

front wheel
roue<sup>F</sup> pivotante

cross brace
croisillon<sup>M</sup>

tipping lever
dispositif<sup>M</sup> anti-bascule

footrest
repose-pied<sup>M</sup>

# forms of medications

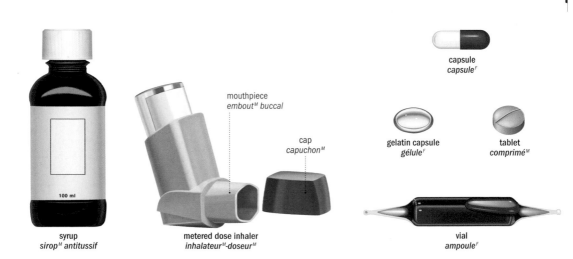

capsule
capsule<sup>F</sup>

mouthpiece
embout<sup>M</sup> buccal

cap
capuchon<sup>M</sup>

gelatin capsule
gélule<sup>F</sup>

tablet
comprimé<sup>M</sup>

100 ml

syrup
sirop<sup>M</sup> antitussif

metered dose inhaler
inhalateur<sup>M</sup>-doseur<sup>M</sup>

vial
ampoule<sup>F</sup>

SOCIETY

# dice and dominoes

*dés*[M] *et dominos*[M]

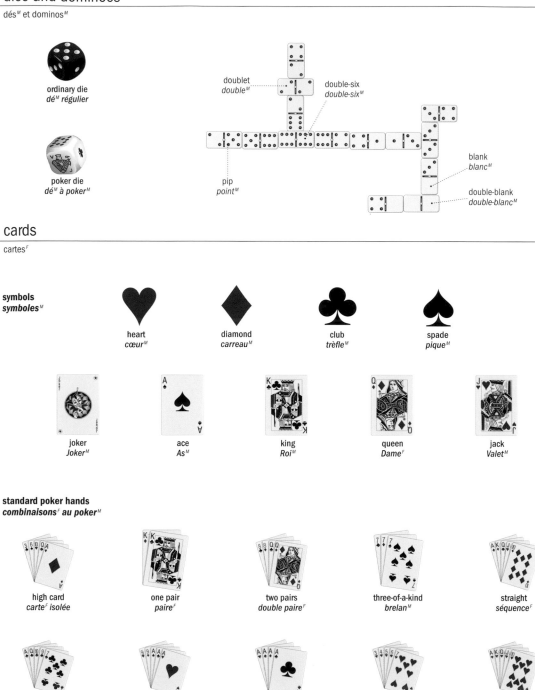

ordinary die
*dé*[M] *régulier*

poker die
*dé*[M] *à poker*[M]

doublet
*double*[M]

double-six
*double-six*[M]

blank
*blanc*[M]

double-blank
*double-blanc*[M]

pip
*point*[M]

# cards

*cartes*[F]

**symbols**
***symboles***[M]

heart
*cœur*[M]

diamond
*carreau*[M]

club
*trèfle*[M]

spade
*pique*[M]

joker
*Joker*[M]

ace
*As*[M]

king
*Roi*[M]

queen
*Dame*[F]

jack
*Valet*[M]

**standard poker hands**
***combinaisons***[F] ***au poker***[M]

high card
*carte*[F] *isolée*

one pair
*paire*[F]

two pairs
*double paire*[F]

three-of-a-kind
*brelan*[M]

straight
*séquence*[F]

flush
*couleur*[F]

full house
*main*[F] *pleine*

four-of-a-kind
*carré*[M]

straight flush
*quinte*[F]

royal flush
*quinte*[F] *royale*

# board games
jeux<sup>M</sup> de plateau<sup>M</sup>

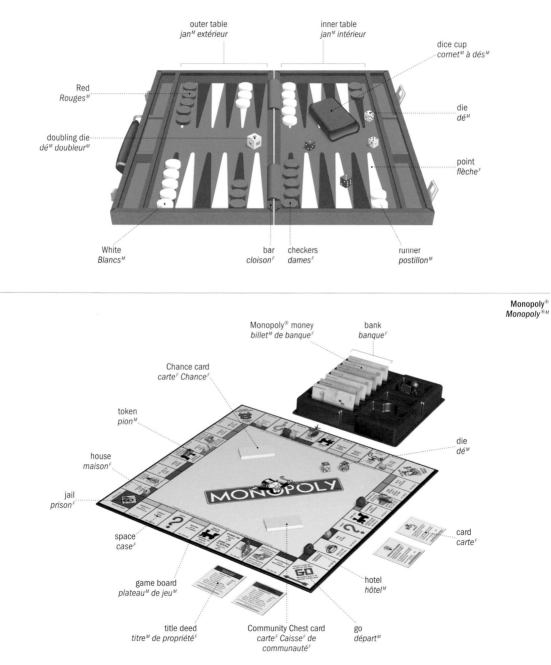

backgammon
jacquet<sup>M</sup>

outer table
jan<sup>M</sup> extérieur

inner table
jan<sup>M</sup> intérieur

dice cup
cornet<sup>M</sup> à dés<sup>M</sup>

Red
Rouges<sup>M</sup>

die
dé<sup>M</sup>

doubling die
dé<sup>M</sup> doubleur<sup>M</sup>

point
flèche<sup>F</sup>

White
Blancs<sup>M</sup>

bar
cloison<sup>F</sup>

checkers
dames<sup>F</sup>

runner
postillon<sup>M</sup>

Monopoly®
Monopoly<sup>®M</sup>

Monopoly® money
billet<sup>M</sup> de banque<sup>F</sup>

bank
banque<sup>F</sup>

Chance card
carte<sup>F</sup> Chance<sup>F</sup>

token
pion<sup>M</sup>

die
dé<sup>M</sup>

house
maison<sup>F</sup>

jail
prison<sup>F</sup>

card
carte<sup>F</sup>

space
case<sup>F</sup>

game board
plateau<sup>M</sup> de jeu<sup>M</sup>

hotel
hôtel<sup>M</sup>

title deed
titre<sup>M</sup> de propriété<sup>F</sup>

Community Chest card
carte<sup>F</sup> Caisse<sup>F</sup> de
communauté<sup>F</sup>

go
départ<sup>M</sup>

SPORTS AND GAMES

469

# board games

## chess
### échecs<sup>M</sup>

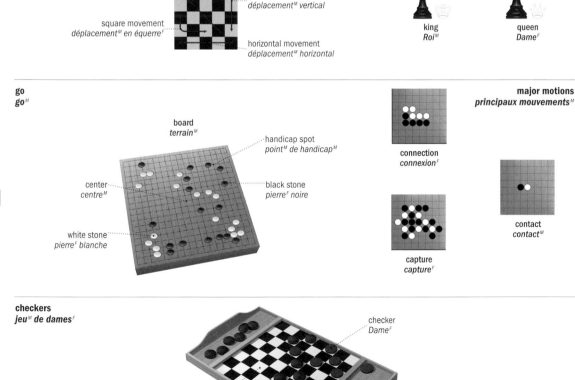

queen's side
aile<sup>F</sup> Dame<sup>F</sup>

king's side
aile<sup>F</sup> Roi<sup>M</sup>

**chess pieces**
***pièces***<sup>F</sup>

chessboard
échiquier<sup>M</sup>

Black
Noirs<sup>M</sup>

white square
case<sup>F</sup> blanche

black square
case<sup>F</sup> noire

chess notation
notation<sup>F</sup> algébrique

White
Blancs<sup>M</sup>

pawn
Pion<sup>M</sup>

rook
Tour<sup>F</sup>

bishop
Fou<sup>M</sup>

knight
Cavalier<sup>M</sup>

types of movements
types<sup>M</sup> de déplacements<sup>M</sup>

diagonal movement
déplacement<sup>M</sup> diagonal

vertical movement
déplacement<sup>M</sup> vertical

square movement
déplacement<sup>M</sup> en équerre<sup>F</sup>

horizontal movement
déplacement<sup>M</sup> horizontal

king
Roi<sup>M</sup>

queen
Dame<sup>F</sup>

## go
### go<sup>M</sup>

**major motions**
***principaux mouvements***<sup>M</sup>

board
terrain<sup>M</sup>

handicap spot
point<sup>M</sup> de handicap<sup>M</sup>

center
centre<sup>M</sup>

black stone
pierre<sup>F</sup> noire

connection
connexion<sup>F</sup>

white stone
pierre<sup>F</sup> blanche

contact
contact<sup>M</sup>

capture
capture<sup>F</sup>

## checkers
### jeu<sup>M</sup> de dames<sup>F</sup>

checker
Dame<sup>F</sup>

checkerboard
damier<sup>M</sup>

SPORTS AND GAMES

# video entertainment system

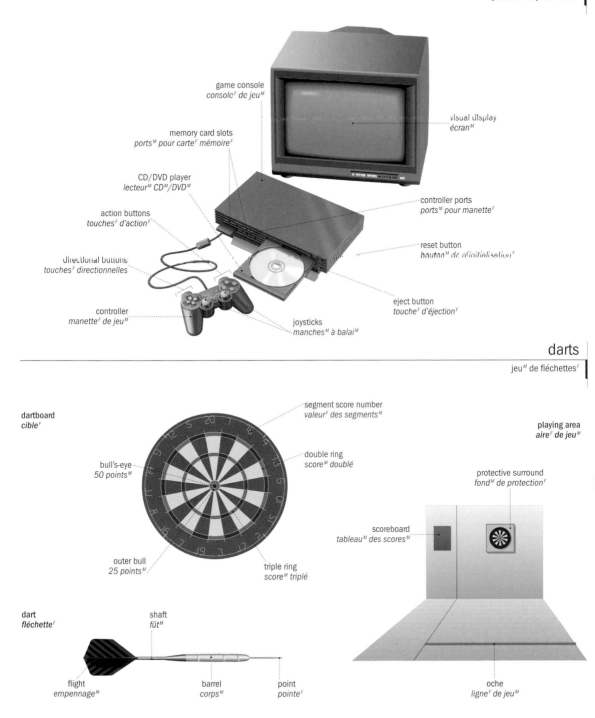

game console
consolc<sup>F</sup> dc jeu<sup>M</sup>

visual display
écran<sup>M</sup>

memory card slots
ports<sup>M</sup> pour carte<sup>F</sup> mémoire<sup>F</sup>

CD/DVD player
lecteur<sup>M</sup> CD<sup>M</sup>/DVD<sup>M</sup>

controller ports
ports<sup>M</sup> pour manette<sup>F</sup>

action buttons
touches<sup>F</sup> d'action<sup>F</sup>

reset button
bouton<sup>M</sup> de réinitialisation<sup>F</sup>

directional buttons
touches<sup>F</sup> directionnelles

controller
manette<sup>F</sup> de jeu<sup>M</sup>

eject button
touche<sup>F</sup> d'éjection<sup>F</sup>

joysticks
manches<sup>M</sup> à balai<sup>M</sup>

# darts

dartboard
cible<sup>F</sup>

segment score number
valeur<sup>F</sup> des segments<sup>M</sup>

playing area
aire<sup>F</sup> de jeu<sup>M</sup>

bull's-eye
50 points<sup>M</sup>

double ring
score<sup>M</sup> doublé

protective surround
fond<sup>M</sup> de protection<sup>F</sup>

scoreboard
tableau<sup>M</sup> des scores<sup>M</sup>

outer bull
25 points<sup>M</sup>

triple ring
score<sup>M</sup> triplé

dart
fléchette<sup>F</sup>

shaft
fût<sup>M</sup>

flight
empennage<sup>M</sup>

barrel
corps<sup>M</sup>

point
pointe<sup>F</sup>

oche
ligne<sup>F</sup> de jeu<sup>M</sup>

SPORTS AND GAMES

# arena

stade<sup>M</sup>

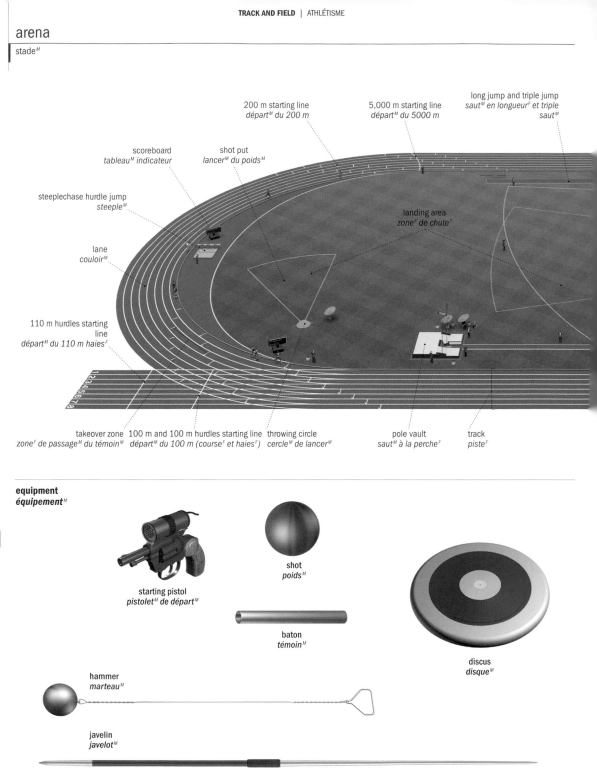

200 m starting line
départ<sup>M</sup> du 200 m

5,000 m starting line
départ<sup>M</sup> du 5000 m

long jump and triple jump
saut<sup>M</sup> en longueur<sup>F</sup> et triple
saut<sup>M</sup>

scoreboard
tableau<sup>M</sup> indicateur

shot put
lancer<sup>M</sup> du poids<sup>M</sup>

steeplechase hurdle jump
steeple<sup>M</sup>

landing area
zone<sup>F</sup> de chute<sup>F</sup>

lane
couloir<sup>M</sup>

110 m hurdles starting
line
départ<sup>M</sup> du 110 m haies<sup>F</sup>

takeover zone
zone<sup>F</sup> de passage<sup>M</sup> du témoin<sup>M</sup>

100 m and 100 m hurdles starting line
départ<sup>M</sup> du 100 m (course<sup>F</sup> et haies<sup>F</sup>)

throwing circle
cercle<sup>M</sup> de lancer<sup>M</sup>

pole vault
saut<sup>M</sup> à la perche<sup>F</sup>

track
piste<sup>F</sup>

## equipment
équipement<sup>M</sup>

starting pistol
pistolet<sup>M</sup> de départ<sup>M</sup>

shot
poids<sup>M</sup>

baton
témoin<sup>M</sup>

discus
disque<sup>M</sup>

hammer
marteau<sup>M</sup>

javelin
javelot<sup>M</sup>

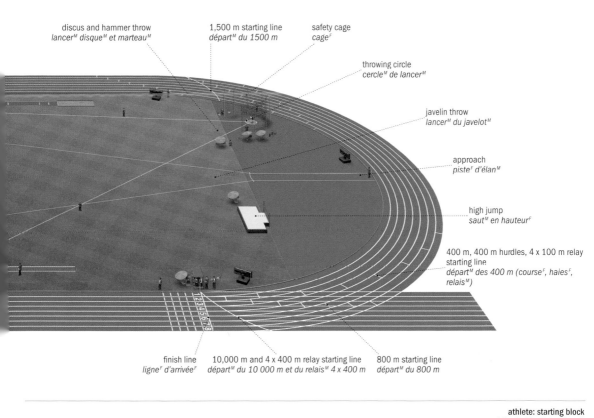

discus and hammer throw
lancer^M disque^M et marteau^M

1,500 m starting line
départ^M du 1500 m

safety cage
cage^F

throwing circle
cercle^M de lancer^M

javelin throw
lancer^M du javelot^M

approach
piste^F d'élan^M

high jump
saut^M en hauteur^F

400 m, 400 m hurdles, 4 x 100 m relay
starting line
départ^M des 400 m (course^F, haies^F,
relais^M)

finish line
ligne^F d'arrivée^F

10,000 m and 4 x 400 m relay starting line
départ^M du 10 000 m et du relais^M 4 x 400 m

800 m starting line
départ^M du 800 m

athlete: starting block
athlète^F : bloc^M de départ^M

singlet
maillot^M

number
dossard^M

shorts
short^M

pedal
sabot^M

track shoe
chaussure^F de piste^F

notch
cran^M

starting line
ligne^F de départ^M

anchor
fixation^F

lane line
ligne^F de couloir^M

rack
crémaillère^F

spike
pointe^F

block
bloc^M

base
embase^F

SPORTS AND GAMES

473

# baseball

baseball[M]

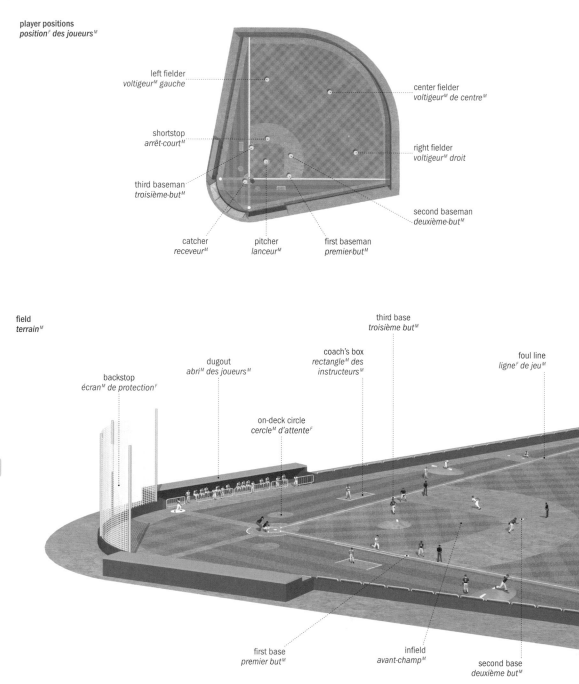

**player positions**
*position[F] des joueurs[M]*

left fielder
*voltigeur[M] gauche*

center fielder
*voltigeur[M] de centre[M]*

shortstop
*arrêt-court[M]*

right fielder
*voltigeur[M] droit*

third baseman
*troisième-but[M]*

second baseman
*deuxième-but[M]*

catcher
*receveur[M]*

pitcher
*lanceur[M]*

first baseman
*premier-but[M]*

**field**
*terrain[M]*

third base
*troisième but[M]*

coach's box
*rectangle[M] des instructeurs[M]*

foul line
*ligne[F] de jeu[M]*

dugout
*abri[M] des joueurs[M]*

backstop
*écran[M] de protection[F]*

on-deck circle
*cercle[M] d'attente[F]*

first base
*premier but[M]*

infield
*avant-champ[M]*

second base
*deuxième but[M]*

pitch
*lancer*<sup>M</sup>

home-plate umpire
*arbitre*<sup>M</sup> *en chef*<sup>M</sup>

batter
*frappeur*<sup>M</sup>

pitcher
*lanceur*<sup>M</sup>

catcher
*receveur*<sup>M</sup>

home plate
*marbre*<sup>M</sup>

pitcher's mound
*monticule*<sup>M</sup>

pitcher's plate
*plaque*<sup>F</sup> *du lanceur*<sup>M</sup>

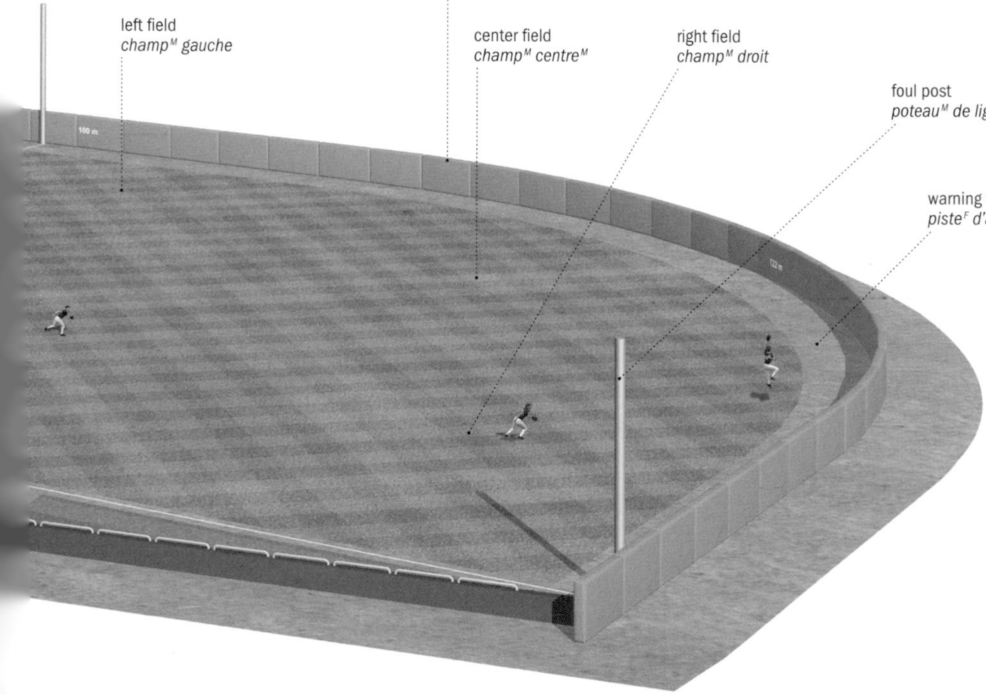

outfield fence
*clôture*<sup>F</sup> *du champ*<sup>M</sup>
*extérieur*

left field
*champ*<sup>M</sup> *gauche*

center field
*champ*<sup>M</sup> *centre*<sup>M</sup>

right field
*champ*<sup>M</sup> *droit*

foul post
*poteau*<sup>M</sup> *de ligne*<sup>F</sup> *de jeu*<sup>M</sup>

warning track
*piste*<sup>F</sup> *d'avertissement*<sup>M</sup>

baseball

**baseball**
*balle<sup>F</sup> de baseball<sup>M</sup>*

bat
*bâton<sup>M</sup>*

batter's helmet
*casque<sup>M</sup> de frappeur<sup>M</sup>*

batter
*frappeur<sup>M</sup>*

catcher
*receveur<sup>M</sup>*

throat protector
*protège-gorge<sup>M</sup>*

mask
*masque<sup>M</sup>*

frame
*grille<sup>F</sup>*

chest protector
*plastron<sup>M</sup>*

catcher's glove
*gant<sup>M</sup> de receveur<sup>M</sup>*

team shirt
*maillot<sup>M</sup> d'équipe<sup>F</sup>*

undershirt
*maillot<sup>M</sup> de corps<sup>M</sup>*

batting glove
*gant<sup>M</sup> de frappeur<sup>M</sup>*

pants
*pantalon<sup>M</sup>*

stirrup sock
*chaussette<sup>F</sup>-étrier<sup>M</sup>*

spiked shoe
*chaussure<sup>F</sup> à crampons<sup>M</sup>*

toe guard
*protège-orteils<sup>M</sup>*

leg guard
*jambière<sup>F</sup>*

knee pad
*genouillère<sup>F</sup>*

ankle guard
*protège-cheville<sup>M</sup>*

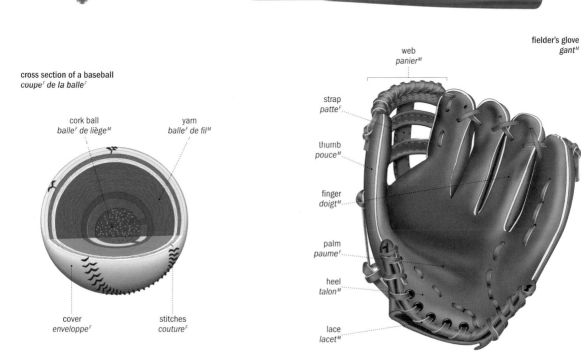

bat
*bâton*<sup>M</sup>

knob
*pommeau*<sup>M</sup>

handle
*manche*<sup>M</sup>

crest
*écusson*<sup>M</sup>

hitting area
*surface*<sup>F</sup> *de frappe*<sup>F</sup>

fielder's glove
*gant*<sup>M</sup>

cross section of a baseball
*coupe*<sup>F</sup> *de la balle*<sup>F</sup>

web
*panier*<sup>M</sup>

cork ball
*balle*<sup>F</sup> *de liège*<sup>M</sup>

yarn
*balle*<sup>F</sup> *de fil*<sup>M</sup>

strap
*patte*<sup>F</sup>

thumb
*pouce*<sup>M</sup>

finger
*doigt*<sup>M</sup>

palm
*paume*<sup>F</sup>

heel
*talon*<sup>M</sup>

cover
*enveloppe*<sup>F</sup>

stitches
*couture*<sup>F</sup>

lace
*lacet*<sup>M</sup>

softball
softball<sup>M</sup>

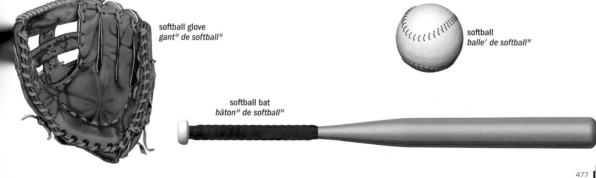

softball glove
*gant*<sup>M</sup> *de softball*<sup>M</sup>

softball
*balle*<sup>F</sup> *de softball*<sup>M</sup>

softball bat
*bâton*<sup>M</sup> *de softball*<sup>M</sup>

SPORTS AND GAMES

# cricket

cricket[M]

**cricket player: batsman**
*joueur[M] de cricket[M] : batteur[M]*

**cricket ball**
*balle[F] de cricket[M]*

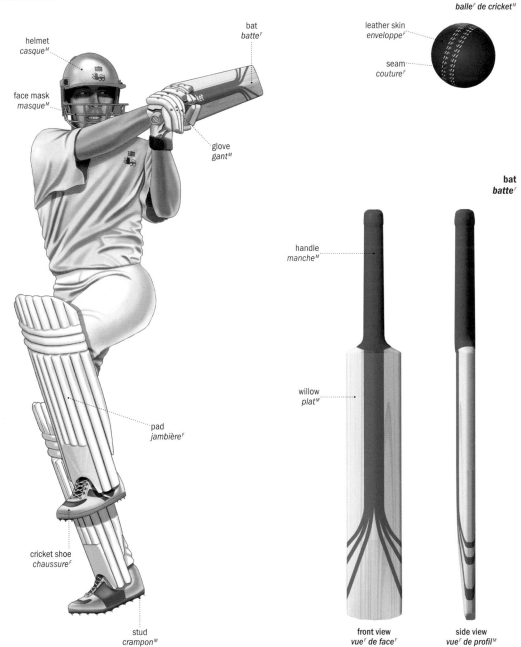

helmet
casque[M]

face mask
masque[M]

bat
batte[F]

glove
gant[M]

leather skin
enveloppe[F]

seam
couture[F]

**bat**
*batte[F]*

handle
manche[M]

willow
plat[M]

pad
jambière[F]

cricket shoe
chaussure[F]

stud
crampon[M]

front view
vue[F] de face[F]

side view
vue[F] de profil[M]

**field**
*terrain*<sup>M</sup>

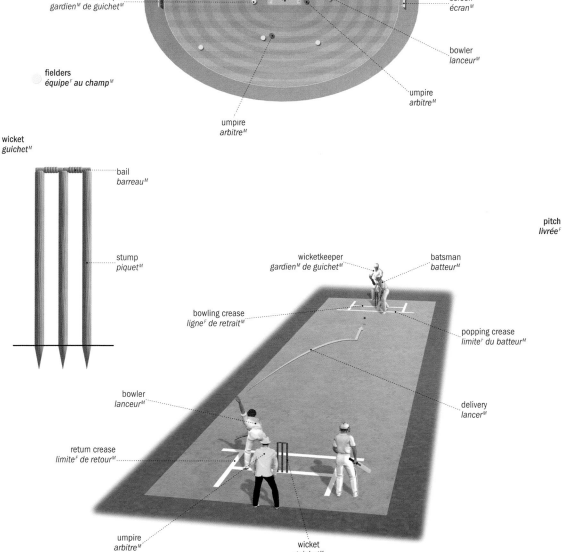

pitch
*livrée*<sup>F</sup>

wicketkeeper
*gardien*<sup>M</sup> *de guichet*<sup>M</sup>

screen
*écran*<sup>M</sup>

bowler
*lanceur*<sup>M</sup>

fielders
*équipe*<sup>F</sup> *au champ*<sup>M</sup>

umpire
*arbitre*<sup>M</sup>

umpire
*arbitre*<sup>M</sup>

wicket
*guichet*<sup>M</sup>

bail
*barreau*<sup>M</sup>

stump
*piquet*<sup>M</sup>

pitch
*livrée*<sup>F</sup>

wicketkeeper
*gardien*<sup>M</sup> *de guichet*<sup>M</sup>

batsman
*batteur*<sup>M</sup>

bowling crease
*ligne*<sup>F</sup> *de retrait*<sup>M</sup>

popping crease
*limite*<sup>F</sup> *du batteur*<sup>M</sup>

bowler
*lanceur*<sup>M</sup>

delivery
*lancer*<sup>M</sup>

return crease
*limite*<sup>F</sup> *de retour*<sup>M</sup>

umpire
*arbitre*<sup>M</sup>

wicket
*guichet*<sup>M</sup>

# soccer

football[M]

**soccer player**
*footballeur*[M]

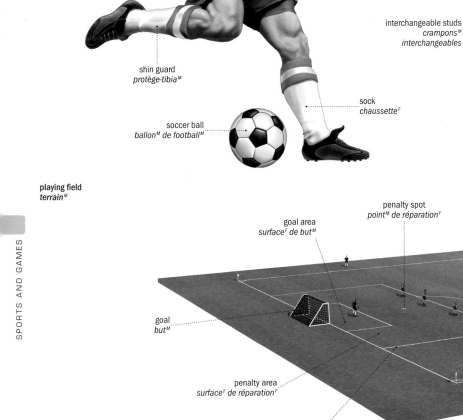

**team shirt**
*maillot*[M] *d'équipe*[F]

**goalkeeper's gloves**
*gants*[M] *de gardien*[M] *de but*[M]

**shorts**
*short*[M]

**interchangeable studs**
*crampons*[M]
*interchangeables*

**soccer shoe**
*chaussure*[F] *de football*[M]

**shin guard**
*protège-tibia*[M]

**sock**
*chaussette*[F]

**soccer ball**
*ballon*[M] *de football*[M]

**playing field**
*terrain*[M]

**center flag**
*drapeau*[M] *de centre*[M]

**penalty spot**
*point*[M] *de réparation*[F]

**goal area**
*surface*[F] *de but*[M]

**goal**
*but*[M]

**penalty area**
*surface*[F] *de réparation*[F]

**penalty marker**
*ligne*[F] *de surface*[F] *de*
*réparation*[F]

**penalty arc**
*arc*[M] *de cercle*[M]

SPORTS AND GAMES

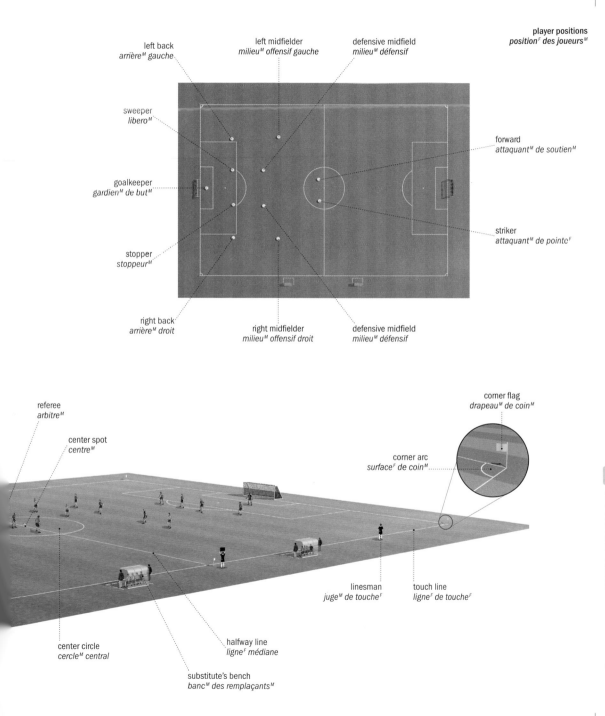

player positions
position<sup>F</sup> des joueurs<sup>M</sup>

left back
arrière<sup>M</sup> gauche

left midfielder
milieu<sup>M</sup> offensif gauche

defensive midfield
milieu<sup>M</sup> défensif

sweeper
libero<sup>M</sup>

forward
attaquant<sup>M</sup> de soutien<sup>M</sup>

goalkeeper
gardien<sup>M</sup> de but<sup>M</sup>

striker
attaquant<sup>M</sup> de pointe<sup>F</sup>

stopper
stoppeur<sup>M</sup>

right back
arrière<sup>M</sup> droit

right midfielder
milieu<sup>M</sup> offensif droit

defensive midfield
milieu<sup>M</sup> défensif

corner flag
drapeau<sup>M</sup> de coin<sup>M</sup>

referee
arbitre<sup>M</sup>

center spot
centre<sup>M</sup>

corner arc
surface<sup>F</sup> de coin<sup>M</sup>

linesman
juge<sup>M</sup> de touche<sup>F</sup>

touch line
ligne<sup>F</sup> de touche<sup>F</sup>

center circle
cercle<sup>M</sup> central

halfway line
ligne<sup>F</sup> médiane

substitute's bench
banc<sup>M</sup> des remplaçants<sup>M</sup>

SPORTS AND GAMES

# rugby

rugby<sup>M</sup>

players' positions
*position<sup>F</sup> des joueurs<sup>M</sup>*

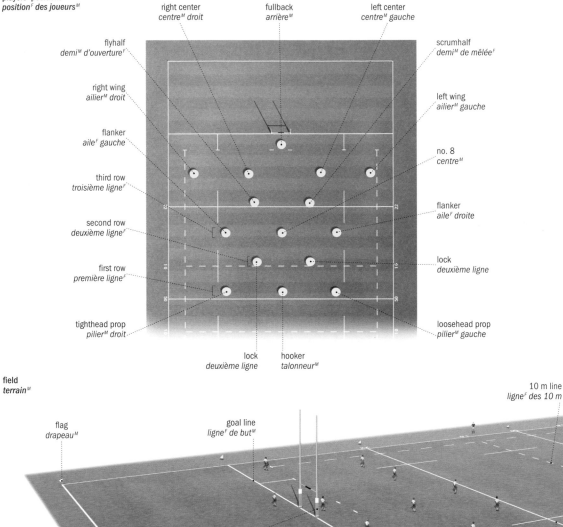

right center
*centre<sup>M</sup> droit*

fullback
*arrière<sup>M</sup>*

left center
*centre<sup>M</sup> gauche*

flyhalf
*demi<sup>M</sup> d'ouverture<sup>F</sup>*

scrumhalf
*demi<sup>M</sup> de mêlée<sup>F</sup>*

right wing
*ailier<sup>M</sup> droit*

left wing
*ailier<sup>M</sup> gauche*

flanker
*aile<sup>F</sup> gauche*

no. 8
*centre<sup>M</sup>*

third row
*troisième ligne<sup>F</sup>*

flanker
*aile<sup>F</sup> droite*

second row
*deuxième ligne<sup>F</sup>*

lock
*deuxième ligne*

first row
*première ligne<sup>F</sup>*

lock
*deuxième ligne*

tighthead prop
*pilier<sup>M</sup> droit*

loosehead prop
*pilier<sup>M</sup> gauche*

lock
*deuxième ligne*

hooker
*talonneur<sup>M</sup>*

field
*terrain<sup>M</sup>*

10 m line
*ligne<sup>F</sup> des 10 m*

flag
*drapeau<sup>M</sup>*

goal line
*ligne<sup>F</sup> de but<sup>M</sup>*

goalpost
*but<sup>M</sup>*

dead ball line
*ligne<sup>F</sup> de ballon<sup>M</sup> mort*

22 m line
*ligne<sup>F</sup> des 22 m*

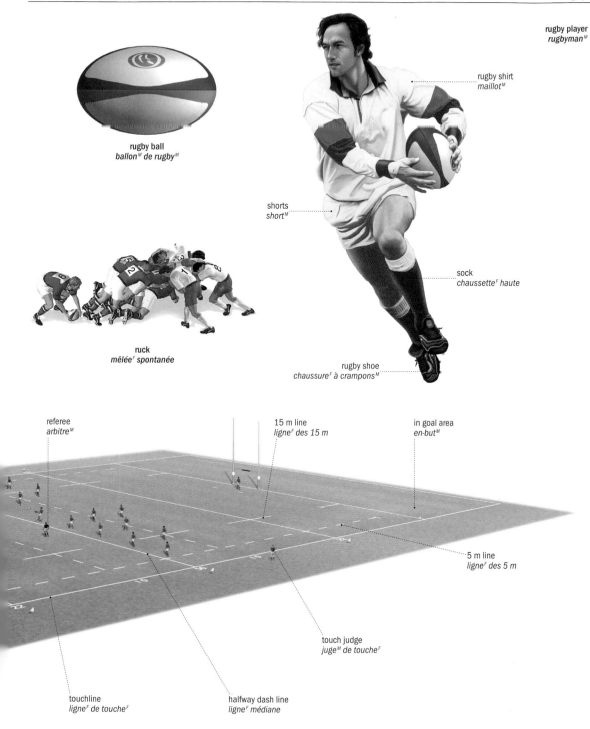

rugby player
rugbyman[M]

rugby shirt
maillot[M]

shorts
short[M]

sock
chaussette[F] haute

rugby ball
ballon[M] de rugby[M]

ruck
mêlée[F] spontanée

rugby shoe
chaussure[F] à crampons[M]

referee
arbitre[M]

15 m line
ligne[F] des 15 m

in goal area
en-but[M]

5 m line
ligne[F] des 5 m

touch judge
juge[M] de touche[F]

touchline
ligne[F] de touche[F]

halfway dash line
ligne[F] médiane

# American football

football<sup>M</sup> américain

**scrimmage: defense**
*mêlée<sup>F</sup> : défense<sup>F</sup>*

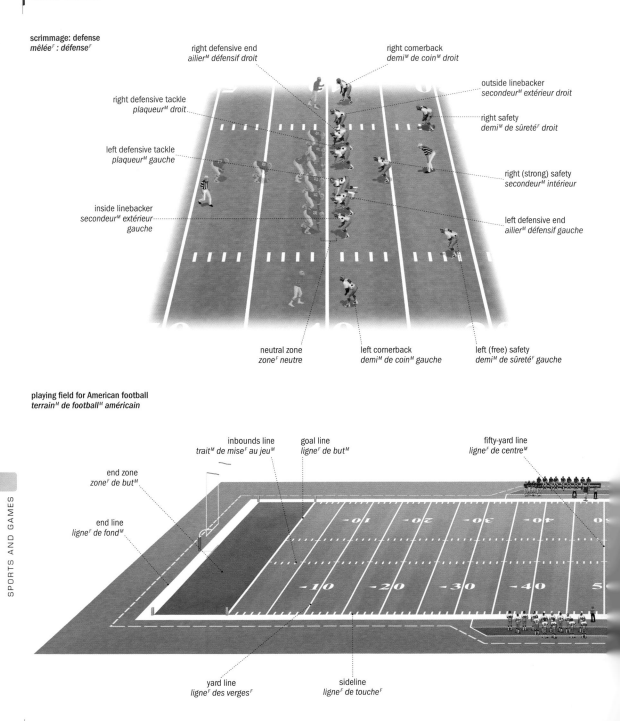

right defensive end
*ailier<sup>M</sup> défensif droit*

right cornerback
*demi<sup>M</sup> de coin<sup>M</sup> droit*

outside linebacker
*secondeur<sup>M</sup> extérieur droit*

right defensive tackle
*plaqueur<sup>M</sup> droit*

right safety
*demi<sup>M</sup> de sûreté<sup>F</sup> droit*

left defensive tackle
*plaqueur<sup>M</sup> gauche*

right (strong) safety
*secondeur<sup>M</sup> intérieur*

inside linebacker
*secondeur<sup>M</sup> extérieur gauche*

left defensive end
*ailier<sup>M</sup> défensif gauche*

neutral zone
*zone<sup>F</sup> neutre*

left cornerback
*demi<sup>M</sup> de coin<sup>M</sup> gauche*

left (free) safety
*demi<sup>M</sup> de sûreté<sup>F</sup> gauche*

**playing field for American football**
*terrain<sup>M</sup> de football<sup>M</sup> américain*

inbounds line
*trait<sup>M</sup> de mise<sup>F</sup> au jeu<sup>M</sup>*

goal line
*ligne<sup>F</sup> de but<sup>M</sup>*

fifty-yard line
*ligne<sup>F</sup> de centre<sup>M</sup>*

end zone
*zone<sup>F</sup> de but<sup>M</sup>*

end line
*ligne<sup>F</sup> de fond<sup>M</sup>*

yard line
*ligne<sup>F</sup> des verges<sup>F</sup>*

sideline
*ligne<sup>F</sup> de touche<sup>F</sup>*

American football

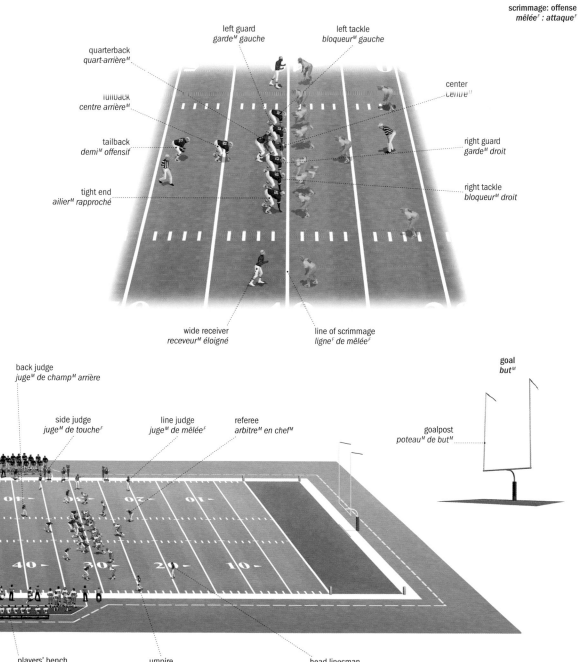

scrimmage: offense
mêlée<sup>F</sup> : attaque<sup>F</sup>

left guard
garde<sup>M</sup> gauche

left tackle
bloqueur<sup>M</sup> gauche

quarterback
quart-arrière<sup>M</sup>

center
centre<sup>M</sup>

tailback
centre arrière<sup>M</sup>

right guard
garde<sup>M</sup> droit

tailback
demi<sup>M</sup> offensif

right tackle
bloqueur<sup>M</sup> droit

tight end
ailier<sup>M</sup> rapproché

wide receiver
receveur<sup>M</sup> éloigné

line of scrimmage
ligne<sup>F</sup> de mêlée<sup>F</sup>

back judge
juge<sup>M</sup> de champ<sup>M</sup> arrière

goal
but<sup>M</sup>

side judge
juge<sup>M</sup> de touche<sup>F</sup>

line judge
juge<sup>M</sup> de mêlée<sup>F</sup>

referee
arbitre<sup>M</sup> en chef<sup>M</sup>

goalpost
poteau<sup>M</sup> de but<sup>M</sup>

players' bench
banc<sup>M</sup> des joueurs<sup>M</sup>

umpire
arbitre<sup>M</sup>

head linesman
juge<sup>M</sup> de ligne<sup>F</sup> en chef<sup>M</sup>

SPORTS AND GAMES

# American football

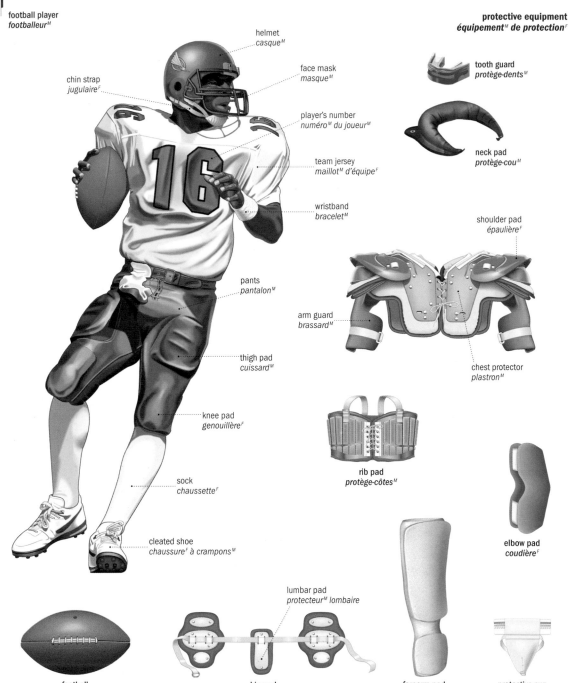

football player
*footballeur*<sup>M</sup>

**protective equipment**
**équipement**<sup>M</sup> **de protection**<sup>F</sup>

helmet
*casque*<sup>M</sup>

face mask
*masque*<sup>M</sup>

chin strap
*jugulaire*<sup>F</sup>

player's number
*numéro*<sup>M</sup> *du joueur*<sup>M</sup>

team jersey
*maillot*<sup>M</sup> *d'équipe*<sup>F</sup>

wristband
*bracelet*<sup>M</sup>

tooth guard
*protège-dents*<sup>M</sup>

neck pad
*protège-cou*<sup>M</sup>

shoulder pad
*épaulière*<sup>F</sup>

pants
*pantalon*<sup>M</sup>

arm guard
*brassard*<sup>M</sup>

chest protector
*plastron*<sup>M</sup>

thigh pad
*cuissard*<sup>M</sup>

knee pad
*genouillère*<sup>F</sup>

rib pad
*protège-côtes*<sup>M</sup>

elbow pad
*coudière*<sup>F</sup>

sock
*chaussette*<sup>F</sup>

cleated shoe
*chaussure*<sup>F</sup> *à crampons*<sup>M</sup>

lumbar pad
*protecteur*<sup>M</sup> *lombaire*

football
*ballon*<sup>M</sup> *de football*<sup>M</sup>

hip pad
*protège-hanche*<sup>M</sup>

forearm pad
*protecteur*<sup>M</sup> *d'avant-bras*<sup>M</sup>

protective cup
*coquille*<sup>F</sup>

SPORTS AND GAMES

# volleyball
*volleyball*<sup>M</sup>

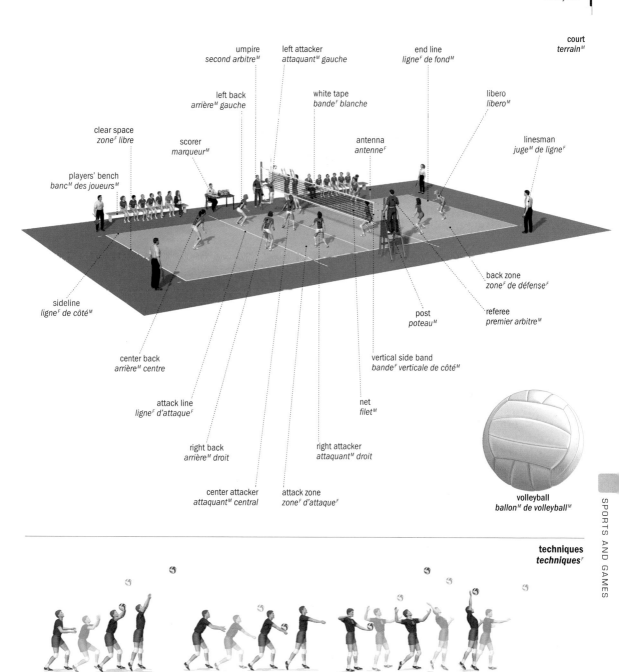

**court**
*terrain*<sup>M</sup>

umpire
*second arbitre*<sup>M</sup>

left attacker
*attaquant*<sup>M</sup> *gauche*

end line
*ligne*<sup>F</sup> *de fond*<sup>M</sup>

left back
*arrière*<sup>M</sup> *gauche*

white tape
*bande*<sup>F</sup> *blanche*

libero
*libero*<sup>M</sup>

clear space
*zone*<sup>F</sup> *libre*

scorer
*marqueur*<sup>M</sup>

antenna
*antenne*<sup>F</sup>

linesman
*juge*<sup>M</sup> *de ligne*<sup>F</sup>

players' bench
*banc*<sup>M</sup> *des joueurs*<sup>M</sup>

sideline
*ligne*<sup>F</sup> *de côté*<sup>M</sup>

back zone
*zone*<sup>F</sup> *de défense*<sup>F</sup>

post
*poteau*<sup>M</sup>

referee
*premier arbitre*<sup>M</sup>

center back
*arrière*<sup>M</sup> *centre*

vertical side band
*bande*<sup>F</sup> *verticale de côté*<sup>M</sup>

attack line
*ligne*<sup>F</sup> *d'attaque*<sup>F</sup>

net
*filet*<sup>M</sup>

right back
*arrière*<sup>M</sup> *droit*

right attacker
*attaquant*<sup>M</sup> *droit*

center attacker
*attaquant*<sup>M</sup> *central*

attack zone
*zone*<sup>F</sup> *d'attaque*<sup>F</sup>

**volleyball**
*ballon*<sup>M</sup> *de volleyball*<sup>M</sup>

**techniques**
*techniques*<sup>F</sup>

tip
*touche*<sup>F</sup>

bump
*manchette*<sup>F</sup>

serve
*service*<sup>M</sup>

SPORTS AND GAMES

# basketball

basketball<sup>M</sup>

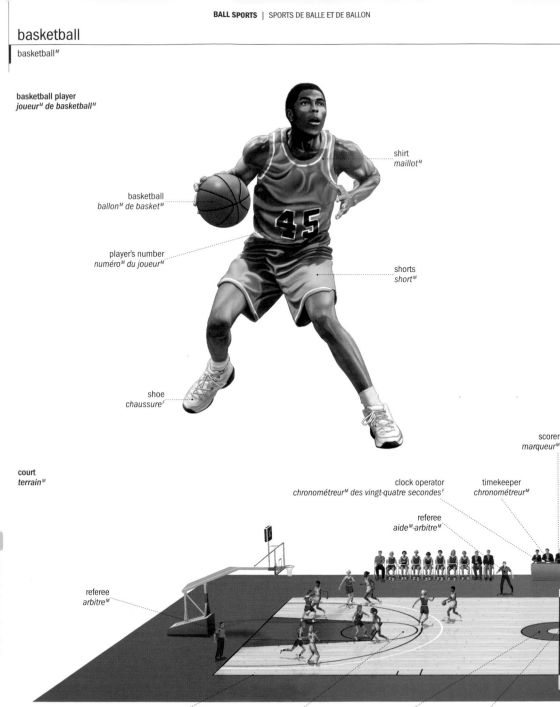

**basketball player**
*joueur<sup>M</sup> de basketball<sup>M</sup>*

shirt
*maillot<sup>M</sup>*

basketball
*ballon<sup>M</sup> de basket<sup>M</sup>*

player's number
*numéro<sup>M</sup> du joueur<sup>M</sup>*

shorts
*short<sup>M</sup>*

shoe
*chaussure<sup>F</sup>*

scorer
*marqueur<sup>M</sup>*

**court**
*terrain<sup>M</sup>*

clock operator
*chronométreur<sup>M</sup> des vingt-quatre secondes<sup>F</sup>*

timekeeper
*chronométreur<sup>M</sup>*

referee
*aide<sup>M</sup>-arbitre<sup>M</sup>*

referee
*arbitre<sup>M</sup>*

sideline
*ligne<sup>F</sup> de touche<sup>F</sup>*

key
*demi-cercle<sup>M</sup>*

restricting circle
*cercle<sup>M</sup> restrictif*

center line
*ligne<sup>F</sup> médiane*

center circle
*cercle<sup>M</sup> central*

SPORTS AND GAMES

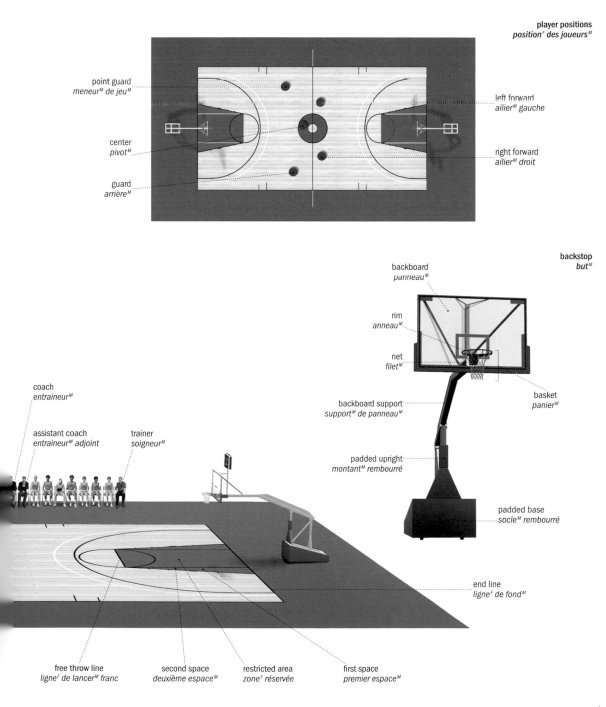

point guard
*meneur*M *de jeu*M

left forward
*ailier*M *gauche*

center
*pivot*M

right forward
*ailier*M *droit*

guard
*arrière*M

backboard
*panneau*M

rim
*anneau*M

net
*filet*M

coach
*entraîneur*M

backboard support
*support*M *de panneau*M

basket
*panier*M

assistant coach
*entraîneur*M *adjoint*

trainer
*soigneur*M

padded upright
*montant*M *rembourré*

padded base
*socle*M *rembourré*

end line
*ligne*F *de fond*M

free throw line
*ligne*F *de lancer*M *franc*

second space
*deuxième espace*M

restricted area
*zone*F *réservée*

first space
*premier espace*M

# tennis
tennis<sup>M</sup>

**court**
*court<sup>M</sup>*

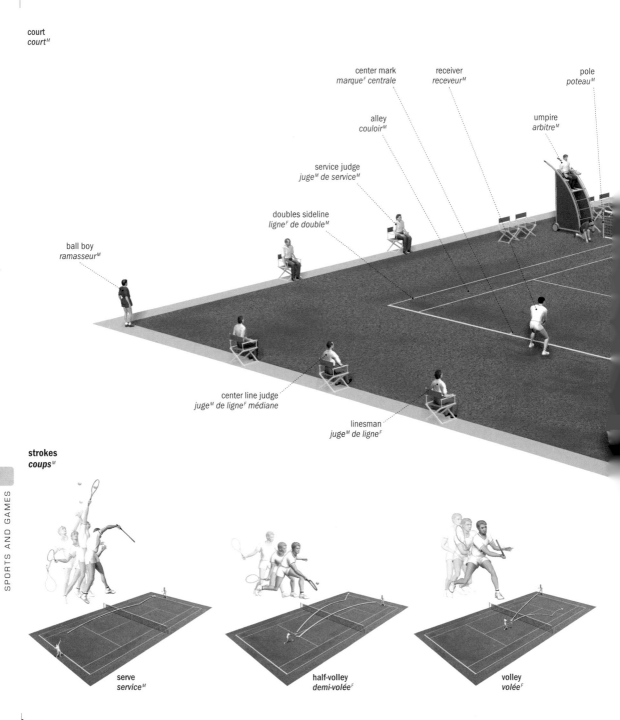

center mark
*marque<sup>F</sup> centrale*

receiver
*receveur<sup>M</sup>*

pole
*poteau<sup>M</sup>*

alley
*couloir<sup>M</sup>*

umpire
*arbitre<sup>M</sup>*

service judge
*juge<sup>M</sup> de service<sup>M</sup>*

doubles sideline
*ligne<sup>F</sup> de double<sup>M</sup>*

ball boy
*ramasseur<sup>M</sup>*

center line judge
*juge<sup>M</sup> de ligne<sup>F</sup> médiane*

linesman
*juge<sup>M</sup> de ligne<sup>F</sup>*

**strokes**
*coups<sup>M</sup>*

serve
*service<sup>M</sup>*

half-volley
*demi-volée<sup>F</sup>*

volley
*volée<sup>F</sup>*

SPORTS AND GAMES

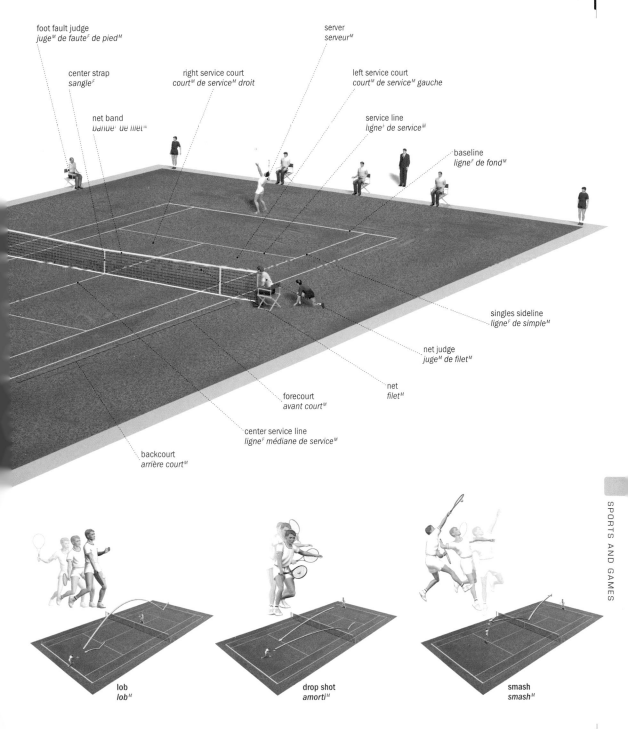

foot fault judge
*juge<sup>M</sup> de faute<sup>F</sup> de pied<sup>M</sup>*

server
*serveur<sup>M</sup>*

center strap
*sangle<sup>F</sup>*

right service court
*court<sup>M</sup> de service<sup>M</sup> droit*

left service court
*court<sup>M</sup> de service<sup>M</sup> gauche*

net band
*bande<sup>F</sup> de filet<sup>M</sup>*

service line
*ligne<sup>F</sup> de service<sup>M</sup>*

baseline
*ligne<sup>F</sup> de fond<sup>M</sup>*

singles sideline
*ligne<sup>F</sup> de simple<sup>M</sup>*

net judge
*juge<sup>M</sup> de filet<sup>M</sup>*

net
*filet<sup>M</sup>*

forecourt
*avant court<sup>M</sup>*

center service line
*ligne<sup>F</sup> médiane de service<sup>M</sup>*

backcourt
*arrière court<sup>M</sup>*

lob
*lob<sup>M</sup>*

drop shot
*amorti<sup>M</sup>*

smash
*smash<sup>M</sup>*

SPORTS AND GAMES

# tennis

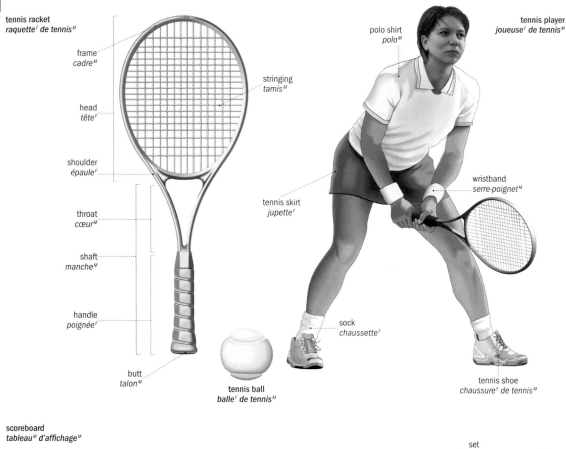

**tennis racket**
*raquette^F de tennis^M*

frame
*cadre^M*

head
*tête^F*

shoulder
*épaule^F*

throat
*cœur^M*

shaft
*manche^M*

handle
*poignée^F*

butt
*talon^M*

stringing
*tamis^M*

tennis ball
*balle^F de tennis^M*

polo shirt
*polo^M*

tennis player
*joueuse^F de tennis^M*

wristband
*serre-poignet^M*

tennis skirt
*jupette^F*

sock
*chaussette^F*

tennis shoe
*chaussure^F de tennis^M*

**scoreboard**
*tableau^M d'affichage^M*

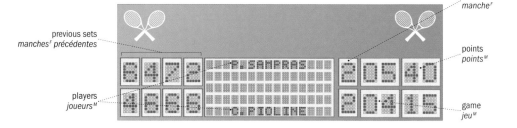

previous sets
*manches^F précédentes*

players
*joueurs^M*

set
*manche^F*

points
*points^M*

game
*jeu^M*

## playing surfaces
*surfaces^F de jeu^M*

grass
*gazon^M*

clay
*terre^F battue*

hard surface (cement)
*surface^F dure (ciment^M)*

synthetic surface
*revêtement^M synthétique*

# table tennis
tennis<sup>M</sup> de table<sup>F</sup>

**table**
*table<sup>F</sup>*

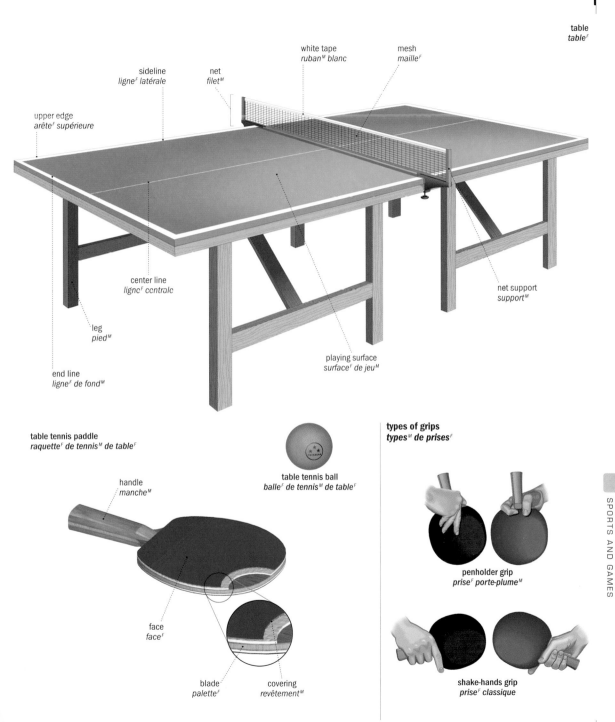

upper edge
*arête<sup>F</sup> supérieure*

sideline
*ligne<sup>F</sup> latérale*

net
*filet<sup>M</sup>*

white tape
*ruban<sup>M</sup> blanc*

mesh
*maille<sup>F</sup>*

center line
*ligne<sup>F</sup> centrale*

leg
*pied<sup>M</sup>*

end line
*ligne<sup>F</sup> de fond<sup>M</sup>*

playing surface
*surface<sup>F</sup> de jeu<sup>M</sup>*

net support
*support<sup>M</sup>*

**table tennis paddle**
*raquette<sup>F</sup> de tennis<sup>M</sup> de table<sup>F</sup>*

handle
*manche<sup>M</sup>*

face
*face<sup>F</sup>*

blade
*palette<sup>F</sup>*

covering
*revêtement<sup>M</sup>*

**table tennis ball**
*balle<sup>F</sup> de tennis<sup>M</sup> de table<sup>F</sup>*

**types of grips**
*types<sup>M</sup> de prises<sup>F</sup>*

penholder grip
*prise<sup>F</sup> porte-plume<sup>M</sup>*

shake-hands grip
*prise<sup>F</sup> classique*

SPORTS AND GAMES

493

# badminton
badminton<sup>M</sup>

court
terrain<sup>M</sup>

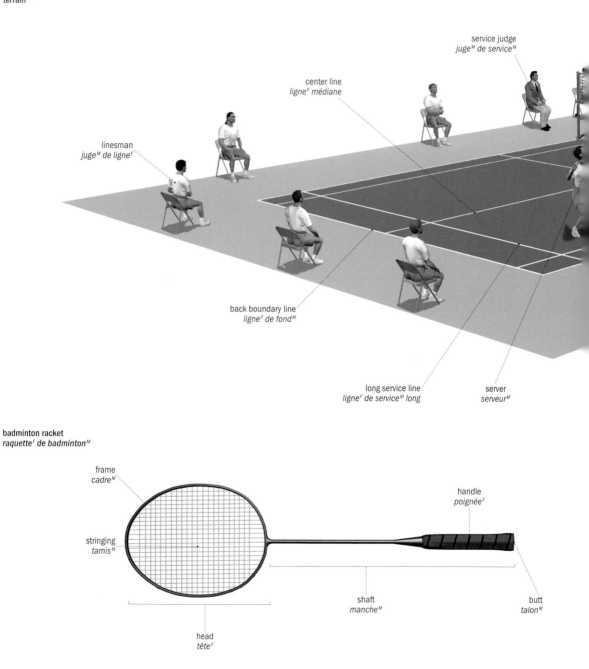

service judge
juge<sup>M</sup> de service<sup>M</sup>

center line
ligne<sup>F</sup> médiane

linesman
juge<sup>M</sup> de ligne<sup>F</sup>

back boundary line
ligne<sup>F</sup> de fond<sup>M</sup>

long service line
ligne<sup>F</sup> de service<sup>M</sup> long

server
serveur<sup>M</sup>

badminton racket
raquette<sup>F</sup> de badminton<sup>M</sup>

frame
cadre<sup>M</sup>

handle
poignée<sup>F</sup>

stringing
tamis<sup>M</sup>

shaft
manche<sup>M</sup>

butt
talon<sup>M</sup>

head
tête<sup>F</sup>

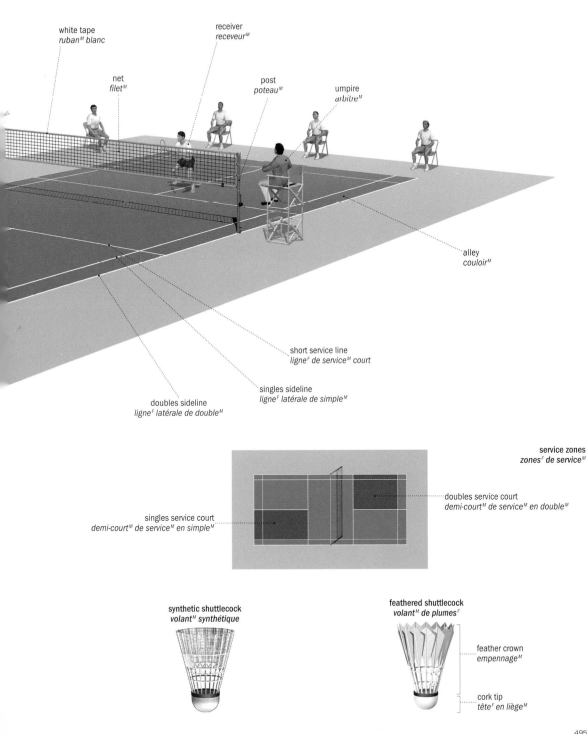

white tape
*ruban*ᴹ *blanc*

receiver
*receveur*ᴹ

net
*filet*ᴹ

post
*poteau*ᴹ

umpire
*arbitre*ᴹ

alley
*couloir*ᴹ

short service line
*ligne*ᶠ *de service*ᴹ *court*

singles sideline
*ligne*ᶠ *latérale de simple*ᴹ

doubles sideline
*ligne*ᶠ *latérale de double*ᴹ

service zones
*zones*ᶠ *de service*ᴹ

doubles service court
*demi-court*ᴹ *de service*ᴹ *en double*ᴹ

singles service court
*demi-court*ᴹ *de service*ᴹ *en simple*ᴹ

synthetic shuttlecock
*volant*ᴹ *synthétique*

feathered shuttlecock
*volant*ᴹ *de plumes*ᶠ

feather crown
*empennage*ᴹ

cork tip
*tête*ᶠ *en liège*ᴹ

# gymnastics

gymnastique<sup>F</sup>

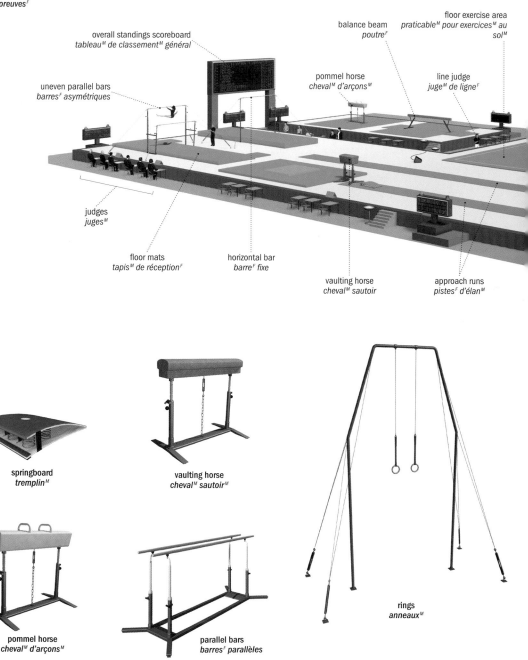

**event platform**
**podium<sup>M</sup> des épreuves<sup>F</sup>**

overall standings scoreboard
tableau<sup>M</sup> de classement<sup>M</sup> général

balance beam
poutre<sup>F</sup>

floor exercise area
praticable<sup>M</sup> pour exercices<sup>M</sup> au
sol<sup>M</sup>

pommel horse
cheval<sup>M</sup> d'arçons<sup>M</sup>

line judge
juge<sup>M</sup> de ligne<sup>F</sup>

uneven parallel bars
barres<sup>F</sup> asymétriques

judges
juges<sup>M</sup>

floor mats
tapis<sup>M</sup> de réception<sup>F</sup>

horizontal bar
barre<sup>F</sup> fixe

vaulting horse
cheval<sup>M</sup> sautoir

approach runs
pistes<sup>F</sup> d'élan<sup>M</sup>

springboard
tremplin<sup>M</sup>

vaulting horse
cheval<sup>M</sup> sautoir<sup>M</sup>

rings
anneaux<sup>M</sup>

pommel horse
cheval<sup>M</sup> d'arçons<sup>M</sup>

parallel bars
barres<sup>F</sup> parallèles

gymnastics

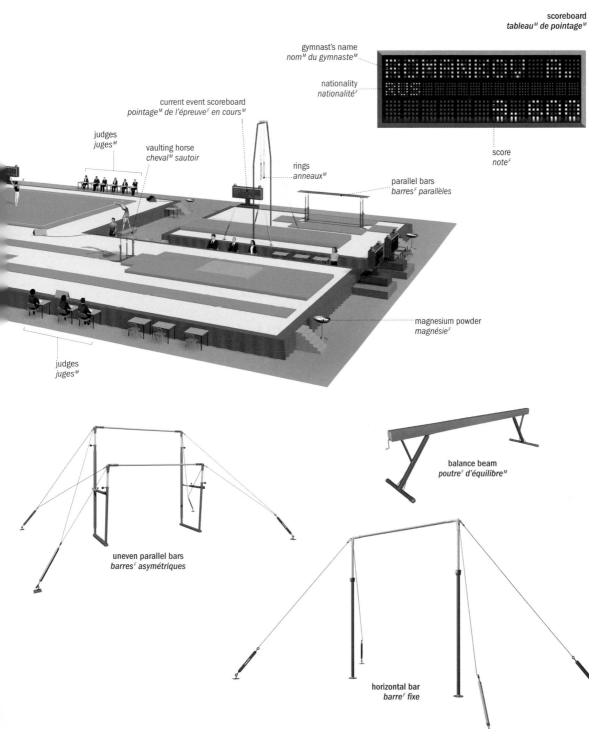

**scoreboard**
*tableau<sup>M</sup> de pointage<sup>M</sup>*

gymnast's name
*nom<sup>M</sup> du gymnaste<sup>M</sup>*

nationality
*nationalité<sup>F</sup>*

current event scoreboard
*pointage<sup>M</sup> de l'épreuve<sup>F</sup> en cours<sup>M</sup>*

judges
*juges<sup>M</sup>*

vaulting horse
*cheval<sup>M</sup> sautoir*

rings
*anneaux<sup>M</sup>*

parallel bars
*barres<sup>F</sup> parallèles*

score
*note<sup>F</sup>*

magnesium powder
*magnésie<sup>F</sup>*

judges
*juges<sup>M</sup>*

uneven parallel bars
*barres<sup>F</sup> asymétriques*

balance beam
*poutre<sup>F</sup> d'équilibre<sup>M</sup>*

horizontal bar
*barre<sup>F</sup> fixe*

SPORTS AND GAMES

497

# boxing

boxe<sup>F</sup>

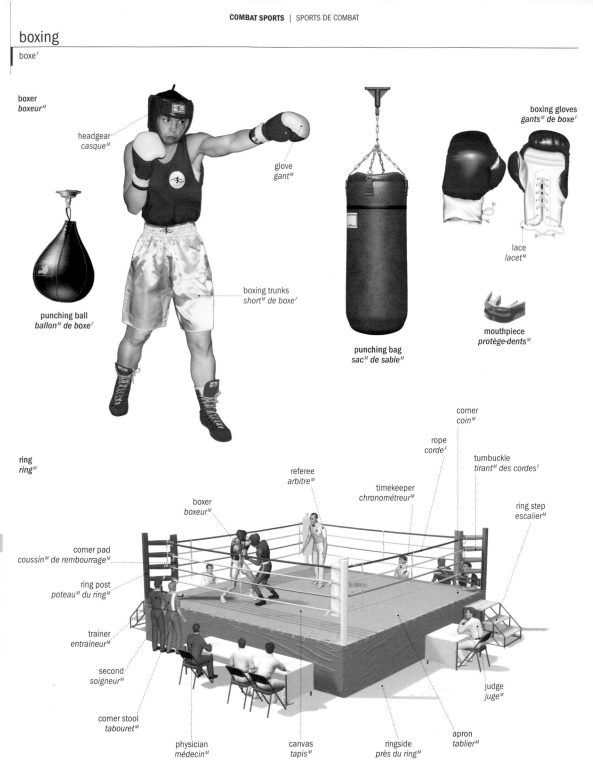

boxer
boxeur<sup>M</sup>

headgear
casque<sup>M</sup>

glove
gant<sup>M</sup>

boxing gloves
gants<sup>M</sup> de boxe<sup>F</sup>

lace
lacet<sup>M</sup>

boxing trunks
short<sup>M</sup> de boxe<sup>F</sup>

punching ball
ballon<sup>M</sup> de boxe<sup>F</sup>

mouthpiece
protège-dents<sup>M</sup>

punching bag
sac<sup>M</sup> de sable<sup>M</sup>

corner
coin<sup>M</sup>

rope
corde<sup>F</sup>

turnbuckle
tirant<sup>M</sup> des cordes<sup>F</sup>

ring
ring<sup>M</sup>

referee
arbitre<sup>M</sup>

timekeeper
chronométreur<sup>M</sup>

ring step
escalier<sup>M</sup>

boxer
boxeur<sup>M</sup>

corner pad
coussin<sup>M</sup> de rembourrage<sup>M</sup>

ring post
poteau<sup>M</sup> du ring<sup>M</sup>

trainer
entraîneur<sup>M</sup>

second
soigneur<sup>M</sup>

judge
juge<sup>M</sup>

corner stool
tabouret<sup>M</sup>

physician
médecin<sup>M</sup>

canvas
tapis<sup>M</sup>

ringside
près du ring<sup>M</sup>

apron
tablier<sup>M</sup>

# judo
judo<sup>M</sup>

scorers and timekeepers
*marqueurs<sup>M</sup> et chronométreurs<sup>M</sup>*

medical team
*équipe<sup>F</sup> médicale*

mat
*tapis<sup>M</sup>*

contestant
*combattant<sup>M</sup>*

safety area
*surface<sup>F</sup> de sécurité<sup>F</sup>*

danger area
*zone<sup>F</sup> de danger<sup>M</sup>*

scoreboard
*tableau<sup>M</sup> d'affichage<sup>M</sup>*

contest area
*surface<sup>F</sup> de combat<sup>M</sup>*

referee
*arbitre<sup>M</sup>*

judge
*juge<sup>M</sup>*

judogi
*judogi<sup>M</sup>*

jacket
*veste<sup>F</sup>*

trousers
*pantalon<sup>M</sup>*

belt
*ceinture<sup>F</sup>*

**examples of holds and throws**
**exemples<sup>M</sup> de prises<sup>F</sup>**

holding
*immobilisation<sup>F</sup>*

stomach throw
*projection<sup>F</sup> en cercle<sup>M</sup>*

sweeping hip throw
*hanche<sup>F</sup> ailée*

major outer reaping throw
*grand fauchage<sup>M</sup> extérieur*

major inner reaping throw
*grand fauchage<sup>M</sup> intérieur*

naked strangle
*étranglement<sup>M</sup>*

arm lock
*clé<sup>F</sup> de bras<sup>M</sup>*

one-arm shoulder throw
*projection<sup>F</sup> d'épaule<sup>F</sup> par un côté<sup>M</sup>*

SPORTS AND GAMES

499

# weightlifting

haltérophilie<sup>F</sup>

barbell
haltère<sup>M</sup> long

wristband
poignet<sup>M</sup> de force<sup>F</sup>

weightlifting belt
ceinture<sup>F</sup> d'haltérophilie<sup>F</sup>

sleeveless jersey
maillot<sup>M</sup> de corps<sup>M</sup>

trunks
culotte<sup>F</sup>

knee wrap
genouillère<sup>F</sup>

strap
lanière<sup>F</sup>

weightlifting shoe
chaussure<sup>F</sup> d'haltérophilie<sup>F</sup>

clean and jerk
épaulé<sup>M</sup>-jeté<sup>M</sup>

snatch
arraché<sup>M</sup>

# fitness equipment

appareils<sup>M</sup> de conditionnement<sup>M</sup> physique

dumbbells
haltères<sup>M</sup> courts

handgrips
poignées<sup>F</sup> à ressort<sup>M</sup>

ankle/wrist weights
bracelets<sup>M</sup> lestés

jump rope
corde<sup>F</sup> à sauter

bar
barre<sup>F</sup>

weight
poids<sup>M</sup>

twist bar
ressort<sup>M</sup> athlétique

chest expander
extenseur<sup>M</sup>

tension spring
ressort<sup>M</sup> de tension<sup>F</sup>

grip
poignée<sup>F</sup>

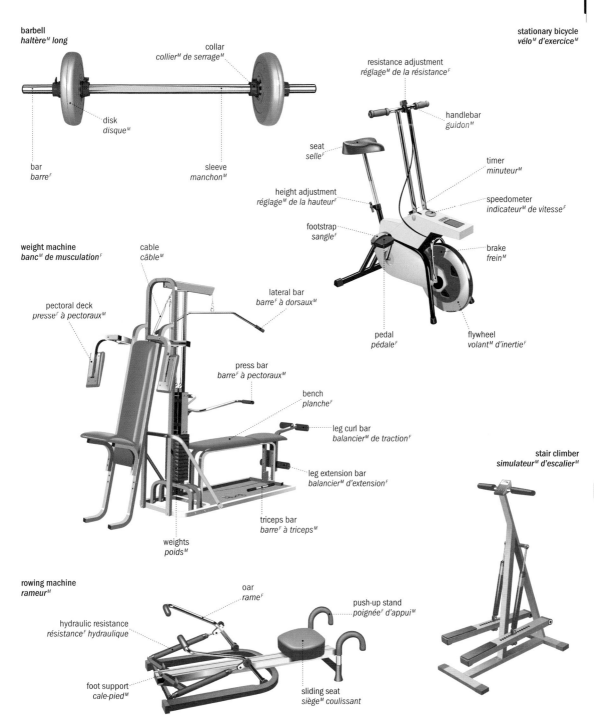

barbell
*haltère*M *long*

collar
*collier*M *de serrage*M

disk
*disque*M

bar
*barre*F

sleeve
*manchon*M

stationary bicycle
*vélo*M *d'exercice*M

resistance adjustment
*réglage*M *de la résistance*F

handlebar
*guidon*M

seat
*selle*F

timer
*minuteur*M

height adjustment
*réglage*M *de la hauteur*F

speedometer
*indicateur*M *de vitesse*F

footstrap
*sangle*F

brake
*frein*M

pedal
*pédale*F

flywheel
*volant*M *d'inertie*F

weight machine
*banc*M *de musculation*F

cable
*câble*M

lateral bar
*barre*F *à dorsaux*M

pectoral deck
*presse*F *à pectoraux*M

press bar
*barre*F *à pectoraux*M

bench
*planche*F

leg curl bar
*balancier*M *de traction*F

leg extension bar
*balancier*M *d'extension*F

triceps bar
*barre*F *à triceps*M

weights
*poids*M

stair climber
*simulateur*M *d'escalier*M

rowing machine
*rameur*M

oar
*rame*F

push-up stand
*poignée*F *d'appui*M

hydraulic resistance
*résistance*F *hydraulique*

foot support
*cale-pied*M

sliding seat
*siège*M *coulissant*

# billiards

billard<sup>M</sup>

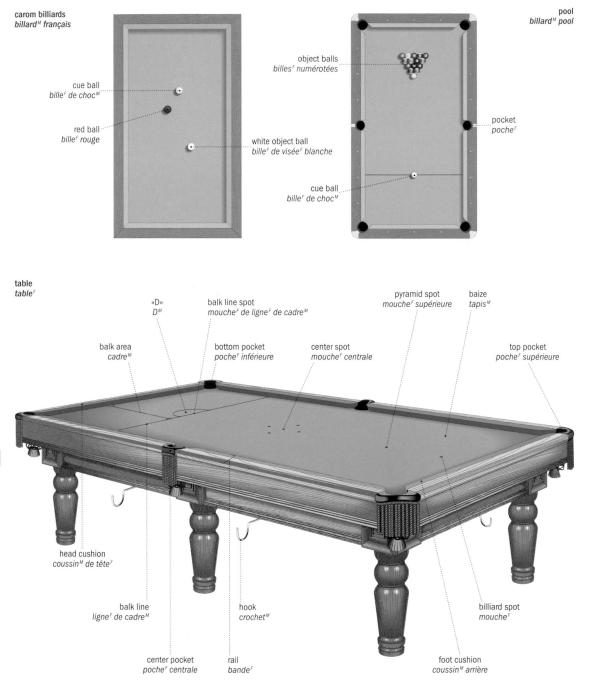

**carom billiards**
*billard<sup>M</sup> français*

**pool**
*billard<sup>M</sup> pool*

cue ball
*bille<sup>F</sup> de choc<sup>M</sup>*

red ball
*bille<sup>F</sup> rouge*

white object ball
*bille<sup>F</sup> de visée<sup>F</sup> blanche*

object balls
*billes<sup>F</sup> numérotées*

pocket
*poche<sup>F</sup>*

cue ball
*bille<sup>F</sup> de choc<sup>M</sup>*

**table**
*table<sup>F</sup>*

«D»
*D<sup>M</sup>*

balk line spot
*mouche<sup>F</sup> de ligne<sup>F</sup> de cadre<sup>M</sup>*

pyramid spot
*mouche<sup>F</sup> supérieure*

baize
*tapis<sup>M</sup>*

balk area
*cadre<sup>M</sup>*

bottom pocket
*poche<sup>F</sup> inférieure*

center spot
*mouche<sup>F</sup> centrale*

top pocket
*poche<sup>F</sup> supérieure*

head cushion
*coussin<sup>M</sup> de tête<sup>F</sup>*

balk line
*ligne<sup>F</sup> de cadre<sup>M</sup>*

hook
*crochet<sup>M</sup>*

billiard spot
*mouche<sup>F</sup>*

center pocket
*poche<sup>F</sup> centrale*

rail
*bande<sup>F</sup>*

foot cushion
*coussin<sup>M</sup> arrière*

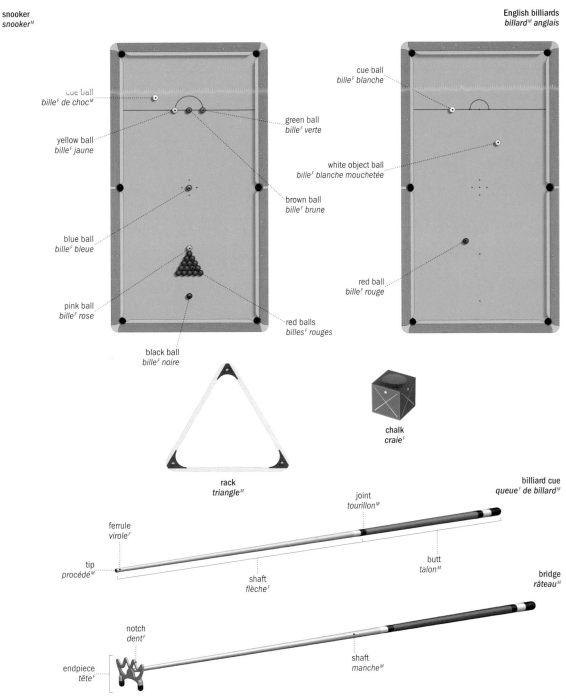

snooker
*snooker*<sup>M</sup>

English billiards
*billard*<sup>M</sup> *anglais*

cue ball
*bille*<sup>F</sup> *de choc*<sup>M</sup>

cue ball
*bille*<sup>F</sup> *blanche*

green ball
*bille*<sup>F</sup> *verte*

yellow ball
*bille*<sup>F</sup> *jaune*

white object ball
*bille*<sup>F</sup> *blanche mouchetée*

brown ball
*bille*<sup>F</sup> *brune*

blue ball
*bille*<sup>F</sup> *bleue*

pink ball
*bille*<sup>F</sup> *rose*

red ball
*bille*<sup>F</sup> *rouge*

red balls
*billes*<sup>F</sup> *rouges*

black ball
*bille*<sup>F</sup> *noire*

chalk
*craie*<sup>F</sup>

rack
*triangle*<sup>M</sup>

billiard cue
*queue*<sup>F</sup> *de billard*<sup>M</sup>

joint
*tourillon*<sup>M</sup>

ferrule
*virole*<sup>F</sup>

butt
*talon*<sup>M</sup>

tip
*procédé*<sup>M</sup>

shaft
*flèche*<sup>F</sup>

bridge
*râteau*<sup>M</sup>

notch
*dent*<sup>F</sup>

shaft
*manche*<sup>M</sup>

endpiece
*tête*<sup>F</sup>

SPORTS AND GAMES

503

# golf

golf^M

**course**
*parcours*^M

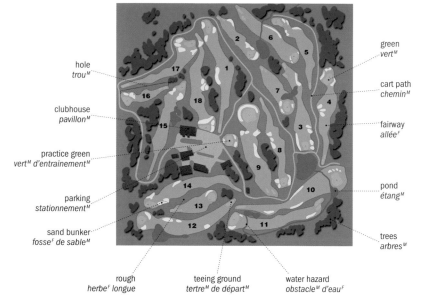

hole
*trou*^M

clubhouse
*pavillon*^M

practice green
*vert*^M *d'entraînement*^M

parking
*stationnement*^M

sand bunker
*fosse*^F *de sable*^M

green
*vert*^M

cart path
*chemin*^M

fairway
*allée*^F

pond
*étang*^M

trees
*arbres*^M

rough
*herbe*^F *longue*

teeing ground
*tertre*^M *de départ*^M

water hazard
*obstacle*^M *d'eau*^F

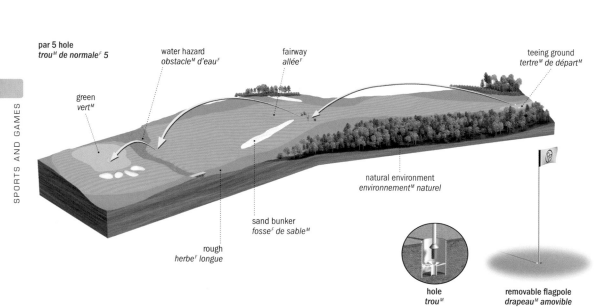

**par 5 hole**
*trou*^M *de normale*^F *5*

water hazard
*obstacle*^M *d'eau*^F

fairway
*allée*^F

teeing ground
*tertre*^M *de départ*^M

green
*vert*^M

natural environment
*environnement*^M *naturel*

sand bunker
*fosse*^F *de sable*^M

rough
*herbe*^F *longue*

hole
*trou*^M

removable flagpole
*drapeau*^M *amovible*

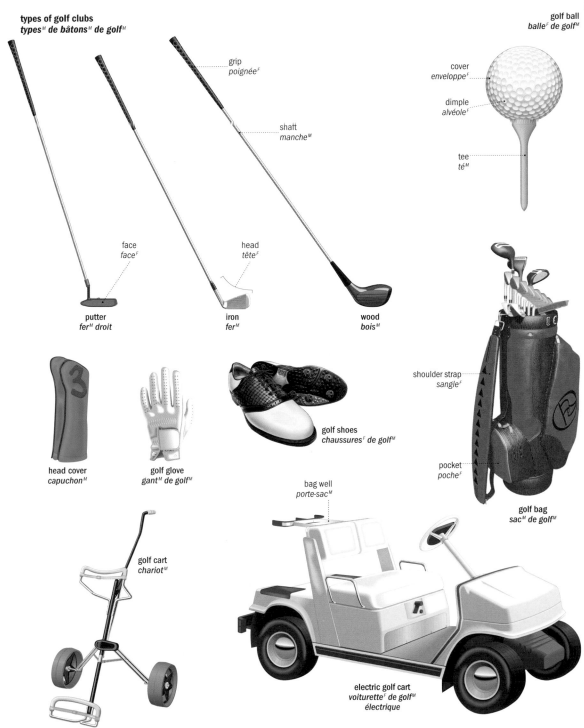

**types of golf clubs**
*types^M de bâtons^M de golf^M*

grip
*poignée^F*

shaft
*manche^M*

face
*face^F*

head
*tête^F*

putter
*fer^M droit*

iron
*fer^M*

wood
*bois^M*

**golf ball**
*balle^F de golf^M*

cover
*enveloppe^F*

dimple
*alvéole^F*

tee
*té^M*

head cover
*capuchon^M*

golf glove
*gant^M de golf^M*

golf shoes
*chaussures^F de golf^M*

shoulder strap
*sangle^F*

pocket
*poche^F*

golf bag
*sac^M de golf^M*

bag well
*porte-sac^M*

golf cart
*chariot^M*

electric golf cart
*voiturette^F de golf^M*
*électrique*

SPORTS AND GAMES

# ice hockey

hockey^M sur glace^F

**ice hockey player**
*hockeyeur^M*

helmet
*casque^M*

visor
*visière^F*

player's number
*numéro^M du joueur^M*

team's emblem
*emblème^M d'équipe^F*

glove
*gant^M*

pants
*culotte^F*

stocking
*bas^M*

skate
*patin^M*

blade
*lame^F*

butt end
*embout^M*

**player's stick**
*crosse^F de joueur^M ; bâton^M de joueur^M*

shaft
*manche^M*

heel
*talon^M*

blade
*lame^F*

**rink**
*patinoire^F*

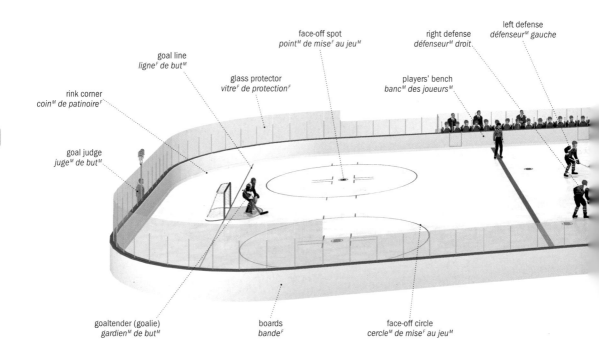

goal line
*ligne^F de but^M*

face-off spot
*point^M de mise^F au jeu^M*

right defense
*défenseur^M droit*

left defense
*défenseur^M gauche*

glass protector
*vitre^F de protection^F*

players' bench
*banc^M des joueurs^M*

rink corner
*coin^M de patinoire^F*

goal judge
*juge^M de but^M*

goaltender (goalie)
*gardien^M de but^M*

boards
*bande^F*

face-off circle
*cercle^M de mise^F au jeu^M*

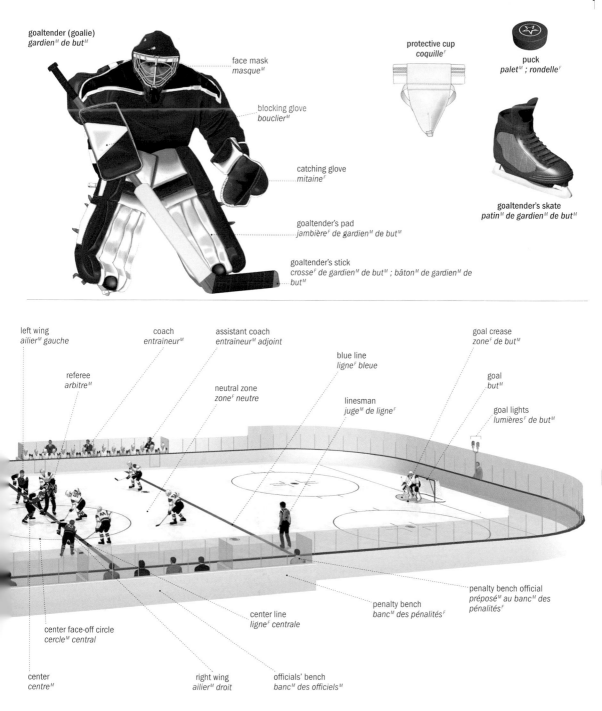

goaltender (goalie)
*gardien<sup>M</sup> de but<sup>M</sup>*

face mask
*masque<sup>M</sup>*

blocking glove
*bouclier<sup>M</sup>*

catching glove
*mitaine<sup>F</sup>*

goaltender's pad
*jambière<sup>F</sup> de gardien<sup>M</sup> de but<sup>M</sup>*

goaltender's stick
*crosse<sup>F</sup> de gardien<sup>M</sup> de but<sup>M</sup> ; bâton<sup>M</sup> de gardien<sup>M</sup> de but<sup>M</sup>*

protective cup
*coquille<sup>F</sup>*

puck
*palet<sup>M</sup> ; rondelle<sup>F</sup>*

goaltender's skate
*patin<sup>M</sup> de gardien<sup>M</sup> de but<sup>M</sup>*

left wing
*ailier<sup>M</sup> gauche*

coach
*entraîneur<sup>M</sup>*

assistant coach
*entraîneur<sup>M</sup> adjoint*

referee
*arbitre<sup>M</sup>*

neutral zone
*zone<sup>F</sup> neutre*

blue line
*ligne<sup>F</sup> bleue*

linesman
*juge<sup>M</sup> de ligne<sup>F</sup>*

goal crease
*zone<sup>F</sup> de but<sup>M</sup>*

goal
*but<sup>M</sup>*

goal lights
*lumières<sup>F</sup> de but<sup>M</sup>*

penalty bench official
*préposé<sup>M</sup> au banc<sup>M</sup> des pénalités<sup>F</sup>*

penalty bench
*banc<sup>M</sup> des pénalités<sup>F</sup>*

center line
*ligne<sup>F</sup> centrale*

center face-off circle
*cercle<sup>M</sup> central*

center
*centre<sup>M</sup>*

right wing
*ailier<sup>M</sup> droit*

officials' bench
*banc<sup>M</sup> des officiels<sup>M</sup>*

SPORTS AND GAMES

# speed skating

patinage$^M$ de vitesse$^F$

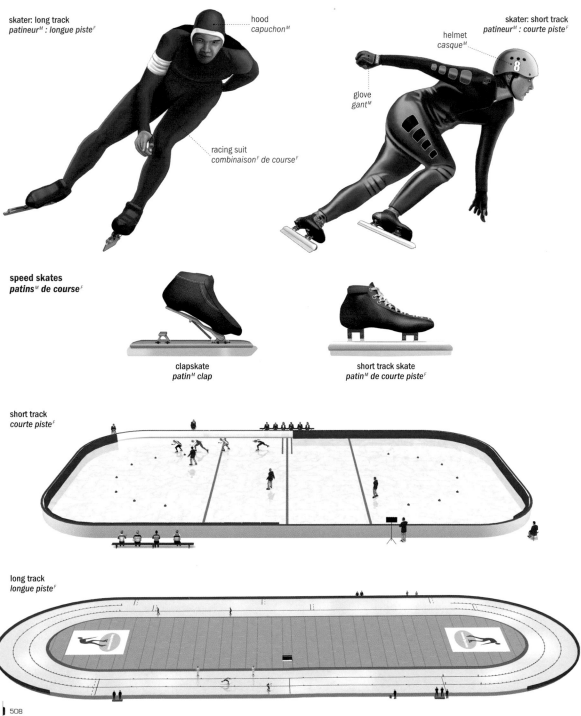

skater: long track
*patineur$^M$ : longue piste$^F$*

hood
*capuchon$^M$*

skater: short track
*patineur$^M$ : courte piste$^F$*

helmet
*casque$^M$*

glove
*gant$^M$*

racing suit
*combinaison$^F$ de course$^F$*

**speed skates**
*patins$^M$ de course$^F$*

clapskate
*patin$^M$ clap*

short track skate
*patin$^M$ de courte piste$^F$*

short track
*courte piste$^F$*

long track
*longue piste$^F$*

# figure skating
patinage<sup>M</sup> artistique

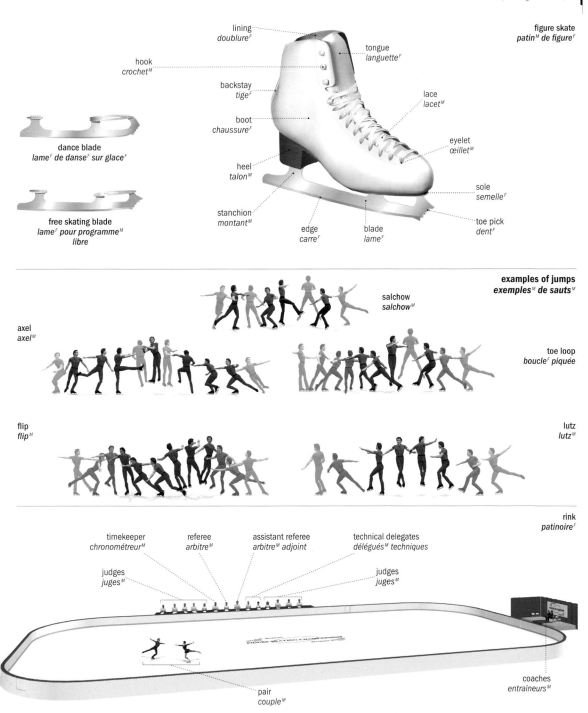

**figure skate**
*patin<sup>M</sup> de figure<sup>F</sup>*

lining
*doublure<sup>F</sup>*

tongue
*languette<sup>F</sup>*

hook
*crochet<sup>M</sup>*

backstay
*tige<sup>F</sup>*

lace
*lacet<sup>M</sup>*

boot
*chaussure<sup>F</sup>*

eyelet
*œillet<sup>M</sup>*

**dance blade**
*lame<sup>F</sup> de danse<sup>F</sup> sur glace<sup>F</sup>*

heel
*talon<sup>M</sup>*

sole
*semelle<sup>F</sup>*

**free skating blade**
*lame<sup>F</sup> pour programme<sup>M</sup>
libre*

stanchion
*montant<sup>M</sup>*

edge
*carre<sup>F</sup>*

blade
*lame<sup>F</sup>*

toe pick
*dent<sup>F</sup>*

**examples of jumps**
*exemples<sup>M</sup> de sauts<sup>M</sup>*

salchow
*salchow<sup>M</sup>*

axel
*axel<sup>M</sup>*

toe loop
*boucle<sup>F</sup> piquée*

flip
*flip<sup>M</sup>*

lutz
*lutz<sup>M</sup>*

rink
*patinoire<sup>F</sup>*

timekeeper
*chronométreur<sup>M</sup>*

referee
*arbitre<sup>M</sup>*

assistant referee
*arbitre<sup>M</sup> adjoint*

technical delegates
*délégués<sup>M</sup> techniques*

judges
*juges<sup>M</sup>*

judges
*juges<sup>M</sup>*

coaches
*entraineurs<sup>M</sup>*

pair
*couple<sup>M</sup>*

SPORTS AND GAMES

509

# alpine skiing

ski^M alpin

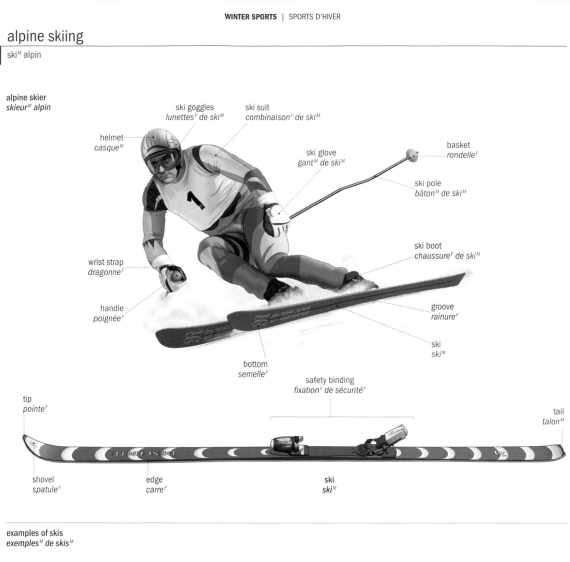

alpine skier
*skieur^M alpin*

ski goggles
*lunettes^F de ski^M*

ski suit
*combinaison^F de ski^M*

helmet
*casque^M*

ski glove
*gant^M de ski^M*

basket
*rondelle^F*

ski pole
*bâton^M de ski^M*

ski boot
*chaussure^F de ski^M*

wrist strap
*dragonne^F*

groove
*rainure^F*

handle
*poignée^F*

ski
*ski^M*

bottom
*semelle^F*

safety binding
*fixation^F de sécurité^F*

tip
*pointe^F*

tail
*talon^M*

shovel
*spatule^F*

edge
*carre^F*

ski
*ski^M*

examples of skis
*exemples^M de skis^M*

slalom ski
*ski^M de slalom^M*

giant slalom ski
*ski^M de grand slalom^M*

downhill and Super-G ski
*ski^M de descente^F/super-G^M*

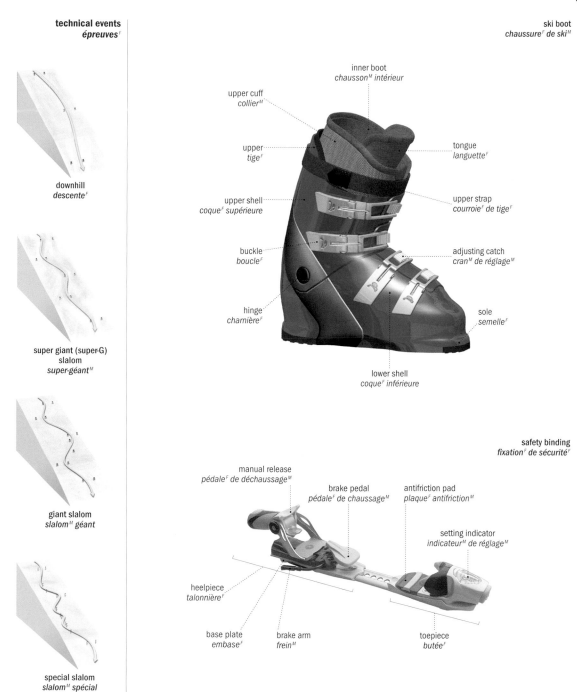

**technical events**
*épreuves*<sup>F</sup>

downhill
*descente*<sup>F</sup>

super giant (super-G)
slalom
*super-géant*<sup>M</sup>

giant slalom
*slalom*<sup>M</sup> *géant*

special slalom
*slalom*<sup>M</sup> *spécial*

ski boot
*chaussure*<sup>F</sup> *de ski*<sup>M</sup>

inner boot
*chausson*<sup>M</sup> *intérieur*

upper cuff
*collier*<sup>M</sup>

upper
*tige*<sup>F</sup>

tongue
*languette*<sup>F</sup>

upper shell
*coque*<sup>F</sup> *supérieure*

upper strap
*courroie*<sup>F</sup> *de tige*<sup>F</sup>

buckle
*boucle*<sup>F</sup>

adjusting catch
*cran*<sup>M</sup> *de réglage*<sup>M</sup>

hinge
*charnière*<sup>F</sup>

sole
*semelle*<sup>F</sup>

lower shell
*coque*<sup>F</sup> *inférieure*

safety binding
*fixation*<sup>F</sup> *de sécurité*<sup>F</sup>

manual release
*pédale*<sup>F</sup> *de déchaussage*<sup>M</sup>

brake pedal
*pédale*<sup>F</sup> *de chaussage*<sup>M</sup>

antifriction pad
*plaque*<sup>F</sup> *antifriction*<sup>M</sup>

setting indicator
*indicateur*<sup>M</sup> *de réglage*<sup>M</sup>

heelpiece
*talonnière*<sup>F</sup>

base plate
*embase*<sup>F</sup>

brake arm
*frein*<sup>M</sup>

toepiece
*butée*<sup>F</sup>

# ski resort

station^F de ski^M

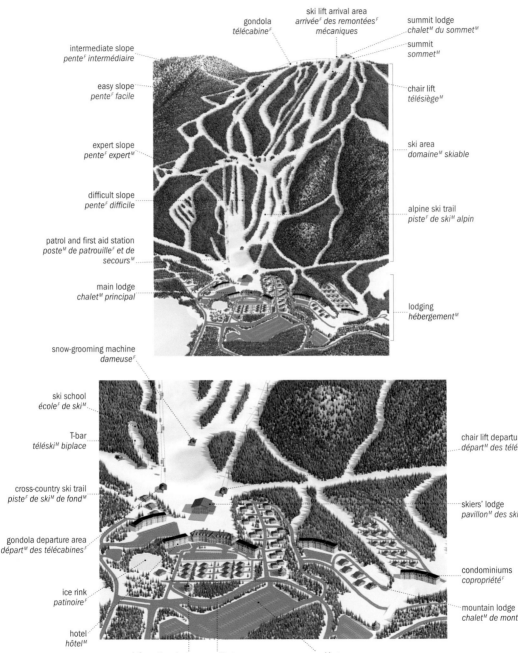

intermediate slope
pente^F intermédiaire

easy slope
pente^F facile

expert slope
pente^F expert^M

difficult slope
pente^F difficile

patrol and first aid station
poste^M de patrouille^F et de
secours^M

main lodge
chalet^M principal

gondola
télécabine^F

ski lift arrival area
arrivée^F des remontées^F
mécaniques

summit lodge
chalet^M du sommet^M

summit
sommet^M

chair lift
télésiège^M

ski area
domaine^M skiable

alpine ski trail
piste^F de ski^M alpin

lodging
hébergement^M

snow-grooming machine
dameuse^F

ski school
école^F de ski^M

T-bar
téléski^M biplace

cross-country ski trail
piste^F de ski^M de fond^M

gondola departure area
départ^M des télécabines^F

ice rink
patinoire^F

hotel
hôtel^M

information desk
renseignements^M

village
village^M

parking
parc^M de stationnement^M ;
stationnement^M

chair lift departure area
départ^M des télésièges^M

skiers' lodge
pavillon^M des skieurs^M

condominiums
copropriété^F

mountain lodge
chalet^M de montagne^F

# snowboarding

surf<sup>M</sup> des neiges<sup>F</sup>

snowboarder
*surfeur<sup>M</sup>*

helmet
*casque<sup>M</sup>*

goggles
*lunettes<sup>F</sup>*

coveralls
*combinaison<sup>F</sup>*

shin guard
*protège-tibia<sup>M</sup>*

glove
*gant<sup>M</sup>*

snowboard
*surf<sup>M</sup> des neiges<sup>F</sup>*

hard boot
*botte<sup>F</sup> rigide*

flexible boot
*botte<sup>F</sup> souple*

freestyle snowboard
*surf<sup>M</sup> acrobatique*

alpine snowboard
*surf<sup>M</sup> alpin*

# ski jumping

saut<sup>M</sup> à ski<sup>M</sup>

ski jumper
*sauteur<sup>M</sup>*

ski jumping suit
*combinaison<sup>F</sup> de saut<sup>M</sup> à ski<sup>M</sup>*

helmet
*casque<sup>M</sup>*

glove
*gant<sup>M</sup>*

ski jumping boot
*chaussure<sup>F</sup> de saut<sup>M</sup> à ski<sup>M</sup>*

jumping ski
*ski<sup>M</sup> de saut<sup>M</sup>*

binding
*fixation<sup>F</sup>*

SPORTS AND GAMES

513

# cross-country skiing

ski<sup>M</sup> de fond<sup>M</sup>

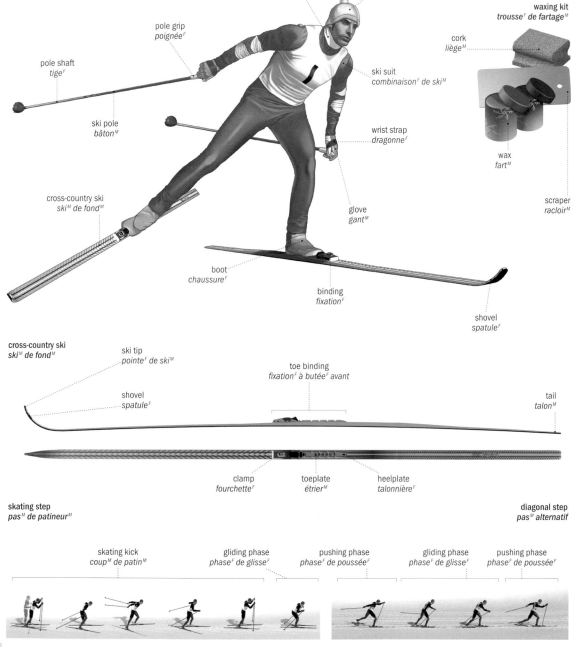

**cross-country skier**
*skieur<sup>M</sup> de fond<sup>M</sup>*

turtleneck
*col<sup>M</sup> roulé*

ski hat
*bonnet<sup>M</sup> ; tuque<sup>F</sup>*

**waxing kit**
*trousse<sup>F</sup> de fartage<sup>M</sup>*

pole grip
*poignée<sup>F</sup>*

cork
*liège<sup>M</sup>*

pole shaft
*tige<sup>F</sup>*

ski suit
*combinaison<sup>F</sup> de ski<sup>M</sup>*

ski pole
*bâton<sup>M</sup>*

wrist strap
*dragonne<sup>F</sup>*

wax
*fart<sup>M</sup>*

cross-country ski
*ski<sup>M</sup> de fond<sup>M</sup>*

glove
*gant<sup>M</sup>*

scraper
*racloir<sup>M</sup>*

boot
*chaussure<sup>F</sup>*

binding
*fixation<sup>F</sup>*

shovel
*spatule<sup>F</sup>*

**cross-country ski**
*ski<sup>M</sup> de fond<sup>M</sup>*

ski tip
*pointe<sup>F</sup> de ski<sup>M</sup>*

toe binding
*fixation<sup>F</sup> à butée<sup>F</sup> avant*

tail
*talon<sup>M</sup>*

shovel
*spatule<sup>F</sup>*

clamp
*fourchette<sup>F</sup>*

toeplate
*étrier<sup>M</sup>*

heelplate
*talonnière<sup>F</sup>*

**skating step**
*pas<sup>M</sup> de patineur<sup>M</sup>*

**diagonal step**
*pas<sup>M</sup> alternatif*

skating kick
*coup<sup>M</sup> de patin<sup>M</sup>*

gliding phase
*phase<sup>F</sup> de glisse<sup>F</sup>*

pushing phase
*phase<sup>F</sup> de poussée<sup>F</sup>*

gliding phase
*phase<sup>F</sup> de glisse<sup>F</sup>*

pushing phase
*phase<sup>F</sup> de poussée<sup>F</sup>*

SPORTS AND GAMES

# curling
curling<sup>M</sup>

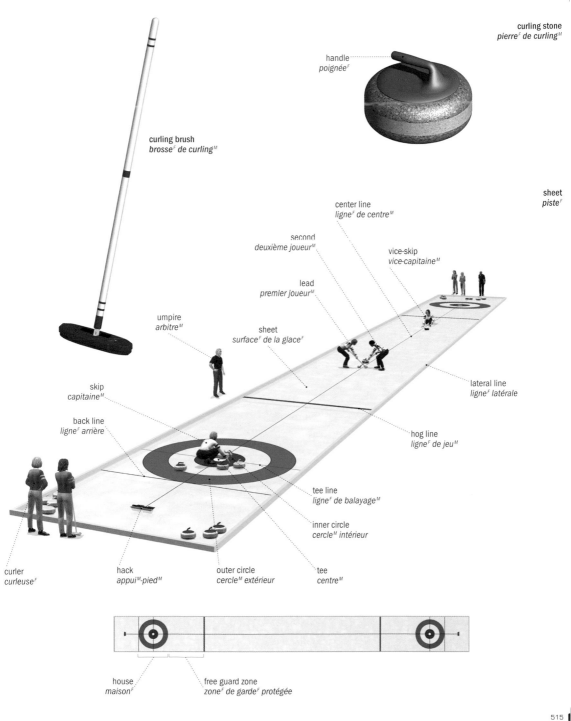

**curling stone**
*pierre<sup>F</sup> de curling<sup>M</sup>*

handle
*poignée<sup>F</sup>*

**sheet**
*piste<sup>F</sup>*

**curling brush**
*brosse<sup>F</sup> de curling<sup>M</sup>*

center line
*ligne<sup>F</sup> de centre<sup>M</sup>*

second
*deuxième joueur<sup>M</sup>*

vice-skip
*vice-capitaine<sup>M</sup>*

lead
*premler joueur<sup>M</sup>*

umpire
*arbitre<sup>M</sup>*

sheet
*surface<sup>F</sup> de la glace<sup>F</sup>*

lateral line
*ligne<sup>F</sup> latérale*

skip
*capitaine<sup>M</sup>*

back line
*ligne<sup>F</sup> arrière*

hog line
*ligne<sup>F</sup> de jeu<sup>M</sup>*

tee line
*ligne<sup>F</sup> de balayage<sup>M</sup>*

inner circle
*cercle<sup>M</sup> intérieur*

curler
*curleuse<sup>F</sup>*

hack
*appui<sup>M</sup>-pied<sup>M</sup>*

outer circle
*cercle<sup>M</sup> extérieur*

tee
*centre<sup>M</sup>*

house
*maison<sup>F</sup>*

free guard zone
*zone<sup>F</sup> de garde<sup>F</sup> protégée*

SPORTS AND GAMES

515

# swimming

natation<sup>F</sup>

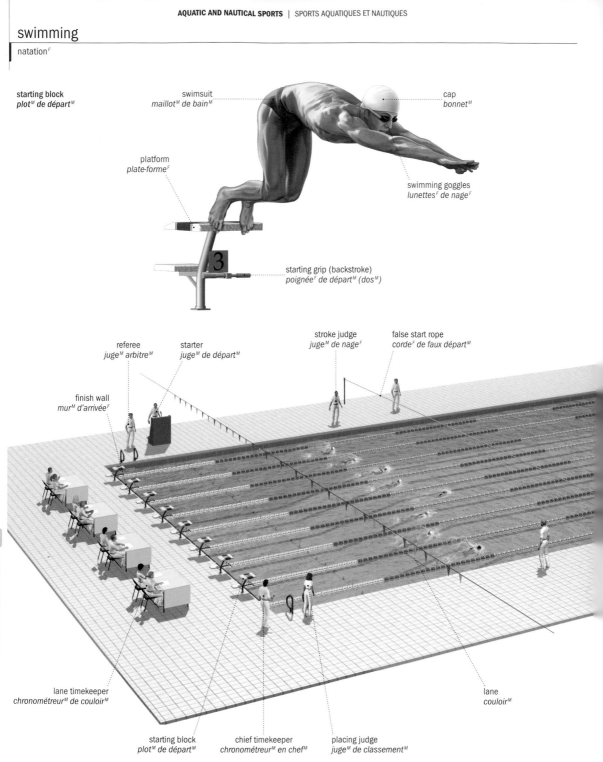

**starting block**
*plot<sup>M</sup> de départ<sup>M</sup>*

**swimsuit**
*maillot<sup>M</sup> de bain<sup>M</sup>*

**cap**
*bonnet<sup>M</sup>*

**platform**
*plate-forme<sup>F</sup>*

**swimming goggles**
*lunettes<sup>F</sup> de nage<sup>F</sup>*

**starting grip (backstroke)**
*poignée<sup>F</sup> de départ<sup>M</sup> (dos<sup>M</sup>)*

**referee**
*juge<sup>M</sup> arbitre<sup>M</sup>*

**starter**
*juge<sup>M</sup> de départ<sup>M</sup>*

**stroke judge**
*juge<sup>M</sup> de nage<sup>F</sup>*

**false start rope**
*corde<sup>F</sup> de faux départ<sup>M</sup>*

**finish wall**
*mur<sup>M</sup> d'arrivée<sup>F</sup>*

**lane timekeeper**
*chronométreur<sup>M</sup> de couloir<sup>M</sup>*

**lane**
*couloir<sup>M</sup>*

**starting block**
*plot<sup>M</sup> de départ<sup>M</sup>*

**chief timekeeper**
*chronométreur<sup>M</sup> en chef<sup>M</sup>*

**placing judge**
*juge<sup>M</sup> de classement<sup>M</sup>*

**types of strokes**
*types<sup>M</sup> de nages<sup>F</sup>*

front crawl
*crawl<sup>M</sup>*

butterfly stroke
*papillon<sup>M</sup>*

breaststroke
*brasse<sup>F</sup>*

backstroke
*nage<sup>F</sup> sur le dos<sup>M</sup>*

backstroke turn indicator
*repère<sup>M</sup> de virage<sup>M</sup> de dos<sup>M</sup>*

sidewall
*mur<sup>M</sup> latéral*

turning wall
*mur<sup>M</sup> de virage<sup>M</sup>*

turning judges
*juges<sup>M</sup> de virages<sup>M</sup>*

competitive course
*bassin<sup>M</sup> de compétition<sup>F</sup>*

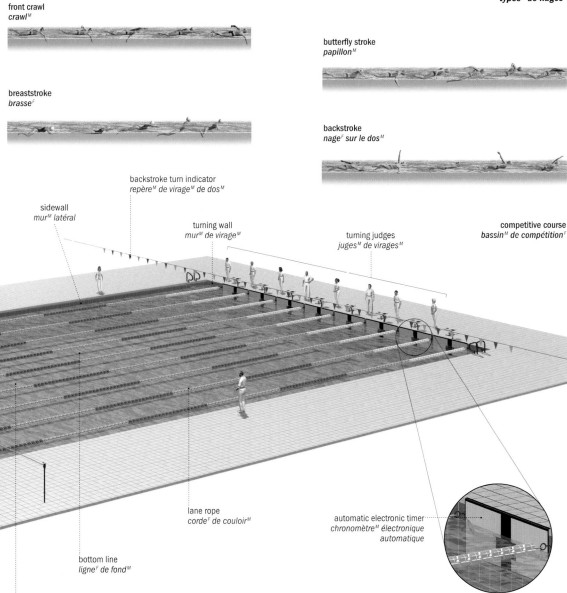

lane rope
*corde<sup>F</sup> de couloir<sup>M</sup>*

automatic electronic timer
*chronomètre<sup>M</sup> électronique automatique*

bottom line
*ligne<sup>F</sup> de fond<sup>M</sup>*

swimming pool
*bassin<sup>M</sup>*

SPORTS AND GAMES

# diving

plongeon<sup>M</sup>

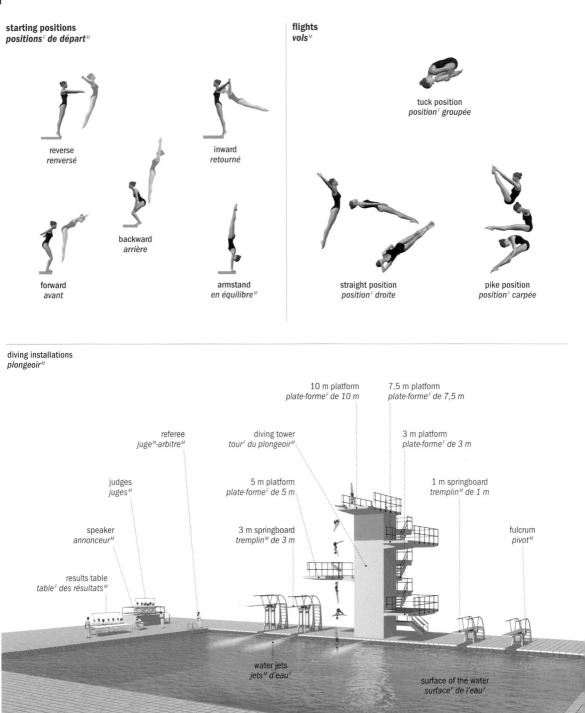

**starting positions**
*positions<sup>F</sup> de départ<sup>M</sup>*

reverse
*renversé*

inward
*retourné*

forward
*avant*

backward
*arrière*

armstand
*en équilibre<sup>M</sup>*

**flights**
*vols<sup>M</sup>*

tuck position
*position<sup>F</sup> groupée*

straight position
*position<sup>F</sup> droite*

pike position
*position<sup>F</sup> carpée*

**diving installations**
*plongeoir<sup>M</sup>*

10 m platform
*plate-forme<sup>F</sup> de 10 m*

7.5 m platform
*plate-forme<sup>F</sup> de 7,5 m*

referee
*juge<sup>M</sup>-arbitre<sup>M</sup>*

diving tower
*tour<sup>F</sup> du plongeoir<sup>M</sup>*

3 m platform
*plate-forme<sup>F</sup> de 3 m*

judges
*juges<sup>M</sup>*

5 m platform
*plate-forme<sup>F</sup> de 5 m*

1 m springboard
*tremplin<sup>M</sup> de 1 m*

speaker
*annonceur<sup>M</sup>*

3 m springboard
*tremplin<sup>M</sup> de 3 m*

fulcrum
*pivot<sup>M</sup>*

results table
*table<sup>F</sup> des résultats<sup>M</sup>*

water jets
*jets<sup>M</sup> d'eau<sup>F</sup>*

surface of the water
*surface<sup>F</sup> de l'eau<sup>F</sup>*

SPORTS AND GAMES

# sailboard
planche<sup>F</sup> à voile<sup>F</sup>

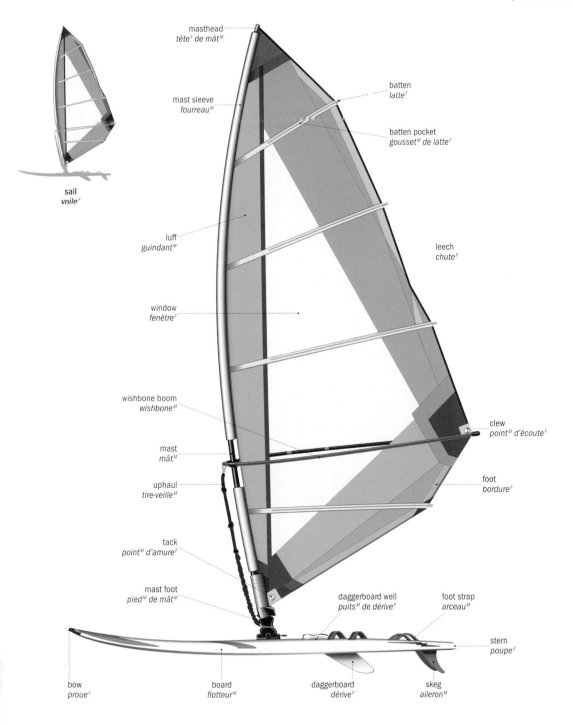

sail
voile<sup>F</sup>

masthead
tête<sup>F</sup> de mât<sup>M</sup>

mast sleeve
fourreau<sup>M</sup>

batten
latte<sup>F</sup>

batten pocket
gousset<sup>M</sup> de latte<sup>F</sup>

luff
guindant<sup>M</sup>

leech
chute<sup>F</sup>

window
fenêtre<sup>F</sup>

wishbone boom
wishbone<sup>M</sup>

clew
point<sup>M</sup> d'écoute<sup>F</sup>

mast
mât<sup>M</sup>

foot
bordure<sup>F</sup>

uphaul
tire-veille<sup>M</sup>

tack
point<sup>M</sup> d'amure<sup>F</sup>

mast foot
pied<sup>M</sup> de mât<sup>M</sup>

daggerboard well
puits<sup>M</sup> de dérive<sup>F</sup>

foot strap
arceau<sup>M</sup>

stern
poupe<sup>F</sup>

bow
proue<sup>F</sup>

board
flotteur<sup>M</sup>

daggerboard
dérive<sup>F</sup>

skeg
aileron<sup>M</sup>

SPORTS AND GAMES

# sailing

*voile*<sup>F</sup>

**sailboat**
*dériveur*<sup>M</sup>

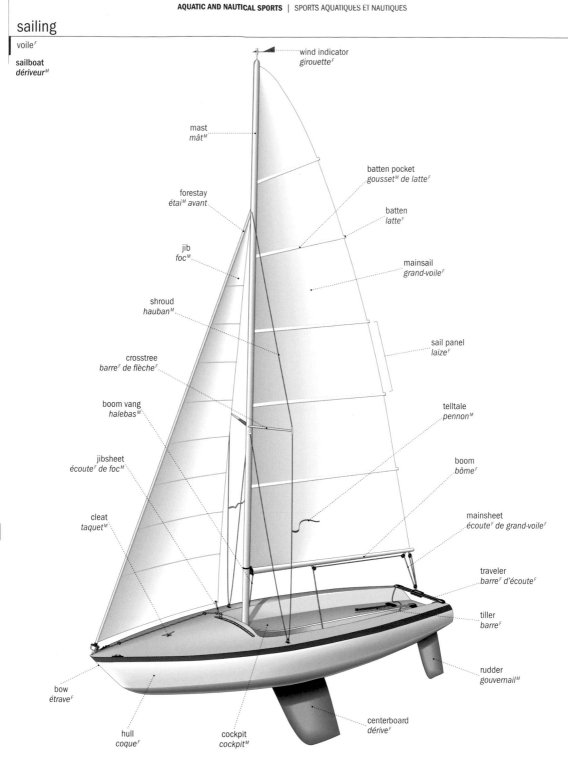

wind indicator
*girouette*<sup>F</sup>

mast
*mât*<sup>M</sup>

batten pocket
*gousset*<sup>M</sup> *de latte*<sup>F</sup>

forestay
*étai*<sup>M</sup> *avant*

batten
*latte*<sup>F</sup>

jib
*foc*<sup>M</sup>

mainsail
*grand-voile*<sup>F</sup>

shroud
*hauban*<sup>M</sup>

sail panel
*laize*<sup>F</sup>

crosstree
*barre*<sup>F</sup> *de flèche*<sup>F</sup>

boom vang
*halebas*<sup>M</sup>

telltale
*pennon*<sup>M</sup>

jibsheet
*écoute*<sup>F</sup> *de foc*<sup>M</sup>

boom
*bôme*<sup>F</sup>

cleat
*taquet*<sup>M</sup>

mainsheet
*écoute*<sup>F</sup> *de grand-voile*<sup>F</sup>

traveler
*barre*<sup>F</sup> *d'écoute*<sup>F</sup>

tiller
*barre*<sup>F</sup>

bow
*étrave*<sup>F</sup>

rudder
*gouvernail*<sup>M</sup>

hull
*coque*<sup>F</sup>

cockpit
*cockpit*<sup>M</sup>

centerboard
*dérive*<sup>F</sup>

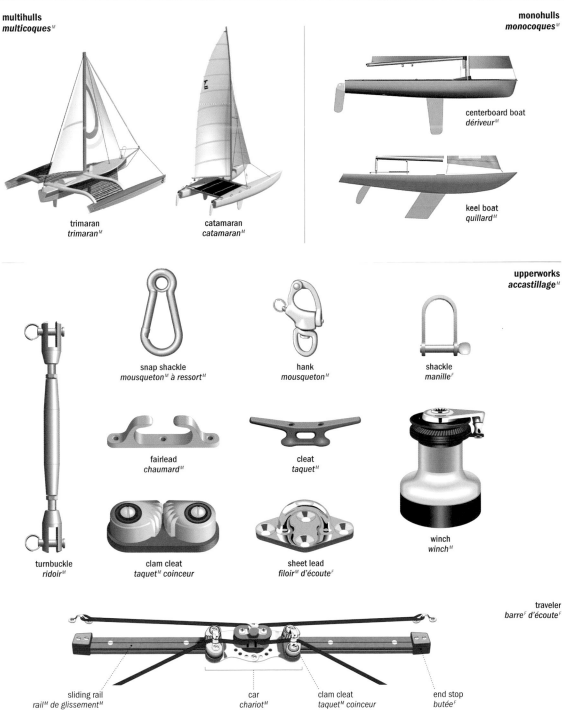

**multihulls**
*multicoques* M

**monohulls**
*monocoques* M

centerboard boat
*dériveur* M

keel boat
*quillard* M

trimaran
*trimaran* M

catamaran
*catamaran* M

**upperworks**
*accastillage* M

snap shackle
*mousqueton* M *à ressort* M

hank
*mousqueton* M

shackle
*manille* F

fairlead
*chaumard* M

cleat
*taquet* M

turnbuckle
*ridoir* M

clam cleat
*taquet* M *coinceur*

sheet lead
*filoir* M *d'écoute* F

winch
*winch* M

traveler
*barre* F *d'écoute* F

sliding rail
*rail* M *de glissement* M

car
*chariot* M

clam cleat
*taquet* M *coinceur*

end stop
*butée* F

SPORTS AND GAMES

# road racing

cyclisme<sup>M</sup> sur route<sup>F</sup>

**road-racing bicycle and cyclist**
*vélo<sup>M</sup> de course<sup>F</sup> et cycliste<sup>M</sup>*

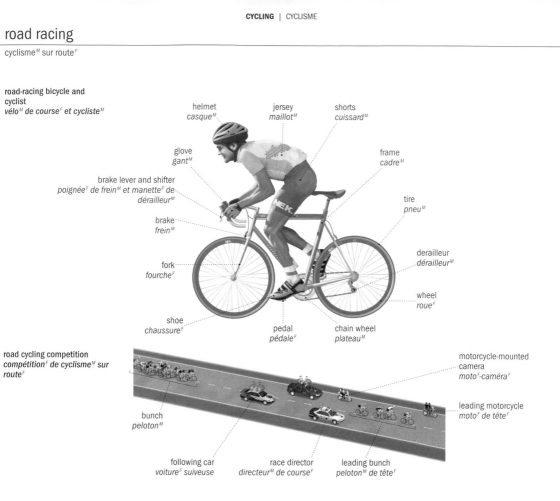

helmet
casque<sup>M</sup>

jersey
maillot<sup>M</sup>

shorts
cuissard<sup>M</sup>

glove
gant<sup>M</sup>

frame
cadre<sup>M</sup>

brake lever and shifter
poignée<sup>F</sup> de frein<sup>M</sup> et manette<sup>F</sup> de dérailleur<sup>M</sup>

tire
pneu<sup>M</sup>

brake
frein<sup>M</sup>

derailleur
dérailleur<sup>M</sup>

fork
fourche<sup>F</sup>

wheel
roue<sup>F</sup>

shoe
chaussure<sup>F</sup>

pedal
pédale<sup>F</sup>

chain wheel
plateau<sup>M</sup>

**road cycling competition**
*compétition<sup>F</sup> de cyclisme<sup>M</sup> sur route<sup>F</sup>*

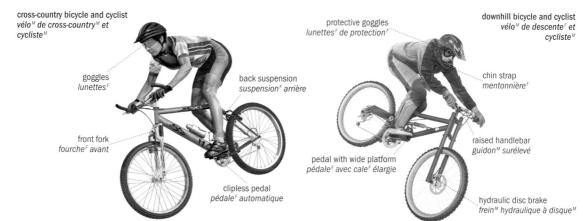

motorcycle-mounted camera
moto<sup>F</sup>-caméra<sup>F</sup>

leading motorcycle
moto<sup>F</sup> de tête<sup>F</sup>

bunch
peloton<sup>M</sup>

following car
voiture<sup>F</sup> suiveuse

race director
directeur<sup>M</sup> de course<sup>F</sup>

leading bunch
peloton<sup>M</sup> de tête<sup>F</sup>

# mountain biking

vélo<sup>M</sup> de montagne<sup>F</sup>

**cross-country bicycle and cyclist**
*vélo<sup>M</sup> de cross-country<sup>M</sup> et cycliste<sup>M</sup>*

protective goggles
lunettes<sup>F</sup> de protection<sup>F</sup>

**downhill bicycle and cyclist**
*vélo<sup>M</sup> de descente<sup>F</sup> et cycliste<sup>M</sup>*

goggles
lunettes<sup>F</sup>

back suspension
suspension<sup>F</sup> arrière

chin strap
mentonnière<sup>F</sup>

front fork
fourche<sup>F</sup> avant

raised handlebar
guidon<sup>M</sup> surélevé

pedal with wide platform
pédale<sup>F</sup> avec cale<sup>F</sup> élargie

clipless pedal
pédale<sup>F</sup> automatique

hydraulic disc brake
frein<sup>M</sup> hydraulique à disque<sup>M</sup>

# personal watercraft

scooter<sup>M</sup> de mer<sup>F</sup> ; *motomarine*<sup>F</sup>

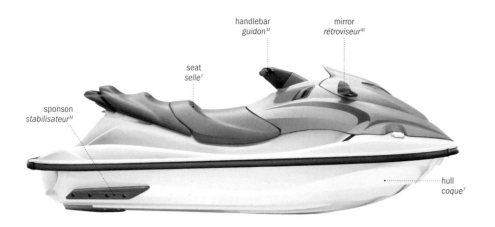

handlebar
*guidon*<sup>M</sup>

mirror
*rétroviseur*<sup>M</sup>

seat
*selle*<sup>F</sup>

sponson
*stabilisateur*<sup>M</sup>

hull
*coque*<sup>F</sup>

# snowmobile

*motoneige*<sup>F</sup>

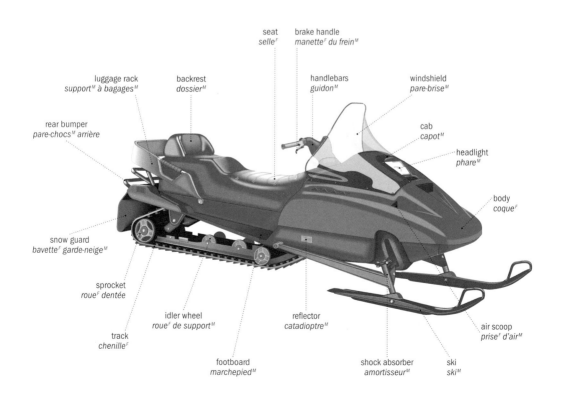

seat
*selle*<sup>F</sup>

brake handle
*manette*<sup>F</sup> *du frein*<sup>M</sup>

luggage rack
*support*<sup>M</sup> *à bagages*<sup>M</sup>

backrest
*dossier*<sup>M</sup>

handlebars
*guidon*<sup>M</sup>

windshield
*pare-brise*<sup>M</sup>

rear bumper
*pare-chocs*<sup>M</sup> *arrière*

cab
*capot*<sup>M</sup>

headlight
*phare*<sup>M</sup>

body
*coque*<sup>F</sup>

snow guard
*bavette*<sup>F</sup> *garde-neige*<sup>M</sup>

sprocket
*roue*<sup>F</sup> *dentée*

idler wheel
*roue*<sup>F</sup> *de support*<sup>M</sup>

reflector
*catadioptre*<sup>M</sup>

air scoop
*prise*<sup>F</sup> *d'air*<sup>M</sup>

track
*chenille*<sup>F</sup>

footboard
*marchepied*<sup>M</sup>

shock absorber
*amortisseur*<sup>M</sup>

ski
*ski*<sup>M</sup>

SPORTS AND GAMES

# car racing

course<sup>F</sup> automobile

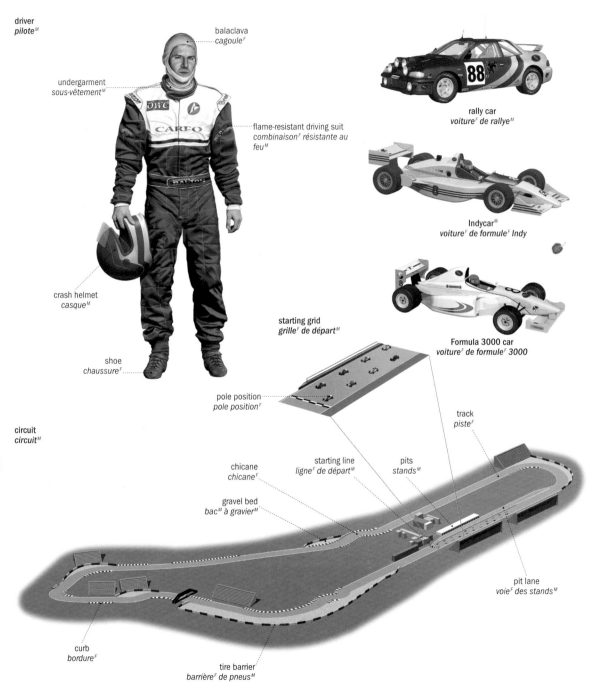

driver
pilote<sup>M</sup>

balaclava
cagoule<sup>F</sup>

undergarment
sous-vêtement<sup>M</sup>

flame-resistant driving suit
combinaison<sup>F</sup> résistante au
feu<sup>M</sup>

crash helmet
casque<sup>M</sup>

shoe
chaussure<sup>F</sup>

rally car
voiture<sup>F</sup> de rallye<sup>M</sup>

Indycar®
voiture<sup>F</sup> de formule<sup>F</sup> Indy

Formula 3000 car
voiture<sup>F</sup> de formule<sup>F</sup> 3000

starting grid
grille<sup>F</sup> de départ<sup>M</sup>

pole position
pole position<sup>F</sup>

circuit
circuit<sup>M</sup>

track
piste<sup>F</sup>

chicane
chicane<sup>F</sup>

starting line
ligne<sup>F</sup> de départ<sup>M</sup>

pits
stands<sup>M</sup>

gravel bed
bac<sup>M</sup> à gravier<sup>M</sup>

pit lane
voie<sup>F</sup> des stands<sup>M</sup>

curb
bordure<sup>F</sup>

tire barrier
barrière<sup>F</sup> de pneus<sup>M</sup>

SPORTS AND GAMES

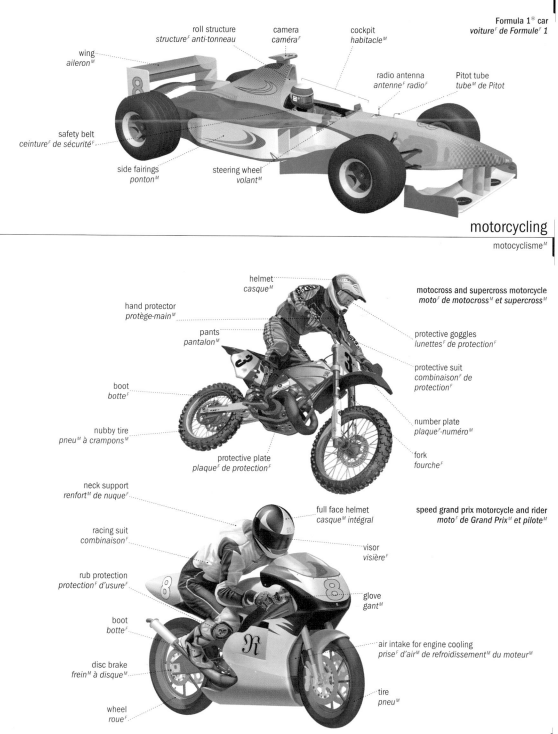

Formula 1 ® car
*voiture*F *de Formule*F *1*

wing
*aileron*M

roll structure
*structure*F *anti-tonneau*

camera
*caméra*F

cockpit
*habitacle*M

radio antenna
*antenne*F *radio*F

Pitot tube
*tube*M *de Pitot*

safety belt
*ceinture*F *de sécurité*F

side fairings
*ponton*M

steering wheel
*volant*M

# motorcycling

*motocyclisme*M

helmet
*casque*M

hand protector
*protège-main*M

pants
*pantalon*M

boot
*botte*F

nubby tire
*pneu*M *à crampons*M

protective plate
*plaque*F *de protection*F

motocross and supercross motorcycle
*moto*F *de motocross*M *et supercross*M

protective goggles
*lunettes*F *de protection*F

protective suit
*combinaison*F *de protection*F

number plate
*plaque*F-*numéro*M

fork
*fourche*F

neck support
*renfort*M *de nuque*F

racing suit
*combinaison*F

rub protection
*protection*F *d'usure*F

boot
*botte*F

disc brake
*frein*M *à disque*M

wheel
*roue*F

full face helmet
*casque*M *intégral*

visor
*visière*F

glove
*gant*M

air intake for engine cooling
*prise*F *d'air*M *de refroidissement*M *du moteur*M

tire
*pneu*M

speed grand prix motorcycle and rider
*moto*F *de Grand Prix*M *et pilote*M

SPORTS AND GAMES

# skateboarding

planche^F à roulettes^F

skateboard
*planche^F à roulettes^F*

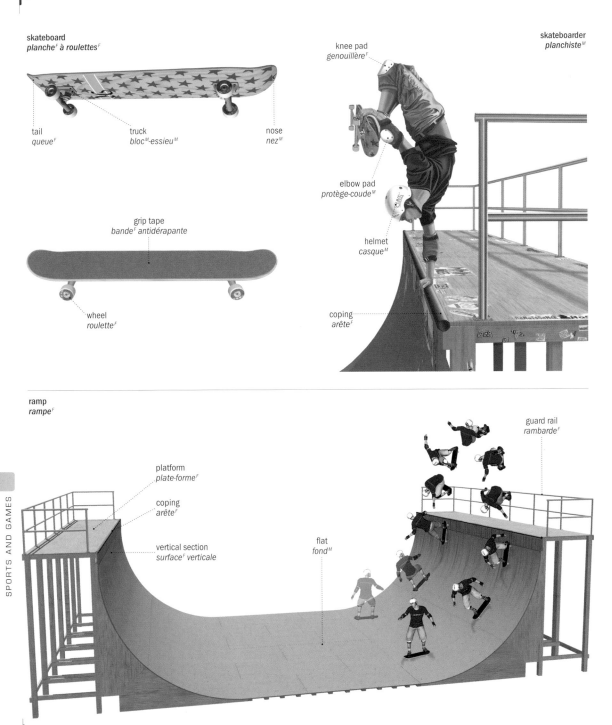

knee pad
*genouillère^F*

skateboarder
*planchiste^M*

tail
*queue^F*

truck
*bloc^M-essieu^M*

nose
*nez^M*

elbow pad
*protège-coude^M*

grip tape
*bande^F antidérapante*

helmet
*casque^M*

wheel
*roulette^F*

coping
*arête^F*

ramp
*rampe^F*

guard rail
*rambarde^F*

platform
*plate-forme^F*

coping
*arête^F*

vertical section
*surface^F verticale*

flat
*fond^M*

# in-line skating

patin<sup>M</sup> à roues<sup>F</sup> alignées

acrobatic skate
*patin*<sup>M</sup> *acrobatique*

inner boot
*chausson*<sup>M</sup> *intérieur*

upper shell
*coque*<sup>F</sup> *supérieure*

skater
*patineuse*<sup>F</sup>

helmet
*casque*<sup>M</sup>

frame
*platine*<sup>F</sup>

wheel
*roue*<sup>F</sup>

elbow pad
*coudière*<sup>F</sup>

knee pad
*genouillère*<sup>F</sup>

wrist guard
*protège-poignet*<sup>M</sup>

in-line speed skate
*patin*<sup>M</sup> *de vitesse*<sup>F</sup>

in-line skate
*patin*<sup>M</sup> *à roues*<sup>F</sup> *alignées*

upper shell
*coque*<sup>F</sup> *supérieure*

inner boot
*chausson*<sup>M</sup> *intérieur*

adjusting buckle
*boucle*<sup>F</sup> *de réglage*<sup>M</sup>

in-line hockey skate
*patin*<sup>M</sup> *de hockey*<sup>M</sup>

boot
*chaussure*<sup>F</sup>

axle
*essieu*<sup>M</sup>

heel stop
*frein*<sup>M</sup> *de talon*<sup>M</sup>

wheel
*roue*<sup>F</sup>

truck
*bloc*<sup>M</sup>*-essieu*<sup>M</sup>

SPORTS AND GAMES

527

# camping

camping<sup>M</sup>

**examples of tents**
*exemples<sup>M</sup> de tentes<sup>F</sup>*

rainfly
double toit<sup>M</sup>

two-person tent
tente<sup>F</sup> deux places<sup>F</sup>

door
porte<sup>F</sup>

canopy
auvent<sup>M</sup>

guy line
hauban<sup>M</sup>

stake
piquet<sup>M</sup>

strainer
tendeur<sup>M</sup>

elastic strainer
Sandow<sup>®M</sup>

zipper
fermeture<sup>F</sup> à glissière<sup>F</sup>

inner tent
tente<sup>F</sup> intérieure

**family tent**
*tente<sup>F</sup> familiale*

window canopy
auvent<sup>M</sup> de fenêtre<sup>F</sup>

living room
séjour<sup>M</sup>

guy line
hauban<sup>M</sup>

elastic strainer
Sandow<sup>®M</sup>

bedroom
chambre<sup>F</sup>

sewn-in floor
tapis<sup>M</sup> de sol<sup>M</sup> cousu

wall
mur<sup>M</sup>

stake loop
boucle<sup>F</sup> de piquet<sup>M</sup>

canvas divider
cloison<sup>F</sup>

frame
armature<sup>F</sup>

screen window
fenêtre<sup>F</sup> moustiquaire<sup>F</sup>

**wagon tent**
*tente<sup>F</sup> grange<sup>F</sup>*

**wall tent**
*tente<sup>F</sup> rectangulaire*

SPORTS AND GAMES

pup tent
*tente*F *canadienne*

rainfly
*double toit*M

roof pole
*mât*M *de toit*M

elastic strainer
*Sandow*®M

inner tent
*tente*F *intérieure*

door
*porte*F

stake loop
*boucle*F *de piquet*M

sewn-in floor
*tapis*M *de sol*M *cousu*

stake
*piquet*M

one-person tent
*tente*F *individuelle*

dome tent
*tente*F *dôme*M

pop-up tent
*tente*F *igloo*M

**propane or butane accessories**
*accessoires*M *au propane*M *ou au butane*M

lantern
*lanterne*F

globe
*globe*M

burner frame
*bâti*M *du brûleur*M

pressure regulator
*régulateur*M *de pression*F

pump
*pompe*F

leakproof cap
*bouchon*M *antifuite*

heater
*chaufferette*F

tank
*réservoir*M

double-burner camp stove
*réchaud*M *à deux feux*M

burner
*brûleur*M

tank
*réservoir*M

wire support
*grille*F *stabilisatrice*

single-burner camp stove
*réchaud*M *à un feu*M

control valve
*robinet*M *relais*M

SPORTS AND GAMES

529

camping

**examples of sleeping bags**
*exemples^M de sacs^M de couchage^M*

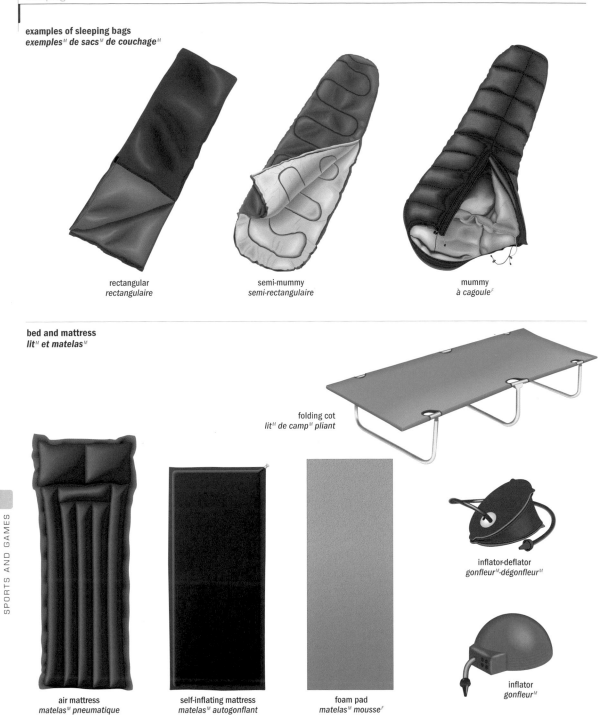

rectangular
*rectangulaire*

semi-mummy
*semi-rectangulaire*

mummy
*à cagoule^F*

**bed and mattress**
*lit^M et matelas^M*

folding cot
*lit^M de camp^M pliant*

inflator-deflator
*gonfleur^M-dégonfleur^M*

inflator
*gonfleur^M*

air mattress
*matelas^M pneumatique*

self-inflating mattress
*matelas^M autogonflant*

foam pad
*matelas^M mousse^F*

SPORTS AND GAMES

cutlery set
*ustensiles*^M *de campeur*^M

**cooking set**
**popote**^F

spoon
*cuiller*^F

belt loop
*ganse*^F

plate
*assiette*^F *plate*

sheath
*étui*^M

fork
*fourchette*^F

knife
*couteau*^M

saucepan
*faitout*^M

handle
*queue*^F

frying pan
*poêle*^F

coffee pot
*cafetière*^F

cup
*tasse*^F

**camping equipment**
**matériel**^M **de camping**^M

scissors
*ciseaux*^M

fish scaler
*écailleur*^M

ruler
*règle*^F *graduée*

magnifier
*loupe*^F

file
*lime*^F

**Swiss Army knife**
**couteau**^M **suisse**

pen-blade
*petite lame*^F

cross-tip screwdriver
*tournevis*^M *cruciforme*

bottle opener
*décapsuleur*^M

screwdriver
*tournevis*^M

screwdriver
*tournevis*^M

large blade
*grande lame*^F

nail nick
*onglet*^M

can opener
*ouvre-boîtes*^M

awl
*poinçon*^M

corkscrew
*tire-bouchon*^M

# camping

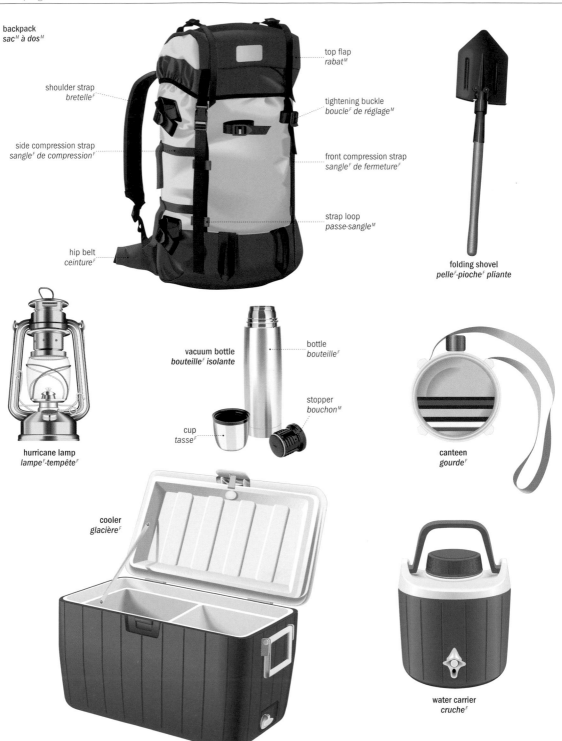

backpack
*sac*<sup>M</sup> *à dos*<sup>M</sup>

top flap
*rabat*<sup>M</sup>

shoulder strap
*bretelle*<sup>F</sup>

tightening buckle
*boucle*<sup>F</sup> *de réglage*<sup>M</sup>

side compression strap
*sangle*<sup>F</sup> *de compression*<sup>F</sup>

front compression strap
*sangle*<sup>F</sup> *de fermeture*<sup>F</sup>

strap loop
*passe-sangle*<sup>M</sup>

hip belt
*ceinture*<sup>F</sup>

folding shovel
*pelle*<sup>F</sup>*-pioche*<sup>F</sup> *pliante*

hurricane lamp
*lampe*<sup>F</sup>*-tempête*<sup>F</sup>

vacuum bottle
*bouteille*<sup>F</sup> *isolante*

bottle
*bouteille*<sup>F</sup>

stopper
*bouchon*<sup>M</sup>

cup
*tasse*<sup>F</sup>

canteen
*gourde*<sup>F</sup>

cooler
*glacière*<sup>F</sup>

water carrier
*cruche*<sup>F</sup>

SPORTS AND GAMES

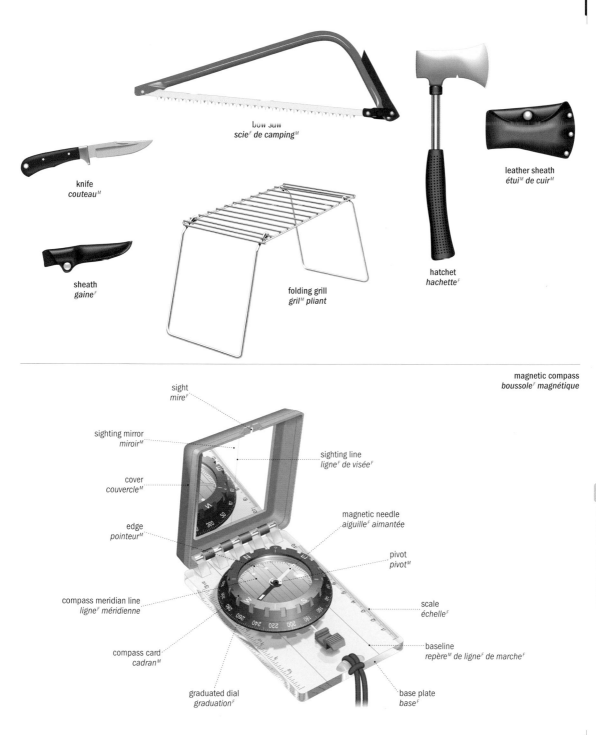

bow saw
*scie*<sup>F</sup> *de camping*<sup>M</sup>

knife
*couteau*<sup>M</sup>

sheath
*gaine*<sup>F</sup>

folding grill
*gril*<sup>M</sup> *pliant*

hatchet
*hachette*<sup>F</sup>

leather sheath
*étui*<sup>M</sup> *de cuir*<sup>M</sup>

magnetic compass
*boussole*<sup>F</sup> *magnétique*

sight
*mire*<sup>F</sup>

sighting mirror
*miroir*<sup>M</sup>

cover
*couvercle*<sup>M</sup>

edge
*pointeur*<sup>M</sup>

compass meridian line
*ligne*<sup>F</sup> *méridienne*

compass card
*cadran*<sup>M</sup>

graduated dial
*graduation*<sup>F</sup>

sighting line
*ligne*<sup>F</sup> *de visée*<sup>F</sup>

magnetic needle
*aiguille*<sup>F</sup> *aimantée*

pivot
*pivot*<sup>M</sup>

scale
*échelle*<sup>F</sup>

baseline
*repère*<sup>M</sup> *de ligne*<sup>F</sup> *de marche*<sup>F</sup>

base plate
*base*<sup>F</sup>

SPORTS AND GAMES

# hunting

chasse<sup>F</sup>

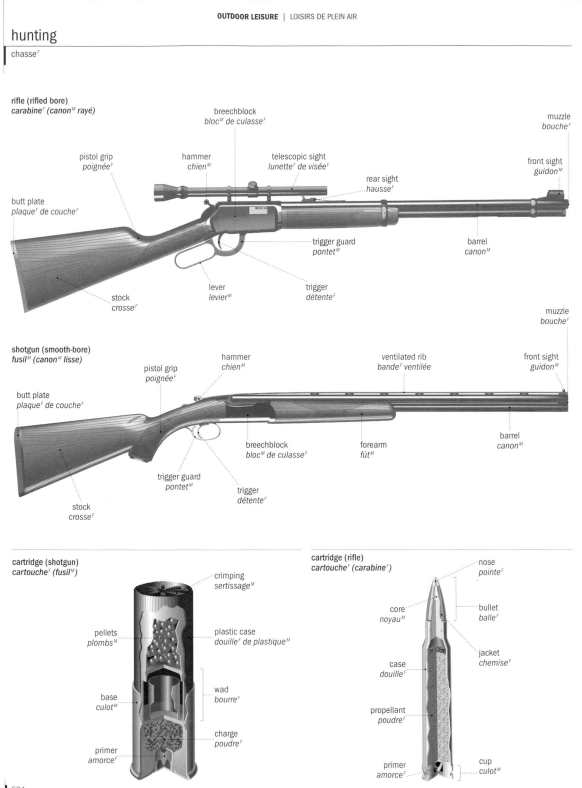

rifle (rifled bore)
carabine<sup>F</sup> (canon<sup>M</sup> rayé)

breechblock
bloc<sup>M</sup> de culasse<sup>F</sup>

muzzle
bouche<sup>F</sup>

pistol grip
poignée<sup>F</sup>

hammer
chien<sup>M</sup>

telescopic sight
lunette<sup>F</sup> de visée<sup>F</sup>

rear sight
hausse<sup>F</sup>

front sight
guidon<sup>M</sup>

butt plate
plaque<sup>F</sup> de couche<sup>F</sup>

trigger guard
pontet<sup>M</sup>

barrel
canon<sup>M</sup>

stock
crosse<sup>F</sup>

lever
levier<sup>M</sup>

trigger
détente<sup>F</sup>

shotgun (smooth-bore)
fusil<sup>M</sup> (canon<sup>M</sup> lisse)

hammer
chien<sup>M</sup>

ventilated rib
bande<sup>F</sup> ventilée

front sight
guidon<sup>M</sup>

muzzle
bouche<sup>F</sup>

pistol grip
poignée<sup>F</sup>

butt plate
plaque<sup>F</sup> de couche<sup>F</sup>

breechblock
bloc<sup>M</sup> de culasse<sup>F</sup>

forearm
fût<sup>M</sup>

barrel
canon<sup>M</sup>

trigger guard
pontet<sup>M</sup>

trigger
détente<sup>F</sup>

stock
crosse<sup>F</sup>

cartridge (shotgun)
cartouche<sup>F</sup> (fusil<sup>M</sup>)

crimping
sertissage<sup>M</sup>

pellets
plombs<sup>M</sup>

plastic case
douille<sup>F</sup> de plastique<sup>M</sup>

base
culot<sup>M</sup>

wad
bourre<sup>F</sup>

primer
amorce<sup>F</sup>

charge
poudre<sup>F</sup>

cartridge (rifle)
cartouche<sup>F</sup> (carabine<sup>F</sup>)

nose
pointe<sup>F</sup>

core
noyau<sup>M</sup>

bullet
balle<sup>F</sup>

jacket
chemise<sup>F</sup>

case
douille<sup>F</sup>

propellant
poudre<sup>F</sup>

primer
amorce<sup>F</sup>

cup
culot<sup>M</sup>

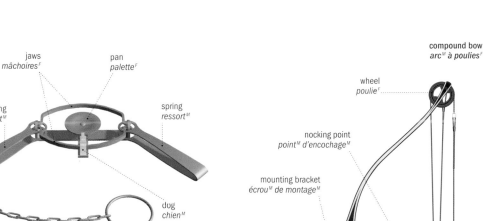

jaws
mâchoires^F

pan
palette^F

spring
ressort^M

spring
ressort^M

dog
chien^M

**leghold trap**
**piège^M à patte^F à mâchoires^F**

compound bow
arc^M à poulies^F

wheel
poulie^F

nocking point
point^M d'encochage^M

mounting bracket
écrou^M de montage^M

sight
mire^F

arrow rest
appui^M-flèche^F

grip
poignée^F

cable guard
espaceur^M de câbles^M

bowstring
corde^F

cable
câble^M

limb
branche^F

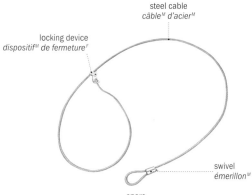

steel cable
câble^M d'acier^M

locking device
dispositif^M de fermeture^F

swivel
émerillon^M

**snare**
**collet^M**

clip
attache^F

**decoy**
**appeau^M**

# fishing

pêche<sup>F</sup>

**flyfishing**
*pêche<sup>F</sup> à la mouche<sup>F</sup>*

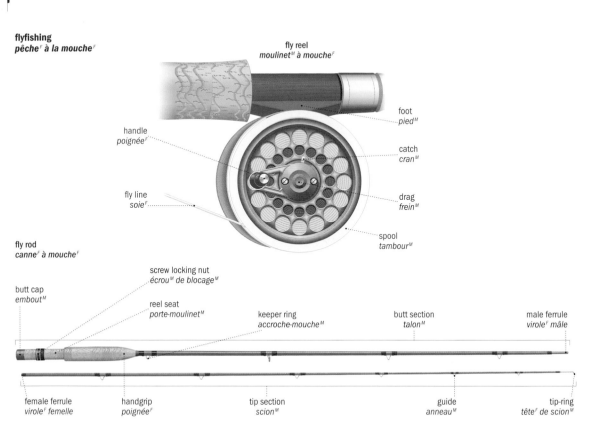

fly reel
*moulinet<sup>M</sup> à mouche<sup>F</sup>*

foot
*pied<sup>M</sup>*

handle
*poignée<sup>F</sup>*

catch
*cran<sup>M</sup>*

fly line
*soie<sup>F</sup>*

drag
*frein<sup>M</sup>*

spool
*tambour<sup>M</sup>*

**fly rod**
*canne<sup>F</sup> à mouche<sup>F</sup>*

screw locking nut
*écrou<sup>M</sup> de blocage<sup>M</sup>*

butt cap
*embout<sup>M</sup>*

reel seat
*porte-moulinet<sup>M</sup>*

keeper ring
*accroche-mouche<sup>M</sup>*

butt section
*talon<sup>M</sup>*

male ferrule
*virole<sup>F</sup> mâle*

female ferrule
*virole<sup>F</sup> femelle*

handgrip
*poignée<sup>F</sup>*

tip section
*scion<sup>M</sup>*

guide
*anneau<sup>M</sup>*

tip-ring
*tête<sup>F</sup> de scion<sup>M</sup>*

**artificial fly**
*mouche<sup>F</sup> artificielle*

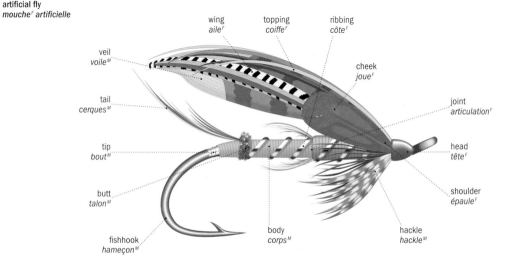

wing
*aile<sup>F</sup>*

topping
*coiffe<sup>F</sup>*

ribbing
*côte<sup>F</sup>*

veil
*voile<sup>M</sup>*

cheek
*joue<sup>F</sup>*

tail
*cerques<sup>M</sup>*

joint
*articulation<sup>F</sup>*

tip
*bout<sup>M</sup>*

head
*tête<sup>F</sup>*

butt
*talon<sup>M</sup>*

shoulder
*épaule<sup>F</sup>*

fishhook
*hameçon<sup>M</sup>*

body
*corps<sup>M</sup>*

hackle
*hackle<sup>M</sup>*

**casting**
*pêche<sup>F</sup> au lancer<sup>M</sup>*

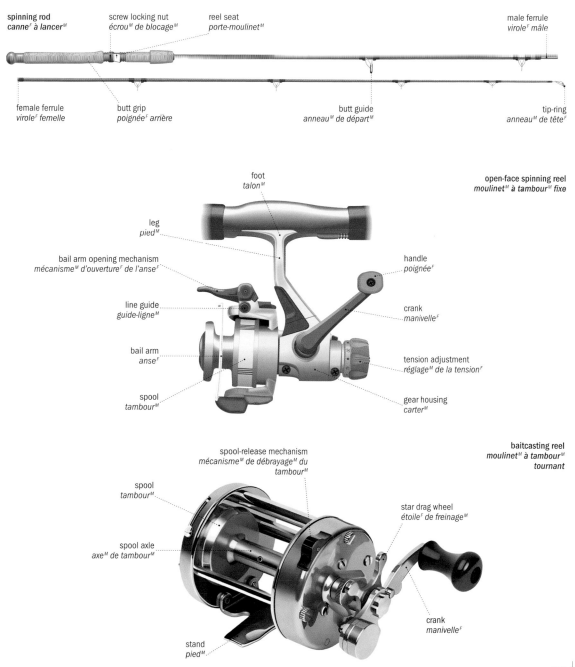

spinning rod
*canne<sup>F</sup> à lancer<sup>M</sup>*

screw locking nut
*écrou<sup>M</sup> de blocage<sup>M</sup>*

reel seat
*porte-moulinet<sup>M</sup>*

male ferrule
*virole<sup>F</sup> mâle*

female ferrule
*virole<sup>F</sup> femelle*

butt grip
*poignée<sup>F</sup> arrière*

butt guide
*anneau<sup>M</sup> de départ<sup>M</sup>*

tip-ring
*anneau<sup>M</sup> de tête<sup>F</sup>*

foot
*talon<sup>M</sup>*

open-face spinning reel
*moulinet<sup>M</sup> à tambour<sup>M</sup> fixe*

leg
*pied<sup>M</sup>*

bail arm opening mechanism
*mécanisme<sup>M</sup> d'ouverture<sup>F</sup> de l'anse<sup>F</sup>*

handle
*poignée<sup>F</sup>*

line guide
*guide-ligne<sup>M</sup>*

crank
*manivelle<sup>F</sup>*

bail arm
*anse<sup>F</sup>*

tension adjustment
*réglage<sup>M</sup> de la tension<sup>F</sup>*

spool
*tambour<sup>M</sup>*

gear housing
*carter<sup>M</sup>*

baitcasting reel
*moulinet<sup>M</sup> à tambour<sup>M</sup>
tournant*

spool-release mechanism
*mécanisme<sup>M</sup> de débrayage<sup>M</sup> du
tambour<sup>M</sup>*

spool
*tambour<sup>M</sup>*

star drag wheel
*étoile<sup>F</sup> de freinage<sup>M</sup>*

spool axle
*axe<sup>M</sup> de tambour<sup>M</sup>*

crank
*manivelle<sup>F</sup>*

stand
*pied<sup>M</sup>*

SPORTS AND GAMES

**fishhook**
*hameçon*^M

eye
*œillet*^M

gap
*ouverture*^F

shank
*hampe*^F

point
*pointe*^F

barb
*ardillon*^M

throat
*gorge*^F

bend
*courbure*^F

**spinner**
*cuiller*^F

swivel
*émerillon*^M

treble fishhook
*hameçon*^M *triple*

split link
*anneau*^M *brisé*

blade
*palette*^F

**float tackle**
*bas*^M *de ligne*^F

bobber
*flotteur*^M

swivel
*émerillon*^M

leader
*avançon*^M

sinker
*plomb*^M

snap
*mousqueton*^M

snelled fishhook
*hameçon*^M *monté*

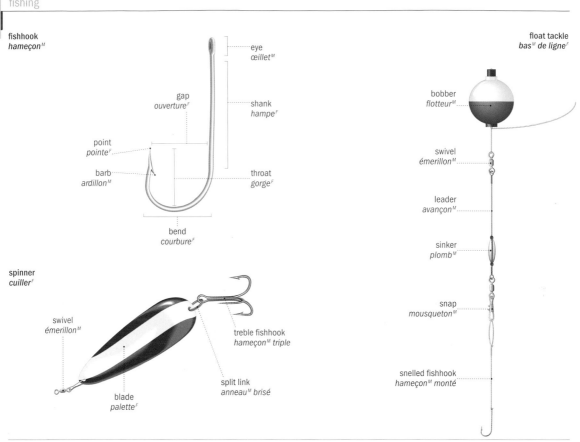

**clothing and accessories**
*vêtements*^M *et accessoires*^M

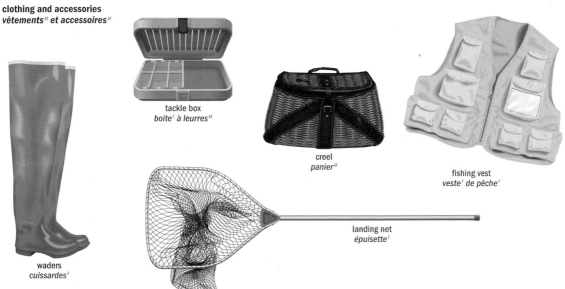

tackle box
*boîte*^F *à leurres*^M

creel
*panier*^M

fishing vest
*veste*^F *de pêche*^F

waders
*cuissardes*^F

landing net
*épuisette*^F

# English Index

1 astronomical unit 3
1,500 m starting line 473
1/10 second hand 424
10 m line 482
10,000 m relay starting line 473
100 m hurdles starting line 472
100 m starting line 472
110 m hurdles starting line 472
15 m line 483
200 m starting line 472
22 m line 482
35 mm still camera 10
4 x 400 m relay starting line 473
5 m line 483
5,000 m starting line 472
50 astronomical units 2
50,000 astronomical units 2
800 m starting line 473

## A

A 298
abalone 157
abdomen 67, 68, 70, 71, 78, 92, 94
abdominal aorta 102, 107
abdominal cavity 111, 112
abdominal segment 67
ablutions fountain 447
aboveground pipeline 404
aboveground swimming pool 184
abruptly pinnate 55
ABS 357
absorbed solar radiation 46
absorbent cotton 461
absorbing plate 410
absorption by clouds 46
absorption by Earth's surface 46
absorption of carbon dioxide 54
absorption of water and mineral salts 54
abutment 284, 344
abyssal hill 33
abyssal plain 33
Abyssinian 87
acanthus leaf 200
acceleration lane 343
accelerator cable 237
accelerator control 235
accent mark 299
access door 423
access gallery 407
access road 388
access server 335
access window 333
accessories 356, 372
accessory pocket 352
accessory shoe 314

accidentals 299
accordion 296
accordion bag 276
accordion pleat 253
account identification 443
accumulator 357
ace 468
achene 59, 60
acid rain 47, 48
acid snow 48
acorn nut 223
acorn squash 129
acoustic ceiling 293
acoustic guitar 302
acoustic meatus 115, 116
acrobatic skate 527
acromion 99
acroterion 279
action buttons 471
actor 290
actors' seats 290
actress 291
acute angle 428
Adam's apple 92
add key 337
add to memory 337
additive color synthesis 418
adductor longus 96
adductor magnus 97
Aden, Gulf 19, 20
adhesive bandage 461
adhesive disk 75
adhesive tape 461
adipose tissue 113, 114
adjustable channel 222
adjustable clamp 206
adjustable frame 226
adjustable lamp 206
adjustable strap 260
adjustable thermostat 179
adjustable waist tab 244
adjuster 466
adjusting band 324
adjusting buckle 527
adjusting catch 511
adjusting screw 222, 224
adjustment knob 353
adjustment slide 246
administration 445
adobe house 288
Adriatic Sea 18
adult skull, lateral view 100
adventitious roots 52
advertisement 313
advertising panel 378
advertising poster 380

adzuki beans 131
Aegean Sea 18
aerial cable network 316
aerial ladder truck 455
aerocyst 51
aerodynamic brake 412
affluent 32
Afghanistan 452
Africa 14, 20, 34, 451
African Plate 27
Afro pick 268
aft shroud 7
afterbay 406, 407
aftershave 271
agar-agar 123
agglomeration 430
agitator 212
agricultural pollution 47
aileron 392
air bag 354
air bag restraint system 354
air bubbles 339
air communications 317
air compression unit 376
air concentrator 270
air conditioner 361
air conditioner compressor 360
air conditioning equipment 386
air conditioning system 46
air filter 235, 350
air filter pre-cleaner 401
air hole 312
air horn 364
air inlet 367, 395
air inlet control 192
air intake 362, 383
air intake for engine cooling 525
air mass, type 39
air mattress 530
air pollutants 47
air pollution 47
air pre-cleaner filter 398
air pump 346
air relief valve 385
air scoop 523
air shaft 278
air space 79
air temperature 39
air transport 388
air unit 262
air vent 214
air-inlet grille 270
air-outlet grille 270
air-pressure pump 461
air-supply tube 454
aircraft weather station 38
airliner 37

airplane, movements 395
airport 25, 388, 430
aisle 120, 285
ajowan 139
ala 117
alarm/charge indicator light 337
Alaska, Gulf 16
Albania 450
albatross 80
albumen 79
alcohol bulb 424
alcohol column 424
Aleutian Islands 16
Aleutian Trench 34
alfalfa sprouts 130
alga, structure 51
algae 51
algae, examples 51
Algeria 451
alkaline manganese-zinc cell 417
alkekengi 132
all-purpose flour 144
all-season tire 358
all-terrain vehicle 369
alley 490, 495
alligator 77
allspice 138
alluvial deposits 32
almonds 133
alphabetical keypad 338
alphanumeric keyboard 346, 442, 443
alphanumeric keypad 327, 330
alpine ski trail 512
alpine skier 510
alpine skiing 510
alpine snowboard 513
Alps 18
Alsace glass 165
altar cross 446
altarpiece 446
alternate 330
alternate: level 3 select 330
alternating-current power cord 336
alternative key (Alt) 330
alternator 350, 360, 413
alternator fan belt 360
alternator warning light 355
alternator/fan belt 350
altitude clamp 8, 9
altitude fine adjustment 8, 9
altitude scale 37
altocumulus 42
altostratus 42
alula 78
aluminum foil 162
aluminum recycling container 49

alveolar bone 101
amaranth 143
Amazon River 17
ambulance 460, 462
ambulatory 285
ambulatory care unit 465
American bacon 156
American corn bread 145
American football 484
American football, playing field 484
American mustard 140
American outlet 198
American plug 198
Americas 448
Amery Ice Shelf 15
ammunition pouch 456
amoeba 66
amorphous solid 414
amount of substance, unit 426
ampere 426
amphibians, examples 75
amphibious firefighting aircraft 394
amphitheater, Roman 281
ampli-tuner 322, 325
amplitude 418
ampulla of fallopian tube 113
anal clasper 67
anal fin 74
analog camcorder 320
analog watch 424
analytical balance 423
anatomy 96
anatomy of a bivalve shell 73
anatomy of a male lobster 71
anatomy, human being 96
anchor 473
anchor pin 357
anchor point 70
anchor-windlass room 383, 387
anchorage block 344
anchovy 159
anconeus 97
Andes Cordillera 17
andirons 193
Andorra 449
andouillette 156
anemometer 413
anesthesia room 464
angles, examples 428
Angola 452
Anik 317
animal cell 66
animal dung 48
anise 142
ankle 92, 94
ankle boot 241
ankle guard 476

ASTRONOMY > 2-13;    EARTH > 14-49;    VEGETABLE KINGDOM > 50-65;    ANIMAL KINGDOM > 66-91;    HUMAN BEING > 92-119;    FOOD AND KITCHEN > 120-181;    HOUSE > 182-215;
DO-IT-YOURSELF AND GARDENING > 216-237;    CLOTHING > 238-263;    PERSONAL ADORNMENT AND ARTICLES > 264-277;    ARTS AND ARCHITECTURE > 278-311;    COMMUNICATIONS AND
OFFICE AUTOMATION > 312-341;    TRANSPORT AND MACHINERY > 342-401;    ENERGY > 402-413;    SCIENCE > 414-429;    SOCIETY > 430-467;    SPORTS AND GAMES > 468-538

539

ASTRONOMY > 2-13;   EARTH > 14-49;   VEGETABLE KINGDOM > 50-65;   ANIMAL KINGDOM > 66-91;   HUMAN BEING > 92-119;   FOOD AND KITCHEN > 120-181;   HOUSE > 182-215;
DO-IT-YOURSELF AND GARDENING > 216-237;   CLOTHING > 238-263;   PERSONAL ADORNMENT AND ARTICLES > 264-277;   ARTS AND ARCHITECTURE > 278-311;   COMMUNICATIONS AND
OFFICE AUTOMATION > 312-341;   TRANSPORT AND MACHINERY > 342-401;   ENERGY > 402-413;   SCIENCE > 414-429;   SOCIETY > 430-467;   SPORTS AND GAMES > 468-538

541

ENGLISH INDEX

ASTRONOMY > 2-13;   EARTH > 14-49;   VEGETABLE KINGDOM > 50-65;   ANIMAL KINGDOM > 66-91;   HUMAN BEING > 92-119;   FOOD AND KITCHEN > 120-181;   HOUSE > 182-215;
DO-IT-YOURSELF AND GARDENING > 216-237;   CLOTHING > 238-263;   PERSONAL ADORNMENT AND ARTICLES > 264-277;   ARTS AND ARCHITECTURE > 278-311;   COMMUNICATIONS AND
OFFICE AUTOMATION > 312-341;   TRANSPORT AND MACHINERY > 342-401;   ENERGY > 402-413;   SCIENCE > 414-429;   SOCIETY > 430-467;   SPORTS AND GAMES > 468-538

545

ENGLISH INDEX

ENGLISH INDEX

ENGLISH INDEX

ASTRONOMY > 2-13; EARTH > 14-49; VEGETABLE KINGDOM > 50-65; ANIMAL KINGDOM > 66-91; HUMAN BEING > 92-119; FOOD AND KITCHEN > 120-181; HOUSE > 182-215;
DO-IT-YOURSELF AND GARDENING > 216-237; CLOTHING > 238-263; PERSONAL ADORNMENT AND ARTICLES > 264-277; ARTS AND ARCHITECTURE > 278-311; COMMUNICATIONS AND
OFFICE AUTOMATION > 312-341; TRANSPORT AND MACHINERY > 342-401; ENERGY > 402-413; SCIENCE > 414-429; SOCIETY > 430-467; SPORTS AND GAMES > 468-538

549

ENGLISH INDEX

ENGLISH INDEX

ASTRONOMY > 2-13;   EARTH > 14-49;   VEGETABLE KINGDOM > 50-65;   ANIMAL KINGDOM > 66-91;   HUMAN BEING > 92-119;   FOOD AND KITCHEN > 120-181;   HOUSE > 182-215;
DO-IT-YOURSELF AND GARDENING > 216-237;   CLOTHING > 238-263;   PERSONAL ADORNMENT AND ARTICLES > 264-277;   ARTS AND ARCHITECTURE > 278-311;   COMMUNICATIONS AND
OFFICE AUTOMATION > 312-341;   TRANSPORT AND MACHINERY > 342-401;   ENERGY > 402-413;   SCIENCE > 414-429;   SOCIETY > 430-467;   SPORTS AND GAMES > 468-538          555

ASTRONOMY > 2-13;    EARTH > 14-49;    VEGETABLE KINGDOM > 50-65;    ANIMAL KINGDOM > 66-91;    HUMAN BEING > 92-119;    FOOD AND KITCHEN > 120-181;    HOUSE > 182-215;
DO-IT-YOURSELF AND GARDENING > 216-237;    CLOTHING > 238-263;    PERSONAL ADORNMENT AND ARTICLES > 264-277;    ARTS AND ARCHITECTURE > 278-311;    COMMUNICATIONS AND
OFFICE AUTOMATION > 312-341;    TRANSPORT AND MACHINERY > 342-401;    ENERGY > 402-413;    SCIENCE > 414-429;    SOCIETY > 430-467;    SPORTS AND GAMES > 468-538

557

ASTRONOMY > 2-13;   EARTH > 14-49;   VEGETABLE KINGDOM > 50-65;   ANIMAL KINGDOM > 66-91;   HUMAN BEING > 92-119;   FOOD AND KITCHEN > 120-181;   HOUSE > 182-215;
DO-IT-YOURSELF AND GARDENING > 216-237;   CLOTHING > 238-263;   PERSONAL ADORNMENT AND ARTICLES > 264-277;   ARTS AND ARCHITECTURE > 278-311;   COMMUNICATIONS AND
OFFICE AUTOMATION > 312-341;   TRANSPORT AND MACHINERY > 342-401;   ENERGY > 402-413;   SCIENCE > 414-429;   SOCIETY > 430-467;   SPORTS AND GAMES > 468-538

561

ENGLISH INDEX

# Index français

ASTRONOMIE > 2-13;  TERRE > 14-49;  RÈGNE VÉGÉTAL > 50-65;  RÈGNE ANIMAL > 66-91;  ÊTRE HUMAIN > 92-119;  ALIMENTATION ET CUISINE > 120-181;  MAISON > 182-215;  BRICO-
LAGE ET JARDINAGE > 216-237;  VÊTEMENTS > 238-263;  PARURE ET OBJETS PERSONNELS > 264-277;  ARTS ET ARCHITECTURE > 278-311;  COMMUNICATIONS ET BUREAUTIQUE > 312-341;
TRANSPORT ET MACHINERIE > 342-401;  ÉNERGIES > 402-413;  SCIENCE > 414-429;  SOCIÉTÉ > 430-467;  SPORTS ET JEUX > 468-538

563

INDEX FRANCAIS

INDEX FRANÇAIS

ASTRONOMIE > 2-13; TERRE > 14-49; RÈGNE VÉGÉTAL > 50-65; RÈGNE ANIMAL > 66-91; ÊTRE HUMAIN > 92-119; ALIMENTATION ET CUISINE > 120-181; MAISON > 182-215; BRICO-LAGE ET JARDINAGE > 216-237; VÊTEMENTS > 238-263; PARURE ET OBJETS PERSONNELS > 264-277; ARTS ET ARCHITECTURE > 278-311; COMMUNICATIONS ET BUREAUTIQUE > 312-341; TRANSPORT ET MACHINERIE > 342-401; ÉNERGIES > 402-413; SCIENCE > 414-429; SOCIÉTÉ > 430-467; SPORTS ET JEUX > 468-538

565

INDEX FRANÇAIS

ASTRONOMIE > 2-13;  TERRE > 14-49;  RÈGNE VÉGÉTAL > 50-65;  RÈGNE ANIMAL > 66-91;  ÊTRE HUMAIN > 92-119;  ALIMENTATION ET CUISINE > 120-181;  MAISON > 182-215;  BRICO-
LAGE ET JARDINAGE > 216-237;  VÊTEMENTS > 238-263;  PARURE ET OBJETS PERSONNELS > 264-277;  ARTS ET ARCHITECTURE > 278-311;  COMMUNICATIONS ET BUREAUTIQUE > 312-341;
TRANSPORT ET MACHINERIE > 342-401;  ÉNERGIES > 402-413;  SCIENCE > 414-429;  SOCIÉTÉ > 430-467;  SPORTS ET JEUX > 468-538

567

INDEX FRANCAIS

INDEX FRANÇAIS

ASTRONOMIE > 2-13; TERRE > 14-49; RÈGNE VÉGÉTAL > 50-65; RÈGNE ANIMAL > 66-91; ÊTRE HUMAIN > 92-119; ALIMENTATION ET CUISINE > 120-181; MAISON > 182-215; BRICO-
LAGE ET JARDINAGE > 216-237; VÊTEMENTS > 238-263; PARURE ET OBJETS PERSONNELS > 264-277; ARTS ET ARCHITECTURE > 278-311; COMMUNICATIONS ET BUREAUTIQUE > 312-341;
TRANSPORT ET MACHINERIE > 342-401; ÉNERGIES > 402-413; SCIENCE > 414-429; SOCIÉTÉ > 430-467; SPORTS ET JEUX > 468-538

571

INDEX FRANÇAIS

ASTRONOMIE > 2-13; TERRE > 14-49; RÈGNE VÉGÉTAL > 50-65; RÈGNE ANIMAL > 66-91; ÊTRE HUMAIN > 92-119; ALIMENTATION ET CUISINE > 120-181; MAISON > 182-215; BRICO-
LAGE ET JARDINAGE > 216-237; VÊTEMENTS > 238-263; PARURE ET OBJETS PERSONNELS > 264-277; ARTS ET ARCHITECTURE > 278-311; COMMUNICATIONS ET BUREAUTIQUE > 312-341;
TRANSPORT ET MACHINERIE > 342-401; ÉNERGIES > 402-413; SCIENCE > 414-429; SOCIÉTÉ > 430-467; SPORTS ET JEUX > 468-538

573

INDEX FRANÇAIS

ASTRONOMIE > 2-13; TERRE > 14-49; RÈGNE VÉGÉTAL > 50-65; RÈGNE ANIMAL > 66-91; ÊTRE HUMAIN > 92-119; ALIMENTATION ET CUISINE > 120-181; MAISON > 182-215; BRICO-
LAGE ET JARDINAGE > 216-237; VÊTEMENTS > 238-263; PARURE ET OBJETS PERSONNELS > 264-277; ARTS ET ARCHITECTURE > 278-311; COMMUNICATIONS ET BUREAUTIQUE > 312-341;
TRANSPORT ET MACHINERIE > 342-401; ÉNERGIES > 402-413; SCIENCE > 414-429; SOCIÉTÉ > 430-467; SPORTS ET JEUX > 468-538

577

ASTRONOMIE > 2-13; TERRE > 14-49; RÈGNE VÉGÉTAL > 50-65; RÈGNE ANIMAL > 66-91; ÊTRE HUMAIN > 92-119; ALIMENTATION ET CUISINE > 120-181; MAISON > 182-215; BRICO-LAGE ET JARDINAGE > 216-237; VÊTEMENTS > 238-263; PARURE ET OBJETS PERSONNELS > 264-277; ARTS ET ARCHITECTURE > 278-311; COMMUNICATIONS ET BUREAUTIQUE > 312-341; TRANSPORT ET MACHINERIE > 342-401; ÉNERGIES > 402-413; SCIENCE > 414-429; SOCIÉTÉ > 430-467; SPORTS ET JEUX > 468-538

581

INDEX FRANÇAIS